Introduction to Artificial Intelligence

Introduction to Artificial Intelligence

Eugene Charniak
Brown University

Drew McDermott
Yale University

ADDISON-WESLEY PUBLISHING COMPANY

Reading, Massachusetts ● Menlo Park, California ● Don Mills, Ontario
Wokingham, England ● Amsterdam ● Sydney ● Singapore ● Tokyo ● Mexico City
Bogotá ● Santiago ● San Juan

Mark S. Dalton/Sponsoring Editor

Hugh J. Crawford/Manufacturing Supervisor
Martha K. Morong/Production Manager
Dick Morton/Art Editor
Margaret Pinette/Production Editor
Patti O'Hare Williams/Text and Cover Designer
Kenneth Wilson/Illustrator
William J. Yskamp/Copy Editor

This book is in the Addison-Wesley Series in Computer Science.
Michael A. Harrison/Consulting Editor

Credits
Fig. 1.1: © Tom McHugh.   Fig. 1.2: Adapted from Woods, William A., "An experimental parsing system for transition network grammars," in R. Rustin, *Natural Language Processing.* New York: Algorithmics Press, Inc., 1972.   Fig. 1.3: Reprinted by permission of Westview Press from *Artificial Intelligence in Medicine,* edited by Peter Szolovits. Copyright © 1982 by the American Association for the Advancement of Science.   Fig. 1.4: Reprint permission from *AI Magazine.* Vol. 2, No. 2, (1981) published by the American Association for Artificial Intelligence.   Fig. 1.6: (right) Leonard Lee Rue; (left) Ylla. © 1978.   Fig. 3.34: From Stevens, K.A., "Computation of locally parallel structure," *Biol. Cybernetics* pp. 19–28 (1978).   Fig. 3.40: From *Vision* by David Marr. W.H. Freeman and Company. Copyright © 1982.   Figs. 3.45–3.50: From Schatz, Bruce R., "The computation of immediate texture discrimination." Memo 426. MIT Artificial Intelligence Lab (1977).   Fig. 3.57: From Barrow, H.G., and Tenenbaum, J.M., "Recovering intrinsic scene characteristics from images," in Hanson, A., and Riseman, E. (eds.), *Computer Vision Systems.* New York: Academic Press (1978).   Fig. 3.63: From Barrow, H.G., and Tenenbaum, J.M., "Recovering intrinsic scene characteristics from images," in Hanson, A., and Riseman, E. (eds.), *Computer Vision Systems.* New York: Academic Press (1978).   Fig. 3.81: From Shepard, Roger N., and Metzler, Jacqueline, "Mental rotation of three-dimensional objects," *Science* **171**:701–703 (1971). Copyright 1971 by the American Association for the Advancement of Science.   Fig. 3.82: From Hinton, Geoffrey, "Some demonstrations of the effects of structural descriptions in mental imagery." *Cognitive Science,* **3**(3): 231–251 (1979).   Fig. 4.2: Courtesy of Professor Harvey Silverman, Department of Engineering, Brown University.   Fig. 9.38: From Wilkins, David, "Using patterns and plans in chess," *Artificial Intelligence* **14**(2):165–203 (1980).   Fig. 9.40: RISK® game equipment used by permission of Parker Brothers © 1975, 1980. RISK is Parker Brothers' registered trademark for its world conquest board game equipment.   Fig. 11.20: Lew Merrim/Monkmeyer Press Photo Service, Inc.

Library of Congress Cataloging in Publication Data

Charniak, Eugene.
  Introduction to artificial intelligence.

  Includes bibliographies and index.
  1. Artificial intelligence.   I. McDermott, Drew V.
II. Title.
Q335.C483   1984   001.53'5   84-14542
ISBN 0-201-11945-5

For Judi, Lynette, and Aaron

Preface

While we have no evidence, we suspect that most professors write textbooks because they are going to teach a course for which none of the existing texts are suitable. Whether or not this is typically the case, it was certainly the reason for the book you are now holding. There were three things we wanted from a text on Artificial Intelligence (from now on "AI").

- It had to include those aspects of the field that we felt would prove to be enduring (for example, low-level vision research, which is given short shrift in most AI textbooks).
- It should present AI as a coherent body of ideas and methods, drawing on the work of the last twenty years, but translating it into a more uniform set of concepts, favoring clarity over journalistic accuracy.
- It should acquaint the student not only with the classic programs in the field, but the underlying theory as well: mathematical logic for knowledge representation and inference, linguistics for language comprehension, etc.

In brief, our belief was that AI is distinguished by its subject matter, not its history or methods. Its subject matter is the mind, considered as an information processing system.

When each of us became aware that the other was thinking along these lines, we decided to pool our efforts and write a textbook to reflect our view of the field. Four years later, here is the result.

Writing a textbook turned out to be a good way to develop humility about the shortcomings of other textbooks. For one thing, a general-purpose textbook must cover the significant results in *all* aspects of the field, including some its authors know little about. So we had to do some reading and writing we hadn't anticipated.

Second, we have been made aware just how hard it is to extract coherent and lasting theories from a field developing as rapidly as AI. While we have succeeded to some degree in finding some unifying concepts and notations, the book still has aspects of the usual AI "grab-bag." We managed to throw out a few dusty programming techniques, but there are many areas where there is no satisfactory theory as yet, so we have had to present the traditional, unsatisfactory one instead. We have felt free to "editorialize" at several points about the inadequacies of current theories.

On balance, however, we are pleased by our book. We have some strong opinions about what good AI is, and we were gratified about how much of it there is to report on, and how often our opinions meshed into a coherent framework for reporting on it. We hope the audience sees the same coherence we did.

While we wrote this book for introductory undergraduate AI courses, at the second to fourth year level, there is wide variety in the kinds of students who might take such a course. "Ideal" students would come to the study of AI with a rather long list of previous courses. From computer science they would have had introductory programming (including recursion), data structures, logic (including the first order predicate calculus), and a smattering of formal language theory. From linguistics, they would have had a course in generative grammar, and perhaps one in semantics as well. Naturally, it would help if they had the calculus, a first course in physics (so as to better understand the work in low-level vision) and a course in statistics (for the treatment of medical diagnosis).

Naturally, *no* student will have this panoply of prerequisites. Furthermore, since we wanted the book to be usable in a variety of classroom situations, we did not want to absolutely assume *any* of the prerequisites, except some programming experience. So, while a course in AI for cognitive scientists should have people with linguistics backgrounds, they may or may not know much about logic. On the other hand, while upper level undergraduates in computer science will have had most of the computer science background, they may not have had formal language theory, and, if our experience has been typical, their grasp of predicate calculus will be tenuous.

Our solution to this problem has been to try to explain everything. However, typically our explanations will be fast, and thus instructors would be well advised to give extra material on those areas in which their students will be unprepared. One exception is the differential and integral calculus, which, for obvious reasons, we did not want to summarize. Fortunately, the calculus is only needed in one section on vision, and it can be skipped if need be. We have also tried to separate more advanced material into optional subsections. Thus we hope that this book can find a home in many climates.

Everything in the book depends on Chapter 1, in which we introduce the idea of "internal representation" for facts and rules. The need to devise flexible and efficient representations occurs in almost all subfields of AI.

Chapter 2 is an introduction to the programming language Lisp and is optional since we have made the rest of the text pretty much independent of the language. Thus it should be possible to teach the course using another symbol-manipulation language, like Prolog. If you do, let us know. Indeed, one could read the book and profit from it without touching a computer, but it wouldn't be much fun. Part of the attraction of AI is getting a machine to exhibit some "mental" faculty, and readers shouldn't deny themselves this experience.

Chapters 3 and 4 examine transduction of information into internal representation for sight and language, the two senses most intensively studied by AI researchers.

The central chapters of the book are 6 and 7, which deepen the ideas sketched in Chapter 1 on internal representation and reasoning. We recommend doing one of 3 and 4 before these chapters, to see where the internal representations come from. Chapter 5, on search, presents the notion of a goal tree, which is used in many of the subsequent chapters.

Chapters 8, 9, 10, and 11 cover four important topics, reasoning under uncertainty, robot planning, language understanding, and learning. For the most part they are independent of each other, except that the work in Chapter 10 on motivation analysis depends on Chapter 9.

In summary, the order to do the book in is this:

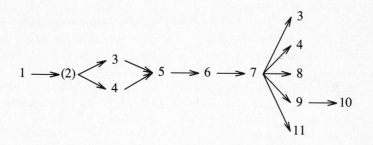

Chapter 2 is in parentheses because readers not interested in programming can skip it. Chapters 3 and 4 appear twice because they can be done in either place, although at least one of them ought to be done before 5. There are some local interchapter dependencies not shown in this diagram. These are indicated in the opening material at the front of each chapter.

Through out all of the chapters we have tried to give the reader some idea of the history of the field, as well as the intellectual filaments that connect AI to related disciplines. For this reason we have included various "boxes" covering topics which, while connected to the main body of the text, are nevertheless excursions. There are boxes on the history of AI, its relation to cognitive science, its relation to the rest of computer science, details of Lisp, etc. Often diversions are the most enjoyable parts of class lectures, and we hope these boxes give something of the same flavor.

Naturally, the most important way to make connections is through references, and we know from experience that many textbooks find their greatest use as reference works later. We have provided as many pointers into the AI literature as possible, but no effort has been made to find the earliest references to some idea for the sake of giving credit. Rather we have tried to confine our references to those that would be useful to someone today, and that are published in accessible places, such as books, journals, and conference proceedings. We probably have not succeeded at this, but have come close enough to offend someone who, if this were a research paper, would have had his out-of-print, but seminal, technical report mentioned. We apologize on both counts.

Acknowledgements

This book benefited from the advice of many people. Early drafts were read and constructively criticized by James Allen, James Beisaw, Mark Burstein, Ernie Davis, Tom Dean, Michael Gavin, Fernando Gomez, Jim Hendler, Graeme Hirst, Lewis Johnson, Janet Kolodner, Michael Lebowitz, Stan Letovsky, Barbara Meier, David Miller, Ashfaq Munshi, Chris Riesbeck, Yoav Shoham, Jim Spohrer, Peter Wegner, and Steve Zucker. We got general advice and other help from Larry Birnbaum, Mike Brady, David Byrne, Greg Collins, Eric Gold, Matt Kaplan, Wendy Lehnert, Steve Reiss, and Chris Riesbeck. The brevity of our thanks should not belie the real impact all of these folks have had on the form and content of the book.

We would like to take this opportunity to note that the order of the names on the cover is alphabetical, and has no other significance.

E.C.
D.V.M.

Contents

1

Notes in this position at the beginning of chapters give the reader guidelines on what previous material is required for the chapter, and to what degree it is important that the chapter be read in sequence. Obviously, this chapter requires no previous material. All subsequent chapters make use of material covered here.

AI and Internal Representation

1.1 Artificial Intelligence and the World

As with many branches of computer science, it is unlikely that the average reader will come to this book with no idea of what Artificial Intelligence (AI) is, or what it is good for. At times it seems that one cannot read a newspaper or weekly magazine without some reference to the field, and the interest is certainly understandable. AI researchers are trying to create a computer which thinks. The very idea is intriguing, and reflection does not lessen the hold that such ideas have. What would the world be like if we had intelligent machines? What would the existence of such machines say about the nature of human beings and their relation to the world around them? Would college professors become obsolete?

We raise these questions not because this book will answer them; it will not. Ultimately these are questions about economics, psychology and, at the deepest level, the nature of human values. Rather we mention them to illustrate the ramifications of the science we will be describing in this book.

But even at a more mundane level of everyday economics, AI has tremendous implications. One subarea of AI is robotics. Figure 1.1 shows the use of robots to weld car bodies together. Many of the issues that arise in the construction of such robots are more properly in the domain of mechanical engineering than AI (e.g., can one create a motor which will allow a mechanical arm to move in certain ways?). Nevertheless questions like how to get a robot arm from one place to another without killing anybody are standard AI problems.

Another area of AI research is *natural language comprehension*. (We say "natural" language to distinguish it from computer languages.) Figure 1.2 shows examples of the kinds of question answered by a database system which

Figure 1.1 Robot welding machines

```
** (How many samples contain chromite?)   ; The English query.
Interpretations:                          ; The translation into the
(printout                                 ; database query language.
 (number x6 / (seq samples) :             ; Asked to print out the
    (and T (contain x6 'chromite))))      ; number of things x6 that are
                                          ; samples containing chromite.

Executing: (3)                            ; There were three.
** (What are those samples?)              ; Second query.
Interpretations:                          ;
(for every x6 / (seq samples) :           ; For every sample x6 that
    (and T (contain x6 'chromite))        ; contains chromite
    (printout x6))                        ; print it out.
Executing: s10020                         ; The samples are s10020
           s10045                         ; s10045
           s10084                         ; and s10084.
```

Figure 1.2 Examples of the Lunar database query system

has a *natural language front end*. That is, there is a program which translates the query from natural language to some database query language — an artificial language designed to be used by computer databases. The particular front end we show is a relatively old one, the *Lunar* system [Woods72]. This program answered questions about the rock samples which were brought back from the moon.

Other researchers have been trying to get machines to do medical diagnosis. Figure 1.3 shows some output from the *Caduceus* program [Miller82]. This is a program which, given the symptoms of the patient, will suggest other tests to be performed, and once it has enough information will suggest what disease or diseases the patient has. According to its creators this program knows about two-thirds of the diseases which go under the heading of *internal medicine* (medicine of the internal organs, as opposed to, say, the eyes or the bones). Admittedly, doctors are still better than the machine, but progress has been considerable.

One AI program that has replaced people in its domain of expertise is the *Xcon* program [McDermott81] (originally called R1). Xcon *configures* computers (and in particular, the Digital Equipment Corporation's Vax^{TM} computer).

```
(Doctor)
Internist-1 consultation Sumex-aim    ; Caduceus was originally named
version                               ; Internist. Sumex-aim is a group
                                      ; of researchers in AI medicine who
                                      ; share computational resources.
Please enter findings                 ; The program first asks the
* sex male                            ; doctor to enter the facts about
* race white                          ; the patient.
* age 26 to 55                        ; There is a fixed vocabulary of
* alcoholism chronic                  ; symptoms which must be followed.
* go                                  ; This tells Caduceus to take over.
Disregarding:                         ; Caduceus finds a set of diseases
   exposure to rabbits                ; of which it suspects the patient
   leg weakness                       ; has one.  Symptoms not explained
   creatinine blood increased         ; by these diseases are put aside.
Considering:                          ; These are the symptoms that are
   age 26 to 55                       ; explained by the diseases
Ruleout:                              ; that it is considering.  It will
   hepatitis chronic                  ; try to rule out all but one of
   alcoholic hepatitis                ; the diseases.
Abdomen pain generalized?             ; In order to do this it asks
* no                                  ; for further information.
Abdomen pain right upper
        quadrant?
```

Figure 1.3 Output from the Caduceus program

Buying a computer is something like buying a stereo outfit. One orders components separately, and must then connect them up at installation time. Because of the greater complexity, configuring computers (as the connection process is called) requires experience. The Xcon program now configures all orders for Vax computers. Figure 1.4 shows an order for a Vax and a small part of the output of the Xcon program.

We could go on in this vein for some time. There are AI programs to do mathematics, predict the presence of mineral deposits, use TV cameras to see the world and identify what is there, verify the designs of electronic components, play backgammon, and much more. Nevertheless, such examples are misleading in two ways. First, the uninitiated tend to read too much into their capabilities. To us, the difference between, say, the ability to weld car bodies together and the ability to do light housework does not seem that great. Welding, if anything, seems more difficult. Yet while there are car-welding robots already at work, there will not be a general household robot for a long time. Similarly, while there are programs that will understand database queries, there is no program which will read and interpret medical reports, or college applications, and none are visible on the horizon. What accounts for these differences?

We will come back to this question, but first let us mention the second way in which this listing of AI programs is misleading. Naturally some people in AI work on programs such as the ones we just mentioned, but this is not the sort of thing which the majority of people do most of the time. Rather one finds AI researchers working on such seeming minutiae as

- writing a program that takes two pictures of a scene, taken from slightly different viewpoints, and finds points in the two pictures which correspond to the same place in the scene.
- worrying about the use of the word "and" in English. ("And" is a *conjunction*, but exactly what sorts of things can it combine?)
- trying to puzzle out the way fluids behave. (If you pour your cup of coffee into two containers, do you now have two "coffees"? What if you pour them back again? What if you pour all but one-tenth of a cup back?)

Why should AI researchers worry about such things anyway? The answer is intimately bound up with our earlier question, why tasks that seem roughly similar in intellectual demands are so different in their prospects for automation. Let us take one example. Going back to the photograph of the robot welders, one should notice that there is no evidence that the robots have any ability to *see* what they are doing. Indeed, they have no such ability, and it is not needed because the positions of the cars as they come by is so fixed that the arms can simply go to the same location each time and make a weld there. If the cars are in the wrong place, then the welds will do little good, but it is up to the assembly line manager to make sure that this will not happen.

No such precision is found in housework. A robot that will make your bed cannot depend on the sheets being in exactly the same place every morning. Therefore our household robot will need the ability to see the world around it, and recognize what it sees (a robot that confused your grand piano with your

Components ordered:

1	SV-AXHHA-LA	; [packaged system]
1	FP780-AA	; [floating point accelerator]
1	DW780-AA	; [unibus adapter]
1	BA11-KE	; [unibus expansion cabinet box]
6	MS780-DC	; [memory]
1	MS780-CA	; [memory controller]
1	H9602-HA	; [cpu expansion cabinet]
1	H7111-A	; [clock battery backup]
1	H7112-A	; [memory battery backup]
1	REP05-AA	; [single port disk drive]
4	RP05-BA	; [dual port disk drive]
1	TEE16-AE	; [tape drive with formatter]
2	TE16-AE	; [tape drive]
8	RK07-EA	; [single port disk drive]
1	DR11-B	; [direct memory access interface]
1	LP11-CA	; [line printer]
1	DZ11-F	; [multiplexer with panel]
1	DZ11-B	; [multiplexer]
2	LA36-CE	; [hard copy terminal]

Output:

DEC-NUMBER V0-7 12-1-79

Cabinet Layout

			BA11-KE* UPA 1			
Console LA36-CE*	011780-CA*	H9602-HA*1	H9602-DF1	TE16-AE*	TE-16-AE*	TE-16-AE*
			BA11-KE* UPA 0	TM03-FA*		

Figure 1.4 Input and a fraction of the output of the Xcon program

bed could go through a lot of pianos). But getting a robot to recognize its sur-
roundings is no easy matter. We will discuss such issues at some length in
Chapter 3. One thing our robot will have to do is recognize how far away
something is. Stereo vision is useful here because objects will appear at slightly
different places to the two eyes, and the discrepancy (the *disparity*, to use the
technical term) is a good clue to how far away something is. In Chapter 3 we

will discuss how disparity is measured. For the moment we simply note that this was the first of the minute technical issues in the above list.

1.2 What Is Artificial Intelligence?

While we have said that most readers will come to this book with a reasonable idea of what AI is, it is traditional to begin an introductory text by defining the topic, so we will essay a definition:

> Artificial intelligence is the study of mental faculties through the use
> of computational models.

The occurrence of the word "intelligence" in the name of this field is misleading. When talking about what other people do, we tend to reserve the word for mental feats of unusual creativity or cleverness. As a consequence, it sounds as if "artificial intelligence" were a technique for producing an abundance of clever insights. In fact, the most interesting problems for AI arise in attempts to duplicate the mental faculties of "ordinary" people, such as vision and natural language. Nonhandicapped people find tasks like seeing and talking easy, and so don't attach much significance to them. Tasks like multiplication of 10-digit numbers, on the other hand, are hard for most people.

The use of computers to study mental faculties — which has been possible, obviously, only since the invention of the computer in the 1940s — provides some immediate insights into how hard vision and multiplication really are. It turns out that for a computer to do the simplest act of vision requires several million multiplications. The fact that we can do the harder task with less conscious effort than the easier one is merely an evolutionary accident.

There is an unspoken premise in the previous paragraph: that the way brains work is something like the way computers work. Obviously, brains and computers are built out of different components, with different properties, so this premise is on the face of it false. However, we can weaken this assumption to make it more plausible. The fundamental working assumption, or "central dogma" of AI is this:

> What the brain does may be thought of at some level as a kind of
> computation.

Exactly what kind of computation is the subject of this book. To the extent that this dogma is true, the application of computational models to the study of mental faculties will pay off.

The use of the term "mental faculties" in our definition of AI may make the field sound like part of psychology. But while there is much cross-fertilization between the two fields, most AI workers see their field as distinct. For one thing, AI is concerned with working programs, whereas psychologists feel more comfortable with experimental confirmation. But more importantly, while AI is concerned with the general behavior that goes along with intelligence, it is not committed to any particular way of producing the results (and in particular, the methods may not be exactly those that people use).

Despite this disclaimer from time to time we will help justify a decision for taking one option over another by using information about how people do things. In AI we are constantly faced with choices in how we will design our programs, and most of the time there is very little evidence as to how such choices should be made. If we have reasonable evidence that people do things in a particular fashion, then we have some reason to believe that it is at least *possible* for an intelligent organism to operate in this way. Admittedly, this does not say that it would be the best way for our programs to work, but lacking any superior reasons for our choice, an argument from "possibility" is better than nothing.

The ultimate goal of AI research (which we are very far from achieving) is to build a person, or, more humbly, an animal. We hypothesize that this creature has various modules, shown in Figure 1.5. Some of the boxes are labeled with the number of the chapter where we concentrate on the associated module. The overall structure of our diagram is INPUT → INTERNALS → OUTPUT. The connections to the internals are labeled *internal representation*. This concept will drive much of what we do in the book, and we will justify it next.

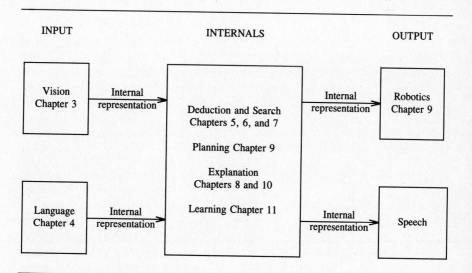

Figure 1.5 Mental faculties

1.3 Representation in AI

A *representation* is a stylized version of the world. Depending on how it is to
be used, a representation can be quite simple, or very complex. Suppose we
were building a program to identify objects visually as they came, down an
assembly line so that they can be shunted in various directions. Let us concentrate on the output sent by this program to the shunting equipment. If the only
kinds of object that can come along are, say, bells, books, and candles, then the
output can be restricted to the symbols, bell, book, or candle. Indeed, we
really do not even need the words; we could do just as well with the symbols 1,
2, or 3, or just electronic signals to the shunting machinery. This is a representation, albeit a very simple one.

Unfortunately, if we want to build a creature more elaborate than a slug,
we can't get away with such a simple approach. Suppose our animal were given
the two scenes shown in Figure 1.6. Here, of course, the complexity of the
scene has increased from the assembly-line case, but we are not concerned with
that at the moment. Rather we are interested in a more restricted question,
namely, what should the output of the visual recognition faculty be? Clearly, if
in both cases it just output lion, it would somehow be missing the point, not that
it would matter to our animal, or at least not for very long.

The conclusion is that the output of the vision program must, at least in
principle, be able to express almost any aspect of the *content* of the scene.
Different aspects will be interesting in different situations, but the output must
never be at a loss to express the presence of a crucial object or relationship.

Figure 1.6 Not all pictures of lions are created equal.

From this point on we will use the term *representation* only for schemes with this degree of flexibility.

In Figure 1.5 we have embodied a key assumption we will be making, that all representations produced by the vision and language modules, used by the inference and planning modules, and acted on by the muscle and speech systems, are essentially the same, or easily intertranslatable. This is not a vacuous requirement. A reflex arc is a good counterexample. This is a simple nerve pathway that causes a bit of behavior as a result of a stimulus. For instance, touching something hot causes one's hand to jerk away. We can think of this system as being able to represent two facts: "touching something hot," and "not touching something hot." If the first is recognized, then a bit of behavior (jerking) occurs. When one reflex is triggered, no other reflex is involved. Some simple animals may actually work this way. But complex animals cannot afford to. What they see or hear must be integrated with other inputs, stored, pondered, and, when acted upon, coordinated with other goals. So, even when a complex animal has a reflex arc, it also has a slower circuit to notify the main nervous system that it has burned its hand. This slower circuit continually reminds the creature to include "take care of the hand" on its agenda of things to do.

The common language produced or operated on by various modules we will call the *internal representation*. As we will see, the existence of this representation is to some extent an abstraction. The same representation may be embodied in a variety of different data structures, to make different operations efficient. But we will assume that it is easy to translate from one to another, and, in a sense to be explained, they are all variants of the same abstract internal representation.

Box 1.1

AI to the Dartmouth Conference

Unlike most fields you study in college, computer science, and in particular, artificial intelligence, does not have a long and distinguished history. Not long, at any rate. Most of the basic ideas and, perhaps even more important, the basic sets of preconceptions that make up AI can be traced back only to the middle years of this century.

This is not to say, of course, that these ideas sprang into being full blown, without any intellectual forebears. The idea of creating an artificial intelligence is an old one. European literature is replete with stories of one person or another accomplishing this goal, and it is presumably not coincidence that *Frankenstein* [Shelley81], one of the great horror stories of all time, deals with a Dr. Frankenstein who builds an artificial person, to a rather dreadful end.

If we want more scientifically respectable ancestors, we may press into service the many logicians and philosophers who have labored to formalize, and ultimately to mechanize, the "laws of thought." One of the

classic names here is that of George Boole (1815-1864) who invented
boolean algebra, in which we find what today are the standard logical
definitions of and, or, etc. Today, Boole's ideas have been incorporated
into both mathematics and philosophy. But his concerns were, if anything, more in the direction of artificial intelligence. The book upon
which his fame is based is titled *An Investigation of the Laws of Thought
on Which Are Founded the Mathematical Theories of Logic and Probabilities* (1854), and in his preface he says this:

> The laws we have to examine are the laws of one of the most important of
> our mental faculties. The mathematics we have to construct are the
> mathematics of the human intellect.

Nor is Boole the only name we could cite. But the plain fact of the
matter is that it was only in the twentieth century that the intellectual tools
(logic and the study of formalism) and the physical devices (from vacuum
tubes, to transistors, to chips) have been available.

Within this century, perhaps the first person to see clearly the possibility of computer intelligence was Alan Turing (1912-1954). Turing
worked with precursors of modern computers during World War II. After
the war, in 1950, he published his famous article *Computing Machinery
and Intelligence* [Turing63] in which he explicitly puts forward the idea
that a computer could be programmed so as to exhibit intelligent behavior.
He also examines, and rejects, arguments as to the impossibility of
artificial intelligence. But probably the most famous contribution of the
article is the so-called *Turing test*. Turing first envisions a test in which
you have typewriter communication to two rooms, one of which has a man
in it and one of which has a woman. Both the man and the woman would
claim to be a woman, and it would be your problem to decide which was
telling the truth. Similarly, Turing suggests we could have a person in
one room and a computer in the other, both claiming to be a person, and
you would have to decide on the truth. Obviously, if you failed at this
task (or could only guess at chance level), then one would be inclined to
say that the computer was intelligent, the alternative being out of the question in polite company. (Actually, the paper makes it sound as if Turing
had in mind the computer pretending to be a woman in the man/woman
game, but the point is not completely clear, and most have assumed that
he intended the test to be a person/computer one, and not
woman/computer.)

While this paper came out in 1950, as did another influential paper
by Claude Shannon on the possibility of computer chess, most observers
give 1956 as the start of artificial intelligence as we know it today, for
1956 was the date of the so-called Dartmouth Conference. The conference
was organized by a young assistant professor of mathematics at Dartmouth
named John McCarthy with the help of a friend of his at M.I.T., Marvin
Minsky. McCarthy proposed that

a two-month, ten-man study of artificial intelligence be carried out during the summer of 1956 at Dartmouth College in Hanover, New Hampshire. The study is to proceed on the basis of the conjecture that every aspect of learning or any other feature of intelligence can in principle be so precisely described that a machine can be made to simulate it.

To the best of anyone's knowledge, this is the first time the term "artificial intelligence" saw print. McCarthy seems to have invented the term, although he is not sure that he had not heard it from someone else, and he used it despite the fact that it seemed rather inflammatory at the time. In an earlier attempt to solicit papers on the topic he had used the "more respectable" term "automata studies," but had received, naturally enough, papers on automata theory.

This conference was also the first meeting of the four men who would lead artificial intelligence, at least in the United States, for the next twenty years: McCarthy and Minsky whom we have already mentioned, plus Allen Newell and Herbert Simon. The latter two seemed to be the most advanced of the group, already having a working AI program, the Logic Theorist. These were not the only participants, but they proved to be the most influential, with Minsky establishing a group at M.I.T., McCarthy one at Stanford, and Newell and Simon already working in the area at what was then the Carnegie Institute of Technology (now Carnegie-Mellon University).

But aside from founding the field of artificial intelligence, relatively little was accomplished at the conference, certainly little compared to the hopes of the organizers. Although those who visited the Dartmouth campus that summer did not realize it, artificial intelligence is a very difficult field, for intelligence is a complicated business.

1.4 Properties of Internal Representation

To get a better handle on internal representation and the properties it must have, let us change our task somewhat. Rather than looking at a vision program, consider, instead, a program that accepts information in simple English sentences and later will answer questions based upon this information. So, we might tell it that Dave caught a cold, and then later ask if he is ill, and expect to get back some answer like yes, or perhaps even better, "Yes, he has a cold."

We will assume that this task can be broken up into four steps.

- When the program gets a statement, it translates it into an internal representation and stores it away.
- When it gets a question, it translates it into an internal representation as well.

- It uses the internal representation of the question to fetch statements from its memory.
- It translates the answer back into English.

This breakdown may seem pretty obvious, but we have already made several important choices. For example, we could simply store the English, and then use the English to answer the question when it is asked. The idea would be that if we are never asked, we have saved the effort that would have gone into the translation. But there are good reasons for rejecting such an approach. First, there is good evidence that people do not do things this way. We tend to remember the "gist" of what we are told long after we have forgotten the exact words.

Second, from a strictly AI point of view, consider a situation in which our program is talking to Fred, and Fred, pointing to Dave says, "He has a cold." If the program simply saves the English, then later on it will be stuck when it tries to figure out who the "he" is referring to. Thus we must conclude that we determine such referents while listening, rather than when answering. From here it is a short step to concluding that we determine at least part of the internal representation. This, of course, assumes the following principle of internal representation:

Internal representation makes the choice of referent explicit.

The situation in which a referent in a sentence is not clear is called *referential ambiguity*. It is "referential" in that the problem is determining the reference of, say, "he," and it is "ambiguity" in that there is more than one interpretation. Thus another way of stating our first principle of internal representation is "the internal representation must eliminate all referential ambiguity."

So our representation must have some way to indicate reference unambiguously. In day-to-day conversation, if we were asked what the referent for "he" is in the example above, we would reply "Dave." But this is not sufficient. We happen to know several people named Dave. If we put "Dave" in the internal representation there would be no way to decide which one was meant. Of course, we could go to last names as well, but often this will not work either. (We happen to know two John Andersons.)

The solution is to *make up* names for each individual so that we can guarantee that the names we assign will be unique. That is, there is only one individual per name. We will call such unique names *instances*. They are also often called *tokens*. Typically we create instances by using some convenient symbol and adding a number after it, where the number guarantees that the symbol is unique. So, we could represent two Daves by dave-1 and dave-2. Note that these symbols are not English words. Rather they are symbols in our internal representation, and to distinguish them we use a different typeface. Naturally, there will be problems in going from English (or visual) input to such symbols, but we will have to simply grit our teeth and try to do it.

Thus our internal representation for a sentence like "Jack caught a ball" will use unique symbols for "Jack" and "a ball" and hence might come out like this:

jack-2 caught ball-17.

While this is better, the meaning of this revised version is still not completely clear. In particular, the meaning of "caught" is not clear. Suppose we have already told our program that "Dave caught a cold." When we ask "Who is ill?" we might be told, "Dave caught a cold and Jack caught a ball." This is called *word-sense ambiguity* because the word "caught" in English has more than one *word sense* (that is, it has more than one meaning). If our internal representation is to explicate meaning, this too should be removed. Thus we should distinguish between the two meanings of "catch" by using two symbols, say catch-illness and catch-object. Our representation then becomes this:

jack-2 catch-object ball-17.

More generally we have the following:

All predicates in a internal representation must be unambiguous.

A *predicate* is simply something that asserts a fact about one or more entities. In this case we are asserting a catching relation between Jack and the ball.

At this point we have removed everything from the original sentence except one thing, the period at the end. The period is used to separate one sentence from the next, and in much the same way, we need to keep pieces of internal representation separate. While we could use periods, for historical reasons people have tended to delimit individual pieces of internal representation by parentheses, giving us this:

(jack-2 catch-object ball-17)

Actually, there is still one thing remaining from the original sentence, namely word order. English uses word order to express what we will call *functional structure*. In the example at hand, we depend on word order to distinguish the following:

Jack caught a ball.
A ball caught Jack.

When we talk about the "functional structure" we mean distinguishing the "catcher" from the "caught."

We do not have to modify our internal representation, since we can simply use the order of symbols there in exactly the same way that English does. However, we should be aware that English is not consistent in this ordering. So we have in English so-called *passive sentences* where the *direct object* of the sentence (in "Jack caught a ball" this would be the "a ball") is put at the front of the sentence, as in: "A ball was caught by Jack." It is possible to distinguish passive from nonpassive sentences, and we will discuss the issue in greater length in Chapter 4 when we discuss language. Our point now is the general principle:

Internal representation must clearly indicate functional structure.

Thus the order we use in our internal representation is purely a conventional order, and has nothing to do with the original sentence. Again for historical reasons internal representations are typically written with the predicate coming first. Thus we would have

    (catch-object jack-2 ball-17)

One more point before going on. So far we have been dealing with very simple cases, where one English sentence translates into one piece of internal representation. (From now on we will call these pieces of internal representation *formulas*. When we want to stress that they are stored in some database, we will call them *assertions*.) In general, however, a single sentence will become several formulas. For example, suppose we have "Jack caught a green ball." It is quite possible, indeed, even likely, that the "ball" in this sentence has not been mentioned previously, and hence we would have to create a new instance to represent this object. To do this would require stating that this instance is an instance of a ball, and that the color of this object is green. Thus we would have

    (catch-object jack-1 ball-3)
    (inst ball-3 ball)
    (color ball-3 green)

The second formula states that ball-3 is an instance (inst) of a ball, while the third states that its color is green. (We will be using the inst predicate throughout this book to state that some particular individual is an instance of some general type of entity.) The result is that a single sentence was translated into three formulas.

1.5 The Predicate Calculus

When we divided AI programs up as illustrated in Figure 1.5 we did not pay much attention to the central box — the processes that used the incoming internal representation. While it is difficult to characterize these topics in any detail, one thing that all of them require is the ability to draw inferences. To draw an inference is to come to believe a new fact on the basis of other information. There are many kinds of inference. The best understood is *deduction*, which is "logically correct inference." This means that deduction from true premises is guaranteed to result in a true conclusion. Although we rarely notice, we need to make deductions all of the time. Earlier when we were told that someone came down with a cold, and then asked if that person were ill, we were making a deduction (if a person comes down with a cold then the person *has* a cold, and since a cold is an illness, therefore the person was ill.)

The standard way to characterize deduction is by using a system called the *predicate calculus*. The word "calculus" in "the predicate calculus" has little to do with what we normally think of as "the calculus." "The calculus" refers to the differential and integral calculus, and is so called because it gives us a way of "calculating" differentials and integrals. The "calculus" in "the predicate calculus" tells us that this gives us a way of calculating the truth of propositions. As such, the predicate calculus consists of a language for expressing propositions, and rules for how to infer new facts (propositions) from those we already have. We will start by describing the language.

1.5.1 Predicates and Arguments

The language of the predicate calculus is an extension of that we constructed for our internal representation. Here too we will have *formulas*, and the formulas we saw in the last section are of the simplest type in the predicate calculus.

```
(catch-object jack-1 block-1)    ; jack-1 caught an object block-1
(inst block-1 block)             ; that happens to be a block
(color block-1 blue)             ; colored blue.
```

To make up these formulas we need a set of *predicates*, e.g., inst, color, and catch-object. If we were going to be really formal, we should list all of the legal predicates, but we will feel free to introduce new ones at the slightest pretext, provided only that the intent of the predicate should be reasonably clear.

Each predicate requires one or more *arguments*. In the above examples they all require two. It is important to realize that the predicate calculus does not specify what predicates we may have, or how many arguments they should take. For example, to say that block-1 is a block, in the example above we used this formula:

```
(inst block-1 block)
```

While this will be our convention throughout the book, it is not part of the definition of the predicate calculus. We could have used this instead:

```
(block block-1)
```

In this version we have a one place (i.e., one argument) predicate block. There may be reasons for preferring one of these representations over the other, but the predicate calculus itself does not dictate the choice.

Each of the arguments to a predicate must be filled by a *term*. Terms come in three varieties, *constant symbols*, *variables*, and *function applications*. Constant symbols include things like block-1 jack-1 and blue. Again, we should really give a complete list of the ones we will use, but we won't.

Function applications are things like (son-of clyde). They consist of a function, here son-of, that will take zero or more arguments. Son-of is a function of one argument. The arguments of functions are themselves terms. Since these are not programming language functions we should not think of them as "evaluating" to some individual. Rather they are simply a complicated way of naming somebody. For the moment we will ignore functions completely, and return to them only in Chapter 6.

The last sort of term is a variable, which we will come back to later.

A predicate plus the proper number of arguments (terms) is the simplest kind of formula, called an *atomic formula*.

1.5.2 Connectives

To be able to reason about our formulas we need to be able to say things like "if this is true, then that will be true" or "if both this and that are true, then this other thing is true" or "this is not true." To do this we we can build more complicated formulas from atomic formulas by combining them with so-called *connectives*. These are and, or, not, and if. So, if p and q are formulas in our language then (and p q), (or p q), (not p), and (if p q) are also formulas. (Because we want to talk about what is allowable in general, we have started to use variables in place of actual propositions. That is, in the above p and q could be any propositions, and thus we are describing the general case. This is essentially similar to the use of variables in standard mathematical arguments: "Let n be a number, then $2n$ will be an even number." However p and q range over statements in the predicate calculus rather than numbers.)

The connectives and, or, etc. are sometimes called "truth-functional predicates" because we can determine the truth or falsity of one of these combinations by simply knowing the truth of the formulas from which it is made. For example, (or p q) is true if and only if at least one of p and q is true. (Actually, we will allow and and or to take more than two formulas. In this case or is true if at least one of its subformulas is true.) Here are some examples of formulas that use these predicates.

(and (color block-1 yellow)	; *Block-1 is a yellow*
(inst block-1 elephant))	; *elephant.*
(if (supports block-2 block-1)	; *If block-2 supports block-1*
(on block-1 block-2))	; *then block-1 is on block-2.*
(if (and (inst clyde elephant)	; *If clyde is an elephant*
(color elephant gray))	; *and an elephant is gray*
(color clyde gray))	; *then clyde is gray.*

More formally, we can express the relation between a connective predicate and its arguments in terms of a *truth table*. The truth tables for the standard predicate calculus connectives are given in Figure 1.7. A truth table gives the truth of a combination in terms of the truth of the components. We have already noted the rule for or. (and $p_1 \ldots p_n$) is true if and only if all of the p_j are true. Naturally (not p) is true if and only if p is false.

Most people find the rules for if more difficult to understand than those for the other connectives. To some degree the rule for if makes sense. Note that if

(if p q)

p	q	(and p q)	p	q	(or p q)
t	t	t	t	t	t
t	f	f	t	f	t
f	t	f	f	t	t
f	f	f	f	f	f

p	(not p)	p	q	(if p q)
t	f	t	t	t
f	t	t	f	f
		f	t	t
		f	f	t

Figure 1.7 Truth tables

is true, and p is also true, then the truth table tells us that q is true, which is exactly what we want.

However, there are other aspects of if that are more confusing. If we take the truth table literally, which is, of course, how we should take it, then a statement like "If R2D2 is a cabbage, then $2+2 =4$" is a true statement, simply because we know (a) R2D2 is not a cabbage, (b) $2+2$ does equal 4, and (c) (if f t) is true. Somehow this seems odd.

Actually, the real problem here is not so much the exact way that we fill out the truth table for if, but rather the fact that we consider if a truth-functional predicate at all. In common English we typically use "if" in situations where there is some sort of causal connection. So, when we say "I will go if you do" we mean that your going will influence me to go as well. Thus in English "if" is not a truth-functional predicate in that the truth of the entire statement is not simply a function of the truth of the two connected statements. But in the predicate calculus if is a truth value predicate, and hence has no connotation of causation.

Once one has accepted that the predicate calculus if does not express causality, it is not to hard to convince oneself that the truth table must be filled out the way it is. For example, consider the rule that (if f t) is true. Suppose we were told that if anyone gets caught in the rain, then that person will be wet.

(if (*anyone is caught in the rain*) (*that person is wet*))

One day we note that Dave is wet, but he was not caught in the rain (suppose that he was sprayed with a hose). In this case we have (if f t). But clearly our experience with Dave does not invalidate our rule, so in this case the if-then rule must still be true. So, (if f t) is true.

1.5.3 Variables and Quantification

With connectives we can say things like "if Clyde is an elephant, then Clyde is gray." But really, we want to be able to say something much more general: "If anything is an elephant, then it is gray." To do this we need to introduce predicate calculus *variables* and *quantifiers*. There are two kinds of quantifier, *existential quantifiers* and *universal quantifiers*. Universal quantifiers say that something is true for all possible values of a variable. We indicate that x is a universally quantified variable in the formula *f* with this:

(forall (x) *f*)

We say here that *f* is in the *scope* of the variable x. If there are several universal variables we can write it this way.

(forall (x y z) *f*)

Using universal quantification we can express the rule that "all elephants are gray."

(forall (z) (if (inst z elephant) (color z gray)))

More precisely, this states that for all objects, if the object is an elephant, then the color of the object is gray. Note that we had to translate "all elephants are gray" into this slightly different form, using an if. This particular translation is a very common "idiom" in the predicate calculus.

The other kind of quantification is existential quantification. We indicate that a variable is existentially quantified like this:

(exists (x) *f*)

For example, to say that every person has a head, we would say

(forall (x) (if (person x) (exists (y) (head-of x y))))

More literally this says that for anything, if it is a person, then there exists something that is the head of this person. At this point we have defined all of the constructs of the predicate calculus. Figure 1.8 summarizes the entire language.

1.5.4 How to Use the Predicate Calculus

So far our presentation of the predicate calculus has been rather abstract. Throughout this book we will be using it as a tool for AI, and while this should eventually give the reader a feel for how the predicate calculus is used, a preview might be in order.

Initially in our discussion of internal representation we considered the task that of taking statements in English and answering questions based upon the information received. Let us consider this task again.

The initial problem for the system upon receiving some input is to translate from the English to the predicate calculus equivalent. Doing this in

The language of the predicate calculus consists of these:
- A set of constant terms.
- A set of variables.
- A set of predicates, each taking a specified number of arguments.
- A set of functions, each taking a specified number of arguments.
- The connectives if, and, or, and not.
- The quantifiers exists and forall.

The terms of the language are these:
- constant terms.
- variables.
- functions applied to the correct number of terms.

The formulas of the language are these:
- A predicate applied to the correct number of terms.
- If p and q are formulas then (if p q), (and p q) (or p q), and (not p).
- If x is a variable, and p is a formula, then (exists (x) p), and (forall (x) p).

Figure 1.8 The predicate calculus

general is a difficult problem (as Chapters 4 and 10 will emphasize), but now we want to concentrate on the end result. We have stipulated that it will be a statement in the predicate calculus. The point we want to make is that this still tells us hardly anything about the output. Presumably it will be a collection of statements, so somewhere in the representation we might find this:

```
(and (                            )      ; Some collection of
     (                            )      ; statements will be true.
     . . .
     (                            ))
```

But what predicates should we use, how many arguments should they take, what constants do we have? The predicate calculus says nothing about this. It is up to you, the AI researcher, to decide. For example, if the sentence were "Fran smoked a cigarette," one might suggest a smoking predicate (we use the "ing" form to distinguish it from the noun "smoke") that would take two arguments, a *smoker* and a *smoked* in that order. On the other hand, *conceptual dependency*, a theory of representation which we will discuss at length in Chapter 6, has an ingest predicate. This predicate is intended to capture the similarities between eating, drinking, and smoking. To represent smoking would require a series of statements saying, in effect, "Fran ingested smoke from a cigarette through the mouth." One may argue about which is better, but the only point we want to make here is that the predicate calculus leaves the decision to you. *These decisions, the choices of predicates, functions, and constants, are probably the most important ones to be made in AI.*

If the input sentence is a question, then once the internal representation is found, it is necessary to look for the answer in the database. In general it will not be there explicitly. Rather it will be necessary to infer the answer from other facts. The example we used earlier was inferring that Jack was ill through the chain of reasoning "Jack caught a cold. Therefore he had a cold. Therefore he had an illness."

Inference, or at least deduction, is predicate calculus's strong point. In the predicate calculus the initial facts which drive the deductions are called *axioms*. These are the things we assume and are to be distinguished from the things we deduce using the axioms, which are *theorems*. In mathematics we normally think of the axioms as being set out in advance, and never changed. However, in AI we have a different view. We will be using the predicate calculus to represent the information we gain from vision, or language. Every time we turn around (or hear a new sentence) we get in new information. This information will be further axioms for our system. (In general the new facts will not be deducible from previous facts, and since all formulas are either axioms or theorems, the new facts must be axioms.) Thus, in contrast to mathematics, our set of axioms will not be stable, but rather will change over time. But there is nothing wrong with that.

To deduce new facts from the axioms, the predicate calculus has *rules of inference*. The most famous of the rules of inference is *modus ponens*, which says that given (if *p q*) and *p* we are allowed to deduce *q*. Another such rule is *universal instantiation*:

If something is true of everything, then it is true for any particular thing.

We will not attempt a formal axiomatization of the predicate calculus. That is, we will not specify exactly which rules of inference are needed. There are many possible axiomatizations. In Chapter 6 we will give one that is particularly suited to computer implementation.

Given these rules, one can infer new facts using the standard techniques of mathematical proofs. One starts with already established information and deduces new information using the rules of inference until, at the end, one has deduced the fact one wanted. The trouble with this technique, as most students will remember from taking geometry, is that it is all too possible to keep deducing new facts, without apparent progress toward the fact one wants. Many important problems in AI stem from this troublesome observation.

As a simple example of deduction, we will deduce that Tweety is yellow, given that Tweety is a canary, and all canaries are yellow.

(inst tweety canary)	; *Assumption 1.*
	; *Tweety is a canary.*
(forall x (if (inst x canary)	; *Assumption 2. All*
(color x yellow)))	; *canaries are yellow.*
(if (inst tweety canary)	; *Using universal instan-*
(color tweety yellow))	; *tiation on assumption 2.*
(color tweety yellow)	; *Using modus ponens on*
	; *the above instantiation*
	; *plus assumption 1.*

This may seem like a rather ponderous way of coming to such a simple conclusion. In part this is simply the common feeling that things we do without much thought ought to be inherently simple for the machine. Whether or not this *ought* to be the case, we will repeatedly observe that it *isn't*. However, for deductions of this sort there is a simpler method — one that we will lay out in Chapter 6.

1.6 Other Kinds of Inference

The predicate calculus gives us rules for making deductions. As we have said, deduction is "legal inference" because given true axioms the inferences drawn will also be true. Deduction, however, is only one kind of inference among many.

A second kind of inference is called *abduction*. Abduction is the process that generates explanations. To a first approximation, abduction has the following paradigm:

> From: *b*
>
> (if *a b*)
>
> Infer: *a*

As we will see in Chapter 10, this is not exactly what we want, but it is close enough for now.

Unlike deduction, abduction is *not* a legal inference. Abduction allows false conclusions, as in

> From: (feels-terrible Bill)
>
> (forall (x) (if (has-cancer x) (feels-terrible x)))
>
> Infer: (has-cancer Bill)

Assuming that Bill feels terrible, then the two premises are true, yet the conclusion we have drawn is a rather drastic one.

Although abduction can lead us to wrong conclusions, it is nevertheless very useful, and even necessary. So, while a doctor who made the inference above would rapidly lose patients, medical diagnosis is really just the careful use of abduction. Typically a doctor might conclude that a person has, say, a lung problem if several of the symptoms of lung problems are present. The logic here is that we know that the patient is short of breath, the patient has loud breathing sounds, etc. We also know these two facts:

> (forall (x) (if (has-lung-problem x) (is-short-of-breath x)))
>
> (forall (x) (if (has-lung-problem x) (has-loud-breathing-sounds x)))

Given such facts we can account for the symptoms by postulating that the patient has a lung problem. Alternatively, we would say that we have "explained" the symptoms by assuming the lung problem.

Thus we see that abduction is really explanation, and medical diagnosis is simply a well-controlled form of explanation. Furthermore, other well-known explanatory tasks involve abduction as well. For example, when we say that you have "understood" a story that you have read, we typically mean that you have abduced the correct explanatory facts. So, if we read "The guests tied streamers and tin cans to the car," we would normally assume that we are reading about a wedding. Again, this is abduction, since we know that these activities take place at weddings, and from these clues we abduce "wedding." Chapters 8 and 10 will look at abduction in great detail, with medical diagnosis and story comprehension given particular emphasis.

The last kind of inference we want to discuss is *induction*. While induction can take several different forms, the most common is this:

From: (P *a*), (P *b*), . . .
Infer: (forall (x) (P x))

Obviously this is not sound inference either, but as with abduction, induction is very useful in our everyday lives, where it is more commonly known as learning. So, if we see a lot of leaves, and all of them are green we might infer (induce) that all leaves are green. In this case we have the following:

From: (if (inst leaf-1 leaf)   ; *We have one leaf*
          (color leaf-1 green))   ; *that is green.*

      (if (inst leaf-2 leaf)   ; *We have a second leaf*
          (color leaf-2 green))   ; *that is also green.*

Infer: (forall (x) (if (inst x leaf)   ; *Infer that all leaves*
           (color x green)))   ; *are green.*

Learning is perhaps the most important thing in our repertoire of abilities, and has proved to be the most difficult for computers to do. We will discuss this issue in detail in Chapter 11.

1.7 Indexing, Pointers, and Alternative Notations

In the preceding sections we have proposed the predicate calculus as a plausible candidate for an internal representation. One should keep in mind which are the important and which are the trivial aspects of this decision. For example, the particular *notation*, or way in which we represent the predicate calculus on a page, is comparatively unimportant. We mention this because in the AI literature the student will come across notations that, on the surface, look quite different. In this section we will show that they can be understood as alternative notations for the same underlying representation.

Several popular AI representations have been members of a family of representations that go under the name of *associative networks* (or *associative nets*). (They have also been referred to as *semantic networks*.) From the viewpoint of the predicate calculus, associative nets replace terms with *nodes* (typically drawn as small ovals) and relations with *labeled directed arcs*. (A "directed arc" can be thought of as a line connecting two nodes, with an arrow-head indicating direction.) To take a simple example, Figure 1.9 shows a scene, a linear predicate calculus rendition, and the same set of facts in an associative net format.

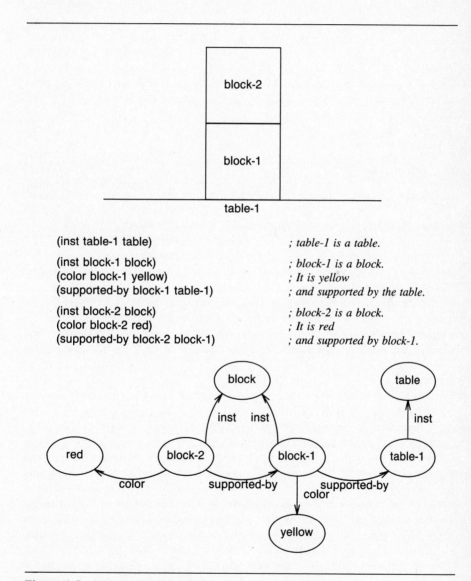

(inst table-1 table)   ; *table-1 is a table.*

(inst block-1 block)   ; *block-1 is a block.*
(color block-1 yellow)   ; *It is yellow*
(supported-by block-1 table-1)   ; *and supported by the table.*

(inst block-2 block)   ; *block-2 is a block.*
(color block-2 red)   ; *It is red*
(supported-by block-2 block-1)   ; *and supported by block-1.*

Figure 1.9 A blocks world scene

The two representations may look radically different on the printed page, but they contain the same information.

1.7.1 Indexing

There does seem to be one way in which the associative net and the original linear notations differ however. When one looks at the associative nets, the visual format suggests that information about instances, like block-1, is clustered in a particular place. Any fact that mentions block-1 has an arrow going into or out of the block-1 node. So having found block-1 we will then have access to all of the information about it. This is an issue of *indexing*, and is obviously important. If some process in our program wants to know the color of block-1, it would seem silly to have to search all over creation to find the fact. Much more plausible is to have block-1 point to the information directly.

For those to whom indexing is an unfamiliar concept, the most familiar analogy would be with the indexing scheme in a library. Books are arranged according to a numbering system, like Dewey Decimal or Library of Congress. To find the book one wants, one consults the index (or catalogue), which indexes books by author, title, subject etc. Naturally, finding the book in the index does not immediately give you the book. Rather it gives you the number of the book, which makes getting the book comparatively easy. In computer terminology we speak of *addresses* (or *pointers*) rather than library numbers, but the idea is just the same.

Thus an indexing scheme gives us *pointers* from one node to another. For example, in order to state that block-2 is supported by block-1 we need a pointer from block-2 to block-1. However, pointers are one-directional. That block-2 has block-1's address does not ensure that block-1 has block-2's. But typically this will be needed as well, because otherwise we will have no way to efficiently retrieve the answer to the question "What does block-1 support?" What we need is a *back pointer* because it gives us the ability to follow the arrow in the backward direction.

Armed with our new terminology, we can restate the point we earlier made intuitively. Associative networks suggest a scheme of pointers and back pointers that would seem to make accessing information very easy. The linear notation does not seem to do this for us, at least not on the surface. On the surface the predicate calculus gives us a long list of formulas, and to find a particular fact, like the color of a block, could involve a rather long search. However, we can add an indexing scheme to the predicate calculus as well. There are many ways we can arrange such a scheme, and in Chapter 7 we will take a look at several alternatives. For the moment we can simply note that if the indexing scheme suggested by the associate networks seems useful, we could adopt that.

Thus the linear notation plus an appropriate indexing scheme gives us everything in the associative net formalism shown above. Indeed, it gives us more than the simple version of associative nets we have presented so far, because the latter has no capacity for representing logical connectives (e.g., if) or quantification. Work has been done to add these to the associative net formalism [Schubert76, Hendrix75] making the two notations equivalent in expressive power.

1.7.2 The Isa Hierarchy

Given that the two notations are equivalent, we have the option of using either in the course of this book. For the most part we will stick to the linear notation, as it is more concise, especially for formulas with quantification. However, very often it helps to be able to think of a set of facts in several different notations, since different notations tend to have different "associations" attached to them. (One way to tell a "pro" from an amateur in AI is how well the person can switch notations in the middle of a discussion.) Our earlier discussion of indexing was one such association.

Another key idea in AI that has sprung from the thinking of things as associative networks is the *isa hierarchy*. We can represent the idea that Clyde is an elephant in two ways, as shown in Figure 1.10. Although we have not stressed this point, the obvious reason why we want such statements is to enable us to deduce various facts about Clyde that we assume to be true because he is an elephant. Clyde is gray, has a trunk, etc. This ability is called the *inheritance of properties*. Looking at things as an associative network gives us Figure 1.11. In this particular case both **clyde** and **fred** inherit the properties of **elephant**.

But there is no reason to stop here. We know properties of elephants by virtue of the fact that they are higher animals. For example, they have heads, hearts, etc. And, in turn, higher animals have a lot in common with animals in general. Thus we would want **clyde** to inherit properties not only from

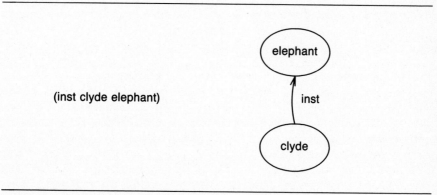

(inst clyde elephant)

Figure 1.10 Clyde's elephanthood as an associative net

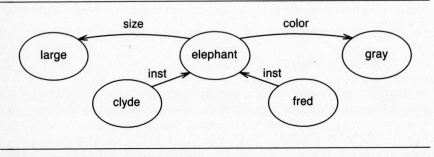

Figure 1.11 Inheritance of properties

elephant, but **higher-animal** and **animal** as well. This is usually portrayed as in Figure 1.12. There we used the predicate **isa** ("is a") to represent the relation between **elephant** and **higher-animal**. While **inst** says that a particular individual is a member of some class, **isa** says that one class is a more general version of another. Roughly speaking, the distinction is like that in set theory

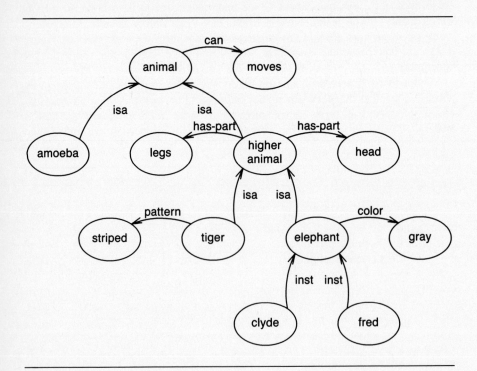

Figure 1.12 An isa hierarchy

between *element* and *subset*. As with inst, isa and its hierarchy will be with us throughout the book.

1.7.3 Slot-Assertion Notation

As we have already seen, in predicate calculus we indicate functional relations within a formula by the linear order of the arguments within the parentheses. For example, a catch-object formula distinguishes the "catcher" from the "caught" by the order of the arguments.

(catch-object jack-2 ball-5)

The order chosen is initially arbitrary. We could have, if we had wanted to, used the reverse order. But once we have decided on a convention we have to stick to it, or we will end up with a different (and bizarre) meaning.

Another notation found in AI uses a different method of indicating functional relations. We will call it the *slot-assertion notation*. In a slot-assertion notation the various arguments (or *slots*) of a predicate are expressed as separate assertions. A possible slot-assertion representation of the catch statement above would look like this:

(inst catch-22 catch-object)   *; There is an instance of catching.*
(catcher catch-22 jack-2)   *; Jack did the catching.*
(caught catch-22 ball-5)   *; He caught a certain ball.*

In this example we have given the two slots the names catcher, and caught.

The first thing we should note here is that this is still the predicate calculus. We still have predicates and arguments, and the normal syntax of the predicate calculus still applies. However, we are using the predicates in a slightly different way. We have created names for the different slots, and made these into predicates, e.g., caught. Also, we have created a new object, catch-22, that is intended to denote a particular act of catching. Having this object allows us to refer to this action in a way we could not do with our original version:

(catch-object jack-2 ball-5)

So to some degree these two notations are not precisely equivalent. Nevertheless, they are both the predicate calculus.

As we have expressed it, the names catcher and caught are arbitrary, serving, as far as the formalism is concerned, simply to distinguish the two. Of course, we have used names that have meaning to people, so that it will be easy for the reader to remember which argument is which. But you should keep in mind that these do not have meaning to the computer. In Chapter 4 we will consider representations in which the names we use are not arbitrary, but rather are intended to have meaning in themselves, thus contributing to the overall meaning of the formula.

1.7.4 Frame Notation

As a final example of a new garb for predicate calculus, we will look at *frame* or *slot-and-filler notation*. This notation is much like our slot-assertion notation, since it too uses named slots, but now rather than creating separate assertions, we combine them into one larger statement. In this notation, rather than this:

```
(catch-object catch-22)
(catcher catch-22 jack-2)
(caught catch-22 ball-5)
```

we write this:

```
(catch-object    catch-22
                 (catcher jack-2)
                 (caught ball-5))
```

The correspondences should be clear.

As with the earlier example of associative nets, while this can be viewed as an alternative notation for the predicate calculus, it too suggests a different implementation. Now, rather than creating several independent assertions, we instead create one structure (often called a *frame*) that includes all of the information. This implementation is frequently handy when we do not intend to add new pieces of information to the structure often, or when we always want to access all of the information associated with a particular concept. This is often true in vision programs, and this notation will be used in Chapter 3 frequently. Slot and filler notation also suggests an indexing scheme somewhat like that of associative networks, but without the back pointers.

1.8 References and Further Reading

Throughout the book we will be pointing the reader to places where he or she can get further information on the topics discussed. The major topic of this chapter is logic, so we will simply mention that there are innumerable textbooks on the subject. One of the standard texts is Mendelson's *Introduction to Mathematical Logic* [Mendelson64]. While this is an "introduction," it presumes a fair amount of mathematical sophistication. In particular, the logic we covered in this chapter takes only a page or two. For a more leisurely treatment, see [Suppes57].

For more on the history of AI, probably the best book is that by McCorduck [McCorduck79].

We will also take this opportunity to give some general pointers to books and articles on AI. There are any number of textbooks on AI. Comparing them should give the reader an idea of how unsettled the field is. There are several texts that are less formal than this one, ranging from Boden's [Boden77] (the least formal) to Winston's [Winston84] to that by Rich [Rich83]. For a more formal treatment than is given in this book, the reader might take a look at the text by Nilsson [Nilsson80].

After you have finished this book (and perhaps a more advanced text on a particular topic), if you still want to know more, it will be time to consult the research literature. There are three major journals that publish articles on general AI, *Artificial Intelligence*, *Cognitive Science*, and the *IEEE Transactions on Pattern Analysis and Machine Intelligence*. There are also several journals on subspecialties: *Computational Linguistics*, *Computer Graphics and Image Processing*, *IEEE Transactions on Systems, Man, and Cybernetics*, and *International Journal of Robotics Research*.

There are two major conferences in the field that publish proceedings. They are the *International Joint Conference on Artificial Intelligence* (also known as the Ijcai) and the *National Conference on Artificial Intelligence* (also known as the AAAI because it is run by the *American Association for Artificial Intelligence*). The AAAI also publishes a magazine, *The AI Magazine*. There is also a European Association for Artificial Intelligence (which is older than the American version) that publishes a newsletter, the *AISB Quarterly*. (AISB stands for Artificial Intelligence and the Simulation of Behaviour.) The Association for Computing Machinery (the *ACM*) has a special interest group (Sig) in artificial intelligence, *Sigart*, that also publishes a newsletter. In Canada, the main AI organization is the *Canadian Society for Computational Studies of Intelligence* which sponsors a conference every two years.

Exercises

1.1 For each of the following formulas, state if it is true, false, or cannot be determined based only on the axioms in Figure 1.13.

   a) (not (is-sane Alex))
   b) (is-genius Clyde)
   c) (is-genius Alex)
   d) (is-genius Gerry)
   e) (female Clyde)
   f) (forall (x) (if (not (is-sane x)) (inst x AI-course-instructor)))
   g) (forall (x) (if (inst x AI-course-instructor) (not (is-sane x))))

1.2 Represent the information in Figure 1.14 in an associative network notation.

1.3 This exercise links up with several exercises in Chapter 2 to create a simple deduction program. The raw data for this program is given in Figure 1.14. Using this knowledge we would like to be able to infer new facts, while not inferring anything silly. Some examples of the behavior we are interested in are given in Figure 1.15. The nils in Figure 1.15 indicate that

```
(forall (x)
  (if (is-sane x)
    (not (inst x AI-course-instructor)))))    ; Anyone sane does not
                                              ; teach an AI course.
(inst Alex AI-course-instructor)              ; Alex is an AI instructor,

(inst Gerry AI-course-instructor)             ; as is Gerry.

(not (inst Clyde AI-course-instructor)        ; Clyde is not.

(inst Clyde circus-elephant)                  ; Clyde is a circus
                                              ; elephant.
(forall (x) (if (is-genius x)                 ; Every genius is
            (inst x circus-elephant)))        ; a circus elephant.

(not (exists (y)                              ; Nothing is both
        (and (male y)                         ; male and a circus
            (inst y circus-elephant)))))      ; elephant.

(male Alex)                                   ; Alex is a male.

(forall (x) (if (not (male x))                ; Anything not male
            (female x)))                      ; is female.
```

Figure 1.13 Axioms for Exercise 1.1

```
(isa circus-elephant elephant)    ; Circus elephants are elephants.
(has-part elephant head)          ; Elephants have heads
(has-part elephant trunk)         ; and trunks.
(has-part head mouth)             ; Heads have mouths.
(isa elephant animal)             ; Elephants are animals.
(has-part animal heart)           ; Animals have hearts.
(isa circus-elephant performer)   ; Circus elephants are performers.
(has-part performer costume)      ; Performers have costumes.
(isa costume clothes)             ; Costumes are clothes.
```

Figure 1.14 Knowledge for an inference program

we may not infer that the formula is true, but neither could we prove that it is false. Some facts that would allow us to make some of these deductions are also given in Figure 1.15.

a) As we did in Figure 1.15, give one or more predicate calculus facts that would enable us to infer the facts about isa given in Figure 1.15.

b) The two facts in Figure 1.15 are not sufficient for making all of the has-part inferences shown there. Identify the inference that will not be made, and add a general rule that will allow us to infer this class of fact.

```
                        (isa circus-elephant animal)          →    t
                        (isa circus-elephant clown)           →    nil
                        (has-part circus-elephant trunk)      →    t
                        (has-part circus-elephant mouth)      →    t
                        (has-part circus-elephant leg)        →    nil
                        (has-part elephant costume)           →    nil
                        (has-part circus-elephant clothes)    →    t
         (forall (x y z) (if (and (has-part x y)   ; If x has a part y, and
                             (has-part y z)) ; y has a part z,
                    (has-part x z)))        ; then x has a part z.

         (forall (x y z) (if (and (isa x y)        ; If all x's are y's and
                             (has-part y z)) ; y's have a part z,
                    (has-part x z)))        ; then x's have a part z.
```

Figure 1.15 Rules for the elephant world

2

Naturally, if you intend to do the Lisp programming exercises scattered throughout this book, this chapter is indispensable. But even if you intend to do no Lisp programming, it would be a good idea to look this chapter over. We have tried to make the rest of the book independent of Lisp, but ideas from Lisp pervade many parts of AI.

Lisp

2.1 Why Lisp?

In the study of Artificial Intelligence the reason for learning Lisp is roughly that for learning French if you were going to France — it's the native language. There are occasional programs in AI written in languages other than Lisp, but if one were to take, say, the 100 best-known programs in the field, probably 95 would be in Lisp, and of the remaining five, four were written before Lisp was available on most computers. (The last might have been written in Prolog, a recent competitor to Lisp, which we talk about briefly in Chapter 6.)

However, this reason for learning Lisp really only pushes the question back one level. Why is it that everyone uses Lisp, as opposed to, say, Pascal, or, heaven forbid, Fortran? This is hard to explain until one has had more experience with both AI and Lisp, but roughly speaking we can distinguish two basic reasons. First, Lisp is much more flexible than most languages. Users have such total control over what goes on that if they do not like the syntax of the language, they may change it to suit themselves. Suppose that you do not like the method for defining programs in, say, Fortran, can you do anything about it? Short of switching to another language the answer is clearly no. Indeed, the very idea seems absurd. But not to Lisp users.

The second reason for choosing Lisp is the way in which Lisp is oriented toward the manipulation of symbols as opposed to, say, numbers. Lisp gives us automatic facilities for associating information with symbols. For example, we might associate with "canary" the fact that its color is yellow. Also, Lisp has facilities for easily constructing new data structures and, should these data structures outlive their usefulness, taking them apart again and using the storage space for something else. All of this is without the programmer needing to think very much about what is going on. This reclamation facility is called *garbage collection*.

2.2 Lisps

One troublesome aspect of Lisp, at least to a textbook writer, is its lack of standardization. There is no document or committee that can tell you, officially, what is and what is not Lisp. This has some advantages. The freedom to experiment has kept Lisp young at heart. But the large number of dialects means that whatever we teach in all probability will not correspond to the Lisp you will be using on your computer.

The Lisp we use here corresponds most closely to *Franz Lisp*, a common subdialect of *Maclisp*. However, we have felt free to smooth over a few of Lisp's idiosyncrasies. Where we do, we will note the fact, and in general we will try to indicate the places where Lisps are most likely to differ from one another. However, before using any function in the definition of a larger function, it is a good idea to try it out first by itself. Fortunately, the interactive nature of Lisp makes this easy.

2.3 Typing at Lisp

The first thing to understand about Lisp is that it is primarily an *interpreted language* (as opposed to a compiled language). Technically this means that rather than first translating everything you write into machine language, and then running your program, Lisp looks at what you have written line by line, figures out what you have requested, and then does it. (It is possible to compile Lisp, but this is a more advanced topic and will not be covered in this book.)

From a more personal point of view, however, the difference between Lisp and most languages is that Lisp provides not just a language, but rather an *environment*, and to use Lisp you must enter this environment. (In this respect it is like APL.) Indeed, the relation between Lisp and the Lisp environment is so close that from now on, rather than saying "enter the Lisp environment" we will simply say, "enter Lisp."

Assuming you have already logged in, to enter Lisp on most machines you simply type this:

   lisp < cr >

The < cr > here stands for "carriage return" and simply means that you should type carriage return at the end of the line. From now on we will not bother to indicate this explicitly. Once you are in Lisp whatever you type will be processed by Lisp. In particular, Lisp will read whatever you type, *evaluate* it, print out the results, and then wait for you to type something else. This is called the *read-eval-print loop*. Reading and printing are about what you would expect, so getting familiar with Lisp really amounts to learning what Lisp does when it evaluates something. To start with a really simple case, numbers evaluate to themselves. That is, the value of 5 is 5. So, when you enter Lisp, Lisp will initially be waiting for you to type something. It will indicate this with a *prompt*, which typically differs from Lisp to Lisp, and in some Lisps can be changed by the user. We will use -> as our prompt. After Lisp has read, evaluated, and printed out its response, it will give you another prompt to indicate that it is ready to do something else.

Eventually you will want to stop. Again, how this is done will vary depending on the Lisp you are using. For our Lisp we type (exit). Franz Lisp uses lowercase for all predefined functions, some other Lisps use uppercase, or allow both. A very simple session with Lisp would go as follows (anything following a ";" up to the next carriage return is a comment and is ignored by Lisp. We will use this to give asides to the reader as well as to comment our programs):

```
lisp
-> 5                    ; We ask Lisp to evaluate 5.
5                       ; It does so and prints out the value.
-> 106
106
-> -33
-33
-> 2.71
2.71
-> (exit)
```

This isn't very exciting, so let us now describe the ability to ask Lisp to perform arithmetic. To call a function in Lisp we enclose the name of the function and its arguments inside parentheses. So, to add 3 and 4 together we call the function + with the arguments 3 and 4.

```
-> (+ 3 4)
7
```

In general, the syntax of the + instruction is this:

(+ *-nums-*)

Here the *-nums-* indicates that + may take any number of arguments, each of which is a number. If + took exactly two arguments we would have written the following:

(+ *num1 num2*)

The spacing here is not too critical. That is, one could put spaces between the left parenthesis and the + and everything would still be fine. Or again, one could have put more spaces between the arguments, or between the final argument and the right parenthesis. For that matter, we could have put in extra lines, since Lisp would treat them like extra spaces. However, normal Lisp style is to do exactly what we did above — put no spaces between the left parenthesis and the name of the function, one space between each pair of arguments, and no spaces between the final argument and the right parenthesis. Neither function names nor arguments may contain embedded blanks.

Here are some other Lisp arithmetic functions:

```
(* -nums-)       ; num1*num2* · · ·
(- -nums-)       ; num1-num2- · · ·
(/ -nums-)       ; num1 / (num2*num3* · · · )
```

As examples of the results one can expect from these functions we would have:

```
-> (+ 2.3 3.7 1)
7.0
-> (* 2 3 -1)
-6
-> (/ 12 3 2)
2
```

You should check these functions to see if your Lisp uses the same names. Arithmetic is comparatively unimportant in Lisp because most of the things one wants to do are concerned with the manipulation of symbols, not numbers. Hence the naming of arithmetic functions is particularly uncoordinated in Lisp. In many cases English versions of the symbols are used instead, e.g., plus. In other cases (e.g., Franz Lisp), both versions are available, but only the spelled out versions work for floating-point numbers.

When Lisp evaluates a function, such as the ones above, it first evaluates all of the arguments. In the cases we have seen so far, all of the arguments have been numbers, and hence evaluated to themselves. However, we may, if we like, embed a call to one function within a call to a second. In this case the embedded function call will be evaluated first, and the results used by the outer function call. So, if we wanted to compute (81 + 12) / 3, we could write this:

```
-> (/ (+ 81 12) 3)
31
```

Here Lisp is obeying a simple rule. If it sees a left parenthesis, it assumes that you are giving it a function, and it proceeds to interpret what follows as a function with arguments until it sees a balancing right parenthesis. So, when it sees the (+ 81 12) it interprets it as a second function call inside the first, and proceeds to evaluate 81 and 12, the arguments of this second function. Once it has done this, it calls the + routine on the answers, and + returns the answer 93. This, in turn, is passed on as the first argument to /, etc. There is no theoretical limit on how far you may continue such embedding, although any real computer will eventually run out of space.

Like most of us, you will make mistakes from time to time. As computer languages go, Lisp is quite tolerant of mistakes and offers numerous facilities for finding out what went wrong, and correcting it. Here is a simple example in which we type "__" (underscore) instead of "−" (minus).

```
-> (* 2 (__ 15 8))
Error: eval: Undefined function __      ; Lisp complains about "__"
<1>: (return '-)                        ; You have a chance to correct
14                                      ; yourself, at which point Lisp
->                                      ; will finish the computation.
```

When Lisp comes across the underscore it complains that it is an undefined function. It then leaves you off in a *break loop*. A break loop is just a read-eval-print loop but one that occurs in the middle of a previous computation. There are various facilities for looking around to see what went wrong, but in the case at hand the error is simple enough. Note that the prompt for input has changed to <1>:, from its normal ->. This is to remind you that you are in a break loop, and not in the *top-level read-eval-print loop*. (This is the read-eval-print loop that greeted you when you first got into Lisp.) If you make a mistake while typing in the break loop, you will be put into a second break loop, whose prompt will be <2>:.

To get out of the break loop you can do one of several things. Calling exit will, as before, get you out of Lisp. Typically, however, this is done only for quite serious errors. Alternatively, the function reset will return you to the top-level read-eval-print loop. The function return when given with no argument is like reset in that it aborts the computation it was doing, but it returns you to the next highest-level break loop. Thus if you were at a second-level break, (return) would bring you back to the first-level break loop — not the top level. Last, the function return *with an argument* will tell Lisp to continue the computation, but to substitute for the offending object (in our example the underscore) the argument to return. (Again, this is an area that varies from Lisp to Lisp; find out how your Lisp works.) Note that we actually put a single quotation mark prior to the minus sign. This is important, and it must be there. Its significance will be explained later.

Another useful thing to know is the *break character* that will interrupt Lisp, in case you give Lisp a program that goes into an infinite loop. This differs from Lisp system to Lisp system. On ours it is the "delete" key, but as likely as not it will be different on yours.

2.4 Defining Programs

In Lisp, all programs are functions. That is, all programs expect that you will be giving them zero or more arguments, and they will return exactly one value. Sometimes, of course, this value may not be of much interest, the *side effects* of evaluation being of primary interest, but for the sake of uniformity, it will be there. So to write a program we must define a function. You can do this while in Lisp. For example, to define the function square you would write:

```
-> (defun square (num) (* num num))
square
```

Here defun tells Lisp that you are about to define a function. Note that defun is a function, pretty much like other functions. Its value is the name of the defined function. Its syntax is this:

(defun *"fn-name"* (-*"args"*-) -*"exps"*-)

The quotation marks around the argument names here indicate that the argument will be taken "as is." That is, the arguments to defun will *not* be evaluated. So defun is first given the name of the function you are defining (in this case square), followed by zero or more variables, which will be bound to the arguments of the function (here the only variable is num). These variables are the *formal parameters* of the function. (We will also refer to them as *local variables*, although this is a more general term.) They form a *list*, which in Lisp is a sequence of zero or more Lisp objects preceded by a left parenthesis and ending with a right parenthesis. Such variables are said to be *defined* or *declared* inside the function. Following the formal parameters come one or more expressions which will be evaluated when we call the function (in square there is only one such expression, namely the call to *). If we had wanted a function with no arguments we would replace the list of arguments by the *empty list*.

(defun no-argument-function () . . .)

In Lisp the empty list is a very common construct, and has a special name, nil. It can be written as either nil or as (). Lisp will normally print nil, but you can use either.

The value of a function which you define is always the value of the last of the expressions within the definition. Because our function square has only one such expression, its value is the value of that expression.

Once we have defined square, we use it just like any other function.

-> (square 9)
81

There is no difference in the way you call a built-in function, such as +, and the way you call a function which you yourself have created.

When we call square, the value of its argument, in this case 9, gets assigned to the local variable, in this case num. While Lisp is within a function, all of its formal parameters will continue to have their initial values, unless we explicitly change them. Furthermore even if num had a value outside of square, this would have no effect on the function, and the variable would be given back its old value when the function is finished.

While you can, if you like, write all of your functions while in Lisp, in many Lisps the function definition will go away as soon as you leave the Lisp environment. Hence if you want to keep your creations around, write your function definitions in a file. To use these functions when you are in Lisp, you must tell Lisp to read the file. Lisp then treats what you have written in the file as if you had typed it at Lisp directly, and hence your functions will be defined. Again, the function to read a file into Lisp will have different names in different Lisps. In ours it is load, as in (load *filename*).

2.5 Basic Flow of Control in Lisp

So far our functions have not had any branching or loops. Obviously we are going to need both of these abilities. To illustrate looping, we have here the function **add-nums**, which takes a number and adds together it plus all of the numbers smaller than it (down to zero). So if given 5, it will produce $5+4+3+2+1$ ($=15$).

```
(defun add-nums (num)
    (loop (initial (sum 0))            ; sum ← 0
          (while (> num 0))            ; loop while num > 0
          (do (setq sum (+ sum num)))) ;   sum ← sum + num
          (next (num (- num 1)))       ;   num ← num - 1
          (result sum)))               ; return sum
```

As before we define our function with **defun**, which is followed by the function name and a single argument. After that, things get more complex. We have introduced here the basic looping function we will use in this book, **loop**. Unfortunately, **loop** is not standard, so again it will be necessary to determine what looping capabilities your Lisp provides (we will be getting to the standard parts of Lisp soon). Basically, **loop** takes any number of lists, each one of which will start with one of the following key words: **initial**, **while**, **until**, **next**, **do**, and **result**. All sections are optional, and except for **initial** and **result**, all may appear any number of times. The **initial** section defines (or declares) local variables. As with the formal parameters to functions, these variables are defined only within the loop and, in general, will not have values outside of it. (If they do have a value outside of the loop, this value will be saved, and the variable will get it back when the loop has finished.) The **initial** section also gives variables their initial values. The form of the **initial** section is this:

(initial ("var_1" val_1) $\cdots$ ("var_n" val_n))

In the example above, the variable **sum** is given an initial value of **0**.

In a similar way, the **result** section is performed only when Lisp is about to break out of the loop. It specifies the value to be returned by **loop**.

(result *expression*)

In our example, the value of the loop is specified by

(result sum)

which simply says to return the value of **sum** as the value of the loop. Note that since our **add-nums** function only has one expression to evaluate (the **loop** function itself), whatever value the loop returns will also be the value of **add-nums**.

All of the other sections may appear any number of times, and will be performed once each time through the loop, in the order they are presented within **loop**. The **while** and **until** sections take one argument, that is expected to return a value of true or false.

(while *expression*)
(until *expression*)

So, in an until section, the loop will be broken if the argument returns "true." In a while section the convention is the opposite. Again, in **add-nums** we have one while section that looks like this:

(while (> num 0))

Here the expression within the while is a call to the Lisp function >.

(> *num1 num2*)

This function tests whether its first argument is greater than its second. If it is, it returns t, which is the Lisp symbol representing "true" (and which, like numbers, evaluates to itself). If the test is false, > returns nil which, besides being the empty list, also is Lisp's symbol for false. Thus in our **add-nums** loop, once the value of num becomes less than 1, the loop is broken.

The do section of the loop specifies the "body" of the loop. It consists of one or more expressions to be evaluated. In the case at hand we have this:

(do (setq sum (+ sum num)))

Here we have introduced a new function, **setq**.

(setq *"atom" expression*)

Here *atom* is the name of a variable (it is not evaluated) and the variable is set to the value of *expression*. In **add-nums** the expression is (+ sum num) and its value will be the sum of the two numbers. The effect will be to reset the value of sum to this new value.

Last, the next section of the loop specifies how to update the loop variables for the next iteration. We will usually place it at either the beginning or end of the loop, but it may appear anywhere, and the updating will take place at the point in the loop where it is specified. So, if it appears before, say, a while section, the while will get the new values, and not the old (assuming it looks at the loop variables at all). The syntax of next is this:

(next ("*var*$_1$" *val*$_1$) · · · ("*var*$_n$" *val*$_n$))

Let us look again at our function **add-nums**.

```
(defun add-nums (num)
        (loop (initial (sum 0))              ; sum ← 0
              (while (> num 0))              ; loop while num > 0
              (do (setq sum (+ sum num)))  ;    sum ← sum + num
              (next (num (− num 1)))        ;    num ← num − 1
              (result sum)))                 ; return sum
```

If we called the function with the argument 2, Lisp would behave as follows. First num would be set to 2, as part of calling **add-nums**. Then the loop would be evaluated. This would first cause the new variable sum to be defined, and initialized with the value 0. Next num would be checked to see if it is greater than 0. It is, so the loop continues, and sum will be set to the sum of it and num, giving 2. The next section of the loop will reset num to 1, and the loop will repeat. Again num will be checked against 0; it is still larger, so sum will be reset to (+ sum num) which will give us 3. Then num will be set to 0 for the next time around the loop. This time it will not be greater than 0, so the loop breaks and the loop function will return the value specified by the result section, which is sum, i.e., 3. Since the loop function is the last (and only) expression inside add-nums, its value will be the value of the entire function. Assuming that add-nums was called from the top level, the value of add-nums, 3, would be printed out as a response.

The values of none of the the functions called within add-nums will have their values printed out. People new to Lisp initially play around with simple functions at the top level, and get used to having their values printed out. They are then confused about what will happen when these functions appear within larger ones. Their values will not be printed out (unless you do something special to change that) since the reason they are printed out at the top level is *because* they are at the top level. This will not be the case when they are within a function.

One final point about our function add-nums. The formal parameter num is changed by setq in the course of executing add-nums. It is important to note that this has no effect on any variables outside add-nums, as shown by:

```
-> (setq v1 5)
5
-> (add-nums v1)
15
-> v1
5
```

The variable v1 in the example above was not changed by add-nums. In some programming languages v1 would be changed in such circumstances, but this does not happen in Lisp.

The other major flow-of-control function we need to look at is cond — Lisp's equivalent to the if-then-else statements of other languages. The prototypic use of cond looks like this:

```
(cond (test₁ action₁)
      (test₂ action₂)
      . . .
      (testₙ actionₙ))
```

Each test is evaluated until one of them is true. Then the action associated with that test is performed, and the value of the cond will be the value of the action performed. Once one of the tests has been found true, and the action performed, no further test (or action) within the cond will be tried. If none of the tests are true, the value of the cond will be nil. As an example, the following is a home-grown version of the absolute-value function.

```
(defun abs-val (x)              ; Return the absolute value of x.
    (cond ((< x 0) (* x −1))    ; Multiplying by −1 gives the
          (t x)))               ; absolute value of a neg num.
```

In the first test/action pair (or *cond clause*), x is compared to 0. If it is less, then the second element of the pair multiples it by −1 to get the positive version. This will be the value of the cond. If x is not less than 0 then Lisp will continue on to the second cond clause. Here the "test" is the symbol t. As already mentioned, t evaluates to itself, so this test comes out true, and the cond will return x (which at this point must be positive).

Actually, the format of cond is somewhat looser than we have described. Cond pairs need not have any action at all following the test, and there may be more than one such action. In either case, the value of the last expression of the cond clause whose test evaluates to true will be the value of the cond. Furthermore, there is really no distinction between tests and other Lisp functions. A test (or *predicate*) is any Lisp function which returns true or false. False, as we have noted, is simply nil. However, true is not simply t in Lisp, but rather *anything other than* nil. Here is a version of abs-val which takes advantage of this fact.

```
(defun abs-val (x)              ; Return the absolute value of x.
    (cond ((< x 0) (* x −1))    ; Multiplying by −1 gives the
          (x)))                 ; absolute value of a neg num.
```

Here, the second possibility within the cond says, in effect, just return the value of x. Thus the actual definition of cond is this:

```
(cond (test -actions-)
      . . .
      (test -actions-))
```

To give you another example of what a Lisp function looks like, in-order takes three numbers, and returns t if first is greater than second which in turn is greater than third. Otherwise it returns nil.

```
(defun in-order (first second third)
    (cond ((> first second) (> second third))))
```

If first is not greater than second, then the cond will have none of its tests succeed, so it will return nil and hence in-order will return nil. If first is greater than second, then the cond will return the value of

```
(> second third)
```

and hence we will only return t if *first* > *second* > *third*.

2.6 Lisp Style

As you probably noticed when we wrote add-nums, Lisp is much easier to read if we indent the code to reflect the level of nesting of parentheses. You should do this too when you write Lisp code. The following is a general rule for indentation. If you want to know where to indent to on line *n*, look at line *n-1*. Find the left parenthesis which matches the outermost right parenthesis on line *n-1*. Suppose it appears in column *c*. If you are in no danger of running off the right hand side of the page due to excess indentation, the best place to start line *n* is in column *c*. If you are afraid of getting squeezed, then start to the left of *c*, provided that you do not start at the same place or to the left of any currently open parenthesis.

What this boils down to in the typical cases is this:

```
(  (              )         ; previous line
   X                        ; place to start if you have lots of room
X                           ; the farthest left you may properly start
```

There are, however, some exceptions to this rule, the most prominent being the arguments to **defun**. If we followed this rule for **defun** as well we would get this:

```
(defun add-nums (num)
                 (loop (initial (sum 0))
                       (while (> num 0))
                       . . .))
```

Usually this places the code too far to the right, so the standard format lines the body of the function directly under the name. With this exception, however, the rule works quite well for anything you are currently doing.

As with all programming languages, there will always be many ways in Lisp of accomplishing a given task, so the exact way in which a function is expressed will differ from person to person. The sum of these decisions defines one's programming style. Most of the rules for deciding between alternatives in Lisp are equally applicable to other programming languages.

- Try to make your program reasonably efficient.
- Try to make your code reflect the way you think about the problem (even if this leads to minor inefficiencies).
- Include extensive comments in your code. (Strictly speaking this is not a stylistic matter, but it is so important that we could not leave it out.)

There are, however, other rules of Lisp style that are peculiar to Lisp. For example, the following would be a commonplace in many languages:

```
d := a + b          ; We assume that a, b, and c are
e := a + c          ; input variables to the function.
d := d * e
return d
```

Lisp tends to stress functional embedding instead, so that this example would usually be written as follows:

```
(* (+ a b) (+ a c))
```

Because of this, the need for extra temporary variables tends to be less in Lisp than other languages. However, there are occasions when you need a temporary variable to store an intermediate result.

```
d := a / b
e := c * d
d := d + e
return d
```

Here we need to store the results of the a / b computation in a temporary variable. The standard way to get a temporary variable in Lisp is with the function let.

```
(let (("variable" value) . . . ("variable" value))
    -expressions-)
```

Each variable is given a *value* as its initial value. (If no value is given, the default is nil, and no parentheses are needed around the variable.) After the variables are bound, each *expression* is evaluated. Within the body of the let each *variable* will have the value given to it in the declaration, or by a previous setq within the let. As before, variables defined outside the let with the same names will not be affected by what happens inside the let. The value of the let will be the value of the last *expression*. Using let we can create a literal translation of the computation above.

```
(let (d e)                  ; Variables d and e are declared
    (setq d (/ a b))        ; with nil default values.
    (setq e (* c d))        ;
    (setq d (+ d e)))       ; The final value will be d.
```

It is possible to shorten this by using the feature of giving initial values to variables.

```
(let ((d (/ a b)) e)        ; d is given the value (/ a b).
    (setq e (* c d))        ; e is given a default value of nil.
    (setq d (+ d e)))
```

Furthermore, by combining this with functional embedding we get this:

```
(let ((d (/ a b)))          ; d is given the value (/ a b).
    (+ d (* c d))))         ; The final value will be this sum.
```

The judicious use of let and functional embedding can remove the need for most instances of setq. Doing this is considered the mark of an expert Lisp programmer.

2.7 Atoms and Lists

So far we have used examples in which all of the processing has been done on numbers. Lisp is normally not the language of choice for numerical processing, but numbers have a property that makes them convenient in an introduction to

Lisp — they evaluate to themselves. That is, if we type a number at the top-level read-eval-print loop, we get that same number back.

Now let us move on to consider the use of Lisp for symbolic processing — Lisp's forte. For example, suppose we have a variable, sentence, and we want to set this variable to the symbol hello.

    -> (setq sentence hello)   ; *The exact wording of the error*
    Unbound Variable: hello   ; *message will vary between Lisps.*

Unfortunately this did not work. The reason for this is easy to see. The function setq evaluates its second argument. So before, we had this:

    (setq sum (+ sum num))

The second argument to setq is evaluated to get the sum. If Lisp is given a single symbol to evaluate, it is assumed to be a variable, and Lisp tries to find the value of the variable. In the case at hand, a variable hello was never defined, and thus has no value.

We need some way to tell Lisp that we do not want the value of hello, but rather the symbol itself. The way we do this is with the function quote.

    (quote *"anything"*)

The argument to quote is *not* evaluated. Rather, it simply takes it "as is." The value of quote is simply whatever appears in place of the *anything* in the above definition. Hence this is what we should have written at the start of this section in order to set the value of sentence to hello.

    (setq sentence (quote hello))

As you might imagine, quote is a rather frequently used function. As such, it is a bother to keep writing (quote . . .) every time we want to quote something. To reduce the amount of typing, all Lisps have an abbreviation for the function quote, which is normally the single quotation mark.

    (setq sentence 'hello)

We will use this reduced version throughout the book. (This is also why, in Section 2.3, we had (return '-).)

Things like hello are called *atoms* in Lisp. Atoms are either numbers, or *symbols*. A symbol is a string of letters and numbers which starts with a letter and which has no blank spaces. For example, all Lisp function names, like cond, are symbols (and hence atoms). In general, symbols evaluate to the last value they were given, either by setq, or by being bound when Lisp enters a function.

We can group atoms together into *lists* by putting parentheses around them. So, for example (A B) is a list consisting of two atoms. We will speak of each item in a list as an *element* or *member* of the list.

In fact, we have been dealing with lists all along, since (+ sum num) is a list of three atoms. That it also happens to be an expression in the programming language Lisp is of no concern to Lisp, because Lisp programs can be manipulated as data.

Lists may have other lists as elements.

((a b) c (d e f))

This is a list of three elements, the first of which is itself a list of two elements. The phrases *list structure* and *S-expression* (for "symbolic expression") are used to cover symbols, numbers, and the lists built out of them (although later we will redefine them to have slightly different meanings).

We have already mentioned the empty list, (), or nil. The symbol nil is unique in that it is both an atom and a list. You should keep in mind the importance of parentheses to Lisp. () and (()) are not the same thing. The first is the null or empty list, but the second is not an empty list. It is rather a list of one element, which happens to be the empty list. Similarly, ((())) differs from both of the above.

Now that we have lists, we need to be able to take them apart and put them together again. We will start off by taking them apart. Given a list we can look at its elements with the functions car and cdr.

(car *list*)
(cdr *list*)

Car returns as its value the first element of *list* while cdr returns a list with everything but the first element, or the rest of *list*.

```
-> (setq lst1 '(a (b c) ( (d e) ) (f)))      ; Giving lst1 a value
(a (b c) ((d e)) (f))                         ;
-> (car lst1)                                 ; car returns the first
a                                             ; member of the list.
-> (cdr lst1)                                 ; cdr returns the rest
((b c) ((d e)) (f))                           ; of the list.
-> lst1                                       ; car and cdr have not
(a (b c) ((d e)) (f))                         ; changed the value of
-> (setq lst2 (cdr (car (cdr lst1))))         ; lst1.
(c)                                           ;
-> lst2                                       ;
(c)                                           ; the cdr of a one-element
-> (cdr lst2)                                 ; list produces the empty
nil                                           ; list.
```

There are several things to note here. First, the functions car and cdr do not change the list they are looking at. Rather, they return as their values part of that list (the first element, or everything but the first element) without changing the list at all. Second, the last example shows that if we take the cdr of a list with one element we get the rest of the list, which is a list with no elements, or nil.

As an example of how we use car and cdr, the following program returns t if its single argument is a list of consecutive numbers, and nil otherwise. We assume that the input is a list with at least one element.

```
(defun consec (lst)
    (loop (while (cdr lst))                ; Until the last element
          (while (equal (+ (car lst) 1)    ; make sure the second
                        (car (cdr lst))))) ; element = first + 1.
          (next (lst (cdr lst)))           ; Work through the list.
          (result (null (cdr lst)))))))    ; If we got to the end,
                                           ; return t, else nil.
```

We have introduced two new functions here, equal and null.

(equal *exp1 exp2*)

(null *exp*)

The predicate equal returns t if the value of *exp1* is equal to the value of *exp2*, while null returns t if its argument is nil.

The functions car and cdr should not be applied to atoms, only to lists. (Which is not to say that you will necessarily get an error if you do use them on atoms. However the result will differ widely from Lisp to Lisp.) An exception is nil, whose car and cdr are both nil in most Lisps.

One can often be forced to write long strings of embedded cars and cdrs. To save typing, Lisp allows these to be abbreviated. Here is an example and its abbreviation:

(car (cdr (car lst1)))
(cadar lst1)

The general rule is that the first letter is a "c," the last is an "r," and between there are "a"s and "d"s. (Some Lisps limit the number of letters in between the c and the r, typically to four.)

Needless to say, the names car and cdr are not very mnemonic. Box 2.1 on the history of Lisp shows the historical reasons why they have the names they do, but since the historical reasons deal with the architecture of a machine which very few people these days have ever seen, they will not serve very well as a memory aid. Rather you will just have to memorize the two names. (Nor, we should add, is there much hope of changing the names to something more reasonable. These names have become so well established that for many Lisp users they have even become part of normal English vocabulary. For example, since cdr can be used to look at successive portions of a list, some Lisp users talk of a function "cdring" down a list. Needless to say, some care should be exercised in the use of such "words" around the uninitiated.)

Box 2.1

The History of Lisp

Those who have read the earlier box "AI to the Dartmouth Conference" have already encountered John McCarthy as the man who coined the term "artificial intelligence" and the organizer of the Dartmouth conference on the subject. He is also well known as the creator of Lisp.

His interest in such a language arose during the Dartmouth conference. The earliest list-processing language, IPL, had been developed by
Newell and Simon for their Logic Theorist. This had already demonstrated the benefits of list processing for AI, and McCarthy set out to
design a better list processing language. He intended to model it on the
then newly developed Fortran, and his target machine was the IBM 704, a
machine that he had available to him. An instruction on this machine consisted of four sections. Two large ones were used to store memory
addresses. (Those of you who have had an assembly language course will
remember that pointers are really just memory addresses.) These fields
were called the *address* and *decrement* and one could get the contents of
an address stored in them by moving the address stored in them to an
index register. There were also two three-bit sections, called the *prefix*
and *tag*, so in the first design, there were four commands for retrieving
the contents of the memory locations pointed to by these sections, cpr (for
"contents of the prefix part of the register number"), ctr, car, and cdr.
Eventually the first two of these were dropped from the language, leaving
the car and cdr we are blessed with today.

During this time McCarthy was writing a differentiation program,
not because he wanted one, but rather to get a feel for what features were
needed in his yet-to-be-implemented language. He and his students also
wrote the read and print routines for Lisp, but put off tackling the hard
part, a compiler for the language. In the meantime, the language became
so mathematically elegant that McCarthy wrote a paper [McCarthy60]
showing how it could be used to express computations in automata theory,
rather than the more traditional *Turing machine* (a theoretical machine
developed for mathematical purposes by another early AI advocate, Alan
Turing). In his paper extolling the virtues of Lisp for mathematical uses,
he showed that one could write a *universal function* in Lisp that could
interpret any Lisp function. This was necessary if he wanted to convince
mathematicians, since one of the nice features about Turing machines is
that one can write down the description of a universal Turing machine that
can simulate any other Turing machine. McCarthy called his universal
Lisp function eval.

Remember that at this point Lisp still did not really exist because
there was no compiler for it. But one of McCarthy's students, Steve
Russell, pointed out that if he hand-coded eval, they could run the
language. McCarthy's first reaction was to tell Russell that he had theory
and practice mixed up. But eval was written, and Lisp was born.

2.8 Basic Debugging

Earlier we saw that when Lisp catches an error, it goes into a break loop that
sometimes allows you to correct the error. The degree to which errors can be

corrected after you start execution varies from Lisp to Lisp. However, virtually every Lisp has three basic debugging tools: the break loop (which we have seen), the function baktrace (of no arguments), and the function trace

    (trace -"*function-name*"-)

The worth of these functions becomes truly apparent only when one is dealing with a large program. So let us consider a slightly larger program than any we have dealt with so far. This program is a very small question answerer, and the code, with bugs, is in Figure 2.1. It will take two arguments, a list of statements that it knows to be true, and a query. Here is a sample session with the debugged program:

```
; query looks at each truth in truths, and calls matchp to see if this
; truth matches the question.  If one does, it is returned.  Else respond "nil".

(defun query (question truths)
    (loop (while truths)                    ; Look through facts
          (until (matchp question truth))   ; until one matches
          (next (truths (cdr truths)))      ; the query.  Return the
          (result truth)))                  ; matched fact.

; matchp decides if question matches truth.  It does this by looking
; at each atom in question and compares it to that in truth.  If it finds
; a mismatch, it immediately returns nil.  If it gets to the end of both
; question and truth, it returns t.

(defun matchp (question truth)              ; Look at each place of
    (loop (while question)                  ; two patterns in turn
          (while (match-atoms (car question) ; until a mismatch.
                              (car truth))   ;
          (next (question (cdr question))   ; Go to next place.
                (truth (cdr truth)))        ; Truth will be nil
          (result (null truth))))           ; if we reach the end
                                            ; and both lists are
                                            ; the same length.

; match-atoms matches an atom from one pattern against one from the other.
; If it has a variable, or if the subconstituents are equal, it returns t.

(defun match-atoms (item1 item2)            ; Two atoms match
    (cond ((equal item1 item2))             ; if they are equal
          ((equal item1 '*variable))))      ; or variables.
```

Figure 2.1 Code (with bugs) for a simple query answerer

```
-> (setq truths* '((own jack-1 dog-1)        ; Jack owns a certain dog.
                   (love jack-1 ann-1)        ; Jack loves Ann.
                   (love ann-1 *variable)     ; Ann loves everybody.
                   (own ann-1 dog-2)          ; Ann also own a dog.
                   (love dog-2 dog-1)))       ; Ann's dog loves Jack's.
((own jack-1 dog-1) (love..)...)             ; The value of setq.
-> (query '(love jack-1 dog-1) truths*)       ; Does Jack love his dog?
nil                                           ; No.
-> (query '(own ann-1 *variable) truths*)     ; Does Ann own anything?
(own ann-1 dog-2)                             ; Ann owns dog-2.
-> (query '(love ann-1 jack-1) truths*)       ; Does Ann love Jack?
(love ann-1 *variable)                        ; Ann loves everyone.
```

The important thing to note about our system is that the symbol *variable will match anything. This example is also useful because it illustrates the recommended practice of breaking up large functions into several logically self-contained subprograms, each of which is quite short. In Figure 2.1 we have one that looks through the ''database'' for something that matches the query, one that matches a query with a database item, and one that matches an atom in the query with an atom of the database item.

A debugging session for this code is shown in Figure 2.2 and Figure 2.3. In the first test we find that we have an unbound variable truth and we are put into a break loop, as seen by the new prompt, <1>:. To find the location of the unbound variable we call the function baktrace. This function prints out everything that is currently being worked on. Starting from the most recent, it tells us that we are executing a baktrace — true, but not too useful. Then it tells us that we tried to evaluate truth. Again true, since this is what caused the error. Prior to that we tried to evaluate matchp. It is important to know that when Lisp evaluates a function, it starts by remembering the function it is to evaluate, and then works on the arguments. Thus we can see here that most likely the variable truth is an argument to the function matchp. If we look three calls farther down, we see that this must be inside the function query. If we look at the code, we see that, indeed, there are two references to the variable truth, which is undefined in query. (Fixing the bug is left as an exercise.)

Next in Figure 2.2 we have this:

```
-> (query '(own ann-1 *variable) truths*)
(own ann-1 dog-2)
```

This is the desired response. However, when we try

```
(query '(love ann-1 jack-1) truths*)
```

rather than getting the response that Ann loves everyone, we get the answer nil.

This time our break loop does us no good because the function did not stop. It just returned the wrong answer. To find out what happened we use the Lisp function trace, which makes the system inform the user of all calls to the function traced as they occur. It will also give the value that the function returned on each call. By tracing matchp we can find out if it is returning all

```
-> (query '(love jack-1 dog-1) truths*)        ; Does Jack love his dog?
Error: Unbound Variable: truth                 ; It has an unbound variable.
<1>: (baktrace)                                ; Call baktrace to find out
baktrace -- truth -- matchp --                 ; were it happened.
cond -- prog --query                           ; It happened in query
                                               ; as an argument to matchp.

; [Actually fixing the bug is left as an exercise.]

-> (query '(love jack-1 dog-1) truths*)        ; Does Jack love his dog?
nil                                            ; Get the correct answer.
-> (query '(own ann-1 *variable) truths*)      ; Does Ann own anything?
(own ann-1 dog-2)                              ; Ann owns dog-2.
-> (query '(love ann-1 jack-1) truths*)        ; Does Ann love Jack?
nil                                            ; WRONG ANSWER!
-> (trace matchp)                              ; Trace matchp.
***matchp is ready to be traced               ; Response from
(matchp)                                       ; trace function.
-> (query '(love ann-1 jack-1) truths*)        ; Try same thing again.
***ENTERING matchp [lambda]                    ; Called matchp
   *arglist*                                   ; to match query against
   {question} (love ann-1 jack-1)              ; (own jack-1 dog-1).
   {truth} (own jack-1 dog-1)                  ; It should return nil.
***EXITING matchp  Returns=> nil               ; And it does.

***ENTERING matchp [lambda]                    ; Ditto.
   *arglist*                                   ;
   {question} (love ann-1 jack-1)              ;
   {truth} (love jack-1 ann-1)                 ;
***EXITING matchp  Returns=> nil               ;

***ENTERING matchp [lambda]                    ; Call matchp to match
   *arglist*                                   ; query against
   {question} (love ann-1 jack-1)              ; (love ann-1 *variable).
   {truth} (love ann-1 *variable)              ; It should return t.
***EXITING matchp  Returns=> nil               ; IT RETURNS NIL!!!

   ...                                         ; Skipping over stuff
nil                                            ; and get wrong answer again.
-> (trace (matchp break t t))                  ; Now break when matchp
***matchp is untraced                          ; is entered (t t says,
***matchp is ready to be traced                ; in effect, "always break").
(matchp)
```

Figure 2.2 A debugging session — part I

correct answers to the function that called it. We see, as we might have guessed, that it returns the wrong answer when asked to match the query against the data item that should match, namely, (love ann-1 *variable). But why doesn't this match? To find out we could trace match-atoms to see if it is the cause of the error, or if the problem is internal to matchp. However, if we were to trace match-atoms straight off, the number of calls to it would be very

```
-> (query '(love ann-1 jack-1) truths*)        ; Try again.
***ENTERING matchp [lambda]                    ; This is not the error case.
   *arglist*                                    ;
   {question} (love ann-1 jack-1)               ;
   {truth}  (own jack-1 dog-1)                  ; To continue from a broken
Break matchp                                    ; function, use (return).
<1>: (return)                                   ; The function will then
***EXITING matchp   Returns=> nil               ; be evaluated as usual.

***ENTERING matchp [lambda]                     ; Ditto.
   *arglist*                                    ;
   {question} (love ann-1 jack-1)               ;
   {truth}  (love jack-1 ann-1)                 ;
Break matchp                                     ;
<1>: (return)                                    ;
***EXITING matchp   Returns=> nil                ;

***ENTERING matchp [lambda]                      ; This is the crucial case.
   *arglist*                                     ;
   {question} (love ann-1 jack-1)                ;
   {truth}  (love ann-1 *variable)               ;
Break matchp                                      ; So before continuing on, we
<1>: (trace match-atoms)                          ; trace match-atoms to see if
***match-atoms is ready to be traced              ; it is at fault.
(match-atoms)                                     ;
<1>: (return)                                     ; Now continue on.

***ENTERING match-atoms [lambda]                  ; This should return t.
   *arglist*                                      ;
   {item1} love                                   ;
   {item2} love                                   ;
***EXITING match-atoms Returns=> t                ; And it does.

***ENTERING match-atoms [lambda]                  ; Ditto.
   *arglist*                                      ;
   {item1} ann-1                                  ;
   {item2} ann-1                                  ;
***EXITING match-atoms  Returns=> t               ; And it does.

***ENTERING match-atoms [lambda]                  ; Again should return t.
   *arglist*                                      ;
   {item1} jack-1                                 ;
   {item2} *variable                              ;
***EXITING match-atoms  Returns=> nil             ; BUT IT DOES NOT!!!
                                                  ; Skip the rest
```

Figure 2.3 A debugging session — part II

large, and we would get a lot of garbage on the screen. So instead, we again
trace **matchp**, but this time tell **trace** to **break** the function every time it is
called. Thus every time Lisp calls **matchp** it will immediately go into a break
loop. At first we hit cases where it is working properly, so we just type

(return). When we get to the crucial case, we then start tracing match-atoms. As we then watch match-atoms we see that it does not handle the match of jack-1 and *variable correctly. Thus we know *(1)* the bug is in the function match-atoms and *(2)* that it occurs when the second argument is a variable. At this point the bug should be easy to find and fix, and it is left to you as an exercise.

2.9 Building Up List Structure

Next we want to build lists. The most basic way to do this is with cons (for construct).

>   (cons *exp list*)

The function cons creates a new list whose first element (its car) is the first argument to cons, and whose subsequent members (its cdr) are the second argument.

```
-> (setq l2 (cons 'a '(b)))
(a b)
-> l2
(a b)
-> (car l2)
a
-> (cdr l2)
(b)
```

In effect, cons adds the value of *exp* to the front of the value of *list*, which is expected to be a list. (This is not quite true, but it is close enough for now. We will be more accurate in a moment.) It is important to emphasize that cons creates a *new* list. It will not affect any previously created list. For example:

```
-> (setq l1 (cons 'b nil))      ; Consing onto nil creates a 1
(b)                             ; element list (i.e., the cdr is nil).
-> (setq l1 (cons 'a l1))       ; We cons on another atom to
(a b)                           ; get a 2-element list.
-> (setq l1 (cons '(1 2) l1))   ; We may cons on things other than
((1 2) a b)                     ; atoms. Here we cons on a list.
-> (setq l2 (cons 'a l1))       ; If we cons on something else to
(a (1 2) a b)                   ; the list l1, this will not change l1.
-> l1                           ; The value of l1 is unchanged.
((1 2) a b)                     ;
-> (setq l1 'foo)               ; Now change the value of l1.
foo                             ;
-> l2                           ; And we see that the value of l2
(a (1 2) a b)                   ; is not changed.
```

We first added a to the front of the empty list giving us a list with only one element, a. Then we added b to the front of that. Then we added the list (1 2) to the front of the new list we were making. Last, we added **a** to the front of **l1** but since we set a second variable to the answer, **l2**, this had no effect on **l1**, which kept its previous value. Then we changed the value of **l1**, and we see that the value of **l2** is unchanged.

To get an idea of how **cons** is used in functions, we give here a function that takes as input a list, and returns a second list that is the reverse of the input. Most Lisps have such a function already built in, called, naturally, **reverse**, so we will call ours **our-reverse**.

```
(defun our-reverse (lst)
      (loop (initial (ans nil))          ; Loop through
            (while lst)                  ; lst each time
            (next (ans (cons (car lst) ans))  ; adding to front
                  (lst (cdr lst)))       ; of ans.
            (result ans)))
```

Note that **cons**ing each element of the original list onto a new one automatically reverses the list. In this case this is exactly what we wanted to happen, so there was no problem. However, often we do not want such a reversal. In these cases we often will first create the new list in the reverse order and then use **reverse** (or **our-reverse** if we do not have a built-in version) to "re-reverse" the final version. For example, Figure 2.4 shows a function that takes a list and returns a new list that contains every second element of the original, starting with the second.

Now let us correct an untruth we promulgated earlier. It is not really true that the second argument to **cons** must be a list.

```
-> (setq dot-pair (cons 'a 'b))      ; Consing two atoms together
(a . b)                              ; gives us a dotted pair.
-> (car dot-pair)                    ; Both its car
a                                    ;
-> (cdr dot-pair)                    ; and its cdr
b                                    ; are atoms.
```

As we see from this little dialogue, if we **cons** together two atoms, we get what is called a *dotted pair*. They are written as **(a . b)** where the first element is the

---

```
(defun every-other (lst)
      (loop (initial (ans nil))          ; Loop through
            (while lst)                  ; lst until no
            (while (cdr lst))            ; more than one
            (next (ans (cons (cadr lst) ans))  ; element left.
                  (lst (cddr lst)))      ; Add every other
            (result (reverse ans))))))   ; to answer.
```

Figure 2.4 The function **every-other**

car while the second is the cdr. Dotted pairs are rarely used, and we would recommend against your using them. Indeed, we could have just as well ignored them, except if you ever make a mistake and cons together two atoms and get a dotted pair, it is better if you have some idea of what is going on. As for how dotted pairs fit into the overall scheme of things, this will have to wait until we delve deeper into the underlying implementation of Lisp at the end of this chapter.

Often list is a more convenient function than cons for building up lists.

(list -*exps*-)

The function list takes zero or more arguments (like +) and returns a list comprised of the value of each of the *exps*. For example:

```
-> (list 1)                          ; list may take one
(1)                                  ; argument,
-> (list 1 2)                        ; or two,
(1 2)                                ;
-> (list 1 2 3)                      ; or three, etc.
(1 2 3)                              ;
-> (list)                            ; It can even take
nil                                  ; zero.
-> (list (list 'a 'b) 'c)            ; We can make lists
((a b) c)                            ; within lists.
-> (cons (cons 'a (cons 'b nil))     ; This does the same
         (cons 'c nil))              ; thing as the last
((a b) c)                            ; but uses cons.
```

The last example shows how list can be more convenient than cons.

In yet other cases the function append is what you need.

(append -*lists*-)

While list makes a list of its arguments append appends all of its arguments together. That is, all of its arguments must themselves be lists, and then append will strip off the outermost parentheses of each and make a long list of the innards.

```
-> (append '(a) '(b))                ; Appending two lists
(a b)                                ; gives us the contents
-> (append '(a b) '(c d))            ; of each, but in a
(a b c d)                            ; single list.
-> (append '(a) () '(b))             ; Since () has no
(a b)                                ; elements, it
-> (append '(a) () '((a) (b)) '(a b (c)))  ; disappears.
(a (a) (b) a b (c))
```

As with list and cons, append creates a new list and has no effect on its arguments. Note particularly that empty lists, i.e., nil, simply disappear when appended with other lists.

Often one wants to create a piece of list structure that is based upon a template, with certain parts filled in. For example, suppose we wanted a list with the following form:

(If *prop* is true then (and *prop prop*) is true)

The intention is to fill in *prop* with some value, like (on cat mat). While this could be done with list, a much more convenient way is using the *back-quote* function. Like quote, back-quote has a one character abbreviation, which is '. Back-quote works like quote, only any part of the expression preceded by a comma will be evaluated, and its value substituted in. So the example above could be done using back-quote like this:

'(If ,prop is true then (and ,prop ,prop) is true)

Also, anything preceded by a ,@ will be evaluated, and its value *spliced* into the corresponding position. For example:

```
-> (setq v1 '((setq x (+ x y)) (* x (+y 3))))     ; v1 is a list
((setq x (+ x y)) (* x (+y 3)))                    ; of commands.
-> (setq v2 '(let ((x 3) (y 7)) ,@v1))             ; We will splice
(let ((x 3) (y 7)) (setq x (+ x y)) (* x (+y 3)))  ; it into the let.
```

2.10 More on Predicates

We have already seen several Lisp predicates, such as >, equal, and null. As we noted, to indicate false they return nil, while anything other than nil is considered to be "true." For example, the Lisp function member tells us if *exp* is an element of *list*.

(member *exp list*)

But, rather than just return t if it is, member returns the list starting with the element we were looking for.

```
-> (member 'b '(1 2 3))          ; b is not a
nil                              ; member of the list.
-> (member 'b '(a b c))          ; b is a member
(b c)                            ; of the list.
-> (member 'b '(a b c b a))      ; member finds only
(b c b a)                        ; the first occurrence.
-> (member '(1 2) '(1 2 3))      ; The list (1 2)
nil                              ; is NOT a member.
-> (member '(1 2) '(a (1 2) b))  ; Here the list (1 2)
((1 2) b)                        ; is a member.
-> (cond ((member 'b '(a b c)) 'yes)  ; cond works with
        (t 'no))                 ; predicates that
yes                              ; return things other
                                 ; than just t and nil.
```

The function **member** decides on membership by looking down the list element by element until it either finds the element it is looking for, or until it comes to the end of the list. Thus, while it works quite well for short lists, the longer the list, the slower it will be.

That Lisp treats any non-nil value as t effectively means that Lisp makes no distinction between predicates and any other function since, after all, *all* Lisp functions either return nil or something other than nil. However, some functions like + never return nil, so they are obviously not very useful as predicates.

Lisp has two functions for combining predicates, **and** and **or**.

(and *-exps-*)
(or *-exps-*)

The function **and** will keep evaluating expressions until it either reaches the end (in which case it returns the value of the last one) or until one of them returns nil, in which case it returns nil. That is, **and** returns "true" if all of the expressions inside of it return "true" (where again, by "true" we mean anything other than nil.) Naturally, **or** returns true if any of its expressions return true. It stops looking when the first true value is found. The value **or** returns is that of the first expression to have a value other than nil. If all of the expressions evaluate to nil, then **or** returns nil.

```
-> (setq foo '(a b c))
(a b c)
-> (setq bar nil)
nil
-> (and t foo)          ; and returned the value of
(a b c)                 ; its last argument.
-> (and foo t)          ; The same thing occurs here
t                       ;
-> (and bar foo)        ; Since bar is nil this
nil                     ; returns nil.  Once a nil is
-> (and bar bletch)     ; found no further arguments
nil                     ; are evaluated so Lisp
                        ; never notices that bletch
                        ; is an unbound variable.
-> (or foo bar)         ; or returns the first non-
(a b c)                 ; nil value, here foo's.
-> (or t foo bar)       ; Both and and or may
t                       ; take any number of arguments.
-> (or bar t foo)       ; Here the second argument has
t                       ; the first non-nil value.
-> (or t foo bletch)    ; Again, Lisp never notices that
t                       ; bletch is unbound.
```

We noted earlier that **null** returns t if its argument is nil. If you think about it, **null** can also serve as the way to reverse a test.

```
-> (> 5 6)
nil
-> (null (> 5 6))
t
-> (null (> 6 5))
nil
```

In logic the normal name for this function is not, and so Lisp allows not and null to be used interchangeably. For readability we recommend that you use null if you want to test whether a list is empty, and not if you want to reverse the sense of a predicate.

Another class of Lisp predicates helps determine what kind of object Lisp has in front of it.

(numberp *exp*)	*; Returns t if exp evaluates to a number,* *; else nil.*
(consp *exp*)	*; Returns t if exp evaluates to a list or dotted* *; pair, else nil.*
(atom *exp*)	*; Returns t if exp evaluates to an atom.*

2.11 Properties

Every symbol in Lisp may have *properties* associated with it. (For historical reasons properties are said to be found on the symbol's *property list*. However, this name is now misleading since the properties are not necessarily stored in a list.) Using properties we can attach attributes and values to symbols. To use an example we mentioned at the beginning of this chapter, we could add the attribute color to the atom canary with the value yellow. We do this with the function putprop.

(putprop *symbol value attribute*)

This information may be accessed using get, as in (get *symbol attribute*).

-> (putprop 'canary 'yellow 'color)	*; canary gets the*
yellow	*; color yellow,*
-> (putprop 'canary '(wings feathers) 'parts)	*; and gets parts*
(wings feathers)	*; wings and feathers.*
-> (get 'canary 'color)	*; We ask what color*
yellow	*; a canary is,*
-> (get 'canary 'parts)	*; and what parts it*
(wings feathers)	*; has.*
-> (putprop 'canary 'red 'color)	*; If we give a new*
red	*; color for a canary,*
-> (get 'canary 'color)	*; the old one goes*
red	*; away.*

As this last example shows, putting a value as a property under an indicator will clobber any previous value under that indicator. Properties are permanent.

That is, once you add something to a property list, it stays there until you change the value, or explicitly remove the property using remprop.

(remprop *symbol attribute*)

2.12 Pointers, Cell Notation, and the Internals (Almost) of Lisp

Consider the following reasonably obvious conversation with Lisp:

```
-> (putprop 'eagle 'brown 'color)    ; Add a color prop-
brown                                ; erty to eagle.
-> (setq v1 'eagle)                  ; If we set the
eagle                                ; variables v1 and v2
-> (setq v2 'eagle)                  ; both to eagle,
eagle                                ;
-> (get v1 'color)                   ; we can access eagle's
brown                                ; properties via
-> (get v2 'color)                   ; either variable.
brown
```

This may seem very straightforward, but it hides an important idea. The variables v1 and v2 both have the value eagle. However, they must both be "pointing" to the same data structure because, as we see in the example, we can do a get on either of them, and receive the same value. Or to put this another way, there is, in our Lisp, exactly one symbol eagle, and the two variables must both point to this same symbol. Indeed, whenever we assign a value to a variable, what the variable gets is a pointer to the value. We can visualize the situation as shown in Figure 2.5. Each symbol in Lisp has a unique storage location (a unique instance), and all references to it are simply pointers to this same unique storage location. This means that whenever Lisp reads in a symbol, it sees if it knows about this symbol already, and if so, it will not create a new version.

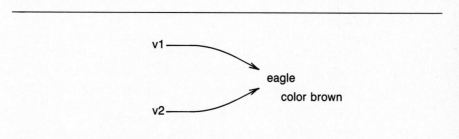

Figure 2.5 Two variables pointing to the same symbol

But this is *not* true of lists. Two lists may look identical, but they may be made up out of different pieces of memory. In particular, whenever Lisp reads in a new list, it will automatically create a new piece of list structure, without any regard to whether or not it has seen such a list before. Therefore we can have the situation shown in Figure 2.6. There v3 and v4 point to different pieces of list structure. However, v5 points to the same list structure as v3 since we set the value of v5 to whatever was the value of v3 and this makes the pointer of v5 the same as the pointer of v3.

Now, let us ask the question, in Figure 2.6 is v3 equal to v4? Both yes and no would be appropriate. We could say yes because they are, after all, item for item the same list, namely (a b c). Alternatively, we could say no because we have two different pieces of list structure. To capture this difference, Lisp has two different equality predicates. One, we have already seen, equal, takes the liberal view. Even if they are not the same piece of storage, things still can be equal if they are made up of the same things. The other, eq, takes the strict view that we must have the same piece of storage, or more technically, that the pointers must be the same.

(eq *exp1 exp2*)
(equal *exp1 exp2*)

So, if we continued the example in Figure 2.6. we would have this:

-> (eq v3 v4)	; *v3 and v4 point*
nil	; *to different things*
-> (equal v3 v4)	; *but they are equal.*
t	;
-> (eq v3 v5)	; *v3 and v5 point*
t	; *to the same thing.*

Some further points are given in the following example:

```
-> (setq v3 '(a b c))
(a b c)
-> (setq v4 '(a b c))
(a b c)
-> (setq v5 v3)
(a b c)
```

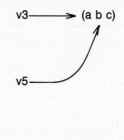

Figure 2.6 Separate but equal lists

```
-> (eq 'a 'a)                 ; An atom is eq to itself
t                             ;
-> (eq 'a 'b)                 ; but not to any other atom.
nil                           ;
-> (setq x (list 'a))         ; Two newly created lists
(a)                           ; which have the same
-> (setq y (list 'a))         ; members will NOT be
(a)                           ; eq to each other.
-> (eq x y)                   ;
nil                           ;
-> (eq x x)                   ; However, a list will
t                             ; be eq to itself.
-> (equal x y)                ; The two lists will be
t                             ; equal to each other.
```

The function **member** (discussed in the last section) uses **equal** when testing whether its first argument is an element of its section argument. Most Lisps also have a function **memq** which is just like **member**, except that it uses **eq** instead.

However, the diagrammatic version used in Figure 2.6 was oversimplified in two important respects. First, as we have already noted, atoms in Lisp are unique, there is only one copy of them, and every occurrence of the atom is a pointer to the same copy. Therefore Figure 2.6 would be better illustrated as Figure 2.7.

The other way in which Figure 2.6 simplified things is that it ignored the fact that lists in Lisp are stored in a ''linked'' fashion, in which each element points to the next one in the list, except for the last one, which points to nil.

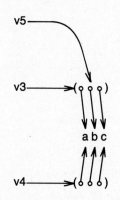

Figure 2.7 Two lists sharing the same elements

Sometimes it is important to have a good visualization of this, and to get it we use an extension of our informal graphical notation, called *cell notation* (or *box notation*). In this notation the list (a b) would be represented as in Figure 2.8. Here we have two rectangles, each rectangle containing two parts. The rectangles are called *cons cells*. The two parts of a cons cell are used to store pointers to the car and cdr, respectively. They are called cons cells because the function cons works by grabbing one and filling in the cell's left and right parts with its two arguments. So, the first cons cell in Figure 2.8 has its left part pointing to the atom a (which is the car of the list), and its right part pointing to the cdr of the list, which is another cons cell. This second cell, shown by itself in Figure 2.9 represents the Lisp list (b). The slash across the right-hand part is a shorthand notation for a pointer to nil. If we have a list with sublists, then we get the car of some cons cell pointing to not an atom but another cons cell, as in the cell notation for (a (b)). (See Figure 2.10.)

You should note the close correspondence between the internal representation and the way in which this structure would be built up using cons. One of the points we made earlier is that cons creates a new cons cell with pointers to its two arguments. If the second argument is an atom, rather than a list, then we get a *dotted pair*, which we introduced earlier, without really explaining what one was. So, the dotted pair (1 . 2) would have the internal representation shown in Figure 2.11. One can even create more complex structures that have dotted pairs in them. Figure 2.12 gives the cell notation corresponding to the dot notation (a b . c).

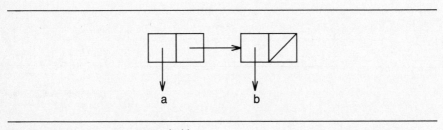

Figure 2.8 Cell structure for (a b)

Figure 2.9 Cell structure for (b)

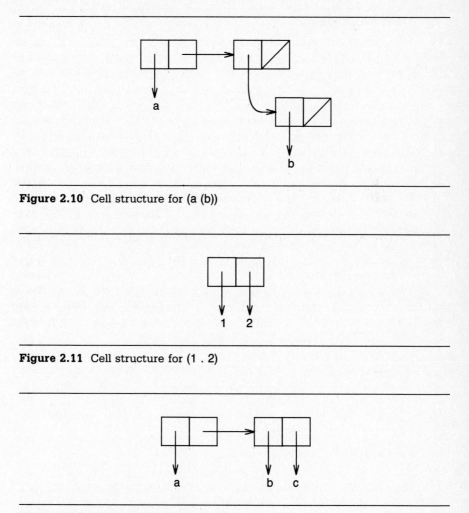

Figure 2.10 Cell structure for (a (b))

Figure 2.11 Cell structure for (1 . 2)

Figure 2.12 Cell structure for (a b . c)

If we think about it, much of what we have been representing as lists could equally well be represented in our dot notation.

(a) = (a . nil)
(a b) = (a . (b . nil))

However, because this representation is so much more complex, we seldom use it.

Box 2.2

Memory Allocation in Lisp

Those of you who have had a computer science data-structures course will have found some of the last section quite familiar. The internal representation for lists discussed there is a very common component of such courses, the *linked list*. A linked list, according to the standard definition, is a data structure with two parts, a "data" part, and a "link" part. In Lisp lists these are the car and cdr respectively.

One thing that comes up in the data structures presentation has, however, been absent from our discussion. We have made no mention of the allocation and recall of the elements of a linked list. Roughly speaking this involves two programs. One, the allocator, keeps track of memory locations that are not being used (typically there is a list of such locations). To add a new element to a list, one asks the allocator for the memory, and the memory to be used is removed from the allocator's list. In Lisp, this is done by the function cons, which, of course, also puts values into the car and cdr portions of the linked list element. The list of free cells kept by cons is called the *free list*.

The other program needed is the "de-allocator." When a cell is removed from a linked list, its memory is freed by handing it over to the de-allocation routine. Essentially all this routine does is to add this memory to the allocator's list of free memory locations. This allows the freed cells to be used by someone else.

However, there is nothing directly corresponding to the de-allocator in Lisp. The reason for this is that one cannot return a cell to the free list whenever a function is done with it. To see why this is the case, consider a situation, such as that in Figure 2.6. Suppose we were to continue the dialogue of Figure 2.6 with this:

    (setq v5 (cdr v5))

As far as v5 is concerned, it would appear that the cell of Figure 2.13 has just been freed. However, the cell is not free because the variable v3 still points to it, and changing v5 should have no effect on v3. Furthermore,

a

Figure 2.13 A cell that lost one spectator

asking the programmer to keep track of the intertwining list structures that Lisp allows would in effect take away much of the freedom that Lisp promises.

Therefore Lisp embodies a more complex way of managing memory, called *garbage collection*. While there are many ways to implement garbage collection, there are two basic schemes. First, one can count the number of pointers to every cell, and record this number in the cell. This is called *reference counting*. Every time Lisp adds or removes a pointer, the number would be incremented or decremented by one. Should the number ever reach zero, the cell would then be declared free. The major problem with this technique is *circular list structure*. (See Section 2.13 on destructive modification of list structure for a definition. As for why this is a problem, that is left as an exercise.)

The second method is called the *mark-and-sweep algorithm*. Basically, the allocator keeps allocating free storage until it runs out. At that point, the garbage collector is called, and it first finds out which cells are still being used. It does this by tracing the list structure being pointed to by every variable (and every property), marking a special bit reserved for this purpose in every cell encountered. This is the *mark phase*. After the mark phase comes the *sweep phase*. Essentially every memory location available for list structure is examined to see if the mark bit is on. If so, it is being used, and is not touched. If not, then it is not being used, and it is recycled. The resulting algorithm is this:

Function: Garbage-collection
Arguments: None
Algorithm: Call mark on every property and variable value.
   For each cell in memory:
      If the cell is unmarked, put it in the free storage list
      Else unmark the cell.

Function: Mark
Arguments: cell - the cell to be examined.
Algorithm: If cell is marked, do nothing
   Else turn on cell's mark bit, and mark its successor.

The major problem with this scheme is that the two sweeps through memory can take a long time. Furthermore, since all other operations must be suspended during this process, mark-and-sweep garbage collection can make real-time applications impossible.

2.13 Destructive Modification of Lists

Both cons and list create new list structures, and hence have no effect on previously built lists. So consider the terminal session shown in Figure 2.14 along with the resulting cell structures. As we can see, putting 0 onto the front of the

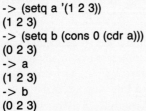

```
-> (setq a '(1 2 3))            ; Setq a to a list.
(1 2 3)                         ;
-> (setq b (cons 0 (cdr a)))    ; Give b a different
(0 2 3)                         ; first element but it
-> a                            ; shares the last two.
(1 2 3)                         ; The a remains
-> b                            ; unchanged.
(0 2 3)
```

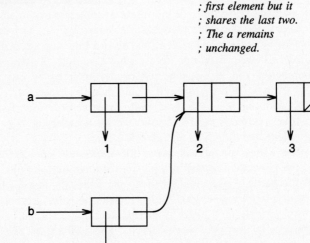

Figure 2.14 Sharing list structure

list b had no effect on the variable a. (Also note the sharing of list structure between a and b.) That cons and list do not modify list structure is most often exactly what we want, but sometimes we really want to modify already existing structures. For this purpose Lisp provides three functions, rplaca (replace car), rplacd (replace cdr), and nconc.

    (rplaca *list exp*)
    (rplacd *list exp*)
    (nconc *-lists-*)

Rplaca replaces the car of *list* with *exp*, while rplacd replaces the cdr of *list* with *exp*. We use the cell notation to show the results of these commands. See Figure 2.15. (In Figure 2.15 the dotted lines show links that were removed by the destructive modification.) The function nconc works just like append, except that all of the arguments (excluding the last one) are destructively changed to make the final list. (See Figure 2.16.) To take a more complicated example, suppose we continued the terminal session shown in Figure 2.14. Note that while the first elements of a and b are distinct, they share the list structure for (2 3). Now, suppose we continue on as shown in Figure 2.17. Here we have destructively modified the piece of list structure pointed to by a but this had no effect on b since it did not share that piece of list structure. Now let us try the manipulations in Figure 2.18. There we modified some list structure that

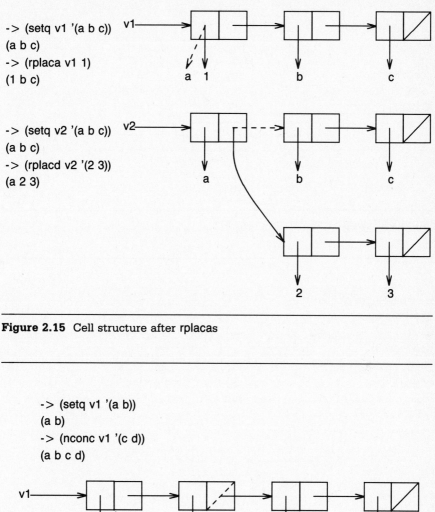

```
-> (setq v1 '(a b c))
(a b c)
-> (rplaca v1 1)
(1 b c)
```

```
-> (setq v2 '(a b c))
(a b c)
-> (rplacd v2 '(2 3))
(a 2 3)
```

Figure 2.15 Cell structure after rplacas

```
-> (setq v1 '(a b))
(a b)
-> (nconc v1 '(c d))
(a b c d)
```

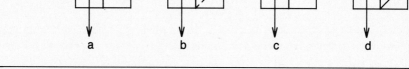

Figure 2.16 Cell structure after an nconc

was shared, and hence we changed both a and b at the same time. Figure 2.19 shows how rplacd can do the same thing.

In general, destructive modification of list structure should be avoided if possible. You may not realize that a given piece of list structure is shared by two separate pieces of your program. The destructive modification by one part

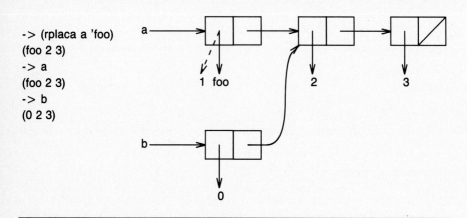

```
-> (rplaca a 'foo)
(foo 2 3)
-> a
(foo 2 3)
-> b
(0 2 3)
```

Figure 2.17 Destruction on one list only

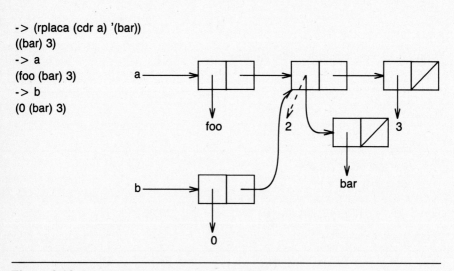

```
-> (rplaca (cdr a) '(bar))
((bar) 3)
-> a
(foo (bar) 3)
-> b
(0 (bar) 3)
```

Figure 2.18 Destruction seen by two variables

may suddenly show up as an inexplicable bug in the other. Also, you can get yourself into all sorts of infinite loops. It is quite easy to do, as in Figure 2.20. This is called a circular list. Graphically it looks like Figure 2.21. Lisp tries to print out the list but, as you might expect, has some difficulty finishing. Indeed, Lisp goes into an infinite loop in trying to print out the answer, and has to be stopped "manually." Before playing around with such things, make sure you know the break character so you can interrupt such loops.

```
-> (rplacd (cdr b) '(99 100))
((bar) 99 100)
-> b
(0 (bar) 99 100)
-> a
(foo (bar) 99 100)
```

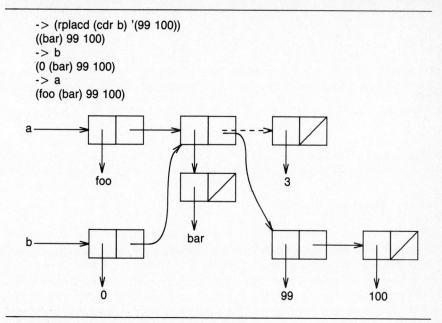

Figure 2.19 A rplacd seen by two variables

```
-> (setq x '(1))
(1)
-> (rplacd x x)
(1 1 1 1 1 1 1 1 1 1 1 1 1 1 1 1 1 1 1 1 1 1 1 1 1 1 1 1 1 1 1 1 1 1 1 1 1
 1 1 1 1 1 1 1 1 1 1 1 1 1 1 1 1 1 1 1 1 1 1 1 1 1 1 1 1 1 1 1 1 1 1 1 1 1 1 1
 1 1 1 1 1 1 1 1 1 1 1 1 1 1 1 1 1 1 1 1 1 1 1 1 1 1 1 1 1 1 1 1 1 1 1 1 1 1 1
 1 1 1 1 1 1 1 1 1 1 1 1 1 1 1 1 1 1 1 1 1 1 1 1 1 1 1 1 1 1 1 1 1 1 1 1 1 1 1
 . . .
```

Figure 2.20 Creating a circular list

Because of these problems, you might ask why *ever* use destructive list modification. There are two basic reasons. Sometimes recopying entire structures (e.g, a large data base) is prohibitively expensive. In other cases a structure is pointed to by several variables (or property lists) and you want all of them to be changed. Destructive modification will do it with one instruction. The alternative is to track down everyone who points at the thing, and change each one separately.

It is convenient to reserve the term ''S-expression'' for a ''well-behaved'' list structure — one that has no circularities or strange elements.

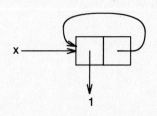

Figure 2.21 A circular list

2.14 The for Function

Because the list is the fundamental way of grouping objects together in Lisp, often we will want to perform the same operation on each member of a list. Lisp provides several functions for doing this, known collectively as *mapping functions*. Unfortunately, they are rather complex and, to keep things simple, we will not introduce them here. Instead we will combine several of them into a single rationalized function, the for function. While many Lisps have some version of for, it is not standardized, and you should check to see if your Lisp has one and, if so, you should learn its exact syntax.

Our for function has the following forms:

```
(for ("variable" in list)
    (do "expression"))

(for ("variable" in list)
    (save "expression"))

(for ("variable" in list)
    (splice "expression"))
```

In each case *variable* is bound to successive elements of *list*. For each element, *expression* is evaluated. The difference between the three is what happens to the value of *expression*. For do, it is ignored; for save, the values are put together into a list; while for splice, the values are spliced (i.e., nconced) together into a list. For example, suppose we wanted to take a list of numbers, and produce a second list of numbers, each number one greater than the corresponding number in the first list. The following would do the job:

```
-> (for (num in '(2 4 5 1))
        (save (+ num 1)))
(3 5 6 2)
```

Here the variable num is set to 2, 4, 5, and 1, respectively. For each number the function (+ num 1) will be executed, and the result will be collected in a list, that is, returned as the value of the for function.

As a second example, suppose we wanted to take a list of pairs of numbers, such as ((1 3) (55 11) (12 1) (18 21)) and output a list of the sums of each pair. We can do this with the following:

```
-> (for (pair in '((1 3) (55 11) (12 1) (18 21)))
        (save (+ (car pair) (cadr pair)))
(4 66 13 39)
```

Naturally, the variable defined by the for function (in the last example, pair) is not defined after we leave the for.

The for function is actually more general than we have indicated. It is not restricted to a single list, but may take any number. For example:

```
-> (for (a in '(1 2 3)) (b in '(2 3 4))
        (save (+ a b)))
(3 5 7)
-> (for (x in '(a b c d)) (y in '(1 2 3))
        (save (list x y)))
((a 1) (b 2) (c 3))
```

The first for adds the successive numbers from each argument. The second for pairs up the elements of the (a b c d) list with the corresponding element of the (1 2 3) list. It stops after three such pairings because at this point the second list has run out of elements.

As we have already noted, different versions of the for function do different things with the values produced in the second clause of the function. A clause headed by save puts all of the values together into a single list. That is, you can think of save as keeping track of all of the outputs and then applying list to all of them. A second option, splice, does the same thing but applies nconc to the outputs. (We really do mean nconc, so watch out for cases where destructive modification of lists can hurt you.) The third option, do, in essence produces no output at all. (Because everything in Lisp must produce an output, different Lisps do different things here. It is a bad idea to make use of the values in such cases.)

Looking at the last of these, do, we would typically use it if we were interested only in the side effect of the function, and not its value. For example, suppose we had two lists, one with objects, and a second with colors. The following function would put the color property on the objects under the indicator color.

```
(defun add-color (obj-list color-list)      ; Adds the color from
    (for (obj in obj-list)                   ; color-list to the
        (color in color-list)                ; object in obj-list
        (do (putprop obj color 'color))))    ; under the indicator
                                             ; color.
```

As for splice, its most common use is getting rid of spurious nils. For example, suppose we were given a list of names, and we wanted to produce a list of just those people in the original list for whom we had an associated age stored as a property. We cannot use **save** because it returns all the results, and we want to ignore some. The solution is to use **splice**.

```
(defun have-age (name-list)          ; For each name in
     (for (name in name-list)        ; name-list, if it has
          (splice                    ; an age on its property
               (cond ((get name 'age) ; list, return it in the
                    (list name))))))   ; final answer.
```

We enclose the successful names in a layer of parentheses so that we return either a list of the desired name, or nil. Suppose we had this input:

(ann mary greg cliff sue)

Assume that the first, third, and fifth have ages. If we simply looked at each individual output of the cond function we would see this:

(ann) nil (greg) nil (sue)

(Remember, in most Lisps if the cond falls off the end without any test being true, the value is nil.) However, this gets spliced together. When we splice nil in with another list, the nil "disappears," and we will be left with this:

(ann greg sue)

2.15 Recursion

One technique that is often useful in advanced programming is *recursion*. We say that a program is recursive if it calls itself as a subfunction either directly (function foo calls function foo) or indirectly (function foo calls function bar, which in turn calls function foo). In some languages, recursion is either not allowed, or hedged with special restrictions, but not in Lisp. In Lisp any function may call itself.

To get some idea of how recursion works, and why it is useful, let us go back to the distinction we made earlier between the Lisp functions eq and equal. As you may remember, we defined equal by saying that to a first approximation two pieces of list structure were equal if they looked the same when printed out. Let us now give a more formal definition.

Two objects *obj1* and *obj2* are **equal** if

1) they are eq, or
2) they are both list structures and
       (equal (car *obj1*) (car *obj2*))
       (equal (cdr *obj1*) (cdr *obj2*))

According to this definition, we first see if the two objects are eq, but if not, we then start decomposing the two objects into parts and look to see if the parts (the cars and cdrs) are themselves equal. So, we would decide that (1 2) is equal to (1 2) by doing the computation illustrated in Figure 2.22. As you should have noticed, this definition of equality is recursive because we define the equality of the whole in terms of the equality of the parts. This does not make the

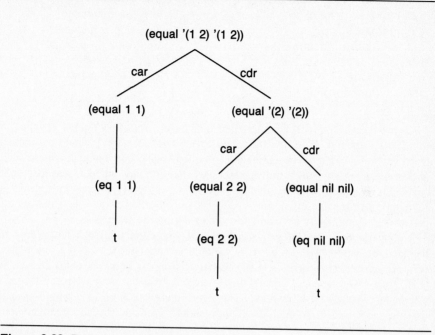

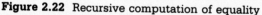

Figure 2.22 Recursive computation of equality

definition invalid because it does not lead to an infinite loop. Rather at some point (when it gets down to the level of atoms) it stops recurring, and uses **eq**. In Lisp we can write this definition of equality as follows:

```
(defun equal (a b)          ; a and b are equal
    (cond ((eq a b))        ; if they are eq
          ((and (consp a)   ; or if both are
                (consp b)   ; lists and their
                (equal (car a) (car b))   ; respective car's
                (equal (cdr a) (cdr b)))))) ; and cdr's are
                            ; equal.
```

This particular kind of recursion, where we break a list up into its **car** and **cdr** and call a function recursively on each part, is very common in Lisp programming, and is called *car-cdr recursion*.

2.16 Scope of Variables

When we first introduced **defun** we noted that any of the formal parameters to a function in Lisp get their new values upon entering the function, and will lose them upon leaving. Now we want to discuss a bit more closely what happens in between. In particular, suppose we have the following:

```
-> (defun function1 (var1)          ; The variable var1
        (function2 17))             ; is local to function1
function1                           ; (where it is defined)
-> (defun function2 (x)             ; and while we may use
        (+ var1 x))                 ; it in function2, it
function2                           ; is not local there.
-> (function1 5)
22
```

Note that the variable var1 while being defined in function1 retains its value in function2. Indeed, if function2 called function3, then var1 would be defined there as well. That is, a variable is defined inside the function where it is declared, and in any function that function calls, and any function that they call, etc. This is called *dynamic scoping* and it is a property of most Lisps. It is "dynamic" in the sense that the *scope of a variable* (i.e., where it is defined) is determined dynamically by who calls whom during the computation.

A variable is said to be a *local variable* (in a function) if it is declared in the function where it is used. If a variable is not local it is said to be a *free variable* or a *special variable*. It is bad style to use special variables because it is difficult to understand a program if variables appear in it whose value and "meaning" are given elsewhere. However, there are occasions where special variables are useful. In such cases they should be made visually distinctive so that a reader of the code will not fruitlessly search for their declaration. We will do this in this book by putting an asterisk at each end of the variable name, as in *important-variable*.

One particular subclass of special variables are those that are defined at the top level of Lisp. That is, they are implicitly defined when we do a setq when typing at Lisp, or if such a setq appears at the top level in a file (that is, not inside a function definition). These are called *global variables* because they are defined everywhere.

Box 2.3

Atoms and Hashing

We have noted that all atoms in Lisp are unique. This presents a problem for the Lisp reader. Whenever you type a new atom at it, Lisp must decide if there is a copy of this atom around, in which case, it should press the copy into service. If there is no copy, a new atom must be created. Naturally, this is done quite a bit, so this process must be fast, even when the number of atoms known to Lisp is large. There are several well-known techniques in the computer science literature for handling such cases. The one used by Lisp is called *hashing*.

Suppose we had an infinite amount of memory. In any computer system, when a new name is typed in, that name is converted into a number because in all digital computers both numbers and characters are represented internally as numbers. For every name, there would therefore be a corresponding memory location (the location with the same number as the name). For example, FOO might have the associated number/location 707979. Then, every time this routine gets in a new atom, it goes to the corresponding memory location, and sees if anything is there (which would indicate that it had seen the atom before). Given the computer's ability to quickly retrieve the contents of a given memory location, this scheme gives a quick way to reuse the same atom every time its name is typed at Lisp.

Of course, computers do not have infinite memory. However, suppose our machine does have more memory locations than past and future atoms. We could then do the same thing, only now we will be restricted to, say, 100,000 memory locations. But what happens if we get a name whose number is greater than 100,000? The solution is simply to reduce all numbers to numbers less than 100,000 by some standard process. For example, dividing by 100,000 and taking the remainder would work fine. The remainder would, of course, be less than 100,000, and we could look at that location.

The only problem is that it could happen that two different atoms lead to the same number. For example, the numbers for FOO (707979) and FFOO (70707979) have the same remainder when divided by 100,000 (7,979). There are various ways to handle this. They all depend on the fact that if we have more spaces than names, there must be *some place* to put the atom. For example, if the routine goes to the memory location, and finds some other atom there, it could go to the next memory location. However, all of these schemes assume that the distribution of atoms throughout the 100,000 or so locations will be even. If not, then one part will be empty, and another will have terrible space conflicts. For this reason, it is important to choose a number-producing function that tends to spread its values throughout all possible locations. Since most people use atoms which are related to words in their language, the incoming atoms will not be spread out. (There will be very few atoms with zzz's in them for most of us.) The standard way to accomplish this is to choose a function that will tend to spread out atoms no matter how similar they are. A common function for doing this (assuming 2^m locations reserved for this purpose) is to use the high-order m bits of this function:

$a *$ input mod W

Here W is the number of bits in the word of the machine being used, and a is a constant chosen to make things work "well." (There are rules of thumb for choosing such constants; see, for example, [Sedgewick83].) The result will be that the atoms will be all mixed up (or *hashed up*) in the directory. In Lisp, this directory is called the *oblist* (for "object list").

Thus when you type an atom at Lisp, it looks the atom up in the oblist to see if it has been encountered before. If not, it will be entered in the oblist. The oblist has all of the atoms known to the Lisp you are working with at any given time.

2.17 Input/Output

Because you as a Lisp user are in a read-eval-print loop at the top level, you need be less concerned with input and output than a programmer in some other language. The top-level reader will read in the values you wish to supply to your top-level function, and the top-level printer will print out the results.

Nevertheless, input and output functions are still needed, and we will mention them briefly. Since we are again dealing with the periphery of Lisp, these functions are not well standardized, so we will not delve very deeply into the topic but simply attempt to give you some idea of the kinds of things which are typically available. Because in all likelihood you will have more use for printing functions, we will start with them.

One of the most important printing functions that the user should be familiar with is pp, which stands for *prettyprinting*. A prettyprinter is a function which takes an S-expression and prints it out in an indented fashion. Thus a typical use for the prettyprinter is looking at functions and data structures during the debugging process.

```
-> (defun foo (x) (cond ((> x 5) 'greater-than-5)    ; Define a function
((< x 5) 'less-than-5) ((equal x 5) 'equal-to-5)))   ; without worrying
foo                                                  ; about spacing.
-> (pp foo)                                          ; The function pp
(def foo                                             ; will print it out
     (lambda (x)                                     ; nicely indented.
        (cond ((> x 5) 'greater-than-5)              ; Do not worry
              ((< x 5) 'less-than-5)                 ; about lambda and
              ((equal x 5) 'equal-to-5))))           ; def at this time.
nil                                                  ; nil is the value
-> (setq v1                                          ; of the pp function.
'(some (highly embedded (piece)) (of (list)          ; Now we use pp
(structure) (which) (for some reason))               ; on a piece of list
(we want to read)))                                  ; structure.
(some (highly embedded (piece)) (of (list)           ; Here we get the
(structure) (which) (for some reason)) (we want      ; value of the setq
to read))                                            ; printed back at us.
-> (pp v1)                                           ; Now try the pp.
(some (highly embedded (piece))
        (of (list) (structure)
                (which)
                (for some reason))
        (we want to read))
```

You might note that the definition of foo printed out by pp looks slightly different from the version we typed in. The reasons for this will be discussed when we discuss the details of Lisp's representation for functions in Box 5.1.

Another major reason for printing out information is to give diagnostic and debugging information during the course of execution. Lisp has any number of functions for printing information. The standard one is print, which prints one S-expression. (Others include printc (prints one character) and patom (prints one atom).) For the moment we will pretend that all of these take one argument, the thing to be printed. In fact, there is a second argument, which is optional. Its significance will be discussed at the end of this section. So, suppose we wanted Lisp to print out a debugging message whenever it enters the function foo above.

```
-> (defun foo (x)
        (print '(Entering foo with x bound to)) ; Add two calls to
        (print x)                               ; print debugging
        (cond ((> x 5) 'greater-than-5)         ; information.
              ((< x 5) 'less-than-5)            ;
              ((equal x 5) 'equal-to-5))))      ;
foo                                             ; The value of defun.
->(foo 4)                                       ; Now let us try it.
(Entering foo with x bound to)4less-than-5      ; We get the infor-
                                                ; mation plus the value.
```

As can be seen from this example, print prints out the information all right, but unless we do something to get it to look reasonable, it comes out in a rather funny-looking way.

Most Lisps these days have special functions for printing formated output. The one in Franz Lisp is msg. Let us repeat the example above using it.

```
-> (defun foo (x)
        (msg "Entering foo with x bound to "
            (or x) N)
        . . .)
foo
->(foo 4)
Entering foo with x bound to 4
less-than-5
```

Essentially msg prints out anything between quotation marks as is. It will evaluate any piece of list structure (in the example above (or x) evaluates to the value of x) and certain atoms like N have special meanings. N says to put in a line feed. There are other things which can be done with msg, but we will ignore them.

For most output functions there are corresponding input functions. The most used is read (reads one S-expression), and others include ratom (reads one atom) and readc (reads one character). For the moment we will assume that they take no arguments. The following is a function to ask the user for an answer to some problem.

```
-> (defun ask ()
        (msg "I give up, what "      ; Print out a nice message
             "is the answer?" N      ; followed by a prompt.
             "* ")                    ; Then read what the user
        (read))                       ; responds, and return
                                      ; it as the value of ask.
ask                                   ;
-> (ask)                              ; Calling ask causes it to
I give up, what is the answer?        ; print out a message,
* foobar                              ; and read what the user
foobar                                ; types to it.
```

So far we have tacitly assumed that all input and output was to the terminal. It is possible to direct it to files instead. In such cases one must first open a file for reading or writing (using the functions infile and outfile). Each of these takes one argument, the name of the file, and returns a *port* which can be thought of as a portal to the file. Earlier we noted that both reading and writing functions took an optional argument. This argument is a port and, if present, the input or output will go to the file, and not to the terminal. However, at this point you would be best advised to consult your friendly Lisp reference manual for further details.

2.18 Macros

So far we have concentrated on the bread-and-butter aspects of Lisp. In this section we will look at one topic which is normally classified as an "advanced" one, but which nevertheless plays a major role in the Lisp programmers toolbox — *macros*. Many programming languages have a *macro facility*. This offers a way for the programmer to have often used chunks of code substituted into programs. Lisp has such a facility as well. A Lisp macro is a Lisp function whose value is itself a Lisp function call. The second function call is substituted in place of the first, and its value will be the one that "counts." To define a macro one uses defmacro. For example, suppose we wanted to define a function sq that does exactly what setq does. Here is how to do it with a macro.

```
-> (defmacro sq (var val)             ; defmacro defines a macro with two
        '(setq ,var ,val))            ; arguments, variable and value.
sq                                    ; Its value is a call to setq.
-> (defun sq-test (a b)               ; Let's try using it
        (sq x a)                      ; in a function.
        (sq y b))                     ;
sq-test                               ;
-> (sq-test 3 4)                      ; Now try the function
4                                     ;
```

```
-> x                          ; x got bound to 3.
3                             ;
-> y                          ; y got bound to 4.
4
```

Probably the easiest way to think about macros is to imagine that when the macro call is found in a function (as sq is found in sq-test) the macro is evaluated at the time the function is defined. This phase is called *macro expansion*. The result of macro expansion is a second piece of Lisp code, which is now put into the function being defined (here sq-test). Later when we call this function the new code will be evaluated just as if you had typed it in originally. A macro can go any place you could put a normal Lisp function, and the code it produces will act as if it had always been there.

In the case of sq, the code produced through macro expansion will be a call to setq. In particular, a call to sq of the form

    (sq z 8)

will produce the code

    (setq z 8)

(You might want to refresh your memory of the back-quote function at this point.) The definition of sq-test after macro expansion will look like this:

```
(defun sq-test (a b)
    (setq x a)          ; The first call to sq is replaced here.
    (setq y b))         ; The second call is here.
```

Note that the arguments to the macro call are *not* evaluated at macro expansion time. This is obviously important for sq because in (sq x 3) the x should not be evaluated.

Another useful feature of macros is that they allow for functions which do not take a fixed number of arguments. For example, suppose we want to generalize our sq function so that it takes any number of variable value combinations, as in:

    (sq x 3 y 'hello)

The following version of sq will allow for this:

```
(defmacro sq lst                      ; Lst will be a list of args.
    (loop (initial (ans nil))         ; Ans collects the setqs
          (while (cdr lst))           ; until no more pairs
          (next (ans (cons            ; e.g., (setq x 3).
                    '(setq ,(car lst) ; Add each seq to ans.
                           ,(cadr lst))
                    ans))
                (lst (cddr lst)))     ; Go on to next pair.
          (result '(progn ,@(reverse ans)))))  ; Put setqs together.
```

Here the expansion of (sq x 3 y 'hello) will be this:

```
(progn (setq x 3)
       (setq y 'hello))
```

The function **progn** evaluates all of its arguments, and returns the value of the last.

The one unusual aspect of this definition of **sq** is the fact that it takes one variable, which does not have parentheses around it. This tells Lisp that this variable should be bound to *all* of the arguments to the macro call (unevaluated). Because all of the arguments are made into a list there is obviously no restriction on how many there are. This ability is useful for top-level user-interaction functions, where it allows for optional arguments.

2.19 References and Further Reading

There are any number of beginning textbooks on Lisp. The grandfather of them all is by Weissman [Weissman67]. Some of the more recent ones are those by Wilensky [Wilensky84], Winston and Horn [Winston80] Siklossy [Siklossy76] and Shapiro [Shapiro79]. For a more advanced treatment of Lisp, and its use in AI, you might look at the book by Charniak, Riesbeck, and McDermott [Charniak80].

Exercises

2.1 Write Lisp code to compute the following:

a) $\dfrac{943+491}{62-21}$

b) $82463*(45-33)-552$

c) $666+\dfrac{\dfrac{144}{6}}{8*7}$

2.2 Define the function **average**, which will take two numbers as arguments and compute their average.

2.3 Write a function that computes the factorial of a number. (Factorial of 0 is 1, and factorial of n is $n*(n-1)* \cdots *1$. Factorial is defined only for integers greater than or equal to 0.)

2.4 Write a function of two integer arguments that computes the first argument raised to the power of the second argument. That is, if we call this function **exponent**, then the arguments 5 and 3 will compute 5^3.

```
-> (exponent 5 3)
125
```

You may assume that the second argument is a nonnegative integer.

2.5 Assume that the variable lst1 has the value (a (b c) ((d e)) (f)).

   a) What is the value of (car (cdr (car (cdr lst1))))?
   b) Write an expression using cars and cdrs which will extract the f
      from lst1.

2.6 Write a function which takes as input a list of numbers and returns their
     sum. That is, if we call the function add-them, we would have

        -> (add-them '(1 2 3 4))
        10

2.7 Fix the bugs in query and match-atoms of Figure 2.1.

2.8 Using just cons and nil build up the list (()).

2.9 What will (cons 1 (cons 2 (cons (cons 3 nil) nil))) evaluate to?

2.10 After each of the following commands, give the value of lst1, and, where
     applicable, lst2.

        (setq lst1 (cons '(a b) nil))
        (setq lst1 (cons 1 lst1))
        (setq lst2 (cons 2 lst1))
        (setq lst1 (cons 3 lst1))

2.11 Write a function pair-off that takes a list of atoms and returns a list with
     each pair of atoms made into a sublist. (If the number of atoms is not
     even, it will return nil.)

        -> (pair-off '(a b c d))
        ((a b) (c d))
        -> (pair-off '(a b c d e))
        nil

2.12 Exercise 1.3 was concerned with inference using a simple set of facts,
     repeated here in Figure 2.23. In this and subsequent exercises found in
     this chapter we will implement several programs that use this information.
     We will assume that the statements are found in a list bound to some vari-
     able, in Figure 2.23, data. (Note the setq in Figure 2.23.) For this exer-
     cise write the function parts that takes two arguments, an object, and a
     list of data.

        (parts *object data-list*)

     The function parts will go through *data-list*, looking for everything that is
     explicitly stated to be a part of *object*. (It need not do any inference.) For
     example, on the data in Figure 2.23 we would expect the following
     behavior:

```
(setq    data
              '((isa circus-elephant elephant)      ; Circus elephants are elephants.
                (has-part elephant head)            ; Elephants have heads
                (has-part elephant trunk)           ; and trunks.
                (has-part head mouth)               ; Heads have mouths.
                (isa elephant animal)               ; Elephants are animals.
                (has-part animal heart)             ; Animals have hearts.
                (isa circus-elephant performer)     ; Circus elephants are performers.
                (has-part performer costume)        ; Performers have costumes.
                (isa costume clothes)))             ; Costumes are clothes.
```

Figure 2.23 Knowledge for an inference program

```
-> (parts 'elephant data)      ; The only explicit parts
(trunk head)                   ; of elephants mentioned
-> (parts 'costume data)       ; are trunk and head.
nil                            ; Costume has none.
-> (parts 'performer data)     ; Performer has only
(costume)                      ; costume.
```

2.13 What are the values of the following three Lisp function calls:

```
(list '(1 2) '(3))
(cons '(1 2) '(3))
(append '(1 2) '(3))
```

2.14 Using the function **loop**, write the function **intersection** that, given two lists, produces the intersection of the two lists. For example:

```
-> (intersection '(a b c d) '(a 1 c 2))      ; Standard case.
(a c)                                        ;
-> (intersection '(a a b c d) '(a a 1 c 2))  ; Repeated elements
(a c)                                        ; are removed.
-> (intersection '(a (b c) d) '(a 1 (b c) 2)) ; The elements may
(a (b c))                                    ; themselves be lists.
```

2.15 Write a function that takes a single list and looks at each element of the list. If the element is a number, it is saved in a list of numbers that have been seen. If the element is a symbol, it is saved in a list of symbols, and if it is neither, it is "thrown away." In particular, if it is a list, it will not look at the elements of the list. The function returns a list comprising the two lists just described: first the list of numbers, then the list of symbols. (The order within these lists is not important.) If there are repeats, they will be listed only once. For example,

```
-> (classify '(a 3 (b 2) 4 c 3 (b 2)))
((3 4) (c a))
```

2.16 If you did Exercise 2.14 (writing an intersection function), the function you wrote probably worked by going through one list and for each item in it, looking at each element of the second list to see if they were the same. This can be "hidden" by using the function **member**, but the principle is the same. To a rough approximation, this technique takes time proportional to $m*n$ where m and n are the lengths of the two lists. For very long lists this can be expensive. The time to intersect two lists of length 100 will be 400 times longer than the time needed to intersect two lists of length 5. We can significantly improve this if we restrict consideration to lists of symbols. The idea is to first go through one list putting a mark on the property list of each element, then go through the second list looking for those elements that are marked, and save them. Finally the function should remove all of the marks. This will take time proportional to $2n+m$. Write this function.

2.17 Define the function **addprop**.

> (addprop *symbol attribute value*)

We want **addprop** to work like the previously encountered **putprop**,

> (putprop *symbol value attribute*)

in that it modifies the properties of *symbol* under the indicator *attribute*. However, rather than putting *value* as the value, it adds *value* to the list of properties already there. Naturally, **addprop** will call **putprop**. Thus we get the following dialogue:

-> (get 'elephant 'has-part)	; *Initially elephant*
nil	; *has nothing under*
	; *has-part.*
-> (addprop 'elephant 'has-part 'head)	; *We then add head*
(head)	; *as a part.*
-> (get 'elephant 'has-part)	; *Now we get a list*
(head)	; *with one element,*
	; *head. If we*
-> (addprop 'elephant 'has-part 'trunk)	; *addprop trunk*
(trunk head)	; *under has-part, we*
-> (get 'elephant 'has-part)	; *will now have both*
(trunk head)	; *it and head there.*

2.18 In this exercise we will create a function named **make-db**.

> (make-db *data-list*)

Here *data-list* is expected to be a list of formulas of the form shown in Figure 2.23. The basic idea behind **make-db** is to put the information in *data-list* into a form more easily accessible to Lisp. This form will use a symbol's properties to store the information about an object. In particular, **make-db** will consider each formula to be a fact about the first argument.

(isa circus-elephant elephant)

is considered to be a fact about **circus-elephant**. Thus **make-db** will add to **circus-elephant**'s properties (under the attribute **isa**) the value **elephant**. The function **addprop** from Exercise 2.17 would be useful here.

(has-part elephant trunk)

would cause **make-db** to add **trunk** to the **has-part** indicator of **elephant**. The result of this should be a database with the following form:

Atom	Properties	
	isa	has-part
circus-elephant	(elephant performer)	
elephant	(animal)	(head trunk)
head		(mouth)
animal		(heart)
performer		(costume)
costume	(clothes)	

2.19 Because the function described in Exercise 2.18 does not store *back pointers*, there is no way of going from, say, **head**, to the things that have heads. Revise the function **make-db** so that it also stores back pointers.

2.20 Explain how the presence of circular lists can cause problems to the reference counting implementation of garbage collection.

2.21 Using the cell notation, show graphically the pointers for **var1**, **var2**, and **var3** after the following conversation.

(setq var1 '(1 2))
(setq var2 var1)
(setq var3 var2)

2.22 Draw the cell notation for the following:

a) (a)
b) ((a))
c) (a (b c d))
d) (a ((b c) d))

2.23 What is the list structure corresponding to the following cell notation in Figure 2.24.

2.24 Draw the cells corresponding to the list structures pointed to by the variables **x** and **y** before and after the **rplacd** command in the following:

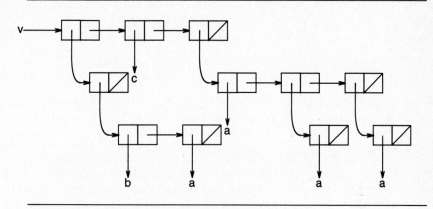

Figure 2.24 Cell notation for an s-expression

```
-> (setq x '(a b c))
(a b c)
-> (setq y (cdr x))
(b c)
-> (rplacd x '(e))
(a e)
```

2.25 If we do not care about screening out repeated elements, a very simple definition of **intersection** can be written using the **for** function. Write such a function.

2.26 Write a function that returns a list of all of the atoms that appear in an expression, no matter at what level of list structure the atoms appear. You may have duplication if you like and the order of appearance is not important.

```
-> (atoms-of '(a (b c) (((d) b))))
(b d c b a)
```

2.27 This is the last of the exercises based upon the facts about elephants, mammals, etc. given in Figure 2.23. For the purposes of this assignment you should have available the function **make-db** described in Exercise 2.18 that takes the list of formulas shown in Figure 2.23 and indexes them on the symbols' properties. In this assignment you are to write two functions: isa-p and has-part-p.

(isa-p *object superclass*)
(has-part-p *object subpart*)

(The -**p** at the end is a common Lisp convention for indicating predicates.) **Isa-p** should return a non-**nil** value if we already have stored in the database that *object* isa *superclass*, or if the program can prove this fact according to the following logical rules:

```
(forall (x, y, z) (implies (and (isa x y)   ; If x isa y
                                (isa y z)); and y isa z,
                    (isa x z)))    ; then x isa z.
                                   ;
(forall (x) (isa x x))             ; Everything isa
                                   ; itself.
```

That is, isa-p returns a non-nil value if *object* = *superclass* (e.g., elephant isa elephant), if *object* isa *superclass* according to the database, or if *object* isa *intermediate* according to the database and

(isa-p *intermediate superclass*)

is true. Otherwise it should return nil. Note therefore that isa-p will be recursive. The other function, has-part-p, should work so as to produce the results given in Figure 1.15. That is, if a has-part predication is true in Figure 1.15, then the corresponding call to has-part-p should return a non-nil value, and if false, it should return nil. Thus we would expect has-part-p and isa-p to work as follows:

```
-> (isa-p 'circus-elephant 'animal)
t
-> (isa-p 'circus-elephant 'clown)
nil
-> (has-part-p 'circus-elephant 'trunk)
t
```

3

This chapter depends on material in Chapter 1, but nothing else depends on it. If you would like to omit the details of low-level vision, skip Sections 3.4.1 to 3.4.5, and Sections 3.4.7 to 3.4.8.

Vision

3.1 Introduction

Sight is our most impressive sense. It gives us, without conscious effort, detailed information about the shape of the world around us. It is also the most intensely studied sense in AI, and a natural place to begin our study of the transduction of physical phenomena into internal representation.

Vision starts with an eye, a device for capturing and focusing the light that bounces off objects. Every point on an object (other than a mirror) scatters incident light out in all directions. An eye has a lens or pinhole that directs the light from one point on an object to just one point on a surface.

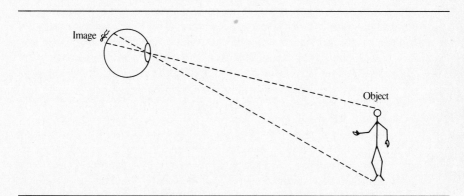

Figure 3.1 Image of a stick man

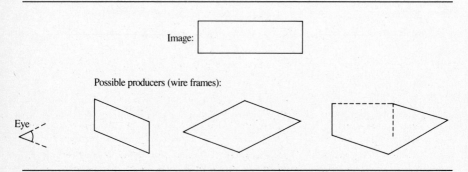

Figure 3.2 Three interpretations of a rectangular image

The pattern of light cast this way is an *image*. See Figure 3.1. The image is upside down and reversed right-to-left, but that's irrelevant: no one is "looking" at it, only performing computations on it. It *is* relevant that the image is two-dimensional, while the object is three-dimensional. It is inevitable that the image is ambiguous. For example, an image in the shape of a rectangle (see Figure 3.2) might be the image of a rectangle, or a square, or even some non-closed curve.

In this chapter, we will usually show images "right-side up." This convention will make reading them easier, but will have the unfortunate side effect that accompanying diagrams showing how an image was formed will look backwards (as in Figure 3.37 and Figure 3.38).

Box 3.1

Upside-down Images

When optics first began to flourish in the seventeenth century, one of the first discoveries made was that the eye contains a lens, much like the lenses being ground by telescope makers. This was exciting, but also confusing. In previous philosophical traditions, such as Scholastic and Aristotelian philosophy, the senses were modeled as receiving some sort of "template" of the sensed object, transmitted through the air by unknown means. The telescope offered a more concrete model: it gathered up light that was already in the environment, and made it into an image. Clearly, the eye did something very similar.

The confusion arose because the telescope is in one respect a terrible model of vision. Having gathered the light and formed an image, it leaves the rest to whoever is looking through it. Inevitably, therefore, early opticians assumed that vision consisted of the "soul" looking at the image cast by the lens on the back of the eye. But the image is upside down and backwards. Why don't we have a subjective impression of this?

The correct explanation is that the processes going on behind the eye are not themselves like ''looking,'' but like ''data processing.'' A data processor does not care where on the retina the patch corresponding to *upper-left* lies; *lower-right* will do fine. Because of the ways neurons communicate, it helps if regions that are close together in the real world are processed close together in the brain, but for many computational devices (like digital computers) even this is not required.

This viewpoint has been obvious only recently. For three hundred years, there was no concept of data processing separate from holistic human experience, and so circular models in which looking was explained in terms of the soul's looking were hard to avoid. It was widely thought that humans *did* perceive the world upside-down at birth, and had to learn that, e.g., raising the right hand would cause downward movement in the left part of the image. Eventually, the ''inversion'' of the image so that all sensory channels were in harmony became so automatic that by adulthood no one could remember the way things ''really'' looked.

Although this whole issue seems silly now, as late as 1975 the New Columbia Encyclopedia (p. 2904) said this: ''The image formed on the retina is . . . inverted . . . . However, the mental image as interpreted by the brain is right side up. How the brain corrects the inverted image to produce normal vision is unknown . . . .''

3.2 Defining the Problem

Unlike many problems in AI, the vision problem may be stated with reasonable precision: Given a two-dimensional image, infer the objects that produced it, including their shapes, positions, colors, and sizes. (One imprecision is that this fails to say what counts as an object; when you look at a beach, you don't have to enumerate the grains of sand.)

An image may be thought of as a function giving the *gray level* at every point on the image plane. The gray level varies from 0, meaning utter blackness, up to some maximum brightness, which we can call 1, corresponding to the maximum response the eye can make. (In this book, we will neglect color vision.)

We can assign coordinates to the surface the image is produced on. We will need two, because surfaces are two-dimensional. The easiest way to do this is to assume the image surface is flat, and use ordinary Cartesian x and y coordinates. This is appropriate for computer vision; for creatures with eyeballs, some other system might be better.

We can approximate the gray-level function by a two-dimensional array image. This approximation amounts to breaking the image into squares, and recording the average gray level over each square. We call the cell (image i j), the smallest unit of the image, a *pixel*, for ''picture element.'' Figure 3.3 gives an example. Note how each cell records the *average* gray level over it, so that details smaller than the size of a pixel are obscured. In this example, the result

(a)

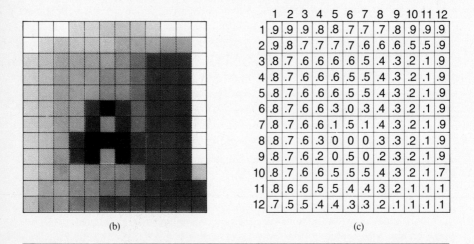

	1	2	3	4	5	6	7	8	9	10	11	12
1	.9	.9	.9	.8	.8	.7	.7	.7	.8	.9	.9	.9
2	.9	.8	.7	.7	.7	.7	.6	.6	.6	.5	.5	.9
3	.8	.7	.6	.6	.6	.6	.5	.4	.3	.2	.1	.9
4	.8	.7	.6	.6	.6	.5	.5	.4	.3	.2	.1	.9
5	.8	.7	.6	.6	.6	.5	.5	.4	.3	.2	.1	.9
6	.8	.7	.6	.6	.3	.0	.3	.4	.3	.2	.1	.9
7	.8	.7	.6	.6	.1	.5	.1	.4	.3	.2	.1	.9
8	.8	.7	.6	.3	0	0	0	.3	.3	.2	.1	.9
9	.8	.7	.6	.2	0	.5	0	.2	.3	.2	.1	.9
10	.8	.7	.6	.6	.5	.5	.5	.4	.3	.2	.1	.7
11	.8	.6	.6	.5	.5	.4	.4	.3	.2	.1	.1	.1
12	.7	.5	.5	.4	.4	.3	.3	.2	.1	.1	.1	.1

(b)   (c)

Figure 3.3 Array of pixels

is quite drastic. In a real image, there would be thousands of pixels, not 144, so that features like the "A" in the figure would not be so obscured. However, the same phenomenon would recur at a smaller scale.

Although it is artificial to model an image as a square array, modeling it as a discrete set of points is quite reasonable. The eye and brain must at some level do a similar discretization, because the back of the eye, the *retina*, is composed of millions of sensory nerve cells called *receptors* that respond to the illumination striking them. Anything whose image is much smaller than a receptor cannot be resolved.

However, it is probably not reasonable to think of the retina as a mere array of gray levels; a lot of information processing goes on there. Hence, although the details of the physiology of the animal visual system will not be of direct concern to us in this book, bear in mind that the computations we discuss may, in many animals, occur in the retina as well as in the brain.

It is unbelievably difficult to reason back from an image to the scene that created it. So much information is lost or obscured in the creation. As Figure 3.1 suggests, each spot in the image corresponds to one spot in the real world, namely, the piece of surface the light bounced off in order to make the image spot. (Two or more surfaces can contribute if transparent surfaces are allowed, but we will neglect this possibility.) Unfortunately, there are an infinite number of *candidate* spots that could have produced this image spot. Look at Figure 3.4. In the figure, we show the formation of an image of a single point, *A*. Its coordinates in the outside world are *x*, *y*, and *z*. The coordinates of the corresponding point in the image are *x'* and *y'*; *z* is called the *depth* of *A*, and is missing from the image, obviously. We measure *z* from the lens to the object. The distance from the lens to the image plane is labeled *f*, the *focal length*. By properties of similar triangles,

$$\frac{x'}{f} = \frac{x}{z} \qquad \frac{y'}{f} = \frac{y}{z}$$

For a given spot on the image, we know its *x'* and *y'*. Its *f* is also known, since it is the same for all points. But an infinite number of values of *x*, *y*, and *z* are compatible with known values of *x'*, *y'*, and *f*. A spot may have been the result of light bouncing off a nearby surface at one elevation, or a faraway surface at a higher elevation. This is why the rectangular image of Figure 3.2 is

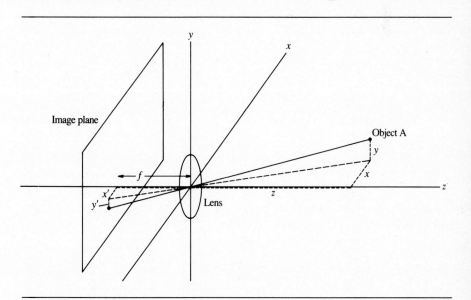

Figure 3.4 Geometry of image formation

ambiguous; each point could have come from a physical location far from those generating its neighbors.

Even when a coherent figure has been identified, the size of the physical object producing it is still ambiguous. The real size depends not only on the size of the figure in the image, but also on the distance ("depth") and orientation of the object as well. In Figure 3.5, f is the focal length of the camera; z is the depth of the object; θ is its orientation; s is its real size, and s' its apparent size. As before, f is known, but z, s, and θ are unknown. Without further information, this equation has lots of solutions, which correspond to very different scenes. A vision system that can't tell the difference between a nearby cat and faraway tiger is in trouble.

All this presupposes that there is a single image region corresponding to an object. What if the tiger is standing among some shrubbery? What if another object (the next victim?) is between the eye and the tiger, as in Figure 3.6?

An important feature of an object is its color. We will ignore true color vision, but we still have the problem of judging the whiteness of an object. The whiteness of an image area is just the percentage of light it reflects, or its *reflectance*. But in the image all we have is the amount of light hitting the eye. This depends on several variables:

- the actual reflectance
- the brightness of incident light

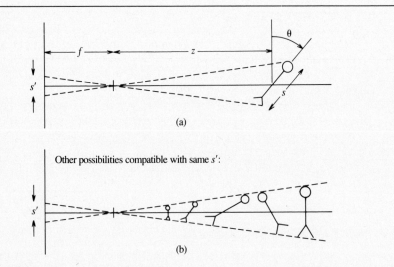

Figure 3.5 Find s, z, θ given s' and f

Figure 3.6 Partly occluded tiger

- the incidence angle: the angle at which the light hits the object (one per light source, and there may be several)
- the surface orientation of the area with respect to the viewer

In general, the light reflected by a surface came from an illumination source. When the light bounced off the surface, it was reflected in all directions. The amount the observer sees depends on two angles: the angle between the incoming light rays and the surface, and the angle between the outgoing light rays and the surface. Some surfaces (such as mirrors) reflect light almost entirely in one direction; these are called *specular* surfaces. Some reflect light equally in all directions; these are *Lambertian* surfaces. See Figure 3.7. In practice, many objects are near-Lambertian reflectors.

Because gray level depends on all these variables, a surface of uniform reflectance may appear as a region of varying gray level. An illuminated sphere will be irregularly shaded, and appear in the image as a disc of varying brightness. And, of course, many brightness variations are due to shadows. How is it that people can tell the difference between a white wall in shadow and a gray wall in sunlight?

3.3 Overview of the Solution

Fortunately, we know it is possible to extract information about objects from their images; we do it all the time. Attempts to explain how to do it began in the 1940s. In the 1950s, this research led to pattern recognition theory, now

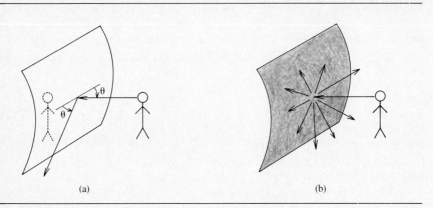

Figure 3.7 Reflecting surfaces

no longer considered part of AI. But very little real progress was made until quite recently.

> Despite considerable progress in recent years, our understanding of the principles underlying visual perception remains primitive. Attempts to construct computer models for the interpretation of arbitrary scenes have resulted in such poor performance, limited range of abilities, and inflexibility that, were it not for the human existence proof, we might have been tempted long ago to conclude that high-performance, general-purpose vision is impossible. [Barrow78]

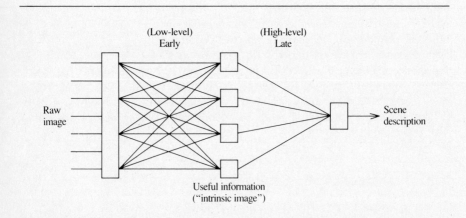

Figure 3.8 Stages of visual processing

We complete this dire observation by remarking that most of the results we will discuss are no more than ten years old. Although they look quite promising, they are fragmentary and not secure.

The overall structure of the emerging solution to the vision problem is of a two-stage process: early and late visual processing. In early processing, the goal is to get useful information from the raw image, and every part of the image is processed in the same way. In late processing, the goal is to find the objects from the useful information. See Figure 3.8. This schematic is intended only to suggest that early processing is parallel and local — lots of identical processing of small regions of the image. Its results are revealing enough that higher-level processes can walk through them sequentially and extract a symbolic description of the scene.

We'll look at both phases. It will help to describe first what the "Useful information" of Figure 3.8 consists of, since that is the destination of early processing, and the starting point of late processing. It is called the *intrinsic image*. (It has also been called the *2.5 dimensional sketch*.) It is a grouping of the image into regions corresponding to real physical surfaces. See Figure 3.9, which extends Figure 3.3. As the legend indicates, each of the 144 cells of the intrinsic image contains four quantities: the *illumination*, *reflectance*, *depth*, and *orientation* at that patch of surface. (The first three are given as somewhat arbitrary numbers; orientation is specified as an arrow, which would be represented as a vector of three numbers in the machine.) This is not an image at all in the sense we have been using, since it gives the values of real physical quantities at every point, rather than light intensities. The intrinsic image also shows physical boundaries between regions. These correspond to abrupt changes in the reflectance, depth, or illumination of the surface. (The terminology will be explained in Section 3.4.6.)

To illustrate the meaning of the intrinsic image, consider two points: A, from row 7, column 5, and B, from row 7, column 11. Both have gray level 0.1, but A is brightly illuminated and dark colored, while B is dimly illuminated and light colored (and their depths and orientations differ as well). In order to produce the intrinsic image, the vision system has had to "factor" 0.1 into a set of aspects of the physical situation that combined to give just this gray level. As we have emphasized, an infinite number of combinations can do this.

"Factoring" of this sort appears to be quite a feat. We should emphasize that to keep the example small we have used absurdly coarse pixels. It would not be practically possible to produce such a perfect intrinsic image from this gray-level image. But there is hope for doing it on more realistic images.

This hope is still controversial, but becoming less so. Computing intrinsic images is certainly difficult, in two senses: it is a difficult research problem to figure out how to accomplish the task; and it seems now that the solution, once obtained, will be costly to apply, measured in computing cycles. Fortunately, most of this cost is for early processing, where many of the computations are parallel and can be done simultaneously. The human visual system works in parallel, so if it is computing an intrinsic image, it has a big advantage over a serial computer, which must simulate the work of those millions of loosely

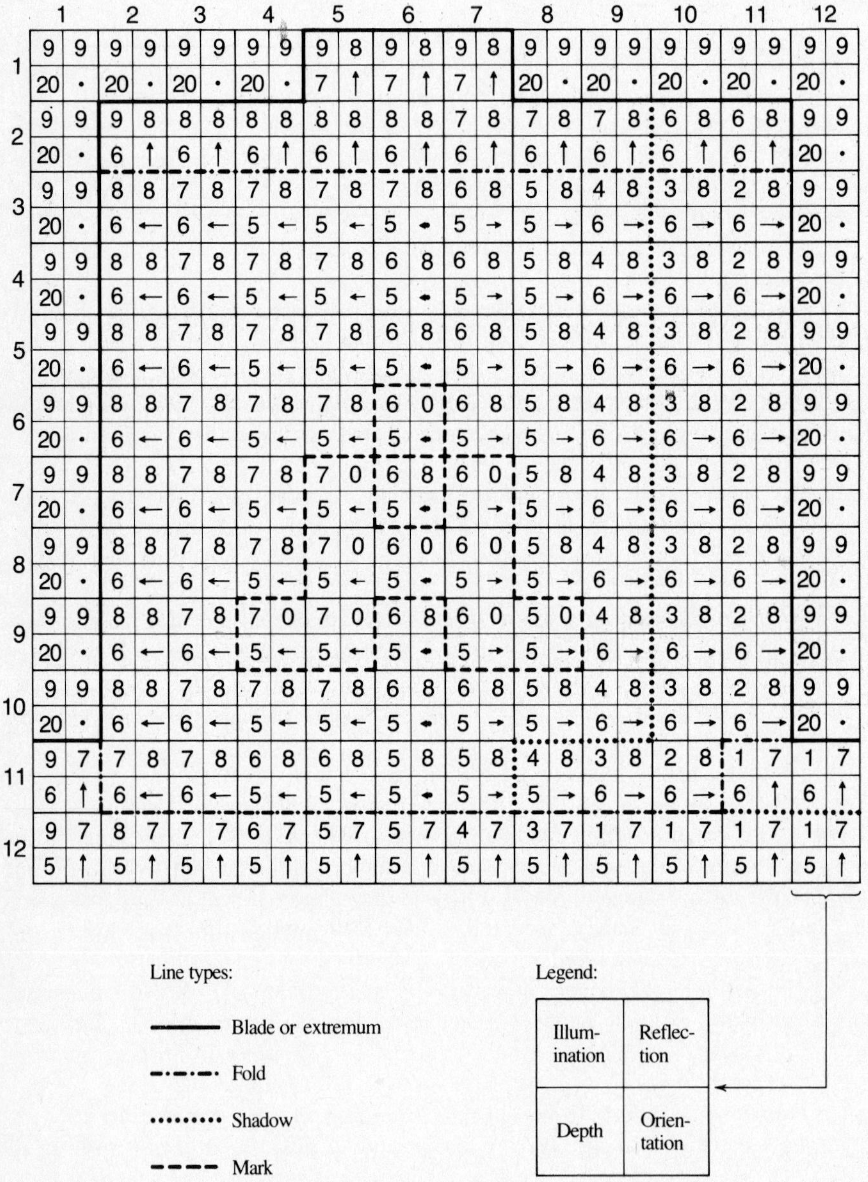

	1	2	3	4	5	6	7	8	9	10	11	12
1	9 9 / 20 ·	9 9 / 20 ·	9 9 / 20 ·	9 9 / 20 ·	9 8 / 7 ↑	9 8 / 7 ↑	9 8 / 7 ↑	9 9 / 20 ·	9 9 / 20 ·	9 9 / 20 ·	9 9 / 20 ·	9 9 / 20 ·
2	9 9 / 20 ·	9 8 / 6 ↑	8 8 / 6 ↑	8 8 / 6 ↑	8 8 / 6 ↑	8 8 / 6 ↑	7 8 / 6 ↑	7 8 / 6 ↑	7 8 / 6 ↑	6 8 / 6 ↑	6 8 / 6 ↑	9 9 / 20 ·
3	9 9 / 20 ·	8 8 / 6 ←	8 7 / 6 ←	8 7 / 5 ←	8 7 / 5 ←	8 6 / 5 •	8 5 / 5 →	8 4 / 5 →	8 3 / 6 →	8 2 / 6 →	8 9 / 6 →	9 9 / 20 ·
4	9 9 / 20 ·	8 8 / 6 ←	8 7 / 6 ←	8 7 / 5 ←	8 7 / 5 ←	8 6 / 5 ←	8 6 / 5 →	8 5 / 5 →	8 4 / 6 →	8 3 / 6 →	8 2 / 6 →	9 9 / 20 ·
5	9 9 / 20 ·	8 8 / 6 ←	8 7 / 6 ←	8 7 / 5 ←	8 7 / 5 ←	8 6 / 5 •	8 6 / 5 →	8 5 / 5 →	8 4 / 6 →	8 3 / 6 →	8 2 / 6 →	9 9 / 20 ·
6	9 9 / 20 ·	8 8 / 6 ←	8 7 / 6 ←	8 7 / 5 ←	8 7 / 5 ←	8 6 / 5 •	0 6 / 5 →	8 5 / 5 →	8 4 / 6 →	8 3 / 6 →	8 2 / 6 →	9 9 / 20 ·
7	9 9 / 20 ·	8 8 / 6 ←	8 7 / 6 ←	8 7 / 5 ←	8 7 / 5 ←	0 6 / 5 •	8 6 / 5 →	0 5 / 5 →	8 4 / 6 →	8 3 / 6 →	8 2 / 6 →	9 9 / 20 ·
8	9 9 / 20 ·	8 8 / 6 ←	8 7 / 6 ←	8 7 / 5 ←	8 7 / 5 ←	0 6 / 5 •	0 6 / 5 →	0 6 / 5 →	8 5 / 6 →	8 4 / 6 →	8 3 / 8 2 →	9 9 / 20 ·
9	9 9 / 20 ·	8 8 / 6 ←	8 7 / 6 ←	8 7 / 5 ←	0 7 / 5 ←	0 6 / 5 •	8 6 / 5 →	0 5 / 5 →	0 4 / 6 →	8 3 / 6 →	8 2 / 6 →	9 9 / 20 ·
10	9 9 / 20 ·	8 8 / 6 ←	8 7 / 6 ←	8 7 / 5 ←	8 7 / 5 ←	8 6 / 5 •	8 6 / 5 →	8 5 / 5 →	8 4 / 6 →	8 3 / 6 →	8 2 / 6 →	9 9 / 20 ·
11	9 7 / 6 ↑	7 8 / 6 ←	7 8 / 6 ←	6 8 / 5 ←	6 8 / 5 ←	6 8 / 5 •	5 8 / 5 →	5 8 / 5 →	4 8 / 6 →	3 8 / 6 →	2 8 / 6 ↑	1 7 / 6 ↑
12	9 7 / 5 ↑	8 7 / 5 ↑	7 7 / 5 ↑	7 6 / 5 ↑	7 5 / 5 ↑	7 5 / 5 ↑	7 5 / 5 ↑	7 4 / 5 ↑	7 3 / 5 ↑	7 1 / 5 ↑	7 1 / 5 ↑	7 1 / 5 ↑

Line types:

——— Blade or extremum

—·—·— Fold

·········· Shadow

— — — Mark

Legend:

Illum- ination	Reflec- tion
Depth	Orien- tation

Figure 3.9 Intrinsic image for Figure 3.3

coupled neurons all by itself. This takes a lot of time. If high-quality machine vision ever becomes a reality, it will need parallel computers to be done in real time.

Many vision projects before 1975 tried to avoid such massive computations. They didn't work too well. If there were a cheaper way to do vision, evolution would probably have found it.

3.4 Early Processing

Simple brute force is pointless unless guided by a theory. What we need may be thought of as a theory of how to "invert" the process of image formation. We must assign physical interpretations to the optical features found in the image, in spite of the ambiguities.

In early vision, the machine's basic strategy is to take many image characteristics into account to infer many physical characteristics; there are no one-to-one relationships. This implies that it cannot find the orientation intrinsic image independently of, say, the reflectance intrinsic image. The interpretation of one constrains the other.

There is not enough constraint unless we make plausible assumptions about what the machine is looking at. In some cases, it can guess or even know what it's looking at, and can bring a large number of clues to bear on deciphering its image. This applies most to industrial applications, like a vision-guided car factory. The only thing the machine will ever see there is an auto engine, so all it has to do is figure out exactly where the engine is. But for general-purpose vision, guesses about what the machine is looking at are not available until late vision. So when we talk of assumptions about the scene, we mean general assumptions about the physical world, not assumptions about exactly what the machine is looking at.

These assumptions tend to be instances of what is called the "nonaccidental image properties" heuristic:

> Properties observable in the picture are not by accident, but are projections of some preferred corresponding 3-D properties.

One example of this property is the assumption the eye naturally makes about the object producing the rectangular image of Figure 3.2, namely, that it is a closed curve with straight sides.

Another example is the assumption the eye makes that a texture gradient reflects a surface orientation. A *texture gradient* is a systematic change in the size and shape of the elements making up a texture. See Figure 3.10, in which the surfaces look as if they tilt away from the viewer (which, unless you are holding the book at a funny angle, they do not).

We will see examples of such assumptions repeatedly. As in the texture example, the best evidence that an assumption is worth making by a visual system is often that the human visual system makes it; and the best evidence for

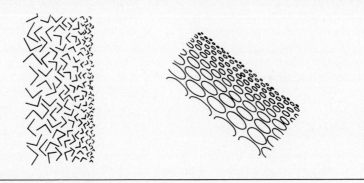

Figure 3.10 Texture gradients

this is that the eye can be fooled, in the absence of other cues, into perceiving what the assumption predicts.

In the rest of this section, we will look at some of the modules of the early-vision system. Figure 3.11 gives an overview of some of them. Each box is labeled with the main phenomenon of interest there. The first step of processing is the production of the *primal sketch*, a description of edges and other

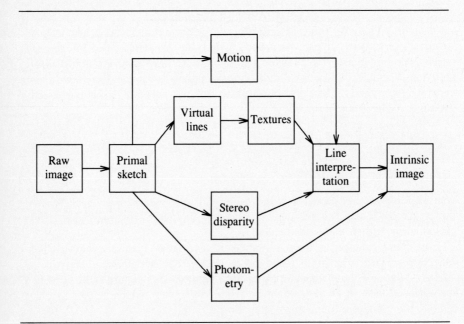

Figure 3.11 An overview of early visual processing

features of interest in the image. See Section 3.4.1. Many processes work with the primal sketch to extract more information. *Grouping processes* organize small features into larger wholes; one example is the *virtual-line* finders of Section 3.4.3. *Texture* analysis finds surface patches that consist of similarly organized elements, and extracts information from the changes in these elements. See Section 3.4.5. *Motion analysis* finds features that appear to be moving together, and derives the shape of the surface they belong to; we will not talk about this topic further. Analysis of *stereo disparity*, the slight differences between two views of the same scene through left and right eyes, reveals the depth and orientation of nearby surfaces. See Section 3.4.4. *Photometry* derives the shape of surfaces from their shading; this is another topic we will have to pass by.

Finally, all the evidence is put together to interpret the *lines* and *regions* found in the image as physical *areas* and *boundaries*, and the intrinsic image is produced. See Sections 3.4.6 through 3.4.8.

3.4.1 Gray-Level Image to Primal Sketch

The first step of early visual processing abstracts away from raw gray levels, analyzing the image as a structure of *changes* in gray levels. The early vision phase produces a database of data structures, each describing a *feature*, assembled from one or more edgelets. We use the term *edgelet* to mean the smallest distinguishable "piece of edge," that is, a small patch where the gray level goes from dark to light. See Figure 3.12. This database of features is called the *primal sketch*. It serves as the basis for all later processing. (It is not clear whether any module ever has to look at the raw image again.)

A typical feature description might look like that shown in Figure 3.13. This expression describes an edge consisting of one or more edgelets found aligned near position $x = 104$, $y = 23$ in the image. The orientation is the angle of the vector from the dark side to the light side.

This sort of data structure uses the *slot-and-filler* notation we described in Chapter 1. It describes an entity as being of a certain basic type (here, **edge**), with characteristics of standard kinds, such as its **position**, **orientation**, and so forth.

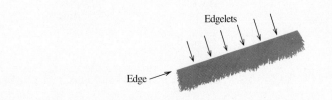

Figure 3.12 Edge assembled from edgelets

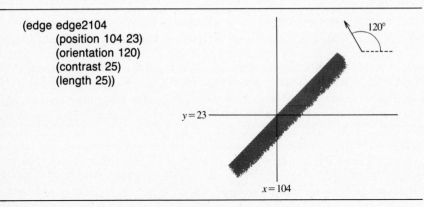

```
(edge edge2104
    (position 104 23)
    (orientation 120)
    (contrast 25)
    (length 25))
```

Figure 3.13 An edge and its description

The primal sketch is easier to work with than the raw image. For one thing, it contains fewer data; each feature description describes a small area of the image, but one made up of many pixels. But the most important reason is that the primal sketch is one step closer to "meaning something" than the gray levels are. A feature like an **edge** could be one of a list of things (a shadow, an object boundary, or some of the other phenomena we will describe below). A single pixel could be anything at all. If you are still doubtful, reflect on how easy it is for people to understand line drawings (e.g., cartoons). In such a drawing, all the normal surface information is missing; only edges remain. Yet we can still pick out the objects, and even recognize familiar faces. This is strong evidence that the primal-sketch features are the most important part of an image.

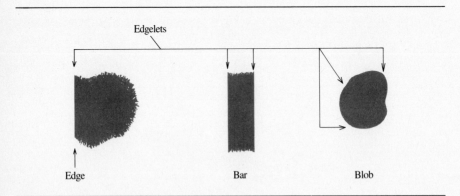

Figure 3.14 The three kinds of primal feature

Primal-sketch features are of three kinds: *edges*, *bars*, and *blobs*. (See Figure 3.14.) An edge is a sequence of edgelets laid end-to-end with roughly the same orientation, which separates a large light area from a large dark one. A bar is a pair of edgelet sequences running along together, bounding a region lighter or darker than the surrounding region. A blob is a small group of edgelets surrounding a small patch. (A big spot is described as the set of edges making up its border.) Figure 3.15 shows examples from a realistic image.

Edgelets and features are found by looking for places where the gray level changes abruptly. For readers with some calculus, the following discussion will sharpen up what we mean by "abruptly."

3.4.2 Convolution with Gaussians (Optional)

Figure 3.16 shows the first and second derivatives of intensity (taken perpendicular to the edgelet). A place where the second derivative crosses zero, or *zero crossing*, is where the first derivative attains its highest absolute values, where the gray levels change fastest. Intuitively, and for good theoretical reasons, such a zero crossing is our criterion for an edgelet.

While taking zero crossings of images may seem reasonable for smooth curves such as that in Figure 3.16, real pictures have *noise*, which complicates things. Figure 3.17 is an example of what light intensities might really look like. (As before, we have reduced the image to one dimension by picking an arbitrary direction to scan along; we will put the other dimension back in later.) Figure 3.17 illustrates a single object, with a significant intensity change on either side. However, if we took the second derivative we would find all sorts of zero crossings, corresponding to the spurious peaks created by the noise.

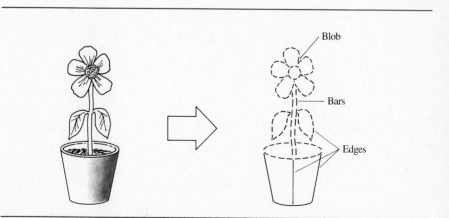

Figure 3.15 Primal features in a potted plant

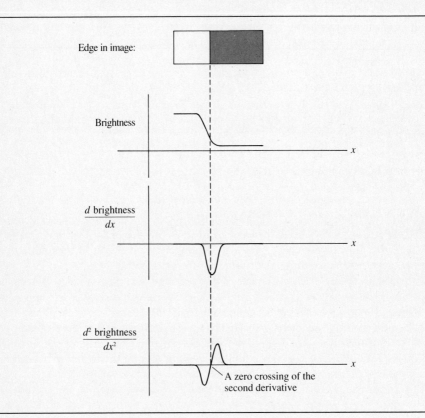

Figure 3.16 Behavior of brightness derivatives at an edgelet

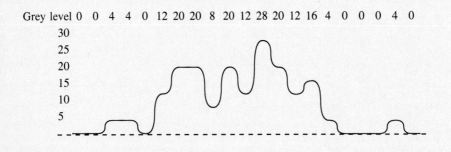

Figure 3.17 A one-dimensional image

The solution is to *smooth* the curve out by averaging each point with its neighbors. There are an infinite number of possible arrangements of weights one can use in taking this average. We can illustrate a particular one with a graph that uses the vertical axis to indicate the weight given to the value at a point, and the horizontal axis to indicate the position of the point. The zero position on the horizontal axis corresponds to the point whose value we are smoothing using the values from nearby points. For example, in Figure 3.18, the diagram indicates that we will smooth by averaging a point with the light intensity of the point immediately to its right, and giving each value equal weight. Another, symmetric scheme would weight the center point as 50%, while the points one over on each side would be counted 25%. So a gray level of 6, with a 2 to its left and a 4 to its right, would get smoothed to 4.5 thus:

$$2 \times 25\% + 6 \times 50\% + 4 \times 25\% = .5 + 3 + 1 = 4.5$$

Figure 3.19 shows the diagram for this set of weights. The weight diagrams can themselves be considered functions; in our one-dimensional illustrations,

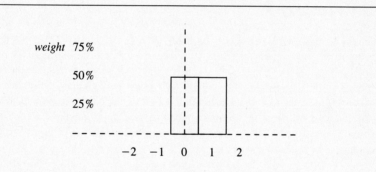

Figure 3.18 A simple set of weights for smoothing

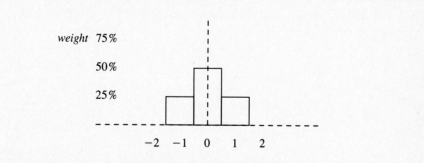

Figure 3.19 A symmetric set of weights for smoothing

they are functions of one discrete variable *w(i)*. The gray level is also a function, which we may denote *g(i)*. The general formula for weighting *g* is then:

$$Smoothed \ g(i) = \sum_{j=left}^{j=right} g(i-j)w(j) \tag{3.1}$$

The sum is taken over the bounds *left* to *right*. We can think of this as the range over which *w(j)* is nonzero. For the *w* of Figure 3.19, *left*=−1, *right*=1. However, we could just as well take *left*=−∞, *right*=∞, because all but three of the terms are zero anyway. (In case you have noticed that *g(i−j)* starts off at the *right* and moves left, see Exercise 3.2.) At the boundaries of the image, *g(i−j)* will denote a pixel off the image. Hence the values obtained at boundary pixels are meaningless, and must be discarded. In other words, the smoothed image is smaller than the original by the "width" of the weight diagram.

Figure 3.20 shows how a sequence of gray levels is smoothed into a less bumpy sequence. To get the smoothed version we take each point and apply the smoothing function to it and its two neighbors. We then move to the next point and do the same thing.

This is still rather bumpy, primarily because we have been lazy and shown changes that occur over only two or three pixels. If we had a system as sensitive as a human eye, we might have twenty, or perhaps two hundred light receptors picking up the changes for a single edgelet. When we are talking about numbers in this magnitude, we can smooth over a much larger number of elements — perhaps in the tens or hundreds of elements. How should we do it? Clearly we want the center point to count the most, and clearly the further away from the center a point is, the less weight it should have. We might want something like the weights shown in Figure 3.21.

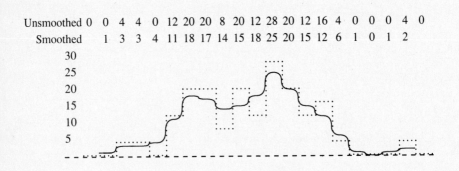

Unsmoothed 0 0 4 4 0 12 20 20 8 20 12 28 20 12 16 4 0 0 0 4 0
Smoothed   1 3 3 4 11 18 17 14 15 18 25 20 15 12 6 1 0 1 2

Figure 3.20 Smoothing a sequence of light intensities

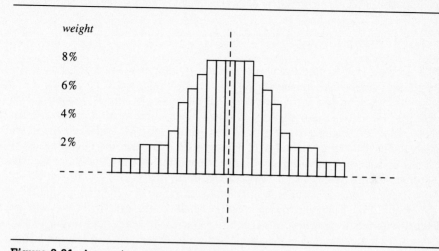

Figure 3.21 Averaging over many points

If we had even more points, rather than drawing it discretely, we would simply draw a curve and get something like the curve of Figure 3.22. This particular curve is called a *Gaussian curve* and it occurs frequently in statistics and probability. But that is not of particular concern to us here. For our part we use it because it is a curve with the shape we intuitively want. (This intuition can be backed up technically.) As before, we will apply this curve to each point in the scene, thus doing a weighted average of its gray level with the values at the neighboring points. This is called *convolving* the scene with the Gaussian curve. The process is known as *convolution*.

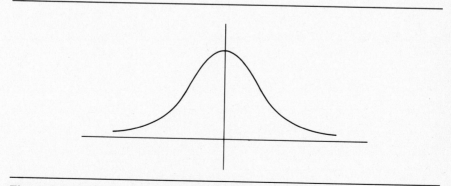

Figure 3.22 Continuous smoothing weights

The mathematical definition of convolution in the continuous case is a natural extension of our previous definition of smoothing in the discrete case:

$$smoothed\ g(x) = \int_{-\infty}^{\infty} g(x-u)w(u)du \qquad (3.2)$$

The notation $g*w$ is used to indicate the convolution of g and w to create a new function, a smoothed version of g.

To extend all this to two-dimensional pictures, we need a two-dimensional analogue to our Gaussian curve, and a two-dimensional version of convolution. The curve is obtained by rotating the one-dimensional version around the "weight" axis, giving the curve of Figure 3.23. Note that the three dimensions in this figure are the two image dimensions and the weight dimension; we have not introduced anything like a "three-dimensional image."

Generalizing the definition of convolution requires weighting a point by all the points around it, and hence requires another integral sign. We will not bother with this technicality.

Let us back up and remind ourselves how we got here. We noted that the machine could find the lines in a scene by taking the second derivatives of the light intensities and looking for zero crossings. We then commented that if it used the raw light intensities, the noise would create lots of spurious bumps, and hence lots of spurious zero crossings. Hence we decided to first smooth the light intensities by convolving the scene with the Gaussian, and then taking the second derivative of the result. Symbolically we can represent this process as follows:

$$\frac{\partial^2}{\partial x^2} Gaussian*Image$$

This formula says to convolve each image with the Gaussian curve, and then take the second derivative. However, there is a mathematical result (which you

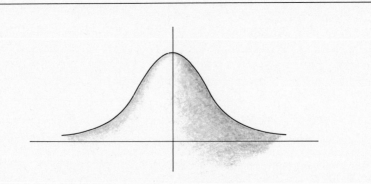

Figure 3.23 Two-dimensional continuous smoothing

can prove or accept on faith) that states:

$$\frac{\partial^2}{\partial x^2} Gaussian*Image = \frac{\partial^2 Gaussian}{\partial x^2}*Image \qquad (3.3)$$

This says that the machine can convolve the image, not with the Gaussian, but rather with the second derivative of the Gaussian. We show this curve for the one dimensional case in Figure 3.24. Using this approach is clearly to our advantage. Rather than having to do two separate operations on each scene (first Gaussian, then second derivative), the machine need only do one operation, convolving with the second derivative of the Gaussian. Of course, we must find this curve, but only once, when we program the machine, and

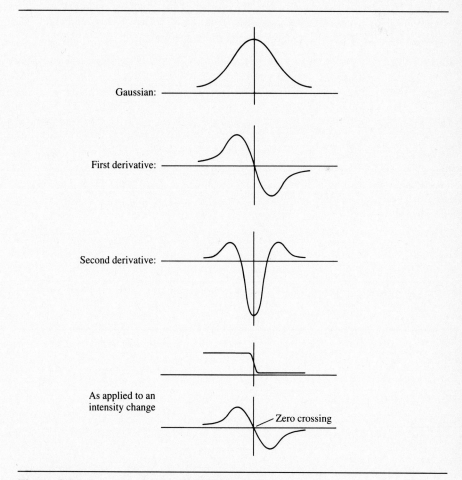

Figure 3.24 Derivatives of a Gaussian curve

thereafter it can use this same curve on each new scene. An example of how this curve will react with a light intensity change is illustrated in Figure 3.24. It indicates that we get a zero crossing at exactly the spot where we would expect it.

The two-dimensional analogue of this curve is again found by revolving its curve around the vertical axis. The result looks a little like a sombrero, as shown in Figure 3.25.

Even though we have settled on Gaussians for use in smoothing images, there is one degree of freedom left: the width of the Gaussian. Figure 3.26 shows several alternatives. The high-peaked, narrow Gaussian averages in only a few neighbors with the gray level of a pixel; the low-peaked, wide Gaussian averages in many. As we saw in Figure 3.20, averaging in only two points left a few "spurious" peaks. On the other hand, if the machine averages over too wide an area, it could throw away real features of relatively low contrast. The sharp Gaussian is said to have *high resolution*; the wide one, *low resolution*.

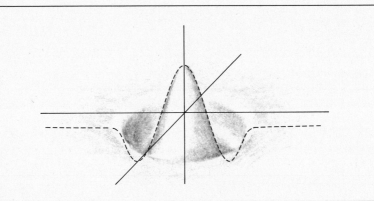

Figure 3.25 Two-dimensional curve to be convolved

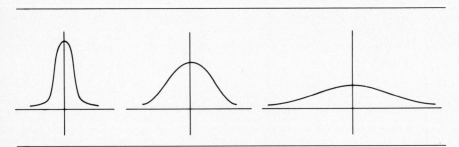

Figure 3.26 Several Gaussians of different widths

One solution to this dilemma is to smooth at two or more resolutions, and take derivatives at all of them. (Five might be a good number.) This procedure produces a set of two or more "maps" of the image, showing edgelets that appear at different resolutions. Then the machine looks for agreement and disagreement among the maps of zero crossings. A vivid, high-contrast edgelet that borders a large patch will appear on every map as an edge. But an edgelet that borders a small patch may be missed in low-resolution maps. That's because the gray levels at the left and right borders of the patch will be swamped by faraway points outside it. See Figure 3.27. At some finer resolution, the small patch will appear as two or more edgelets. If these edgelets are in two parallel lines, pointing in opposite directions, the machine classes the group as a bar. If they all point toward a center, it classes the group as a blob.

We can conclude that an edgelet will always be "corroborated" by other edgelets, either in the same map or maps at other resolutions, or both. An uncorroborated edgelet can be discarded as noise. There is no mathematical theorem to this effect. In fact, there are mathematically possible images that cause the Gaussian operator to report many edgelets at the same place when there is no physical boundary there. However, such images do not normally occur in nature. This is called the *spatial coincidence assumption*:

> If a zero-crossing segment is present in a set of independent [maps of Gaussian convolutions] . . ., and the segment has the same position and orientation in each channel, then the set of such zero-crossing segments indicates the presence of an intensity change in the image that is due to single physical phenomenon (a change in reflectance, illumination, depth, or surface orientation). ([Marr82] p. 70)

In other words, groups of corroborating edgelets are so strongly correlated with physical boundaries that we can ignore the uncorroborated ones.

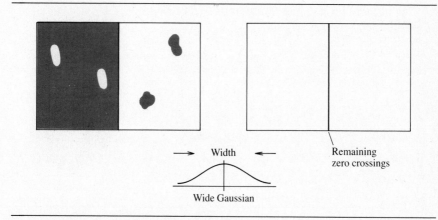

Figure 3.27 Small patches convolved away

Box 3.2

Gaussian Convolution in the Brain

Given the good theoretical properties of Gaussian operators, it is interesting to ask if brains use them. The answer seems to be yes. However, there is one major problem in applying this algorithm to brains. Brains use neurons to process information, and from what we can tell, one neuron passes a value to the next by changing the rate at which it fires. So the faster the neuron is firing, the larger the value it is trying to pass along. The trouble is that in the algorithm described in the text, we need to pass both positive and negative values. While there is no trouble firing faster to get a higher value, there is no obvious way to fire at a rate less than zero.

The solution nature found to this is rather clever. The *visual cortex* is that part of the brain where the information from the eyes ends up. A neuron there integrates information from several different spots on the retina, and thus different neurons will respond to different types of stimuli, occurring at different places on the retina. There are, however, two particular kinds of neuron that are important to our current discussion. They both seem to operate by convolving our "sombrero" Gaussian with a portion of the image, but one kind fires faster when the value is more and more positive, while the other fires faster when the value becomes more and more negative. Both of these are shown in Figure 3.28. Both types of receptors seem to exist in the visual cortex.

If we look back at Figure 3.24, we see that a line is indicated by a high value of the Mexican hat on one side of the line, and a large negative value on the other. In terms of our two neuronal receptors, the positive one would fire in response to the first, and the negative one would respond to the second. Thus if we have positive and negative receptors right next to each other, and both firing, this would indicate that an intensity change occurred between the two.

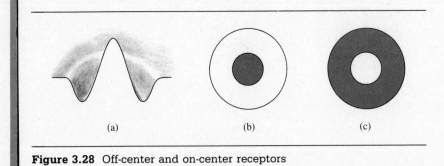

(a)   (b)   (c)

Figure 3.28 Off-center and on-center receptors

3.4.3 Virtual Lines

The next box in Figure 3.11 that we will examine is the one labeled "Virtual lines." For a variety of reasons, including the presence of noise, the machine must add to the features found in the primal sketch some lines found by connecting nearby blobs, bar endpoints, and edge endpoints in the image. People apparently do this, since we have no trouble understanding Figure 3.29. But which nearby features are connected? How does the vision system distinguish the door from the walls? The basic answer is that it connects a point to its nearest neighbors. But what is the cutoff between the "near" neighbors and the not-so-near?

An ingenious answer involves the construction of a *histogram* of line orientations, virtual and real. The machine draws from every point a "virtual line" to each nearby point within some preset distance, as in Figure 3.30. It then categorizes these lines into 10° "buckets" and plots a graph of how many lines appear in each bucket. See Figure 3.31.

A curve showing the proportion of some population of objects is called a *histogram*. Because the nearer neighbors are more important, the machine weights each neighbor by the reciprocal of its distance. (So faraway features can be neglected entirely.)

If there are many objects in the population, the chart will be almost a continuous curve. In the typical virtual-line case, however, there are only a few neighbors for each point, so the histogram is fairly lumpy. To compensate for this, the algorithm adds in the histograms for each neighbor, which gives a smoother curve, as shown in Figure 3.32. The peaks in the histogram represent where the "overall flow" of virtual lines should be in the neighborhood of this point.

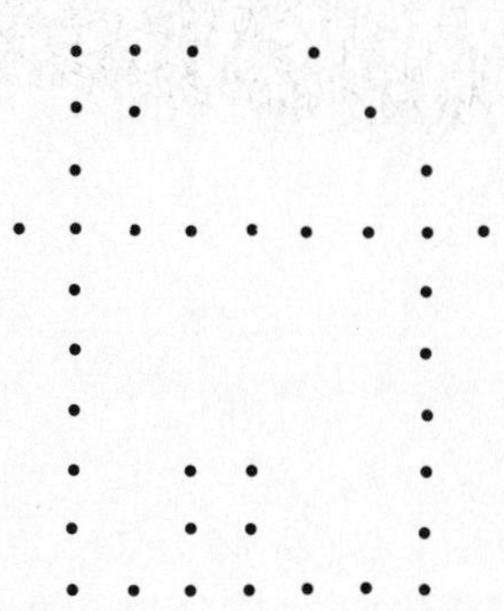

Figure 3.29 What is this?

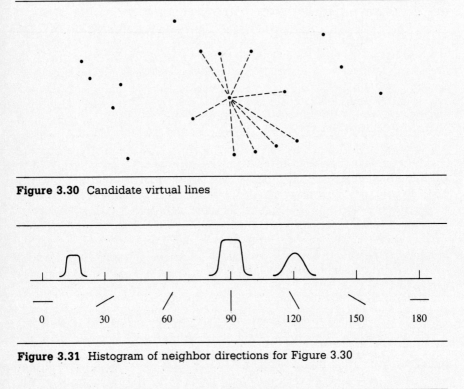

Figure 3.30 Candidate virtual lines

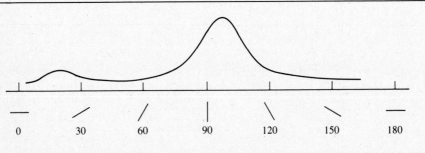

Figure 3.31 Histogram of neighbor directions for Figure 3.30

Figure 3.32 Smoothed histogram of near neighbors

Now the machine throws away all the virtual lines except those in the buckets coinciding with the peak of the histogram. It does this for every blob or edge termination in the primal sketch. For our "dot-house" example (in Figure 3.29), the result is as shown in Figure 3.33. Some more interesting examples are shown in Figure 3.34. These patterns were obtained by taking a random set of dots and making a double exposure by superimposing the same set displaced

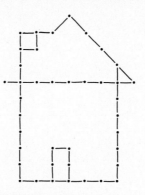

Figure 3.33 Virtual lines drawn by algorithm

slightly. In Figure 3.34(a), the picture was expanded slightly; in Figure 3.34(c), rotated. Figure 3.34(b) and Figure 3.34(d) show the results of the line-proposing algorithm in each case. The expansion generates a set of lines radiating outward, while the rotation generates a whorl of lines around the center. For both humans and this algorithm, it is easy to pick out adjacent dots that follow a global trend, ignoring local distractors.

3.4.4 Stereo Disparity

Another process that occurs at this level is the use of "stereo disparity" to measure the depths of objects in a scene. Some animals, like horses and rabbits, use their two eyes as almost independent information channels. Two eyes enable them to survey twice as big an area as they could survey with only one. If they see danger, they can run away from it; if they see food, they can amble toward it. But predators and primates have to be able to grab nearby objects (horses, rabbits, or branches) quickly and reliably. Their eyes point in approximately the same direction, so they get two slightly different views of about the same thing. For example, Figure 3.35 shows two different views of a row of rectangular objects. The left eye sees the front rectangle displaced to the right, and vice versa.

The advantage of this *stereoscopic* vision is that it can tell the vision system the distance of points that appear in both images, as demonstrated by the construction in Figure 3.36. In Figure 3.36, z is the depth of the point P; θ_1 and θ_2 are the directions to it; and b is the "baseline" distance between the two eyes. The law of sines then tells us that

$$\frac{R_1}{\sin(\theta_2)} = \frac{R_2}{\sin(\theta_1)} = \frac{b}{\sin(180° - \theta_1 - \theta_2)} \tag{3.4}$$

(The *law of sines* says that the ratio of side length to the sine of the opposite

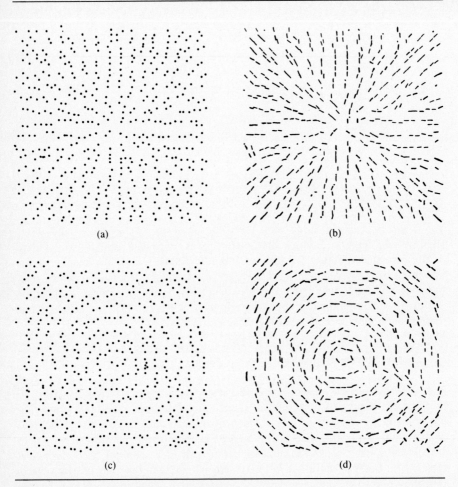

Figure 3.34 Random-dot flow patterns

angle is the same for all three sides of a triangle.) But $z = R_1\sin(\theta_1) = R_2\sin(\theta_2)$, so

$$z = \frac{b\sin(\theta_1)\sin(\theta_2)}{\sin(180° - \theta_1 - \theta_2)} \tag{3.5}$$

The depth can be determined from the two angles and the baseline.

If the distance z to point P is large compared to b, then the sum of θ_1 and θ_2 will be about 180°, and the denominator will be close to 0. In this case, the result will be unreliable.

This looks easy, but there is a problem, namely, how θ_1 and θ_2 are computed. Consider the two images in Figure 3.37. The machine can get θ_1 and θ_2 by observing how far P's image lies from the midline, as shown in Figure 3.38.

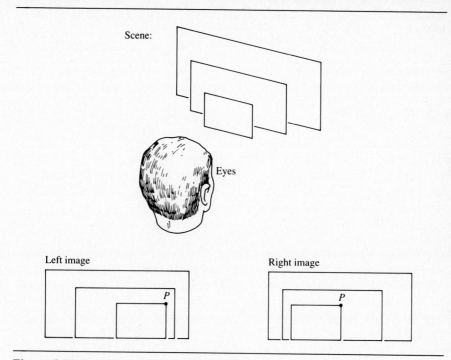

Figure 3.35 Two views of a rectangle row

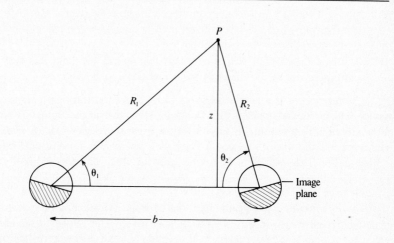

Figure 3.36 Geometry of stereo vision

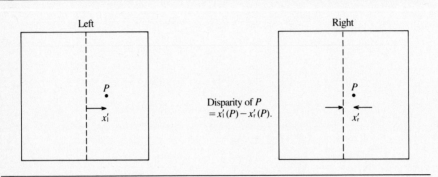

Figure 3.37 Disparate images of P

Unfortunately, in real images, there are no little Ps that uniquely identify points in the image. There are only gray levels. The machine must figure out which pixel in one image corresponds to which pixel in the other. The displacement of P in one image from its counterpart in the other is called its *disparity*. Such a value is assigned to every point in the image from each eye. Finding the match between images is equivalent to calculating the disparity for each point.

A key issue is whether this matching up occurs early or late in visual processing. It seems plausible at first that it occurs later. In Figure 3.39, if the machine waits until it has recognized the arrow (twice), then it will have an excellent idea which points match up. However, there are two reasons to place stereo matching in early processing:

1. It will help a lot in recognizing objects if we have depth information about their surfaces. If the information is to be available *for* recognition, it must be computed *prior* to recognition.
2. Humans provide an existence proof that it can be done this way. They can figure out stereo disparity for "random-dot stereograms."

A *stereogram* is a pair of pictures to be looked at through a *stereoscope*, a device which channels one picture to the left eye, one to the right. The two pictures are slightly different, in such a way that each eye sees what it would see if you were looking at a real scene. There is a vivid three-dimensional effect. (A "Viewmaster" toy is a stereoscope for viewing three-dimensional still cartoons. Before *Life* magazine and television, people would use stereoscopes to see realistic pictures of faraway places.)

A *random-dot* stereogram, like that of Figure 3.40, is a pair of computer-generated pictures made up of thousands of dots. The two pictures are identical, except that a square region in the middle of the left picture has been displaced a few millimeters in the right one. It is virtually impossible to tell this by examining the pictures. Clearly, no object recognition occurs, except for classing the two patterns as having similar textures.

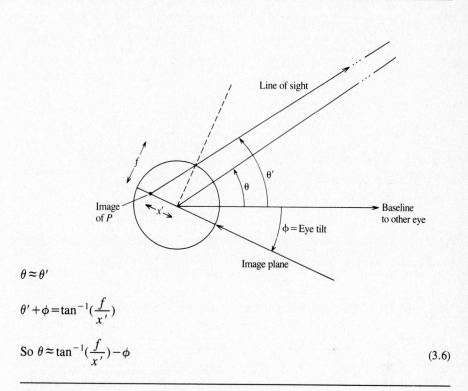

$\theta \approx \theta'$

$\theta' + \phi = \tan^{-1}(\dfrac{f}{x'})$

So $\theta \approx \tan^{-1}(\dfrac{f}{x'}) - \phi$ (3.6)

Figure 3.38 Getting θ from x' and eye tilt

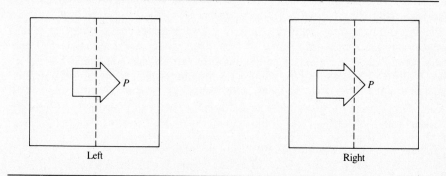

Figure 3.39 Disparate images of an arrow

Nonetheless, most subjects see a ghostly square hovering above or below a background plane when they view the two pictures through a stereoscope. (Whether it is seen above or below depends, of course, on which way the central square is shifted.)

(a)   (b)

Figure 3.40 Random-dot stereogram

The compelling conclusion is that object recognition is not necessary for stereo matching. The matching must occur at an earlier level. In fact, it is now known that matching can take place between the primal sketches from the two images. That is, what gets matched are edges, bars, and blobs (and hence these are what disparity values are assigned to). This is easier than matching gray levels, because a blob can match only a blob; but there are still a lot of blobs.

The matching algorithm exploits two properties of images in the real world: *uniqueness* and *continuity*. Uniqueness means that a given image pixel comes from a single physical surface patch, and hence has one disparity value. Continuity means that disparity varies smoothly almost everywhere, because the image was produced from a continuous physical surface that jumps in depth only at physical boundaries between objects. Two nearby image points probably came from the same surface, and so must have similar disparity values. (These are corollaries of the "nonaccidental image properties" assumption.)

We will not describe this algorithm in great detail. It operates iteratively, refining initial guesses as to the disparity values for primal-sketch features. For each primal-sketch feature, the machine keeps a vector of plausibility of possible disparities:

$$-1 \quad\quad 0 \quad\quad 0.5 \quad\quad 0.8 \quad\quad 0.5 \quad\quad \leftarrow \quad\quad \text{plausibilities}$$
$$-2 \quad\quad -1 \quad\quad 0 \quad\quad 1 \quad\quad 2 \quad\quad \leftarrow \quad\quad \text{possible disparities}$$

Here we assume plausibilities range from -1, meaning "ruled out," to 1, meaning "decided." Each element of the vector is initialized with a number that depends purely on how well this feature matches the feature at the given disparity value. The numbers are improved by taking continuity into account. Although a feature at one location might match two or more features in the other image, its neighbors' disparities might cast doubt on some of them, and vice versa. Eventually the vectors are brought into agreement on the most likely interpretation.

This process is made more efficient by carrying it out at more than one resolution. As we described in the previous section, the primal sketch is found at different levels of coarseness. There we emphasized how this helped give noise immunity. It also helps with stereo matching. The matching is cheaper at a coarse resolution, where there are fewer features to match. Indeed, if the disparity values are not great compared to the size of feature picked up, there will be at most two candidates to match any given feature. The coarse match gives an approximate answer about the disparity of the images being matched, which provides enough information for the high-resolution match to preserve the assumption that the disparities are small compared to resolution. That is, each feature in the high-resolution sketch can be shifted by the disparity from the coarse match before being matched itself, and, as before, there will be only one or two candidates for this match. (In a computer, the shifting can be done computationally. There is some evidence that the human eye does it physically, by swiveling the eyes successively toward different points in the real world, giving rise to a series of images, each of which has minimal disparity in the part focused on.)

Stereo-disparity analysis can tell the machine something about surface orientation as well as depth. Indeed, people seem to extract more reliable surface-orientation information than depth information from stereo vision. If a surface is tilted away from the viewer, then the disparity will decrease in the direction of tilt; this decrease and its magnitude tell the tilt and slant of the surface.

The terms "tilt" and "slant" may be defined precisely as follows: The *tilt* is defined as the direction of a line perpendicular to the surface (the "surface normal") in the image. Another quantity, the *slant*, is defined as the angle between the surface normal and the line of sight; it is the amount of tilt in the direction of tilt. These concepts will be important in the next section. See

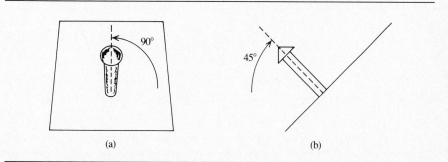

(a)   (b)

Figure 3.41 A surface with tilt = 90°, slant = 45°

Figure 3.41. In Figure 3.9, each arrow points in the direction of tilt; its length
is proportional to the slant.

3.4.5 Texture

Texture is the organization of a surface as a set of repeated *elements*. It is
of importance because distortions of a texture in an image are likely to
correspond faithfully to orientation and depth changes in the original scene. See
Figure 3.42.

Several methods have been proposed for extracting information about surface orientation and depth from textures. Some of them depend on prior recognition of the texture, that is, analysis of it as consisting of a set of elements that
are basically the same. For example, the direction in which texture *density*
increases fastest (the *density gradient*) should correspond to the tilt of the surface. See Figure 3.43.

We can distinguish three kinds of texture difference. In a region where
density is changing linearly, we perceive a slanted surface. But at the border

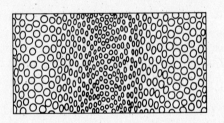

Figure 3.42 Surface orientation changes suggested by texture distortions

Figure 3.43 Finding tilt from texture density gradient

between two places with different perceived slants, we see two surfaces meeting, or a curving surface. (See Figure 3.42.) In Figure 3.44, we see one surface on top of another. Thus the visual system should class texture differences as one of:

1. Same elements at the same orientation, but different sizes. (Indicates tilted surface.)
2. Same elements, but viewed from a different orientation. (Indicates curved surface.)
3. Different elements. (Indicates different surfaces.)

Unfortunately, techniques like this rely on classifying different patches of the surface as having the "same" texture even when their elements are of different size. You can't recognize one patch of an image as having a texture that is a distortion of that of another patch unless you can recognize that the two textures are basically the same. Classifying textures as "the same" or "different" is called *texture discrimination*. For texture to be a useful clue, this classification must occur early in vision.

Consider Figure 3.45, Figure 3.46, and Figure 3.47. These three patterns just look like a repetition of one "cell" with a little jiggle in each. This is the standard way to produce idealized textures for psychological studies. Now look at Figure 3.48, Figure 3.49, and Figure 3.50. In each of these three artificial textures, there is a randomly placed rectangle with a different texture. This may seem a trivial observation, since the unit cell is different in the region of different texture. Couldn't we just test for equality of unit cells to test for sameness of texture?

Look again closely at Figure 3.45 through Figure 3.47. In each case, there is a rectangle containing a pattern made up of a different unit cell from the rest of the picture. But these differences are harder to see than those of Figure 3.48 through Figure 3.50. So something else besides a test for equality must be going on in the process of texture discrimination. A moment's thought will show that it had to be this way, because if *every* difference in unit cell made a

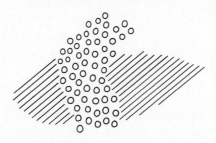

Figure 3.44 One texture occluding another

⋈ ⋈ ⋈ ⋈ ⋈ ⋈ ⋈ ⋈ ⋈ ⋈ ⋈ ⋈
⋈ ⋈ ⋈ ⋈ ⋈ ⋈ ⋈ ⋈ ⋈ ⋈ ⋈ ⋈
⋈ ⋈ ⋈ ⋈ ⋈ ⋈ ⋈ ⋈ ⋈ ⋈ ⋈ ⋈
⋈ ⋈ ⋈ ⋈ ⋈ ⋈ ⋈ ⋈ ⋈ ⋈ ⋈ ⋈
⋈ ⋈ ⋈ ⋈ ⋈ ⋈ ⋈ ⋈ ⋈ ⋈ ⋈ ⋈
⋈ ⋈ ⋈ ⋈ ⋈ ⋈ ⋈ ⋈ ⋈ ⋈ ⋈ ⋈
⋈ ⋈ ⋈ ⋈ ⋈ ⋈ ⋈ ⋈ ⋈ ⋈ ⋈ ⋈
⋈ ⋈ ⋈ ⋈ ⋈ ⋈ ⋈ ⋈ ⋈ ⋈ ⋈ ⋈
⋈ ⋈ ⋈ ⋈ ⋈ ⋈ ⋈ ⋈ ⋈ ⋈ ⋈ ⋈
⋈ ⋈ ⋈ ⋈ ⋈ ⋈ ⋈ ⋈ ⋈ ⋈ ⋈ ⋈
⋈ ⋈ ⋈ ⋈ ⋈ ⋈ ⋈ ⋈ ⋈ ⋈ ⋈ ⋈
⋈ ⋈ ⋈ ⋈ ⋈ ⋈ ⋈ ⋈ ⋈ ⋈ ⋈ ⋈

Figure 3.45 An artificial texture

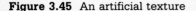

⊔ ⊔ ⊔ ⊔ ⊔ ⊔ ⊔ ⊔ ⊔ ⊔ ⊔ ⊔
⊔ ⊔ ⊔ ⊔ ⊔ ⊔ ⊔ ⊔ ⊔ ⊔ ⊔ ⊔
⊔ ⊔ ⊔ ⊔ ⊔ ⊔ ⊔ ⊔ ⊔ ⊔ ⊔ ⊔
⊔ ⊔ ⊔ ⊔ ⊔ ⊔ ⊔ ⊔ ⊔ ⊔ ⊔ ⊔
⊔ ⊔ ⊔ ⊔ ⊔ ⊔ ⊔ ⊔ ⊔ ⊔ ⊔ ⊔
⊔ ⊓ ⊓ ⊓ ⊔ ⊔ ⊔ ⊔ ⊔ ⊔ ⊔ ⊔
⊔ ⊓ ⊓ ⊓ ⊔ ⊔ ⊔ ⊔ ⊔ ⊔ ⊔ ⊔
⊔ ⊓ ⊓ ⊓ ⊔ ⊔ ⊔ ⊔ ⊔ ⊔ ⊔ ⊔
⊔ ⊓ ⊓ ⊓ ⊔ ⊔ ⊔ ⊔ ⊔ ⊔ ⊔ ⊔
⊔ ⊓ ⊓ ⊓ ⊔ ⊔ ⊔ ⊔ ⊔ ⊔ ⊔ ⊔
⊔ ⊓ ⊓ ⊓ ⊔ ⊔ ⊔ ⊔ ⊔ ⊔ ⊔ ⊔
⊔ ⊔ ⊔ ⊔ ⊔ ⊔ ⊔ ⊔ ⊔ ⊔ ⊔ ⊔

Figure 3.46 An artificial texture

discriminable texture, there wouldn't be any texture. Human eyes attend only to some differences.

A lot of work has been done on the problem of texture discrimination. However, good computational answers to the question of how textures are classified as "different" or "the same" have been slow in coming.

Recently, it has been pointed out that surface orientation could be extracted from texture without prior recognition of texture elements. Note that the distribution of tangents to an ellipse is different from that of a circle. The

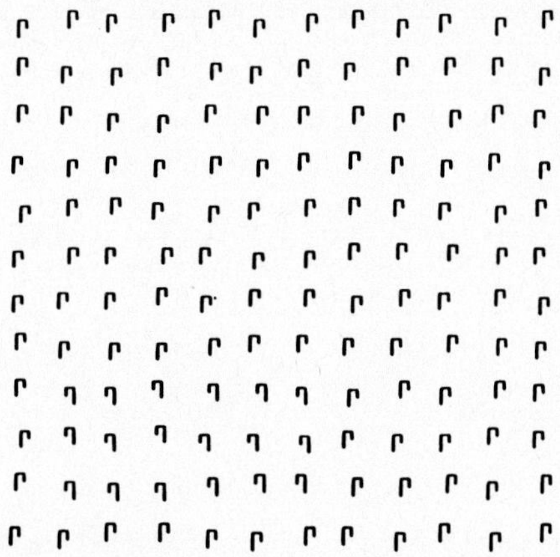

Figure 3.47 An artificial texture

ellipse has tangents pointing mainly along the major axis, while the circle has tangents uniformly distributed, as shown in Figure 3.51. A randomly produced curve would have about the same number of lines (virtual and real) in all directions. Perhaps the eye assumes that

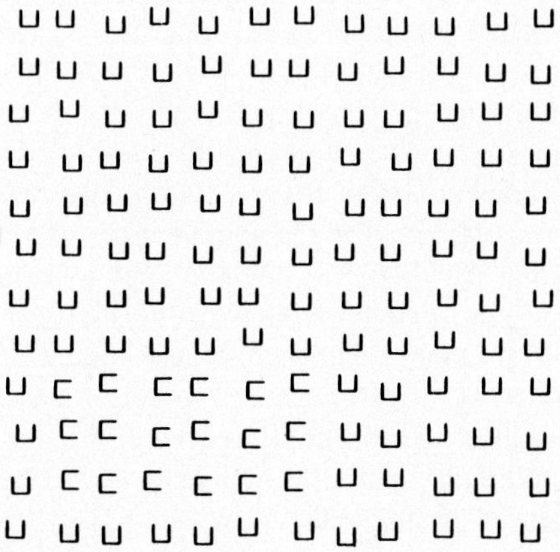

Figure 3.48 An artificial texture

Figure 3.49 An artificial texture

> Any large, regular departure from uniformity is due to a tilt toward or away from the observer [Witkin80].

Under this assumption, the eye can recover the tilt by finding the histogram of line directions. The direction of tilt is then 90 degrees *away from* the peak in the histogram. See Figure 3.52.

Using this approach, one can detect regions of approximately constant orientation (i.e., approximately constant line orientation), *then* look for texture elements and check their density (and other properties) to refine the computation of tilt and slant.

One piece of confirming evidence for this kind of theory is that the human visual system seems to attend to orientation differences more than other kinds [Beck82]. It seems significant that in Figure 3.45 to Figure 3.47, the number of line segments at a given orientation is the same for the two different texture elements. (See Figure 3.53a.) In Figure 3.48, one kind of texture element has two vertical lines, the other kind two horizontal ones. (See Figure 3.53b.) Unfortunately, the whole story is more complex, because Figure 3.49 and Figure 3.50 have the same distribution of orientations and are still discriminable. In Figure 3.49, it seems plausible that the strong differences in orientations of *virtual lines* account for the discrimination, but it is not known whether virtual lines will account for all the observed phenomena.

```
L  L  L L  L  L L L L  L L L L
L  L L L  L  L L L  L  L L  L L
L  L  L L  L  L L  L L L  L  L L
L  L L  L  L L L  L L L  L  L L  L
L  L  L L  L  L L L L  L  L L  L
L  L  L  L L L  L  L L L L  L  L L
L L  L L  L  L L L L  L  L  L L
L L L  L  L L L  L L L L  L  L
L  L  J  J  J  J  J  J L  L  L L L
L  J  J  J  J  J  L  L  L L  L L
L  J  J  J  J  J  J L  L  L L L
L  L L  L  L L  L  L L  L  L L L  L
```

Figure 3.50 An artificial texture

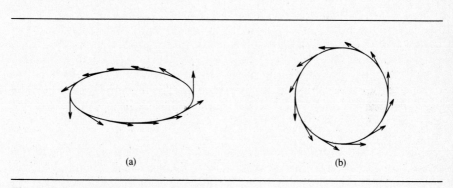

(a)   (b)

Figure 3.51 Distributions of tangents

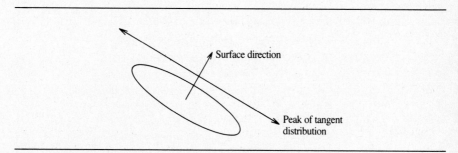

Surface direction

Peak of tangent
distribution

Figure 3.52 An ellipse analyzed as a tilted circle

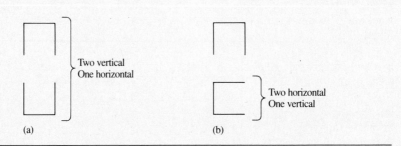

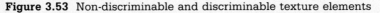

Figure 3.53 Non-discriminable and discriminable texture elements

3.4.6 Intrinsic Image

We have been working our way through the processes shown in Figure 3.11, which are aimed at finding the *intrinsic image*. This database specifies the values of illumination, reflectance, surface orientation, and depth at each point. In addition, it explicitly localizes physical *boundaries* between different areas of objects.

The notion of "boundary" must be kept separate from the concept of "line" that we have worked with so far. In fact, we have a whole hierarchy of concepts here, as shown in Figure 3.54. The *line* is the most abstract entity we have found so far. We use this term to denote any one-dimensional phenomenon extracted from the image, such as the virt·ɔl lines we examined in Section 3.4.3.

We use the term *boundary* to refer to a real physical entity, where two areas meet. The two areas may differ in orientation, illumination, or

Where Defined	Concept	Definition
Image	Edgelet	Unit intensity change
Image	Edge	Primal-sketch feature, composed of several edgelets
Image	Line	Sequence of primal-sketch features, *or* texture-region boundary, *or* . . .
World	Boundary	Place where two surfaces meet, or where illumination or reflectance changes abruptly

Figure 3.54 Hierarchy of "linear" concepts

reflectance. The first we call a *fold*, the second a *shadow*, and the third a *mark*. Much of the work of the last stage of early vision can be thought of as deciding what the true physical interpretation should be for the lines that have been found.

We can make a similar distinction for two-dimensional entities. A *region* is a two-dimensional patch of image that is uniform in some way. An *area* is a piece of physical surface with uniform reflectance and illumination.

We need two different sets of terms because the correspondence between image entities and physical entities is imperfect. Consider the edge of a cube. In our terminology, this is a boundary between two areas, the faces of the cube. But, in an image, the corresponding line might divide a cube face and the background, as in Figure 3.55.

As we mentioned, there are three kinds of boundary — folds, marks, and shadows. But there are five kinds of line — those three, plus *blades* and *extrema*. See Figure 3.56 (and compare Figure 3.9). A fold may appear as a blade in the image, in which case the region on one side of the blade will not be the same as the one on the other side of the corresponding physical boundary, as in Figure 3.55. In the case of extrema, there is no boundary at all corresponding to the line.

Therefore, the problem is to classify each line as a physical phenomenon, either a boundary viewed a certain way or a self-occlusion, and to figure out the physical characteristics of the areas corresponding to the regions between the lines. To carry out this task, what we have so far are the following data:

- From virtual-line analysis: a set of lines
- From texture analysis: a set of regions of similar texture
- From stereo analysis: the approximate depth of each surface element
- From texture and stereo analysis: the approximate orientation of surface elements

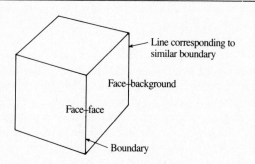

Figure 3.55 Differences between world terms and image terms

*	Fold	two surfaces meet, both visible
	Blade	two surfaces meet, just one visible
	Extremum	self-occlusion by a curved object, like a cylinder or sphere
*	Shadow	an abrupt change in illumination
*	Mark	an abrupt change in reflectance or texture

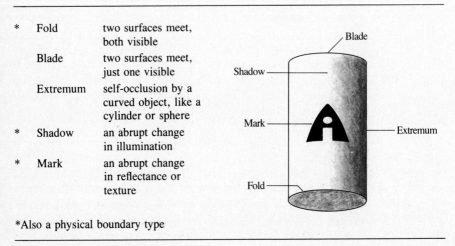

*Also a physical boundary type

Figure 3.56 Types of image line

Unfortunately, putting all this together is not easy. For one thing, each analysis is incomplete. If a region has little texture, we may not be able to tell its orientation. If an object is far away, stereo will be of little help. On the other hand, each source of information constrains the others. Presumably all the information sources cooperate in some way to arrive at the correct answers for all intrinsic images.

The kind of *continuity* assumption we used in the stereo disparity calculation is important for mediating this cooperation. As before, such an assumption depends upon the fact that the image was produced from ordinary physical surfaces, and hence each quantity varies continuously over a region. The discontinuities occur at lines. At every line, some quantity or its derivative changes discontinuously. But not every quantity changes at every line. The table in Figure 3.57 shows what can and cannot change at each type of line.

A continuity assumption is useful because it strongly constrains the joint interpretation of nearby points. Once we have interpreted one part of the image, nearby parts fall into place. Such constraint propagation starts and stops at lines. It stops there because of the discontinuities. For instance, information about one surface bounded by an extremum tells you nothing at all about the surface on the other side.

Lines often are the starting point for information propagation, too. At an extremum, the orientation of the surface is perpendicular to the observer. (Its slant is 90°.) So, if a line can be classed as an extremum, we can propagate this information into one of the regions it bounds. At a blade, surface orientation is constrained only to be perpendicular to the orientation of the blade. See Figure 3.58.

	Must Stay the same	May change
Fold	Depth	Orientation, reflectance, Illumination
Extremum	Nothing	Depth, illumination, orientation, reflectance
Blade	Nothing	Depth, illumination, orientation, reflectance
Shadow	Depth, orientation, reflectance	Illumination
Mark	Depth, orientation, illumination	Reflectance

Figure 3.57 Changes possible at various line types

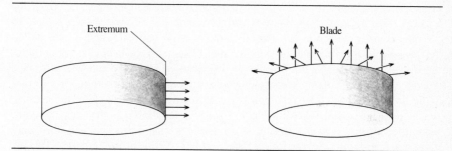

Figure 3.58 Surface orientation constraints at blades and extrema

Distinguishing between blades and extrema is an open problem. Note that in the table of Figure 3.57, these two are not distinguished by predictable changes in any image property. It can be argued [Barrow78] that in some cases the measured uniformity of illumination can be used to verify that a line has surface orientation perpendicular to the line of sight, making it an extremum, but a more general method is unknown.

Together, blades and extrema are called *occluding lines* (because one of the surfaces they border lies in front of the other). Humans have a strong disposition to see an occluding line as lying in a plane if possible. Furthermore, they tend to perceive nonuniform distributions in tangent direction as due to surface orientation. (This is analogous to the idea of determining the orientation of texture elements from tangent directions, but extended to regions the size of an entire object. See Figure 3.52, but now visualize the edge of the ellipse as an occluding line rather than a texture element.)

Together, these constraints tend to suggest an orientation for the boundary of an area. Then one can infer the detailed orientation of parts of the interior by reconciling the orientations found so far with the constraints provided by the necessity that orientation, illumination, and other quantities vary smoothly in most places.

There are other constraints besides the continuity constraints. These constrain different quantities at the same point rather than the same quantity at neighboring points. For example, with one light source and an ideally diffusing surface, the reflected light, surface orientation, illumination, and angle of incidence of the light must obey the constraint:

reflected light = reflectance × illumination × cos(angle of incidence)   (3.7)

No one has proposed an explicit algorithm for "solving" all the constraints, finding a solution that "fits best." We will look at a sketch of such an algorithm below, but it will be only a sketch. First, to convince you that the constraints are solved as a group in the human visual system, we will present a psychological experiment done by Alan Gilchrist [Gilchrist77]. This experiment involved setting up two large surfaces, each with a small tab in front. See Figure 3.59. The two surfaces met, one being nearly horizontal and the other vertical. One tab extended out from the horizontal surface; the other, up from the vertical. Surfaces and tabs were textureless, and the tabs were trapezoidal, so that an observer with one eye closed, looking from one particular angle, would be misled into thinking the tab was parallel to the surface behind it, rather than the one it was attached to. (Since, in the absence of other clues, the skewed tangent distribution of the trapezoid would suggest this orientation.) To further baffle the subject, the horizontal surface and vertical tab were white; the vertical surface and horizontal tab were black. That is, each tab was the opposite color from the surface it was attached to. The horizontal surface and tab were illuminated strongly; the vertical surface and tab were kept in the dark. The ink

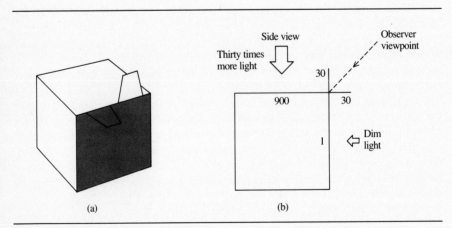

Figure 3.59 Gilchrist's experiment

and light were coordinated so that a black patch in light reflected the same light as a white patch in darkness.

Binocular observers could see the correct orientation of the tabs using stereo disparity cues. The illumination-continuity assumption then told them that each tab was getting the same illumination as its attached surface. So they correctly identified the line between a surface and its coplanar tab as a "mark," or reflectance discontinuity.

Monocular observers were misled into thinking that the tabs were coplanar with the surfaces that in reality they occluded. So they saw a tab reflecting very little light lying in the horizontal, brightly illuminated surface. The real reason it was so dim was that it was in the dark. But the subjects saw it as black. Similarly, they saw the illuminated, hence moderately bright horizontal black tab as protruding down into the (very dark) vertical black surface, and saw the tab as white.

We summarize these results in Figure 3.60. The two subjects each see the lines differently, and hence impose different continuity assumptions on them. In particular, notice where they put the "mark" lines, across which there is illumination continuity. Across a mark, a difference in reflected light cannot be a difference in *illumination*, so must reflect a difference in *reflectance*, or whiteness.

3.4.7 Cooperative Algorithms

Gilchrist's results should convince you that the interpretation assigned to a line plays a large role in the interpretation assigned to its interior. However, the information flow is not just one way. An eccentric ellipse tends to be seen as a tilted circle, but if its interior is filled with a uniform texture, it will be

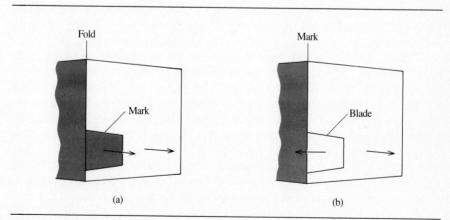

Figure 3.60 Results of Gilchrist's experiment

seen as a nontilted ellipse. The two sources of information "argue" about the best overall interpretation, or, stated more optimistically, they "cooperate" in arriving at this interpretation. Such algorithms turn up in several places in vision. They are characterized by

- A set of elements to be interpreted. In this case, the elements are the small "surface patches" the intrinsic image consists of (as in Figure 3.60). The interpretation is an assignment of surface orientation, boundary classification, and other physical properties to each patch.
- A set of constraints between adjacent elements. In this case, continuity is the main constraint: two adjacent patches should not be drastically different in any characteristic (unless a boundary runs between them).

Given these two characteristics, an algorithm is *cooperative* if it repeatedly adjusts the interpretation of each element to be in greater harmony with its neighbors until global harmony is attained. By "harmony" we mean *constraint satisfaction*. If the interpretation assigned to every element obeys all constraints, then we have reached a satisfactory overall interpretation. The term *relaxation algorithm* is also used.

Cooperative algorithms are attractive in vision applications because they can exploit parallelism in a natural way. It is easy to envisage special-purpose computers with one processor per interpretation element (implemented as a large integrated circuit, or, in the brain, a group of neurons). The processors talk only to their neighbors, and yet arrive at a global solution.

The indefinite iteration is a crucial feature of this style of algorithm. We do not classify a system as cooperative if its processors arrive at an interpretation after a small, bounded number of consultations with their neighbors. The same processor architecture can often be used for both cooperative and noncooperative applications. For example, the stereo matcher of Section 3.4.4 was studied in two versions. The first operated cooperatively, iterating until a disparity was found for each surface patch. Later, it was realized that by using additional information the number of consultations between neighbors could be reduced to one or two, yielding a more efficient noncooperative algorithm.

Many cooperative algorithms can be thought of as solving *labeling problems*. Formally, such a problem consists of a set of *elements*, as before, and a set of possible labels for each element. In the problem of finding a surface interpretation, each possible label might specify a different surface orientation. (We assume a discrete set of candidate labels because that's the traditional assumption.) For simplicity, we assume that the candidate labels are the same for each element. So there are n elements $e_1, \ldots, e_n$ and each has m candidate labels, $\lambda_1, \ldots, \lambda_m$. The constraints between elements are represented by a matrix of *compatibilities* $r_{ij}(\lambda, \lambda')$ whose sign indicates the direction of the evidence that element i's label is λ given that element j's label is λ':

If $r_{ij}(\lambda, \lambda') > 0$
  then λ at element i is supported by λ' at element j.

If $r_{ij}(\lambda,\lambda') < 0$
   then λ at element i is contradicted by λ' at element j.
If $r_{ij}(\lambda,\lambda') = 0$
   then λ' at element j provides no evidence about λ at element i

The magnitude of the value indicates the degree of support. The magnitude must lie between -1 and 1.

In our example, the r_{ij} come from constraints such as that of equation (3.7), and from continuity. If the λs are alternative surface orientations, for instance, $r_{ij}(\lambda,\lambda')$ is highest when $\lambda = \lambda'$. In other words, the ideal case is for two nearby surface orientations to be identical, and there is a penalty when they are very different.

The goal of the labeling algorithm is to find the correct label λ for each element. What the machine keeps track of along the way are *weights* for each label, a set of numbers $p_i(\lambda)$ for each i and λ. For instance, if the possible labels are A, B, and C, element 3 might at some point have weights

$p_3(A) = 0.0$
$p_3(B) = 0.8$
$p_3(C) = 0.2$

which indicates that A is definitely not the correct label, while B probably is. The weights at an element must be nonnegative and sum to 1, like probabilities. However, there is no theoretical justification for thinking of them as actual probability values.

On every iteration, the algorithm changes the weights to reflect constraints from neighboring elements. Different algorithms call for different recipes for updating the weights. One general formula [Rosenfeld76], first computes

$$q_i(\lambda) = \sum_{j=1}^{n} c_{ij} \sum_{all\lambda} r_{ij} p_j(\lambda')$$

for each element i, where the c_{ij} are weights that sum to 1. The quantity q_i measures the amount by which λ's weight ought to increase as indicated by evidence from neighboring elements, those with nonzero $r_{ij}(\lambda,\lambda')$. (If we take $c_{ij} = 1/$*number of neighboring elements*, we get a simple average.) Since each r_{ij} is between -1 and 1, and each p_j is between 0 and 1, the q_i values lie between -1 and 1.

Now, the actual updating formula is this:

$$p_i(\lambda) := \frac{p_i(\lambda)[1 + q_i(\lambda)]}{\sum_{all\lambda} p_i(\lambda)[1 + q_i(\lambda)]}$$

(This is an assignment statement ($:=$), not an equation. It gives the new values of p_i as a function of the old values.) This formula seems to work in several cases empirically, although it has no real theoretical justification. Note that $1 + q_{ij}(\lambda)$ lies between 0 and 2, so that the formula does two things: it changes p in the right direction, and it makes sure that p always lies between 0 and 1.

For example, suppose that we let each element represent the orientation of a patch of surface in an intrinsic image. The λs are possible orientations. To be utterly simplistic about it, suppose there are only two labels, up and dn (for "down"). Figure 3.61 shows one patch element, surrounded by four neighbors. The r_{ij} are such that it is absolutely impossible to have a dn next to an up. (This is an extreme form of continuity.) All of the orientations have been determined except the one in the middle (element 1). On the next iteration, its new weights are computed as follows. First, we have

$$q_1(\text{up}) = 0.25 \times 4 \times [1 \times 1 + -1 \times 0]$$
$$= 1$$
$$q_1(\text{dn}) = 0.25 \times 4 \times [-1 \times 1 + 1 \times 0]$$
$$= -1$$

And then

$$p_1(\text{up}) = 1 \times \frac{1+1}{2} = 1$$

$$p_1(\text{dn}) = 1 \times \frac{1-1}{2} = 0$$

That is, after one iteration the middle element has joined its fellows as an up. From then on, every element remains an up.

A crucial issue for a scheme like this is whether it *converges*, that is, reaches a stable set of weights after a while. Usually this is a matter of tuning the r_{ij} weights to get convergence to happen.

In the rest of this section, we will examine a more realistically sized example, a cooperative algorithm for finding intrinsic images, proposed by

3 up 1
dn 0

2 up 1   1 up .5   4 up 1
dn 0   dn .5   dn 0

5 up 1
dn 0

Parameters: $c_{ij} = \begin{cases} .25 & \text{for the four neighbors} \\ 0 & \text{for everyone else.} \end{cases}$

$$r_{ij}(\text{up, up}) = 1$$
$$r_{ij}(\text{up, dn}) = -1$$
$$r_{ij}(\text{dn, up}) = -1$$
$$r_{ij}(\text{dn, dn}) = 1$$

Figure 3.61 Example cooperative labeling problem

Barrow and Tenenbaum [Barrow78]. It has not been implemented, and its convergence properties are completely unknown. Barrow and Tenenbaum's algorithm is intended to run on a computer composed of thousands of processors,
one for every property (illumination, depth, etc.) at every patch of the intrinsic
image. We will call these *patch managers*. In the terminology we used above,
an "element" is a pair < *patch, property* >. Each patch manager has the job of
keeping track of the weights on possible values of its property, and adjusting
them to satisfy constraints. To this end, it communicates with two groups of
other processors: those managing the same quantity at nearby points, and those
managing different quantities for the same point. Neighboring processors compare their weights and adjust them if constraints are violated. This process is
intended to continue until agreement is reached. At that time the contents of
each processor's "property register" constitutes the intrinsic image. In Figure
3.62, there are three vertical planes, each containing processors responsible for
a single type of quantity (depth, orientation, or reflectance) over the entire
image. The vertical connections have to do with continuity constraints; processors communicating within a plane try to make each other differ as little as possible. Horizontal connections have to do with interquantity constraints such as
equation (3.7).

Lines are handled by another, more complex processor called the *line proposer*. It is able to modify a horizontal link between two patch managers by
labeling that link as a discontinuity, thus turning off the dialogue between them
(or, in our previous terminology, changing the corresponding r_{ij} value to 0).

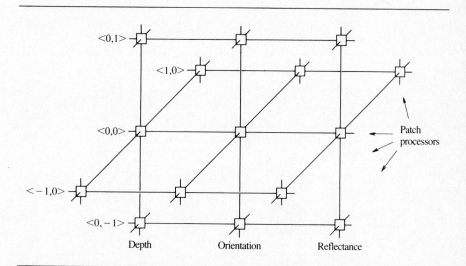

Figure 3.62 Barrow and Tenenbaum's cooperative processor array

For instance, a mark is proposed between two patches by labeling the link between the reflectance managers for those two patches as a discontinuity.

Lines are initially proposed from the primal sketch, in all the ways we examined in Sections 3.4.1 through 3.4.5. But these processes are not foolproof. A large enough gap in a line will prevent proper interpretation of the regions on either side, because continuity of all surface properties will be enforced across the gap. Usually, in fact, no interpretation will be possible. When the line proposer detects a failure of the array of patch managers to converge on a single interpretation, it attempts to find plausible places for such gaps, and hypothesizes lines there that the lower-level system missed. This continues until a single interpretation emerges. The line proposers could get used when either neighboring elements failed to converge at all (their weights oscillated), or when they converged to an ambiguous weight vector (with large weights attached to quite different values of the intrinsic property at that point).

One nice thing about this model is that it provides a framework for explaining *subjective contours*, lines that are perceived but correspond to nothing real in the scene, like those in Figure 3.63. In this figure, it is hard not to feel that there is a boundary separating the point-side-up triangle from the background. If you look closely, though, this border goes away. Barrow and Tenenbaum's model of this situation is that the sharp breaks in the circle and point-side-down triangle signal a line, in particular a blade, lying in front of the cutoff figures. So the depth of the point-side-up triangle is less than the depths of the figures behind it, which is less than or equal to the depth of the background. Now the system attempts to propagate these conclusions away from the original lines, into the interior of the triangle and the rest of the picture. Everything goes fine until propagation reaches both sides of the gaps in the proposed line; here the continuity constraint demands that the depths be equal. Depending on exactly how the algorithm is implemented, it will at this point either fail to converge at all, or converge to ambiguous weight vectors around the ''gap.'' So

Figure 3.63 A subjective contour

at this point, according to the model, the line proposer proposes a line there to make the constraint go away and allow things to settle down.

3.4.8 Vertex Analysis and Line Labeling

So far we have examined constraints on lines and regions. Another important set of constraints arises from consideration of vertices. For example, in Figure 3.63, why doesn't the eye see the "nicks" in the circles as marks? The reason may be because of the way in which the straight line of the bite meets the curved line of the circle. Usually if a mark extends to the line bordering a region, then there is a continuation of the border that borders the mark. See Figure 3.64.

Another example is shown in Figure 3.65. Even in the absence of all other information, the presence of T-shaped junctions between lines strongly indicates the presence of a blade. When the shafts of two Ts line up, it indicates the continuation of an occluded surface on the other side of the occlusion.

So far, there is no general theory of vertex types. But a fair amount is known if we make certain restrictions on the objects in the scene. Consider the

Figure 3.64 What a mark would look like

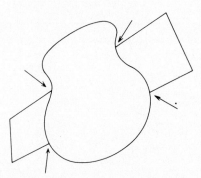

Figure 3.65 Occlusions suggested by **T** junctions

drawing in Figure 3.66. None of us have any trouble interpreting this as a picture of a scene with four blocks, as opposed to, say, three or five. Furthermore, we can assign the various regions (closed connected parts of pictures) to the various hypothesized objects. But how do we do this? How, for example do we decide that Region 1 does not correspond to the surface of any block, but Region 2 does? Clearly, we are not using any stereo or texture information, since we are looking at a single, textureless picture.

For some time it was thought that it is simply our assumption that the world consists of regular blocks which enables us to perform this task. However, this cannot be so, because we have no trouble with oddly shaped blocks or nonpolyhedral shapes (as in Figure 3.67). Perhaps even more striking evidence is provided by visual illusions. One popular example is given in Figure 3.68. That we fairly quickly decide that this picture could not denote a real object indicates that we have knowledge of a much more categorical nature than "the world often consists of blocks." We seemingly also have knowledge of what sorts of things the world cannot have.

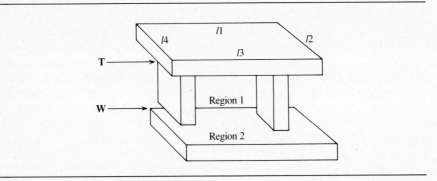

Figure 3.66 A four-block configuration

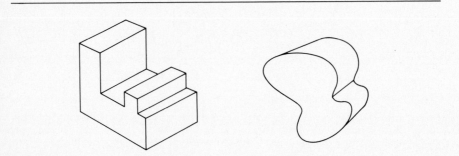

Figure 3.67 Oddly shaped objects

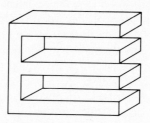

Figure 3.68 The three or four prong illusion

But what is this knowledge? It cannot be any of the constraints we have considered so far. In line drawings we have no motion, or texture, and the light intensity information indicates where the lines are, but no more. Thus we must have information about how lines must join together if they are to denote real objects, independently of texture and other visual properties.

We will continue our bilateral terminology in this section, using the term *vertex* for the point where two physical boundaries meet, and the term *junction* for the point where two image lines meet.

What people have found is that the junctions in a picture tell us a lot about the lines which make up the junction. For example, a junction that looks like a Y (naturally called a Y junction) often denotes a vertex where three visible planes meet, as in Figure 3.69. If this were always the case, then all lines which go into a Y junction must be folds, and not blades, again as in Figure 3.69. Remember our earlier definition of these terms. A fold is a line on an object where the regions on both sides of the fold are visible; a blade is a fold physically, but in such a position that we can only see one of the two sides. In Figure 3.66, lines l1 and l2 are blades, whereas l3 and l4 are folds. Unfortunately, Y junctions sometimes appear in other situations. (See Exercise 3.12.)

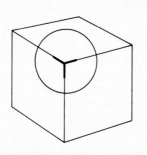

Figure 3.69 A Y junction in a picture of a cube

To try to bring some order into this, let us simplify by considering only line drawings in a world with no shadows, no surface markings, and only polyhedral objects. (A *polyhedron* is a shape bounded entirely by flat faces. Cubes and pyramids are examples of polyhedra; spheres and cylinders are not.) Thus the only two kinds of lines in this world are blades and folds. If any of the lines surrounding a region are folds, then clearly the region is part of a block. If all of the lines are blades, then the region may be background. (Not always, however; see Exercise 3.13.)

To simplify even more, we will make two other restrictions on our scenes. First, we will assume that none of the junctions we see are the result of coincidences. That is, if we changed our point of view slightly we would not change the basic structure of any of the junctions. In Figure 3.70a, the circled junction becomes two separate junctions when we change our point of view, as in Figure 3.70b. We will assume that nothing of this sort happens in our pictures. Actually, this is just the "nonaccidental properties heuristic" once again.

Furthermore, we will also restrict consideration to scenes in which all vertices are *trihedral vertices*. A trihedral vertex is one which is created by the meeting of three, and only three planar areas. In the image, not all of these planes may be visible (and so would not correspond to any regions), but they count anyway. So, both Figure 3.66 and Figure 3.67 can be interpreted as arising from scenes in which all of the vertices are trihedral. The normal interpretations we assign to the scenes in Figure 3.71 have non-trihedral vertices.

By making these restrictions we have limited the possibilities sufficiently to enable us to enumerate all the ways in which lines may come together at junctions. To begin with, there are only four types of junction, shown in Figure 3.72. Formally, a **Y** junction is one in which three lines intersect at a point, and the angles between each of the lines and the others is less than 180 degrees. If one of the angles is exactly 180 degrees then we call the junction a **T** junction because it looks like a T. If one of the angles is more than 180 degrees we call it a **W** junction. A junction with two lines is called an **L** junction.

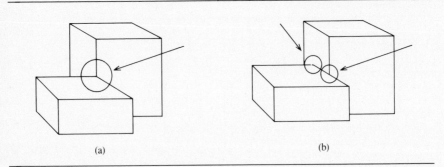

(a)   (b)

Figure 3.70 A product of coincidence

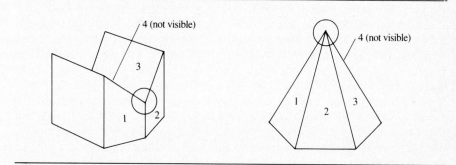

Figure 3.71 Non-trihedral vertices

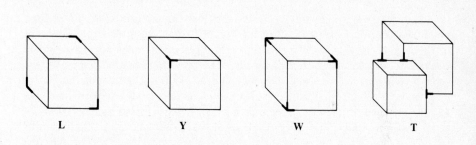

Figure 3.72 Junction types in trihedral scenes

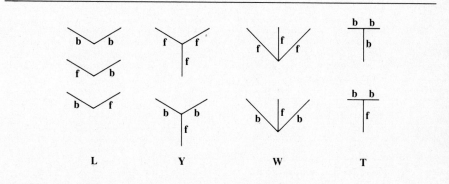

Figure 3.73 A catalogue of possible junction labelings

Only certain combinations of blades and folds can occur at a given junction type. Figure 3.73 gives all the possibilities. Note, for instance, that there are only two configurations allowed at a **Y** junction. (See Exercise 3.14.)

Let us now add one simple additional rule: Any line which has the background on one side of it must be a **b** (the background has no folds). Now, assuming the background is easy to find, we can in many cases deduce the correct interpretation for every line in the image. To take a simple case, for the cube in Figure 3.74a we can immediately label six lines as **b**, because they have the background on one side. If we now look at, say, the upper left-hand side **W** junction, then by looking at the possible labelings we can immediately see that the remaining unlabeled line must be an **f**, as in Figure 3.74b. In the same way, the other two **W** junctions require that their third lines must also be **f**s, giving us the completed labeling in Figure 3.74. (See Exercises 3.15 and 3.16.)

Because these constraints purport to hold for all possible scenes consisting of trihedral vertices, if a scene has no consistent labeling, it is not a possible scene. Thus it is interesting to note that Figure 3.68 has no consistent labeling. (See Exercise 3.19.)

Unfortunately, this simple scheme does not capture all of the information one might like. For example, consider Figure 3.75a. When we apply our rules to the hole, as in Figure 3.75, we find that three of the lines are not uniquely determined, despite the fact that we are hard pressed to see how the left one could be anything but a **b** and the other two **f**s. Indeed, this is correct, but to prove it requires labeling the lines with more information. In particular, not only do we need to know if a line is a **b** or an **f**, but we also need to know, in the case of a **b**, which side corresponds to the occluding object. To indicate this we will require that the **b** symbol always appears on the side of the line corresponding to the occluding object.

Having made this distinction, we must now go back to our catalogue of junction types, and find out if any of them require blades on one side or

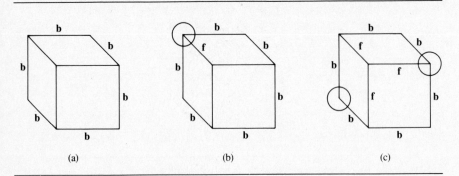

(a)   (b)   (c)

Figure 3.74 Labeling a cube

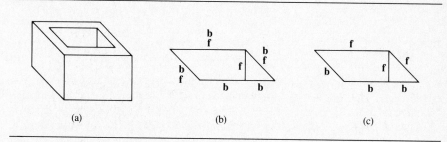

Figure 3.75 A block with a hole

another. When we do this we get the catalogue in Figure 3.76. Figure 3.75c shows the hole labeled using this new catalogue.

This has been a quick look at line labeling. Even to handle our trihedral world we could usefully add new labels. (For example, we could distinguish between concave and convex folds.) Furthermore, the world does not consist of polyhedral scenes with only trihedral vertices, and no shadows or surface markings. Thus much work has been done on extending this technique for more complicated scenes. But we will stop here.

3.5 Representing and Recognizing Scenes

The next step in visual processing is scene description. This is a vague term. A program that counted the trees it could see would output "7" or some other number, and that would be a description. But we want to be able to construct descriptions with considerably more complexity, such as this one:

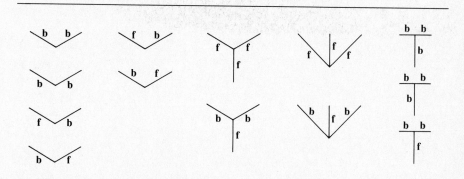

Figure 3.76 A junction catalogue with two blade types

There is a tiger, ready to pounce in this direction. There is a tiger trap between me and the tiger. The trap is not set.

In the terms we introduced in Chapter 1, we need an *internal representation*. The problem of late vision is to produce a description in such a powerful notation starting from an intrinsic image.

The algorithm to perform this transformation operates in three stages. See Figure 3.77. The first stage is to switch from a region-oriented (intrinsic-image) representation to an object-oriented (3-D) one. Then the machine looks in a "catalogue" of known object types to find familiar objects that resemble those it has found in the image. Finally, the stored descriptions must *match* the description of what the machine is looking at. To produce the "tiger" description, the machine must produce a description of the object it is looking at, then find a description of the typical tiger in the catalogue, and match the two, to produce a final description of the form **tiger** plus slot values.

3.5.1 Shape Description

To make this work, we need a *shape notation*. It will be used in two places: in the catalogue, to represent the shapes of "typical" tigers, airplanes, buildings, etc.; and as the input to the matcher, to represent the shape of the particular object seen now. As we will see, these require somewhat different treatments. For now, we will focus on the second, the description of a given object.

There are a wide variety of shape-description notations. They fall into two basic categories: surface descriptions and volume descriptions. The former describe the surfaces bounding the object; the latter, the pieces of the object. For example, in Figure 3.78, we can describe the object as a parallelepiped, or as a set of six faces.

Volume and surface descriptions might seem equivalent, since a volume and its surface completely constrain each other. Nonequivalence arises for

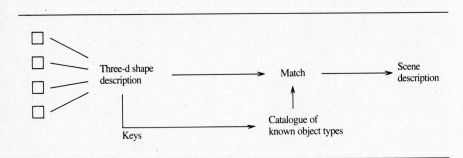

Figure 3.77 Late visual processing

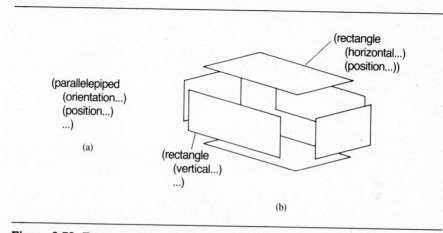

Figure 3.78 Two representations of a brick

several reasons. The first is the fact that almost any shape description is only approximate. Consider a beach: at the finest resolution, its shape consists of trillions of tiny bumps, created by grains of sand. At a coarser resolution, it consists of features like dunes, each a meter or two across. At the coarsest resolution, it is a ribbon running alongside the ocean. The "right" resolution depends entirely on the use we want to put the object to. It is important in describing sandpaper to talk about its bumps, but usually only dunes matter on a beach. Hence a shape description will not describe the geometry of an object exactly; the geometry it describes will "come close" to the real geometry.

A related consideration is the requirement that objects that are similarly shaped should have similar shape descriptions. That is, some differences are less important than others; if two objects differ only in unimportant ways, their shape descriptions should be nearly identical. For instance, a smooth banana and a rough banana should have similar shape descriptions, even though their boundaries, examined under a microscope, are completely different.

One appealing way to satisfy these requirements is to represent a given object at more than one resolution. The overall shape of a banana, rough or smooth, is a cylinder. So the shortest possible description of any banana is: cylinder. If this is the only description, then all bananas come out identical.

Since we want similarity, not identity, we add to this basic description some modifications, such as:

1. Pointy ends
2. Length 20 cm
3. Curved axis
4. Color yellow
5. Surface smooth

A slot-and-filler notation does a good job of expressing a shape as a basic shape plus modifications:

```
(cylinder shape55
        (end1 cone)
        (end2 cone)
        (length (20 cm))
        (width (4 cm))
        (axis-curvature 0.1)
        (color yellow)
        (surface-roughness 0))
```

We will use the term *shape primitive* for basic shapes like cylinder. The shape primitives we choose will determine which shapes are simple and which similarities are obvious.

Armed with this concept, we can reconsider whether to represent shapes by surfaces or volumes. We can now rephrase the question as, Are shape primitives volume elements or surface elements? In the banana example, the basic shape is cylinder, a volume element. To describe it as a surface, we would have to form a collection of surfaces that together bound the banana. This seems too complex. Furthermore, it would make it harder to notice that two bananas have a similar shape. For most three-dimensional objects, volume primitives seem to make descriptions simpler. On the other hand, if intricate, possibly concave polyhedra were the principal objects encountered by the machine, describing each as a collection of faces might be the simplest thing to do.

Our banana description needs more work. We specified that each end of the banana is a cone. What role is the symbol cone playing here? In fact, it is another shape primitive, and we can if we want flesh out the description with further information:

```
(cylinder shape55
        (protrusion
                (cone end1 (length (4 cm))
                       (width (4 cm))
                       . . . )
                (location bottom))
        . . . )
```

Allowing shape descriptions inside shape descriptions makes the notation *hierarchical*. At the highest level, there is a single shape primitive. Slot fillers modify this with parameters like axis-curvature and length. Some fillers mention further shape primitives and their modifiers, then descriptions of subshapes, and so forth, as far down as necessary. So our beach description could mention dunes, and sand grains if we felt like it. Different programs would process a shape description to different levels of resolution.

Shape description is simplified if we allow parts of an object to consist of empty space. Otherwise, the description of an object with an indentation would be quite messy. Consider a bowling ball. This is essentially a sphere, but a closer look shows three holes. The simplest way to describe the overall shape is as shown in Figure 3.79. Each indentation is described as a shape. Furthermore, we must describe its location in the frame of reference of the bowling ball. (We have made up some ''spherical'' coordinates here; don't worry about whether they make sense. In a realistic system, more care would have to be given to describing the location and orientation of subshapes.) Together, indentations and protrusions will be labeled *shape parts*.

We now have the equipment for describing what the machine is looking at, an individual bowling ball, banana, or whatever. Of course, the machine does not yet realize what it is looking at; it has only a description of the shape of an unknown thing. To verify that the thing is actually a banana, this description must be *matched* against the description of a ''typical'' banana. If all bananas are identical, the typical description could be an ordinary description, but not all bananas are identical. For instance, suppose that the length of a banana can vary from 10 cm to 30 cm. We can express this particular constraint by using an interval instead of a single number in the **length** slot. But, for greater generality, we must replace some of the slot fillers with variables, and augment the description with *constraints* on those variables. An example of what we need, and the general form, are shown in Figure 3.80. The idea is describe a shape using *shape-descrip*, an ordinary shape description, but with some of the constants replaced by the variables in *vars*. The intent is to describe all and only the shapes obtained by substituting in values of the *vars* that satisfy *constraints*. Each constraint is just a predicate-calculus formula involving the *vars*.

```
(sphere shape595
        (diameter . . . )
        . . .
        (indentation (cylinder thumb-hole
                        (length (3 cm))
                        (width (2.5 cm))
                        . . . )
                (location (0.1 0.1)))
        (indentation (cylinder ring-finger-hole
                        (length (3 cm))
                        (width (2.5 cm))
                        . . . )
                (location (0 0)))
        (indentation (cylinder middle-finger-hole
                        (length (3 cm))
                        (width (2.5 cm))
                        . . . )
                (location (−0.1 −0.1))))
```

Figure 3.79 Shape description for a bowling ball

Example:

```
(constrained (l w c)
        (cylinder (length l)
                  (width w)
                  (color c)
                  . . . )
        (≥ l (10 cm))
        (≤ l (30 cm))
        (≥ (/ l w) 3)
        (≤ (/ l w) 7)
        (or (= c yellow) (= c green)))
```

General form:

```
(constrained vars
        shape-descrip
        -constraints-)
```

Figure 3.80 Constrained shape descriptions

We will call this a *parametrized shape description*; the variables are called *parameters* of the description. An ordinary shape description will be called a *constant* shape description.

Box 3.3

Imagery and Internal Representation

While we have, by and large, adopted propositional representations in this book, many have hypothesized that people store visual information in imagery. If asked, people can conjure up images of all sorts of things in their heads. But are there really images in the head? In some sense the answer has to be yes. After all, virtually everyone reports seeing images, and hence they are clearly "there." But what is the underlying form and process which gives rise to these reports? In particular, could it simply be our "standard" propositional representations?

This debate has been sharpened in the recent past by a series of psychology experiments supporting the idea of imagery. The classic example here is one by Shepard on mental rotation [Shepard71]. In this experiment people are shown two pictures, like those in Figure 3.81. They are asked to indicate if the object shown in the left can be rotated so that it will look like the object on the right. In half the cases the objects are identical in shape, so that such a rotation can be found; in the remaining cases the two objects are mirror images, so that there is no such rotation.

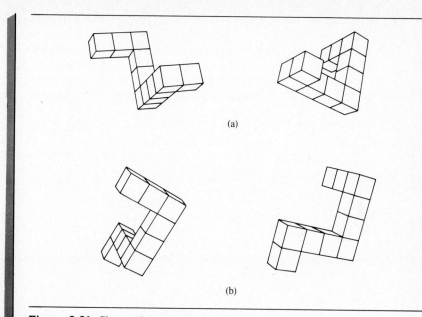

(a)

(b)

Figure 3.81 Shepard rotation pictures

The basic result is that the time taken to perform the task is directly proportional to the angle of rotation separating the two objects. Furthermore, when asked how they perform the task, the subjects report that they "mentally rotate" the first object until it coincides with the second. When asked to show how fast the object rotates, they indicate an angular velocity which exactly corresponds to the reaction times.

This is certainly a striking result, and there have been other interesting experiments pointing in the same direction. People have images, and they have the ability to manipulate them to solve tasks, just as any other kind of representation.

But others find this sort of thing very problematic. For starters, exactly what is an "image"? The most obvious representation would be an array of light intensities, although if any of the theories in this chapter are correct, an image might be a primal sketch or an intrinsic image. But even the most refined of these, the intrinsic image, is still a long way from the more propositional representation which we suggest, and the reasons we have put forward for the more abstract representation still hold. In a propositional representation of a lion coming at you, we get, separated out, notions like lion, **stance**, tree, or whatever happens to be around. By getting a separate and distinct representation for lion we have something upon which we can hang, and hence retrieve, our knowledge of lions. An intrinsic image does not give this to us. Instead, everything is blended together to make up the entire scene. Computationally it simply makes more sense to unblend this once and for all than to store the blend, and have to decode it in order to remember "once a lion was coming at me . . . ."

However, most modern theories of imagery do not claim that images replace propositional representation, but rather supplement it. Thus arguments of the above form are beside the point, and instead we should ask questions like, "What is the nature of such images?" and "Of what use are they?" We cannot explore this in any depth here, and we will only look at one experiment that indicates that if there are images, they are nothing remotely like "pictures." This experiment is by Hinton, and it too uses mental rotation, but this time to a different end [Hinton79]. The task he gave his subjects follows.

> Imagine a wire-framed cube resting on a table top with the front face directly in front of you and perpendicular to your line of sight. Imagine the long diagonal that goes from the bottom, front, left-hand corner to the top, back, right-hand one. Now imagine that the cube is reoriented so that this diagonal is vertical and the cube is resting on one corner. Place one fingertip about a foot above a table top and let this mark the position of the top corner on the diagonal. The corner on which the cube is resting is on the table top, vertically below your fingertip. With your other hand point on the spatial locations of the other corners of the cube.

Before going on, you might try this yourself (the correct picture is Figure 3.82). The results are striking. Virtually nobody is able to do this mental rotation and get the correct results. Even more bizarre is the fact that most people do not even get the right number of corners, most indicating that there will be four, whereas in fact there are six. This is a most unusual kind of picture.

But this is simply a piece of negative evidence. As for what actually corresponds to a mental image, nobody knows.

3.5.2 Matching Shape Descriptions

We now have two entities: a description of what the machine is looking at, and a (parametrized) description of the typical banana. If they can be made to match, then it is plausible that this thing being looked at is indeed a banana.

Of course, there is a big question here: How did the machine think to try matching the typical banana, instead of the typical whale? We will talk about that in the next section. For now, just assume that "banana" has come to mind.

The first step in matching is to verify that the two objects are described by the same basic shape primitive. If so, then the constraints on slots are checked. We said that a constraint was an arbitrary predicate-calculus formula; hence, an arbitrary deduction might be necessary to test that a constraint was satisfied. (See Chapter 6.) However, usually the constraints involve only predicates like equality and inequality, which can be tested by just comparing numbers and symbols.

Of course, it is not enough that the overall characteristics match: the shape parts of the two objects must match as well. The machine must find a correspondence between the parts of the two shape descriptions that makes all the constraints come out true. Two parts can be put in correspondence if they are both **indentations** or both **protrusions**, and if their shape descriptions otherwise match.

For example, consider the parametrized description of the shape of a camel. It will specify three protrusions (on top): the head and two humps. The two humps will have very similar descriptions (as **cones** modified appropriately). Hence, there are two possible matches against an actual camel: the correct correspondence, and one in which the humps are switched. One of these will be discarded when the camel constraints are tested.

In some cases, more than one correspondence survives until the end of the match process. For instance, some sheep dogs look about the same at each end. A match of the parametrized sheep dog description with an actual sheep dog can produce two matches: head = "lump1," tail = "lump2," and vice versa. In other words, it may not be possible from matching alone to tell which way the sheep dog is pointing.

The matching process we have described so far is independent of vision. We might as well be matching corporate organization charts (where the constraints would be on things like yearly budget instead of orientation and position). But the vision context introduces some special problems.

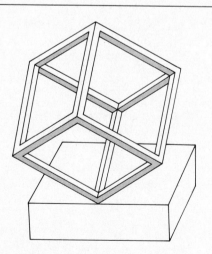

Figure 3.82 A wire-frame cube resting on one corner

First, one shape may be described more finely than the other. The shape catalogue may describe "rabbit" in detail, whereas the machine only got a glimpse of a thing with a fluffy tail. Fortunately, our shape notation is hierarchical, so that small details can be ignored in cases like this. All we have to do is give the matcher a variable "tolerance," a size below which mismatches do not matter. Then as soon as the machine tries to match a part smaller than the tolerance, it can just assume the match will succeed.

A more serious problem is *occlusion*: the object may be partially hidden by another object. For example, our camel might be standing behind a tree that completely hides its humps, as in Figure 3.83. We would still like it to be seen as a camel (or at least not be rejected). There is as yet no known answer to this problem. One idea is to take a proposed match, and use it to transform the parametrized shape description to image coordinates. That is, once the machine has decided that the major axis of the thing it is looking at should match the major axis of the stored camel description, and matched a couple of legs as well, then it has enough information to transform the stored camel description back to the image, asking, in effect, "What would a camel seen from this angle look like?" From this point on, it could match the two-dimensional visible patches instead of continuing to reason in terms of three-dimensional shape descriptions. Alternatively, it could use the predicted image as a guide to the

Figure 3.83 Camel behind a tree

three-dimensional match, ignoring parts whose predicted images lay behind surfaces (as retrieved from the intrinsic image).

3.5.3 Finding a Known Shape to Match Against

Now we confront the big problem we mentioned: deciding that the object the machine is looking at *might* be a banana. There are two phases, as shown in Figure 3.77. In phase 1, we produce a description of the object. In phase 2, we use this description to suggest objects that might match. That is, we use it as a *key* into the shape-description catalogue.

We will assume that the index is organized as a *discrimination net*, a structure useful in several places in AI. It is essentially a tree with a question at each node, such as, "What is the shape primitive?" For each possible answer ("sphere," "cylinder," etc.), there is a *child* node, which organizes all of the objects corresponding to that answer. For instance, the cylinder child of the root node leads to all the stored descriptions of objects that are cylinders. See Figure 3.84.

The "cylinder" node begins another tree of discriminations. The first question it asks is, "What is the orientation of the main axis?" The answer "vertical" leads to a net for objects like buildings, silos, humans, and trees. The answer "horizontal" leads to a net for animals and airplanes.

This is a tiny fragment of a realistic net. Note that it does not take very long to get down to substantive descriptors, like "animal," which have parametrized shape descriptions associated with them. The machine can match the animal description with what it is looking at, and verify that it is an animal (and find its head, etc.).

Suppose the match fails. The only way this can happen is if the object differs from an animal is some respect other than being cylindrical, horizontal, having one vertical protrusion, and no flat side protrusions. Suppose, for example, that an object matches the description of an elephant, except that it is only 30 cm high. There are three possibilities:

1. The vision module up to this point has made a mistake, and the object is actually further away than it concluded, so it's really 3 m high.
2. This is a new kind of animal, that differs from ordinary elephants in size.
3. It is a toy elephant. We could store a toy- *x* description for every sort of animal *x*, but it seems easier to handle this case specially by classifying all unusually small *x*s as toy *x*s (especially if they seem unusually placid as well). Unfortunately, our notation is not robust enough to work up a generic description of toy-*x*.

In Figure 3.84, the discrimination net continues below the animal node. Having verified that the thing is an animal, the next step is to figure out *which* animal. At the beginning of Section 3.4, we pointed out that general-purpose vision would have to make do with only general assumptions about physics; that guesses about what the machine was looking at were normally not available.

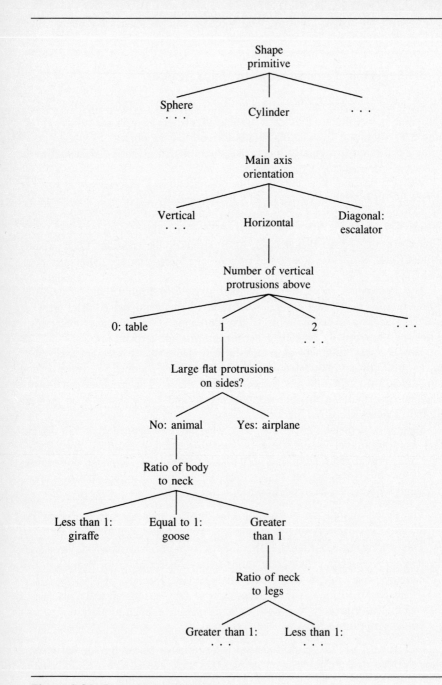

Figure 3.84 Example discrimination net

Here is where that begins to be false. Once it has decided it is looking at an animal, it has more specific assumptions to work with. For instance, if the legs had not been found yet, it would know where in the image to look harder for them. This is "top-down" image understanding, in which a hypothesis (e.g., "animal") guides processing, as opposed to "bottom-up," in which the data lead to hypotheses. The occlusion trick we described in Section 3.5.2 is another example.

So far our discrimination nets are just trees. Although Figure 3.84 does not show it, it is useful to allow more than one path from the top to a subordinate node. Suppose the machine is looking at an elephant head on, so it sees a head with tusks, and a body behind it. The body looks more like a sphere than a cylinder, so the machine fails to retrieve the appropriate description. Nonetheless, it may still recognized one piece of this object as an elephant's head, and the catalogue entry for head may suggest looking for an animal attached to the back of it, oriented in a certain way. Thus the machine finds the animal entry by a nonstandard route. Having found it, however, everything else is the same. It takes the animal description and transforms it by the unusual viewing angle to find what it would look like in the image. Having verified that it would look rather spherical, and that the hind legs would be occluded by the body, matching can proceed as usual.

An issue that arises in discrimination-net design is how the questions are to be ordered. Why not start with asking about color at the top, and only get around to the shape primitive at the end? The answer is that the first questions to ask are those whose answers are almost always available in the image, are strongly discriminatory, and tend to divide the world up in "meaningful" ways. There is a "natural class" of objects that have the same geometry as animals (namely, animals), but no such class of objects with the same color as a banana. (A person who had never seen a sunflower before would not classify it as just like a banana except for shape differences.)

3.5.4 Describing a Seen Shape

In the course of Section 3.5 we have been working "backward" through Figure 3.77. First we described matching two shape descriptions (one of them parametrized). Then we described how a discrimination net was used to retrieve the description of a known type of object from the catalogue. Now we must describe what is actually the first step, producing a description of the object or objects from the intrinsic image. The reason we have postponed this discussion is that the object-description phase should be designed to make the later steps work well.

The key requirement is that the description produced must be syntactically similar to the stored one, or else the discrimination net will not find anything. Consider Figure 3.85. Should this object be described as a cube with half its top cut off, or as a parallelepiped with a parallelepiped on top? It makes a difference, because (assuming there is a familiar object with this shape) the

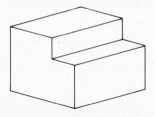

Figure 3.85 A cube with a notch? Or a brick with a bump?

shape will be in the catalogue either under this description

(cube (indentation . . .))

or under this completely different description

(parallelepiped (protrusion . . .)).

No plausible indexing scheme will find one of these given the other as what to look for.

Of course, even if the indexer succeeded, the matcher we sketched in the previous section would fail to match. However, it is easy to imagine a matcher that would work harder to see the two shapes as the same. Sometimes the matcher is called to match two *constant* object descriptions. If a robot wanders by the same building twice (and knows it is the same because of an inscription on the door), then it might try to match the description it remembers with what it is seeing now. It might well want a matcher extended to be able to convert cube descriptions into parallelepiped descriptions in this case if all else fails. But such an extension won't help in the discrimination net; if the building is misdescribed the second time it is seen, the robot won't realize it is the same building as before.

It will help avoid this problem if the vocabulary of shape primitives does not make distinctions that are too subtle. If both ovoid and ellipsoid are in the vocabulary, we run the risk of misdescribing one as the other, and failing to recognize it.

The misdescription problem is in theory inevitable in a system that classifies all objects into a few "qualitative" classes, which is what shape primitives amount to. Suppose sphere and cube are used as shape primitives. Since a sphere can be continuously deformed into a cube, there must be borderline objects that could be described either way. Either the machine can produce multiple descriptions for such borderline objects, or we can try to choose the vocabulary so that borderline objects are rare, or we can try to capture as much as possible of the variation among objects quantitatively, so that it is more obvious to the machine that one descriptor is "close" to another.

One shape primitive that works in many domains is the *generalized cylinder*, the volume obtained by sweeping a cross section along an axis. See Figure 3.86. Of course, we have to describe the differences between objects as

Figure 3.86 Objects consisting of generalized cylinders

well, but we are more likely to get most of the description approximately right if it has lots of pieces, and if many of these pieces are described by numbers rather than symbols. So we can describe *object1* as being a **generalized-cylinder** with a square cross section and a vertical axis, about 100 meters long and 20 meters wide. *Object2* we describe as a **generalized-cylinder** with a circular cross section and a curving horizontal axis, about 1 meter long and 4 centimeters wide. Even if we get some of the details wrong, the first strongly suggests "building," and the second strongly suggests "snake."

Unfortunately, real objects rarely consist of one cylinder. Except for snakes, animals have legs and tails; even snakes have heads cluttering things up. This is not a problem for our notation; we can describe appendages as protrusions from the basic shape. The problem is that the machine has to be able to do this in a way that matches a catalogue entry, without knowing what it's looking at yet. In Figure 3.87 how does the machine know to describe a thing as a body plus a neck, instead of a single curved object, before it knows the thing is

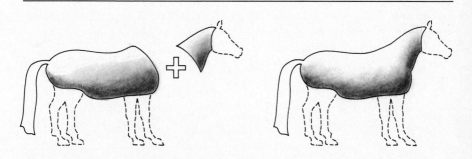

Figure 3.87 Two ways to segment a horse

a horse? This is called the *segmentation* problem. It is not yet solved, although
there are some promising approaches. One possibility is to segment an object at
concavities and points opposite such concavities, as in Figure 3.88.

The machine's task is made much easier by the fact that it is working with
the intrinsic image, not a raw image. Each segment that is proposed has to
make sense as a cylinder, given its silhouette and the surface orientations of the
region bounded by the silhouette.

Once segmentation is complete, the machine takes the largest cylinder, and
describes the object as a cylinder of that size and orientation, with the other
cylinders as protrusions. Indentations arise from small concavities which are
ignored in the first-order segmentation.

There is some evidence that generalized cylinders are used by the human
visual system. When you think about it, the fact that our crude figures look like
horses at all to you is remarkable. In fact, Figure 3.89 demonstrates that
humans can classify as a familiar shape a crude stick figure that preserves only

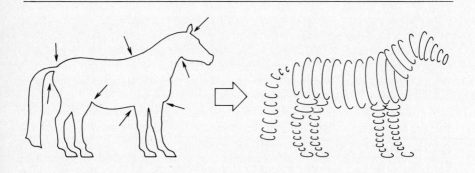

Figure 3.88 Segmenting a horse

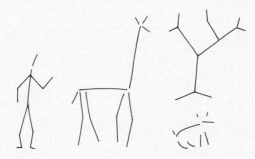

Figure 3.89 Stick figures

the relative orientation and lengths of the axes of an object's various component cylinders. This suggests that the numbers, positions, and relative sizes of cylinders in an object determine what it is seen as. Details are relatively unimportant. What you need to see a typical mammal is just the pattern shown in Figure 3.90. The discrimination net we showed in Figure 3.84 reflected this idea.

3.6 References and Further Reading

There are several books devoted to vision. Marr's book [Marr82] is the most unified treatment. It is oriented toward explaining the human visual system. The book by Ballard and Brown [Ballard82] is about computational techniques. Rather than attempting to explain how the human visual system actually works, it provides a rich source of algorithms of all sorts. A special issue of the journal *Artificial Intelligence*, all of Volume 17 (1981), is devoted exclusively to vision. It has also been made into a book. Earlier work in vision is described in [Winston75].

A lot of the terminology we used comes from Marr, such as *2.5 dimensional sketch* and *primal sketch*. The term *intrinsic image set*, which we shortened to *intrinsic image*, is from the work of Barrow and Tenenbaum. In a series of articles [Barrow78, Barrow80, Barrow81] they have put forth a theory similar to Marr's, but not tied so closely to psychological results.

The idea of smoothing at several levels of resolution is presented in [Marr80]. Connecting primal sketch features using a histogram is due to David Marr and Kent Stevens [Stevens78]. In the area of stereo vision, and in particular, random-dot stereograms, see [Julesz71] for a wealth of experimental results. (The phenomenon was discovered by Bela Julesz.) The matching algorithms we put forward for finding corresponding points in the two images are due to Marr and Poggio [Marr79]. Two areas of low-level vision we were not able to cover are motion analysis (see [Ullman79]) and photometry (see [Horn77]).

There has been a fair amount of work on texture discrimination starting with the pioneering work of Gibson [Gibson50], and the psychological experiments and theories of Julesz. [Julesz75]. Several methods have been proposed for extracting information about surface orientation and depth from textures.

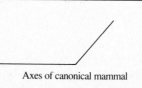

Axes of canonical mammal

Figure 3.90 Axes of canonical mammal

See [Stevens79, Kender80]. (We also borrowed the term *nonaccidental image properties* from this last paper.) The idea that orientation of virtual lines accounts for texture discrimination is from [Schatz77]. That surface orientation could be determined from texture prior to texture recognition is from [Witkin80].

Our catalog of line types, and in particular Figure 3.57, is from [Barrow78]. For more information on determining line labels from vertices, see [Freuder80, Waltz75] and [Chakravarty79]. See [Hummel83] for an analysis of labeling problems. This last article presents a labeling algorithm more complex than the one presented here, but with more predictable convergence properties.

Turning to high-level vision, for more on representing typical object shapes, see [Marr78] and [Brooks81]. A discussion of generalized cylinders is found in [Agin72]. This work also describes an algorithm for segmentation. The idea of segmenting at concavities is due to Vatan and is described in [Marr82]. The suggestion that the numbers, positions, and relative sizes of cylinders in an object determine what it is seen as is from [Marr78]. For some ideas on the representation of large scale objects (entire scenes, rather than individual objects), see [Davis84]. For more on the idea of imagery see [Kosslyn75, Kosslyn77] (for the "pro-image" side) and [Pylyshyn73] (for the "anti-image" position).

Exercises

3.1 (Requires calculus) Prove that the derivative of a convolution is the same as the convolution of a derivative, as in equation (3.3).

3.2 Explain why the formulas in equations (3.1) and (3.2) are correct only if the weighting function w is symmetric. How would they have to change if the weighting function were asymmetric, as in Figure 3.18? (The less general formulation is used so that $f*g$ will come out the same as $g*f$, which is technically convenient. For those who know some calculus, the proof of this commutativity is easy; figure it out.)

3.3 In this exercise we will study the properties of Gaussian convolution by using a discrete approximation to the second derivative curve of Figure 3.24, as shown in Figure 3.91. Note that this function is defined only on integer values of x, and it generates weights 1, 2, 3, 2, . . . for coordinates -8, -7, -6, -5, ...

   a) The sum of the 17 weight values in Figure 3.91 is 0 ($1 + 2 + 3 + 2 + 1 + -2 + . . .$). Explain why this means that convolving this curve with a one-dimensional gray-level curve of constant slope over a range larger than 17 will yield 0 for any point in the middle of that range. (This is what you expect, because the second derivative is zero over an interval of constant slope.)

   b) We will define the *width* of the curve in Figure 3.91 to be 18. Draw similar approximations with widths 6 and 60. Make sure that

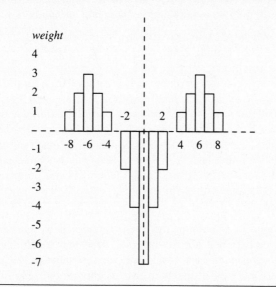

Figure 3.91 Discrete linear approximation to Gaussian second derivative

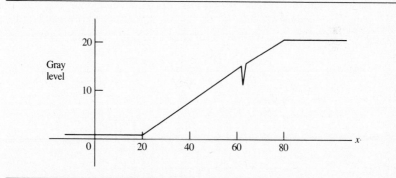

Figure 3.92 Example gray-level curve

their weight values sum to 0. Why is it irrelevant exactly what the vertical scale is so long as the weights sum to 0?

c) Consider the gray-level curve of Figure 3.92. Derive the result of convolving this curve with the discrete Gaussians of widths 6 and 60. Where are the zero crossings in each case? In the wide-Gaussian version, you should see a zero crossing at about 40 corresponding to the gradual illumination change. In the narrow-Gaussian version, you should see two zero crossings at about 63 corresponding to the small dip. If you do not have access to a real computer, use the cruder but more manageable approximation of Figure 3.93, and simulate the computer manually.

3.4   A *binary image* is an image with just two "gray levels," 0 and 1.   You can picture such a thing being produced by a television camera with poor brightness resolution, so that each pixel is either "turned on" or not. (Alternatively, you can produce a binary image from an ordinary image by *thresholding*, turning each pixel into a 1 if it is above the threshold, 0 if below. Different choice of threshold leads to a different image.) Binary images take less space to store, and suggest simpler algorithms than ordinary images, even though they do not contain as much information. Write a program to find edgelets in binary images. It should take as input an array of 1s and 0s (or "trues" and "falses" if you prefer), and output an array of the same size with each cell labeled with whether an edgelet occurs there.

3.5   The analogue of *smoothing* for binary images is to ignore blobs that are too small or bars that are too narrow. One way to do this is to examine the neighborhood of each pixel, and set the value in the pixel to be the same as the majority of pixels in that neighborhood. For instance, in Figure 3.94, if the neighborhood is taken as the set of 9 points around a point (including itself), then the central 1s will change to 0s. The larger the neighborhood, the larger the feature that will be smoothed away. Change the program of Exercise 3.4 so that it takes a "neighborhood size" parameter, and smooths using it. Using a large neighborhood is like doing low-resolution convolutions. Explain why, in a binary image, you can

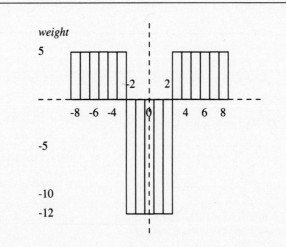

Figure 3.93 Square approximation to Gaussian second derivative

```
0  0  0  0  0          0  0  0  0  0
0  1  1  1  0    →     0  0  0  0  0
0  0  0  0  0          0  0  0  0  0
```

Figure 3.94 Smoothing a binary image

never have an edgelet appear in the low-resolution map that does not appear in higher-resolution maps.

3.6 Write the algorithm to find virtual lines. (Section 3.4.3.) It should take a list of point coordinates, and do the following:

1. Find each point's nearby neighbors
2. Compute the histogram of vector orientations for each point and its near neighbors.
3. Add each histogram to all the neighbors
4. Find peaks in each histogram, and return vectors near the peaks.

3.7 If the algorithm of Exercise 3.6 is applied to a large set of points, you will find that the first step, finding nearest neighbors, takes the longest, because it requires n^2 distance computations for n points. For this algorithm and many others, it would be desirable to be able to find just the features near a given feature of interest. One can do this by keeping the data base in an array, such that (features $i\ j$) is the list of features found at location (i, j). (Presumably the size of this array is less than that of the original image, but it's still pretty big.) Now, to find features near a feature at (i, j), you examine cells $(i-1, j-1)$ $(i-1, j)$, and so on. Alter the algorithm to take advantage of this idea.

3.8 In Section 3.4.4, we said that stereo disparity was defined for every point on each image. This is not quite true. Give some examples of points that have no disparity. (*Hint*: Look at a stereo pair like Figure 3.35.)

3.9 Consider two images made by a pair of eyes 5 cm apart, facing straight ahead, with a focal length of 1 cm. Suppose that a point P is seen with coordinate $x = -0.1$ in one eye, and $x = 0.1$ in the other. Use equations (3.6) and (3.5) to estimate the depth of the object containing point P. Plot the depth for a few other values of x'. At what depth does x' become so small that it is comparable to the size of a receptor?

3.10 A student is puzzled by the claim in Section 3.4.6 that all boundaries are either folds, shadows, or marks. "Some boundaries, such as the edge of a sphere, do not correspond to any of them," she points out. Explain what this student has misunderstood.

3.11 In the example of Figure 3.61, verify that the weights of elements 2 to 5 do not change on the first iteration, and none of the weights change thereafter.

3.12 Find a **Y** junction in Figure 3.67 which has two lines coming into it that are normally interpreted as blades rather than folds.

3.13 Construct a scene containing a region bounded on all sides by blades, which is nonetheless not to be interpreted as a part of the background.

3.14 Prove that under our assumptions Figure 3.73 gives all the legal combinations of folds and blades that can occur at the four junction types.

3.15 In the example of Figure 3.74, we did not look at the constraints for the **L** vertices, or the **Y** vertex at the center. Show that these are consistent with what we learned from the other constraints.

3.16 Figure 3.95 has all of its lines and junctions labeled. Starting with the same scene unlabeled, explain how all the labels could be deduced.

3.17 In the same way, label the lines and junctions in Figure 3.66.

3.18 The problem of line labeling (Section 3.4.8) can be expressed as a cooperative labeling problem (Section 3.4.7), if we make a few adjustments. Let each line be an element. Two lines are neighbors if they share a junction. The first adjustment required is that the machine might have to take into account more than one neighbor per constraint. At **Y** junctions, for instance, all three lines create a constraint. The second adjustment is to make the algorithm *discrete*, by making the constraints absolute instead of weighted. A label on line *l* is *rejected* if there is some constraint *l* takes part in such that there is no selection of labels from the other lines in the constraint that combine with this label to make a

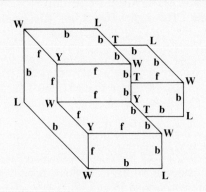

Figure 3.95 A scene with junction types

legitimate junction (that is, one in Figure 3.73). For instance, Figure 3.96 shows the rejection of a **b** label at a **Y** junction.

a) Simulate a few iterations of the resulting algorithm. Try implementing it.
b) If in Figure 3.96 the horizontal line had started with labels **b**, **f**, no rejection would have occurred. But some conclusion can be drawn (given Figure 3.73), namely that one of the two ambiguous labels must be a **b** and the other an **f**. Give an example where this failure to draw a conclusion leads the algorithm to leave in some ambiguities that could be eliminated by deeper analysis.

3.19 Try to give Figure 3.68 as complete a labeling as possible, using our first catalogue of legal junction labels, Figure 3.73. As you would hope, a completely consistent labeling is impossible. However, note that in one portion of the picture we get a consistent labeling that does not correspond to our interpretation of the scene, and that seems, in fact, inconsistent at that point. Now relabel the figure using the revised catalogue of Figure 3.76. Show that with this new labeling, the portion of the scene that formerly received an undeserved consistent labeling is no longer consistent.

3.20 Figure 3.97 shows the description of an unknown object. The orientations of <0,0,0> indicate that the parts are aligned with the large parallelepiped. The location fields give the coordinates of the *centers* of the parts with respect to the *centers* of the large parallelepiped. (That is, if a part had location <0,0,0> with respect to thing1, their centers would coincide.) What is this object?

3.21 Write a program that takes a shape description and tests whether it contains a cone at any level. (*Hint*: This program is most easily written using recursion (Chapter 2). Explain why.)

3.22 It seems tedious, in the parametrized camel description of Section 3.5.1, to repeat the hump description twice; or, in the description of the bowling ball, to repeat the definition of "finger hole" three times. Propose a way to provide for "subroutines" in shape descriptions, so that hump or

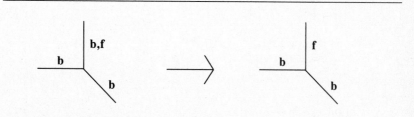

Figure 3.96 Cooperative line labeling

```
(parallelepiped thing1
    (length 2 cm)    ; where length, width, and height
    (width 2 cm)     ; are measured against the x, y, and z
    (height 1 cm)    ; axes, respectively.
    (protrusion
        (parallelepiped part1
            (length 2 cm)
            (width 0.1 cm)
            (height 0.5 cm))
        (orientation <0,0,0>)
        (location <2 cm, -0.5 cm, 0 cm>))
    (protrusion
        (parallelepiped part2
            (length 2 cm)
            (width 0.1 cm)
            (height 0.5 cm))
        (orientation <0,0,0>)
        (location <2 cm, 0.5 cm, 0 cm>)))
```

Figure 3.97 What is this the shape of?

finger-hole could be defined separately, as a cone or cylinder with modifications, and then used as often as convenient, with further modifications on each use.

3.23 A "typical picket fence" cannot be described in our shape notation, nor, for that matter, can an individual picket fence if the number of pickets is not known precisely. Suggest an extension that will make this possible. (*Hint*: it will help to have thought about Exercise 3.22.)

3.24 Write a function to test whether a parametrized shape description matches a constant shape description. Assume no indentations or protrusions.

For simplicity, you may make the assumption that, outside of the constraints, a variable occurs as exactly one slot filler in a parametrized structural description. For instance, to state that the length and width of the object must be the same, you must write

```
(constrained (. . . x y . . . )
    (. . .
     (length x)
     (width y)
     . . .)
    . . .
    (= x y)
    . . . )
```

instead of this somewhat shorter version:

```
(constrained ( . . . x . . . )
    (cylinder (length x)
              (width x)
              . . . )
    . . . )
```

The one slot where the variable occurs is called its *declaration*. E.g., in the example, x is declared to be the length, and y the width of the object.

Given this convention, the first step of the algorithm is to extract variable declarations. That is, for each bound variable in the parametrized description, find the slot that declares it. Then find its value in the constant shape description. When all the values have been collected, check the constraints.

3.25 Alter the program of Exercise 3.24 to handle shapes with parts. It should look like this:

- Extract declarations and constraints for variables not declared inside part descriptions. (It is legal for the one "declaring" occurrence of a variable to be inside a part description. E.g., x may occur as the length of the third protrusion.)
- If those constraints are not satisfied, the match fails.
- Otherwise, generate sets of "internally consistent" pairings of parts. A pairing is internally consistent if the two subshape-descriptions match, without regard to constraints from the overall shape. (Note: matching subshape-descriptions is a recursive call to the matcher.)
- For each set of pairings, verify the remaining constraints on the overall shape.
- Return verified part correspondences.

3.26 Explain why a ten-humped camel would cause the algorithm of Exercise 3.25 to go crazy. (This is a good exercise to do even if you have not implemented the program described in Exercise 3.25.)

3.27 The discrimination net of Figure 3.84 has one major problem. If the object the machine sees is a banana, then the question about "Main axis orientation" is inappropriate, because the main axis of the banana might be seen in a variety of orientations. Propose a better organization for the net so that objects like bananas are dealt with appropriately.

3.28 Make up some sample discriminations to add to the discrimination net of Figure 3.84 to allow it to distinguish among ten different types of animal, like giraffe, pig, hippo, dog, cat, etc. How many discriminations did it take? In principle, it could take just one, if there were ten different answers. What's the minimum number it could take if each question has exactly two answers?

4

This chapter requires the material in Chapter 1. Later chapters do not depend on this one, except for Sections 10.4 and 11.6. Those sections marked optional are not needed by subsequent sections in this chapter (excepting subsequent optional sections). A little bit of Lisp enters into this chapter in the discussions of the ATN grammar, and the associated semantic functions. This is less true of the nonoptional sections, which can probably be read without knowledge of Lisp.

Parsing Language

4.1 Levels of Language

If vision is the most impressive of our senses, it is probably language which most clearly identifies us as human. As with vision, the problem here is to take the information provided by the outside world and translate it into a precise internal representation. (To a large degree, those studying language tend to use the term *semantic representation* for what we have been calling internal representation. We will continue with our previous usage.) The reasons for making this translation are those we gave in Chapter 1 when we discussed the need for an internal representation in the first place: the structural ambiguity of language (or other kinds of input), the referential ambiguity of noun phrases, and the word sense ambiguity of most English words. If we do not know what the words in a sentence mean, or who a pronoun refers to, it is impossible to infer anything of interest from what we are given.

The analogy between language and vision is flawed in one respect — we not only gather information with language, but we use it for communication as well. However, to keep the discussion focused, we will concentrate on the understanding of language, and ignore all of the fascinating issues that arise in its production.

Most of us understand both written and spoken language, but reading is learned much later, so let us start with spoken language. We can divide the problem into three areas — acoustic-phonetic, morphological-syntactic, and semantic-pragmatic processes, as shown in Figure 4.1. The first of these processes, acoustic-phonetic, is responsible for taking the sounds (presumably represented as a plot of how much energy is coming in at various sound frequencies) and translating the input into words. The second takes these words and establishes the syntactic form of the utterance, while the third tries to tease

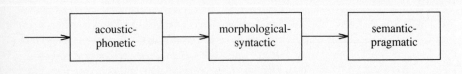

Figure 4.1 The three levels of linguistic analysis

out the meaning from the syntactically analyzed utterance. As with vision however, the process is complicated by ambiguity at each level. It is not possible to accomplish any of these tasks on the basis of local information.

The actual input might be represented as in Figure 4.2. In the ideal world one would segment this stream of information into words by looking for places where there is silence, and assuming that these represented pauses between words. One might then analyze the input between two successive silences in order to try to find the individual sounds which make up the word. So, for example, if we found a "k" sound, as in "kite," followed by an "a" sound, as in "apple," followed by a "t" sound, then we would be reasonably disposed to believe that we had heard the word "cat."

While this is the basic idea, the reality is not so simple. Just consider the problem of figuring out where the words are. To see that this can be difficult,

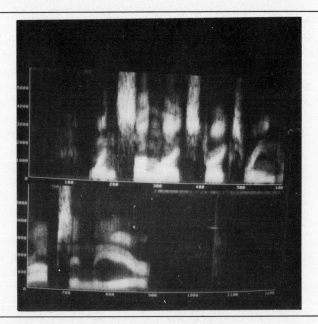

Figure 4.2 Frequency vs. time plot for a sentence

consider the story of a young woman who visited New York for the first time. Later she asked a relative what a "nominal egg" was. In response to the puzzled look on the relative's face, she said that everything in New York cost "a nominal egg." The phrase, of course, was "an arm and a leg." In the transition between what the speaker intended to say and what she heard a number of word boundaries were lost, and the boundaries that remained did not correspond to any of the original words. The point is that the pauses in speech have only occasional relations to word boundaries.

At the next level, the syntax of a language helps us decide how the words are being combined to make up larger meanings. This is what we meant when we spoke of "functional structure" in Chapter 1. So, when we consider the meaning of a sentence like "The dealer sold the merchant a dog," it is important that we keep clear about what is being sold to whom.

Here too ambiguity is a problem. Some common examples are:

I saw the Golden Gate bridge flying into San Francisco.
(Is the bridge flying?)

I ate dinner with a friend.
I ate dinner with a fork.

Can companies litter the environment
(Is this a statement or a question?)

Finally, assuming we have overcome the problems at the previous levels, we must create an internal representation, and then, and most mysterious of all, somehow "use" the information in an appropriate way. This is the level of semantics and pragmatics. Here too ambiguity is rampant. One problem at this level is to determine the referents of pronouns. Normally this is easy. About 90% of the time a pronoun in English refers to the last-mentioned object of the appropriate type (masculine, feminine, neuter). But the other 10% can be difficult indeed.

Jack went to the store. He found the milk in aisle three.
He paid for it and left.

Here the problem is deciding whether the "it" in the last sentence refers to aisle three, the milk, or even the store. Other cases can be considerably more complex, requiring the reader to have absorbed many pages of information.

As for the "use" of a sentence, it can vary even more widely. A sentence like

There will be a big earthquake in San Francisco next year.

can "mean" anything from "you had better get earthquake insurance for your house" to "I don't want to have the convention held there" or even, "If it doesn't happen, my AI geology program will look rather silly."

In this chapter we will concentrate on the role of syntax and semantics in going from a typed sentence to an internal representation of that sentence. Thus on one hand we will not go into the separate problems of speech comprehension. On the other, we will not look at how language is used. Naturally, divorced from its use, the internal representation is of no interest. However, a discussion of how one might use the knowledge provided by language must wait until later chapters, when we will have more logical machinery at our command. However, assuming that we can agree on an internal representation as a useful and plausible intermediate point between words and actions, it is reasonable to work on the process of translating into the internal representation, and worry about applications later.

To make things more concrete in the course of this chapter we will develop a program to translate English into internal representation. We will not show the actual program because explaining it would take too much time. Rather we will look at the major data structures the program uses; that is, how it represents the meanings of words, the grammar of English, and so forth.

Box 4.1.

The Sad Story of Machine Translation

One possibility that any scientist must take into account is that he or she has made a poor choice of problem. A poor scientific problem is one that cannot be solved with the knowledge and tools available at the time. The ''classic'' example of this is the alchemists' attempts to change lead into gold. A more recent example, and one directly related to the concerns of this chapter, is the attempt to do automatic machine translation in the late 1950s and early 1960s.

Very soon after the invention of the digital computer, it was realized that one might use a computer to automate a two-language dictionary. That is, one would type in a word in one language and get out the translation. Of course, there might be more than one translation. As we have already noted, words tend to be ambiguous, and typically there will not be a word in the target language that shares all of the ambiguity of the word with which you started. However, in such cases one could simply print out all of the possibilities.

Quickly, however, machine translation researchers became more ambitious. On one hand, they realized that it might be possible to analyze the morphology of the words. (See section 4.2.5.3.) By doing this one could save on dictionary space. Furthermore, some researchers hoped that by providing word-for-word translations, one might be able to understand what was going on without recourse to a human translator. However, this latter hope remained unrealized. Instead, researchers started working on phrase-by-phrase, and sentence-by-sentence translations — translations that used rudimentary syntactic rules to analyze the sentences. The earliest work was done in the USSR, followed by work in the United States, where one of the first experiments was a machine translation project at Georgetown University. In 1954, using a dictionary of 250 words, and six syntactic rules, a program developed there translated some sentences from Russian. Here are some of the translations.

> The quality of crude oil is determined by calorie content.
> The quality of saltpeter is determined by chemical methods.
> TNT is produced from coal.
> They obtain dynamite from nitroglycerine.

This experiment was perceived as demonstrating that machine translation was feasible, and within a few years money started flowing into projects that were aimed at this goal. Projects at Harvard, M.I.T., the University of Pennsylvania, and other places soon started up. The goal of these projects was to produce usable translations, typically from Russian, possibly with *post-editing* (a process in which a person who knows only English would tidy things up). By 1966, the United States government had spent about $20 million on machine translation and closely related topics, but long before this, people were having doubts about the work. These doubts were well placed, since now, nearly twenty years later, we still are a long way from automatic translation. Furthermore, we recognize obstacles on many fronts, from syntax (there is still no program that can handle all, or nearly all, of English syntax), to referent determination (which can come into play in translation), to word sense disambiguation. However, in the early 1960s it was the word-sense disambiguation problem which seemed the most critical. To see why, consider the following fragment of a machine-produced translation of an article in Russian about space biology. This was done about 1966. In places where the machine could not decide on the appropriate word or phrase, all possibilities are given, separated by slashes.

> Biological experiments, conducted on various/different cosmic aircraft, astrophysical researches of the cosmic space and flights of Soviet and American astronauts with the sufficient/rather persuasiveness showed/indicated/pointed, that momentary/transitory/short orbital flights of lower/below than radiation belts/regions/flanges of earth/land/soil in the absence of the raised/increased/heightened sun/sunny/solar activity with respect to radiation are/appear/arrive report safe/not-dangerous/secure.
> (As reprinted in [Pierce66].)

Perhaps the most influential critic of this work was a linguist, Bar-Hillel, who in 1964 published a critique that pointed out that there was no way to do word sense disambiguation without a deep understanding of what a sentence meant.

This was the beginning of the end for the work on machine translation. The end of the end came with the publication of a report, requested by the National Science Foundation, on how machine translation work was going. The *Pierce Report* [Pierce66] came out in 1966, and said what we would now consider obvious. There was no way that the work on machine translation could be justified in terms of practical output. The translations they were producing were very hard to read, with concomitant increases in reading time, and decreases in comprehension. Furthermore, even post-editing did not bring the machine versions up to the levels of human translators (and when post-editing was added in, the machine versions were just as expensive as the human variety).

It is sobering to consider the difference in quality between the experimental translations done in 1956, and the "real" ones done nearly ten years later. The experimental versions are much clearer. The reason, of course, is the very limited domain, vocabulary, and syntax used in the experiment. That simple ideas do not necessarily scale up to real-world problems is a lesson we in Artificial Intelligence have been taught many times. The trick is to remember the lesson each time before investing too heavily in a particular bag of ideas.

4.2 Expressing the Rules of Syntax

4.2.1 Why We Need Rules of Syntax

In vision, the most natural way to get information into the computer is to use a TV camera or similar device; the process starts with raw light intensities. For language, however, there is a simpler way than using a microphone to capture the raw sounds; we can type in the words at a computer terminal. For this reason, most AI work in language has started from written language, and so shall we.

In Chapter 1, we argued that we needed some form of internal representation to express the knowledge that our programs would use. One of the points we made in passing was that English does not explicitly indicate its functional structure; rather, this structure must be inferred. Much of the knowledge used to make this inference is syntactic in nature — for example, our knowledge of normal word order in a sentence. So, if we reverse the order of "the boy" and "the frog" in "The boy ate the frog." we get a very different meaning. That is, we use word order to indicate the eater and the eaten.

But word order is not sufficient to make such distinctions. The words "boy" "frog" and "eat" occur in a different order in each of the following sentences, yet the underlying relations between these words stay the same.

The boy ate the frog.
The frog was eaten by the boy.
The frog which the boy ate died.
The boy whom the frog was eaten by died.

The second of these examples is referred to in English grammar as a *passive* sentence. Passive sentences are marked by the object of the sentence appearing in the normal spot for the subject. The main verb is preceded by a form of the verb "to be" (in this case, the past tense form "was") and the verb itself, "eaten," is in a special form, called the *past participle*. The knowledge used here is knowledge of syntax, and thus such examples suggest that in a program that translates from English to internal representation, a good first thing to do would be to syntactically analyze (or *parse*) the sentence.

While this is exactly what we will be doing, this is not a completely uncontroversial approach. Everyone agrees that some syntactic knowledge is needed, but many would argue that this information should be integrated with knowledge of a semantic nature. Otherwise, they argue, how could it be that people (and one day, perhaps, our programs) understand ungrammatical sentences? Those that favor a separate syntactic phase have counterarguments, and we will return to this issue later in this chapter. But for the moment, whatever the merits of the two positions, it is simply easier to explain things if we separate out syntax so that we can look at the components of language one at a time. That is what we will do.

Thus to parse a sentence in, say, English, we need to know the rules of syntax for the language. Then we need some way to apply the rules to actually do the parsing — the *parser*. The distinction between the rules and the ability to apply them is referred to as that between *competence* (the abstract rules expressing our knowledge of language) and *performance* (how we actually use these rules to do something). While it could be that there is no neat separation between the two, the fact that children are capable of learning a wide variety of languages has led people to assume that we have some sort of built-in language capability (the parser) and all we need learn are the particular rules for our own language. Once again, it is easiest to explain things if we make this assumption, so we will first concentrate on the rules of grammar, and only later ask how a parser could use them to build up structure from input.

Rules of syntax, then, specify the legal syntactic structures for a sentence. (Naturally, if a sentence does not have a legal syntactic structure, then it is ungrammatical, so the rules of grammar also distinguish the grammatical from the ungrammatical). Thus syntax is bounded at one end by the single word, and at the other by the sentence.

4.2.2 Diagraming Sentences

The study of English syntax presupposes some knowledge of the structure of English. Most of us get this through diagraming sentences, one of those funny things teachers have us do in grammar school. It is not clear that this ever helped us with our English, the purported reason for such exercises, but it will help us in AI. Such diagrams, at least the version your authors learned as children, looked like this:

Jack |ate |a frog

Here the long vertical line separates the *grammatical subject* ''Jack'' from the *grammatical predicate* ''ate a frog.'' The short vertical line divides the predicate into two parts, the verb ''ate'' and the *direct object* ''a frog.''

Another way of indicating the same information is in a tree structure, as in Figure 4.3, which expresses the same information, and uses the same terminology, but indicates the internal organization of the sentence by the tree structure, rather than by vertical lines. This notation is widely used in both linguistics and AI. A variant, using slightly different names, is shown in Figure 4.4. Terms like "subject" and "predicate" refer to the role the words play in the sentence. In Figure 4.4 we have used terms like np (which stands for *noun phrase*) and vp (for *verb phrase*). These terms indicate not the role in the sentence (note that both the subject and the direct object are noun phrases) but rather the structure of the items themselves. For example, noun phrases are built around *nouns* (like "Jack" or "frog"). If we wanted to be more precise, we would note that the noun phrase "a frog" was built out of a *determiner*, "a" and a noun, "frog." Other common determiners are "the," "some," and "every." (These syntactic categories for words are called *parts of speech*.) We might also note that the noun phrase "Jack" consisted only of a special kind of noun called a

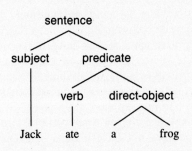

Figure 4.3 Tree notation for a diagrammed sentence

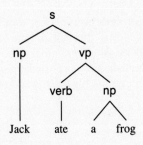

Figure 4.4 Tree notation using syntactic categories

proper noun, which is the name of a person, place, or thing. We can put this information in the tree, too, giving us Figure 4.5. We will call such structures *parse trees* or *phrase markers*. (The latter term comes from the fact that they serve to mark or delimit the phrases of the sentence.)

4.2.3 Why Do We Care about Sentence Structure?

Most, but not all, AI researchers in this area believe that phrase markers are an important intermediate structure between the sentence and the internal representation. So far our only justification for them was the comment that we all learned about this sort of thing in school. Do phrase markers really matter? They do, and this can be shown in many ways. At an immediately intuitive level, these diagrams say formally things English speakers know intuitively, such as the fact that the determiner "a" in the example above relates more to "frog," the word after it, than to "ate," the word before it.

If we want a more formal demonstration, suppose we wanted to write a program that generated English sentences in appropriate circumstances, and suppose one sentence we wanted to generate was:

Is Jack going to the store?

There are many issues to consider, but look just at the first two words. Most English sentences start out with a noun phrase, but here we start out with the verb "is." Of course, we know from our knowledge of English that this is no fluke. This sentence is called a *yes-no question* because we expect either a yes or no as an answer. (Questions like "Who went to the store?" are called *wh-questions*.) Yes-no questions in English typically start with a verb, and in particular the verb must be an *auxiliary verb* — that is, a verb that is secondary to the

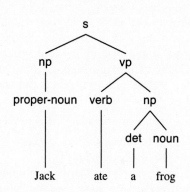

Figure 4.5 A parse tree

main verb in the sentence (in the case above "going"). We might wonder about the rule governing the structure of such sentences. One guess might be

A yes-no question is just like a normal statement, except
the first auxiliary verb of the sentence appears at the front.

Note that while such a rule would require knowing the parts of speech of every word, it would not require knowing the internal structure of the sentence. We could imagine a routine that generated yes-no questions from statements by scanning from the front until it hit an auxiliary verb, and then putting the verb at the front.

However, such a rule will not work. Consider the sentence

The boy who was sleeping was wakened.

If we apply the rule as just stated we would get

* Was the boy who sleeping was wakened?

instead of the correct

Was the boy who was sleeping wakened?

The asterisk on the incorrect sentence is a common notation to indicate that the sentence is considered ungrammatical by native speakers. Of course, if we accept the idea that sentences do have an internal structure, then the failure of the rule above is no longer puzzling. We intuitively recognize that there is a *subordinate clause* in this sentence, namely "who was sleeping." Once we admit to this bit of internal structure, we can then reformulate our rule to say that the auxiliary that is moved is the first one of the main sentence. That is, our sentence would have a structure as shown in Figure 4.6. The first auxiliary of the topmost **s** node, namely, "was," is the one that gets moved, giving

Was the boy who was sleeping wakened?

You might pay some attention to the fact that we have used an **s** node to represent the phrase "who was sleeping." Previously we used **s** nodes only to indicate complete sentences, but there is a great similarity between complete sentences and subordinate clauses. For example, a complete sentence can take a *prepositional phrase* (**pp**) at the end of it, as diagrammed in Figure 4.7. A prepositional phrase consists of a *preposition*, or **prep** (in this case "on") followed by a noun phrase. But subordinate clauses can take prepositional phrases as well:

The boy who was sleeping on the table was wakened.

Typically the main sentence is referred to as a *major sentential clause* while a subordinate clause is a *minor sentential clause*.

There are, of course, some differences between major and minor **s**'s. The most obvious is that only major **s**'s have a period (or other final punctuation) after them. Thus we will often distinguish between an **s-maj** and an **s**. An **s-maj** consists of an **s** followed by a **final-punc**.

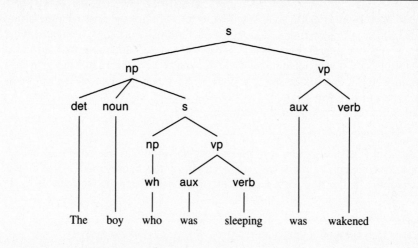

Figure 4.6 Parse tree for multi-clause sentence

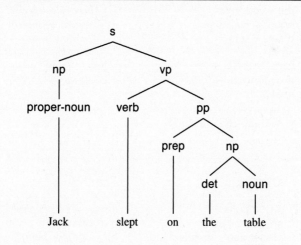

Figure 4.7 Prepositional phrases in clauses

4.2.4 Context-Free Grammars

So far our method of specifying the structure of a sentence has been intuitive. A standard way to formalize our knowledge of the structure of a language is to provide a series of *rewrite rules* (also known as a *grammar*) that will generate the sentences of the language. Probably the best known of such systems are the *context-free grammars*. A simple context-free grammar for a very small fragment of English might look like Figure 4.8. We always start with the s-maj node, which is a nonterminal node (or a nonterminal constituent) A *nonterminal node* is one that appears only in the interior of our tree structures, and not in the final sentence. Each nonterminal node is replaced by the right-hand side of a rule in which it appears on the left, until we have only *terminal nodes* (or *terminal constituents*) which are the nodes that appear in the final sentence. An example of the derivation of the sentence

>   Bill loves the frog.

is given in Figure 4.9. The result here does not show the tree structure, but we could have that too simply by keeping track of the intermediate stages of the derivation. In the tree form each nonterminal constituent is attached to lower

---

s-maj → s final-punc	; *Jack ate the candy |.*
s → np vp	; *Jack |ate the candy*
vp → verb np	; *ate |the candy*
np → det noun	; *the |candy*
np → proper-noun	; *Jack*
det → the	; *These rules specify*
noun → boy	; *the parts of speech*
noun → frog	; *of various words.*
verb → ate	; *For example, "ate*
verb → loves	; *and "loves" are*
proper-noun → Bill	; *both verbs.*
final-punc → .	

Figure 4.8 A context-free grammar

Sentence	Rule used
s-maj	
s final-punc	s-maj → s final-punc
np vp final-punc	s → np vp
proper-noun vp final-punc	np → proper-noun
proper-noun v np final-punc	vp → v np
Bill v np final-punc	proper-noun → Bill
Bill loves np final-punc	v → loves
Bill loves det noun final-punc	np → det noun
Bill loves the noun final-punc	det → the
Bill loves the frog final-punc	noun → frog
Bill loves the frog.	final-punc → .

Figure 4.9 A context-free derivation

constituents via lines and this indicates how it was broken down. So, the derivation in Figure 4.9 could be summarized in Figure 4.10. For example, we can see that the last np was broken down into a det and a noun.

Such grammars are called context-free because the rules state how to replace a nonterminal without any reference to the context in which the nonterminal finds itself.

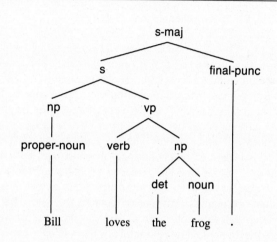

Figure 4.10 The result of a context-free derivation

Box 4.2

Context-Free Languages

Those readers who have taken a course in the theory of computation will have been introduced to context-free languages as one way of characterizing the complexity of certain tasks. If you have taken a course in compiler construction, then you may well have seen context-free languages used to parse programming languages. The question of how to parse context-free languages efficiently is standard fare in algorithm courses. Context-free languages, and the parsing thereof, are topics that run throughout computer science.

A context-free language is one which has a context-free grammar that will produce all of the strings of that language, and no string that is not in the language. In theory of computation courses these "languages" are not necessarily the variety we normally think of, but rather arbitrary strings. For example, consider the language that consists of a string of "a"s followed by a string of "b"s, where the two strings are of equal length. So, ''aabb'', and ''aaaaabbbbb'' are strings in the language, but ''aabbb'' ''ba'' and ''abc'' are not. This is a context-free language because the following context-free grammar characterizes it.

S → aSb
S → ab

This language is normally referred to as $a^n b^n$. The language $a^n b^n c^n$ on the other hand is not context free. There are techniques for proving this, but we will not go into them here.

A natural question to ask is if English or other natural languages are context-free. This question presupposes that we have a firm idea of what strings are (and are not) English, and that such decisions are independent of the surrounding sentences (or situation). It is not obvious that these presuppositions are true. For example, without any context, a sentence like ''Mary thinks vanilla.'' seems very strange, and probably ungrammatical. As such it would be judged not part of English. However, coming after a question like, ''Does anyone know what flavor ice cream Joe wants?'' this statement seems not only grammatical, but commonplace.

Ignoring issues like that, there is probably agreement that English is a context-free language in the sense described above. However, one can place a more stringent constraint on context-freeness. Rather than considering a language as a collection of strings, one could consider a language to be a collection of phrase-structure trees. Each phrase structure would specify not only the string, but also the grouping of the constituents. One can then distinguish between ''weakly'' and ''strongly'' context-free language. A language is weakly context-free if there is a context-free grammar that produces the right strings. It is strongly context-free if there is also a context-free grammar that captures exactly the same groupings. So, the context-free grammar given earlier produces trees of the sort shown in Figure 4.11. These trees imply pairings between as and bs

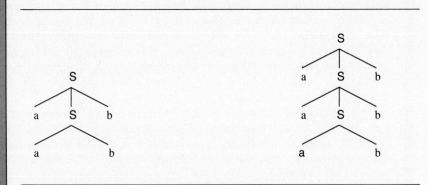

Figure 4.11 Tree structures produced by context-free grammar

which are indicated by the trees shown in Figure 4.12. But suppose we wanted pairings which were more like those of Figure 4.13. It turns out that there is no context-free language that will produce such pairings.

There is currently debate about whether various languages are strongly context free. For example, a sentence like "Jake, Norm, and Van like apples, oranges, and pears, respectively." seems to require pairings like the second ones just mentioned. On the other hand, after a few "respectively" pairs, people have a hard time too.

4.2.5 Dictionaries and Features

4.2.5.1 Subject-verb Agreement.   In many cases it is difficult to express a rule of grammar with context-free rules. Suppose we want to worry about *number agreement* between noun and verb. That is, in English we may say

The boys are hungry.

but not

* The boys is hungry.

This is ungrammatical because "is" is a third-person singular form of the verb "to be" while "the boys" is a third-person plural noun phrase. The possible number types in English are shown in Figure 4.14.

Figure 4.12 Pairings implied by context-free parse trees

Figure 4.13 Pairings unattainable by a context-free grammar

	Singular		Plural	
	Abbrev.	Example	Abbrev.	Example
first person	1s	I am hungry.	1p	We are hungry.
second person	2s	You are hungry.	2p	You are hungry.
third person	3s	He is hungry.	3p	They are hungry.

Figure 4.14 Person and number features in English

It is, of course, true that people can understand sentences in which agreement is not present, as in "The boys is sleeping." But to reject the rule on this account would be unwise. First, we do at least *notice* that the sentence is ungrammatical, and second, some sentences can only be completely understood with the constraints given by such a rule. Consider:

The fish is hungry.
The fish are hungry.

It is only by enforcing number agreement that we know if we have one fish or more than one.

We will call things like "first person singular" (or 1s) *syntactic features*. Such features are divided up into different *feature dimensions*. In the case at hand, the dimension is syntactic number, or simply *number*, and the possible values along this dimension are 1s, 2s, 3s, 1p, 2p, and 3p. Another dimension of feature which we will eventually need is sentence mood, which has the possible values question, statement, and command.

Now, to return to our rule of subject-verb agreement, incorporating it into a context-free grammar tends to be inconvenient. The only way to do it is to have two rules for expanding s nodes:

s → np-singular vp-singular
s → np-plural vp-plural

We would then have to have two sets of rules for noun phrases, one which would expand the np-singular node, and one for the np-plural node. Having to virtually double the size of our grammar hardly seems very convenient.

However, if we allow our rules to explicitly manipulate features we can then state our rule of subject-verb agreement, at least informally, as follows:

The subject np and the main verb must have
the same feature value along the number dimension.

We will state this rule more formally in section 4.2.6.

4.2.5.2 Features. In Figure 4.15 we have indicated the feature dimensions we will need for the grammar we develop in this chapter. As we mentioned

	Dimension	Default values	Other values	
(def-feature	n-number	(3s)	1s 2s 1p 2p 3p)	
(def-feature	v-number	(1s 2s 1p 2p 3p)	3s)	
(def-feature	tense	(tenseless present)	past progressive pastp)	*; Tenseless =* *; infinitive form.* *; Progressive* *; = "ing form."* *; Pastp =* *; past participle* *; = "en form."*
(def-feature	mood	(statement)	question command)	*; "Mood" indi-* *; cates type* *; of sentence.*
(def-feature	dative	(no)	yes)	*; Few verbs* *; allow dative* *; movement. (See* *; section 4.3.4.)*

Figure 4.15 Features and feature indicators for our parser

earlier, we develop a parser in the course of this chapter and we frequently will show the data structures it needs. Figure 4.15 is the first example of this. It uses a Lisp function **def-feature**, the exact workings of which are unimportant to us. All we need know is that it defines the features and dimensions which the parser can use. We have included only enough dimensions and features for the grammar we will be developing later. A more complete grammar would need many more. You should note that in Figure 4.15 we have also indicated *default values*, so that if no value for a feature is indicated, the default can be assumed.

Along a particular dimension, any individual word or phrase may have at most one value. That is, a particular occurrence of a noun is either singular or plural, but not both. However, as we have already seen, some nouns, like "fish" may be either, and while any particular instance will be one or the other, initially we may not be able to tell which. In these cases we will allow a feature dimension to have more than one value, but we understand this as implying an *exclusive or* (either one, or the other, but not both).

4.2.5.3 Morphology. Next we need a way for our parser to tell which words take which features. This is the role of a dictionary. The dictionary will specify for each word of English its part of speech, any nondefault values for its features, and presumably something about its meaning, although this will have to wait until later in this chapter. However, in English, as in all other languages, individual words often can be given different prefixes and suffixes. So, for example, the verb "love" can appear in various guises, such as "loves," "loved," "loving," "unloving," etc. Both the spelling and our intuition tell us that there is one basic (or *root*) form, "love," and various derived forms. It would be wasteful if our dictionary had to include all of these. The solution, of course, is to have our parser use explicit knowledge of the structure of words (their *morphology*) and have it figure out when a word is simply a variant of one that is already in the dictionary. So we would want "boys" to be recognized as a plural variant of "boy." Some common patterns are exemplified in Figure 4.16. Of course, we must be careful in generalizing these patterns, or we could get errors like these:

kiss → kis + (number = 3p)
definition → definitio + (tense = pastp)

To some degree, such mistakes can be prevented by installing more stringent checks on which endings are allowed in which circumstances. For example, a singular noun ending in "s" will never form its plural by adding "s," but rather by adding "es." It also helps to first ensure that a word is not already in the dictionary before attempting to remove "endings," and that the end product, after the parser has removed all of the supposed endings, is itself in the dictionary.

If we assume that we have such a procedure, then our dictionary can be reasonably compact, because the morphology unit will take care of the standard examples. Furthermore, having default values for features will mean that for the root words, like singular nouns, the dictionary need not even indicate that the word is singular, since this is the default case. A few sample dictionary entries are shown in Figure 4.17. As with our earlier illustration of features, we use a special-purpose Lisp function to make this information available to a parsing program; the name of the function is just dictionary. A dictionary entry has one of two forms

(*word part-of-speech -feature-assignments-*)
(*word root-form part-of-speech -feature-assignments-*)

---

boys	→	boy	+ (n-number = 3p)
dishes	→	dish	+ (n-number = 3p)
playing	→	play	+ (tense = progressive)
			+ (v-number = 1s 2s 3s 1p 2p 3p)
taken	→	take	+ (tense = pastp)
			+ (v-number = 1s 2s 3s 1p 2p 3p)
loves	→	love	+ (tense = present) + (v-number = 3s)
played	→	play	+ (tense = past)
			+ (v-number = 1s 2s 3s 1p 2p 3p)

Figure 4.16 Morphological analyses of typical words

```
(dictionary (a det)
            (be auxverb (tense = tenseless))
            (is be auxverb (tense = present)
                        (v-number = 3s))
            (block noun)
            (block verb)
            (can modal
                (v-number = 1s 2s 3s 1p 2p 3p))
            (can noun)
            (do modal)
            (did do modal (tense = past)
                    (v-number = 1s 2s 3s 1p 2p 3p))
            (fish noun
                (n-number = 3s 3p))
            (frog noun)
            (jack proper-noun)
            (move verb)
            (story noun)
            (stories story noun (n-number = 3p))
            (tell verb (dative = yes))
            (told tell verb
                (tense = past)
                (v-number = 1s 2s 3s 1p 2p 3p))
            (will modal (tense = future)
                (v-number = 1s 2s 3s 1p 2p 3p))
```

Figure 4.17 Sample dictionary entries

Box 4.3

Atoms in Lisp

Those doing Exercise 4.3 will need to know a bit more about how Lisp handles atoms. In particular, since the morphology of the word depends on getting the spelling of the word, it will be necessary to break an atom up into its individual letters. This can be done with the Lisp function **explode**, which takes an atom, and returns a list of its letters.

(explode *atom***)**

Letters are represented as one-character atoms. For example:

```
-> (explode 'boys)
(b o y s)
-> (explode 'some%rndm*1stuf3f)
(s o m e % r n d m * 1 s t u f 3 f)
```

(In many modern Lisps, characters are a separate data type. Many Lisps allow **explode** to take things other than atoms, e.g., lists, and will do something reasonable with them, like spelling out the spaces and parentheses. We will assume a simple, traditional dialect like Franz Lisp.)

Next, suppose you have taken the atom "boys," exploded it, and then want to ask the dictionary if it knows about "boy," that is, "boys" without the final "s." This can be done with the Lisp function **implode**.

(**implode** *list-of-letters*)

```
-> (implode '(b o y))
boy
```

Another Lisp feature is the ability to create new atoms. A function for doing this in Lisp is **newsym**, which produces a new atom modeled on the one it was given, but with a number appended to the end.

(**newsym** *atom*)

```
-> (newsym 'foo)     ; Ask newsym to produce an atom based upon
foo1                 ; "foo." We get back the atom foo1.
-> (newsym 'foo)     ; If we repeat the request we get back a new
foo2                 ; atom, differing in the final number.
-> (newsym 'bar)     ; For each atom the numbers start at 1.
bar1
```

Note however that not all Lisps have **newsym**. If your Lisp doesn't, it will certainly have the function **gensym**. In some cases this will operate just as we described **newsym**. However, you should check your manual to make sure that **gensym** puts the new symbol on the oblist (see the discussion in Box 2.3, "Atoms and Hashing.")

4.2.6 Transformational Grammar (Optional)

4.2.6.1 Subject-Verb Agreement as a Transformational Rule. We introduced the topic of subject-verb agreement in English because it was a good way to lead into a discussion of features. However, subject-verb agreement is also a standard test case for rule formalisms for English. Indeed, in our discussion we established that context-free rules were not, at least in their present form, convenient for the representation of subject-verb agreement. We then presented an informal rule, which simply said that the number feature of subject and verb had to be the same. We will now introduce a rule formalism in which we can express this rule. This new kind of rule is called a *transformational rule*, and the study of grammar based upon such rules is called *transformational grammar*.

However, we should note that there is no agreement among linguists as to the best way to represent the rules of grammar. Indeed, there is currently a resurgence of interest in context-free grammars for describing natural languages. (They have always been useful for computer languages.) These ideas are still quite controversial, and the techniques used to overcome the kind of objection we made earlier tend to be complicated. Instead, we will adopt the more traditional way of expressing facts like number agreement, which uses context-sensitive rules. In particular, we will retain our original rule:

s → np vp

but now we will add a transformational rule, which looks quite different. See Figure 4.18. Here **number** is a variable ranging over the possible number indicators shown previously. The rule specifies that the **verb** should be replaced by a **verb** which has a feature on it that gives it the same number as the subject of the sentence.

Generally speaking, we will allow transformational rules to do the following:

1. Put features on constituents of the sentence
2. Move constituents
3. Add constituents
4. Delete constituents

Actually, we have already seen another example of a transformational rule. The informal rule we proposed for handling the placement of auxiliaries in questions is actually a transformational rule. It accounts for the phenomena by assuming that there is one version of the sentence (where the auxiliary comes just before the verb), which is transformed into the other version. This rule is often called *aux-inversion*.

Like our context-free rules, transformational grammar specifies the legal sentences of a language by giving rules that generate them. Indeed,

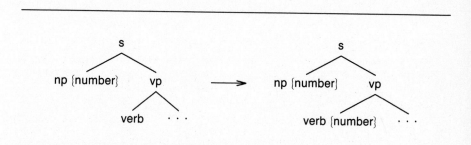

Figure 4.18 A transformational rule

transformational grammar in its most common form starts out with context-free rules to build up the basics of the sentence, but then modifies the basic sentences with the transformational rules, such as the one above for subject-verb agreement. A basic sentence (complete with tree structure) built by the context-free rules is called a *deep structure*. When we have applied the transformational rules to a deep structure, we end up with a legal English sentence (again with tree structure), called the *surface structure*. See Figure 4.19.

4.2.6.2 Reflexivization. Another instance where a transformational rule is useful is illustrated by the following paradigm:

*I washed me	I washed myself
I washed you	*I washed yourself
I washed him	*I washed himself
You washed me	*You washed myself
*You washed you	You washed yourself
You washed him	*You washed himself

Pronouns such as "myself" or "yourself" are called *reflexive pronouns*. It is easy to see that we have a complementary distribution here, which suggests that we could formulate a rule that transforms one form into the other. Somewhat arbitrarily taking the left-hand side sentences as more basic (we could justify it, but we won't), we can formulate a transformational rule that takes the left-hand sentences and makes the direct object into a reflexive when it and the subject are (roughly) the same pronoun. This rule is called *reflexivization*. A first crack at this rule is shown in Figure 4.20, where np1 and np2, are both pronouns of the same person (e.g., both first person pronouns).

However, this rule is not quite correct, as seen when we expand the paradigm above to the third person singular case.

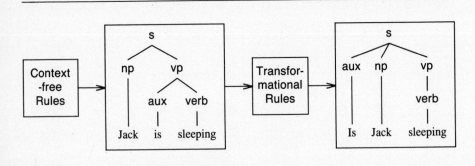

Figure 4.19 Transformational grammar

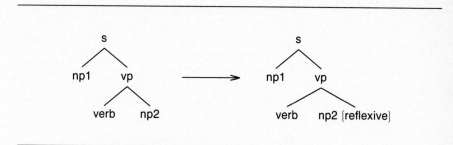

Figure 4.20 Reflexivation rule (version 1)

Jack washed me.   *Jack washed myself.
Jack washed you.   *Jack washed yourself.
Jack washed him.   Jack washed himself.

First, there is no need for both np's to be pronouns. Secondly, for the final case, both "Jack washed him." and "Jack washed himself." are correct. However, they do not have the same meaning. In "Jack washed him." we understand the "Jack" and the "him" as referring to different people, something not true when we use a reflexive pronoun. This suggests a modification of our rule so that it only makes the transformation when the subject and object refer to the same individual. The modified version is shown in Figure 4.21. The use of i in np_i indicates that the two noun phrases refer to the same individual. Note that this rule would also account for our understanding "Jack hit him" as having Jack hitting someone else.

4.2.6.3 Imperatives.
Another case where we could use a transformational rule is *imperative sentences* in English, as in:

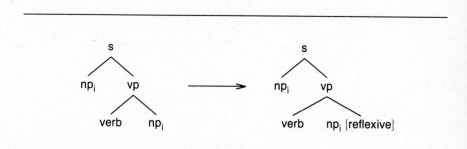

Figure 4.21 Reflexivation rule (corrected)

Buy a loaf of bread!

Imperatives differ from most other English sentences in that they do not have an explicit subject. We might try to account for this by assuming that we have a special context-free rule for imperative sentences, in which the **s** node only gets expanded to a verb phrase — no initial noun phrase. An alternative, however, would be to use the regular context-free rule, and assume that the subject is deleted by a transformational rule when the sentence is imperative. Figure 4.22 shows a rule that will perform this deletion. Some support for assuming the existence of such a rule comes from sentences like:

Wash me!   *Wash myself!
*Wash you!   Wash yourself!
Wash him!   *Wash himself!

This looks just like our earlier examples, for which we proposed a rule that says if subject and object refer to the same thing, then the object should be replaced by a reflexive pronoun. The trouble here is that, at least in the surface structure, there is no subject. However, if we were to assume that in the deep structure there is a subject, and furthermore that the subject is "you," then the examples above would fall out from the normal rule for handling reflexive pronouns. For this reason the imperative rule is often called *you-deletion*. We will make the "you" explicit in later versions of the rule.

4.2.6.4 Passive and Cases.   Yet another example of a transformational rule is the passive construction. Here we want to capture the relation between the two sentences:

Jack hit Bill.
Bill was hit by Jack.

Figure 4.23 shows a rule that transforms actives into passives. It is interesting to note how the passive construction interacts with pronouns. So, for example, contrast the following two sentences.

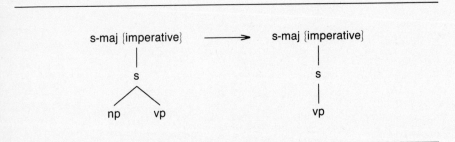

Figure 4.22 The rule of you-deletion (version 1)

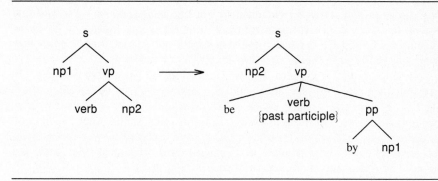

Figure 4.23 The passive transformation

> He hit Bill.
> Bill was hit by him.

We had to change the "he" of the first sentence to "him" in the second. However, this is not directly the effect of passive, since we always use "him" rather than "he" when we have the pronoun in anything other than the subject position. For example:

> He loves Jane.
> Jane loves him.

> She loves Bill.
> Bill loves her.

In situations like this where the form of the noun phrase changes depending on the role it plays in the sentence, we say that there are different *cases* in the language. In English, there is very little such variation in noun phrases, but pronouns do vary somewhat, and in particular they distinguish between the subject role, called the *nominative case* and the object role, called the *accusative case*.

4.2.6.5 Deep Structure and Internal Representation. We started this section by claiming that an understanding of the syntactic structure of a natural language would help us to translate it into an internal representation. From looking at the results of the transformations suggested in this section, it should be clear that we have justified this claim, at least in part. While we initially postulated a deep structure for syntactic reasons, it would seem that our deep structure is closer to our idea of what an internal representation should be (as expressed in Chapter 1) than the original English sentences. In our deep structure the understood "you" of imperative sentences is made explicit. We do not have both active and passive sentences to contend with, but only active ones, with the passive versions created by transformations. Initial auxiliaries in yes-no questions are straightened out, and the identity of referents is indicated in order to handle reflexive pronouns. Indeed some researchers in linguistics have suggested that deep structure and internal representation are one and the same. We will not assume this (our deep structures still have English words instead of predicate calculus predicates and constants) but this should not detract from the fact that deep structure is a step in the right direction.

Implicit in this is the idea that transformations do not change meaning. If they did, then the deep structure could not represent *all* of the meaning since some of it would be created by the transformations. This is a controversial assumption, but we will make it since it will drastically simplify our handling of *semantic interpretation* (the process of going from a phrase marker to the internal representation). It will allow us to ignore transformational rules when we consider how semantic interpretation is done.

4.3 Syntactic Parsing

In the last section we concentrated on the problem of describing the structure of English with both context-free and transformational rules. However, the rules we postulated were not directly relevant to the problem of parsing. Rather, they were intended as an abstract characterization of the rules of English. In this section we will try to rectify this situation, and explicitly consider the problems of parsing.

4.3.1 Top-Down and Bottom-Up Parsing

Our problem is, given just the words in a sentence, to find the syntactic tree associated with the sentence. Restricting our attention to context-free grammars for the moment, there are two basic methods — *bottom-up parsing* and *top-down parsing*. We will consider bottom-up parsing first.

The basic idea of bottom-up parsing is simply to use the rules "backwards." We start with our sentence, for example "He ate the frog," and try to match a part of it against the right-hand side of some rule. As we see in Figure 4.24 and Figure 4.25, we can match the "he" against the right-hand side of "pronoun → he." Having done this, we replace the part matched by the left-hand side of the rule, giving us "pronoun ate the frog." In the diagram, we have left the "he" hanging off the pronoun node. By consistently doing this, we generate the complete tree, which is what we really want. However, in doing the matching, we look only at the topmost line. The rest is there just to give us the desired final result.

This looks pretty easy, but our example is deceptive. A problem occurs with any parsing method when a given construct can fit two different rules.

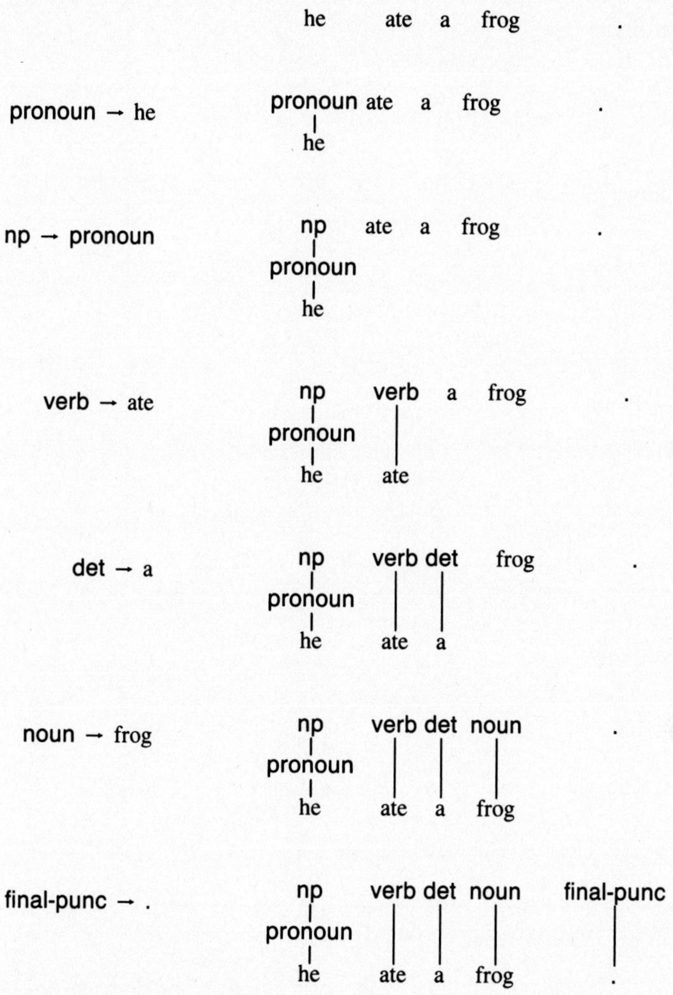
he ate a frog .
pronoun → he
pronoun ate a frog .
he
np → pronoun
np ate a frog .
pronoun
he
verb → ate
np verb a frog .
pronoun
he ate
det → a
np verb det frog .
pronoun
he ate a
noun → frog
np verb det noun .
pronoun
he ate a frog
final-punc → .
np verb det noun final-punc
pronoun
he ate a frog .

Figure 4.24 Bottom-up parsing — part I

Consider the two sentences:

> That can made him sick.
> That can make him sick.

Depending on whether we find "made" or "make" in the sentence above, the noun phrase will be "that can" or simply "that." In the second of these two

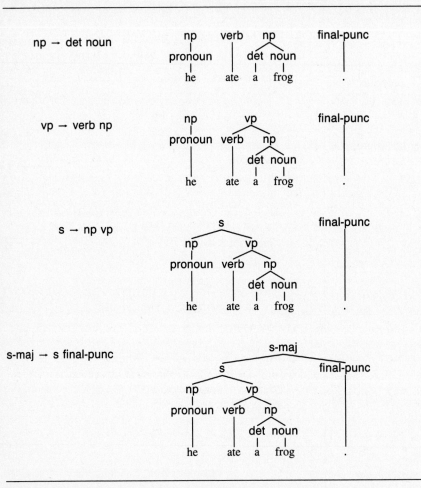

np → det noun

vp → verb np

s → np vp

s-maj → s final-punc

Figure 4.25 Bottom-up parsing — part II

cases, the "can" will be interpreted as part of the verb phrase. (In particular, things like "can" are called *modals*. They are part of the *auxiliary system* in English.) To handle both sentences there must be two rules for both of the first two words:

    det → that
    pronoun → that

    noun → can
    modal → can

At the time when we try to apply these rules, we will not know which to use. Only later will it be possible to weed out incorrect guesses, when they lead to a position in which analysis must halt because no rules apply. For example, if we guess that the "that" is a pronoun and that the "can" is a noun, we will eventually discover that we have made a mistake, because there are no rules that will allow for the sequence **pronoun noun** at this point in the sentence. However, there is no way to tell that this sequence is illegal before analyzing the rest of the sentence; there are grammatical English sentences with pronouns and nouns juxtaposed.

The point here is that in situations in which more than one rule may apply, we have no alternative other than trying them one by one until we find a combination of rules that will assign a structure to the sentence. If we have several different ambiguities (places where more than one rule may apply), and if they are independent of each other, then the number of tracks we will have to follow will grow exponentially with the number of ambiguities. In some cases this can strain our computing resources.

In the situation we just gave, there is no way we could have predicted the correct way to go on the basis of the sentence up to the point where the ambiguity occurred. Sometimes, however, earlier parts of the sentence can predict the structure, as in

He can make you sick.

On the basis of the previous words, namely, "He," we should know that "can" cannot be a noun. Unfortunately, strict bottom-up parsing will not allow us to make use of this information. Again, we will have to start on one trail, and then give it up later.

In cases like this, a second method, called *top-down parsing* works better. Top-down parsing works much as our earlier method of starting with an **s** node and continually replacing it by possible right-hand sides. Again taking the sentence "He ate the frog," we have illustrated the process in Figure 4.26 and Figure 4.27.

Unfortunately, while top-down parsing does better on some sentences, it does worse on others. For example, consider:

Did you hit Bill?

For a bottom-up parser, there should be no trouble recognizing that the "Did" is an auxiliary verb, and hence that this is a yes-no question, since only yes-no questions can start with a tensed auxiliary verb. (A *tensed verb* is one with a tense, such as past or present tense. The opposite is a *tenseless* or *infinitive verb*.) However, a strict top-down parser could not handle things so nicely. It might well start by assuming **s → np vp** and try all possible expansions of the **np** node before it gave up.

4.3.2 Transition Network Parsers

We have seen that neither top-down nor bottom-up parsing is foolproof. However, the tendency has been to prefer top-down parsing as the lesser of two evils. In this section we will look at one version of top-down parsing called a *transition network parser*. While virtually nobody uses transition network

s-maj → s final-punc	We start by looking for an **s**.
s → np vp	In turn we look for an **np** (followed by a verb etc).
np → det noun	So we look for a **det**, but do not find one.
np → pronoun	Find "he", giving us

```
        s
        |
        np
        |
     pronoun
        |
       he
```

s → . . . vp	Having found our **np**, we look for a **vp**
vp → verb np	Now we are looking for a **verb**, get "ate"

Figure 4.26 Top-down parsing of "He ate a frog." - part I

parsing, a modified version of it, called an *augmented transition network parser* or *ATN* is probably the best-known parsing mechanism in AI. The unaugmented version will give us the basic flavor without having to initially introduce the complexities of transformational rules.

4.3.2.1 Transition Nets in Graphical Notation. Note that in the simple-minded top-down parsing method we considered, there will be an inefficiency if we have two rules like these:

A → B C D
A → B C E

If the first one fails, we throw out the results and start on the next rule, in which we duplicate the parsing of B and C. A better method would be to combine the two rules into one, in a manner that shows the parts they have in common:

A → B C {D/E}

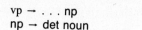 vp → ... np   Now we are looking for an np
np → det noun   So we look for a **det,** and find one

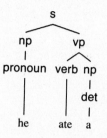

np → ... noun   Now look for a **noun,** and find one
s-maj → ... final-punc   Then look for and find final punctuation.

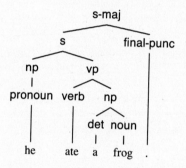

Figure 4.27 Top-down parsing of "He ate a frog." - part II

An alternative notation for this rule is this:

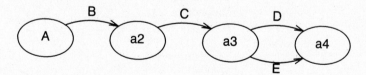

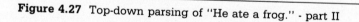

The name of the first node (or *state*) **A** indicates that this is for parsing an **A,** while the arcs indicate the next thing to be found (first a **B,** then a **C,** etc.). These should be thought of as tests. That is, an arc with the label **B** on it says, that the parser may follow this arc if the next thing in the sentence passes the test "Is this a **B?**" If the test comes out true, we will often speak of the test (or arc) *succeeding*; if the test on an arc comes out false, we speak of the test (or arc) *failing*. From the node **a3** the parser can follow either of two different arcs, indicating two alternative rules. A node like **a4** which has no arcs leading

out of it to other nodes is a *done node*. Should the parser reach it, it has succeeded in parsing the constituent named by the first node (in the example above,
an A).

   This notation for grammars is called a *transition network*. Another example of the notation, this time used on our context-free grammar for a fragment
of English, is given in Figure 4.28. In it we have adopted the informal (but
common) convention of labeling a node in a network with the name of the network, followed by a "/," followed by the last constituent parsed. So vp/v is a
node in the vp network which is reached upon finding a v. This is an "informal" convention because nothing requires that we use it. It does, however,
make the status of the nodes clear.

   There are two basic ways in which the tests on the arcs operate. If the
parser is testing for a part of speech, like noun, then the test works by looking
at the input stream, and seeing if the next symbol is indeed a noun. If it is, it

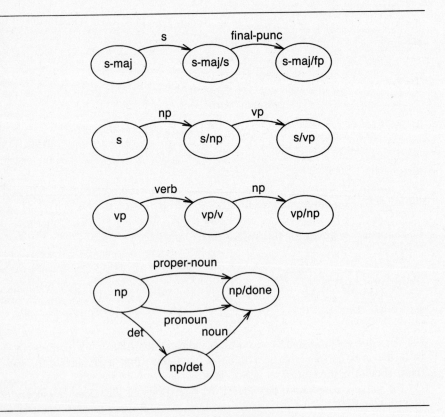

Figure 4.28 Informal transition network grammar

will be removed from the input stream and the test will have succeeded. We will call this a **category** test, and denote it thus:

> (category *terminal-symbol*)

(Henceforth we will refer to the parts of speech as the terminal symbols of the grammar, and the larger units as the nonterminal symbols. Strictly speaking this is not correct, because the words themselves are the terminal symbols, but the distinction is small.) On the other hand, if the parser wants to find a nonterminal, like an **np**, then it can instead go to the network for **np**s, and follow it. If the parser can follow the **np** network to a done node, then it will have found an **np**, so the original test for an **np** succeeds. We will call such a test a **parse** test;

> (parse *nonterminal-symbol*)

Naturally, if the subnetwork, e.g., **np**, cannot reach a done node, the **parse** test fails. In Figure 4.29 we take the context-free grammar shown previously in Figure 4.28, but now substitute the formal tests just discussed.

We will also allow two other kinds of tests. The test **peek** acts just like the test **category**, except that it does not remove the word from the input stream:

> (peek *terminal-symbol*)

The **word** test looks to see if the next word from the input has the root *root*.

> (word *root*)

This differs from **category**, which looks to see if the next word is in a particular category. For example, **(word be)** would succeed if the incoming word were "be" or "is" or "was." Figure 4.30 summarizes the tests that an arc may have in our transition network grammar.

Having more than one arc coming out of a node of a network corresponds to our earlier situation of having several different rules that might apply. Such situations are called *choice points*. Should the parser reach a state in which all of the outgoing arcs fail, it is said to have a *failure*, in which case it probably made an incorrect decision at a previous choice point. In such cases it goes back to a previous choice point (we may also speak of *failing back* to the choice point) and try another path. This is called *backtracking*. In simple transition net parsers, the parser always fails back to the last choice made. In such cases the parser is said to be using *chronological backtracking*, because its decision about where to backtrack to is based upon the time when the decisions occurred, the last decision being the first one to redo. (Later in this chapter we consider alternative strategies. In Chapter 5 we will talk about backtracking from a more general point of view.)

In this way our transition network grammar can, in principle, handle the earlier examples:

> That can make you sick.
> That can made you sick.

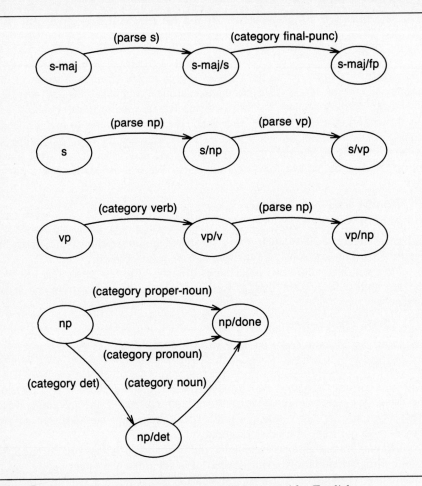

Figure 4.29 A graphical transition network grammar for English

The parser would make a guess about which arcs to take, and would interpret the words "that" and "can" depending on what the particular arc was expecting. If, when it gets to "make" or "made," it finds it cannot go any further, it will then backtrack, and try the alternative arcs, leading to the correct parse.

4.3.2.2 Nongraphical Notations for Transition Networks. While the graphical notation we have been using for representing networks is quite striking for small examples, it tends to get clumsy with large ones. It is also obviously true that we cannot directly give our computer a grammar in this format. For both of these reasons, we will mostly omit the graphical notation in favor of one more like a computer language. We will do this with four new flow-of-control terms: seq (for "sequence"), either, optional, and optional*. Figure 4.31 illustrates the correspondences between these terms and the graphical notation. In it we

Test	Succeed condition	Success side effects
(category *terminal-symbol*)	Next word of input is a *terminal-symbol*	Removes next word from input
(parse *nonterminal-symbol*)	The network named *nonterminal-symbol* finishes	None
(peek *terminal-symbol*)	Next word of input is a *terminal-symbol*	None
(word *root*)	Next word of input has the root *root*	Removes next word from input

Figure 4.30 Tests on arcs in a transition network grammar

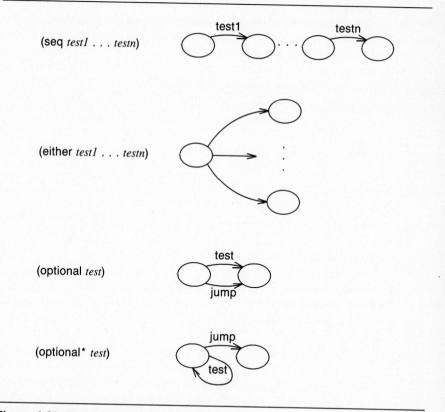

Figure 4.31 Flow-of-control terms for ATNs

have used the notion of a "jump," which allows one to go from one state to another without a test. Note that we have used this only to help establish the relations between **optional** and **optional*** and the graphical notation. In our nongraphical notation we will have no **jump** "test," because we can use the optional commands instead.

The connective **seq** is used to represent a sequence of nodes, each of which has only one test. For example:

(seq (parse np) (parse vp))

The connective **either** is used when we have several tests coming out of the same node. For example, part of our **np** network will now look as follows:

```
(either (category proper-noun)          ; np → proper-noun
        (category pronoun)              ; np → pronoun
        (seq (category det)             ; np → det . . .
             (category noun)))          ; np → . . . noun
```

As this example shows, we can nest control terms (here **either** and **seq**) within one another. This is allowed to any level.

The **optional** test is used for something that may or may not be there. If it may occur more than once, we use **optional***. (Asterisks are commonly used to indicate "zero or more times.") So, if we wanted to allow our noun phrases to have any number of adjectives (as in "The big upright orange banana") followed by any number of prepositional phrases (as in "The banana with a black spot on the table") we could replace our **np** net with this:

```
(either (category proper-noun)          ; np → proper-noun
        (category pronoun)              ; np → pronoun
        (seq (category det)             ; np → det . . .
             (optional* (category adj)) ; np → . . . (adj)*
             (category noun)            ; np → . . . noun
             (optional* (parse pp))))   ; np → . . . (pp)*
```

This would correspond to the network shown in Figure 4.32.

To give networks names (e.g., the **np** network) we use the Lisp function **def-net**.

(def-net *net-name network*)

```
(def-net s (seq (parse np)              ; s → np . . .
                (parse vp)))            ; s → . . . vp
```

4.3.2.3 Remembering the Past in Transition Networks. As our transition network parser is currently set up, it is not possible to get as output the parse tree for the sentence because the parser has no memory of what it has done. It does not need such a memory, because the rules it is designed to handle are context-free rules. Nevertheless, it would be nice to see the tree, and later on, when we start adding semantic routines to our network, these routines will have to examine this tree. So we will add the capability to remember what has happened in the parser. This capacity will also be needed when we generalize to an *augmented* transition network parser.

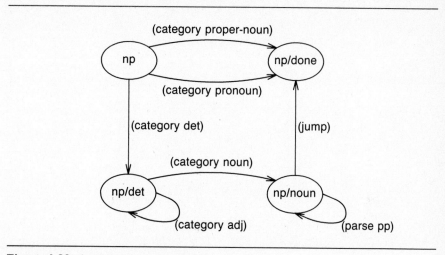

Figure 4.32 A noun phrase network

First, we will have our parser build a parse tree as it proceeds. This involves starting an empty tree at the beginning of the sentence, and adding to it as we go along. With this in mind, we redefine **parse**, **category**, and **word** so that they automatically attach the parsed constituent to the tree (but **peek** will not).

To keep track of the tree structure, we must have a format for it which can be represented on a computer. Because most ATN parsers are written in Lisp, the obvious candidate is a list notation where each constituent is represented by a list. The first element of the list names the kind of constituent, and the subconstituents are represented by sublists. Figure 4.33 shows an example parse tree and a possible Lisp representation. However, exactly how phrase markers are stored and printed out will vary from program to program.

We also need a way to access the tree structure created. The modifier $, as in $s, refers to the constituent of type s currently above where the parser is working at the moment. So if it is parsing an np within an s, then $s will return the s node above the np. Also, $last will access the last constituent looked at by either **parse**, **category**, **word**, or **peek**. Thus except for $last, $ references can be only to constituents directly above the one being worked on. See Figure 4.34 for some examples of how $ works.

For more complicated situations we have the function **the**.

(the {first} *"category"* **of** *constituent***)**

This function will return the last (rightmost in tree) node of type *category* that is found directly under *constituent*. If there are more than one such constituent (for instance, more than one noun phrase in a verb phrase), we will get the last one, unless the optional **first** appears. Figure 4.34 also gives examples of the workings of the **the** function. The **the** function can also be used to access features of constituents. (We discussed features in section 4.2.5.2.)

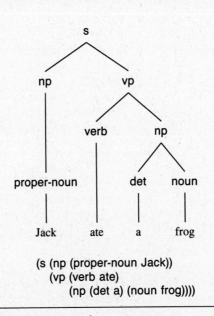

```
(s (np (proper-noun Jack))
   (vp (verb ate)
       (np (det a) (noun frog))))
```

Figure 4.33 Lisp representation of a parse tree

(the *"dimension"* of *constituent*)   ; *Returns the features of*
                                          ; *constituent along the dimension*
(the n-number of $last)
(the mood of $s-maj)

Last, while the parse tree is built up automatically, we do need a way to set features of nodes. This can be done with the function :=.

(:= *"left-hand-side" right-hand-side*)

will cause future evaluations of *left-hand-side* to produce *right-hand-side*. For example, to set the mood of the sentence to be question we would execute this:

(:= (the mood of $s-maj) 'question)

4.3.3 Augmented Transition Networks (Optional)

As developed so far, both our graphical and Lisp-like notations for transition networks are equivalent to context-free rules of grammar. That is, any language that we can describe with our transition networks can equally well be described by a context-free grammar. As we have seen, however, context-free grammars are not the most obviously suitable formalism for describing languages. Hence we now want to augment our transition networks to handle transformational rules as well. The result will be an *augmented transition*

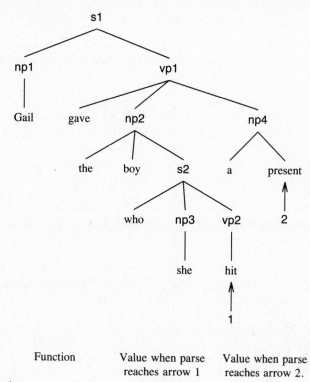

Function	Value when parse reaches arrow 1	Value when parse reaches arrow 2.
$s	s2	s1
$vp	vp2	vp1
$np	np2	np4
$last	hit	present
(the np of $vp)	nil	np4
(the first np of $vp)	nil	np2
(the np of $s)	np3	np1
(the verb of $vp)	hit	gave

Figure 4.34 Examples of tree-accessing functions

network or *ATN*. Roughly speaking, we need to add the following abilities:

- Remembering what already appeared in the sentence
- Manipulating features on constituents
- Adding and deleting constituents

The functions for remembering the past we have already introduced, along with :=. The rest we will introduce now.

4.3.3.1 Feature Manipulation in an ATN.   There are two functions for manipulating features. := we have already seen. The other one we need is =.

> (= *"left-hand-side" right-hand-side*)

This function tests whether the features described on the *right-hand-side* are also present on the *left-hand-side*. Some uses for it are the following:

(= (the dative of $last) 'yes)	; *Does the last constituent allow dative?*
(= (the n-number of	; *Does the np attached to s have the*
(the np of $s))	; *same number feature as the verb we*
(the v-number of $last))	; *just looked at?*
(= (the tense of	; *Is the verb of the constituent*
(the verb of $vp)) 'tenseless)	; *we are parsing a tenseless verb?*

Essentially, = checks to see whether the features on the left-hand side have any overlap with those on the right-hand side. As we mentioned in our earlier discussion of features, having more than one feature is taken as indicating an exclusive or. If there is an overlap, the features of the left-hand side will be replaced by the intersection of the two feature lists. If the feature is not there, the test fails. If the appropriate feature dimension is missing, the default feature list is assumed.

4.3.3.2 Adding and Deleting Constituents in an ATN.   Besides the ability to manipulate features, our transformational rules also allowed us to add, and delete constituents.

(detach *constituent location*)	; *constituent is found directly under*
	; *location, and is removed from there.*
(insert *constituent*)	; *constituent is inserted into the*
	; *input stream.*

An example of insert is seen in the rule of *"you-insertion,"* which is our ATN equivalent of the transformational rule *you-deletion*. (Remember, transformational grammar rules were written as if going from deep structure to surface structure, while in parsing we do the opposite. A deletion in one direction is an insertion in the other.) The *you-deletion* transformation was given in Figure 4.22. A corrected version, with the "you" made explicit, is shown in Figure 4.35. This rule transforms "You go to sleep" into "Go to sleep." Our ATN rule will look to see if a verb starts the sentence. If one does, then the rule will insert "you" into the input stream. We will make our rule even more careful by having it test that the verb is tenseless. A verb form is classed as tenseless if it is in the same form as its infinitive; "go" is tenseless because its infinitive form is "to go." Note that we cannot say:

> *Going to the store!
> *Went to the store!

Later on, when we consider *aux-inversion* again, we will consider sentences like

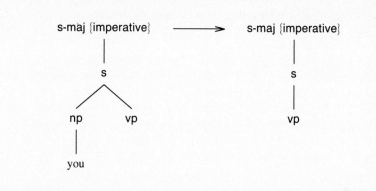

Figure 4.35 The rule of you-deletion

"Did Jack sleep?" This too starts with a verb, but not an infinitive verb (the infinitive form is "to do"), so this extra test will prevent the rule from applying here. Our ATN rule is this:

```
(optional
   (seq (peek verb)            ; See if the sentence starts with
        (= (the tense of $last) ; a verb which is in the
           'tenseless)          ; infinitive form.
                                ; The construct (the word you)
        (insert                 ; produces a new word
           (the word you))      ; which is put into the input stream
        (:= (the mood           ; $s-maj refers to the current s-maj
             of $s-maj)         ; node. This indicates that the
            'command)))         ; sentence is a command.
```

Naturally, this rule does not stand by itself, but rather must be inserted into the ATN at the appropriate spot. Since *you-insertion* can only occur in major clauses, and since the "you" gets put in at the front of the sentence, this rule goes into the s-maj network before it parses an s. So our ATN network for an s-maj node would now look like this:

```
(def-net s-maj
   (seq (optional                      ; ------------------
        (seq (peek verb)               ;            |
             (= (the tense of $last)   ;            |
                'tenseless)            ; You-insertion rule
             (insert (the word you))   ;            |
             (:= (the mood of $s-maj)  ;            |
                 'command)))           ; - ----------------
        (parse s)                      ; s-maj → s. . .
        (category final-punc)))        ; s-maj → . . . final-punc
```

4.3.4 Movement Rules in ATN Grammars (Optional)

4.3.4.1 The Rule of Aux-inversion.   The remaining functions we need for our ATN — drop, save-last, and use— handle movement rules. In Section 4.2.3 we described the transformation of "The boy will sleep" into "Will the boy sleep?", although we didn't give the name of this transformation, which is *aux-inversion*, until Section 4.2.6. Figure 4.36 spells the rule out. Because our transformational rule moves the aux to the left, our ATN rule must, in effect, undo this by moving it to the right, past the intervening np. Our rule to do this is this:

```
(optional
    (seq (category aux)              ; First parse the aux.
         (parse np)                  ; Then parse the intervening np.
         (drop (the aux of $s-maj))  ; Drop the aux into input stream.
         (drop (the np of $s-maj))   ; Drop the np, reversing np and
         (:= (the mood of $s-maj)    ; aux. Note that the sentence
            'question)))             ; is a question.
```

As an example, suppose the ATN parser were working on "Will the girl kiss Bill?", and had already parsed the aux "will" and the np "the girl," arriving at the state shown in Figure 4.37. Subsequent events are shown in Figure 4.38 and Figure 4.39. First the parser drops the aux back into the input stream, giving Figure 4.38. Then it drops the np into the input stream, giving Figure 4.39. Here np is the constituent parsed by the (parse np) command. Note that our ATN parser is able to drop a piece of the tree structure back into the input stream, just as easily as dropping a single word. At this point the constituents

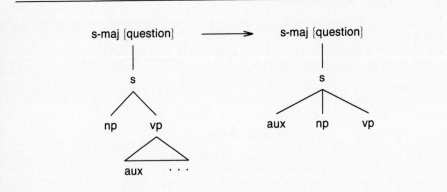

Figure 4.36 The rule of aux-inversion

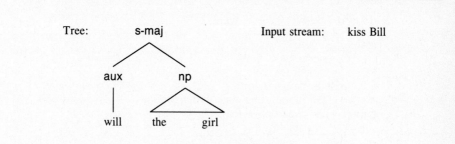

Figure 4.37 State of the parser after "Will the girl . . ."

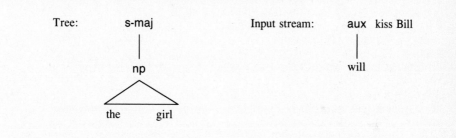

Figure 4.38 State of the parser while undoing aux-inversion

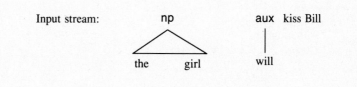

Figure 4.39 State of the parser after undoing aux-inversion

have been returned to their standard order, **np aux vp**, so when the ATN applies the normal rules for parsing declarative sentences they will work, assuming, of course, that we have sufficient rules to parse the equivalent declarative sentence, "The girl will kiss Bill." (Some required extensions to our grammar are discussed in Exercise 4.7.) Naturally, *aux-inversion* must apply before the rules for declarative sentences, so it should be inserted early in our **s-maj** network. The revised **s-maj** network is shown in Figure 4.40.

```
(def-net s-maj
  (seq (either
            (:= (the mood of $s-maj) 'statement)      ; A sentence is either
                                                       ; a statement
            (seq (peek verb)                           ; --------------------
                 (= (the tense of $last)               ; or a command
                    'tenseless)                        ;
                 (insert (the word you))               ; You-insertion rule
                 (:= (the mood of $s-maj) 'command));  ; --------------------
            (seq (:= (the mood of $s-maj)              ; or a question
                     'question)                        ;
                 (optional (seq (category wh)          ;
                                (save-last)))          ; Wh-movement rule
                 (optional                             ;
                   (seq (category aux)                 ;
                        (parse np)                     ;
                        (drop (the aux of $s-maj))     ; Aux-inversion rule
                        (drop (the np of $s-maj))))))  ; --------------------
       (parse s)                                       ; s-maj → s . . .
       (category final-punc)))                         ; s-maj → . . . final-punc
                                                       ;
(def-net s (seq (parse np) (parse vp)))                ; s → np vp
                                                       ;
(def-net np                                            ;
  (either (category proper-noun)                       ; np → proper-noun
          (category pronoun)                           ; np → pronoun
          (seq (category det)                          ; np → det . . .
               (optional* (category adj))              ; np → . . . (adj)* . . .
               (category noun)                         ; np → . . . noun . . .
               (optional* (parse pp)))                 ; np → . . . (pp)*
          (use)))                                      ; np → gap for wh
                                                       ;
(def-net vp                                            ;
  (seq (category verb)                                 ; vp → verb . . .
       (optional                                       ; --------------------
         (seq (= (the dative of $last) 'yes)           ;
              (parse np)                                ;
              (parse np)                                ; Dative movement
              (drop (the first np of $vp))             ;
              (insert (the word to))                   ;
              (drop (the np of $vp))))                  ; --------------------
       (parse np)                                       ; vp → . . . np . . .
       (optional* (parse pp))))                         ; vp → . . . (pp)*
                                                       ;
(def-net pp                                            ; pp → prep np
    (seq (category prep) (parse np)))
```

Figure 4.40 An ATN for a fragment of English

Figure 4.40 also includes two other new rules. One rule, *wh-movement*, is studied in Section 4.3.4.2 The other new rule is *dative movement*. This is the transformational rule that relates the following pairs of sentences.

Jack gave the book to Mary → Jack gave Mary the book.
Jack told the story to Mary → Jack told Mary the story.
Jack threw the ball to Mary → Jack threw Mary the ball.

(In these sentences, "Mary" is said to be in the "dative case," hence the name of this transformation.) In both of the top pair of sentences the noun phrase "the book" is the direct object of the sentence. In those cases, such as the right-hand side sentences, where we have a second noun phrase directly under the verb phrase (that is, without a preposition, as on the left), we call that noun phrase the *indirect object*. In these sentences we see that there seems to be a rule that causes the formation of indirect objects from prepositional phrases like "to Mary." This is the rule of *dative movement*. Not all verbs allow this rule, however:

Mary dedicated the book to Jack → * Mary dedicated Jack the book.
Mary set the words to music → * Mary set music the words.

To account for this we will mark the verbs that allow dative movement as yes for dative, and our ATN rule checks to see if the verb is so marked before it allows the rule to apply. Later we will look at this rule more closely.

4.3.4.2 Unbounded Movement Rules.
So far, all of the movement rules we have looked at are *bounded movement rules*. In bounded movement rules there are strict limits on how far the constituent may move. These are specified by the rule itself; that is, the rule gives both the starting and ending location in detail. For example, in *aux-inversion* the rule specifies that the auxiliary is initially after the subject noun phrase, and moves to a position before it. There are, however, other movement rules called *unbounded movement rules*. The primary example of such a rule in English is the rule of *wh-movement*. This rule is responsible for the formation of wh-questions in English, taking

Jack has given what to Bill?

and creating

What has Jack given to Bill?

(You might note that we also have *aux-inversion* here. However, because this is not a yes-no question, the auxiliary does not move to the front of the sentence. If we are careful, we can use the same rule of aux-inversion to handle these cases as well.)

Wh-movement is unbounded because the wh may be moved arbitrarily far from where it originates.

Jack did say that he wants Fred to buy what?
What did Jack say that he wants Fred to buy?

Previously, when a constituent like our aux in *aux-inversion* had to be moved, we simply parsed the intervening constituents (for *aux-inversion* this was just a noun phrase), dropped the moved constituent back into the input stream, and then dropped the intervening constituents back into the input stream as well. This puts the moved constituent in the standard location. But we cannot do that here, because the "what" could have come from virtually anywhere. Indeed, the only way to find out where it came from is to start parsing the sentence as if the "what" were not moved, and look for a place where the sentence is missing a noun phrase. Such places are called *gaps*. To find such gaps, the parser initially parses the "what" (using a normal **category** test), and then saves it for future gap-filling with the function **save-last**. When the parser needs it to fill in, the grammar will use the function **use**. The **use** function looks to see if anything has been saved by **save-last**. If not, the function fails. If there is something, it is used at that point in the parse (as if it had appeared in the input stream), and "unsaved," so that it cannot be used a second time.

> (save-last)   ; *Puts the last parsed object into a special*
>   ; *list, which the* **use** *command knows about.*
> (use)   ; *Puts the last item* **saved** *into the parse*
>   ; *tree. Fails if nothing* **saved**.

A simple version of *wh-movement* requires two changes to our ATN, one at the beginning of the **s-maj** net to parse and save a **wh** and a second in the **np** net to state that one way to parse an **np** is to use one saved up by a previous **save-last**. The ATN of Figure 4.40 includes these changes. Figure 4.41 summarizes all of the commands for our ATN.

When trying to understand how the ATN parser works on the grammar in Figure 4.40 it is important to remember how ATN parsers backtrack when they have made an incorrect choice. So, using the grammar of Figure 4.40 on a sentence like "Take your vitamins!" the ATN parser would first have to make a choice in the **either** in the **s-maj** network. Assuming the parser tries choices from top to bottom, it would start working on a statement. It would first mark the **s-maj** as a **statement** and then execute the **(parse s)** command, which would take it to the **s** network, where it would execute a **(parse np)** command. In the **np** network it would look for words that could begin a noun phrase. Because "take" will match none of these, backtracking must start. Since the only **either** command occurred in the **s-maj** network, at the very beginning, the parser will go back to that point and try one of the alternative choices. Indeed, the next choice handles commands, and the parse will go through.

4.4 Building an ATN Interpreter (Optional)

Our discussion to this point has been focused on building a grammar for an ATN. But how does one construct the actual parsing mechanism? We will consider this now.

Ability	Function
Basic context-free tests on arcs	(category *terminal-symbol*) (parse *nonterminal-symbol*) (peek *terminal-symbol*) (word *root*)
Flow-of-control functions	(seq *-tests-*) (either *-tests-*) (optional *test*) (optional* *test*)
Remember past	$category (the {first} "*category*" of *constituent*) (the "*dimension*" of *constituent*)
Manipulate features	(= "*left-hand-side*" *right-hand-side*) (:= "*left-hand-side*" *right-hand-side*)
Add constituent	(detach *constituent location*) (the word "*word*")
Delete constituent	(insert *constituent*)
Bounded movement	(drop *constituent*)
Unbounded movement	(save-last) (use)

Figure 4.41 Commands for our ATN

ATN interpreters are fairly simple devices, at least in their "pure" state. The only real complexity in them is their backtracking ability, and this is a conceptual complexity — the additional code is minuscule. This is not to say that we have shown everything needed. A full-fledged system would have a dictionary, plus associated functions, a morphology unit, and a fair amount of code for functions like the and =. But these functions are icing on the basic ATN cake, and differ from implementation to implementation; the underlying technology of ATNs does not.

4.4.1 A Non-Backtracking ATN Interpreter

The high-level description of our ATN interpreter is given in Figure 4.42. We have ignored a large number of things, such as remembering the parse tree, or determining whether the next input corresponds to a particular category of word. We have also left out the commands optional and optional*. But, most important, we have left out backtracking. As we shall see, however, this will be easy to add.

Function: atn

Arguments: `*s*`, the input sentence — a nonlocal variable.

Algorithm: Call atn-main, starting it with a (parse s-maj) command.
          If successful, print out resulting tree. Otherwise report failure.

Function: atn-main

Arguments: actions - A list of actions to be performed. An
                     action might be one like seq that has many
                     subactions to perform. If this is the case,
                     put the subactions on this list.

Algorithm:
Loop: Until either no actions are on actions, or an action fails.

      Remove first action from actions and evaluate it.

      Case: category, word, peek, = etc.: If test is successful,
            then continue. Otherwise report failure to atn.

            seq: Put all of the subactions on actions at front.
            Thus next thing done will be first of the subactions.

            either: Pick one of the possibilities "at random"
            and put it on the front of actions.

            parse: Add a done action to actions
            (see next case). Add the network associated with the
            constituent to be parsed to actions.

            done: The parser has completed a constituent.
            If there are more actions, keep looping;
            if there are no further actions, then if `*s*` is
            empty, report back success, but if `*s*` has things
            left on it, report back failure.

      Endloop.

Figure 4.42 A nonbacktracking ATN interpreter

To see how our preliminary ATN interpreter works, consider the action of
the Lisp function atn on the sentence "Jack sleeps," with this simplified grammar:

```
(def-net s-maj (seq (parse np)
                    (category verb)))

(def-net np (either (category proper-noun)
                    (category pronoun)))
```

Initially atn will call atn-main and it will have:

```
*s* = "Jack sleeps"
actions = (parse s-maj)
```

Because the action is a **parse**, an **s-maj** node for the parse tree is created, and a **done** action is put on the list of further actions to be performed. Whenever the ATN interpreter reaches a **done** action, this signifies that a constituent has been completed. We will see how this works later.

The **parse** action also resets the current action to be the network associated with **s-maj**. This will leave the interpreter in this state:

```
*s* = "Jack sleeps"
actions = (seq (parse np)               ; The action associated with
              (category verb))          ; the s-maj network.
         (done s-maj)
```

This completes one loop around **atn-main**, which now repeats. Because the next action is a **seq**, the actions indicated inside of it are added to the front of **actions**.

```
*s* = "Jack sleeps"
actions = (parse np)
         (category verb)
         (done s-maj)
```

Next comes the **parse** action, which puts another **done** action on the list of things to do, and sets the interpreter to work on the **np** network.

```
*s* = "Jack sleeps"
actions = (either (category proper-noun)
                  (category pronoun))
         (done np)
         (category verb)
         (done s-maj)
```

Next, the **either** action picks one of the possibilities "at random." Naturally, when we look at backtracking, we will modify this so that it remembers the other possibilities as a choice-point. Assuming that it "guesses" correctly and chooses to pick up a proper noun, the parser will have the following as the next state:

```
*s* = "Jack sleeps"
actions = (category proper-noun)
         (done np)
         (category verb)
         (done s-maj)
```

The **category** action is executed next, succeeding, and (as a side effect) removing "Jack" from ***s***. It will also add "Jack" to the parse tree, but we will ignore this. Then the **category** test is removed from **actions**, leaving us with this state:

```
*s* = "sleeps"
actions = (done np)
          (category verb)
          (done s-maj)
```

Next the interpreter performs the done action. This indicates the end of the np, so, for example, the next things to be parsed should not be added to the np node of the parse tree. The done action is removed from actions, and the next one, the category test for a verb, is taken. By this time you should have a general idea of what is going on.

4.4.2 A Backtracking ATN Interpreter

To add backtracking to our interpreter we need to be able to store choice-points. A choice-point is a data structure that contains enough information to allow the parser to restart a computation where it was left off. Every time the parser comes to a choice-point, which for us means any time it has to execute an either action, it remembers the situation by storing away a choice-point. It will store these in a variable called *agenda*. If we continue to ignore the parse tree, and a few other issues as well, all that has to be remembered is (1) the value of *s* and (2) the value of actions.

The only other change we need is to modify the top-level program, atn, so that if atn-main returns failure, then, rather than giving up, atn will restart atn-main using one of the choice-points from *agenda*. Remember, these contain all of the information atn-main needs for its workings. The revised version of atn is given in Figure 4.43. It is virtually identical to the previous version. New sections are given in *italics*.

To see how this will work, let us pick up our previous example at the point where the parser was about to do an either command. The only thing new we need to add is that at this point *agenda* is empty.

```
*s* = "Jack sleeps"
actions = (either (category proper-noun)
                  (category pronoun))
          (done np)
          (category verb)
          (done s-maj)
*agenda* = nil
```

Now, rather than picking one possibility and throwing the others away, we will store the other possibilities on the agenda. So, to make things interesting, suppose that our parser guesses wrong, and decides to look for a pronoun, storing the other option away. Figure 4.44 shows the resulting state of the parser, including the choice-point store in *agenda*. The parser will now try to pick up a pronoun, and fail. Thus atn-main will report failure back to atn. Now, atn will look on *agenda*, and take the first element (in this case the only element) from this list. This will be the last element added to the list. These

Function: atn

Arguments: *s*, the input sentence — a nonlocal variable.
Variables: *agenda* — *stores the choice-points put on by the*
                either *command. Initially it is set to the*
                (parse s-maj) action, and *s* *to the input*
                sentence. A nonlocal variable.

Algorithm:
Loop: Until either a successful parse, or *agenda* *is empty.*
    Call atn-main *choosing the first choice-point from*
    agenda, *and removing it from the list.*
    If successful, print out resulting tree; else try next choice-point.

End Loop.

Function: atn-main

Arguments: actions - A list of actions to be performed. An
                 action might be one like seq that has many
                 subactions to perform. If this is the case,
                 put the subactions on this list.

Loop :   Until either no more actions on actions , or an action fails.

     Remove first action from actions and evaluate it.

     Case: category, word, peek, = etc: If
        test is successful, then continue.
        Otherwise report failure to atn.

        seq: Put all of the subactions on front of actions.
        Thus next thing done will be first of the subactions.

        either: pick one of the possibilities "at random"
        and put it on the front of actions.
        For each alternative action, store a choice-point
        with (a) the current *s* *and (b) the alternative added*
        to actions. *Thus if the* either *branches, say,*
        three ways, add two choice-points to *agenda*.

        parse: Add a done action to actions.
        (See next case.) Put the network associated with the
        constituent to be parsed on actions.

        done: The parser has completed a
        constituent. If there are more actions, keep looping;
        if there are no further actions, then, if *s* is
        empty, report back success, and if *s* has things
        left on it, report back failure.

Endloop.

Figure 4.43 A backtracking ATN interpreter

```
*s* = "Jack sleeps"
actions = (category pronoun)
            (done np)
            (category verb)
            (done s-maj)
*agenda* = [ *s* = "Jack sleeps"
              actions = (category proper-noun)
                        (done np)
                        (category verb)
                        (done s-maj)        ]
```

Figure 4.44 Use of an agenda for backtracking by an ATN

values will be used when **atn-main** is called again, giving this:

```
*s* = "Jack sleeps"
actions = (category proper-noun)
            (done np)
            (category verb)
            (done s-maj)
*agenda* = nil
```

This time our ATN parser will try the other possibility, namely, looking for a **proper-noun**. This will be found, and it will go on to parse the sentence as before.

Box 4.4

Efficiency of Parsing

Programming languages are often context-free, or sufficiently close to context-free that it pays to think of them as such, but with an exception or two. Because of this, compilers use context-free parsers to establish the syntactic structure of the input. Naturally, there has been some study of how to do such parsing efficiently.

Work in analysis of algorithms characterizes the efficiency of an algorithm by abstracting away from its implementation on some particular machine, and instead specifying how the time the algorithm takes increases as a function of the size of the input. A context-free parser takes two inputs, the grammar, and the particular sentence to be parsed. Most analyses have assumed that the size of the grammar is fixed, and have concentrated on how the time to parse depends on the length of the input. There have been many results in this area, but the "standard" algorithm for parsing context-free languages is the *Cocke-Kasami-Younger algorithm* for context-free parsing (later improved by Earley). This algorithm has the property that in the worst case, the time to parse an input goes up with the cube of the length of the sentence (or program), and in the best case goes up only linearly. That is

$$time = constant \times length^3$$

Naturally, unless we know the constant in front, we do not actually know how fast the algorithm will be. Indeed, it turns out that there are other algorithms which in some sense are "better" in that the exponent is less than 3. However, these algorithms have very large constants in front, and for typical inputs this constant would more than wipe out any gain due to the exponent. Thus the Cocke-Kasami-Younger algorithm is the one of choice for context-free parsing.

We might now ask how this compares to our ATN parser. First, the two are not strictly comparable, because ATNs handle noncontext-free languages. However, we can make them comparable by removing the ATN's context sensitivity (which ultimately boils down to the ability to remember, and make use of, the history of the sentence). Having done this, our ATN implementation is much worse because the time it will take goes up exponentially with the length of the input.

$$time = constant \times 2^{length}$$

Intuitively, the reason the ATN parser can take so long is that upon reaching the end of the sentence it may find out that it can't parse the last word, and backtrack. It will then try a different way of parsing the last two words, but each time fail, so it will then try the third-to-last word, etc. The point is that constituents will be parsed over and over again, even when the problem is somewhere else. To take one example:

Is the terminal in my office?
Is the terminal in my office broken?

Assume it is the second sentence that requires backtracking. To fix things requires going back to just after the word "terminal" and assuming that the prepositional phrase "in my office" is now attached to the noun phrase "the terminal." Thus both the noun phrase "my office" and the prepositional phrase of which it is a part, "in my office," will have to be reparsed, *despite the fact that neither has changed.*

The obvious way to fix this would be to save completed constituents like prepositional phrases and noun phrases so that if the ATN parser backtracks over them, when it starts forward again it can, as it were, pick them up whole, rather than recreating them. This is exactly what the Cocke-Kasami-Younger algorithm does. It keeps track of constituents in a table so that it creates them only once. For example, some of the constituents for the sentence "The boys eat leaves" are indicated in Figure 4.45. This table indicates, for example, that there is a well-formed s starting at word 2 and ending at word 3, "boys eat."

Exactly the same technique has been used in ATNs, and is called a *well-formed substring table.* (This is also related to Kay's *chart*

		Constituent starts at:			
		1	2	3	4
Consti-					
tuent	2	np	np		
ends	3	s	s	vp,s	
at:	4	s	s	vp,s	np

Figure 4.45 Table of constituents for "The boys eat leaves"

parsing [Kay80].) If we introduce a well-formed substring table into our ATN implementation then our ATN parser will work in times comparable to the standard algorithm. Indeed, it could be considered a notational variant of it. The main difference is that the Cocke-Kasami-Younger algorithm works bottom-up in that it first tries to create low-level constituents, and then builds up to higher ones, whereas an ATN parser starts looking for an s and works down to looking for lower ones. But this affects only the order in which constituents are entered into the table, not the efficiency of the algorithm.

Unfortunately, this technique will not work if we re-extend our ATN to context-sensitive languages. With context sensitivity, what constitutes a valid constituent will change with the surrounding context. Because backtracking can modify the earlier analysis, it can change the context, and thus what was earlier, say, a noun phrase, may no longer be one. To take a simple example, the word "tell" normally would not be considered a valid verb phrase, because it requires a direct object. However, in the context of a sentence which has undergone *wh-movement*, "Who did Jack tell?", it is perfectly fine as a verb phrase.

In general, context-sensitive languages allow this to happen all over the place. However, as we have already noted, English, if not context-free, is very close to it. We can take advantage of this fact and modify the table so that it records some of the context surrounding saved constituents (such as whether *wh-movement* had occurred). The result is almost as useful as in genuine context-free languages.

4.4.3 Alternative Search Strategies

Our ATN parser can be thought of as searching through partial parses of the sentence looking for a complete parse. We will be talking about search in some detail in Chapter 5. For the moment, we just note that our ATN parser follows the backtracking strategy mentioned earlier. It tries to keep on parsing, making a "guess" at choice-points, until it encounters a failure. At that point it backs up to the last choice-point, and restarts, this time using an alternative arc out. This search pattern is called *depth-first search*.

It is possible, however, to get very different behaviors out of our ATN with only minor changes. To see how this can be done, we need first remind ourselves that each choice-point contains all of the information needed to restart the computation. Thus there is no need to restart the computations in some clearly "logical" order. If we wanted it to, our ATN parser could pick a random number, and select some random choice-point to investigate next. (Of course, this would make our ATN a bit hard to understand, and it would appear quite scatterbrained to an observer.)

More logically, rather than always picking the last choice, the ATN parser could always pick the earliest unexplored choice-point. This is called *breadth-first search,* because all early arcs out of a node will be explored before any of them will be extended past another choice-point.

Finally, as we will note later in our discussion of semantics, there are good reasons for considering more complicated systems for choosing which choice-point to use next. In these, each possibility is ranked by semantics and the most highly ranked is taken next.

4.5 From Syntax to Semantics

Our discussion so far has concentrated on going from a natural language sentence to a syntactic tree, and has looked only at the role syntax plays in this process. Now we will discuss how a program might go from the syntactic tree to an internal representation, a process called *semantic interpretation*. For our discussion of semantics we will simplify the grammar we use. In general we will use only the context-free rules from the preceding sections. As we will point out later, while this might seem like a major limitation, it is not.

In general, producing internal representations requires that we disambiguate words and references, as well as convert to the particular logical form specified by our internal representation. In this section we will concentrate primarily on the latter. Even a basic treatment of disambiguation requires a more detailed analysis of the world knowledge that lies behind the words, and is therefore deferred until Chapter 10.

4.5.1 The Interpretation of Definite Noun Phrases

A particularly simple case of semantic interpretation is that which occurs when, looking at the scene in Figure 4.46, we interpret the phrase "the red block" as referring to the red block that appears on top of the blue block. Such noun phrases are called *definite noun phrases* or *definite descriptions* because they are expected to pick out a particular, or *definite*, referent.

Presumably, in looking at Figure 4.46 our visual system has created a group of facts that represent the scene. Whether these facts are represented in

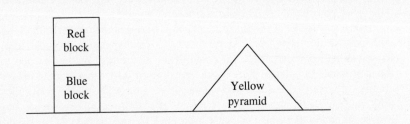

Figure 4.46 A blocks-world scene

the slot and filler notation used in Chapter 3, or in the assertional notation introduced in Chapter 1, is not important. We will assume an assertional notation,
giving us this set of facts:

(inst block-1 block)	*; Block-1 is a block*
(color block-1 red)	*; and is red.*
(inst block-2 block)	*; Block-2 is a block.*
(color block-2 blue)	*; It is blue, and*
(support block-2 block-1)	*; it supports block-1.*
(inst block-3 pyramid)	*; Block-3 is a pyramid*
(color block-3 yellow)	*; and is yellow.*

Let us suppose that we have a mechanism for searching this database for an
object that is both red and a block. We will describe in Chapter 6 how such a
mechanism can be built; here we will simply assume it exists. Finding the
referent of "the red block" can then be reduced to a request of the following
form:

(retrieve-val '?x '(and (inst ?x block)	*; Find a ?x that is a block*
(color ?x red)))	*; and is red.*

Here ?x is a logical variable that may range over any object in our database.
The prefix ? will be reserved for such variables. The idea here is that we want
to end up with ?x bound to some object from the database about which both of
the conjoined assertions are true. (See Chapter 6 for more on this.) Thus if the
Lisp function retrieve-val can do this job for us, the problem of deciding that
"the red block" refers to block-1 can be divided into two parts — first, realiz-
ing that the meaning of "the red block" is the retrieve-val request above, and
then executing the request.

However, even at this low level of detail there are already problems with
what we have described. In particular, this process will work only in very narrow and unrealistic situations. More commonly, we have a noun phrase like
"the steering wheel" and are expected to pick out a unique steering wheel.
Since most of us have encountered many steering wheels, the noun phrase itself
does not provide enough information. It must be the context that narrows down
the choice, presumably since only one steering wheel was referred to recently.

(In fact, it need not have even been referred to. If we were talking about a unique car, then we would assume that the phrase referred to the steering wheel of the car.)

However, whatever processes are responsible for such abilities, they would seem to be on top of our ability to create a logical description of the object, such as we did for "the red block." Thus we will look at this subproblem in this chapter, and return to the larger problem of including contextual clues later, in Chapter 10.

If a program is to go from the phrase marker to a logical description, words like "red" and "block" must have associated with them "meanings" that specify how to build up part of this description. These meanings are specified in the dictionary or lexicon. In particular, the one for "red" must contribute this clause:

(color ?x red)

Our semantic routines will then build up the internal representation for the entire noun phrase out of the internal representations for the individual words. Thus if the meaning of "block" is something like (inst ?x block), then combining this with the meaning of "red" will give us this:

(and (inst ?x block) (color ?x red))

In the same fashion, "the" will contribute the information that we want to call retrieve-val, and the parser will have then built up the meaning of the entire phrase.

This process is called *compositional semantics*. The assertion that semantics is, in fact, compositional is a theory about how we understand. This theory claims that the reason we are able to understand an arbitrarily large number of sentences, most of which we have never heard before, is that, first, we are able to parse them syntactically using a relatively small number of syntactic rules, and second, we can derive the meaning of the whole from the meanings of the parts. To do this we need to specify three things:

- The meaning of individual words;
- How the meanings of individual words combine to form the meaning of groups of words; and
- How all this hooks up with our syntactic parser.

Our previous discussion touched upon the first two of these, and while later sections will go into them in greater detail, let us now consider the last of the three, how semantic rules link to the syntactic parser. Typically this is done in one of two ways. One is to create the internal representation after we have already done the syntactic parse. This has several advantages, such as not wasting time on creating an internal representation for a parse that eventually fails. However, as should be clear from earlier examples, in cases where a sentence may have more than one syntactic form, it is often possible for semantics to guide the parser. To give yet another example of this, consider:

I read an article about the Vietnam war in the newspaper.

Here the prepositional phrase "in the newspaper" may be part of the noun phrase "the Vietnam war," or else it may modify the verb "read." Only semantics can tell us that the phrase "the Vietnam war in the newspaper" is odd, and thus unlikely to be correct.

Thus to facilitate the interaction of semantics and syntax, we will build up the internal representation at the same time that we are establishing the syntactic relations. We will do this by interleaving the two processes, which in turn can be done by adding to our ATN grammar new actions that actually create the internal representation.

Given this model of the semantic interpretation phase, we can now see why restricting consideration to the context-free part of the ATN is no real limitation. Those who read the sections on transformational grammar will remember that our transformational rules transformed the sentence into the form expected by the context-free rules without changing its meaning. Thus when we add semantics, the process will be this: transformational rules translate into the form expected by the context free rules, the context free rules create the phrase marker, and the semantic rules (which were developed to handle the context free part) will create the internal representation.

4.5.1.1 Semantic Features for Our ATN (Optional). In the previous section we saw that our ATN will need to be told the meanings of words, and how these meanings combine. To do this we will have to add two new properties to constituents, the **referent** property, which stores a symbol used to represent the referent of the constituent, and the **sense** property, which stores the internal representation itself. The **sense** property will, by the time the constituent is complete, store what we would normally think of as the meaning of the phrase. For our earlier example, "the red block," this was:

```
(retrieve-val '?x '(and (inst ?x block)
                        (color ?x red)))
```

The **referent** property of a constituent is used to store a symbol that, within the meaning, represents the referent of the phrase or, should that not be known, a variable that will eventually be bound to the referent. So in our "red block" example, the variable **?x** will eventually be bound to the correct object **block-1** and thus **?x** is stored in the **referent** property of this noun phrase.

The idea is that when the ATN parser starts a noun phrase it will let the referent be a new variable. It will then build up the sense of the noun phrase from the meanings of the constituents. This will require the variable that was created at the start. At the end of the noun phrase the semantic procedures can find the referent from the sense just built up.

Our use of the terms *sense* and *referent* is taken from the philosopher Frege who used them to distinguish the two different ways in which a phrase like "the morning star" had a meaning. In ancient astronomy, the "morning star" was a star seen near the sun in the morning, while the "evening star" was a star seen near the sun in the evening. It was discovered even in ancient times that both were the same object, the planet Venus. According to Frege, both phrases *refer to* Venus, but they must have some other component to their meaning as well, otherwise the "discovery" that "the morning star is the same as the evening star" would be equivalent to "Venus is the same as Venus", which is a logical truth, and not much of a discovery at all. Frege called this other meaning the *sense* of a word or phrase.

4.5.1.2 Combining Meanings (Optional).   Next we have to figure out how to combine meanings. Looking at the first word of our noun phrase, "the," we can get some idea of the contribution of this word to the total meaning by sub-tracting the contributions of the other words. So, if "red ball" contributes

> (and (color ?x red) (inst ?x ball))

and we want to end up with

> (retrieve-val '?x '(and (color ?x red)
> (inst ?x ball)))

then the meaning of "the" should be something like

> (retrieve-val (the referent of $np)   ; *(the referent of $np)* = ?x
> (the sense of $np))   ; *(the sense of $np)* = *(and . . .)*

This looks reasonable, but it does pose a problem. In order to use this, the pro-cedure must have available the sense of the rest of the noun phrase, which will be retrieved by the expression:

> (the sense of $np)

This cannot be had until the parser has completed the noun phrase. Thus in our instructions about the meaning of "the," we need to specify that the meaning should not be constructed until the noun phrase is complete. This will give us something like this:

> Wait until you have the sense of the rest of the noun phrase,
> and then evaluate this:
>
> > (retrieve-val (the referent of $np)
> > (the sense of $np))
>
> When you have found the value, reset the referent of the np
> to the value found.

More formally, we will have associated with each word a Lisp function that will specify how the meaning of the word is to be combined with the meaning of the rest of the phrase. For "the" this will be the following:

> (def-semantics the   ; *Define the meaning of "the."*
> (: = (the referent of $np)   ; *Reset the referent of np*
> (retrieve-val   ; *to the value retrieved*
> (the referent of $np)   ; *by* retrieve-val.
> (the sense of $np))))

But again, this function can be called only after we already have the sense of the rest of the np. Thus we will introduce a function that serves as an intermediate between the syntax and the semantics functions — **semantics**.

(semantics *"when" "where"*)

When indicates when the semantic function associated with *where* should be evaluated. There are three possibilities, **immediate** (immediately), **end** (only at the end of the current constituent, e.g., at the end of the current np) and **wait** (waits until there is a **semantics immediate** call on the current constituent). Using these functions, our ATN grammar for noun phrases will take the appearance of Figure 4.47. (In this figure we use the ' (back-quote) function which

```
(def-net np
  (either
  (seq
    (:= (the referent of $np)           ; The variable to
        (make-mvar $np))                ; represent the entity
    (either                             ;
    (category proper-noun)              ; proper-noun and pronoun
    (category pronoun)                  ; semantics not defined
    (seq (category det)                 ; np -> det . . .
         (semantics end $last)          ;
         (optional*                     ;
         (seq (category adj)            ; np -> . . . (adj)* . . .
              (semantics wait $last)))  ;
         (category noun)                ; np -> . . . noun . . .
         (semantics immediate $last)    ;
         (optional* (parse pp)))))      ; np -> . . . (pp)*
    (use)))                             ; np -> gap for wh
                                        ;
(def-semantics the                      ; Set the referent
  (:= (the referent of $np)             ; of the np to the
      (retrieve-val                     ; object that
        (the referent of $np)           ; matches the sense
        (the sense of $np))))           ; of the np.
                                        ;
(def-semantics red                      ; "Red" says to
  (add-sense $np                        ; add a statement
    '(color ,(the referent of $np) red))) ; that color=red.
                                        ;
(def-semantics block                    ; "Block" says to
  (add-sense $np                        ; add a statement
    '(inst ,(the referent of $np) block))) ; that np is a block.
```

Figure 4.47 An np grammar with semantics

produces a copy of the expression that follows, except that anything preceded by a comma is replaced by its value. (See Section 2.9.)

To get a feel for this, let us trace through the semantic operation for "the red block." Before looking at the noun phrase, the parser creates a variable to serve as the referent of the noun phrase. This is done by the statement:

(: = (the referent of $np) (make-mvar $np))

Then the parser sees "the" and calls semantics with an argument telling it to use the semantic function for "the," but only after the np is finished. Next comes "red," and now our semantics does roughly the same thing, but this time it will only wait until it gets the next immediate call to semantics. At this point our np will have a variable associated with it, say ?np1, and the following functions waiting to be executed:

(semantics wait red)
(semantics end the)

Next comes "block." Seeing the head noun of a noun phrase causes the ATN to call semantics immediately on the function associated with "block." The function called there, add-sense, says to add its argument to the sense associated with the $np. Since there is nothing there at the moment, this simply creates this new sense:

(inst ?np1 block)

Next, since there is a call to (semantics wait red) waiting around, this call gets processed. This in turn calls the semantic function for "red," giving the following as the sense of the noun phrase.

(and (color ?np1 red) (inst ?np1 block))

(We are assuming here that the function add-sense will add the and when it has to combine two or more atomic predicate calculus formulas.) Finally comes the end of the noun phrase, and the semantics function of "the" will be evaluated, giving:

(: = (the referent of np1)
       (retrieve-val (the referent of np1)
                     (the sense of np1)))

which becomes

(: = (the referent of np1)
       (retrieve-val '?np1 '(and (color ?np1 red)
                                 (inst ?np1 block))))

4.5.1.3 Complicated Semantic Functions (Optional). The semantic functions we have defined so far, particularly those for "red" and "block," are quite simple, just adding new facts on to the sense of the np. Many semantic functions will be this simple, but not all. Consider for example:

> "a former congressman"   is not a congressman
> "an alleged criminal"   may or may not be a criminal
> "a toy elephant"   is not an elephant

So, while a real elephant has lungs, and eats peanuts, a toy one generally has neither property; rather it is a toy in the shape of an elephant. Note, however, that this can be handled by our semantics. The semantics will first do the semantic analysis of "elephant," giving us:

> (inst ?np2 elephant)

However, the semantics for "toy" can say, in effect

1) Find the current inst property in the semantics.
2) Add a statement of the form:
   (shape *the-variable the-inst-property*)
3) Delete the inst property.
4) Add an inst property saying that it is an inst of a toy.

Thus the sense of "the toy elephant" would be this:

```
(retrieve-val '?x          ; Comes from the meaning of "the."
   '(and (inst ?x toy)     ; Comes from the meaning of "toy."
       (shape ?x elephant)))  ; Comes from "elephant"
                           ; as modified by "toy."
```

4.5.2 Case Grammar and the Meaning of Verbs

We have seen that we created the meaning of a definite description by combining the meanings of the parts of the definite description into something that we could then use to retrieve the desired object from our database. Now we want to do something similar, but for sentences as a whole. We will simplify matters initially by just considering the special case of declarative sentences.

4.5.2.1 The Representation of Optional Arguments.

When discussing the meaning of "red," we noted that it had to create a piece of assertional representation that claimed that whatever it was that we were talking about must be red. In the same way, the verbs of a sentence must also create such representations, but because verbs are more complicated than adjectives, their representations will be more complicated as well. So, to start, consider a verb like "buy." We must have associated with "buy" several pieces of information: (1) the related predicate, say buy, and (2) how the various noun phrases found in the sentence map into the argument structure for this predicate. Suppose we want our translation to look something like this:

> Jack bought a car.
> (buy jack-1 car-1)

(Here jack-1 and car-1 are the database objects retrieved by the corresponding nps.) To create this, the semantic function for "buy" might include a template like this:

```
'(buy ,(the referent of (the np of $s))
      ,(the referent of (the np of $vp)))
```

Given our analysis in which an s contains a np and vp, then

```
(the referent of (the np of $s)) = (the referent of subject) = jack-1
(the referent of (the np of $vp)) = (the referent of direct obj) = car-1
```

However, this analysis ignores certain problems. We must also contend with sentences like these:

Jack bought a car from Fred.
Jack bought a car for fifty dollars.
Jack bought a car from Fred for fifty dollars.

Each of these sentences includes an optional component of the act of buying. Such optional components present us with two problems. The first is representing the new information within the internal representation. The second is telling the parsing system how to translate the optional slot or argument into the internal representation decided upon. We will start with the first of these.

One obvious way to include the new information would be to add extra slots to buy, which will be filled by the object denoted by the corresponding noun phrase in the sentence. So we might have this structure:

(buy *subject direct-object from-pp for-pp*)

There are, however, many other prepositional phrases that can also be added to further describe the action:

Jack bought the car on Friday. (time)
Jack bought the car in Chicago. (location)
Jack bought the car with a friend. (accompaniment)
Jack bought the car for a friend. (beneficiary)
Jack bought the car with a check. (instrument)

Because of the sheer number of arguments that would be needed, most of which would not be filled for any particular instance of the verb, people tend to use another of the notation schemes mentioned in Chapter 1, slot-assertion notation. So rather than having a separate place in the "buy" statement for, say, the cost "for fifty dollars," we instead have this:

```
(buy buy-1 jack-1 car-1)        ; Jack bought a car
(cost buy-1 fifty-dollars)       ; for fifty dollars.
```

The first statement says, as before, that jack-1 bought car-1, but now we also give a name to this event, buy-1. We can then use this name in giving further information, such as the cost assertion, where cost is now serving as the name of a slot.

We could also, for that matter, use slot-assertion notation for indicating that jack-1 did the action. That is, we could have something like this:

```
(inst buy-1 buy)
(buyer buy-1 jack-1)
(buyee buy-1 car-1)
(cost buy-1 fifty-dollars)
```

At the moment, however, this is simply notation fiddling, as we have no real reason for preferring one notation or the other. We will return to this point later, however.

4.5.2.2 Cases as Meaningful Argument Names.

If some of our slots will be named, then we might ask which names to use. The names above are arbitrary; they have meaning to the reader but, as far as the machine is concerned they are meaningless symbols. Also, the names are unique to the buy predicate, and different verbs could have different names for their slots; the person who performed a sing action could be indicated by, say,

```
(singer sing-33 pavarotti-2)
```

An alternative is suggested by *case grammar*. Case grammar claims that there is a small fixed number of so-called *deep cases*. These are the basic ways that a noun phrase or prepositional phrase can relate to a verb. All verbs must select their cases from this set. Rather than the two distinct named slots buyer and singer, we would indicate the similarity of these roles (they both indicate the person who is doing the action) thus:

```
(agent buy-1 jack-1)           ; Jack did the buying.
(agent sing-33 pavarotti-2)    ; Pavarotti did the singing.
```

Here agent is the role (or *case*) indicating the person or thing responsible for the action. Note that in saying this we mean to imply that agent will *not* be a meaningless symbol to the system; rather it will have the distinct meaning that whoever or whatever fills the agent case of an action is the person or thing responsible for it. How this meaning gets enforced is an important, but distinct, issue; presumably there would be rules that would allow the system to infer things about something that fills the agent slot. For example:

```
(if (and (agent ?action ?agnt)   ; An agent that does something
         (results ?action bad))  ; that has bad consequences,
    (will-be-sued ?agnt))        ; will be sued.
```

This rule states that an agent will be sued for doing anything which turns out badly.

Some other proposed cases are the *beneficiary case*— a person who benefits from an action:

Mary moved the rock *for Jack*.
Jack wrote the letter *for Mary*.
Mary diagonalized the matrix *for Jack*.

the *instrument case*— something used in the performance of the action:

Mary moved the rock with *a lever.*
Jack wrote the letter *with a pen.*
Mary diagonalized the matrix *with a computer program.*

the *source* and *destination* cases — where objects or information originated or ended up:

Mary moved the rock *from the gorge to the river bank.*
Jack heard the story *from Bill.*
Mary told the story *to Frank.*

and the *patient case*— an object affected in some way by the action:

Jack bought *the car.*
Mary diagonalized *a matrix.*
Jack wrote *a poem.*

While we have not been concerned with how a program is to decide in which case a noun phrase belongs, it should be clear from the previous examples that both sentence position and prepositions tend to indicate (or "flag") the relevant cases. For example, subject noun phrases tend to be agents, while both "to," as in "fly to Boston," and indirect-object position, as in "gave Mary the book," tend to indicate destination. Furthermore such flags tend to hold across verbs at a much greater than chance level. (Just review the previous examples.) Naturally, this is a plus for case theory, because it means that we will not have to repeat this information in the dictionary entry for each verb. As we will see, however, we do not have complete uniformity in this regard.

Also, by assuming the reasonable rule that no action may have a given case filled more than once, we can account for the oddness of sentences such as:

*The oven warmed Jack with a flame. (two instruments)
*Jack threw the catcher the ball to home plate. (two destinations)

(This rule has some problems, however. See Exercise 4.19.)

Despite these nice features, case grammar is nevertheless a controversial theory. Probably the major problem is the inability of people to, in fact, come up with a small set of cases that will work for all verbs. To take but a minor example of this, what case is the noun phrase "fifty dollars," in the sentence "Jack bought the car for fifty dollars"? Often it is considered to be in the instrumental case, since it serves as an instrument to the buying action. But is the "fifty dollars" "something used in the performance of the action"? To see that it is not, consider

Jack bought the car for forty dollars with a new fifty-dollar bill.

Here it seems clear that "a new fifty-dollar bill" is in the instrument case, but that "forty dollars" is in some other, yet undefined, case. Perhaps we can answer this one, but examples of this sort come up with depressing frequency.

But whether or not we can come up with a small number of such cases, the following statements do seem to be true:

- We need some way of representing the optional slots to verbs, and slot-assertion notation is a plausible method.
- Many slots of distinct verbs seem to relate to their verbs in semantically similar ways.
- In many of these, the same prepositions are used to express the relation in the surface structure.

One possible way out would be simply to keep most of the ideas of case grammar, but to relax the assumption that the number of cases is finite and small. The use of slot-assertion notation does not in itself commit us to case theory, and in those situations where we do have similar relations, we can use the same slot name. If, further, we have inference rules that give meaning to these names, then we have much of the substance of case theory without committing ourselves to a particular small set of cases. We will adopt this model.

Now let us return to the problem of building the internal representation of a sentence. In a sentence like "Jack slept in the house," our semantics would build up the sense of the sentence as follows. First we assume that the noun phrases "Jack" and "the house" will have been reduced to jack-1 and house-1 by the noun phrase semantics described earlier. The verb "slept" will contribute something like this:

(inst ?event sleep) ; *There is an instance of sleeping.*

(As you may have noticed, to keep things simple we are steadfastly ignoring the tense of the verb.) Next, the fact that "Jack" is in subject position says that he is the agent of the activity, giving this:

(agent ?event jack-1)   ; *It is Jack doing the event.*

(Really, however, not every subject of a sentence is the agent. See the next section.) As for the prepositional phrase "in the house," the "in" suggests location.

(location ?event house-1)   ; *The event happened in the house.*

Putting all three together results in this:

(and (inst ?event sleep)   ; *A sleeping event was*
     (agent ?event jack-1)   ; *done by Jack*
     (location ?event house-1)) ; *in the house.*

4.5.2.3 Determining Cases in a Sentence. In introducing our discussion of case grammar we mentioned two problems: one, the representation of arguments to a verb, we have already discussed; the other, how we tell our parsing system about which arguments of a verb go into which cases, we will discuss next.

Given a noun phrase argument to a verb, we want to identify its case. We have three particular sources of information, the verb, the noun phrase, and (if the noun phrase is in a prepositional phrase) the preposition. It is easiest (and most traditional) to think of the verb as determining the mapping between syntactic roles and cases. For each verb, we will indicate which cases it takes, how these cases are flagged (e.g., which preposition is used), and whether the case is optional or obligatory. For example, in "buy" the agent and patient cases are obligatory, while cases like source (e.g., "from Jack") are optional. The standard method of representing this information is with a *case frame*:

```
[buy agent = subject          ; e.g., Jack bought the ball.
     patient = direct-object   ; Jack bought the ball.
     {source} = from           ; Jack bought the ball from Bill.
     {cost} = for]             ; Jack bought the ball for one dollar.
                               ;
[fly {agent} = subject         ; Fred flew the plane.
     {patient} = direct-object ; Fred flew the plane.
     {source} = from           ; The plane flew from New York.
     {destination} = to ]      ; The plane flew to New York.
```

We use the "{}" braces to indicate optionality. We have also used the terms subject and direct-object as *pseudoprepositions* to indicate that something appeared in the subject or direct object position, just as from indicates that something appeared in a prepositional phrase headed by the word "from."

However, these examples ignore the comparatively ubiquitous cases, like instrument and beneficiary cases. These are optional here as well, but to include all of the optional cases would be rather time- (and space-) consuming. On the other hand, not all verbs can take an instrumental case:

*Ralph knew the story with a book.
*Ralph has a book with a rock.

While it would be possible to have every verb state its position on every case, it would be nice if we could get a more parsimonious representation. One possibility is based upon the common AI idea of an *isa hierarchy*. In Chapter 1 we saw how we could break the animal domain up into different levels of generality, and save space by expressing information at the right level. We can do the same thing here, but for verbs. Such a hierarchy is given in Figure 4.48. Here we have defined a very general notion of a *relation* which can be anything denoted by a verb. Then we have divided relations up into *stative* relations, like "to know" and *events*, which are things that take place over time. We also indicated what cases each class can take. The idea is that a verb in a lower class inherits the cases of the higher classes, making it unnecessary to constantly restate, "Yes, I can take a locative" (where *locative* is the case indicating location). There are a lot of exceptions to these general rules, but as with the standard isa hierarchy, we will assume that information put at the level of an individual verb will override the general information about a class of verbs.

We will assume from this point on that there is a function get-case of two arguments, the verb of the sentence, and the case indicator (either a preposition, or syntactic role, such as subject). It will have access to the case hierarchy in Figure 4.48 and will return the appropriate case for that case indicator.

```
-> (get-case 'fly 'subject)     ; The subject of fly
   agent                        ; is the agent of the verb.
```

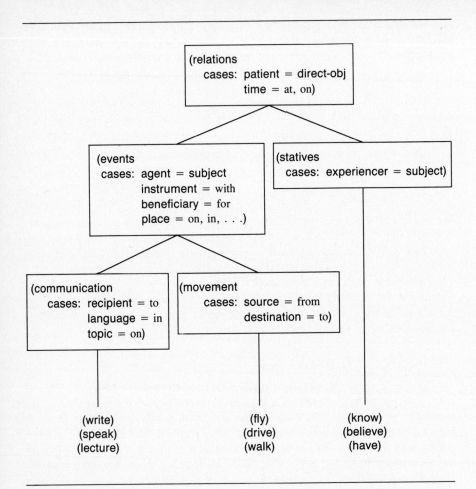

Figure 4.48 A hierarchy for cases

-> (get-case 'believe 'subject)	*; The subject of believe*
experiencer	*; is the experiencer*
-> (get-case 'speak 'on)	*; In "speak on . . ." the case*
topic	*; is the topic.*

See the next section for how **get-case** is used in the parser. (Exercise 4.20 suggests how such a function might be implemented.)

You may have noticed in Figure 4.48 that a given flag may indicate more than one possible case, even for a single verb. For example, "on":

Jack lectured on Lisp on Friday.

We could distinguish these by knowing that certain cases are expecting noun phrase fillers that refer to particular kinds of things. So the **time** case is expecting a filler that refers to a unit of time, while **beneficiary** is expecting an animate object, such as a person or pet. To add this ability to our model, we would first need be able to retrieve a fact like "the time case requires a time noun phrase," and then determine whether the noun phrase fits the requirements. We will not consider exactly how this could be accomplished.

4.5.2.4 Adding Sentence Semantic Functions to Our ATN (Optional).   To close this section, we need only sketch how the semantic mechanisms discussed earlier can be used to implement the case theory. Thus, for a sentence like

> Jack flew the plane to Chicago.

we want to get this representation:

```
(assert '(and (inst event-1 fly)          ; Assert that there is
                                           ; a flying event
              (agent event-1 jack-1)       ; with jack-1 as agent,
              (patient event-1 plane-1)    ; flying plane-1,
              (destination event-1 chicago-1)))  ; with chicago-1 as
                                           ; destination
```

Here **assert** is intended to be some Lisp function which adds a predicate calculus statement to the database. Here it will be asserting that there is some flying event **event-1** that has **jack-1** as the agent, and so forth.

To create this, we first need to create a "referent" for the action described by the sentence, in the above example **event-1**. Then after seeing the subject we need a function that will add an appropriate case statement to our sense. Figure 4.49 shows how this can be done. Note in this example **semantics** does not refer to the semantic function associated with the last word (as in all previous examples), but rather to the semantic function **subject***. To see how all of this works, take the example "Jack moved the block." Initially the parser will guess that the sentence is a statement and will create a referent for the sentence, say **s-3** (this is done by instructions which we have not shown). Then the parser finds the noun phrase "Jack" and the verb "move"; it gives

---

```
(def-net s (parse np)
           (semantics wait 'subject*)      ; Subject adds
           (parse vp))                      ; the subject np
                                            ; to the sense of the s.
                                            ;
(def-semantics subject*                     ;
  (add-sense $s                             ; Add to the sense of s
     '(,(get-case (the verb of the vp of $s) ; that the case for the
                  'subject)                  ; subject is filled
       ,(the referent of $s)                ; by the referent
       ,(the referent of the np of $s))))   ; of the subject np.
```

Figure 4.49 Adding semantic functions to the s network

internal names like np-3 and move-3, respectively, to these syntactic entities. Next it calls semantics of subject, which will give this:

(add-sense 's-3 '(,(get-case 'move-3 'subject) s-3 jack-1))

Then, if get-case says that the noun in the subject position of "move" is the agent, the result will be:

(add-sense 's-3 '(agent s-3 jack-1))

Naturally, we will need further semantic functions for verbs, direct objects, and prepositional phrases, plus the hooks in the ATN to call them. These are left as exercises.

4.6 When Semantics, When Syntax?

When we started our discussion of syntax, we noted that the decision to start with a syntactic parse was a controversial one. Let us now return to this controversy.

4.6.1 The Syntactic Use of Semantic Knowledge

If one looks back at the last section, the one on case grammar, there is an interesting bifurcation in its concerns. Primarily, we were interested in establishing the internal representation of sentences by seeing how the slots of the verb related to the verb itself. At the same time, some of the evidence we used had an almost syntactic ring to it:

*Ralph knew the story with a rock.
*Ralph fell down with a rock.

These were examples we used to illustrate the fact that not all verbs could take instrumental cases. But we can turn this around. By knowing which verbs take instrumental cases, we can account for the unacceptability of certain sentences. So are we doing syntax, or are we doing semantics? Probably the best answer is to finesse the question, and simply say that in the course of trying to parse the sentence we tried to establish the case of the prepositional phrase "with a rock" and had trouble. This trouble was reflected at a conscious level by the feeling that the sentence is unacceptable, for some reason or other.

There are many more examples where semantics seem to influence our syntactic processing. For example, let us consider again the transformational rule of *dative movement*, which was discussed earlier in this chapter. All we need to remember about this rule is that some, but not all, of the verbs that take a "to" prepositional phrase allow a sentence to be rearranged as follows:

Mary gave the book to Jack.	→ Mary gave Jack the book.
Jack told the story to Mary.	→ Jack told Mary the story.
Mary threw the ball to Jack.	→ Mary threw Jack the ball.
Jack dedicated the book to Mary.	→ * Jack dedicated Mary the book.
Mary set the words to music.	→ * Mary set music the words.

What is striking from our current viewpoint is that all of the prepositional phrases that can be moved by dative movement are ones that specify the recipient of the direct object. Furthermore, there are other prepositions that can also indicate the recipient case, and we find dative movement there as well:

Jack knitted a sweater for Sue.	→ Jack knitted Sue a sweater.
Sue bought the car for Fred.	→ Sue bought Fred a car.

Admittedly, not all examples of recipient allow dative movement, so we will still have to indicate **dative-movement** as a feature on particular verbs. Yet even so, the correlation is striking.

I produce the parts for XYZ Corp.	→ * I produce XYZ Corp. the parts.
John carried a book to Bill.	→ * John carried Bill a book.
Ross mentioned the news to Nadia.	→ * Ross mentioned Nadia the news.

What makes *dative movement* interesting is that a decision on whether or not a transformational rule may apply seems to rest, in part, on semantic information.

In examples like these, we interpret the failure of the required semantic relations to hold as creating an ungrammatical sentence. We can imagine implementing this in our ATNs by including the requisite semantic test, intermingled with the various syntactic tests. Should the semantic test fail, then we backtrack, and look for an alternative path. To be more concrete, consider again one of our examples:

*Jack fell down with a rock.

When we process "with a rock" we will be attempting to attach a prepositional phrase to our verb phrase, so we will be at the point in the **vp** network indicted by the arrow.

```
(def-net vp
    (category verb)                    ; vp → verb . . .
    (parse np)                         ; vp → . . . np . . .
    (optional* (parse pp)))  ←         ; vp → . . . (pp)*
```

We want to prevent ungrammatical sentences from getting through our ATN parser, so we can put in a check at this point looking to see if the verb of the sentence will take an argument in the case indicated by the prepositional phrase. With this modification, the **vp** net will look like this:

```
(def-net vp
    (category verb)                          ; vp → verb . . .
    (parse np)                               ; vp → . . . np . . .
    (optional*                               ; vp → . . . (pp)*
        (seq (parse pp)  ←                   ;
            (the verb of $vp takes           ; --------------------
             the case indicated              ; semantic check on case
             by $last))))                    ; --------------------
```

Here we have not worried about how this test would really be programmed. Nor have we considered how this would interact with the semantic routines for constructing the logical form.

However, many, if not most, semantic failures do not produce such a sharp feeling of ungrammaticality. Rather they push us toward one interpretation over another. To take a slight variation on an earlier example, consider the following:

I read an article about the war in the local paper.

Our tendency is to interpret "in the local paper" as modifying "read," and not "war." But we would hardly say that the sentence would be ungrammatical if it modified "war." Indeed, it is not too hard to make up a situation in which we would so interpret the sentence. For example, if we knew that there was a big dispute between the editor and the reporters of the local paper, we might talk about "the war going on in the local paper."

Or consider the two sentences:

Who did Fran give the flowers?
What did Fran give the boy?

Why is it that most people interpret the "who" as the receiver of the flowers in the first sentence, and not vice versa? It cannot be a syntactic fact, because the second sentence has the same syntactic form, but a different interpretation. Presumably it has to do with the fact that giving flowers to people is reasonable, but giving people to flowers is not. Thus we would be tempted to put checks in our ATN not only seeing if the verb can take a prepositional phrase (or direct object, or whatever) of the appropriate variety, but also looking to see if the argument to the verb is the right kind. So "give" might say that its recipient case must be filled by an animate being.

But these rules cannot be absolute, as were our rules of grammar. It is perfectly possible to say

Who did Jack give the dog?
What did Jack give the dog?

Dogs, it would seem, can serve either as the recipient, or the patient of "give." In the first sentence we assume that the "who" refers to a person, and thus the dog makes a *better* patient than does the person, and a *worse* recipient. Thus we would like our rule in some sense to compare the possibilities, and proceed with the parse that has the highest semantic rating.

The problem is how we can do such things within our ATN framework. Up until now a test, semantic or otherwise, returned either a yes or no. If the response was "no," then the test failed, and backtracking started. Now we seem to need responses like "well, I suppose so," or "not too good, but ok."

The solution to our problem is something we said in passing in our discussion of how ATN parsers explore paths when they reach a branch point in a grammar. Initially we did a depth-first search with chronological backtracking. We pointed out, however, that it would be perfectly feasible to do a breadth-first search. There is also a slightly more complicated possibility. Suppose we had associated with each partially completed parse on the agenda a number that represented how "good" the parser thought the partial parse was. How we assign such numbers is a separate issue, but the motivation is that they would reflect semantic reasonableness. Then every time we come to a choice point, we select the partial parse that has the highest goodness rating.

Assuming, then, that we had semantic tests that could provide such goodness numbers, the net effect would be that at any time we would pursue more plausible paths over less plausible ones. Or, to put it slightly differently, by allowing semantic tests to return a goodness number, rather than simply a "go/no-go" decision, we in effect allow comparisons between possible parses, with the most plausible going first.

With this in mind, consider our last examples:

Who did Jack give the dog?
What did Jack give the dog?

Suppose that we have a routine that given the verb and the proposed recipient, returns a number indicating how well the proposed recipient fits the requirements of the verb. Here "who" might rank a +5 since it presumably refers to a person. On the other hand "dog" might rank a 0, since it is animate, but not human. On the other hand, "what" would have a negative value, since it is presumably inanimate. While we will not go into any of the details, at some point in the first of these two sentences we should choose "who" as the recipient, while "dog" becomes the patient, simply because the parses that place these words in those positions will receive higher semantic ranking, and thus whenever the parser has to choose what partial parse to work on next, those will be chosen in preference over the opposite assignments. This sort of behavior has been called *semantic preference* by Wilks [Wilks75].

4.6.2 The Organization of Parsing

We started out by assuming that we initially apply syntactic information to the sentence to get a syntactic parse. However, it quickly became apparent that semantics had to play a role, and thus we opted for a model in which the syntactic parser often called semantic routines for guidance (although exactly how this would work we left vague). We adopted this model for several reasons, including the fact that it is the most popular parsing model within the AI community. There are competitors however. Of the competitors, the strongest is the model in which no distinction is made between syntax and semantics at all. There is instead one component that does the work of both.

We have already mentioned some of the issues that make such an integrated model appealing. Our ability to understand ungrammatical sentences is an obvious one. The ATN model presented here cannot understand ungrammatical sentences, because the discovery of an ungrammaticality will cause a failure, which in turn causes the grammar interpreter to back up, leading to no parse, and thus no internal representation.

To overcome this problem, people have been attempting to modify existing parsing mechanisms to allow for ungrammaticality. There are two general approaches. One is to loosen the reins of grammar by explicitly incorporating into the ATN grammar the ways sentences may differ from the strict grammar found in books. Another possibility is to keep the strict grammar, but modify the parsing mechanism so that if things cannot go through according to the strict rules, the rules are automatically relaxed until something can be done with the sentence. To give a quick hint as to how this could be done, remember that in the previous section we allowed semantic tests to return numbers rather than yes-no decisions. Suppose *all* tests did this. Normal syntactic tests would return very low numbers if the input did not match them, and thus would go to the end of the agenda, most likely never to be seen again. However, if the sentence were ungrammatical, then all partial parses will have suffered from one failed syntactic test or another, and the parser would be forced to continue on with the best of a bad lot.

However, ungrammaticality is just one problem. Another might be called *agrammaticality*, the property exhibited by "sentences" with no grammatical structure whatsoever. An example:

arson hotel explosion

Such strings of nouns are frequently easy to "understand," even though they supply not a scrap of syntax. Semantics must approach such examples without any syntactic unraveling.

The meanings of some sentences are only partially dependent on their syntax. For example, the following was heard on a radio weather forecast:

It's 45 partly cloudy degrees out today.

The phrase "partly cloudy" works fine as an adjective phrase, but it makes no literal sense modifying "degrees." Of course, none of us take "partly cloudy" as really modifying "degrees," but rather the weather in general. Thus we get a legal syntactic structure, but our semantics should, to at least some degree, ignore it.

In still other examples the meaning we finally get out of a sentence is directly opposite to what the sentence literally says. One such example, this time from a TV commercial, has an astronaut telling the viewer how good a particular manufacturer's airplanes are. He tells us:

> The airplanes of the XYZ corporation!
> I would not stake my reputation on anything less.

We are to understand the second line as saying that these planes are very fine, but strictly speaking, the sentence says that if they were the tiniest bit worse, he would not do the commercial.

> The impact of this textbook cannot be underestimated.

This may sound like a boast, but taken literally it is a rather damning comment.

Such examples speak clearly to the issue of enforcing a syntactic parse upon sentences, and make a combined syntax/semantics parser look attractive. However, there are alternatives. One is a model in which syntax and semantics are separate, but working in parallel. The advantage of such a model is that we would no longer have any problem explaining why we are able to do one (semantics) without the other (syntax), since the model assumes that this is, in some sense, the norm.

One particular method here is called the *blackboard model*. In this model, messages are left in a common area, called a blackboard, distinct from both syntax and semantics (and any other source of knowledge, like "context"). Probably the most famous program using this model is the Hearsay speech understanding program. (See Figure 4.50.) This program had many sources of knowledge, including acoustic and phonological information as well as syntax

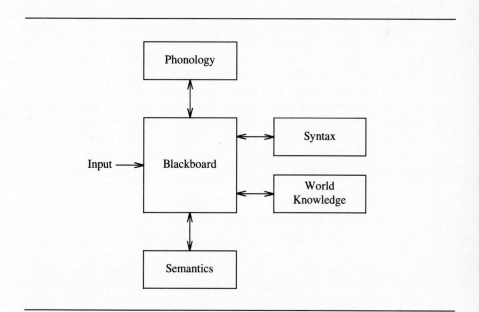

Figure 4.50 A blackboard model for language comprehension

and semantics. Each source of information would write its results on the blackboard, where other sources could see them and possibly extend them.

In practice, however, communication between knowledge sources was restricted. Most could accept messages from only one or two others, because it was not obvious how, say, acoustics could give anything meaningful to, say, context. In particular, and most importantly for our current discussion, the semantics component could accept messages from only one other component, namely syntax. Thus, in the Hearsay implementation, the blackboard model reduces to our previous interleaving model in which syntax calls semantics.

It should not be too hard to see why the program would be designed this way. If some "lower" source of knowledge such as phonology is to talk directly to semantics, then it means that semantics can "understand" such messages without the aid of syntax. But if this is the case, then what use is syntax? Well, we already know the use of syntax: it helps find the logical structure of a sentence. Thus, semantics would have to be able to determine the logical structure without syntax. We already know that this cannot be done in general (the passive construction was the example we used), but perhaps it can be done in some special cases. How this might be accomplished is a current area of research.

Box 4.5

Reversible Passives

One source of information on the relation between syntax and semantics in an overall model of parsing would be psychological evidence on how people do things. Unfortunately, the evidence is ambiguous, and psychologists are as much in the dark as AI researchers. To get a feel for what this evidence looks like, let us consider one well-known experiment, on *nonreversible passives*. Early experiments in the psychology of language seemed to show that passive sentences took longer to understand than active sentences. The experimenter would read sentences to the experimental subjects.

The cat chased the dog.
The dog was chased by the cat.
The dog chased the cat.
The cat was chased by the dog.

Then the subjects would be shown a picture of either the dog or the cat doing the chasing. The subject was asked if the sentence and picture corresponded, and the time to respond (the *reaction time*) was measured. It was found that the reaction time for the passive sentences was longer than that for the active versions.

However, Slobin [Slobin66] tried the same experiment, but distinguished two kinds of passives. On one hand there were the *reversible passives*, in which either noun phrase in the sentence can logically serve as the initiator of the action. The dog and cat examples above are of this type. On the other hand, *nonreversible passives* do not have this property. Some examples Slobin used were these:

> The girl watered the flowers.
> The flowers were watered by the girl.
> The man ate the watermelon.
> The watermelon was eaten by the man.

These passives are nonreversible because of the strangeness of these:

> The flowers watered the girl.
> The girl was watered by the flowers.
> The watermelon ate the man.
> The man was eaten by the watermelon.

The experiment showed that nonreversible passives took no longer to understand than their active counterparts.

The results of this experiment were a shock to many because the earlier work showing that passives took longer to understand had been interpreted as showing that people really do "untransform" sentences in their heads, and the extra time required for passive sentences was the time to untransform. But Slobin's work ruled this out. Furthermore, it seemed to suggest to some that people were using semantics without syntax to get the answer. However, clearly this is reading too much into the results. Remember that the experiment asked the subjects to say if the sentence matched the picture. Adult subjects make very few mistakes at this task. But if they were using only semantics, then in a sentence like "The man was eaten by the watermelon" the semantics would still have the man eating the watermelon, and they should get the matching question wrong. That they didn't suggests that the subjects did syntactic processing.

To summarize: Because people answered the questions correctly, they must have been doing some form of syntactic processing — at least enough to distinguish passive from active sentences. However, since non-reversible passives take no longer than active sentences, the time difference between active and passive for reversible sentences is probably not due to solely to the presence of extra syntactic processing. What does cause the difference is anybody's guess.

4.7 References and Further Reading

The study of syntax in its modern guise starts with Chomsky's classic *Syntactic Structures* [Chomsky57], and his equally influential *Aspects of the Theory of Syntax* [Chomsky65]. Now, however, there are any number of good textbooks that systematize this research, and the student interested in this work might start with one of these [Bach74, Keyser76, Perlmutter79]. Alternatively, you could just take a course from your friendly local linguistics department.

As mentioned in the text, there is little agreement among linguists about the form a grammar for English should take. To get some feel for the variety of grammatical formalisms currently under investigation, you might consult [Moravcsik80]. The renewed interest in context-free grammars for English has been sparked by the work of Gazdar [Gazdar81]. Most work on context-free grammars has been on computer programming languages. The parsing algorithms by Earley and by Cocke, Kasami, and Younger are for this application. See [Aho72] and [Hopcroft69] for details.

The ATN parsing method discussed here has its earliest roots in work by several researchers [Thorne68, Bobrow69]. However it was Woods [Woods72] who popularized the idea, and put it into the current form. The particular primitive rules, and the form of the English grammar, presented here do not stem directly from Woods's work, but rather are grounded in the work of Marcus [Marcus80] and some extensions to Marcus's work by Charniak [Charniak83]. The handling of syntactic features was patterned to some degree after that of Winograd [Winograd83]. This latter book is also a good guide to the varieties of ways in which syntactic theories have been incorporated into AI language processing work. Also, [Charniak76] contains several chapters on the relations between AI language work and syntactic and semantic theories.

The discussion of semantics derives from several sources. The most obvious is the work of Winograd [Winograd72], with influence from Woods [Woods68], Hirst [Hirst83, Hirst83a], and Montague (for whom the best introduction is [Dowty81]). Case grammar is the work of Fillmore. The classic work here is *A Case for Case* [Fillmore68]. The literature spawned by this article has been tremendous. A more recent article by Fillmore is [Fillmore77]. Bruce has written a survey article on the role of case grammar in AI. [Bruce75]. The use of the isa hierarchy in case grammar is taken from Charniak [Charniak81].

The most active opponents to the syntactic approach to parsing have been Roger Schank and his students [Riesbeck75, Riesbeck78, Schank80].

Exercises

4.1 It may seem odd that in Figure 4.15 the default value for the number and person of a noun is **3s** while for a verb it is everything *but* **3s**. Why should this be?

4.2 Write the program **dictionary**, which is illustrated in Figure 4.17. This program takes an (unevaluated) list of dictionary entries, each containing a word, and stores each entry as a property of the word it contains. Because a single word may be more than one part of speech, the program must actually store a list of entries on each word. That is, it must put on the word under the property **features** a structure of the following form:

```
( (part-of-speech1 root1 -feat-pairs1-)
  (part-of-speech2 root2 -feat-pairs2-)
  . . . )
```

For example, under "can" there would be:

```
( (modal nil (v-number = 1s 2s 3s 1p 2p 3p))
  (noun nil) )
```

Normally, the root section is nil as for the "can" example, but sometimes a dictionary entry may define a word in terms of a previously defined word, as with "do" and "did" in Figure 4.17. Then the root section will indicate what it is. In such cases, the features should combine those on the secondary form with those on the root. In case of conflict, the features on the secondary form should prevail. You may assume that roots appear before any of the secondary forms.

4.3   Write a program that, given a word (represented as an atom) finds the root word in the dictionary, and assigns features (e.g., plural) depending on the endings that were removed. You may restrict consideration to suffixes (that is, you need not worry about prefixes such as "un" in "unloving"). The output of your program should be an atom representing the word. Unfortunately, it cannot be the exact atom which came in. This is because a word like "blocks" can be both a noun and a verb, with different properties. While it is fine for our dictionary to say that it is both, within a sentence we need to know which role it plays. Therefore, the output of the morphology unit must be a list of new atoms, one for each part of speech that the word might be. (The box "Atoms in Lisp" specifies how to create these atoms.) Each atom should have the properties type, which indicates the part of speech, lex, which points to the original input word, root, which points to the root form (if different from the original input) and features, which has a list of features, in the same format as the internal dictionary. (See Exercise 4.2.)

4.4   The final version of the reflexivization rule given in Section 4.2.6.2 still has problems, in that it does not account for the use of "itself" in a sentence like "I locked the chain to itself." Explain why the rule does not work. Propose an alternative rule.

4.5   In the sentence "Jack washed his car," the "his" is called a *possessive pronoun*. There is a class of such pronouns that are like the typical possessive pronouns, but have the addition of "own" as in "his own" or "my own."

   a) Propose a transformational rule that will account for the use of "own" in sentences like "Jack washed his own car."

b) Relate this analysis to that for imperative sentences by considering the behavior of imperative sentences in which own-type possessive pronouns are used.

4.6   Consider the dative movement rule in Figure 4.40. Explain what each test of the rule does, and how it works overall. Hand-simulate our grammar on the sentence "Jack told Bill the story," where we assume "told" to have the feature **yes** for **dative**.

4.7   In our discussion of *aux-inversion*, we showed how it would enable the ATN to parse "Will the girl kiss Bill?" provided that it could parse "The girl will kiss Bill." Our current grammar cannot handle this sentence because it has no knowledge of the English *auxiliary system*, the auxiliary verbs that may precede the main verb. Fix this problem, at least for the case of "will" preceding the main verb. Presumably this should be an optional rule, and should go at the beginning of the **vp** network. There, before the **category** test for the verb, we insert an optional sequence starting with a test to see if the next input is a modal. If so we should then **peek** at the next input to make sure that it is another verb. Does the next verb have to have any special property? If so, have the grammar test for it.

4.8   Extend our ATN to handle passives. The passive rule given in our discussion of transformational grammar is a complicated rule because it has both rightward movement and leftward movement. To simplify matters, let us just consider passive to take the surface object and move it to the subject position. See Figure 4.51. Note that in the "reverse" version the deep structure would have no noun phrase in subject position. This might be odd, but it keeps the transformation simple to implement with our ATN. *(1)* Add to the grammar's knowledge of the auxiliary system by including early in the **vp** network a check for a form of the verb "to be" followed

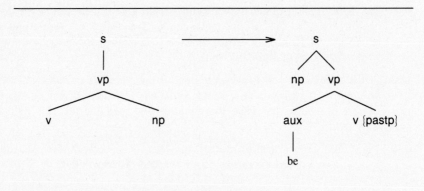

Figure 4.51 Simplified passive transformation

by a past participle. *(2)* If the grammar sees this construction it should also drop the np of $s into the input stream after the past participle. *(3)* Passive sentences require that their main verb be in the past participle form (above noted as pastp.) You may assume that the morphology unit will mark the incoming word as having a tense of pastp. This will be done before the ATN parser looks at it. As another simplification, note that it not necessary to actually modify the tense of the verb. In a real ATN parser the words would be marked with both the root form and whatever tenses were added on. Thus in some sense the words present are in ''both forms.''

4.9 In our discussion of transformational grammar, we noted that some wh-questions also show *aux-inversion*. Explain how well the grammar in Figure 4.40 will handle the following sentences:

> Who did Jack hit?
> Who hit Jack?
> Who will hit Jack?

(For the first and last of these, assume that our grammar has been extended to handle the declarative versions.) If it cannot handle one or more of these sentences, suggest how you might extend the grammar so that it can.

4.10 Explain how it is that our grammar of Figure 4.40 assigns *two* parses to the sentence ''Jack caught a fish.''

4.11 A *particle* is a preposition that combines with a verb, modifying its sense. For example, ''up'' is a particle in the sentence:

> (1) John looked up the phone number.

On the other hand, ''in'' acts like a normal preposition in:

> (2) John looked in the box.

The parse trees for these two sentences are quite different, as shown in Figure 4.52. The rule of *particle movement* allows a particle to move to later in the clause, for instances, sentence (1) may become:

> (3) John looked the phone number up.

We cannot, however, make (4) from (2):

> (4) *John looked the box in.

- a) Extend the grammar of Figure 4.40 to handle particles, as in sentence (1). The rule may be crude in that it need not ensure that the particle seen is one that can legitimately go with the verb.
- b) Will the extended grammar handle sentence (2)? Explain.
- c) Extend the grammar again to handle particle movement, as in sentence (3). (Again, don't worry about checking that the verb and particle match.)

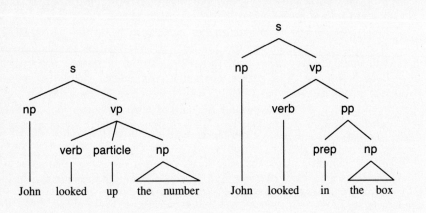

Figure 4.52 Particles and prepositions

4.12 We have already noted that enforcing subject-verb agreement will allow us
to understand

> The fish love Mary.
> The fish loves Mary.

as referring to many fish and one fish respectively. This is because the
word "fish" will have as its **person** property both **3s** and **3p**, meaning
that it can be either third person singular or plural. To incorporate
subject-verb agreement we need this rule:

> (= (the n-number of (the np of $s))
>   (the v-number of (the verb of $vp)))

a) Put this into the appropriate place in the grammar of Figure 4.40.
   Hint: Because of the limitations on $, there are only certain places
   where it even is legal to place the above test.

b) The rule in (a) assumes that the subject noun phrase has an **n-
   number** feature. The grammar of Figure 4.40 does not give it one.
   Extend the grammar so it does.

c) This rule will fail on imperative sentences, which, as we have
   already noted, have tenseless verbs. Naturally, these will not agree
   with the subject, but we do not want this to prevent these sentences
   from being parsed. Modify the Figure 4.40 grammar to take this
   into account.

4.13 Write a semantic function for the word "big."

4.14 Why do we have adjectives wait to impose their meaning on the sentence
until after the head noun is seen as opposed to doing it immediately, or

only after the constituent is finished? (That is, why do we have (**semantics wait $last**) in the adjective portion of our ATN.)

4.15 Define a semantic function for the word "Jack." It will use **retrieve-val** to enable it to find **jack-1** as the referent of the noun phrase "Jack," provided that it knows the fact

   (name jack-1 Jack)

Add the necessary call to **semantics** to the ATN grammar.

4.16 The semantics for our ATN cannot handle a word which has two parts of speech, and a different meaning for each, such as "can." Why not?

4.17 In our discussion of more complicated semantic functions (Section 4.5.1.3) we described one for the word "toy," as it is used in the phrase "toy"elephant. Write this function, and associate it with "toy." (To make this work with our current grammar we will have to assume that "toy" is an adjective. Of course, in phrases like this, it is really a noun, but modifying our parser to handle nouns modified by nouns would be difficult.)

4.18 Discuss what changes would be necessary to handle the syntax of Exercise 4.17 properly. This is an open-ended problem in that it is unlikely that you will come up with a solution that is completely general. Whatever modifications to our grammar and semantics you suggest, show how they will or will not handle similar examples of nouns modifying nouns.

4.19 In our discussion of case grammar, we suggest a rule that a sentence may only specify one filler for any given case. This rule is not problem-free. Try to construct reasonable-sounding sentences that seem to break the rule. At the same time, suggest how a defender of the "only one filler rule" might try to respond. Rank your examples as to how difficult it would be to "explain away" the supposed counterexamples.

4.20 In Section 4.5.2.3 we suggested how the case of a noun might be determined from its role in the syntactic structure and information about the verb. For the semantic routines to take advantage of this theory, you will need to program a few things. First, design data structures to represent the various verb classes, which cases they can take, the default indicator for each case, and how one class relates to the other in the isa hierarchy. Presumably these will be property-list structures. You might consider writing a function that takes some simplified notation, such as the one used in Figure 4.48, and creates the appropriate property-list entries. Also, write the function **get-case**, which takes two arguments, a verb and a case indicator, and produces the name of the appropriate case. Eventually, **get-case** will be called from within semantic functions that hook noun phrases to verbs. Assume that the ATN does not hand over the actual preposition or actual verb to **get-case** but rather nodes of the parse tree, which have the words "hanging off them." The reasons for this were noted in Exercise 4.3 As specified there, given a terminal node of a parse tree, the associated lexical item can be found on the **lex** property of the node. If the lexical item has a root form that differs from the surface form, as "moved" is the surface form of the root "move," then the root can be obtained from the **root** property.

4.21 In Section 4.5.2.3 we saw that different cases required that their fillers have certain semantic properties. In fact, things can get even more complicated than this. Give examples that demonstrate that the same case may have different semantic requirements for different verbs. Also show that in situations in which two prepositions may be used to indicate the same case, they can nevertheless be restricted to fillers with slightly different semantic properties.

4.22 Write semantic functions, and modify the ATN, to handle the following sentences.

> Jack flew the plane to Chicago.
> Jack moved the block to the table.
> Jack told the story to Mary.
> Jack moved the red block from the table.

This will require you to do the following:

a) Write a semantic function **object*** that will be like that for **subject*** given in Section 4.5.2.4, and add a call to this function to the ATN.

b) Do the same for prepositional phrases, and for particular prepositions such as "to," "from," and any others you might wish to handle.

c) Write a semantic function **statement*** which bundles up the sense created by the sentence, and adds a call to **assert** the existence of the action. Modify the ATN to call this function.

d) Add any other semantic functions for words that do not have one yet, such as "table," "story," and "Mary."

4.23 We said at the outset of our work on semantics that it would be necessary to deal only with the context-free portion of our grammar, and the transformational part would take care of itself. Verify that you did the last exercise correctly, by showing that your ATN automatically handles the semantics of dative movement sentences like

> Jack told Mary the story.

4.24 Add capabilities to convert the following sentences into the internal representations given:

You moved the block. (assert '(and (agent move-1 me)
                                                    (inst move-1 move)
                                                    (patient move-1 block-1)))

Move the block. (do-it '(and (agent move-2 me)
                                                    (inst move-2 move)
                                                    (patient move-2 block-1)))

Did you move the block? (retrieve-val '?s
                                                       '(and (agent ?s me)
                                                           (inst ?s move)
                                                          (patient ?s block-1)))

What did you move? (retrieve-val '?what
                                                    '(and (agent ?s me)
                                                           (inst ?s move)
                                                          (patient ?s ?what)))

In the second example, do-it is intended to be a call to a planner and executer, such as described in Chapter 9. It is not the intent here that you produce *exactly* this output. Rather the output you produce should have predicate calculus statements with the same meaning as the above. Thus the order of the conjuncts is irrelevant, as are the variable names. Also the constant names we used here (e.g., block-1, move-1) are arbitrary, so they may be different as well.

4.25 In our discussion of the influence of semantics on syntax, we showed semantic regularities governing which verbs could undergo *dative movement*. On the other hand, we ended up saying that the semantic regularities did not account for all of the facts, and thus we would still have to mark which verbs triggered this rule. It might be argued that because we need to mark a verb yes for dative-movement anyway, the semantic regularities are pointless. Construct a counterargument by showing that the marking on the verb is not sufficient, and that one must also check that the thing moved is the recipient of the direct object.

4.26 In our discussion of case grammar, we suggested the need for a routine that would decide on the case for a noun phrase, based upon the verb, the place in which the noun phrase appears in the sentence, etc. On the other hand, in our discussion of the relations between syntax and semantics we casually added a semantic check to our pp network that would ensure that the verb accepted a case indicated by the preposition. Discuss the relations and interactions between these two routines.

4.27 A fellow student comes to you with the following question.

I understand why we need to go from English to our internal representation. But when you look at the ATN and the associated semantic functions, it seems to be the semantic functions which are doing everything. They find out the cases for things, put everything into the correct logical format, etc. Why do we even need the syntax at all?

Give a brief answer.

5

Although we recommend that this chapter follow either Chapter 3 or Chapter 4, there is little in Chapter 5 that depends on the specifics of either. One exception is Section 5.3.4 which discusses search in ATN parsers. This can be skipped if Chapter 4 has not been read. Chapter 5 is needed primarily for its discussion of goal trees, which come up again in Chapters 6, 9, and 10. The discussion of Strips in Chapter 9 depends on the section here on GPS.

Search

5.1 Introduction

5.1.1 The Need for Guesswork

Some of the most interesting problems in AI have the frustrating property that there is no good way to solve them. It often happens that, although the solution can be generated piece by piece, a partial solution falls apart and some or all of the work to get it must be redone.

As an example, consider the problem of scheduling the activities of a mobile robot. A good schedule will (say) leave the robot idle as seldom as possible, or keep its travel time below some threshold. The activities to be scheduled involve initiating processes at various spatially separated workstations; and coming back to attend to them periodically. There may be deadlines to meet [Miller83].

At first glance it might be hard to appreciate how difficult the scheduling problem can be. A rule like "go next to a work station near where you currently are" would seem to work wonders. But by itself it could lead to problems, as Figure 5.1(a) shows. In this diagram we are looking down on the workplace. The various workstations have times specified when the activity located there must start. (We will assume that each task can be done in ten minutes and that the time to get from one to another is negligible.) In Figure 5.1(a) going to the nearby workstations will mean missing the deadline on the workstation in the right-hand corner. On the other hand, a simple rule like "go next to the work station whose deadline is next" will lead to inefficiencies in Figure 5.1(b). Here the robot would cross the workspace several times, when a nearest neighbor policy would have worked fine.

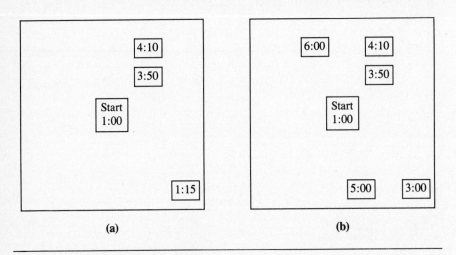

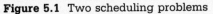

Figure 5.1 Two scheduling problems

So simple rules will not work. In fact, much work has been done on scheduling, but except for some special cases, such problems are thought to be *intractable*. That is, as the size of a scheduling problem (as measured by number of activities or the like) increases, the number of possible schedules to consider, and hence the time required to find an optimal schedule, increase exponentially. This phenomenon is called *combinatorial explosion*. More precisely, consider any algorithm which will solve all scheduling problems. With this algorithm we can associate a function ke^n such that for all integers n there is a problem of size n (that is, n things to schedule) that requires at least ke^n steps for this algorithm to produce the schedule. The exact shape of the function is immaterial; the point is that it grows too fast for us to hope to ever build a computer that can solve all problems of size n for any substantial n.

Note the loophole: for any n, *some* problem of size n will be exponentially hard to solve. Suppose such problems never come up in practice. Then a practical algorithm may be possible after all. That is, the *expected-case complexity* of a problem may be much less than the *worst-case complexity*. Unfortunately, "expected-case" is not a precisely definable term the way "worst-case" is. Consequently, most studies of expected-case complexity are empirical. You write an algorithm and see if it works.

Many of the intractable problems have the feature that a series of correct guesses would suffice to solve them. (There are problems that are even worse. For them guessing does little good because just confirming that the proposal is a solution would take too much time.) In our scheduling example, if you picked the first activity, then the second, then the third, and so on, and at the end the travel time was below the desired threshold, you would be done. Of course, there is no way in general to guess right, but a lot of AI programs are based on doing better than chance. The theory of such guessing is the theory of *search*.

5.1.2 Search Problems

At this point, we will introduce the standard terminology. A *search problem* is characterized by an *initial state* and a *goal-state description*. The "guesses" are called *operators*: a single operator transforms a state into another state, which we hope is closer to a *goal state* (a state satisfying the goal-state description). The objective may be to find a goal state, or to find a sequence of operators to a goal state. In addition, the problem may require finding just any solution, or an *optimal solution*: the "best" solution, measured some way. Sometimes we are not sure whether there is any solution; the object is then to search until a solution is found or we are satisfied that no solution exists.

We will use the term *successor of S* to mean a state S' reachable from a state S by a sequence of operator applications. If the sequence is of length 1, that is, if S' may be reached from S by applying one operator, then S' is said to be an *immediate successor* of S. (Sometimes rather than talking of S' being reached immediately from S we will say that S *generates* S'.) The set of all states that can be reached by applying operators in sequence starting at the initial state is called the *search space*. The scheduling problem may be thought of in this way. The initial state is "nothing scheduled," the goal state description is "completely scheduled with not too much travel time planned," and the operators add one more activity to the schedule. The search space is the set of all schedules. Traditionally a search space is diagrammed as a tree with the initial state at the top and a state connected to its successors by lines. The search space for the scheduling problem presented in Figure 5.1a is given in Figure 5.2. In this figure the boxes indicate schedules of what to do 1st, 2nd, etc. It is instructive to see how large a space is created by such a small problem. There are 120 (5!) possible schedules for the tasks in Figure 5.1b.

A commonly cited class of search problems is *puzzles*. For example, in the "missionaries and cannibals" puzzle, the problem is this:

> Three missionaries and three cannibals are trying to cross a river. As their only means of navigation, they have a small boat, which can hold one or two people. If the cannibals outnumber the missionaries on either side of the river, the missionaries will be eaten; this is to be avoided. Find a way to get them all across.

The initial state has all the travelers on one side of the river and the goal state description has them all on the other. In this case, the goal state is described by being specified completely and the objective is to find the sequence of moves that gets to the end. By contrast, in the scheduling problem the objective is a good schedule and the sequence of moves that gets to it is of little interest.

This distinction, between searching for a state and searching for a path, is important to remember in writing programs, but is of little theoretical significance, so we usually neglect it. This is because the path can always be included in the state. For example, in the missionaries and cannibals problem, a program which searched for the goal state could be made to remember the path

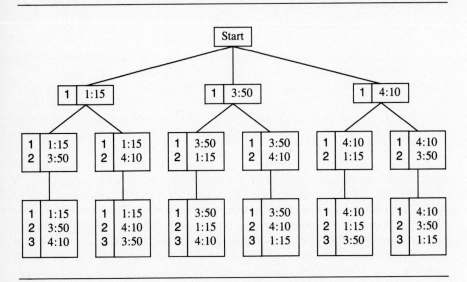

Figure 5.2 Search space for a simple scheduling problem

by changing the definition of the state to include not only who was where, but also the steps taken so far. The latter would be modified each time a step was taken.

The distinction between programs that find any solution and those that find an optimal solution is more interesting. We will talk about it briefly later.

Another example of a search problem is a *memory search*. Here the initial state is a place or set of places to start looking for something in memory, and the goal-state description is a description of a piece of information. The search takes place in a memory structure of some kind. For example, if something unanticipated occurs, you might want to search for a previous time when something similar happened [Schank82]. Consequently, an operator takes the form of a movement from one part of the structure to another ("pointer chasing"). The search space is potentially the whole of memory. An example is given in Figure 5.3. There we are looking for a memory of your losing to your spouse in some competition. We have limited the diagram to some of the more profitable places to look. (There are a lot of assumptions about the nature of memory implicit in the diagram, none of which we care to argue about.) Memory searches are formally like other searches, with the twist that we can design the memory structures to make anticipated searches as cheap as possible. (We will talk more about memory searches in Chapters 7 and 11.)

In the rest of this chapter, we will look at algorithms for attacking search problems. In Section 5.2 we will look at the most general case. Later, we will examine special cases that come up, in which there is more structure given to the operators or the search space.

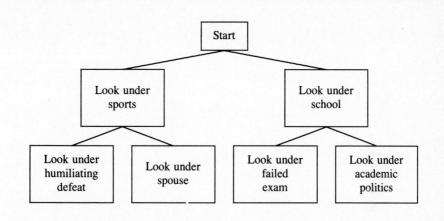

Figure 5.3 Memory search for a time when you lost to your spouse

5.2 A Search Algorithm

In addition to the bare formal specification of a problem, we must have some *hints* to make it tractable. There are two sorts of hint:

1. An *operator-ordering function* (often called a *plausible-move generator*): an algorithm that orders the applicable operators at each state from best to worst.
2. A *state-evaluation function*: an algorithm that gives the estimated distance of each state (usually as a number) from the nearest goal state.

In each case, the function is not guaranteed to be accurate; it can order the operators incorrectly, or call a worse state better. But it ought to do better than chance to be of any use.

We will see uses for both of these kinds of hint. But, for the time being, the second is easier to deal with. An operator-ordering function can go badly wrong if unaided by a state-evaluation function, since once it gets off the correct path there may not be any way back. (To take an extreme example, suppose you want to find someone's house, and you have no address but only a list of places where you should turn. If there is a mistake in the list you will never find the place.) Furthermore, an operator-ordering function can be simulated (at least in principle) by classifying operator A as better than operator B if the state that A leads to is closer to the goal than the state operator B leads to, as measured by the state-evaluation function.

A state-evaluation function gives us a chance to revise our estimates later. In Figure 5.4 we have several snapshots of a search. The nodes in the tree have the numbers returned by the state-evaluation function when applied to that node. The node with the doubled box in each snapshot is that which looks the best at

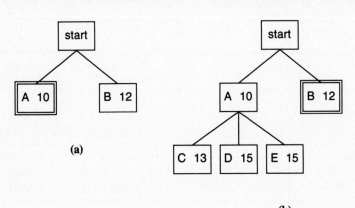

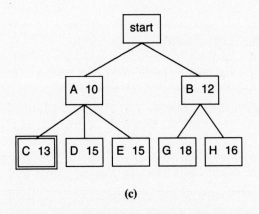

Figure 5.4 Search tree with state evaluation numbers

that point. Since the numbers are the estimated distance to the nearest goal node, the lower the number, the better the state. In Figure 5.4(a) we see that node A looks better than node B. Thus it makes sense to start exploring from A first. If the evaluation function is right, then pushing on from one of A's successors will wind up justifying the rosy assessment at A, but in Figure 5.4(b) we see that the estimate at A has proven to be wrong, because it leads to states that look worse than B. Consequently, the search algorithm should go back to B and try again from there. What if B's estimate was too rosy also? Suppose, to be specific, that some state reachable from A, say C, looks better than every state reachable from B. Then the machine should switch back to C. This is what we see happening in Figure 5.4(c).

In fact, the guiding principle should be to keep track of the most attractive state as states are generated. On each cycle, operators should be applied to that state, and the resulting new states sorted by evaluation-function values. So long as the new most attractive state is an immediate successor of the previous one, the algorithm pursues a single path through the search space. However, the algorithm can at any time switch back to any previously generated state, so long as it looks promising. The phrase *heuristic search* is often used to describe an algorithm of this kind. A *heuristic* is a "rule of thumb" used in problem solving. This kind of search is called heuristic search because the evaluation functions are typically based upon heuristics, and are thus often called *heuristic evaluation functions*.

As a concrete example, consider the problem of coloring a map with a set of *n* distinct colors, such that no two adjacent countries have the same color. For our purposes, a map is a list of lists of country names such that the first element of the list is the name of a country and the rest of the list has all the countries adjacent to this country. For instance, the table

```
((hackiland mungolia conswana brackot)
 (mungolia hackiland conswana predico kalkuli brackot)
 (conswana hackiland mungolia brackot predico)
 (predico mungolia conswana brackot kalkuli)
 (kalkuli mungolia predico brackot)
 (brackot mungolia kalkuli predico conswana hackiland)))
```

is one representation of the map shown in Figure 5.5.

Colorings are represented as lists of pairs: ((*country color*) (*country color*) . . .). For the map of Figure 5.5 if the colors to be used are red, white, green, and yellow, then one legal coloring is this:

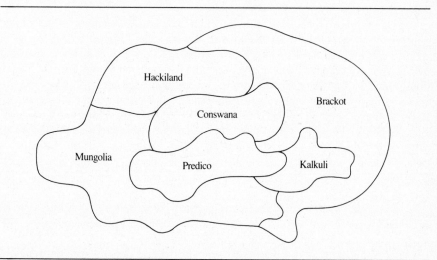

Figure 5.5 A map to be colored in four colors

```
((hackiland yellow)
 (mungolia red)
 (conswana green)
 (predico yellow)
 (kalkuli green)
 (brackot white))
```

There is no coloring of this map with fewer than four colors. Of course, there is a famous theorem that any map can be colored using no more than four colors, but it applies only to maps that can be drawn in the plane. Our list representation allows adjacency graphs that do not correspond to any drawable map. By making the map complex, and limiting the number of colors, it is easy to pose coloring problems with no solution.

Every known method for finding map colorings involves search. To cast the problem in our terms, we choose as our states partial colorings, that is, lists that assign colors to some of the countries. The initial state is obtained by picking an arbitrary color for some country, for instance, ((hackiland yellow)). (This will save some search in the case where there is no solution.) Each operator adds one more color assignment to a partial map. In many cases, there will be no legal operators to apply. For instance, in the map of Figure 5.5, this partial coloring

```
((hackiland yellow)
 (conswana red)
 (predico white)
 (kalkuli green))
```

cannot be extended, because any choice of color for brackot would leave it adjacent to a country with the same color.

The simplest state evaluation function would use "number of uncolored countries" as the measure of distance to a goal state. Figure 5.6 shows what might happen if we used this state evaluation function to search for a coloring. The search was stopped when one was found. Both countries and colors are abbreviated to one letter in the figure. Each node indicates the color assignments at that point, and the value of the state evaluation function. As often happens, a human looking at the tree can see "obvious" stupidities in the evaluation function, which gives the same score, 3, to ((h y)(c r)(p y)) and ((h y)(c r)(p w)), even though the latter "wastes" a color. Exercise 5.3 suggests that a better function would take the number of color options available into account. If a function like this had been used, the search would have been shorter than that of Figure 5.6.

We could write a program to color maps, but it is more revealing to write a general-purpose search function that can be given information about any particular problem. We give this algorithm in Figure 5.7.

To apply search to a particular domain, several domain-specific functions need to be provided.

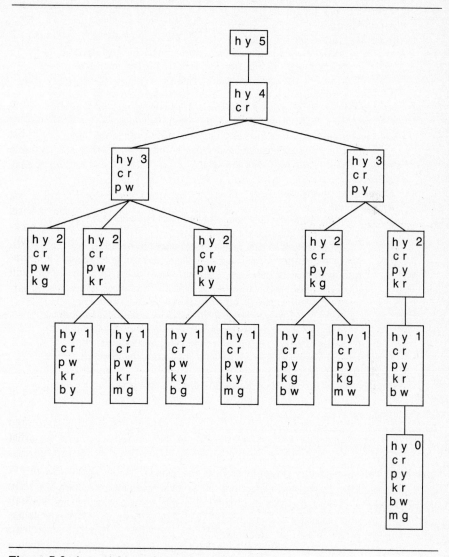

Figure 5.6 A partial search tree for a map coloring

- **goal-test**, a function that tests whether a state is a goal state.
- **successors**, a function that applies all operators to the current state **expl**, returning all the new states.
- **estimator**, a function that takes a state, and returns (as a nonnegative number) the estimated "distance" from that state to the nearest goal state.

These functions are passed as arguments to **search**. For those of you not familiar with Lisp it may seem odd to pass a function as an argument to another

Function: search
Arguments: start — the initial state.
            goal-test — a predicate that returns t only for goal states.
            successors — a function that returns a list of immediate
                       successors of a state.
            estimator — a function that estimates the distance to the
                    nearest goal state. It should be zero for a goal
                    state itself, and higher for anything else.
Local vars: queue — a list of states along with their cost. These are
                states that are generated, but not yet explored.
            expl — the next state to explore
Algorithm:
   queue starts out empty
   expl ← start
   Loop: Until the goal-test function says that expl is a goal state,
          in which case return expl as the answer.
          Use successors to find the successor states to expl
          Apply estimator to each successor state, and merge them into
          queue so that the best state is at the front of queue.
          ; (If the queue had states with values (3 17), and the successors
          ; of expl had values (2 33), the resulting queue would be
          ; (2 3 17 33). Remember that the numbers are estimated distance
          ; to a goal state, so low numbers are better than high ones.)
          If queue is empty, break out of the loop, and indicate
          failure, since we have not found a goal state, and there is
          nothing left to do.
          expl ← first member of queue (which is removed
                    from queue).
   Endloop.

Figure 5.7 The algorithm for search

function. This is perfectly possible in Lisp and Box 5.1 talks about how this is done. An analogy might be instructions on a washing machine which say "Do the following . . . and for the next step, see the instructions on the item of clothing." In both cases we are combining instructions from two different places into a single "program" to be executed.

This is a good place to say a few words about finding optimal states and paths. In general, being able to find just any goal state may not help at all in a search for an optimal state. Having found one, you might have to keep going until you found all of them, keeping track of the best so far. However, it is quite common for the evaluation function to encode, not just the distance from the goal, but also the goodness of the solution. Since we have been using lower numbers for better states, let's pose the optimization problem as one of minimizing the "cost" of a state rather than maximizing its "goodness." Then the number associated with a goal state is how much worse it is than the best possible goal state. Now, if we have an evaluation function that can return a good estimate of the "expected cost" of the nearest goal state instead of the distance to it, we can use **search** without change to find optimal or near-optimal solutions.

It is proved in [Hart68] that if the state-evaluation function is accurate for goal states, and never too high (i.e., never thinks the goal state aimed at is worse than it really is) for nongoal states, then the solution is guaranteed to be optimal. In brief, the reason is that **search** will never be fooled into persisting on the path to a suboptimal solution, because eventually (if only when a suboptimal goal state is reached), the state on the optimal path will have a lower estimate. (See Exercise 5.7.) This theorem is usually not as useful as it sounds. In many cases, it is hard to guarantee that the estimation function is always low enough, without making it too low. After all, taking the estimate as zero guarantees that the optimal solution will be found, but only at the cost of examining the entire search space. (See Exercise 5.8.) It is often more efficient to forgo optimality, and use an evaluation function which occasionally overestimates a little.

In some cases, there may not be any useful evaluation function, or the search space may be so small that a brute force approach is better than anything clever. In this case, the approach is to search the space systematically. There are two basic methods: *depth-first search* and *breadth-first search*.

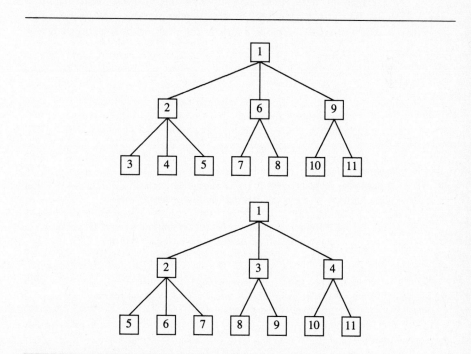

Figure 5.8 Breadth-first and depth-first search

The algorithm in Figure 5.7 kept track of the possible places to search from by using a queue. The queue was sorted according to the estimated cost of a solution. Now we will not have any such values. Depth-first search, or *backtracking*, corresponds to putting new states on the front of the queue, that is, managing it "last-in/first-out." This means that if two states *S1* and *S2* are produced by applying operators to a state *S*, then every state reachable from *S1* will be examined before any reachable from *S2* (unless some are reachable from both). If there are an infinite number reachable from *S1*, then *S2* will never be examined. In this case, some kind of *depth cutoff* can be imposed, that is, a maximum length of operator-application sequence that will be tried. We saw depth-first search used in the ATN parser of Chapter 4. Sometimes the phrase *chronological backtracking* is used to refer to the case where the searcher backtracks only to the most recent state, and the term "backtracking" is reserved for the general case in which once an obstacle is encountered, the searcher may abandon the current state and return to an earlier one, not necessarily the most recent, at which a choice was first made that made the obstacle inevitable. In practice, however, almost all backtrackers are chronological.

Breadth-first search corresponds to always putting new states on the end of the queue, that is, managing it "first-in/first-out." This is called "breadth-first" because it examines all states that are *n* operator applications from the initial state before any that are $n+1$ away. Unlike depth-first search, it has the property that it will eventually explore every state, even without a depth cutoff.

Function: rsearch
Arguments: expl — the state to be explored (initially the root state).
  goal-test — a predicate that returns t only for goal states.
  successors — a function that returns a list of immediate
      successors of a state.
Local vars: queue — a list of states generated, but yet unexplored.
Algorithm:
  If goal-test says that expl is a goal state, then we exit.
  Else   queue ← the states returned by successors when
       applied to expl.
    Loop: Through all members of queue until there
        is nothing left on queue (in which case return
        failure, since none of the successors was on a
        path to a goal state).
      Try rsearch on next member of queue.
      If it returns success, break out of loop and return
        the answer just found.
    Endloop.
  Endif.

Figure 5.9 The algorithm for depth-first search

Figure 5.8 shows a search tree with the order in which states are examined indicated by the numbers in the boxes.

One reason to prefer depth-first in spite of this is that it is simpler to implement. This may seem surprising given the simple symmetry between them, but the "last-in-first-out" character of depth-first search enables us to dispense with the queue altogether, and use a stack. (A *stack* is a sequence of elements that can be altered only by adding a new element at the front, or removing the element at the front.) Because many programming languages use a stack to keep track of function calls and their variables, we can implement depth-first search using the stack itself, and produce a recursive version, like that shown in Figure 5.9.

In many cases this simplicity makes depth-first search the right method, but only if the infinite-search problem can be neglected. It can be neglected only if the search space is finite, or if there are so many goal states that one is likely to be found quickly.

Box 5.1

Functions as Data in Lisp

Functions are defined in Lisp by saying (defun *fun-name* . . .); variables, by saying (setq *var-name* . . .). One can think of both of these operations as assigning a name to something (an algorithm or a data structure, respectively). So why have two distinct operations?

The main reason is historical. When Lisp was first invented (see Box 2.1), the concept of function in programming was poorly understood. Although it was clear that *fun-name* was the name of something, it was less clear what that thing was. Also, it seemed as if the things you could do with functions were quite different from the things you could do with numbers and list structures. The latter could be created, passed as function arguments, altered, combined, and returned as the values of functions. Functions, it appeared, could only be called. Nowadays, it is becoming increasingly clear that it is quite useful to be able to do with functions almost everything you do with any other data type. Newer Lisps have begun incorporating this new viewpoint.

The first step in making functions "first-class citizens" is to make it possible to create one without naming it. (After all, we don't have to give a name to (+ 2 2) when we evaluate it.) The usual notation for such a function is

(lambda (-*args*-) *exp*)

as in (lambda (x y) (cons y x)). This is a function that takes two arguments, x and y, and returns the list obtained by consing y onto x. Lambda is the way Lisp represents the Greek letter λ. (This notation for algorithms is descended from the λ-calculus discussed in Chapter 6.)

All Lisps have some variant of the lambda notation. In fact, functions in Lisp are translated internally into a lambda expression. We saw this in Section 2.17 when we asked Lisp to prettyprint a function, and there was a lambda in it. So you might think that (defun *name args -body-*) would simply be an abbreviation for

(setq *name* (lambda *args -body-*)).

In very modern Lisps (such as Scheme or T) this is exactly the case. Unfortunately, most Lisps are not very modern (including Franz, the version we adopted in Chapter 2). We will start by ignoring this fact. At the end of this section we will mention how more traditional Lisps differ from the ''ideal.''

Since the name of a function is a variable which is bound to the function itself, the evaluation of a function call in Lisp has a very simple form. For example, consider what happens when we ask Lisp to evaluate (cons 1 nil). In Chapter 2 we noted that the arguments 1 and nil would be evaluated (giving 1 and nil, since numbers and nil both evaluate to themselves). Now we want to point out that cons is also evaluated — it evaluates to the function for making a cons cell. When viewed in this light, all of the symbols in a function-call are evaluated, not just the arguments. So for modern Lisps the following would be possible:

```
->(setq foo cons)          ; Foo is set to the function for consing.
{cons}                     ; Functions have funny print names.
-> (foo 1 '(2))            ; Try using foo.
(1 2)                      ; It works just like cons.
-> (setq l (list cons car)) ; Anything can be evaluated to get the
({cons} {car})             ; function, not just atoms.
-> ((car l) 1 '(2))        ; This is ok since (car l) = cons.
(1 2)
```

With this in mind, let us again consider the search function whose algorithm is shown in Figure 5.7. This function requires four arguments: an initial state, a goal tester, a function to produce the successors of a state, and a function to evaluate the goodness of a state. Three of the four are functions. To use search we must supply it the necessary functions. For example, a map-coloring program using search would have the following form:

```
(defun map-color (map colors)
    (search (list (list (caar map)      ; Pick as the initial state
                        (car colors)))  ; one country-color binding.
            (lambda (state) . . .)      ; This is the goal test
                                        ; function.
            (lambda (state) . . .)      ; A successor function.
            (lambda (state) . . .)))    ; A state evaluation
                                        ; function.
```

Actual Lisp code for search is given in Figure 5.10. In particular, note

```
(defun search (start              ; The initial state.
               goal-test-fn       ; A predicate which returns t
                                  ; only for goal states.
               successors         ; Returns a list of immediate
                                  ; successors of a state.
               estimator)         ; Returns a non-negative number
                                  ; which is the estimated distance
  (loop                           ; to the nearest goal state.
    (initial (queue nil)          ; List of alternatives generated
                                  ; but not explored. Each is of
                                  ; the form (value state).
                                  ; state:queued gives the state.
             (done nil)           ; value:queued gives the value.
             (expl start))        ; The next state to explore.
    (until (:= done               ; Loop until we find a goal
              (goal-test-fn expl)))  ; state.
    (do (setq queue               ; Find the successors of expl
             (state-merge         ; and sort them by how well
                (state-sort       ; the estimator thinks of them.
                   (successors expl)  ; Then merge them into the
                   estimator)     ; queue.
                queue)))          ;
    (while queue)                 ; When the queue is empty, stop.
    (next (expl (state:queued     ; Otherwise take the next state
                 (car queue)))    ; from the front of the queue.
          (queue (cdr queue)))    ;
    (result                       ; If done is non-nil we reached
      (cond (done expl)           ; a goal state, so return it,
                                  ; otherwise return the winning
            (t nil)))))           ; state.
```

Figure 5.10 The search algorithm in Lisp

the treatment of the functional arguments. For example, to get the successors of the current state, we have (successors expl). This makes use of the fact that Lisp will treat successors like a variable and expect it to evaluate to a function. If we have called search properly, it will be a function (of one argument), and everything will work just fine. Also notice that search uses two subfunctions that have yet to be defined: state-sort and state-merge. Exercise 5.18 asks you to write them.

As we noted at the start of this discussion, not all Lisps treat function definition on a par with variable assignment. In such Lisps we must remember two things. First, a function name or lambda expression does not evaluate to the function itself. Thus

(search (lambda . . .) . . .)

will not work. The lambda expression must be quoted using a special quote function called function. Thus one would say this:

```
(search (function (lambda . . .)) . . .)
```

The same goes for the name of a function like car. To pass car to the function foo one must say (foo (function car)) and not simply (foo car). The second thing to remember in such Lisps is that only function names may appear in function position — variables, or anything else which evaluates to a function may *not* appear there. Rather one must use the special function funcall. Hence one cannot say (successors expl) (where successors is a variable) as we did in search. Rather one must say this:

```
(funcall successors expl)
```

The function funcall expects its first argument to evaluate to the name of a function, and then uses that function on the rest of the arguments.

There are further complexities that are bound up in all of this. For example, if you pass a function which has a free variable in it, what will the value of this variable be when the function is called? There are two obvious possibilities. It could have the value at the time it was called (this is called *dynamic scoping*) or it could have the value at the time the function was defined (this is *static scoping*). In Chapter 2 we noted that Franz Lisp has dynamic scoping. Dynamic scoping is easier to implement efficiently, but it is generally agreed that static scoping supports more interesting programming styles. However, this gets us into considerably more advanced topics.

5.3 Goal Trees

In this section, we will look at a special case of the general search problem, which arises in searching goal trees. A goal tree describes a situation in which a goal can be satisfied by solving subgoals. If there is more than one method available, an algorithm may have to try several before finding one that works. This brings about a search problem. See Figure 5.11.

Each subgoal may have several pieces, *all* of which must be satisfied, in a consistent way. For example, consider a goal tree for dating. The tree might look like Figure 5.12. First, you have your choice of dating Pat or Terry. Then you must pick dinner and entertainment. To solve the entire problem, you must please your date and spend less than one hundred dollars.

The nodes of a goal tree are of two types: or nodes, which represent choices; and and nodes, which represent simultaneous goals that must have compatible solutions. The tree ends at *success nodes*, which solve the smallest chunks of the problem. For example choosing La Crudité solves the problem of dinner with Terry. Note that there are more possible ways to please Pat than Terry. In fact, since Terry insists on expensive pleasures, there is no solution to the problem of pleasing Terry for less than $100. We could take him or her to La Crudité or to a musical, but we must do both to satisfy the goal "please Terry." So the top choice must be Pat.

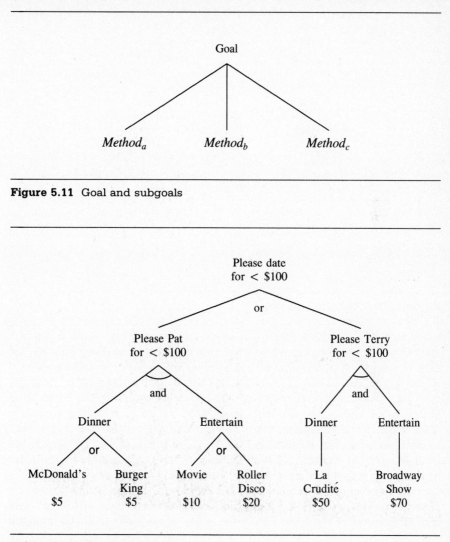

Figure 5.11 Goal and subgoals

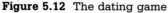

Figure 5.12 The dating game

5.3.1 Formal Definition

To revert to formalism, the general goal tree looks like Figure 5.13. We will use letters to denote **and** nodes, numerals to denote **or** nodes, and these will be concatenated in the obvious way. So the leftmost node in the tree will have the name **a1a1 . . . a1**. The top node has name **0**. The *children* of an **and** node, the nodes just beneath it, will be assumed for formal purposes to be **or** nodes, and the children of **or** nodes are **and** nodes. This requirement is not

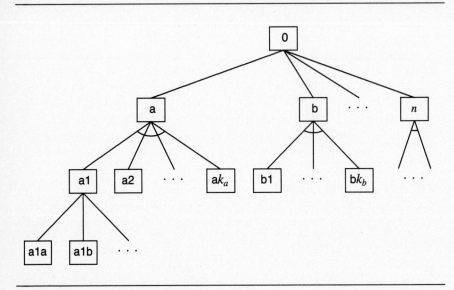

Figure 5.13 Schematic goal tree

too important, because two **and**s in a row can be trivially collapsed, as can two **or**s. In informal examples, we will feel free to violate this requirement for the sake of clarity. A *descendant* of a node is either its child or a descendant of one of its children. The tips of the tree are usually **and** nodes with no children; they are always considered satisfied, and are called *success nodes*. For completeness, we allow **or** nodes with no children, but there is no way to satisfy them; they are called *failure nodes*. Every nonsuccess **and** node has a *constraint* associated with it, C(*node*), which is a function of the solutions to its children. (In our example, "spend less than $100" is a constraint.) If all the constraints in a goal tree are "vacuous," that is, satisfied by any solution at all, then the tree is a (pure) *and/or tree*. We define what it means for a node to be *solved* recursively. An **and** node is solved if all of its children are solved, and their solutions obey the constraint on the node. An **or** node is solved if any of its children are solved. The goal tree is solved if its root is solved.

Here are some examples of goal trees:

1. Map coloring can be thought of as a goal-tree search, in which the goal tree is just two levels deep: there is one **and** node at the top (every country must be colored), and one **or** node beneath it per country (the choice of colors). The constraint at the top is a conjunction of adjacency constraints.

2. Proving a theorem may be thought of as engendering a goal tree. Here the goal is the theorem to be proved. There may be more than one approach to proving it, so it is an **or** node. Each approach may require proving several lemmas, so it is an **and** node. Each lemma is an **or** node

all over again. The leaves of the tree are goals that are identical to axioms (things that don't have to be proved). A solution corresponds to a proof. We will say more about this topic in Chapter 6.

3. Memory searches often produce goal trees. If you need to find an episode in memory in which, say, you were at a party with strangers, you are trying to solve an **and** node like that in Figure 5.14. Finding a party could be an **or** node if there are several places to look for parties. A solution is an episode or object with all of the desired properties.

4. Turning a memory representation into words ("natural-language generation") can be thought of as a goal tree with goals like those in Figure 5.15. For goals like "generate topic" there are several choices how to proceed, so these are **or** nodes.

The constraint at each node is that the lower pieces be stylistically compatible, and that everything be spoken that needs to be. E.g., if the memory structure expresses the idea that "Turing proved this theorem," and "This theorem" is spoken as the "topic" of the utterance, then the predicate must contain the rest of the information (and be in the passive voice). A complete solution is an intelligible utterance.

5. Going the other way, turning natural-language utterances into memory structures can also be thought of as a goal-tree search. The ATN of Chapter 4 is an example. This is a top-down parser, which tries to analyze the sentence as an S, which may be done several ways. One way is to analyze it as an NP followed by a VP. We can think of this as an **and** node, with the constraint that the part of the sentence analyzed as an **np**, when concatenated with the part analyzed as a **vp**, gives the string we

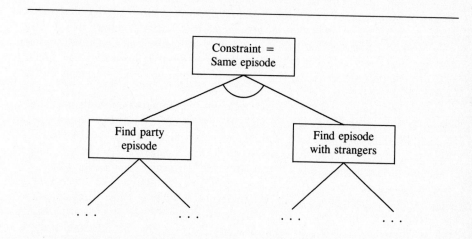

Figure 5.14 Memory-search goal tree

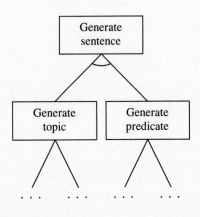

Figure 5.15 Natural-language generation

started with. (There will be other constraints, such as subject-verb agreement.) In general, or nodes arise from eithers and optionals, and and nodes from seqs. We will talk about this more in Section 5.3.4.

5.3.2 Searching Goal Trees

We said at the outset that all of the search algorithms we would look at would be special cases of **search**. At first blush it would seem that this cannot be true. Looking at **search** from our current perspective, we see that it dealt only with or nodes. There was nothing in it to handle cases where all of the children of a node had to be solved. Nevertheless, our original statement holds. As surprising as it may seem, it is possible to recast goal tree searching so that **search** can handle it.

To see how this is done, consider again the dating game problem of Figure 5.12. As is shown in Figure 5.12, the states are actions to be performed. Sometimes these are high-level actions, such as "please Terry" and sometimes they are lower level constructs like "go to the movies." Now let us change things so that the states are not actions to be performed, but rather plans. A plan here will be a tree structure showing things that the planner intends doing to accomplish the topmost goal. A version of the dating game using this new version of the state space is shown in Figure 5.16. So the plan on the bottom left of Figure 5.16 shows us again pleasing Pat by going to McDonald's and a movie. The topmost node in the tree has no plan at all, while the leaf nodes are complete plans. In between we have partial plans in greater or lesser states of completion. In the case of Terry, the tree stops with a partial plan, because there is no complete plan that obeys the constraints.

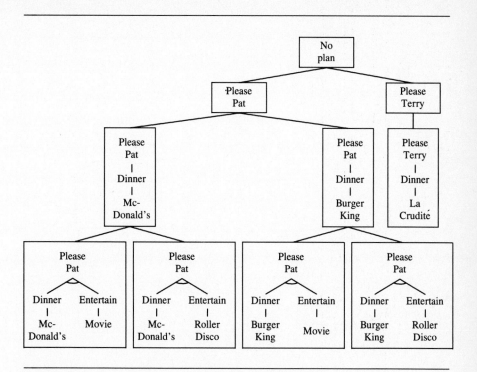

Figure 5.16 Searching through plans for a date

What is crucial from our current perspective is that the tree in Figure 5.16 has only or nodes. The and nodes have gone into the plans. Thus by searching through a space of plans (rather than of actions) we have reduced our goal tree to a normal search space. Having done this we can then apply search as before.

5.3.3 Formalism Revisited

The transformation we performed on our plan goal tree can be performed on any goal tree. To see how this is done, let us again revert to formalism.

To make it clear that we are considering more general objects than simply plans we will talk of *solutions* and *partial solutions*. A *partial solution* to a node *n* is a subtree rooted at *n*, with the property that if it contains an or node *m*, then it contains exactly one child of *m*. A *complete solution* to a node *n* is a partial solution to *n* with the property that if it contains an and node *m*, then it contains every child of *m*, and the solutions to the children satisfy C(*m*), the constraint at *m*. A solution to the entire goal tree is a complete solution to its root, 0. Partial solution *s2* is an *extension* of partial solution *s1* if *s1* is contained in *s2*; that is, *s2* is a tree with all the nodes of *s1*, but with zero or more extra choices made.

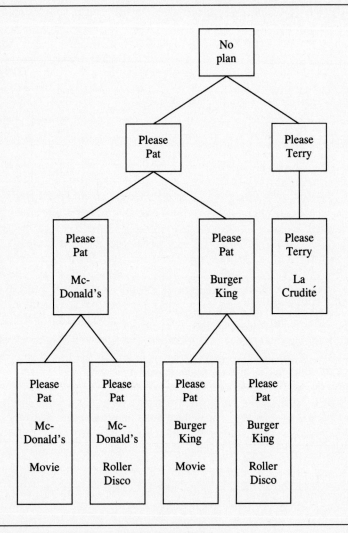

Figure 5.17 Nonredundant revised dating game

The point of these definitions is that we can now define our new search space as a space of partial solutions to the goal tree. The children of a node are those extensions of the node in which exactly one more choice is made. Consider again the revised dating game of Figure 5.16. The node that has "please Pat" is an extension of the "no plan" node and it makes exactly one more choice — that of Pat over Terry. Similarly, the node beneath it with "Burger King" chooses Burger King over McDonald's, and the leaf node with both "Burger King" and "Movie" makes still one more choice.

Actually, the nodes in Figure 5.16 contain redundant information. The elaborate tree structures in the nodes of Figure 5.16 make it clearer what the plan is, but are not really needed. All they really need contain are the choices made. Redone in this style the tree would be Figure 5.17. We should also point out that there are really more possible extensions of the **and** nodes (e.g., "please Pat") than we have indicated. We have only indicated extensions that make choices for the leftmost conjunct (e.g., "dinner"). There are also extensions that make choices for the others (e.g., "entertainment"). In Figure 5.17 and Figure 5.16 these get made after the dinner choices. Thus all the possible plans are covered. As we will note later, the order in which they are generated can sometimes drastically affect the size of the search.

Going back to the general case, consider Figure 5.18. We will use the notation $n:\{l_1, l_2, \ldots, l_k\}$ to refer to the tree rooted at node n and terminating at **and** nodes $\{l_1, l_2, \ldots, l_k\}$ This notation is akin to our last version of the dating game in that it omits the tree structure at each node, and just gives the choices which were made. In this notation, one partial solution to **0** is **0:{a}**. One partial solution to node **a** is **a:{a}**. Another is **a:{a1a, a2b, a3a}**. A complete solution might be **a:{a1a1a, a1a2b, a2b, a3a}** provided that the solution **a1a:{a1a1a, a1a2b}** satisfies the constraint **C(a1a)**, and the entire solution satisfies **C(a)**. In this sequence of three partial solutions to **a**, each is an extension of the previous one; the transition from **a:{a}** to **a:{a1a, a2b, a3a}** makes choices **a1**, **a2**, and **a3**; the next transition makes the further choices **a1a1** and **a1a2**.

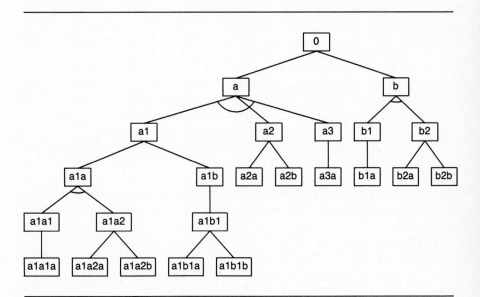

Figure 5.18 Example goal tree

It is important to recognize that a goal tree is an abstract object, not necessarily represented explicitly in the computer. It may often be infinite. Finding
a solution set may be quite difficult.

One way to think about a partial solution is in terms of two things: choices
made so far, and choices left to make. When the second set is empty, the solution is complete. By "choices left to make," we mean "choices you are committed to making by the choices made so far." For instance, in Figure 5.18 the
partial solution 0:{a, a1a, a3a} requires you to make choices at a1a1, a1a2,
and a2. No other choices are forced.

The map-coloring problem discussed earlier may also be thought of as
keeping track of a set of partial goal-tree solutions. At any state, there is a set
of countries colored so far, and a set of countries left to color.

The explicit recording of remaining choices introduces new possibilities
into goal-tree search. One needs an estimate of the distance to a solution and
these recorded choices might be able to provide one. The simplest possibility
would be to say that the more choices to be made, the further the distance to a
solution. For the map coloring problem this would say that one should work on
solutions with more countries colored before ones with fewer.

A better idea is to try to estimate the *difficulty* of the remaining choices.
In some goal tree problems, there is no way to test the constraint at a node until
a complete solution is available for it. But in many cases, it is possible to detect
a constraint violation in advance. For instance, in the map-coloring problem, as
soon as two adjacent countries have the same color, the constraint has been
violated. There is no need to color the remaining countries.

One way to think about this is in terms of choices being *narrowed* by previous choices. Consider the node a in Figure 5.18. The choice of, say, a1a as
the way to solve the a1 node may eliminate some of the choices at the *siblings*
of a1. (Two nodes are *siblings* if they are children of the same *parent*.) That
is, it may be the case that for some choice for a2, say a2a, there is no complete solution to the goal tree that includes a1a. If this is the case then a1a
eliminates a2a as an option. As a more concrete example, in the map of Figure
5.5, once Hackiland, Conswana, and Predico have been painted red, white, and
blue, respectively, all of these choices are eliminated for Mungolia.

If good estimates are available for the number of remaining alternatives at
each remaining choice, then it may make sense to work on the choice with the
fewest remaining alternatives. In the case where the estimate is zero or one,
this is certainly true. In the zero case, if the estimate proves to be accurate,
then the partial solution cannot be extended to a complete solution, and must be
abandoned. In the case where a choice has exactly one alternative, we may as
well take it now; this may constrain other alternatives more quickly.

5.3.4 ATN Parsing as a Search Problem (Optional)

As a more elaborate example, consider the operation of an ATN (such as
we described in Chapter 4) on a grammar with these two rules:

s → np vp
s → aux np vp

(The second rule is for interrogative sentences, of course.) These rules correspond to the goal tree shown in Figure 5.19. Of course, for a reasonable grammar, the entire tree would be infinite, because every English sentence would occur as a complete solution to it. Consider the state of a parser, having made the initial choice of np vp instead of aux np vp. This commits it to two further choices: what kind of np is there, and what kind of vp? The neglected choice, aux np vp, may be thought of as alternative partial solution; it must be saved, because the sentence might actually begin "Will . . .." In this case, the choice we made will eventually lead to a situation in which no further choices are possible.

In Chapter 4 we also considered ways of searching through the space of partial solutions. It is instructive to consider the same problem from the formal search perspective we have developed in this chapter. Our ATN uses backtracking, or depth-first search. For the cases of goal trees, this means that the next partial solution explored is always an extension of the previous one, if there is one. If there isn't, the ATN backtracks to the most recent choice point, and tries an alternative extension.

Other search regimes are possible. Using breadth-first search would mean that all extensions to a partial solution were investigated "in parallel." Having devoted some attention to the np-vp option, it would switch off to explore aux-np-vp, and so on for all other choices.

We also brought up the idea of using semantic guidance for the syntactic search. This would correspond to giving search a state-evaluation function.

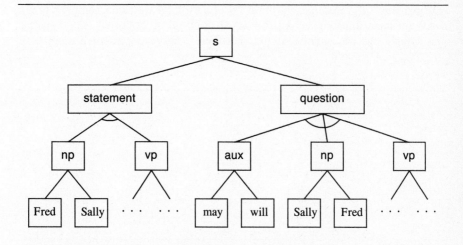

Figure 5.19 Goal tree corresponding to a simple grammar

Recall that such a function had two alternative interpretations — as an estimate of the distance to the nearest goal state, and as an estimate of the cost of the nearest goal state. Suppose that the cost we try to measure is the "semantic implausibility" of the sentence. As the sentence structure emerged, parses that made little sense could be marked as costly, and left at the end of the queue; the ATN would concentrate on partial solutions that made more sense.

Another degree of freedom that we have not yet exploited is whether to parse left to right or in some other order. Consider the grammar rule np → np *and* np; a noun phrase may be made of two conjoined noun phrases. When this rule is used, it sets up three subgoals: find a leading noun phrase, find "and," and find a trailing noun phrase (see Figure 5.20). Suppose that there is no conjunction in the rest of the sentence. Then our ATN could spend a lot of effort finding a lead noun phrase for this rule, only to die for want of a conjunction. An alternative is to first look for the conjunction. Viewing Figure 5.20 as simply a goal-tree search, there is no constraint on the order in which the conjuncts are tried. Admittedly, the normal tendency in parsing is to go left to right, but this is a case where another order would make a lot of sense.

We noted earlier that a partial solution could be thought of as the choices made so far plus the choices still to make and that one could let the number of choices remaining be an estimate of the distance to the solution. This idea has a direct application to ATN parsing. For example, the np network will specify that a noun phrase will have zero or more adjectives. By taking the route which says "there will be an adjective," the ATN adds another choice it needs to make (i.e., the choice of adjective). By equating number of choices to path length, we cause the ATN to try simple sentence constructions before more complex ones (e.g., a sentence without an adjective before one with an adjective). By and large this is a reasonable strategy, and most ATNs use it in an informal way. For example, in the ATN of Chapter 4 we can accomplish pretty much the same thing by saying that at all **optional** or **optional*** choice points first assume that the optional stuff is not there. However, equating number of

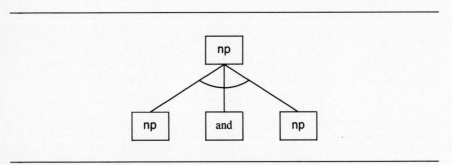

Figure 5.20 A conjoined noun phrase as an **and** node

choices to distance is quite a crude measure. Whether better measures exist for ATNs is not known.

5.4 Game Trees (Optional)

One application of goal trees is to find moves in games, like chess, in which players take discrete turns, and each move leads to a completely predictable, finite set of states. A *game tree* is a tree of alternative courses of play of a game of this kind. See Figure 5.21. Note that the node labels take the viewpoint of a character "me" playing a character "you." The purpose of this is to find out what move the "me" character should make next. Because "you" will be trying to make moves which foil me, I will have to consider your possible responses to my move, and how I can counter them. Thus one can think of the problem as not simply one of deciding on the next move, but rather one of finding a *complete strategy* for winning the game.

5.4.1 Game Trees as Goal Trees

The tree in Figure 5.21 resembles a goal tree. In fact, it *is* a goal tree, a pure and/or tree, to be exact. And just as the goal of a planning goal tree was finding a plan, the goal of a game tree is to find a complete strategy for winning the game. At the leaves of the tree (let's assume it's finite) are final positions in the game, where "I" have either won or not won. A complete strategy is a cookbook telling what to do at every position, or rather, every position that the strategy doesn't rule out. (If the strategy says to play move a first, then we

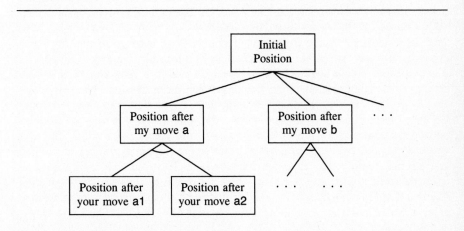

Figure 5.21 A game tree

don't have to think about what we should have done if we had taken move b.)
More formally, a complete strategy is a subtree with the same root as the whole
game tree, such that exactly one branch is selected at "my" nodes, and every
branch is included at "yours." (The strategy must anticipate anything you might
do.)

Clearly, this is syntactically isomorphic to the definitions for goal trees;
"my" nodes play the role of ors, and "yours" the role of ands. There is a
semantic equivalence, too. We can think of a game tree as an attempt to *prove*
that "I" can win. At "my" nodes, it suffices to find one move that can be proven to work; at "yours," we must show that all of your moves fail to stop me.
So a complete strategy can be thought of as a proof that the game is won. (If
there is no strategy guaranteed to win, it is easy to search instead for a
guaranteed draw.)

This would be little more than a curiosity, except that many game-playing
computer programs actually manipulate trees like this. For interesting games
like chess, the tree is too huge for us to consider actually exploring the whole
thing. Instead, moves are explored down a few levels, and then an evaluation
function is applied to judge how "good" the position is. We will call this an
incomplete game tree. (The typical games under discussion are board games, so
the evaluation function is often called a *static board evaluator*.)

It is traditional to have "me" striving for high-rated positions, and the
opponent for low-rated ones, so we can switch to the usual terminology in the
literature, and give the names *MAX* and *MIN* to the two players. (MAX
represents the computer's point of view; this assignment reverses our earlier
convention by which the search routine was trying to find low scores.) The word
ply is used for the levels of a game tree; one move by MAX and one by MIN
make two ply. If we had a really good evaluation function, that is, an absolutely reliable measure of which board positions were better for MAX, we
wouldn't need to explore more than one ply ahead; the correct move would
always be the one that leads to the best position.

Unfortunately, such evaluation functions are hard to come by. For
instance, in chess, we might rate a position by material advantage. But then a
queen sacrifice would always look terrible after one ply. The hope is that such
errors can be compensated for by looking ahead more than one ply. (It is not
easy to explain exactly why this will help; indeed, cases are known where looking ahead further makes estimates worse. But, intuitively, it seems like examining the consequences of moves couldn't hurt, and practice bears this out.) We
will use the phrase *lookahead depth* to refer to the maximum number of ply that
are generated before the evaluation function is applied. Of course, if a position
is encountered before this depth at which the game has ended, the evaluation
function should be applied there (and, of course, it should return a large positive
value if MAX has won, a small negative value if MIN has won, and zero if it is
a draw).

Now, if MIN were cooperating with MAX, instead of opposing him, the
best move would be the one that led to the best position, the one with the
highest value. Unfortunately, the move that leads to the best position could also

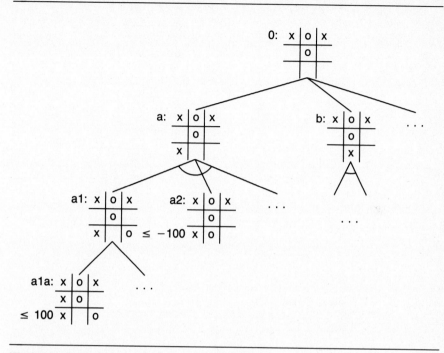

Figure 5.22 Fragment of tic-tac-toe game tree

lead to a terrible position, since the position depends as much on MIN's choices as on MAX's. What we really want is the move that leads to the best position, assuming MIN does her worst.

The *value* of a complete strategy is now defined as the *least* value of any leaf node in the subtree representing that strategy. (That's because the strategy leaves open only MIN's moves, and she can be assumed to pick the worst values for MAX.) The *optimal strategy* is then the complete strategy with the highest value. We will refer to this value as the *minimax value of the tree.*

Note that complete game trees are just a special case of incomplete ones, in which every terminal board position is labeled, say, 100 (win for MAX), 0 (draw), or −100 (win for MIN). An optimal strategy here is one with value 100, if possible, else 0.

To find an optimal strategy, we can use a goal-tree search algorithm in which the estimated value of a partial solution is the value of the least leaf node included in it. For example, Figure 5.22 shows a fragment of a tic-tac-toe (naughts and crosses) game tree, while Figure 5.23 shows the search space corresponding to the game tree of Figure 5.22. Let us first consider the game tree in Figure 5.22. It is MAX's move at node 0, playing x. Consider the move "lower left-hand corner," which leads to position a. If MAX makes this move, MIN has several possible replies, all of which should be considered. One is to put a naught in the lower right-hand corner. This leads to position a1. For this

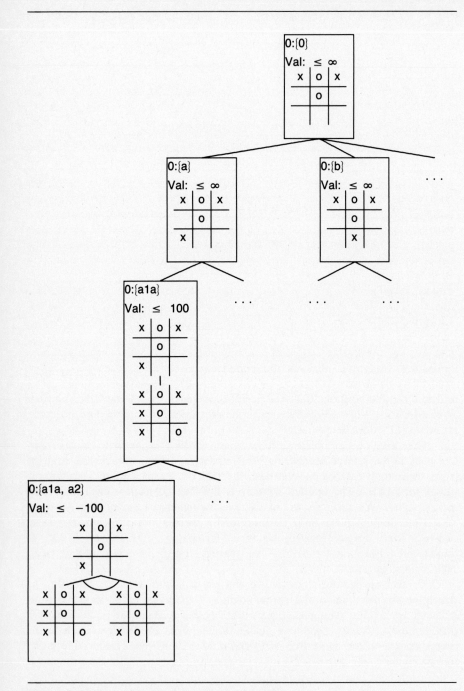

Figure 5.23 Search space for a tic-tac-toe game

MAX has a very good reply, namely, the center-left box. This is position **a1a**, and since it is a win for MAX it suggests a high positive value. But MIN has other possible responses to the move **a**, and before MAX can decide to move there these must be considered as well. One is the move to the bottom-center box, which leads to a win for MIN, and a very low negative value for that board position. At this point the move to **a** is not looking so good.

Now let us consider the same exploration, but from the point of view of the *strategy tree* in Figure 5.23. (We will call search trees over strategies *strategy trees*.) The choice of the lower left-hand corner for MAX, which leads to position **a** corresponds to the partial solution 0:{a} in Figure 5.23. This partial solution contains no leaf nodes, so we give it a ranking of ∞. Actually, we give it a value of $\leq \infty$. The high value ensures that the machine keeps working on it until a leaf node is encountered. The $\leq$ covers us in the very likely case that our opinion will not stay this rosy. The next layer is an **and** node, so we must pursue this strategy for each of the opponent's replies. At **a1**, we contemplate her playing in the lower right-hand corner. Sure enough, MAX wins at the next level, generating position **a1a**, with value ≤ 100. Again, the value is ≤ 100 since MIN may have other choices which will be better (and thus lower the score). This value becomes the value of partial solution 0:{a1a}, and it dominates all other partial solutions obtained by making other choices at **a1**. Unfortunately, we must include in the partial solution what to do if MIN plays in the center of the bottom row (position **a2**). Here there are no further choices; the position is worth ≤ -100. This value is lower than 100, so ≤ -100 becomes the new value of the partial solution 0:{a1a, a2} and the machine loses interest in this partial solution. Unfortunately, the algorithm will continue to check extensions of 0:{a}, even though none will do any better. While in the next section we will consider improvements to our search scheme, without adding more knowledge of tic-tac-toe there is nothing to be done about this particular bug.

By the way, note a subtle change in the meaning of "solution" in going from complete game trees to incomplete trees with position-value estimates. In the latter case, we are looking for optimal solutions, instead of "just any" solution, so it sounds like the answers would be more valuable. Actually, the opposite is true, because the optimal solutions are solutions to a less interesting problem, namely, "Find the apparently best strategy," rather than "Find a guaranteed winner." In each case, we are looking for a "complete" strategy, that is, an exhaustive recipe for what to do at each board position but, of course, the tree no longer represents a complete game. In the previous case, having found the complete strategy, no further thought was necessary. Now, the strategy is complete only with respect to an incomplete tree. Having made the first move, and gotten the opponent's reply, we usually regenerate the entire tree; this is because we will now be looking ahead two more levels, so we may get completely different values for the evaluation function.

5.4.2 Minimax Search

While there are many ways to improve the efficiency of game-tree search procedures, most of them involve adding more knowledge of the game. There is, however, one general method of improving game-tree search, and this has to do with making better use of the values associated with the partial strategies.

Improving the search means considering fewer of the logically possible strategies. The class of algorithms we will discuss in this section are called *minimax search algorithms*. Roughly speaking, they allow the searcher to skip over possible strategies in two cases. The first of these is in Figure 5.24. In this tree there is no need to look at the rightmost branch. Since MIN has the choice of where to go from node b, she can do no worse than get a score of 12 if MAX chooses b. Since MAX is guaranteed 23 if he chooses a, it would be silly of him to choose b. Therefore the final strategy for MAX will not include b, so there is no point in investigating the consequences of such a choice.

The other case where nodes can be skipped over is the converse situation, shown in Figure 5.25. Here MIN would not choose to go to a2 since the choice of a1 guarantees that she will do no worse than a score of 12, while at a2 she can do no better than 25.

While search does not do exactly what we want in either case, it does come close. To see how this comes about, look at Figure 5.26, which is the strategy space representation of Figure 5.25. There in each box we have shown the choices made (in our standard notation), the value of the strategy, and a number indicating the order in which the various strategies were considered. What we see is that we first go down the game tree and look at nodes a1a and a1b, finding that their values are 12 and 11 respectively. This gives us the second and third strategy space nodes. The highest-valued strategy is

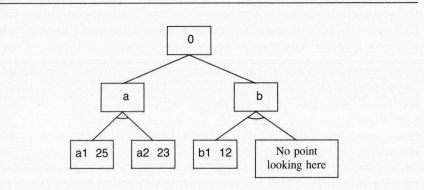

Figure 5.24 A move that is worse for MAX

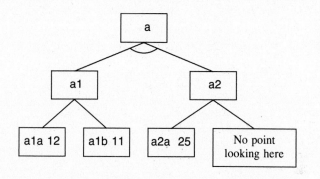

Figure 5.25 A move that is worse for MIN

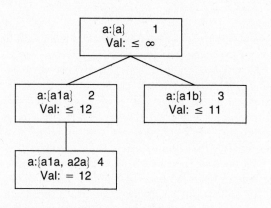

Figure 5.26 A strategy that is worse for MIN

investigated next, which is a:{a1a}. (For the general case we must add a rule which states that if two nodes have the same value, we work on the left-most node.) Then a:{a1a} is expanded by investigating what the strategy should be if MIN had chosen a2. This gives a:{a1a, a2a}. While the value of a2a is 25, the value of a:{a1a, a2a} is still 12, because the value of a strategy is the minimum of the leaf nodes. After a:{a1a, a2a} is found, there is no point in expanding a:{a1a} in a different fashion, or in working on a:{a1b}. In both cases their values are ≤ 12, and since their values could only go down (by including new leaf nodes with values lower than 12), there is no way that they could lead to a strategy better than the complete strategy we already have, a:{a1a, a2a}.

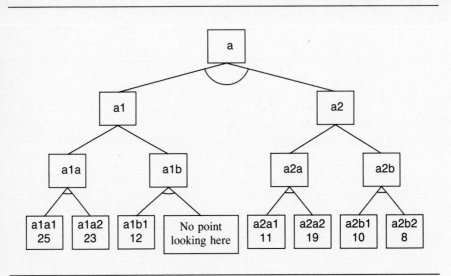

Figure 5.27 A larger case of skipping a node

Unfortunately when we consider larger trees things do not work so well. To see this consider the game tree, shown in Figure 5.27, which includes that of Figure 5.24 as its left-hand branch. In Figure 5.28 we have the start of the search tree for this larger case. If we ignore the two nodes in the bottom row, it shows the situation at the point where we have looked at the nodes **a1a1**, **a1a2**, and **a1b1**. Since it is the left-hand branch that has the highest value, 23, it will be extended next. Furthermore, the way to extend it will be to investigate what happens if MIN chooses **a2**. Thus it would seem that the node labeled "No point looking here" will not be investigated. But this is not correct. As the bottom left-hand node of Figure 5.28 indicates, the investigation of the move to **a2** will show that the two possible responses to this move both lead to partial strategies whose values are 11 and 10. Since they are both lower than 12, the partial strategy that was ignored the previous time will now have the highest value, and will be explored next. But extending this strategy means considering further opponent replies to **a1b**, which, as Figure 5.27 indicates, is pointless. The problem with the continuations 11 and 10 has nothing to do with the choice of move **a1a**. It is simply that MIN has a better move than **a1**, namely **a2**. (A similar extension will have much the same effect on the tree in Figure 5.25. We will not attempt to show this, however.)

The solution to this problem is to introduce the notion of a *solved game tree node*. A solved game tree node is one that no longer deserves any future consideration. Its definition is as follows:

- A terminal node is solved when it has been evaluated.
- A nonterminal MAX node is solved when its highest-valued descendant is solved.

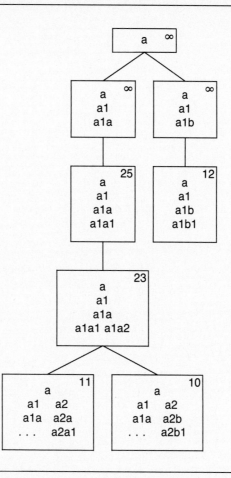

Figure 5.28 Start of search tree for the larger case

- A nonterminal MIN node is solved when its lowest-valued descendant is solved.

In Figure 5.27 the node a1 is solved after looking at a1a1, a1a2, and a1b1 since looking at a1b2 cannot increase the value at a1. In Figure 5.29 we have indicated with asterisks which nodes are solved in each strategy at the point that a1a1, a1a2, and a1b1 have been examined. The idea is that once a node is solved, all other partial strategies which require work on that node are removed from the queue. In Figure 5.29 this has the effect shown by the arrow. The partial solution at the tail has a1 solved, and therefore the partial solution investigating a1b1 will be removed from the queue, since it is still working on a1. Since further work on a1 is barred, the "No point" node cannot be examined.

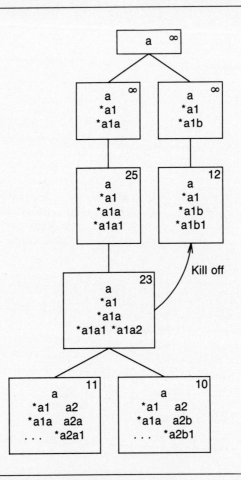

Figure 5.29 A search tree with solved game nodes

The algorithm we now have is known as *SSS**. It is one of a class of algorithms that attempt to avoid exploring board positions that can be guaranteed to be irrelevant. The most famous of this group is called *alpha-beta*. Alpha-beta is quite different, being a depth-first algorithm rather than one that uses the values of partial solutions to guide the search. However, it does calculate minimax values, and uses them to prune the search tree.

5.4.3 Actual Game Playing

It is traditional in textbooks like this to talk about games in terms of game trees. However, it takes some big assumptions to argue that this is the best approach. Human players, while they do ponder consequences of moves, do a lot of other things besides, and even in the worst case they examine only a few positions of the game tree.

For instance, suppose that in thinking about a possible move in chess, a player comes across a "forking" move that the opponent can use in response. A "fork" is an attack on two pieces at once; it is hard to defend against, because only one of the pieces can be moved. The response of a game-tree search program might be to assign a very low value to the board position containing the fork, which will cause it to look at other possible moves. The response of a human player is to look at other moves, but also to think about the fork threat more generally. It may be the case that the opponent has the option of forking for a wide variety of the current player's moves, in which case all of them must be ruled out.

Embarrassingly, however, for games like chess and checkers in which there are not too many legal moves at each position, brute force tree-search methods have done better than methods oriented around pattern recognition and planning (see Box 5.2). However, for games like backgammon, which involves throwing dice, and Go, which has a high branching factor, game-tree methods so far have proved of little value. Hence one would expect more interesting results to emerge from studying them than from studying chess and checkers. We will talk more about planning in games in Chapter 9, where we will talk about the game of Risk^{TM}.

Box 5.2

The History of Chess Playing Programs

It should be no surprise to you that computers play chess, and do it reasonably well. What may not be so clear is that the handheld chess-playing machines that are now sold as consumer items are the fruit of an idea that is centuries old.

Probably the earliest record of a chess playing "automaton" goes back to about 1800, when a man named Von Kempelen exhibited an android dressed up to look like a Turk, seated at a chess board. The Turk won chess games all over Europe, and later in the United States as well. Needless to say, it was a fake, with the android hiding a human chess player.

As for real AI work on chess, two landmark papers independently laid out the basic ideas in terms much like those used in this book. One was by Claude Shannon [Shannon50]. The other, by Alan Turing, [Turing53], was the basis for a program that barely played legal chess, developed at the University of Manchester in England.

In the United States, several groups started working on chess-playing programs during the 50s, with Alex Bernstein being the first to achieve the goal. His program was certainly better than the one at the University of Manchester, but it was still a rank amateur.

Perhaps to get some perspective on this we should discuss the ranking system used in chess. This is a numerical rank by which chess players
can get some idea of how good they are compared to others. The basic
idea is that if you beat someone better than yourself, your rank goes up
and your opponent's goes down, how much depending on the disparity of
rankings prior to the match. About 500 is a beginner playing legal chess,
and 1200 is a good score for the occasional chess player. At 2000 we
enter the realm of the players who are world-ranked, and 3000 would
make you the world champion. According to this scheme, the first program was 500, and Bernstein's a shade higher.

But work on chess was sporadic, and in 1966 John McCarthy
arranged for a chess match between a program developed at Stanford and
one in the USSR. Neither program was much better than that of Bernstein, but McCarthy's point was not to show how good his program was,
but rather to stimulate interest in the subject through the publicity of an
international competition. After a somewhat drawn-out match (it was con-
ducted by mail), the USSR machine won, but it was academic because at
the same time that the match was coming to an end a young programmer
at M.I.T. named Richard Greenblatt developed the first of the modern
chess programs. This was early 1967.

Greenblatt's program, named *MacHack* in honor of *Project MAC*,
the project which housed AI work at M.I.T., was overwhelmingly better
than any other program in existence. While the others were beginners, at
about 600 in the chess rankings, MacHack started out at 1100. But if
MacHack was much better than its competitors, it was not because it had
any new revolutionary ideas. There were some innovations, but the con-
sensus is that Greenblatt succeeded primarily because he was the most
talented (and dedicated) programmer to attack computer chess, and
because he was able to combine the various ideas that had been floating
around into a harmonious whole — no mean feat.

In 1968, several AI researchers (including John McCarthy, Donald
Michie, and Seymour Papert) bet David Levy (an International Master
rated at 2325) that a computer program would beat him within ten years.
But then computer chess again hit the doldrums. Starting in 1970, the
Association for Computing Machinery ran computer chess tournaments,
which were consistently won by Chess 3.0 a program by David Slate and
Larry Atkin at Northwestern University. (By 1972 it had become Chess
3.6.) This program was reasonably conventional, and its rating, while
improving, still stayed around 1400.

In an amusing and informative article [Slate77] they describe what
happened in 1973.

> In April we could no longer push the problem of ACM 1973 out of our
> minds .... We could have tried to improve Chess 3.6 by yet another
> notch. But that would have required expending much effort for rather little
> return. The design deficiencies of Chess 3.6 went much deeper than the

mere fact that it was an old-fashioned program that depended on the searching of large trees filled with unlikely positions. It was poorly documented
and not very modular . . . . No, it had become too painful even to look at
Chess 3.6 any more, let alone work on it.

So they set out to write a better program — one which would be "smar-
ter" and hence do less searching. Certainly conventional wisdom at the
time said that it would only be through such selectivity that progress could
be made. After all, if one used *full-width search* (looking at all the alternatives) then just to look ahead one extra move would require a machine
35 times faster (35 being the average number of legal moves one can make
from a chess position). But to do well with less than full-width search
requires writing a smart plausible-move generator. This is what Slate and
Atkin set out to do.

However, with only a month or two remaining before the tournament we
changed our minds . . . . The principal motivation for switching to full-
width searching was a desire for simplicity. Simplicity was important to
ease the testing and debugging that had to be crammed into a short period of
time. The easiest way to avoid all the complexities of generating plausible
moves is to do away with the plausible-move generator.

The resulting program (Chess 4.0) played better chess, and while it
came in second in 1973, it won the next year. Furthermore, the program
seemed to improve rapidly when put on faster machines, and by 1976
Chess 4.5 had a ranking of 2070. In 1977 it played David Levy, in a
challenge match for the wager made nine years earlier. As would be
expected from the ratings, Levy won the match, but the improvement in
chess programs over the previous nine years was remarkable nevertheless.

At the present time, depending on speed rather than knowledge still
produces the best chess-playing programs. The 1982 computer chess
champion, a program named Belle, used special purpose chess hardware to
speed it up. It had tournament rankings in the 2300 range, although its
lifetime ranking is somewhat lower. In 1983 Belle was deposed by Cray
Blitz, a program developed at the University of Mississippi.

However, sometimes these rankings are misleading. There are cases
where the relative ability of a program compared with its human opponent
seems to rest crucially on whether or not the person has seen earlier
games by the program. If not, then the program plays about even with a
person of its own rank. But a person who has looked over previous
games is likely to win. It seems that at this level of play, players can
diagnose the style of their opponent from previous games, and adjust their
playing to suit. The programs, of course, have no such ability.

This is, of course, a continuing saga. Again it is tempting to say
that sheer speed will no longer suffice, and that more knowledge of chess,
or something else, is needed. But, in fact, nobody knows. Perhaps looking ahead another ply or two will do the job.

5.5 Avoiding Repeated States

To this point we have been steadily following our search trail, starting from the general formulation of search. We then applied this to the special, but important, case of goal-tree search, and in turn applied that to the analysis of game trees. In following this trail we have avoided a lot of interesting and important side routes. It is to these that we will return for the rest of this chapter.

In this section we will discuss an issue that, while it is not literally a part of search theory, is important to practical applications of it. This is the problem of repeated states. Often two different operator sequences will get to the same state from the initial state, and we nearly always want to ignore the second visit. For example, in the missionary and cannibals problem, if at first a missionary and cannibal row over to the other side, and then just row back again, there will be a repeated state. If the second is not ignored, then the search will proceed to rediscover all of the states reached from the initial state. If state duplication is common, or if loops are possible, this can lead to an exponential degree of

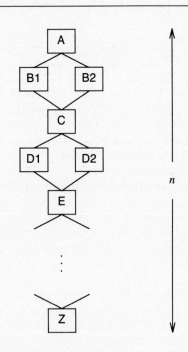

Figure 5.30 State Z will be visited 2^n times

redundancy. Figure 5.30 shows a state which will be visited an exponential number of times.

Consequently, for a realistic system in which state repetition is possible, every generated state must be stored in a table, and every new state must be looked up to make sure it has not been seen before. In principle, this lookup can be expensive, but in practice an efficient scheme can usually be devised by which the lookup can be done in time proportional to the logarithm (or better) of the number of stored states. A simple and efficient way of doing this is the *discrimination tree* (or *net*) pioneered by Newell, Shaw, and Simon in GPS, which we will discuss in Section 5.7. In this scheme, the previously seen states are stored in the leaves of a tree, whose nonterminal nodes are labeled with discriminations. (This is the same idea as the discrimination net of Chapter 3, except that this version will be built on the fly, instead of being a permanent database.)

For example, consider a symbolic integration program, which searches through a space of algebraic formulas in its attempt to transform a formula with an integral sign into one without one. Suppose that formulas $\int (x + sin(x))dx$, $\int x\,dx + \int sin(x)dx$, and $x^2/2 - cos(x)$ are to be *indexed* (stored in the tree). One tree that could do it would be that in Figure 5.31.

One thing to emphasize about this tree is that its structure has nothing to do with the search space or the piece of it examined so far. The discrimination-tree manager, which is responsible for using the tree, does not recognize that one of the stored states is a goal state, for instance.

Now suppose that the machine applies an operator, producing a putative new state S. It must go into the tree, and use answers to the questions at each

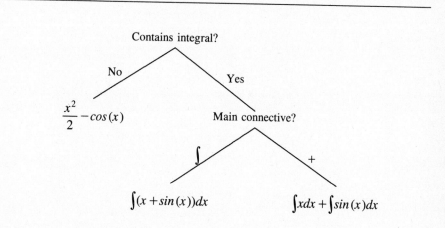

Figure 5.31 Discrimination tree

node to guide it down the arcs. Suppose S is $\int (x - \cos(x))dx$. The answer to question 1, "Contains integral sign?" is "Yes," so the machine goes down the right arc. The answer to "Main connective?" is $\int$, so it goes down the left arc, arriving at the leaf node $\int (x + \sin(x))dx$. When the machine arrives at a leaf, either it has rediscovered the old state S' at that leaf, or it has found a new one that cannot be distinguished from the old one on the basis of the questions leading to it. To tell which of these situations obtains, the machine must call a *match* procedure, which compares S and S', returning one of two results:

1. A report that they are identical; in which case S is normally discarded.
2. A *difference* between them, in the form of a question about them that they answer differently.

In our example, the outcome would be the difference that, for the question "Main connective of integrand?" one formula answers "$+$," the other "$-$." The proper course of action is then to augment the tree, making the node containing S' into a nonterminal asking this question. See Figure 5.32.

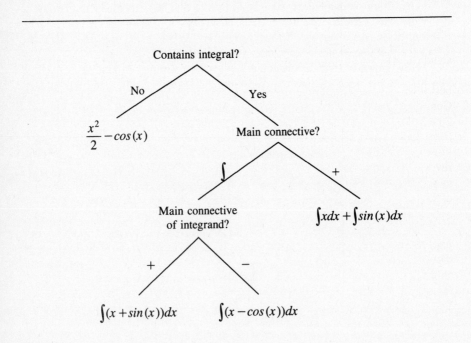

Figure 5.32 Enlarged Discrimination Tree

5.6 Transition-oriented State Representations (Optional)

Let us now return our attention to the basic search algorithm introduced in Section 5.2. It is based on the premise that states in the search space are easy to store. Every time we generate several possible successors, we store the state of the world as each would leave it. In many cases, however, the states are represented by data structures that are large and unwieldy, and it may be prohibitively expensive to keep track of a whole set of them.

Suppose we are trying to write a program to solve a puzzle with complex "board positions." Each operator makes a change to the board (e.g., moves or removes a piece). This change leaves most of the board unchanged. If the board positions were small, we wouldn't mind the waste of recopying most of the information each time.

When the waste is significant, however, we can switch tactics, and represent *changes* to the board position rather than the position itself. We will use the term *transition-oriented* state representation for this strategy, as opposed to the *position-oriented* representation we have been assuming. That is, the representation of a state in search space will be the original position, plus the sequence of operators that led to this state. Actually, the operator itself is not exactly what we want, because the operator says only how to make the change; we also need to be able to unmake it.

Recall that our algorithm had to be able to abandon one approach and switch to another whenever it started to look better. In a position-oriented representation, this was simply a matter of resetting **next** to the state that looked best. In a transition-oriented representation, it is trickier to make the switch. Consider Figure 5.33. Suppose we want to go back to state B from state C. Since we were just pondering C, we had to have an explicit board position there, derived from the original position orig. To go to B, we must re-derive the explicit board position at B, by undoing all the transitions from C (in reverse order, of course), then redoing all the transitions to B. We don't have to go all the way back to orig, but only back to the "latest common ancestor" of B and C, that is, the most recent state that both are derived from (in Figure 5.33, A).

What this sketch shows is that a state transition must be represented as a pair <*forward backward*>, where *forward* is information about how to get to the state from the immediately preceding state, and *backward* is information about how to undo *forward*, that is, how to go back to the immediately preceding state. As an example, consider the peg-jumping puzzle seen in Figure 5.34. The board here consists of an array of holes in the shape of a cross, all but the center one filled with a peg. A move consists of "jumping" one peg over an adjacent peg to an adjacent empty hole, removing the jumped peg. The goal is to remove all pegs but one. The transition between states is represented by the beginning hole and the ending hole; in the forward direction, the peg in between is to be removed; in the backward, to be put back.

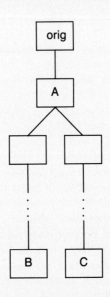

Figure 5.33 Switching states in a transition-oriented representation

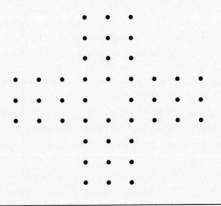

Figure 5.34 Peg-jumping puzzle

In practice, a transition will be represented as a list of three things:

- A *forward function F*.
- A *backward function B*.
- Some *transition data D*.

To apply a transition in the forward direction, we apply *F* to *board* and *D*; to go back, we use *B* and *D* instead. In the peg-jumping puzzle, *D* is a list of two holes, the source and destination. *F* moves a peg from source to destination, removing the peg in between. *B* moves a peg from destination to source, adding a peg in between.

When a transition-oriented representation is combined with depth-first search, an interesting fact emerges. In depth-first search, a given state is never "visited twice"; once it and all its successors have been examined, it is forgotten. This means that the situation of Figure 5.33 never arises except in the special case shown in Figure 5.35. Here B and C are immediate successors of A. B has never been explored, and all of C's successors have been thoroughly explored. That is, in a sense the algorithm never returns to any state except an ancestor of the current state.

Hence, in a depth-first search, both the forward and backward components of a transition may be discarded after the first use. When the machine explores from A in Figure 5.35 it must generate a list of forward transitions. It picks the first, and explores the corresponding immediate successor. As it continues to explore successors, it must retain a sequence of backward transitions that will enable it, if necessary, to go back and try another forward transition from A. In other words, the algorithm must maintain a *stack* of backward transitions, or functions that undo operator applications. Whenever a state is determined to be a loser (have no successors), the last backward transition must be retrieved and executed, taking the algorithm back to the previous state, where something else

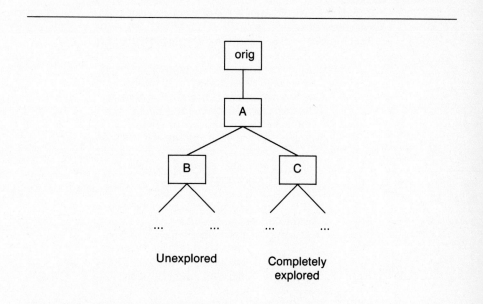

Figure 5.35 Switching states in depth-first exploration

can be tried. (Sometimes the word *backtracking* is used for this kind of search in particular, rather than for depth-first search in general.)

The algorithm for a transition-oriented backtracker, bsearch, is given in Figure 5.36. The stack is not represented explicitly, but is distributed through the various bindings of the local variables of bsearch. The only difference between this function and rsearch is that successors now returns a list of transitions instead of a list of states.

5.7 GPS

GPS was an early search program that has had a tremendous influence on AI research. It is a variant of our search algorithm that uses both state evaluation

---

Function: bsearch
Arguments: expl, goal-test — as for rsearch.
          successors — a function that returns a list of
                 transition triples:
                 <forward, backward, data>.
Local vars: queue — the successors of expl yet unexplored.
          transition — the first member of queue.
Algorithm:
  If goal-test says that expl is a goal state, then exit
  and return expl.
  Else   queue ← the states returned by successors when
              applied to expl.
       Loop: Through all members of queue until there
            is nothing left on queue (in which case
            return failure, since none of the successors
            was on a path to a goal state).
            transition ← first member of queue.
            expl ← the results of applying the forward
                 function from transition to the
                 arguments expl and the data
                 from transition.
            Call bsearch recursively on expl.
            If it returns success, break out of the loop
            and return the answer just found.
            Else expl ← the results of applying the
                 backward function from
                 transition to expl and
                 the data from transition
       Endloop.
  Endif.

Figure 5.36 A transition-oriented backtracker

and operator ordering to guide the search. That is, it does not apply all operators to a state, but only those that look promising.

The letters "GPS" stand for *General Problem Solver.* It was intended to
model human performance in search problems, such as puzzles, and symbolic
integration. Of course, not all problems can be thought of as search problems,
so the "G" in "GPS" seems a little optimistic now. However, under some
assumptions, GPS can be used to produce plans of action (of the sort a robot
might execute), and we will talk about a variant, Strips, used for exactly this
purpose, in Chapter 9.

GPS operates with a technique known as *means-ends analysis.* Given a
state to work on, it *matches* it against the goal-state description. This need not
be the same matcher as used by the discrimination-tree manager of Section 5.5,
but the possible results are the same: either no differences are detected, in which
case the current state *is* a goal state, or there are differences, in which case GPS
tries to "reduce" them. GPS uses such differences two ways. First, the
number of differences serves as a crude measure of global progress toward a
goal. Second, the differences can suggest what action to take next.

Consider the puzzle known as the *Towers of Hanoi,* in which the goal is to
transfer three disks from one peg to another, starting from the initial state
shown in Figure 5.37. The rules are that a disk can be moved only when there
are no disks on top of it, and may not be placed on a smaller disk at the destination peg.

We can think of this as a search problem where the initial state is as
shown in Figure 5.37 and the goal-state description is "All disks on peg C." In
this case, the goal-state description is in the same format as the initial state: the
completely detailed picture shown in Figure 5.38. In the computer we could
represent these as lists, like these:

Initial: ((1 2 3) () ())
Final: (() () (1 2 3))

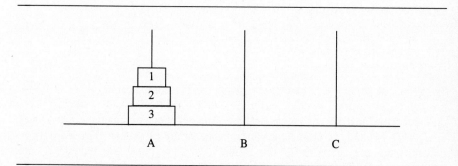

Figure 5.37 Initial state in the Towers of Hanoi puzzle

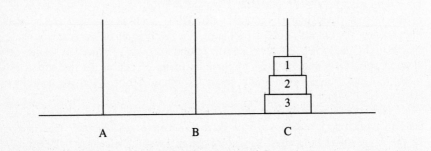

Figure 5.38 Goal state for the Towers of Hanoi puzzle

Now we can apply our match procedure to get three differences between initial and final state:

- 1 is on A, not C
- 2 is on A, not C
- 3 is on A, not C

   Counting differences is only a crude measure of distance to the goal, because it neglects the fact that some differences are more important than others. For example, it counts the two states in Figure 5.39 as equally far from the goal. In fact, disk 3 is "harder to move" than the others, so the second state is actually three moves closer to the goal. We can make GPS realize this by changing the matcher so that it returns only the most important difference, or by changing the evaluation function so that it weights some differences more heavily than others.

   The second use of differences in means-ends analysis is to guide the choice of operators. So far, we have treated operators as "black boxes," functions that could be called to generate zero or more successors to a state. GPS views each operator as consisting of three components:

- Preconditions
- Transformation function
- Differences reduced

The first component is a state description (in the same format as the original goal-state description), which constitutes a necessary (and usually sufficient) condition for the operator to be applicable. The second component is the "black box" part, which, as before, generates zero or more states. The third component links the operator to the differences it is good for reducing. For instance, there are eighteen operators in the three-disk Towers of Hanoi puzzle, each of the form "Move disk i from peg p to peg q." We will use names of the form move-i-p-q for them. So move-1-B-A would move the first disk from the second peg to the first. The precondition of move-i-p-q is that no disk smaller

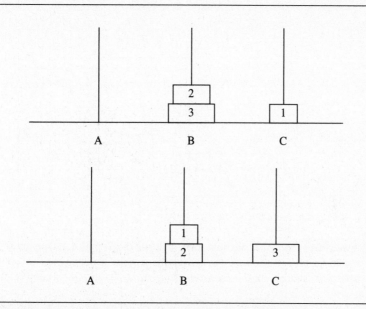

Figure 5.39 Two states in the Towers of Hanoi search space

than i be on peg p or peg q. The transformation function does the actual move. The difference it reduces is of the form "Disk i on peg p, not peg q." The third component of an operator is stored in a data structure called the *table of connections*, or *operator-difference table*. This is provided by the problem poser, and allows GPS, given a difference, to find operators to reduce it.

Continuing with the example, suppose GPS decides to reduce the difference "Disk 3 on peg A, not peg C." The table says **move-3-A-C** is good for this difference. Its precondition is "Disks 1 and 2 both on B." The precondition is not met, but GPS does not give up. Instead, it takes the precondition as a *subgoal* matching it against the current state description just as before. This time, it comes up with two differences: Disk 1 on A not B, and Disk 2 on A not B. Suppose it decides to work on the first. The operator-difference table comes up with **move-1-A-B**, with no preconditions. Applying the operator leads to the state ((2 3) (1) ()).

At this point, GPS has made a mistake. Fortunately, the fact that it is doing a search will save it because it will eventually be able to try other paths. At this early stage, the search is in the situation shown in Figure 5.40. GPS has a choice of working on either of these states, trying something different from the initial state, or pursuing the second one. The fact that GPS has to be able to resume investigation of an earlier state could complicate its control structure compared to our **search** algorithm. In our discussion of **search**, and later **bsearch**, we assumed that the only thing to remember about a state was a list of all its successors or the transitions to those successors. Some of the alternatives for GPS will be operators that cannot in fact be performed on the current state

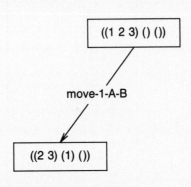

Figure 5.40 Space searched after one move

(like **move-3-A-C** from the starting state in Towers of Hanoi.) Thus as we have formulated it, in GPS search cannot just store successor states, but rather sometimes successor states, and sometimes a current state plus a non-applicable operator.

It is possible to reformulate GPS to make it more compatible with **search**. The trick is to generate all possible subgoals at once. Consider Figure 5.41. The first row is the list of differences between the current state and the goal-state description. The second row is the alternative operators for reducing those differences. The third row is the new differences that arise in attempting to apply each operator; the fourth, operators for reducing these differences, and so on. The operators at the leaves are those whose preconditions match with no differences, so that they can be executed immediately. We will call this the *operator-difference tree*. Figure 5.41 shows the tree for the initial state; every subsequent state has its own tree. (The asterisks in this figure will be explained later.)

The easiest way to implement GPS is to generate this tree exhaustively, and remember only the set of operators at the leaves (here, **move-1-A-C**, and **move-1-A-B**). This is not as painful as it sounds if the number of operators is finite, because we never want to think about the same operator twice. As soon as a duplicate appears, we can forget about it. (Hence the word "tree" is a little inaccurate.)

Using operator-difference trees allows us to treat GPS as a special case of search, in which **successors** works by generating an operator-difference tree, and **estimator** counts differences between a state and the goal description.

The Towers of Hanoi puzzle is easy to describe, but is not really a good illustration of the power of GPS. It is no accident that after the trouble of generating the operator-difference tree, the operators that pop out are *all* the legal ones in that state. The problem is that puzzles are hard precisely because there is no way to make global progress out of a string of local successes (difference

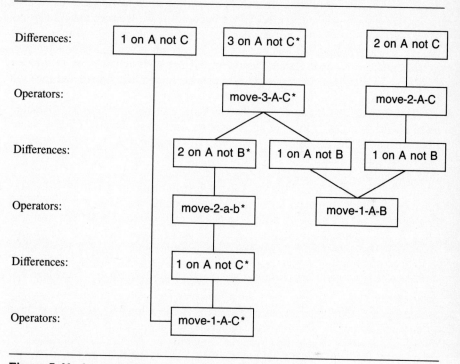

Figure 5.41 An example of an operator-difference tree

reductions). The Rubik's Cube puzzle [Korf82] is perhaps the most horrible example of this phenomenon.

Search is important in AI, but the use of puzzles as examples can mislead you about the *way* it is important. Besides being perversely difficult, puzzles are unusual because they are *presented* as search problems. For most useful applications of search, you have to *discover* how to treat them as search problems. For example, consider the scheduling problem we started with. There are lots of different operator sets. To name three, you could either:

• Start with the empty schedule, and let operators add activities at the end.
• Start with a random permutation of the activities, and let operators interchange activities.
• Start with a partial order, and let operators impose local orderings until the ordering is total.

Each of these will result in a total ordering, but each involves a different search space. The choice can be important. A GPS-style searcher works best if the differences can be ranked in such a way that, having eliminated a high-ranking difference, it can then eliminate all lesser differences without reintroducing a big one.

Actually, as we mentioned, there is such a ranking for the Towers of Hanoi: work on bigger disks first. If we imposed it, we would pursue the asterisked line of Figure 5.41, and would avoid search. The only problem with this insight is that it solves just this one problem. Search is really useful when it is to be applied to an open-ended class of problems, such as the robot scheduling problem. In this case, the more domain-dependent information we can use, the better (the ideal always being to do no search at all).

Of course, the Towers of Hanoi problem can be generalized, by adding more disks. But this is just not an interesting class of problems, if for no other reason than that the length of the *solutions* grows exponentially. To be useful, a search algorithm must be looking for solutions that grow modestly with the size of the problem, and it must not do too much search.

An example of useful search is the Synchem program [Gelernter77]. This program produces syntheses of chemical compounds; you give it the structural description, and it comes up with a sequence of synthesis steps from available compounds. The search space is the set of partial paths ending in the desired compound. A solution is a complete path, starting with available compounds. The program is capable of solving new problems without any tuning.

GPS has been important more as an idea than as a practical program. It drew attention to *matching*, *discrimination trees* and, most importantly, *means-ends analysis*. One aspect of this last idea is that it allows the searcher to think of an operator before it is actually applicable. In some sense, GPS can "plan" to use an operator later, and turn its attention to making it applicable. In Chapter 9, we will make notations for plans more explicit, and separate the planning idea from the search paradigm.

5.8 Continuous Optimization (Optional)

So far we have looked at problems where the search space is *discrete*, that is, where there are countably many states, reachable by applying a finite sequence of operators to an initial state. An entirely different kind of search problem results from considering spaces with a continuum of states, of which only a finite number can be visited by any particular search algorithm. In the abstract, such a problem can be characterized by an *objective function* of several variables: $f(x_1,\ldots,x_n)$. The problem is to find a point $<x_{1M},\ldots,x_{nM}>$ at which f takes on its smallest (or largest) value. This is called a *minimization* or *maximization* problem or, more generally, an *optimization* problem. In what follows, we will put everything in terms of minimization. Sometimes the problem is to find out whether f ever gets below some threshold, but this is attacked by looking for its minimum, and seeing if the threshold is crossed along the way.

One class of examples of this kind of problem is the *relaxation* problems we encountered briefly in Chapter 3. For instance, in the case of stereo disparity, x_i is the ith disparity, and f is a sum of "tensions" due to mismatches and violations of continuity. The object is to find an interpretation — an assignment of values to the x_i that minimizes tension.

Points in the *n*-dimensional space are not defined by an initial state and a set of operators. The *n* may be very large; for relaxation problems of the sort we looked at, *n* could be in the thousands or millions. Hence methods based on enumerating all points, or all points on a fine grid, are out of the question. However, there are several methods for attacking such problems. The classical methods of the calculus depend on finding the derivatives of the function, and then finding a point where all the derivatives equal zero. This requires that we have the objective function written out in standard mathematical notation, in *closed form* as it is called. Typically we do not. Think of the disparity problem again; what we have is a procedure for calculating "tension," and you can't take derivatives of a procedure. Even if we do have a closed-form solution so that we can differentiate it, it may not be possible to solve the equation resulting from setting the result to zero.

In these cases about all we can do with the objective function is plug numbers into it, and see what comes out. Thus the standard methods are all based on the idea of starting at some point and searching for better and better values of *f*. This repeats until no further progress is being made. Such methods are called *iterative*. For iterative methods to work, the following must hold

- The function *f* must be continuous, and, for many continuous-search algorithms, differentiable.
- It must have just one *local minimum* that is, a point surrounded by a neighborhood where *f* takes on larger values.

The reason for these assumptions is that there is no point in looking for gradual improvement in *f* if it is jumping around wildly. For many methods, one needs to have some idea of the rate at which *f* is changing in various directions. Even if *f* is smooth and differentiable, an iterative method will inevitably be fooled by a local minimum that is not a *global minimum*, the true lowest point it attains.

If $n = 1$, that is, the problem is one-dimensional, then these assumptions make the problem fairly easy. The simplest approach is *binary search*. Suppose we have three points, *l*, *m*, and *r* such that the minimum is known to lie between *l* and *r*, and $f(l) > f(m) < f(r)$. See Figure 5.42. The only question is whether the minimum lies between *l* and *m* or between *m* and *r*. To find out, we alternately try points between *l* and *m*, and between *m* and *r*. Consider trying a point between *l* and *m*; call it *x*. If we have $f(x) < f(m)$, then we set *r* to *m* and *m* to *x*. If $f(x) > f(m)$, then we set *l* to *x*. Complementary things happen when *x* is between *m* and *r*. Midpoints can be chosen so that after every two iterations the value of $r - l$ has been at least halved. So the interval within which the minimum is known to lie can be made small after only a few iterations. (Other methods do even better, but depend on more assumptions about *f*.)

Unfortunately, when *n* is greater than 1, there is no analogue to binary search. Instead, we must resort to *hill climbing* (a term more appropriate when looking for maxima, but used for minima as well). Hill climbing requires taking repeated steps through the multidimensional space to the minimum. The simplest idea is called *steepest descent*. On each iteration, we find the direction in which *f* is decreasing fastest. (This direction is called the *gradient vector* of

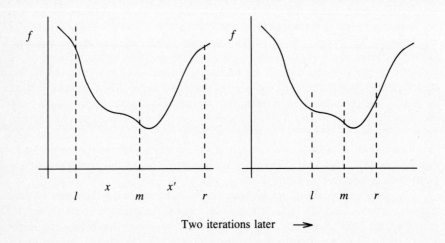

Two iterations later $\longrightarrow$

Figure 5.42 Binary search

f.) Then we apply binary search or some other one-dimensional method to find the minimum along that vector. This is called the "line search" phase. We compute the gradient from the point found by the line search, and repeat.

Although this sounds as if it ought to work well, in fact it has some problems. The main one is the problem of "zig-zagging." Figure 5.43 shows what can happen, using a two-dimensional example. Here the values of f form a long, sloping ravine. The true minimum is at $x_1 = x_2 = 0$; the center of the ravine runs along the line $x_1 = x_2$. Picture starting at any point off the center

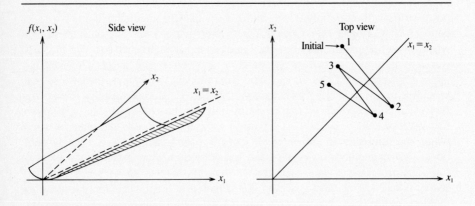

Figure 5.43 Pitfalls of steepest decent

line. Then the steepest-descent direction will be almost perpendicular to the center line, because the slope of f in that direction is much greater than the gentle slope toward the true minimum. You might expect that things would be set right after one iteration, because the first line search would get us to the center of the ravine, from which the direction of steepest descent points right at $<0,0>$. Mathematically, this is true, but slight inaccuracies in the line search will cause the algorithm to miss the center by a little bit, and the same thing will happen all over again. The result is that the algorithm will spend most of its time zigging and zagging past the center line, making only slow progress along it.

Two-dimensional examples like this tend to be misleading. The problem seems so simple — why can't the machine just "look and see" which way to go? The phrase "hill climbing" doesn't help. In fact, an n-dimensional space is a big place. There are improvements to steepest descent, and they are definitely necessary for realistic problems.

So far we have ignored a large class of problems, the *constrained optimization problems*. In these, in addition to the objective function f, there are a set of constraints that must be obeyed. The problem is to find the best value of f that satisfies the constraints. If the constraints are linear inequalities involving the x_i, and f is a linear function of them, then the powerful methods of *linear programming* will work.

5.9 Summary

In this chapter it is easy to miss the forest for the trees, so we will pause here to put it in perspective. This is a "tools" chapter; we needed to pull together some concepts that came up in talking about vision and natural language, and in later chapters we will need to refer to search algorithms, so we stuck this chapter in here. Every practicing AI scientist should be able to write a search algorithm when required, and one is required depressingly often.

It is possible to become too fascinated with the tool, and neglect the work. In practice, it has proven unfruitful to develop very general search programs and apply them to new problems as they come along. What actually happens is this: In the course of doing research, a useful rule, or "heuristic," is discovered, which suggests approaches to some class of problems. The next step is to incorporate the rule into a program. Unfortunately, the rule does not always do the right thing. You can look for a better rule; or you can accept its occasional mistakes; or, in some cases, you can "keep the machine's options open," and try something else when the rule goofs. That's where the techniques of this chapter come in.

We looked at five main classes of search problem:

1. The general search problem: assuming only a search space, some operators, and a state evaluation function. (Section 5.2)

2. Goal-tree search: in which it assumed that a state can be analyzed in terms of a set of *choices* remaining to be made, subject to a *constraint*. This allows us to analyze operators as sets of "choice-making" functions, with some flexibility about which gets to go first. (Section 5.3)

3. Minimax analysis: in which goal trees were used to model two-person games. By adding the notion of a "solved game-tree node" certain partial strategies could be removed from the agenda. (Section 5.4)

4. Means-ends analysis (GPS): here we make further assumptions, that each state in the search space can be *matched* against goal descriptions, and that the resulting *differences* could suggest operators to try. GPS could "plan ahead," and wind up proposing an operator for no reason except to make another operator applicable. (Section 5.7)

5. Continuous optimization: where the search space is a continuum over which an objective function is to be minimized or maximized. (Section 5.8)

If you are a researcher with a heuristic rule, you must survey this set of techniques (and others too numerous to cover in one book), and pick the one that fits your situation best. In most cases, none fits perfectly, and you must be prepared to tinker.

5.10 References and Further Reading

The history of search in AI is a long one. Indeed, at one point some in the field felt that search *was* AI. In part this was due to the central role that problem solving has always had in the field, and the degree to which search seems to be an inevitable aspect of solving problems. Consider *Computers and Thought*, a collection of readings that came out in 1963 [Feigenbaum63], and served to define the early field of Artificial Intelligence. One finds that most of the work tends toward problem solving and search. The impression that GPS made on the field no doubt contributed toward both trends. (While GPS is covered in the Feigenbaum and Feldman book, the most complete reference is [Ernst69].)

The identity of search and AI is no longer a common view. While the best chess programs search through enormous spaces, many game-playing programs do not: the chess endgame program of [Campbell83], a program of [Wilkins80] which makes plans to follow for more than one move (unlike game-tree searches which, as we mentioned, start all over again after every move), the backgammon player of [Berliner80], and the Go project of [Reitman78] (which was never completed).

Indeed, for some time there has been a subsained effort to rid AI of search, or at least all but the most trivial kinds of search. However, this too may be passing, since search seems to be having a rebirth. Again there may be several reasons. For one thing, it is one of the areas of AI that is most susceptible to mathematical analysis. Thus one finds the more mathematically inclined AI practitioners gravitating to the area at least occasionally, and there is also some cross-fertilization from the analysis of algorithms community [Knuth75, Karp83]. It is also the case that the area is producing its own share of interesting results. That looking deeper in the game tree does not necessarily produce more reliable results is hardly expected [Nau82]. The standard algorithm for minimaxing has always been alpha-beta. The SSS* algorithm we presented is a comparatively recent discovery [Stockman79]. We used it because it allows for a unified treatment game-tree search as an application of our **search** algorithm. SSS* also seems to be slightly better than alpha-beta, at least in the abstract. Whether it is actually better for working programs is still an open question. For a discussion of these, and related current research, a good place to start is the special issue of *Artificial Intelligence* on Search.

On the continuous optimization side of things, [Luenberger73] is a good reference. On the particular problem of relaxation, see [Hummel83].

Exercises

5.1 Figure 5.44 shows a search tree with the box for a state indicating the estimated cost for finding a solution from that state (a cost of 0 indicates a goal state). On each iteration of **search**, show the elements of **queue** just before **search** picks the next state to work on. How many states does **search** ultimately consider for this problem? (We will say that **search** "considers" a state when it picks it from the front of **queue**).

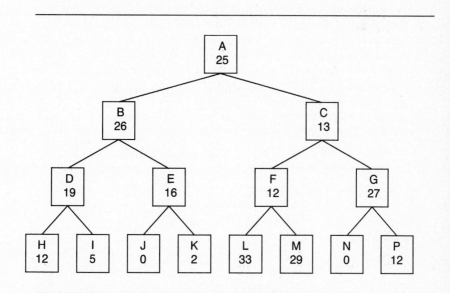

Figure 5.44 Search tree with estimated costs

5.2   Draw out a complete state space for the missionaries and cannibals prob-
      lem. You may assume that repeated states will be detected and cut off so
      that their successors will not be investigated. (However, do put the
      repeated state itself in the tree, suitably marked as such.) For each state
      use Ms and Cs to show where everyone is.

5.3   There are better state-evaluation functions for the map-coloring problem
      than that used in Figure 5.6. For example, of two states with the same
      number of uncolored countries, the one with more "options open" is
      probably better. The "number of options" of a partial coloring might be
      measured by finding the uncolored country with the fewest possible colors,
      and returning the number of possible colors for that country. Give an
      exact algorithm for this state-evaluation function.

5.4   Use the state-evaluation function described in Exercise 5.3 to color the
      map in Figure 5.5. You should assume that the countries are always
      colored in the order h c p k b m and that colors are picked in the order y
      r w g with the next country being colored with the next compatible color
      after the one just used. (That is, if you just used w, for the last country
      and g is not compatible with the country you are now working on, then y
      would be tried next. If that did not work, then r would be tried.)

5.5   Describe in some detail start, goal-test, successors, and estimator for
      the doubly connected planar graph-embedding problem. A doubly con-
      nected graph has at least two disjoint paths between any two nodes. (That
      is, there is no arc such that cutting it causes the graph to separate it into
      two pieces.) Figure 5.45 shows a doubly connected graph and how, by
      removing one arc, it ceases to be doubly connected. A graph is planar if
      it can be laid out on a plane without any of its arcs crossing. Both of the
      graphs in Figure 5.45 are planar, since the layouts in Figure 5.45 have no
      arcs that cross. Figure 5.46 shows a nonplanar graph. The problem is to
      decide if a particular doubly connected graph is planar. We can think of
      this as a search problem where at each step we add one more node, and
      the arcs from it to the nodes to which it must be connected. If we reach

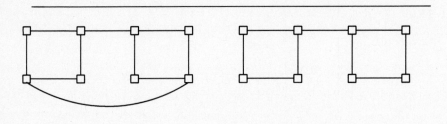

Figure 5.45 Doubly and singly connected graphs

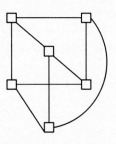

Figure 5.46 A nonplanar graph

the last node without having to cross lines, the graph is planar. A good way to think of planar embeddings of doubly-connected graphs is in terms of regions. Each arc separates two such regions. So in the first graph of Figure 5.45, the arc between the two leftmost nodes separates the inside from the outside of the left-most rectangle. This is a good way to think of the problem because it will be possible to extend a graph if and only if there is a region that has on its boundary all of the nodes to which the new node must be connected. If there is such a region then we just put the new node inside it (thus splitting the region in two). Since all of the nodes to which it must be connected are on the boundary, the arcs to them will not cross any previous arcs. If there is no such region, then putting the new node in any other region will lead to crossings. So finding an embedding requires assigning nodes to regions. A partial solution is a set of nodes and their associated arcs. The algorithm starts by picking an arbitrary node; partial solutions are extended by adding one new node, plus the arcs connecting it to previously embedded nodes; this may divide a region into pieces. The solution cannot be extended if there is no region that has on its boundary all of the nodes to which the newly considered node is attached.

5.6   Give a simple example that shows that if the state-evaluation function can return values which are too high, **search** will not necessarily find the optimal solution.

5.7   Prove carefully that if **estimator** is a cost-estimating function that is accurate for goal states, and never overestimates the cost of the nearest goal state, then **search** is guaranteed to find a least-cost goal state, if it finds any goal state at all. Under what circumstances might it not find any at all (i.e., never halt)?

5.8   Prove that if **estimator** is a cost-estimating function that is accurate for goal states, and returns 0 for nongoal states, then **search** stops only after it has found a zero-cost goal state, or has examined every state in the search space.

5.9 Explain why a depth cutoff would be of little value in the map-coloring problem or the planar-embedding problem of Exercise 5.5.

5.10 Consider an algorithm searching through the space of goal-tree partial solutions. Why is it a good rule for the algorithm to work on the partial solution whose hardest choice is easiest (that is, the partial solution whose maximum evaluation-function value is smaller than the maximum evaluation-function value for all other partial solutions)? Once it chooses a partial solution, why should it then work on the hardest of its choices first?

5.11 Figure 5.47 shows an and/or tree. Show a fragment of the corresponding partial-solution tree that contains all of the nodes visited by **search**. Indicate in what order **search** will consider the various nodes.

5.12 The line-labeling problem mentioned in Chapter 3 can be considered a search problem. Describe how to characterize it in these terms. Make this concrete by describing the search for a solution to the labeling problem of Figure 3.66.

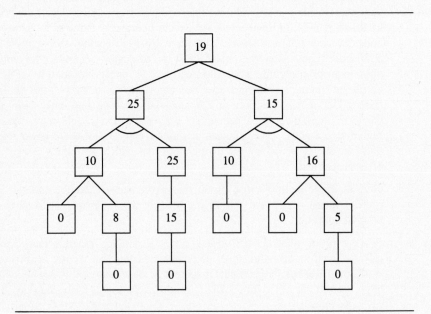

Figure 5.47 An and/or tree

5.13 In Section 5.4.2 we showed how expanding the game tree of Figure 5.24 could result in the node labeled ''No point looking here'' being examined by search. In this exercise we will look at the situation of Figure 5.25.

    a) Show that adding an extra **or** layer on top of the tree in Figure 5.25 will not cause the ''No point'' node to be examined. (We will add it on so that the tree of Figure 5.25 forms the left-hand branch of the enlarged tree.)

    b) Now add both an **or** layer and then an **and** layer above that. Construct a case where the ''No point'' node will be examined.

5.14 Figure 5.48 shows a game tree with the estimated values at the leaves. How many of the nodes of this tree will be investigated by the SSS* algorithm? We will say that SSS* investigates a node of a game tree if that node appears in a strategy that is ranked the highest at some point.

5.15 Considering just the tree dominated by **a1** in Figure 5.48, show the strategy tree as it will be investigated by SSS*.

5.16 We want to enable GPS to solve the following problem.

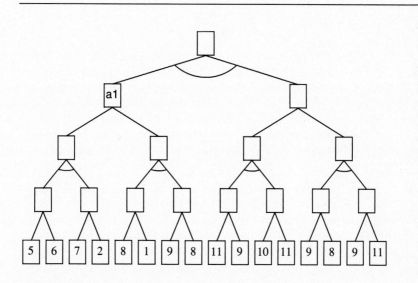

Figure 5.48 A game tree with estimated values of the leaves

In a certain culture, the basic kinship relation is that every child must be the adopted offspring (called a *kyd* in their language) of one and only one adult. At all times, each family must have exactly one kyd which is designated as a *bygshot*. A bygshot is said to *sqysh* each of the other kyds (if there are any) in the family. A kyd who is not a bygshot can trade roles with the bygshot in the same family through a custom called *swyching*. The one who was the bygshot becomes an ordinary kyd in the family, and the other kyd becomes the bygshot. Any adult may adopt a kyd out of its current family by carrying out a custom called *glomming*. The result is that the kyd is in the family of the adult who glommed and no longer in the family it was in previously. A kyd's status as a bygshot (or not) cannot be changed as the result of a glom.

a) Informally describe the data structures that would have to be given to GPS to do the job. Note that in the text, operators were described in such a way that they took no arguments. For this assignment you may assume that they can take arguments. Rather than having a group of operators like **move-1-A-C** we would have one general operator (**move** *peg from-ring to-ring*).

b) Your GPS program will get a goal of the form *get specific kyd X to sqysh specific kyd Y in a family whose adult is Z*. Demonstrate with an informal trace of its behavior how your program would work on the following situation

Family 1: adult = a	Family 2: adult = e
bygshot = b	bygshot = f
other kyds = c, d	other kyds = g

Problem: Get b sqyshing f in family whose adult is e. (This problem appeared in a Stanford University AI comprehensive exam.)

5.17 You are explaining the problem of searching for a move in chess to a fellow student. Your friend notices that the algorithm needs to find the maximum of some function (i.e., the move which is best for you) and suggests that one should simply differentiate the function, set the result to zero, and solve. Explain why this will not work.

5.18 Write **state-sort** and **state-merge**, the functions used in the search algorithm of Figure 5.7. The function **state-sort** takes a list of states and a state-evaluation function, and returns a sorted list of (**value state**) pairs, sorted in increasing order of distance from the goal. The function **state-merge** takes two sorted lists of (**value state**) pairs and produces a new sorted list containing every element of both lists.

5.19 Write **goal-test**, **successors**, and **estimator** for the map-coloring problem. (First read Box 5.1 for subtleties involved in different Lisp implementations.) To avoid excessive search, assume that **successors** picks a single uncolored country and returns all possible ways of coloring it, rather than returning all possible ways of coloring every uncolored country.

5.20 Write a general-purpose goal-tree searcher gsearch. It should represent a partial solution as a *partial object* plus a set of remaining choices. A *choice* is an abstract entity consisting of two parts: an extension function and an evaluation function. The extension function applies to the partial object and returns a list ((*obj -new-choices-*) (*obj -new-choices-*) . . .), each of whose elements contains a new partial object *obj*, and new choices to be added to the old. The evaluation function estimates how hard it is to make the correct choice, given the partial object. This estimate is a nonnegative number, and may be thought of as the number of alternatives the extension function would return if called now; the smaller this number, the harder the choice. For instance, in the map-coloring problem, the partial object is a partial assignment of colors. The remaining choices correspond to uncolored countries. Each extension function generates all consistent new colorings for a single country, and no new choices. Each evaluation function returns the number of available colors for the corresponding country. As mentioned in Exercise 5.10, gsearch should work on the partial solution whose hardest choice is easiest.

5.21 Implement a discrimination tree (Section 5.5) for ordinary S-expressions. Each question should be of the form "What's at the cada. . .ddr?" The answer will be the atom at that position, or *struc if there is a list there.

5.22 This is a term-project-sized assignment to implement a version of GPS that uses search as its back-end. GPS should be a function with these arguments:

- start: the initial state. An arbitrary data structure.
- goal-descrip: a description of the goal state. An arbitrary data structure.
- match: a function that takes a state description and a state, and produces a list of all the differences between them, possibly nil. A difference is represented as a state description, in the same format as goal-descrip. The differences returned by match are intended to be an exhaustive list of the components of a given state description that do not describe a given state.
- file: a function to test for repeated states (see below).
- opdif: a function that takes a difference and returns a list of operators that could reduce it. Each operator is represented as a list (*preconditions ops-fn*), where *preconditions* is a list of differences (state descriptions), and *ops-fn* is a function that that takes a state and returns a list of immediate-successor states, as in search.

Since GPS will call search, it should look like this:

```
(defun gps (start goal-descrip match file opdif)
  . . .
    (search start
      ; goal-test
      (lambda (s)
        . . . match against goal-descrip . . .)
      ; successors
      (lambda (s)
        . . . Construct operator-difference tree using opdif . . .)
      ; estimator
      (lambda (s)
        . . . Count differences using match . . .)
      ; added in previous exercise
      file)  )
```

The version of search you use should be one modified to check for repeated states. That is, search will take another functional argument, file, that takes a state and files it, returning nil if it was seen before, t if new.

Next implement a GPS matcher for the Towers of Hanoi problem. It should take goal descriptions in the form of triples of number lists. If a number is omitted, we don't care where the disk is. If a number is duplicated, it may be on any of the corresponding pegs. So ((()(1 2) (1)) describes the state where 2 is on B and 1 is on B or C (and 3's position is irrelevant). Remember that the matcher returns a list of alternative differences. So matching ((() (1 2) (1)) against ((1 2 3) () ()) should give these differences:

    1 on A, not B
    1 on A, not C
    2 on A, not B

You might also write a symbolic integration program using GPS: a program that takes an expression containing an integral sign, and finds an equivalent expression that does not contain one. For example, $\int x^2 dx$ should get transformed to $x^3/3$. In Lisp notation, we might represent this as this transformation

    (integral (exp x 2) x) => (/ (exp x 3) 3)

To break this down into steps for GPS, we must provide operators that transform expressions. Here are two, expressed informally

    (integral (exp v n) v) => (/ (exp v (+ n 1) n+1)

    (integral (* n e) v) => (* n (integral e v))

To formalize these, we must provide a notation for left-hand sides, and a matcher to compare them with the current expression.

6

Logic and Deduction

6.1 Introduction

In Chapter 1, we discussed the importance of internal representation, and sketched the structure of the predicate calculus and other representation systems. We then turned our attention to the production of representations from inputs, both visual and linguistic. It is time now to justify this analysis by showing how useful these representations can be once they are obtained. We begin in this chapter by studying reasoning processes that can be called "deductive," in that they are concerned with drawing as many useful and probably true inferences as possible from the input.

An important abstraction of this and later chapters is the idea of a *database*, an organized set of data structures that represent what the computer currently "believes." (See Figure 6.1.) Between the database and the program using it is a "gatekeeper," a program responsible for adding and deleting beliefs, and performing certain classes of inference. Some of these inferences are done when facts are added, and some when requests for information arrive at the gatekeeper. The phrase *inference engine* has also been used.

In practice, there is seldom such a clearcut division between the main program and the database, and there is usually not a single database with one central gatekeeper to do inferences. In later chapters, the pluralistic reality will become clear. For the time being, however, such a picture is quite convenient; keep it in mind throughout this chapter. We will explain Figure 6.1 and a simple gatekeeper for it in detail in Section 6.3.

Before that, we will focus on a more abstract level. The word "representation" can be taken in two ways. It refers to conventions for structuring data in a computer program (such as the database we just mentioned), but it also refers to the abstract structuring of expressions denoting facts. We will call

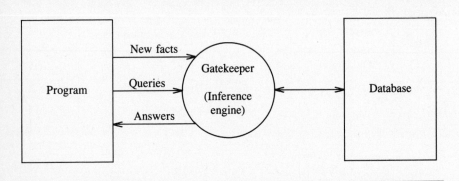

Figure 6.1 Schematic database

these the *concrete representation* and *abstract representation*, respectively. So there are three levels to keep in mind:

Facts

Abstract representation

Concrete representation

The "fact" level refers to the set of possible states of affairs. An abstract representation carves up this rarefied domain into *expressions*, each denoting a different state of affairs. A concrete representation is a way of storing these expressions as data structures. We will use the word *fact base* to mean a set of things a system believes, expressed abstractly, as opposed to a *database*, which is a set of data structures intended to implement a fact base.

Much of the literature on knowledge representation is confusing because it fails to distinguish between these two levels. For instance, it is often claimed that there is a fundamental distinction between *assertion-oriented* representations like predicate calculus, and *object-oriented* representations, like the associative networks we glanced at in Chapter 1. This argument generates a lot of confusion unless distinctions are drawn between the *content* of the representation, an issue at the abstract level, and how it is *indexed*, an issue at the concrete level. Although there is still room for plenty of controversy, it tends to be more productive if divided along this dimension.

Our position, as stated in Chapter 1, is that at the abstract level the predicate calculus has so far served as the most flexible vehicle for capturing content, and that the important problem of knowledge representation is devising good *vocabularies*, or families of useful predicates. In the following section, after a review of predicate calculus, we will talk about this topic.

6.2 Using Predicate Calculus

6.2.1 Syntax and Semantics

Recall that an *atomic formula* in the predicate calculus is written in the form

(*predicate -terms-*)

as in

(loves john mary)
(jealous john mary fred)
(in brick-33 box-104)
(cleartop brick-33)
(kills marlowe (murderer sylvia))

The terms following the predicate are called the *arguments* of the formula. Each formula says that its predicate holds true of its arguments. We will use the term *assertion* for a formula that is currently "believed" by the machine (that is, held in some fact base and used for some purpose). Each term is either a constant (like mary, or 37), or an expression of the form

(*function -terms-*)

as in (murderer sylvia), above. (Later we will introduce variables as terms.) As with predicates, the terms following the function are called its arguments.

A key idea behind the predicate calculus is that every expression *denotes* something, that is, that there is some entity that the expression stands for. This restriction helps ensure that we do not read too much into our formulas. For example, the term sylvia must denote a single object. Presumably, we have a woman named Sylvia in mind when we introduce this term, but this is irrelevant. In fact, it can be misleading, since her actual name plays no role in the notation, and since it discriminates against other women named Sylvia. For this reason, we usually use symbols like sylvia-21 to emphasize that the name is merely mnemonic, and that there may be many other Sylvias, who are not denoted by it.

The individual denoted by a term does not have to be a physical entity like a person. It can be a class, a substance, an event, a cause, a virtue, or any other sort of thing which can be thought of as an individual within the context of the evolving theory. However, once the denotation of a term is determined, it is fixed. Once you decide that sylvia denotes Sylvia Smith, you cannot use the term to denote Sylvia Jones, or the set of all Sylvias, or some woman we know nothing about, except that her name is "Sylvia."

Another key idea of the predicate calculus is that the meaning of a complex term or formula is a function of the meanings of its parts. A function like murderer takes an argument *a*, denoting some entity, and forms a term (murderer *a*), denoting the entity that murdered (or will murder) what *a* denotes. If *a* denotes a nonliving entity or one that dies of natural causes, (murderer *a*) denotes something else. (It seems intuitively more natural to have the term be undefined in such cases, but for technical reasons most logics instead have it denote some unknown thing. However nothing can be inferred about an entity like (murderer carrot-16) so the two options are in practice equivalent.)

The similarity of predicate-calculus syntax to that of Lisp should not mislead you. That murderer is a function does *not* mean that there is a procedure which, when called with the argument sylvia, returns her murderer or nil if sylvia died of natural causes. The same goes for predicates. For instance, we might have a formula (life-on pluto) (which may or may not be true) but there is no general Lisp procedure life-on for deciding whether there is life on a planet.

Terms denote "individuals." What do formulas denote? There are several possible answers to this question. We might take a formula like (on block-33 table-1) to denote "true" or "false"; that is, we might take its *truth value* to be all there is to its meaning. The problem with this approach is that it makes it awkward to embed formulas inside terms and other formulas. Predicates like believe make such embedding necessary. To say "John believes the earth is flat," we will need something like (believe john-22 (flat earth)). If (flat earth) denotes "false," then (believe john-22 (flat earth)) must have the same meaning (that is, truth value) as (believe john-22 (revolves-around sun earth)), because the meaning of each whole proposition depends only on the meanings of its parts, which are the same. But John might believe the earth is flat without believing the sun goes around it.

Logicians are still working on a fully satisfactory answer to this question [Moore80, Montague74]. We will avoid technical problems, and simply say that a formula denotes a "proposition," or "possible state of affairs." So believes takes as arguments a person and a proposition, and the resulting formula denotes the proposition that the person believes the embedded proposition. Under this approach, the truth value of a formula (in the real world) is not the whole of its meaning, but is determined by whether the proposition it denotes is true or not. (See Section 6.5.3 for more information about the issues involved here.)

Because the meaning (denotation) of a predicate-calculus expression depends only on the meanings of its parts, predicate calculus is said to have *compositional semantics*. Because of this compositionality, it is important when introducing a function or predicate to say exactly what the types (and, of course, the number and order) of its arguments are, and exactly what the type and denotation is of the term it constructs. It is okay to use the symbol loves in a construct like (loves bill-22 sylvia-21), or in a construct like (loves bill-22 girls), but not both. In the former case, loves would take two persons as arguments; in the latter, a person and a class of objects. The first sort of predicate is not *a priori* preferable to the second in any way, but if you require both predicates, then you must have two different symbols (e.g., loves-indiv and loves-class).

We combine formulas with connectives (the usual and, or, if, not) to give new formulas:

(or (on brick-33 brick-47) (on brick-47 brick-33))
(if (happen world-war-3)
   (not (happen (second-edition Intro-to-AI))))

The connective if is the most important, because of its role in inference. The formula (if p q) is called an *implication*, with *antecedent p* and *consequent q*. Although if is important pragmatically, we could do without it logically. In the predicate calculus, (if p q) is purely and simply an abbreviation for (or (not p) q). (You can verify this by using the truth tables for if, or, and not in Chapter 1.) This reading of if is reminiscent of the use of the English word in sentences like, "If you sent me that package, it got lost in the mail." This means the same thing as "Either you didn't send it, or it got lost." (As we discussed in Chapter 1, the English word "if" has many other meanings; they are mainly irrelevant in this chapter, but see Section 6.5.2.)

Another derived connective is iff, or "if and only if": (iff p q) is an abbreviation for (and (if p q) (if q p)). It asserts that p and q have the same truth value (either true or false). One role this has is in asserting that p and q mean the same thing, or in defining something in terms of something else.

For computer applications, the Lisp-ish notation we use seems natural, but the traditional notations are different. Figure 6.2 gives a translation table. (We include the quantifiers discussed in Chapter 1, which we will return to in Section 6.2.3.)

6.2.2 Some Abstract Representations

In this section, we will give some examples of abstract representations. Since the syntax of predicate calculus is well understood, we can concentrate on the *vocabulary* for a given domain, the set of predicates, functions, and constants needed to express facts in it. The phrase "set of primitives" is often

Our notation	Traditional notation
(and p q)	$p \land q$
(or p q)	$p \lor q$
(not p)	$\neg p$
(if p q)	$p \supset q$
(iff p q)	$p \equiv q$
(forall (x) p)	$\forall x\, p$
(exists (x) p)	$\exists x\, p$

Figure 6.2 Our notation and the traditional notation

used for this concept. Picking a good vocabulary is a challenging task. A good one enables all the important things to be said cleanly. As Hayes ([Hayes84], p. 8) says,

> The symptom of having got [the vocabulary] wrong is that it seems hard to say anything very useful about the concepts one has proposed . . . . It is easier, fortunately, to recognize when one [has got it right]: assertions suggest themselves faster than one can write them down.

A similar sentiment is voiced by Schank and Carbonell ([Schank79], p. 360):

> The initial choice of [primitives] to represent knowledge in a new domain is necessarily ad hoc. We make an initial, tentative commitment to a new set . . . in the new knowledge domain. In the process of codifying new knowledge, using the knowledge in computing programs that process text and answer questions, and in light of new theoretical considerations, we modify change or even replace our original choice . . . . We believe that this method rapidly converges upon a . . . set of basic units that organizes the knowledge of the domain in a useful and enlightening way.

As a first example, we will look at a representation for shapes and spatial relationships. The vocabulary of this theory embodies a theoretical assumption that metrical relationships among objects are just as important as topological ones. Metrical relationships are those expressible as numerical constraints on coordinates; topological relationships are concerned with containment, overlap, and fitting together, or in general with properties that would remain true even if the objects were stretched out of shape. In this theory, "A is near B" does not get represented as (near a b), but as (≤ (dist a b) (1 meter)). The absence of a vocabulary item for "nearness" is due to a theoretical assumption that the concept of "nearness" can, in a given context, always be expressed as an inequality of this kind. In fact, the assumption holds for many words. "A is between B and C," for instance, gets represented as

(≥ (ang b a c) (160 degree))

So the most important predicates in the theory are ≤ and ≥, "less than or equal" and "greater than or equal." In addition, there are numerical-valued functions like (dist x y), (ang x y z), and (dir x y z). The most primitive such terms are of the form

(*coordinate object frame*)

We construe *coordinate* to include the orientation and scale of objects as well as position. For example, (x a b) denotes the x-coordinate of a with respect to frame b. (tilt eiffel-tower paris) denotes one component of the orientation of the Eiffel Tower with respect to the frame of reference of Paris. Any object can serve as a frame of reference, which means it must have determinate x, y, and z axes. It must also have a determinate scale with respect to any other frame of reference.

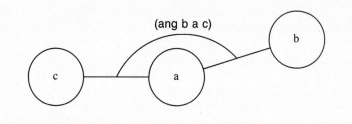

Figure 6.3 A is between B and C

You may have noticed the odd term **(1 meter)** occurring in the "near" example. This term is an abbreviation for **(* 1 meter)**, because (*number* . . .) is an abbreviation for (* *number* . . .). This sort of "syntactic sugar" is often useful.

You may find it implausible that facts involving "near" are represented as inequalities. It is part of the role of an abstract representation to make such disagreements clear. Arguments about a notation tend to be unprofitable if its semantics are inadequately described.

Not everything can be handled in the metric way that "near" and "between" are. For example, there is a sense of "inside" that has nothing to do with metric facts. A mouse inside a snake may be quite close to a mouse outside the same snake. To handle these, we need a separate vocabulary of what we may loosely call "topological" predicates. For instance, (in *x y*) means that the space occupied by *x* is a subset of the space occupied by *y*. (overlap *x y p*) means that the intersection of the space occupied by *x* and *y* is not empty, and is itself occupied by object *p*. (abut *x y p*) says that *x* and *y* fit snugly together, sharing "boundary part" *p*.

In the rest of this section, we will work out in detail a representation for a different domain — that of everyday human actions. This representation is based on Schank's *conceptual dependency* notation, usually called CD, which was devised to serve as a semantic representation for a series of natural-language processing programs. We will use it as an illustration for two reasons. First, no special expertise is required to appreciate the things CD is trying to represent. All people are experts on the domain CD covers, or soon fancy themselves to be. So you may find yourself thinking up improvements to what we present.

Second, to our knowledge, this representation has never been subjected to careful semantic analysis. Even though computer programs have been written that manipulate it, questions still remain about exactly what its symbols mean. We were forced to answer some of them, and in some cases clean up the notation, in order to write this section.

A basic entity in CD is the event, or *conceptualization*. We introduce the predicate **event** to assert that something is an event. For instance, (event ev-29 (do john-22 (ptrans book-3 dunham becton)))

is true if ev-29 is an event consisting of john-22 "ptransing" — causing to move — book-3 from dunham to becton. This is a formula with predicate event and two arguments: ev-29 and (do john-22 . . .). The first is a term denoting a particular event, the second a class of events, namely, those when John does a certain action. We say that ev-29 denotes an event *token*; (do john-22 . . .), an event *type*. (If we simply talk about an "event" we will mean "event token.") The event assertion then says that ev-29 is a token of that type. We can similarly analyze (do john-22 (ptrans book-3 dunham becton)). Here do is a function with two arguments, an agent and an action. The value of a do is an event type, namely, the performance of that action by that agent. Finally, ptrans is a function that takes an object and two locations, and makes a term denoting the action of çausing that object to move from the first location to the second. (The name "ptrans" stands for "physical transfer.") We can assert other things about ev-29:

(speed ev-29 slow)
(vehicle ev-29 golfcart-103)

We adopted a different representation for event descriptions in Chapter 4, which we called "slot-assertion notation." In that notation, we would describe ev-29 more like this:

(inst ev-29 ptrans)
(agent ev-29 john-22)
(patient ev-29 book-3)
(source ev-29 dunham)
(dest ev-29 becton)
(speed ev-29 slow)
(vehicle ev-29 golfcart-103)

These are simply two different but closely related abstract representations. The earlier one treats all parts of an event uniformly, whereas the one in this chapter distinguishes the "agent" slot strikingly by introducing do, and (for ptrans) distinguishes "patient," "source," and "dest" by requiring them to be filled in.

The two representations are almost *notational variants*; that is, it is almost a trivial syntactic transformation to translate from one to the other. The present notation is more concise, and, more important, by separating the agent from the other cases, it provides a term denoting the action performed by the agent. This will be useful when we come to the chapter on managing plans, where plans will be seen to contain many such terms. Of course, the "all-optional" notation has its uses, especially as produced by a natural-language processor, which builds up its output piece by piece as words are parsed; each piece can be a single atomic formula. Rather than force uniformity, we have used both versions, as an illustration of how usage influences even the most abstract levels of representation design.

A major decision at this point is whether (**event** *token type*) asserts that the event actually happened. At first one takes this for granted; what would an event "look like" if it didn't happen? But it is not too hard to think of events that didn't happen, like the Confederacy winning the American Civil War. So our description of **ev-29** remains hypothetical until we add the assertion

> (**happen ev-29**)

The predicate (**actual-event** *token type*) can be defined to mean

> (**and** (**event** *token type*)
>   (**happen** *token*))

The *primitive acts* describe everyday human actions. One, **ptrans**, we have already encountered; the others are:

(**move** *body-part dest*)
> A body part is moved to a place. This is different from **ptrans**, because it normally requires only an act of will.

(**atrans** *object owner-1 owner-2*)
> Control is transferred from one "owner" to another. (A person controls something if that person is able and permitted to use it for current purposes.)

(**propel** *object place-1 place-2*)
> The object is moved by direct physical force, as in throwing or shooting.

(**grasp** *object*)
> The object is grasped. There is no **ungrasp**, although there should be. (See Exercise 6.2.)

(**ingest** *object orifice*)
(**expel** *object orifice*)
> Used to describe all eatings, drinkings, excretings, etc.

(**mtrans** *info place-1 place-2*)
> Information is transferred between physical or mental "places." The information can be a formula or a symbol. We will discuss **mtrans** in more detail below.

(**mbuild** *formula*)
> The actor comes to believe the formula. This is intended to represent sentences like "John proved a new theorem," or "Sally realized who the murderer must be."

(**speak** *sounds*)
> Make a sound. Often the sound will be a string of phonemes in some language. This is the usual way of **mtrans**ing.

(**attend** *sense-organ-type object*)
> An object is attended to as for perception. (**attend eye book-23**) denotes the action of "looking at **book-23**."

The primitive **mtrans** (mental transfer) deserves more discussion. As we noted above, the information transferred can be a formula or a symbol. For

example, this formula is intended to represent the fact, "John gave the name of
the murderer to the police chief":

```
(do john-22 (mtrans (name-of murderer-23)
                (head john-22)
                (head police-chief-7)))
```

It doesn't commit itself to the means by which John performed this communication. It also doesn't say John said *that* this name was the name of the murderer,
although this may be a worthwhile assumption. The thing **mtrans**ed may be
another formula. To say "Jack told Sally that Janet took the kite to the store"
one would have this:

```
(actual-event ev-279
    (do jack-84                        ; Jack informed someone
        (mtrans (actual-event          ; that it actually happened
            ev-303                     ;
            (do janet-50               ; that Janet
                (ptrans kite-3         ; moved the kite
                    house-4            ; from the house
                    store-5)))         ; to the store.
        (head jack-84)                 ; Jack knew this
        (head sally-3))))              ; and now Sally does.
```

Use of **mtrans** assumes that some abstract "information" moves between
"places," such as people's heads. Of course, nobody could take this as a serious theory of mental process; thus their use here raises a thorny issue in
knowledge representation. Is the goal to find a notation to talk about the world
as it really is, or to talk about the world as the average person believes it to be?
For instance, if we want to devise a representation for physical concepts, should
we base it on Newtonian physics, or on "naive" physics, the physics of the
"man on the street"? The difference between the two is rather dramatic: Not
only do we get different conclusions (such as whether all objects eventually stop
moving by themselves), but the very concepts are different; subtle distinctions
between categories like energy and momentum are absent from naive physics. It
may seem that only psychologists could be interested in such a theory, but the
issue is more complex. People often manage to draw useful conclusions from
sketchy premises, where real physics is helpless. For example, in situations
where an object is moving, it almost always *is correct* to conclude that it will
stop moving. For naive physics, this is a trivial conclusion, while a reasoner
using real physics would have to use some otherwise useless information about
frictional forces.

Similarly, the concept of ideas traveling between residences like encyclo-
pedias and people's heads may seem silly. But human beings do use such concepts [Lakoff80], and the correct theory is not available yet. (If it were, this
book would be a lot more systematic.) When it is available, it may still be the
case that the simplest way to draw inferences about communication is by thinking in terms of **mtrans**es and all they entail.

In addition to these functions for describing events, there are functions for describing *states*. These are true or false for stretches of time, often as a result of events. We might try expressing a state as a proposition, like (happy john-22), but then this says John is happy, period. It doesn't allow him to be happy at some times, sad at others. A better idea is to introduce states as a new kind of individual, which can take on different truth values at different times. A particular stretch of time over which a state is true is called a *token* of that state. The predicate state relates the two: (state st-40 (happiness john-22 very)) says that st-40 was or will be a particular stretch of time over which john-22 is happy. Thus state takes two arguments: a *state token* (st-40), and a *state* (happiness john-22 very). Many states are represented as terms of the form (*attribute object value*). In fact, this notation has traditionally been required in CD; we see no reason to insist on it, however. The CD representation does not provide for a set of primitive states the way it does for primitive acts. Some of those that have been used widely include health, happiness, and the like. The *value* argument to many state functions is some kind of intensity measurement. Traditionally numerical scales from −10 to 10 have been used, so that (health john-22 -10) is the state of john-22's being dead.

We now have two sorts of token — event tokens and state tokens. We make a distinction because they have somewhat different properties. A state token is just true over a stretch of time, whereas an event *happens*; it is either instantaneous, or has a beginning, middle, and end. We will use the phrase *time token* to refer to either type.

We also need the distinction between real and possible state tokens. We will use (actual *token*) to mean it actually is true at some time; and (actual-state *token state*) to stand for the conjunction of (state *token state*) and (actual *token*). Two state functions that deserve more mention are loc and mloc, which refer to physical and mental location, respectively. (loc *ob loc*) is the state of object *ob*'s being in location *loc*. (mloc *formula loc*) is the state of the given formula's being in a "mental location" like (head john-22), or encyclopedia-410. Just as locs are the result of ptranses, mlocs are the result of mtranses and mbuilds.

We also have *state change* events. (become *state*) is the event (type) that occurs when *state* goes from false to true. (become (happy john-22 very)), means that John becomes very happy. (To distinguish these from the event types formed from the primitive acts, we will call the latter *primitive events*.) Technically, we cannot represent the state of John's not being very happy as (not (happy john-22 very)). This is because not is a connective, which transforms a proposition into its negation. We need a function state-not that takes a state as argument and denotes the state that is false when and only when the argument is true. We also need state-and, state-or, and so forth. However, to avoid awkwardness, we will use the same names, not, and, and or for connectives between both propositions and states.

In addition to time-token definitions, there are relations among tokens. For instance, one event can precede another or could occur at the same time.

(precede *event-token-1 event-token-2*)
(same-time *event-token-1 event-token-2*)

More specifically we can have

(instr *event-token-1 event-token-2*)

meaning that *event-token-2* was the *way event-token-1* happened, that is, the "instrument" of *event-token-1*. For example,

(actual-event ev-1 (do john-22 (mtrans info-3 book-4 (head john))))
(actual-event ev-2 (do john-22 (attend eye book-4)))
(instr ev-1 ev-2)

That is, "John read the book by looking at it." Often events are hierarchically organized. A given event will consist of several component events. For example, the popping of a bag of popcorn consists of a multitude of subpoppings. We will use the predicate (sub-event *event-token-1 event-token-2*) to state this, as in

(actual-event ev-1 (do john-22 (ptrans john-22 house-31 school-55)))
(actual-event ev-2 (do john-22 (ptrans john-22 house-31 car-54))
(sub-event ev-2 ev-1)

which states that John's going to his car was a subevent (the first step, perhaps) of his going to school.

Events can cause states to be true, and states being true can enable actions to occur. We use the result and enable predicates to express this:

(result *primitive-event-token state-change-event-token*)
(enable *state-change-event-token primitive-event-token*)

One event can prevent another event, meaning that it would have occurred if the preventer had not:

(prevent *event-token-1 event-token-2*)

Here *event-token-2* must not be actual (if it actually happens, it wasn't prevented) and *event-token-1* must be actual. Exercises 6.3 through 6.5 point out some problems with this analysis of prevention. Take a look at them, and think about the questions they raise. These exercises are typical of the sort of dialectic thought process that goes into making up representations. A notation is proposed, and then stretched to its breaking point by thinking up facts that can't be stated in it. Usually a representation is provisionally adopted without all the problems having been solved, because the problems are hard, and because it's not always clear which problems are truly important until more practical experience has been gained.

Getting back to our menagerie of causality types, we also have initiate, in which something causes a mental state (token). Anything can cause a mental state. For instance,

```
(initiate ev-3 ev-4)
(actual-state ev-3 (burning house-42 rapidly))
(actual-state ev-4
   (task john-22
        (mtrans (actual-state ev-3 (burning house-42 rapidly))
               (head john-22)
               fire-dept-5)))
```

(Note that burning is a state, one of many routine states we make up at will.) We have introduced the function task to capture Schank's notion of *goal*. (task *planner act*) denotes a state, the state of affairs in which the *planner* wants to perform *act*. So the three formulas just given say, "John was trying to call the fire department because the house was on fire." We will say more about tasks in Chapter 9. Finally, we have the predicate

   (reason *mental-state-token primitive-event-token*)

as in the following example:

Function	Argument types	Value type
do	(do *agent action*)	event-type
become	(become *state*)	state-change-event-type
mloc	(mloc *formula loc*)	state
loc	(loc *ob loc*)	state
task	(task *agent action*)	mental-state

Predicate	Argument types
event	(event *event-token event-type*)
happen	(happen *event-token*)
actual-event	(actual-event *event-token event-type*)
state	(state *state-token state*)
actual	(actual *state-token*)
actual-state	(actual-state *state-token state*)
precede	(precede *event-token-1 event-token-2*)
same-time	(same-time *event-token-1 event-token-2*)
instr	(instr *event-token-1 event-token-2*)
sub-event	(sub-event *event-token-1 event-token-2*)
result	(result *primitive-event-token state-change-event-token*)
enable	(enable *state-change-event-token primitive-event-token*)
prevent	(prevent *event-token-1 event-token-2*)
initiate	(initiate *time-token mental-state-token*)
reason	(reason *mental-state-token primitive-event-token*)

Figure 6.4 Conceptual dependency predicates and functions

```
(actual-event ev-5
   (do john-22
       (mtrans (actual-state ev-3 (burning house-42 rapidly))
              (head john-22)
              fire-dept-5)))
(reason ev-4 ev-5)
```

which means "John told the fire department about the fire because he intended to."

Except for the primitive acts which were listed earlier, Figure 6.4 gives a summary of the CD predicates and functions.

The CD causal links can be used to construct large networks of events and states, representing entire episodes. For instance, we can have a story of the form, "John was walking through the woods. A lion appeared, hungry and in a rage. John killed it." This could be represented by the fact base of Figure 6.5. The ". . ." in ev-7 is there because we don't know what to put in its place. It means that John did *something* that resulted in the lion dying. We don't know what it is, so we leave it blank. Putting in ". . . " is not the kosher way of doing this. The right way is to use quantifiers, which we will discuss in the next section.

This story (like the one in Exercise 6.6) is moronically simple. As soon as a story involved social actions, or deceit, or complex spatial reasoning by the characters, not to mention surprise or didacticism by the author, the simple vocabulary would fail us. (Of course, Schank's group has developed more

---

```
(actual-event ev-1 (do john-22 (ptrans startplace-1
                                       (part middle woods-2))))
(precede ev-1 ev-2)
(actual-state ev-4 (loc lion-3 (near john-22)))
(precede ev-4 ev-2)
(actual-event ev-2
   (do john-22 (mtrans (actual-state ev-4 (loc lion-3 (near john-22)))
                      eye
                      (head john-22))))
(actual-event ev-3 (do john-22 (attend eye lion-3)))
(instr ev-2 ev-3)
(actual-event ev-5 (hungry lion-3 very))
(actual-event ev-6 (angry lion-3 very))
(same-time ev-5 ev-6)
(actual-event ev-7 (do john-22 . . .))
(actual-event ev-8 (become (dead lion-3)))
(result ev-7 ev-8)
(reason ev-2 ev-7)
```

Figure 6.5 Representation of a simple story

complex vocabularies to handle some of these problems.) Can we just keep on making up predicates and functions to handle these problems? How will we know when the new concepts are reasonable? There are several answers. It ought to be the case that the notation translates smoothly to practical data structures. This sort of consideration underlay the preference for metric concepts in spatial reasoning we described earlier, and the choice of slot-assertion vs. positional notation.

However, there are criteria internal to the abstract level. The representation should provide a way to state any fact in a given domain. It should make intuitively simple facts look simple. It should make intuitively similar facts look similar. Most important, the representations should support useful inferences. This will be our next topic.

6.2.3 Quantifiers and Axioms

We must now introduce *quantifiers* in order to allow a wider range of things to be expressed. As we said in Chapter 1, there are two of them, the *universal* and *existential* quantifiers. A universally quantified formula looks like (forall (-*variables*-) *formula*), as in

(forall (x) (color x green))

which says that everything is green. An existentially quantified formula looks like (exists (-*variables*-) *formula*), as in

(exists (x y) (loves x y))

which says there are two things such that one loves the other, or one thing that loves itself. (forall (x) (P x)) says that any object at all has property P. This might not seem so useful; after all, some things are not green. Usually, though, P is an implication, as in

(forall (x) (if (in x antarctica)
            (temperature x cold)))

This says that any object at all, if located in Antarctica, is cold. Another way to put this is, "Everything in Antarctica is cold." For the implication to be true no matter what x's value is, it must be true when its antecedent, (in x antarctica), is false. And (if *p* *q*) *is* true when *p* is false because it is synonymous with (or (not *p*) *q*). Both kinds of quantifier can bind more than one variable, as in

(forall (x y) (if (on x y) (supports y x))   )

"If one thing is on another, it is supported by it."

There are three reasons why quantifiers are interesting. First, as inputs get more complicated, quantifiers become necessary as part of their internal representation. At the end of Section 6.2.2, we needed to be able to say "John did *something*," and of course an existential quantifier is the right way to say this: (exists (e a) (actual-event e (do john-22 a))). Second, nontrivial inferences are possible only between quantified formulas. This will be our topic in

Section 6.3. Third, and most important, quantifiers are used in writing *axioms*. This may sound as if it would be true only for mathematical applications, but in fact it is of wider importance.

We have stressed that a representation must unambiguously mean something. When you introduce a symbol, you must say what it denotes or, if it is a function, the types of its arguments and the thing denoted by the term it creates. "Saying" means telling it to whomever will write expressions in the notation for the computer. It seems as if you really ought to tell the computer as well. But the whole concept of a computer derives its novelty and power from the fact that complicated symbol manipulations can be done by an agent with no idea what they mean. The manipulations of a formal system depend — by definition — only on the structure of the objects manipulated, and not on any "insight" into the meanings of these objects.

The one thing the machine does have is a set of assertions involving the symbols. The assertions make some inferences possible and not others. Any collection of assertions will therefore exclude some possible meanings of the symbols. For instance, the assertion

(forall (x y) (if (R x y) (not (R y x))))

is a fact about R (namely, that it is "antisymmetric"). Believing this assertion excludes the interpretation that R is the equality relation. It leaves in a large number of other interpretations. (R could mean "heavier than," "above," "contained in," or many other things.) By adding other assertions, we could exclude any interpretation we wanted. What we can't do, it turns out, is narrow the range of interpretations down to one. Mathematically, there will always be an infinite number of interpretations left. At some point, however, the differences between them will have no practical consequences.

So when we use a symbol like in, and tell you that it means "contained in," that is a promise to fill in the details and narrow the range of interpretations by supplying assertions involving the symbol. Sets of assertions are called *theories* by logicians, and the assertions are called *axioms*. The word "theory" sounds a little odd to most people, so we prefer the phrase "fact base" that we have been using all along. The theories studied by logicians are often smaller than those studied by AI theorists. For instance, the theory of partial orders has facts like

(forall (x y z) (if (and (< x y) (< y z))
                  (< x z))

("If x is less than y, and y is less than z, then x is less than z") plus a few others like it.

AI theorists cannot confine themselves to a few axioms this way, because they are interested in pinning down the meanings of more and richer concepts. Their theories will often be open-ended, with hundreds of axioms in principle, of which tens are written down. (In fact, as new information comes in via natural language or some other channel, many new axioms will be added to the fact base.)

For example, the spatial representation discussed in Section 6.2.2, because of its reliance on inequalities, must contain the usual theories of arithmetic and inequalities on real numbers. It also uses a notion of scale. Roughly speaking, the scale of an object is its size with respect to another object. So if obj-1 is 3 times the size of obj-2, the (scale obj-1 obj-2) will be 3. Some axioms about scale are these:

```
(forall (a b)              ; The scale factor of a with
    (= (scale a b)         ; respect to b is
       (/ 1 (scale b a))))) ; the reciprocal of the scale
                           ; factor of b wrt a.

(forall (a)                ; Every frame has a unit scale
    (= (scale a a) 1))     ; with respect to itself.
```

Coordinates in different frames of reference depend on each other in certain ways. For instance,

```
(forall (a b) (if (and (dimension a 1)
                       (dimension b 1))
                  (and (= (x-coord a b)
                          (* (- (x-coord b a))
                             (scale a b))))))
```

"If a and b are one-dimensional, then the position of a with respect to b is the negation of the position of b with respect to a, multiplied by the scale factor between them." For example assume as before (scale obj-1 obj-2) = 3. If obj-2 is left of obj-1 by 3 of obj-2s own units (you could place 3 obj-2s end to end between the two) then obj-1 is to the right of obj-2 by 1 of obj-1s own units. (The one-dimensional case is particularly simple. The axioms for two and three dimensions are more complex.)

```
(forall (a b f1 f2)        ; Except for scale, it does
    (= (dist a b f1)       ; not matter what frame you
       (* (dist a b f2)    ; compute distance in.
          (scale f2 f1))))
```

For the topological predicates, we have axioms like these:

```
(forall (x y z)
    (if (abut x y z)       ; If x abuts y, sharing
        (and (partof z x)  ; boundary part z, then z
             (partof z y)))) ; is part of both x and y.

(forall (x y)              ; An object contains all
    (if (partof x y)       ; of its parts.
        (in x y)))
```

For the conceptual dependency theory, we have general axioms like

```
(forall (e1 e2)
        (if (enable e1 e2)        ; If e1 enables e2, then
            (precede e1 e2)))      ; e1 precedes e2.

(forall (e1 e2)                    ;
        (if (result e1 e2)        ; If e2 is a result of e1,
            (precede e1 e2)))      ; then e1 precedes e2.

(forall (e1 e2)                    ; A prevented event does
        (if (prevent e1 e2)       ; not happen.
            (not (happen e2))))
```

and more specific ones like

```
(forall (e a x p1 p2)
   (if (event e (do a (ptrans x p1 p2)))
      (exist (e1 e2)
         (and (state e1 (loc x p1))
              (event e2 (become (loc x p2)))
              (enable e1 e)
              (result e e2)
              (if (happen e)
                 (and (happen e1)
                      (happen e2)))))))
```

which says, "If a ptranses x from p1 to p2, then it changes state from being at p1 to being at p2." The hardest part of formalizing CD is specifying the relations between a person's state of mind and that person's actions. One reasonable axiom is "If you want to do something (have a task), then you will do something that you believe will accomplish that." Another is that no one does a primitive act except in service of some task. In general, finding good axioms in the domain covered by CD has been quite difficult, because it deals with some deep concepts, like causality and human intention, whose logical structure is unclear.

There is usually not a point-to-point correspondence between a fact base and the database that implements it. Some of the facts will be implicit in the "gatekeeper." (See Figure 6.1.) For example, a program that reasoned about time might need a predicate before and this axiom:

```
(forall (t1 t2 t3) (if (and (before t1 t2)
                            (before t2 t3))
                       (before t1 t3)))
```

(Predicates which have this property are said to be *transitive*.) In the actual implementation it will often pay to implement such transitive rules by special purpose Lisp data structures and programs. Thus the axiom above would not be in the database at all, but buried in the inference engine.

6.2.4 Encoding Facts as Predicate Calculus

Although almost everyone acknowledges that formal languages are the soul of representations, many people have trouble using them. Many papers in AI theory are full of what appear to be formal languages, but are actually just "parenthesized English" — a human being can read it by reading into it, that is, by putting the mnemonic symbols together into a reasonable meaning. Computers can even be made to run two or three canned examples using such a notation. But designing a formal language that is really formal, in that its symbols have consistent, well-defined meanings, is a difficult craft to learn. In this section, we will talk about this craft. The first step is to say more about manipulating quantifiers.

Quantified expressions can occur inside other quantified expressions. The formula

```
(forall (x) (if (lifestyle x hippie)
            (forall (y) (if (inst y person) (loves x y)))))
```

says that hippies love everybody. In detail, it says that, if x is a hippie, then if y is a person, x loves y. One kind of quantifier can occur inside the other kind:

```
(forall (x) (if (is-a-husband x)
            (exists (y) (and (inst y person)
                        (sex y female)
                        (married x y)))))
```

"You can't be a husband without being married to some woman." The word *scope* is used to refer to the parts of a formula where a quantified variable may be referred to. In (forall (*v*) *p*), *p* is the scope of the *bound variable v*. If quantifier *Q1* occurs inside quantifier *Q2*, and they both bind the same variable, then the inner one cancels the outer one. For example, consider

```
(forall (x) (if (inst x university)
            (exists (p)
            (and (occupation p professor)
            (employee p x)
            (exists (x)
            (and (student x p)
            (admire x x))          )))))
```

"At every university there is some professor with a student who admires himself." All the x's inside the innermost exists refer to the same vain student, not to the university.

It is important not to read too much into the English transcriptions of the predicate-calculus formulas. It is tempting, for instance, to read the husband example as implying that to *become* a husband you must get married. But the formula does not mention time at all. In fact, it implies that being a husband is timelessly true or false (in the way that a mathematical statement like the Pythagorean theorem is true or false). This is not necessarily "wrong" because in many applications time can be neglected. For instance, in an income-tax program we can treat a statement as true if it is true (in the real world) on December 31. But if temporal change is important, it must be explicitly noted in the notation.

We should say a bit more about the distinction between these two formulas.

(forall (x) (if (p x) (q x)))   ; *All ps are qs.*

(exists (x) (and (p x) (q x))) ; *Some ps are qs.*

You can't say "All *p*s are *q*s" with (forall (x) (and (p x) (q x))), which means that everything in the universe has properties *p* and *q*. You can't say "Some *p*s are *q*s" with (exists (x) (if (p x) (q x))). This statement is fairly useless, since it means the same thing as (exists (x) (or (not (p x)) (q x))) — "Something is either not *p* or *q*."

When you negate a universal, you get an existential, and vice versa. If it is not true that all *p*s are *q*s, then there must exist a *p* that isn't a *q*. If it is not true that there must exist a *p* that is a *q*, then it must be that all *p*s are not *q*s. But the apparent asymmetry in going from if to and and back takes some getting used to. You can either just accept it, or understand this explanation

(not (forall (x) (p x)))

is equivalent to

(exists (x) (not (p x))).

So

(not (forall (x) (if (p x) (q x))))

is the same as

(exists (x) (not (if (p x) (q x)))).

But (if *a b*) is the same as (or (not *a*) *b*), and (not (or *p q*)) is the same as (and (not *p*) (not *q*)), so (not (or (not *a*) *b*)) is the same as (and *a* (not *b*)). In other words, (not (if *a b*)) is the same as (and *a* (not *b*)), and (not (forall (x) (if (p x) (q x)))) is the same as

(exists (x) (and (p x) (not (q x)))).

Another important thing to remember is that (forall (x) (if (p x) (q x))) does not imply that there are any *p*s or *q*s. E.g.,

(forall (x) (if (and (inst x vegetable) (sentient x))
              (occupation x senator)))

"All sentient vegetables are Senators," is true, because there are no sentient vegetables. If you want to say, "Any sentient vegetable would be a Senator," that's much harder. Such so-called *counterfactual conditionals* require sophisticated methods. (You would have to say something like, "In any possible world in which there is a sentient vegetable, but that world resembles ours enough to have a US Senate, that vegetable would be in the Senate." See Section 6.5.3.)

Fortunately, the only counterfactual conditionals that seem to play an active role in thought are those in which one reasons about actions someone might have done, and these can be handled by Schank's event notation, or some other temporal logic.

Many statements turn into universal implications with an existential in the consequent. For instance, "John hit everyone who was near him yesterday," would be encoded (on July 3, 2009) as

```
(forall (x s1)
   (if (and (inst x person)
            (actual-state s1 (loc x (near john-22)))
            (date s1 july-2-2009))
       (exists (e1 e2 ob p1 a1)
           (and (actual-event e1 (do john-22 (propel ob p1 x)))
                (actual-event e2 (become (in-pain x)))
                (result e1 e2)
                (precede s1 e1)
                (time e1 july-2-2009)))))
```

Note how we handled "yesterday." This English word does not actually signify any particular day, so we can't allow it in the internal representation. If this formula is supposed to be the output of a natural-language parser, then we must assume that it can figure out which day was meant in context. Similar considerations apply to pronouns, and words like "here." Except in specialized applications, such terms will fail to denote a unique individual, and must be avoided.

Getting back to our examples, consider "No one does anything without a reason." This is represented as

```
(forall (x e a)
   (if (and (inst x person) (event e (do x a)))
       (exists (e2) (and (state e2 (task x a))
                         (reason e2 e)))))
```

Note that a sentence talking about "No one" has become a formula beginning "For everyone . . . ." It takes some practice to become adept at these translations. It helps that there are only two choices for the main quantifier of a formula. In a case like this, the existential is clearly inappropriate, so we have to figure out how to use, "For all . . . ." "For all task state tokens . . . ." doesn't seem to go anywhere, so we try "For all persons . . . ." At this point we have to realize that "No one does anything without a reason" is the same as "Everyone does everything for a reason." That leads us to

```
(forall (x e a) (if (and (inst x person) (event e (do x a)))
                    . . .))
```

or, "For all persons and events consisting of their doing an action . . . ." That leaves ". . . for a reason." A word like "a" indicates a quantifier, usually an existential. So we need something like

```
(forall (x e a)
   (if . . . (exists (r) (and (inst r reason) (reason-for e r)))))
```

The fact that we expressed the consequent in terms of another task **e2** instead of a "reason" r reflects our belief that a calculus of tasks will suit most of our purposes more smoothly than a calculus of "reasons," whatever they are. Such a vocabulary decision is important and difficult, but once it is made it starts to have surprising applications, as in this case. A lot of the complexity of English turns out to be redundant for any given problem domain.

Phrases beginning with "a" and "some" are called *indefinite descriptions*. Phrases beginning with "the" and possessive pronouns (like "his") are called *definite descriptions*. (See Chapter 4.) These terms reflect the fact that definite descriptions typically refer to a particular individual the speaker has in mind, and indefinite descriptions typically do not.

Indefinite descriptions usually get formalized as existential quantifiers, but not always. In *Hamlet*, the gravedigger, in answer to the question, "How long will a man lie in the earth ere he rot?" says, "A tanner will last you nine year." We can formalize this as:

```
(forall (t b d) (if (and (occupation t tanner)
                         (event b (burial t))
                         (event d (decompose t)))
                    (≥ (- (date (end d)) (date b)) (9 year))) )
```

That is, we have translated it into "Every tanner . . . ." Definite descriptions give rise to quantifiers in the predicate calculus, but often it doesn't matter which quantifier you use. For instance, the sentence, "Everyone takes good care of their hearts" could become either of the following (where "care for" is left unformalized):

```
(forall (p h) (if (and (inst p person)
                       (inst h heart)
                       (partof h p))
                  (exists (e)
                     (actual-state e (task p (care for h)))) ))
```

or

```
(forall (p) (if (inst p person)
                (exists (h)
                   (and (inst h heart)
                        (partof h p)
                        (exists (e)
                           (actual-state e (task p (care for h))) )))))
```

The first version seems to talk of *all* hearts, and the second of one particular heart. They are equivalent because of one additional fact in the fact base: that everyone has exactly one heart. (We will formalize this shortly.) Although the existential version seems more intuitive, the universal version is usually more useful because inference algorithms like those we present below do better with universals, and because we can avoid dealing with the uniqueness condition. If we were trying to express the exact content of English sentences, an enterprise many philosophers engage in, these practical considerations would be irrelevant.

Sometimes definite descriptions are used to refer to generic concepts. "The water buffalo is a vicious animal" may be taken to mean "All water buffalos are vicious." "The computer revolutionized business" does not refer to a previously mentioned computer. (It cannot be represented by quantifying over all computers, but by talking about the event of computers becoming common.)

Although the vocabulary of predicate calculus varies from domain to domain, there are some predicates that occur again and again. One is equality. $(= x\ y)$ is false for any two objects x and y; it is true only for an object and itself. Equality is useful in theories involving numbers (like the metrical-space theory), but it can also be useful in other domains. A major use is in stating that something is unique, as in our "heart" example:

```
(forall (p x y) (if (and (inst p person)
                         (inst x heart)
                         (inst y heart)
                         (partof x p)
                         (partof y p))
                    (= x y)))
```

That is, if x and y are hearts of person p, then they are the same individual.

It is often necessary to make statements about collections of objects. For this one can use set theory (see Box 6.1), but it is often simpler to use "list theory," that is, use lists the same way Lisp does. We have to be a little careful about how this is done, since the term (a b c) denotes the function a applied to b and c, not a list of three elements. We need a syntax that plays the same role as quote in Lisp. There are three approaches:

1. Just use quote. This is done in the Loglisp system [Robinson80]
2. Introduce other brackets. This is done in Prolog [Warren77] and Duck [McDermott83].
3. Introduce cons as a function.

The last possibility is the most straightforward, and requires no syntax extensions. The list (a b c) is represented as (cons a (cons b (cons c nil))). This looks a little odd to the Lisp eye because it looks like an expression to be evaluated (and it looks like a, b, and c are "unbound variables"). But in predicate calculus this is simply another term. (cons c nil) is an individual, a pair whose first element is the object denoted by c, and whose second element is the object denoted by nil (the empty list). This pair can be an element of another pair, and so on. Once this is grasped, we can introduce special-purpose brackets, as in [a b c], as an abbreviation.

One use of list structures is in stating uniqueness conditions more concisely than with equality alone. Suppose we want to say "The only short friends of Snow White are Happy, Dopey, Sleepy, Sneezy, Bashful, Doc, and

Grumpy." We could use a disjunction of equalities, like this:

```
(forall (x) (if (and (friend x snow-white)
                     (< (height x) (4 feet)))
             (or (= x happy)
                 (= x dopey)
                 . . .)))
```

but it is more concise to say,

```
(forall (x)
    (if (and (friend x snow-white)
             (< (height x) (4 feet)))
        (element x [happy dopey sleepy sneezy bashful doc grumpy])))
```

where (element *x l*) is true if *x* is an element of the list *l*. Of course, we may find it necessary to be more explicit about the meaning of **element**. If so, we can supply some axioms, like these:

`(forall (x y)`	*; x is an element of any*
`    (element x (cons x y))   )`	*; list whose first element*
	; is x.
`(forall (x y z)`	*; If x is an element of z*
`    (if (element x z)`	*; then it is an element of*
`        (element x (cons y z))))`	*; any list with z as tail.*
`(forall (x) (not (element x nil)))`	*; Nothing is an element of nil.*
`(forall (x y z)`	*; If x is an element of a*
`    (if (element x (cons y z))`	*; nonnil list, then either it*
`        (or (= x y)`	*; is equal to the first*
`            (element x z))))`	*; element, or it is a member*
	; of its tail.

Another pair of predicates we have used repeatedly are **inst** and **isa**. (inst *x c*) is true if *x* is an instance of class *c*, as in (inst fido-33 dog). (isa *c1 c2*) is true if *c1* is a subclass of *c2*, as in (isa dog mammal). These concepts are not quite the usual set-theoretical notions of membership and subsethood. They are usually reserved for "natural classes," about which something is known. That's why it is reasonable to construct **isa** hierarchies, as described in Chapters 1 and 7. In fact, we will usually assume that an object is an **inst** of just one class (and its superclasses). Thus given statements like, "Sally is a person," "Sally is a female," and "Sally is a professor," we will usually represent them like this:

```
(inst sally-32 human)
(sex sally-32 female)
(occupation sally-32 professor)
```

That is, we reserve **inst** for Sally's one most natural classification. We use other predicates for her other attributes. As we will see later, this makes it easier to think about answering queries like "What is Sally's occupation?" If we represented all three facts using inst, we would ask, "What occupation-type class is Sally an inst of?" which is more awkward.

Similar arguments can be used to reject representing these facts as

(human sally-32)
(female sally-32)
(professor sally-32)

since then the corresponding query would be "What occupation-type predicate is true of Sally?" The notion that every object is thought of as an inst of one basic class, its "type," seems to be a psychological fact about the way we classify things, which it is convenient to import into the representations we use.

6.2.5 Discussion

This concludes our introduction to predicate calculus as a representation language. We pause here to summarize and comment on its value. One of its assets is that it supports an inference technique, called chaining or resolution, that is in wide use. We will discuss this in Section 6.3. However, to our way of thinking, the main value of logic is as a tool for understanding representation systems. These systems are still rudimentary and prone to error. One reason is the perennial problem of programming: you have to give the computer very precise rules that work in all cases — in this instance, inference rules. Usually you consider a few cases, and make up rules that seem to fit. Then you debug them. If this debugging is done on a working program, then you may be content with getting a couple of examples to work. You may not notice that adding a few more equally plausible rules would allow all sorts of unwanted conclusions to be drawn. For instance, in dealing with CD, we encountered the problem of how to talk about a prevented event. (See Exercises 6.3 through 6.5.) In real programs based on CD, the problem is harder to see and easier to duck; we might casually allow some modules to assume that a named event actually occurs, but make sure the module that deals with prevention never makes that assumption. In a way, this shows the superiority of programs to logic; but a great deal of faith is required to suppose that you or someone else will never change the program so that it, say, calls a subroutine that goes ahead and performs the unwanted inference, because it's normally okay. If, on the other hand, a careful logical analysis of the concepts of *event* and *prevention* is made ahead of time, and all programs are written to respect it, then they are guaranteed not to infer gibberish.

It is easy to confuse this guarantee with a guarantee that all the conclusions of a logic-based system are true. At best, logic guarantees that the conclusions are true if the premises are. Even that is not necessary. Rules can simply have exceptions; rules dealing with the real world almost always do. But there is a difference between a rule that makes occasional mistakes of fact, and one that licenses gobs of logical garbage that we hope programs will overlook.

In summary, the logical stance gives a certain simplicity of viewpoint, abstracted away from implementational details. So you can ask, Is it possible to express a certain fact? How will a proposed rule interact with other rules? How can I get inference A without also getting inference B? This sort of analysis complements and supports the design of practical inference algorithms.

Finally, we should mention an objection to the use of logic to study representation systems. It is often argued that people can tolerate inconsistency in a way that logic cannot. As we know, people often believe inconsistent things. "Government spending should be reduced" and "No particular government program should be cut," for instance. Inconsistency of this kind is deadly for logical systems. It is a fact about logic that if p and (not p) follow from a set of premises, then any conclusion at all follows from those premises. (See Exercise 6.34.) The fallacy is the assumption that people are aware of the contradictions that others perceive in their beliefs, and cheerfully tolerate them. In fact, people are so upset by the idea of contradictions in their own beliefs that they go to great lengths to explain them away. "Useless bureaucracy is draining money away from important government programs." It is certainly true that people are not bothered by contradictions they don't notice. But neither is a computer program, and a program has no guarantee of noticing all contradictions that follow from the facts currently in its database.

Where inconsistency is truly traumatic is in the facts wired into the "inference engine," because there simply is no interesting inference algorithm based on an inconsistent set of axioms. All such inference engines behave the same, answering "yes" to every query. However, this is no argument for not basing inference algorithms on explicit axioms.

6.3 Deduction as Search

Figure 6.1 shows a schematic database with an associated "gatekeeper" for managing additions and deletions, and performing straightforward inferences. Some of the facts believed by the program are embodied as data structures in the database; others are embodied as code in the gatekeeper. The design of these data structures and algorithms depends on which inferences are important to make, and what methods will most efficiently make them.

The simplest design is to use data structures that look just like predicate-calculus formulas, and a gatekeeper that embodies no facts at all, just the basic rules of inference of predicate calculus. The gatekeeper implements three basic commands: **assert**, **retract**, and **query**. The function **assert** puts a proposition into the database while **retract** undoes **assert**. The function **query** takes a pattern and attempts to deduce formulas matching that pattern from formulas in the database.

To take a simple example, suppose the program **assert**s the implication

(forall (x) (if (inst x block) (inst x prism)))

as well as the atomic formula

(inst block-21 block)

and later does a query of (inst block-21 prism). That is, it asks the database, "Is block-21 a prism?" The inference engine should be able to respond yes. The gatekeeper has a choice of when to do this inference. It could do it as soon as (inst block-21 block) is asserted, or it could wait until the query was received. In practice, gatekeepers mix *assertion-time inference* with *query-time inference*; the program using the database doesn't have to know exactly what is done when. For a predicate-calculus system, assertion-time inference is called *forward chaining*; query-time inference is called *backward chaining*. In this section, we will describe these techniques and when they are appropriate.

6.3.1 Forward Chaining and Unification

Traditionally, logicians have not worried about making inferences efficiently, and have instead striven for the simplest mechanism that will make all legitimate inferences. Such mechanisms often fail to suggest how to focus on the interesting ones.

For instance, consider the rule of modus ponens: From p and (if p q), infer q. This rule will not allow us to conclude anything from

(forall (x) (if (inst x block) (inst x prism)))

and

(inst block-21 block)

until we add one more rule: from (forall (-*vars*-) p), infer p with all occurrences of each variable replaced by the same term. From the forall statement we can then infer

(if (inst block-21 block) (inst block-21 prism))

by replacing x with block-21. Now modus ponens can get us to

(inst block-21 prism)

Unfortunately, by applying these inference rules willy-nilly, we can infer many other useless formulas. A generalization of modus ponens called *forward chaining* is more directed. It skips over the intermediate step of inferring things like (if (inst eiffel-tower block) (inst eiffel-tower prism)). Instead, it waits until an assertion of the form (inst *thing* block) is added to the database, and then infers (inst *thing* prism). An essential prerequisite is to represent the quantified facts in the database in *implicit-quantifier form*. We just drop the "forall (x)," and replace every occurrence of "x" by "?x". This gives us

(if (inst ?x block) (inst ?x prism))

which means exactly the same thing as the original, but uses a different notation for universal quantification.

If a formula contains just one existential quantifier, not in the scope of any universals, as in

```
(exists (x) (and (nudist x)
               (polparty x republican)))
```

we can drop the quantifier and replace each variable by a brand-new constant. That is, if there is a nudist Republican, it can't hurt to give this person a name and use that instead. So we pick a hitherto meaningless name like sk-1, and assert

```
(and (nudist sk-1)
     (polparty sk-1 republican))
```

(If there are two or more such people, sk-1 refers to one of them.) For the handling of more complex existentials, see Section 6.3.2.

Now we change modus ponens to the following more general rule:

From p' and (if p q), infer q'.

where p *unifies with* p', and the resulting *substitution* is applied to q to give q'. *Unification* means finding values of variables that make two expressions equal. The two expressions

```
       (inst ?x block)
and    (inst block-21 block)
```

can be unified by the variable value x=block-21. In general the output will be a set of *variable=value* pairs, called a *substitution*. Each *variable=value* pair is called a *variable binding*; each variable is said to be *bound* in this substitution. *Applying* a substitution to a formula means replacing each occurrence of a bound variable with its value; in this case the result of applying the substitution {x=block-21} to (inst ?x prism) gives (inst block-21 prism). This rule of inference is a special case of the *resolution* rule. It is an improvement on other formulations of deduction because it replaces many separate mechanisms with one simple idea. (For the correct, most general statement of it, see Section 6.6.) Given an assertion p, to perform forward chainings requires only that we find assertions (if p' q) whose antecedents unify with it. (Such an implication is said to *resolve with* the assertion p.) As we will see in Chapter 7, there are standard indexing techniques that can make this efficient. However, there are global efficiency problems that the use of resolution does not solve.

We have been using Nevins's convention [Nevins74] that two primed pieces of the inputs can be unified (e.g., p and p'), and a primed output like q' is the result of applying the resulting substitution to the corresponding piece (q) of the input. We will use this convention several times in what follows in order to shorten the statement of inference rules. However, this convention will not always be flexible enough, so we will introduce some further notation. We will use Greek letters for substitutions, as in

$\theta = \{x=a, y=(surface\ ?z)\}$

If p is a formula or term, then $p\theta$ is the result of making the substitution of θ into p. For example, if p is (touching (side ?x) ?y), and θ is the substitution given above, then $p\theta$ is (touching (side a) (surface ?z)). One formula p *subsumes* another formula q if there is some substitution θ such that $p\theta = q$. (not (divine ?x)) subsumes (not (divine fred)), with $\theta = \{x{=}fred\}$. Subsumption may be used to express a simple inference rule: if p subsumes q, then q follows from p. Two formulas that subsume each other are called *variants*. They mean the same thing, but use different variable names in corresponding places. (For example, (p ?x ?x) is a variant of (p ?y ?y).) If p subsumes q but not vice versa, then p *properly subsumes* q. A substitution θ is a *unifier* of a set of formulas or terms $\{p_1,p_2, \ldots ,p_n\}$ if $p_1\theta{=}p_2\theta{=} \cdots {=}p_n\theta{=}P$ that is, if it makes them all the same formula P. A unifier is *most general* if the P it produces is not properly subsumed by the P produced by any other unifier. For example, consider the two formulas

> (above ?z floor-19)
> (if (above ?x ?y) (below ?y ?x))

One unifier of the first formula with the antecedent of the second is $\{x{=}table{-}21,\ y{=}floor{-}19,\ z{=}table{-}21\}$. This leads to the conclusion that (below floor-19 table-21). But the most general unifier is $\{x{=}?z,\ y{=}floor{-}19\}$, which leads to the conclusion (below floor-19 ?z). This conclusion properly subsumes the previous one, and hence is more general. Intuitively, it is better to arrive at more general conclusions, and using the most general unifier (*MGU*) guarantees maximum generality. Note that unification works even when both patterns to be unified contain variables. This is not so important in forward chaining, where it is rare to encounter atomic assertions with variables (note how artificial our examples are), but quite important for backward chaining, as we will discuss.

It can be proved that every set of formulas that can be unified has a unique MGU, but we will not do so here. Figure 6.6 shows an algorithm for finding MGUs. It takes two arguments, the two patterns to be unified, and returns a substitution unifying them, or nix if the two formulas cannot be unified. All the work of unify is done by subunify, which keeps track of the substitution found so far, as it walks through the two patterns in synchrony. When it is through, the final substitution is returned. In the simplest case, the two patterns contain no variables, and unify if and only if they are equal. The result will then be {}.

If there are variables, then the *variable bindings* in the result substitution are generated by function var-unify, shown in Figure 6.7. In var-unify, the check for whether var occurs in $pat\theta$ arises because of cases like this: Suppose we have

> (not (sees ?z ?z))
> (if (not (sees ?x (feet ?x)))
>   (should-diet ?x))

There is no unifier for the forward chain of these two formulas (nor should there be). The algorithm would first call var-unify on ?z and ?x, making $\theta{=}\{z{=}?x\}$. The next call to var-unify would find ?z already bound to ?x, so

Function: unify
Arguments: pat1, pat2 - the two formulas to unify
Algorithm: Call subunify with arguments pat1, pat2, and {}.

Function: subunify
Arguments: pat1, pat2 — two formulas to unify
θ the substitution so far

Algorithm:
    If pat1 and pat2 are equal, return θ.
    If pat1 and pat2 are unequal atoms, return nix.
    If one of the patterns is a variable, call var-unify
        to try to make its value unify with the other pattern.
    Otherwise, the two patterns must be list structures.
    If they are different lengths, return nix.
    Otherwise,
        call subunify on corresponding pieces of pat1 and pat2,
            passing it θ.
        Each such call will return nix or a result substitution θ'.
        As soon as nix is returned, that means some pieces of
            pat1 and pat2 failed to unify, so return nix.
        Otherwise, reset $\theta \leftarrow \theta'$ after each call to subunify.
        When all pieces have been unified, return θ.

Figure 6.6 Unification algorithm

Function: var-unify
Arguments: variable — a predicate-calculus variable
             pat — a pattern to unify with it
             θ —the substitution so far (from previous
                         parts of the patterns)

Algorithm:
    If variable already has a value in θ,
        then return the value of unifying that value with
        pat (found using subunify).
    Otherwise, if pat is the same as variable, return θ
        since a variable trivially unifies with itself.
    Otherwise, check to see if variable occurs in patθ.
        If so, return nix.   *; see text for explanation*
        If not, add variable=pat to θ, and
            return the augmented substitution.

Figure 6.7 Algorithm for unifying a variable

var-unify would be called recursively on ?x and (feet ?x). If the algorithm simply returned $\theta' = \{x = (feet\ ?x)\}$, this would not be a unifier. (Check this for yourself.) But the check for whether ?x occurs in (feet ?x) will catch the circularity, and cause the algorithm to return nix.

So far we have neglected an important issue. Suppose the machine is trying to forward chain on these two formulas:

> (on ?x table)
> (if (on big-bertha ?x) (collapses ?x))

Intuitively, it should be able to conclude (collapses table), but there is no way to unify (on ?x table) with (on big-bertha ?x). The problem is that the occurrence of ?x in both formulas is a coincidence; they are completely different variables. The solution is to rename all the variables in the two formulas that have the same name. (In practice, the simplest way to accomplish this is to rename *all* the variables in one of the formulas with brand-new names. See Exercise 6.16.) This process is often called *standardizing* the two formulas *apart*.

6.3.2 Skolemization

We told you in Section 6.3.1 how to remove simple universal and existential quantifiers, by flagging universals with "?", and replacing existentials with new symbols. More complex quantifier constructions require a more general technique called *Skolemization* to eliminate their quantifiers (after Thoraf Skolem, the logician). For universals, nothing changes in the general case: universally quantified variables are always turned into pattern-matching variables; the universal quantification becomes implicit in the fact that such a variable will match anything.

Existential variables are trickier. In general, every existential variable must be turned into a function term whose arguments are the universal variables from quantifiers whose scopes include that of the existential quantifier. This term then replaces every occurrence of the variable. For example, "Every person has a head" is represented as:

> (forall (x)
>   (if (inst x person)   ; *If x is a person then*
>   (exists (y) (and (inst y head)   ; *there exists a head y*
>   (partof y x)))))   ; *which is part of x.*

or, Skolemized, as:

> (if (inst ?x person)   ; *If ?x is a person, then*
>   (and (inst (head-of ?x) head)   ; *(head-of ?x) is a head*
>   (partof (head-of ?x) ?x)))   ; *and part of ?x.*

where head-of is a new function symbol. As in the simple-existential case, the idea is that, if something exists, we can at least give it a name. In the example, Fred's head is given the name (head-of fred). The trick of making the new symbol a function of some universal variables is a way of generating an infinite supply of object names: (head-of fred), (head-of sally), etc. The original case, where we made up a new constant sk-1, can be seen as making up a function of no arguments when there are no universal quantifiers of wider scope than the existential being eliminated.

Because terms in the predicate calculus denote unique entities, when we introduce the function head-of we must be sure that it is not used in other contexts to mean different things. To ensure such uniqueness, a mechanical Skolemization algorithm would generate ugly-looking terms like (sk-2 fred), using a stream of brand-new symbols of the form sk-*n*. Most of the time, however AI researchers Skolemize "by hand" and then mnemonic functions names make more sense.

This is pretty simple, but unfortunately there is a complication: You can't always tell the type of a quantifier at a glance. (not (exists (x) (divine x))) and (forall (x) (not (divine x))) express the same atheistic thought, that nothing is divine, but one has an existential quantifier and the other a universal quantifier. A moment's thought should convince you that the existential quantifier has no force, since no object's existence is being asserted. (not (divine sk-4)) would mean "There is something that is not divine" when what we want is "Everything is not divine." So the proper Skolemization is (not (divine ?x)). In general, the true type of a quantifier depends on the number of nots that dominate it. What's tricky is to remember that (if *p q*) is the same as (or (not *p*) *q*), so the antecedent of an implication behaves as if negated. That is, an existential in the left-hand side gets treated as a universal, and vice versa. For example, "A car without wheels is not valuable" or

```
(forall (c)
   (if (and (inst c car)
            (not (exists (x) (and (inst x wheel) (attached x c)))))
       (not (valuable c))))
```

would be Skolemized as

```
(if (and (inst ?c car)
         (not (and (inst (sk-5 ?c) wheel) (attached (sk-5 ?c) ?c))))
    (not (valuable ?c)))
```

The existential occurs inside a not *and* inside the antecedent of the implication, so it behaves like an existential. In general, to tell the true type of a quantifier, count the nots and if-antecedents it appears in; if the number is odd, flip the type.

Be aware of another complication — the possibility of name collisions. If the same variable is quantified twice in a formula, you must change one of them before Skolemizing. For example, this formula

```
(forall (y) (if (and (exists (x) (just-left x y))
                      (exists (x) (just-left y x)))
                (crowded y)))
```

which may be read as, "If there is someone to your left and someone to your right (in a movie theater, perhaps), you are crowded," must be Skolemized to

```
(if (and (just-left ?xl ?y) (just-left ?y ?xr))
    (crowded ?y))
```

Because of the delicacy of the interaction between Skolemizing and negation, it is in general hard to form the negation of a Skolemized formula. If the formula contains any free variables or Skolem terms, you must un-Skolemize, negate, and re-Skolemize. For example, the negation of (loves ?x (sk-6 ?x)), where sk-6 is a Skolem function, would be (not (loves sk-7 ?y)), where sk-7 is a Skolem constant. That is, the opposite of "Everybody loves someone" is "Somebody (i.e., sk-7) doesn't love anyone." Figure 6.8 gives a summary of the Skolemization process.

6.3.3 Backward Chaining

Although *forward chaining* is easy to understand, in a typical deductive database most inferences are done at query time, using the rule called *backward chaining*. In this form of inference, the database *gatekeeper* doesn't do anything with the implication (if p q) until it is trying to answer a query of the form q', when it proposes p' as a "*subquery*." We will often use the term *goal* instead of *query*, because from the point of view of the deductive process the aim is to find instances of the query pattern, and such goals will have subgoals and sub-subgoals derived from backward chaining. In fact, the goal-tree idea we developed in Chapter 5 will turn out to be perfect for talking about this process. (See Section 6.3.4.)

In this section, we will talk about the basic mechanics of backward chaining, and worry about the search structure later. Given a goal q' and an implication (if p q), where q and q' have MGU θ, the rule of Backward Chaining says to derive the subgoal $p' = p\theta$, that is, the result of substituting the variable values from θ into p. (Of course, q' and (if p q) are assumed to have been standardized apart, as discussed in Section 6.3.1.) In forward chaining, the assertion resolves with the implication; in backward chaining, we say instead

---

1. Determine which variables are existential and which universal. (They switch for each not which has them in its scope, including the antecedents of if statements.)
2. Replace each existentially quantified variable by a function. The arguments of the function are all the universally quantified variables which include the existential in their scope.
3. If two different universally quantified variables have the same name, rename one of them.
4. Replace each universally quantified v by ?v.

Figure 6.8 Skolemization

that the goal resolves with the implication. For instance, if we are trying to prove (inst block-21 prism), then we can resolve this goal with (if (inst ?x block) (inst ?x prism)) to generate the subgoal (inst block-21 block). If this formula is in the fact base, then we are entitled to infer that block-21 is a prism, our original goal.

It's important to distinguish between formulas that are asserted and formulas used as goals. Where the context does not make our intent clear, we will use the notation (Show: *formula*) for the latter. In the example, the goal (or query) (Show: (inst block-21 prism)) gave rise to the goal (Show: (inst block-21 block)). Show: is not a connective; we use a possibly misleading notation for it because of its close relationship to not, as explained in Section 6.6.

In a goal, the conventions for Skolemizing variables are reversed. A "?"-marked symbol is existentially interpreted; we are looking for a term that satisfies the goal. The goal (Show: (inst ?y prism)) means, "Show that there exists a prism." By contrast, the goal (Show: (forall (y) (inst y prism))) gets transformed into something like (Show: (inst sk-8 prism)), where sk-8 is a brand-new symbol. The intuition is that if you can show that sk-8 is a prism, then you could show that *anything* is a prism. Existential goals have interesting behavior. The goal (Show: (inst ?y prism)) would resolve with our by-now-familiar implication to generate the subgoal (Show: (inst ?y block)). (Here the unification generated the bindings $\{x=?y\}$.) We still get a solution, since this meets with the fact (inst block-21 block) in the fact base. But we get more than that — we get a value for the variable y. The last unification gives us $\{y = block-21\}$. So the original deductive request does not get just the answer "Yes, there is a prism" but "Yes, block-21 is a prism": $\{x=block-21\}$. Another way to put this is that backward chaining ultimately returns one or more *substitutions* as answers. If q unifies with a, giving θ, then the goal (Show: q) has answer θ if a is in the database. Other answers to a goal are derived from the rule of backward chaining, which is revised to read thus:

Given goal (Show: q')
    where (if p q) is in the database,
    and q' and q have MGU θ,
produce subgoal (Show: $p\theta$)
    and if this has answer ψ, then $\theta \cup \psi$ is
    an answer to the original goal.

Conjunctions must be handled specially in backward chaining. The goal (Show: r') will chain through (if (and p q) r) to generate the subgoal (Show: (and p' q')). This is called a *conjunctive goal*. This is to be handled by finding variable bindings that are answers to both (Show: p') and (Show: q'). In practice, as we will see, this is done by generating answers to one conjunct, and throwing away those that don't work on the other conjunct. For example, say we are given the conjunctive goal

(Show: (and (respect ?x ?y) (not (older ?y ?x))))

and the database shown in Figure 6.9. There are two answers to the goal: {x=sally, y=sally}, and {x=fred, y=oswald}. Exercise 6.19 asks you to verify this.

6.3.4 Goal Trees for Backward Chaining

We have been vague so far about the order in which backward chainings are done. Given a nonconjunctive goal, the machine has to find an implication to chain through. Given a conjunctive goal, the machine has to find answers to one conjunct that work on the others. In this section, we will clarify how to find things like this. The resulting algorithm is generically known as a *theorem prover* or *deductive retriever*. Given a goal, one thing we could try is to look for implications whose conclusions unify with the goal. (How to do this efficiently will be dealt with in Chapter 7.) The problem is that we may find more than one. In Figure 6.10, we have shown a schematic example. *P* may be proved using either implication. Each implication will give rise to two subgoals, *both* of which must be proved to prove *P*. Not surprisingly, this is a goal tree, as discussed in Chapter 5. Recall that the and nodes of a goal tree contain *constraints* on the solutions to each of their component or children. For theorem proving, the constraint is that the variable bindings for the subsolutions be identical. To illustrate this, we have to add variables to our problem: Consider the problem of finding a proof for (p ?x) given the implications

(if (and (q1 ?x) (q2 ?x)) (p ?x))　　; *Referred to later as R1*
(if (and (r1 ?x) (r2 ?x)) (p ?x))　　; *Referred to later as R2*

together in a database with these atomic formulas:

(if (older ?x ?z) (respect ?x ?x))	; *If you're older than someone,*
	; *you respect yourself.*
(if (can-do-rubiks-cube ?x)	; *Everyone respects someone who*
(respect ?everyone ?x))	; *can do Rubik's cube.*
(respect fred sally)	; *Fred respects Sally.*
(older sally fred)	; *Sally is older than Fred.*
(not (older ?x ?x))	; *No one is older than himself.*
(if (younger ?x ?y)	; *If x is younger than y, x*
(not (older ?x ?y)))	; *is not older.*
(if (and (inst ?x child)	; *Children are younger than*
(inst ?y adult))	; *adults.*
(younger ?x ?y))	;
(inst oswald child)	; *Oswald is a child.*
(inst fred adult)	; *Fred is an adult.*
(can-do-rubiks-cube oswald)	; *Oswald can do Rubik's cube*

Figure 6.9 An example database

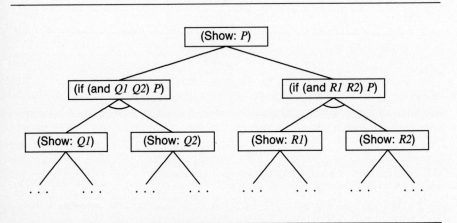

Figure 6.10 Theorem proving goal tree

(q1 a)   (q1 b)   (q2 a)   (q2 b)
(r1 c)   (r2 d)

This problem gives rise to the goal tree shown in Figure 6.11. (For future reference, it is labeled using the convention of Chapter 5; the dotted lines will be explained later.) The ?x used to solve (q1 ?x) must also solve (q2 ?x). Only the left branch is solvable, because the two r solutions are in fact incompatible.

In a sense, predicate calculus is a "universal goal-tree generator." Any goal-tree problem can be expressed as a predicate-calculus problem. For instance, the "Dating Game" goal tree of Chapter 5 might result from the goal

(Show: (and (datable ?p)
            (restaurant ?r)
            (likes ?p ?r)
            (entertainment ?e)
            (likes ?p ?e)
            (< (+ (cost ?e) (cost ?r))
               $100)))

plus facts about restaurants, entertainment, costs, and arithmetic. This universality has been one source of the fascination predicate calculus has held for many AI researchers.

Unfortunately, it is hard to find good general-purpose ways to search goal trees. The problem is that, in the abstract, without knowing more about the application domain, it can be arbitrarily difficult to find a solution to one child of an **and** node that is also a solution to all the others. There is little else to do but generate solutions to one (which can be expensive), and throw away those that don't work out for the others (also expensive, and for nothing if the verdict is "no"). In Chapter 5, we discussed in general terms how to search through

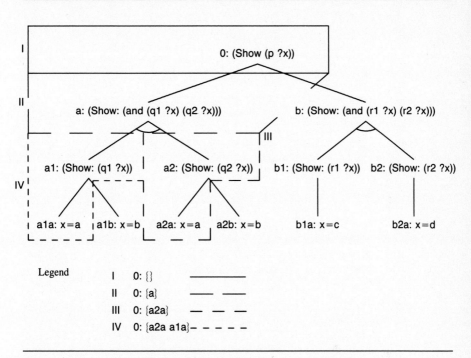

Figure 6.11 Goal tree with conjunctive goals sharing variables

the space of partial solutions to a goal tree. For theorem proving, partial solutions have a simple representation, as the variable bindings discovered so far,
plus the goals that remain. Each goal gives rise to a choice, namely, a choice
of implications to chain through to solve it. The initial partial solution is
"empty substitution, goals = {top-goal}." A partial solution is extended by
picking a goal g to work on, and finding all the assertions in the database of the
form g' or (if p g'). The unification (signaled by the primes) gives the algorithm
new variable bindings to work with. If the assertion is of the form g', then the
chosen goal is just eliminated from the set, and the substitution is plugged into
the remaining goals. If the assertion is of the form (if p g'), then the conjuncts
of p' are added to the goal set as well. At any moment, the set of remaining
goals is called a *sibling goal set*. For example, the sequence of partial solutions
shown in Figure 6.12 might be generated in solving the tree of Figure 6.11. In
Figure 6.12 and future diagrams of this sort "Use:" indicates how the partial
solution was generated, and "Order:" specifies the order in which the partial
solutions are generated. When an empty list of goals is reached, the substitution
represents a complete solution.

In Figure 6.11, these partial solutions are shown as subtrees of the goal
tree. These two representations are complementary. Partial solution III, for
instance, may be thought of as choices already made (at nodes **0** and **a2**), or as

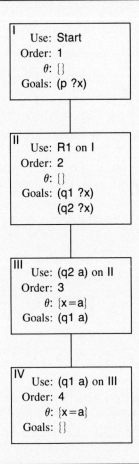

Figure 6.12 Sequence of partial solutions for Figure 6.11

choices remaining to be made (at node a1, which is now the goal (Show: (q1 a)).

Now we have a search space; the next question is what order to search it in. Two obvious alternatives are breadth-first and depth-first search, which are both easy to implement. For example, one depth-first order of exploration of Figure 6.11 is shown in Figure 6.13 (goals only). Note that the attempt to solve (and (r1 ?x) (r2 ?x)) is given up only when all possibilities have been exhausted. In Figure 6.14, one breadth-first order of exploration is shown. In this strategy, we work on (and (r1 ?x) (r2 ?x)) "in parallel" with (and (q1 ?x) (q2 ?x)).

What we really need is a heuristic evaluation function that will tell us when a set of goals is promising. Figure 6.16 and Figure 6.17 show a simple example, the search generated by the query (Show: (and (above ?x table)

(p ?x)	*; (I) Original request.*
(and (r1 ?x) (r2 ?x))	*; (Call this A) Used R2 on I.*
(r2 c)	*; (B) Used (r1 c) on A.*
(and (q1 ?x) (q2 ?x))	*; (II) Dead end, used R1 on I.*
(q1 a)	*; (III) Used (q2 a) on II.*
Success	*; (IV) Used (q1 a) on III.*

Figure 6.13 Depth-first search for proof

(p ?x)	*; (I) Original request.*
(and (q1 ?x) (q2 ?x))	*; (II) Used R1 on I.*
(and (r1 ?x) (r2 ?x))	*; (A) Used R2 on I.*
(q1 a)	*; (III) Used (q2 a) on II.*
(r2 c)	*; (B) Used (r1 c) on A.*
Success	*; (IV) Used (q1 a) on III.*

Figure 6.14 Breadth-first search for proof

1	(if (and (above ?x ?y) (above ?y ?z)) (above ?x ?z))
2	(if (on ?x ?y) (above ?x ?y))
3	(on bl-1 table)
4	(on bl-2 bl-1)
5	(on bl-3 bl-1)
6	(on bl-4 bl-2)
7	(above lamp1 table)
8	(color table beige)
9	(color bl-1 red)
10	(color bl-2 white)
11	(color bl-3 blue)
12	(color bl-4 green)
13	(color lamp1 yellow)

Figure 6.15 Example predicate-calculus database

(color ?x green))) ("Find something green above the table") for the database of Figure 6.15. At any given time there are one or more partial solutions which could be extended. The heuristic we use is to work on the partial solution with the fewest sibling goals. For instance, the boxes labeled 16 and 17 correspond to two alternative partial solutions derived from the partial solution in box 15. Box 17 looks more attractive because it has only one sibling; in this case, the attempt to work on 17 fails immediately, however, so attention is directed back to box 16, producing new solutions 18 and 19. Now box 19 looks more attractive than 18 (since it has two siblings to 18's three), and in fact the evaluation

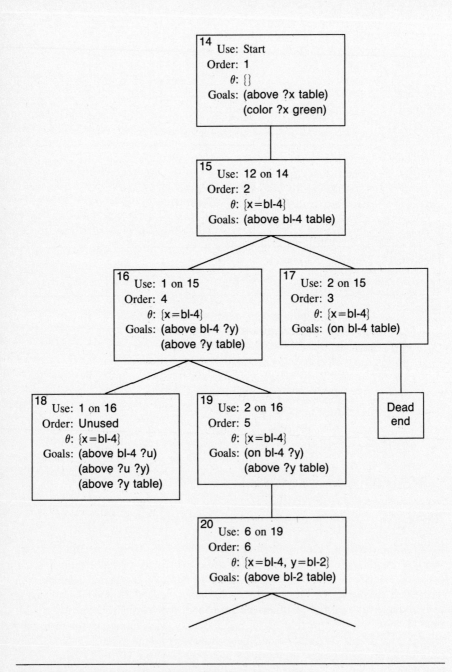

Figure 6.16 Search generated for Figure 6.15 — part 1

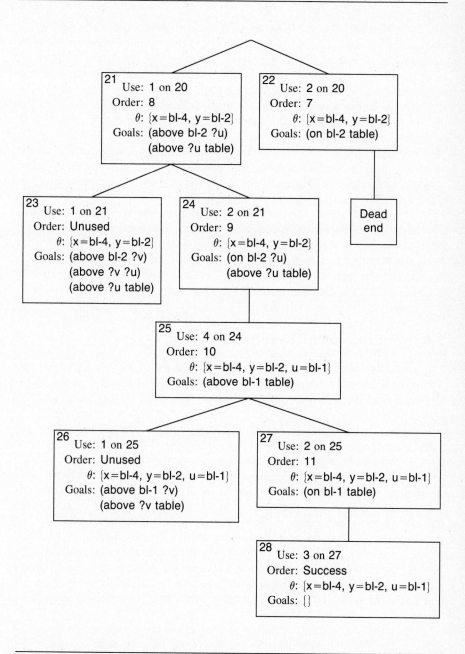

Figure 6.17 Search generated for Figure 6.15 — part 2

function never does find box 18 attractive enough to work on, so its order slot remains marked "unused."

A partial solution can have more than one sibling goal, and you might imagine that in such cases it would pay to explore all the siblings in parallel. As explained in Exercise 6.22, however, there is never any reason to work on more than one sibling goal from a partial solution. Hence in Figure 6.16 and Figure 6.17 we have chosen one goal to work on at each partial solution. The choice is based on a simple criterion: the sibling goal is chosen that resolves with the fewest assertions. All such backward chainings are done, resulting in new partial solutions.

Note that the search space is surprisingly large, even for such a simple problem. Fifteen partial solutions are generated, of which five are "blind alleys" (either they match nothing, or are so large that they get postponed forever). For more on this example, see Exercise 6.23.

Figure 6.17 shows the derivation of just one answer. Of course, there may be others, and there are still partial solutions left to extend. When should the theorem prover keep looking? In general, this is a difficult question. If there were no variables in the original query, then, of course, it can stop after one answer. In some cases [Smith83], it can do a precheck to find the number of possible answers, and stop when that number is reached.

6.4 Applications of Theorem Proving

It is possible to get the impression that the general-purpose deduction techniques we have presented are so good that you need only take axioms like those of Section 6.2.3, put them into the theorem prover, and make all the deductions you need.

In fact, such an approach will almost always get you nowhere. For one thing, many reasoning processes are not deductive. For example, one goal of story understanding is to infer the best hypotheses about the goals of the characters and author. ("Celia is rejecting Donald because she has been self-destructive since childhood. The author is trying to illustrate the *angst* of modern man.") Such an "abductive" reasoning process, while it uses the same representations as deductions, is done differently. See Chapters 8 and 10. We reserve the term "deduction" for reasoning about what conclusions are probably true given current premises, when there is nothing like a "competing" conclusion, as there is in the case of inference to the best explanation. For instance, given a physical system, predicting what it will do (or all the things it might do) is a deductive task. (We call this process *projection*, and we will study it in Chapter 7.)

Even if we restrict attention to deductive tasks, the general-purpose methods described in Sections 6.3 and 6.6 must be used with caution. The problem with them is that they are doing search, with only weak heuristic guidance. This usually leads to poor performance.

If you think about it, it would be a miracle if general-purpose methods always worked well. Think how easy it would be to axiomatize a predicate (chess-win *position player move*). If resolution always worked, we could just input the goal (chess-win *initial-board* white ?move), and find all values of ?move that won for white. In principle, we could do exactly this, but in practice it would be ridiculously expensive. (See Exercise 6.24.)

There are two basic approaches to this problem. One is to make theorem provers more sophisticated, adding better heuristics, and pruning the search space. The other is to tailor the axioms, avoiding intractable problems. In Sections 6.4.1 and 6.4.2, we will briefly sketch where each of these ideas leads.

6.4.1 Mathematical Theorem Proving

One of the most obvious applications of deduction is to mathematical theorem proving. Here the axioms are already known, and few in number. Proofs are typically long and complicated. Because of this, and because blind alleys cause an exponential growth in the goal tree with depth, researchers in this area concentrate on generating as few hopeless subgoals as possible.

Let us illustrate where hopeless subgoals can come from. We will use a nonmathematical example for clarity. Suppose a dating service uses a theorem prover to keep track of facts about people, in particular the "fact" that anyone with a technical interest is incompatible with anyone with a nontechnical one:

(if (and (interest ?p1 ?c1) (technical ?c1)
        (interest ?p2 ?c2) (not (technical ?c2)))
  (not (compatible ?p1 ?p2)))

The problem arises when the theorem prover is given the goal (Show: (not (compatible fred sally))). It generates four sibling subgoals

(Show: (interest fred ?c1))
(Show: (technical ?c1))
(Show: (interest sally ?c2))
(Show: (not (technical ?c2)))

Suppose the first two goals are solved, with c1=computers. Now the machine tries to solve the third and fourth goals. Suppose this attempt fails, because all of Sally's interests are technical. Then the entire rule should fail, and some other way should be tried to show Fred and Sally incompatible. Unfortunately, the original subgoal is still kicking around the goal-tree search; if another interest for Fred is found, in the form of another binding of ?c1, then the tree searcher will try again to show that Sally has a nontechnical interest.

This is called the *independent conjunctive goal* problem. Ignoring it causes a lot of work to be duplicated. There are ways of solving it. One method, called *selective backtracking*, is to analyze a goal failure to determine which variable bindings are responsible. In the example, ?c1 would be exonerated as having nothing to do with the inability to find a nontechnical interest for Sally, so no attempt would be made to find another binding for it.

Another approach is to analyze goal conjunctions in advance, separating them into classes whose failure or success is independent,

A simpler problem is that the same goal can appear many times in a goal-tree search; it wastes a lot of effort if the work of finding answers to it is repeated each time. The solution is to keep track of goals, and avoid working on any one goal more than once. The second time the machine sees a particular goal, it can just generate the answers it found last time. A special case of some interest is when a goal reappears as a subgoal of itself. For instance, in plane geometry, one can prove two triangles congruent by (to name one method) proving corresponding sides equal in length. But you can prove two line segments equal in length by showing they belong to congruent triangles. See Figure 6.18. In the case where the repeated subgoal has no variables, we can just abandon it. (If there is a proof of it, it will be found at the higher level anyway.) If the goal does have variables, then answers to the original occurrence must be fed back into the subgoal. (If you don't follow this last point, see Exercise 6.37.) Keeping track of repeated subgoals is like keeping track of repeated states in ordinary search. In many cases, a discrimination tree is an efficient way of storing them. (See Chapter 5.)

Gelernter's geometry theorem prover [Gelernter59] had a clever way of rejecting useless subgoals. It would be given problems in the form of an implication with universally quantified variables:

(Show: (forall (a b c . . .)
        (if (and $(p_1$ a b . . .) $(p_2$ a b . . .) . . .)
        (q a b . . .))))

In implicit-quantifier form, these would become Skolem constants:

(Show: (if (and $(p_1$ A B . . .) $(p_2$ A B . . .) . . .)
        (q A B . . .)))

We use A, B, etc. instead of sk-9 and sk-10 for aesthetic reasons. The p_i and q would be predicates like "is a line" or "are parallel." In addition, the program would be given a diagram, that is, an assignment of Cartesian coordinates

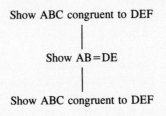

Figure 6.18 Repeated subgoal in geometry theorem proving

to the anonymous constants that made (and (p_1 A B . . .) . . .) true. It would also (in essence) assert each (p_i A B . . .) true, then attempt to prove (q A B . . .). A typical problem might look like this:

Show: (if (and (parallel (line A B) (line C D))
          (parallel (line A C) (line B D))
          (intersect (line A D) (line B C) E))
     (ang= (angle A D B) (angle D A C)))

The diagram is shown in Figure 6.19.

Gelernter's program used the following filtering device: if a subgoal was proposed which was false in the diagram, it would be rejected. For example, in Figure 6.19, suppose that the subgoal (Show: (congruent (triangle A D B) (triangle E A C))) is proposed. The machine would measure the lengths of the sides DB and EC (using the Pythagorean formula on their coordinates), and verify that the triangles are not congruent in the diagram. Then it would never make the attempt to prove them congruent. This is a safe thing to do, because the diagram represents a counterexample to the subgoal; it is a case where (and (p_1 A B . . .) . . .) is true, but the subgoal is false. So it is bound to be pointless to try to prove that the subgoal follows from this conjunction. Furthermore, it is a useful thing to do, because the chances are small that a subgoal is true in the diagram when it does not actually follow from the premises. It is interesting that no theorem prover since then has used a diagram like this. The

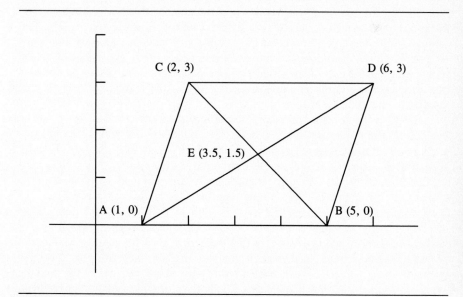

Figure 6.19 A geometry-theorem problem

problem seems to be that there are few domains in which "counterexample generators" like diagrams are available.

Another way in which useless subgoals can be generated is through axioms introducing equality. The straightforward treatment of equality is to add, for every predicate and argument position, an axiom of the form

$$(\text{if } (\text{and } (p \ ?a_1 \ldots ?a_{i-1} \ ?x \ ?a_{i+1} \ldots ?a_n)$$
$$(= \ ?x \ ?y))$$
$$(p \ ?a_1 \ldots ?a_{i-1} \ ?y \ ?a_{i+1} \ldots ?a_n)$$

Unfortunately, these axioms can create a huge number of subgoals. Axioms like these

$$(= (f \ (f \ ?x \ ?y) \ ?z) \ (f \ ?x \ (f \ ?y \ ?z))) \qquad ; f \text{ is associative}$$
$$(= (f \ ?x \ ?y) \ (f \ ?y \ ?x)) \qquad ; f \text{ is commutative}$$

which assert the associativity and commutativity of f, interact with equality axioms to produce more subgoals. Most of them end up being useless. The solution is to treat such axioms using special mechanisms, either altering the unification algorithm to take them into account or using *rewrite rules* to put all terms into a canonical form.

Even after every device has been plugged into resolution theorem provers, there are still some profound problems with them. For one thing, they work best on finite sets of formulas. In mathematical theorem proving (especially in number theory and proofs of program properties), there is often an infinite number of axioms, generated by "axiom schemas." (We will say more about these in Box 6.1 but for those who know some number theory, we have in mind things like mathematical induction, which cannot be expressed as a single axiom.) While there is no problem in principle with interleaving deduction steps with generation of new axioms, most of these new axioms are irrelevant to the problem at hand, and will generate millions of useless subgoals. For domains like these, some control structure is needed above the resolution level to pick out useful axioms [Boyer79].

Even ignoring this problem, resolution theorem provers seem to be doomed to using *generate-and-test*, a very weak method, for solving conjunctive goals that share variables. Given a goal (and (p ?x) (q ?x)), they all work by generating instances of (p ?x) and testing to see if they satisfy (q ?x). It is hard for the former process to take cognizance of the ultimate destination of its answers, so the q goal can wait a long time for a useful answer to pop out.

We don't mean to imply that there is some alternative to resolution. If the theorem-proving problem is thought of as, "Take these axioms, which you've never seen before, and try to derive this theorem," then it's hard to see how to do better. But human mathematicians don't do anything like this. Human mathematicians, given a conjecture to prove or disprove, begin by thinking about the domain of the conjecture, which they are intimately familiar with already. Except in special cases, they probably could not even tell you what the axioms of this domain are. Instead, they do things like exploring what it would mean for the theorem to be true; trying to find lemmas that would prove the theorem, and which "look true"; seeking counterexamples to the theorem and the proposed lemmas. While each of these things has counterparts in the world of resolution theorem proving, they seem to be in a quite different space, of strategies, plans, and domain models, rather than a space of most general unifiers and conjunctive goals. It is somewhat odd that no one has attempted to formalize mathematical theorem proving as a planning problem in this space (using methods like those of Chapter 9). We conjecture that this is because the people writing the programs to duplicate mathematicians are themselves mathematicians, and they can't bear to write a program unless they can prove it has nice, tidy properties. A program that sets about proving theorems in the manner of a human mathematician would be anything but tidy.

A few closing remarks. Although we have ignored this fact, the theorem prover we have presented is not capable of proving all of the theorems which can, in principle, be proved. That is to say, it is *incomplete*. (We will show why this is the case in Section 6.6.) For serious theorem proving, this incompleteness makes our theorem prover unacceptable [Loveland76]. Nonetheless, all the things we said apply to more general (and *complete*) versions.

We should also point out that a distinction is sometimes drawn between "resolution" and "nonresolution" theorem proving (e.g., [Bledsoe77]). We have used the term "resolution" for any rule of inference based on unification. Many would place more stringent conditions. However, no one uses resolution in exactly the pure original form, and there is not much agreement on the number of alterations beyond which it is not resolution any more.

6.4.2 Deductive Retrieval and Logic Programming

One alternative to making the theorem prover more sophisticated is to keep it simple and make sure it never gets problems it can't handle. If we want, we can go all the way, and think of the theorem prover as a language interpreter, which we program by giving it axioms. This is the idea behind the Prolog language and its ancestors, such as Planner.

We will come back to logic programming later in this section. For now, let us instead explore "hints" that can make a theorem prover's job easier. One class of hints concerns whether an implication should be used for backward or forward chaining. Usually it is better to use backward chaining, which waits until an answer is needed before trying to infer it. Forward chaining is fast at query time, but uses up cycles at assertion time — and this time would be spent for nothing if the query never occurs. There are cases, however, when forward chaining is better. The predicate inst supplies the standard example. We have got lots of rules like

    (if (inst ?x dog) (inst ?x mammal))
    (if (inst ?x pig) (inst ?x mammal))
    (if (inst ?x mammal) (inst ?x animal))

In fact, the rules define the classic phylum-genus-species tree, shown in Figure 6.20. If we use these rules in a backward way, then the query (Show: (inst fido

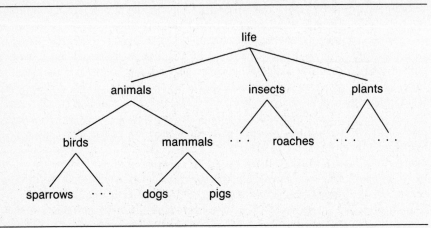

Figure 6.20 Biological taxonomy tree

animal)) will require a large goal-tree search. We will get the subgoals

    (Show: (inst fido bird))
    (Show: (inst fido mammal))
    (Show: (inst fido insect))

and each of these will create many subgoals as well. It will take a long time to realize that Fido is an animal because he is a dog.

If, on the other hand, we use each implication in a forward way, then as soon as we assert (inst fido dog), we will assert (inst fido mammal), (inst fido animal), and (inst fido life). Now the query about whether he is an animal is handled quickly. The price is that representing what Fido is takes several assertions, not one. It seems worth paying in this case.

In general, forward chaining should be used when the following criteria are met:

- Backward chaining would be inefficient.
- The formulas in question are likely to be queried about. (inst is such an important predicate that it is likely our work inferring inst formulas will not go to waste.)
- The forward chaining will terminate quickly.

This last point is crucial. If the inferences in the forward direction are just as inefficient as those in the backward direction, then we are sunk. No general-purpose algorithm will help.

How is the theorem prover to figure out when to use forward and when to use backward chaining? It would be nice if the machine could figure out for each formula how it should be used. Someday this may be a reality. For now, in a practical system, we must tell it. If (if *p* *q*) is to be used forward, we write it in the following form:

$(\rightarrow p\ q)$

If it is to be used backward, we write it in this form instead:

$(\leftarrow q\ p)$

For example,

$(\leftarrow$ (inst ?x mammal) (inst ?x dog))   *; Prove Fido is a mammal*
                                                       ; on demand.

$(\rightarrow$ (inst ?x dog) (inst ?x mammal))   *; Assert Fido is a mammal*
                                                       ; immediately.

Note the reversal. This takes a little getting used to, but has been almost universally adopted. The reason for it is that q is the "trigger pattern" of the backward chainer, the way p is for the forward chainer; so in both formats the pattern right after the arrow is the one that is unified with the assertion or query the theorem prover is working with.

We have discussed how a rule of the form (if (and $p\ q$) r) is handled during backward chaining. Is there a way to use it forward? Clearly, just putting $(\rightarrow$ (and $p\ q$) $r)$ into the database is inappropriate because it is unlikely that (and $p\ q$) will be asserted. What we want instead is for r to be asserted whenever compatible versions of p and q have been asserted, in either order. One way to accomplish this is to put

$(\rightarrow p\ (\rightarrow q\ r))$

into the database. Now if p' is asserted, $(\rightarrow q'\ r')$ will be asserted, and q'' will cause r'' to be asserted. (For this to work, the database manager must make sure that when something of the form $(\rightarrow a\ c)$ is asserted, all currently asserted a' are found, and the corresponding c' asserted. Otherwise, the order in which p' and q'' are asserted might affect the result.)

In addition to requiring such hints, it is quite common to enforce a very simple search order on a theorem prover: depth-first search, with sibling goals being dealt with left to right. The reason is that it is quite easy to implement (and easy for the axiom writer to envision). But this design decision means that many "recursive" axioms (those that mention the same predicate in both antecedent and consequent) will not work. The example at the end of Section 6.3.4 is a case in point. See Exercise 6.25.

At this point, anyone using the theorem prover must to some degree start "programming" it; that is, the user must avoid writing axioms that will cause it to blow up. In the case of Figure 6.15, the offending axiom (number 1) can be rewritten thus (and now we explicitly note that it is to be used for backward chaining):

1 $(\leftarrow$ (above ?x ?z)
      (and (on ?y ?z) (above ?x ?y)))

Now, a goal like (Show: (above ?x table)) will find the correct answers. See Exercise 6.26.

After all this, there are three possible reactions to theorem provers:

- Lose interest in them, since they must be fed so gingerly.
- Stay interested, but confine your attention to domains where axioms that make them sick are rare.
- Become even more interested, and start exploring other ways of programming them.

The last possibility has led to *logic programming*. If we lose our squeamishness, we can start to think of backward chaining as a sort of program-interpretation process. A goal is like a procedure call. An implication is like a procedure body (or a cond clause). Unification is like calling the procedure; variables are passed in one way, and answers come back when the procedure returns. Here is the standard example

    (append nil ?x ?x)

    (← (append (cons ?a ?x) ?y (cons ?a ?z))
       (append ?x ?y ?z))

Each of these axioms may be read as an axiom about the predicate append. The formula (append *l1 l2 l3*) is supposed to mean, "Appending list *l1* to list *l2* gives list *l3*." Under this interpretation, the first axiom says, "Appending nil to any list gives that list." The second says, "If appending ?x to ?y gives ?z, then appending a list with one more element gives ?z with one more element." Thus (append [a b] [foo] [a b foo]) would be true, while (append [a b] [foo] [foo a b]) would be false.

But it is also possible to treat the pair of axioms as a procedure. We can call it with a goal like (Show: (append [how about] [that] ?r)). The resulting stack of subroutine calls is shown in Figure 6.21. Note that since [x y . . .] is just an abbreviation for (cons x (cons y . . . nil)), (cons ?a ?x) unifies with {[how about that]}, giving {a=how, x=[about that]}.

θ: {}
Goals: {(append [how about] [that] ?r)}

    θ: {r=(cons how ?z)}
    Goals: {(append [about] [that] ?z)}

        θ: {r=(cons how (cons about ?z1))}
        Goals: {(append nil [that] ?z1)}

            θ: {r=[how about that]}
            Goals: {}

Figure 6.21 Depth-first execution of append program

We don't have the space to go into logic programming, a rich and rapidly expanding topic. Suffice it to say that unification and backtracking combine to give a powerful and flavorful language. The dialect that is currently most successful is Prolog. (See Exercise 6.29.)

Although logic programming is fascinating, it is getting us off the track. Our interest is in algorithms to do reasoning. A logic-programming language can be used to write an arbitrary algorithm, and hence knowing a program is implemented in such a language tells us nothing about the reasoning algorithm it is using. We will use the term *deductive retriever* for a theorem prover that is a "little bit programmed"; that is, where one expects to be able to add axioms and have them allow new deductions in potentially unpredictable ways, but where one knows to avoid adding certain sorts of axiom. Deductive retrieval may be thought of as "pure" logic programming, since it omits the "dirty stuff" (I/O commands, special control constructs) that is necessary to make a backward chainer into a language interpreter.

The reasoning done by deductive retrievers is not as deep as what we talked about in Section 6.4.1. For instance, many mundane subgoals like (Show: (< 3 10)) come up repeatedly. Rather than handle these with general axioms about numbers, we prefer to program the theorem prover so that, given a goal of the form (< *number number*), it just calls the Lisp function < to do the test. This is called *procedural attachment*. This idea is useful for a variety of predicates.

6.5 Advanced Topics in Representation

6.5.1 Nonmonotonic Reasoning

Suppose that Sue is paid $5000 a year in wages, and makes $7500 a year in tips. What is her total income? Perhaps you concluded it was $12,500. A little reflection will show this isn't necessarily true, since we might have left out another income source. On the other hand, it seems to be a "plausible inference" of a not-too-daring sort that we must make all the time to avoid complete skepticism.

There is, as it happens, no way to get such a plausible inference out of the proof procedures we have looked at. That is, there is no point wasting our time looking for a clever set of formulas that, combined with

(income-source sue wages 5000)

and

(income-source sue tips 7500)

would entail

(total-income sue 12500)

without a crushing side effect. If there were such a set and such a proof, then it would work no matter what other axioms we added. If we added

(income-source sue alimony 10000)

we could still infer that her total income was $12,500. It's possible that we could also infer it was $22,500, but that's no help at all.

A logic in which a conclusion stands no matter what new axioms are added is called *monotonic*. Classical formal systems are all monotonic. This means they can't possibly capture the plausible inference about income, or either of the following:

- Frieda is a professor of computer science. Therefore, Frieda has a Ph.D. Of course, maybe she hasn't. If we are told by a trustworthy source that she hasn't, we just withdraw the conclusion.
- Johnny complains of a fever and has bright purple spots on his feet. A doctor is summoned, and finds that the only explanation is that Johnny has mumbo fever. She concludes that this is what Johnny has, and institutes treatment. Then she finds out Johnny has already had mumbo fever, which confers virtually certain immunity. The doctor withdraws her conclusion.

In all such cases, new information causes an old conclusion to be withdrawn. Such a conclusion is said to be *defeated*. (A conclusion that may later be defeated is *defeasible*.) The entire reasoning system is classified as *nonmonotonic*. The Frieda example illustrates a common pattern, called *default reasoning*. Such a pattern can be analyzed thus

If *x* is a professor of computer science,
and there is no proof that *x* is not a Ph.D.,
then you may infer that *x* is.

The conclusion of such a rule is called a *default*.

The novel part is the "there is no proof" part. Formalizing what this means requires more subtlety than you might expect. However, getting it to work in a practical program is not so hard. We do so by introducing the symbol "consistent." (consistent *p*) is true if (not *p*) cannot be inferred. So this rule can be written

(← (education ?x phd) (and (occupation ?x (prof cs))
                                      (consistent (education ?x phd))))

Now a goal (Show: (education frieda ?what)) will lead to the subgoal (Show: (consistent (education frieda phd))). This subgoal is handled not by further backward chaining, but by having the theorem prover call itself recursively with the goal (not (education frieda phd)). If this goal fails, then the (consistent . . .) goal should succeed. (This is called the *negation as failure* device because it is often thought of as a way of proving something is false by failing to prove it is true. Note that it is implemented by procedural attachment, where the procedure attached to consistent is the theorem prover itself!)

Lest you think this too glib, we will sketch why it will not always work. The attempt to prove Frieda does not have a Ph.D. may well involve a rule with a different default. For instance, we might have the rule

```
(← (not (education ?x phd))
    (and (education ?x md)
         (consistent (not (education ?x phd)))))
```

That is, "M.D.s usually don't also have Ph.D.s." Suppose we know that Frieda has an M.D. Then attempting to show Frieda has no Ph.D. will land us in the subgoal "Show it is consistent that she has no Ph.D.," and hence back in the original goal. Something different must be done to handle such infinite recursions. Exactly what must be done is still not known.

Although the formal theory has a long way to go, we should make it clear that nonmonotonicity is not an unusual property of a reasoning program. On the contrary, most of the inferences done by real programs are defeasible. As the examples suggested, medical-diagnosis and even tax-computing programs must draw conclusions that could be overturned. Even in cases in which the inference is technically monotonic, like playing chess, in practice a program must choose a move after a bounded amount of contemplation; increasing the bound could change its conclusion. The program may be thought of as using a nonmonotonic approximation to the "real" theory.

6.5.2 Using λ-Expressions as Descriptions (Optional)

At several places in this chapter, we have admitted that there are difficulties in translating an arbitrary fact into predicate calculus. In the next two sections, we will sketch approaches to extending the predicate calculus to overcome some of them.

Let's begin with indefinite descriptions. We said in Section 6.2.4 that these usually become existential quantifiers (and occasionally universals). But consider the fact "Jack is trying to build a flying chair." This cannot be translated as "There is a flying chair that Jack is trying to build," and certainly not as "Every flying chair is being built by Jack." The chair doesn't exist yet, and may never exist.

Suppose we analyze the verb of this sentence as try-to-build. (Separating out the try and the build would be better, but a distraction at this point.) try-to-build takes one argument, the object to be built. As we mentioned, however, this is not an object in the sense of an existing entity that can be referred to. Instead, it must be a *description* of an object.

Within the predicate calculus, the standard notation for a description is a λ-*expression*. (λ (-*vars*-) p) denotes a description of a set of objects, namely, that they satisfy property p. So the notation for "flying chair" is

```
(λ (x) (and (inst x chair) (flying-vehicle x))  )
```

and the action Jack is performing is (try-to-build (λ (x) (and . . .))). The predicate describes links descriptions and objects. (describes *description object*) is true if *object* actually satisfies the *description*. Hence if it is true of object A that our λ-expression describes it; i.e.,

```
(describes (λ (x) (and (inst x chair) (flying-vehicle x))   )
           A)
```

then the following must be true:

```
(and (inst A chair) (flying-vehicle A))
```

One problem with λ-expressions is that they contain propositions as parts. We already agreed to allow this, in Section 6.2, so we won't worry too much about it here. (In Box 6.1 we will attempt to conjure the propositions away, with mixed results.)

We can extend the λ notation to allow expressions of the form (λ (-*vars*-) *term*) as well as (λ (-*vars*-) *proposition*). The new kind is a way of introducing new object names, just as the old kind is a way of introducing new object descriptions. The analogue of **describes** is **named**: (named λ-*exp* -*args*-) is the object obtained by substituting in *args* for *vars* in the λ-expression. The expression (λ (x) (father (mother x))) names x's maternal grandfather:

```
(= (named (λ (x) (father (mother x))   )
          fred)
   (father (mother fred)))
```

Now, whenever we need a predicate or name that can be composed out of simpler things, some λ-expression almost always does the job.

For instance, consider the issue of *quantifier scope*. The sentence "Jack wants to beat up a computer science professor" has two possible readings: (1) that there is a particular computer science professor whom Jack wants to beat up (in revenge for a grade, maybe); or (2) that Jack, perhaps because he does this every Saturday night, wants to find a professor and pummel the poor bugger. The first reading may be expressed as

```
(exists (p)
        (and (occupation p (prof cs))
             (task jack (beat-up p))))
```

But what about the second? We must introduce a new connective, (some-act (-*vars*-) *formula action*), which denotes the action of performing *action* using objects that satisfy *formula*. For instance, taking Terry to a movie theater is denoted by

```
(some-act (x) (inst x movie-theater)
              (take-on-date terry x))
```

Beating up a computer science professor is denoted by (some-act (p) (occupation p (prof cs)) (beat-up p)), and the second reading of our sentence about Jack is represented thus:

```
(task jack (some-act (p)
                     (occupation p (prof cs))
                     (beat-up p)))
```

It is a little unnerving that we had to introduce essentially a new quantifier, or "variable binder," to represent this. Actually, we didn't have to, because λ-expressions are enough. We could have made **some-act** a function of two λ-expressions:

> (some-act
>   (λ (p) (occupation p (prof cs)))
>   (λ (p) (beat-up p)))

(λ (p) (beat-up p)) names, given p, the action of beating p up. The term (some-act *d1 d2*) would then denote an action performed whenever an action named by *d2* is performed on an object described by *d1*. Hence, the **some-act** we described is the action of beating up a computer science professor.

We can connect the two readings of the original sentence with an axiom:

> (forall (e a d n)
>   (iff (actual-event e (do a (some-act d n))) *; The some-act happened*
>   (exists (x)   *; iff x (described by*
>   (and (describes d x)   *; d) was acted upon in*
>   (event e (do a (named n x)))))))) *; an actual event e.*

That is, if we're talking about a particular real event token, then the **some-act** and **exists** forms are equivalent. But when we're talking about a **task**, they're not.

Skolemization breaks down whenever such scope issues arise. It "flattens" all quantifiers out, and so cannot make the required distinctions. Hence resolution does not work with λ-expressions.

Box 6.1

Set Theory, Axiom Schemas, and Extensionality

> If we rule out the extensions to predicate calculus of Section 6.5.2 and allow predicates to denote only truth values, then we are left with the *first-order*, *extensional*, *nonmodal* predicate calculus. "First order" means that predicates can occur only as predicates; nothing can be asserted about them. "Extensional" means that we can refer only to things that exist. "Nonmodal" means that propositions cannot occur as arguments; nothing can be asserted about them.
>
> First-order logic is well understood. Furthermore, resolution is defined only for first-order logic (and practical only with a finite number of axioms). As the restrictions on first-order logic are relaxed, the resulting systems of logic get harder and harder to understand. Paradoxes abound. It is easy to argue that the closer one can come to the discipline of first-order predicate calculus, the better.
>
> It turns out that λ-*expressions* can, in a sense, be handled using the first-order predicate calculus. We let (λ (v) p) denote the *set* of all *v* such that *p*. The expression (λ (x) (and (us-senator x) (polparty x republican))) denotes a certain set of 0 to 100 persons. A person fits this description if the person is in this set. In fact, (describes *d x*) just becomes a synonym for the traditional *x∈d*. This approach provides a

straightforward denotation for λ-expressions, but the syntax is illegal; it
has variables and propositions in forbidden places. We get around such
legalities with an axiom that says

> For all *p*,
>   (exists (D) (forall (x)
>   (iff (describes D x) (*p* x))))

That is, because the name we want is technically illegal, we don't actually
use it, but just talk about "the D such that (*p* x) *iff* D *describes* x." This
trick looks just as illegal, since we are quantifying over *p*. One more trick
will get around that problem; we replace this bogus axiom with an infinite
sequence of axioms, one for each *p*, such as these:

```
(exists (d)                      ; There exists some description
   (forall (x)                   ; such that everything it
      (iff (describes d x)       ; describes is red, and
         (color x red) )))       ; vice versa.

(exists (d)                      ; There exists some description
   (forall (x)                   ; such that everything it
      (iff (describes d x)       ; describes is a senator, and
         (senator x) )))         ; vice versa.

(exists (d)                      ; Similarly for red senators.
   (forall (x)
      (iff (describes d x)
         (and (color x red)
            (senator x)))))
```

In each case, we have replaced (*p* x) with a real proposition, like (and
(color x red) (senator x)). An infinite sequence of axioms, produced
according to a well-behaved rule like this, is called an *axiom schema*.
Although, as you might expect, such a thing is a headache for someone
implementing an inference algorithm, it is no problem for a logician. A
finite set of axioms already generates an infinite sequence of theorems in a
well-behaved way, so an axiom schema's contribution is nothing special.

  Now that we have satisfied ourselves that every statement with a λ
can be translated into one without, we can lapse back into this notation
without worrying about it. This approach to representing descriptions is
called *set theory*. It has been of historical importance because of the simple foundation it provides for mathematics. Unfortunately, it is inadequate
for many purposes that arise in AI research. The problem is its "extensionality": Two descriptions are equal if they are true of the same entities.
In particular, if two descriptions are both true of no entities at all, they
have the same meaning. Since there are no flying chairs, and no unicorns
either, we can, in the story about Jack, infer that he is trying to build a
unicorn. (If there were flying chairs, we would be back to the conclusion

we rejected at the outset, that he is trying to build something that already exists.)

So, even though mathematicians are satisfied with extensional logic, philosophers, linguists, and AI researchers are interested in representations in which the meaning of an object depends on more than just the things that currently exist. This is called an *intensional logic*. Such a logic recognizes that every description has two facets: its *extension*, the collection of things that it describes, and its *intension*, which is more mysterious. (See Section 6.5.3.)

6.5.3 Modal and Intensional Logics (Optional)

Alongside the development of ordinary mathematical logic in this century, there also occurred the development of *modal logic*. A modal logic is one that contains connectives like **possibly**, and **entails**. (**possibly** p) is true if p is possible; (**possibly** *"The South won the Civil War"*) might be considered to be true. (There are many senses of "possible"; the one we are getting at is that things might have been otherwise than they actually are, not that the South might in fact have won, in spite of your firm belief that it lost.) (**entails** p q) means that p's truth inevitably involves q's truth. For instance, Nixon's winning the 1960 presidential election might be said to entail Kennedy's not being assassinated in 1963.

Ordinary extensional logic is incompatible with such connectives. It cannot distinguish a false but possibly true statement from a necessarily false one (such as the statement that $2+2=5$). It can't talk at all about whether a false statement would, if true, entail a true one. (Remember that (**if** p q) is true if p is false, so the statement about Nixon and Kennedy, if expressed using **if**, comes out true vacuously.)

Until about 1960, modal logic was in disrepute. Its subject matter was avoidable in mathematics, where statements, if true, are necessarily true. Necessity and possibility are interesting to philosophers, but modal logic seemed to absorb energy from them, rather than give it off. There were lots of different modal logics, and none seemed to have any particular advantages over the others. Most important, there was no semantics for modal logic as there was for extensional logic.

In 1959, Kripke [Kripke63] changed all this by providing the first acceptable semantic analysis of a modal logic. He introduced the notion of a *possible world*. Intuitively, a possible world is a way things might have been. Technically, it is an unanalyzed notion; we simply posit a set of possible worlds, one of which is the one we inhabit — the "real world." We are interested in the truth values of statements in the real world. (**possibly** p) is true if p is true in some possible world. It might be that p is actually false in the real world, but that's no longer a problem. A whole industry has sprung up based on Kripke's idea, producing variations on this. It is now accepted that a modal logic is coherent to the extent that some kind of semantics can be produced for it.

In 1964, Jaakko Hintikka proposed that (knows *a p*), "*a* knows that *p*," can be analyzed modally. We supply our semantics with a set of possible worlds, and we distinguish those compatible with what *a* knows. The meaning of (knows *a p*) is that *p* is true in all worlds compatible with what *a* knows. Although this may sound completely impractical, it turns out that the structure of the semantics can be exploited to produce a resolutionlike proof procedure for reasoning about what someone knows.

Another example is the analysis of *counterfactual conditionals*, of the form, "If *p* were true, then *q* would be true." The simplest analysis of these is that they mean, "In all possible worlds where *p* is true, then *q* would be true." But this analysis is too strong. It seems perfectly reasonable to believe that, "If the earth were much further from the sun, then life would never have evolved on it." But there is presumably a possible world where the earth is further from the sun, and the sun is just enough brighter to compensate. So to preserve the possible-worlds analysis, you must analyze the sentence as meaning, "In any possible world where the earth is much further from the sun, and *as little else is changed from the way things are as possible*, life would never have evolved on the earth."

As we mentioned in Section 6.2, the standard way to describe the meanings of expressions in the predicate calculus is to specify what they denote. The object denoted by a term is its *extension* (see Box 6.1). The "meaning," or *intension*, of a term has traditionally been a less formal concept, but possible-worlds semantics provides a formal proposal, namely, that the intension of a term be taken to be a function specifying its extension in each possible world. Thus, although unicorns and flying chairs are both nonexistent, there are possible worlds in which these drab facts are corrected. In these worlds, the extensions of "flying chair" and "unicorn" are therefore non-empty, and disjoint. Hence the function from every possible world to the extension of "unicorn" in that world is a quite different object from the analogous function for "flying chair," which makes the two concepts different in intension, as they should be.

Although many concepts can be approximated using modal semantics, many of the approximations are unsatisfactory. The logic of knows is a good example. It is an inevitable theorem of this logic that if *a* knows a set of statements, then *a* knows every consequence of that set. This means that anyone who can be persuaded of the truth of Peano's postulates knows everything about number theory that anyone else knows (including Fermat's last theorem, if it follows from those postulates).

The possible-worlds analysis of intension is plagued with the same sort of bug. Two self-contradictory concepts, like "round square" and "married bachelor," have the same extension (namely, the empty set) in all possible worlds. This means that they have the same intension. Many people find it unsatisfying to have "round square" and "unmarried bachelor" mean exactly the same thing; on the other hand, if they are completely meaning*less*, perhaps this is no problem.

Box 6.2

Higher-order Logic and Its Paradoxes

Perhaps we have seemed a little cautious in the text in our analysis of properties and descriptions. We already have a model of properties, namely, predicates themselves. If we simply extend the logic to allow assertions about predicates, then we can treat λ as an operator that takes a proposition and makes a new predicate. Then (try-to-build flying-vehicle) would denote the action of trying to build a flying vehicle, while

(try-to-build
    (λ (x) (and (inst x chair) (flying-vehicle x))))

denotes the action of trying to build a flying chair. We don't have to write

(describes (λ (x) (and (inst x chair) (flying-vehicle x)))
          a)

to say that a is a flying chair, any more than we have to say (describes flying-vehicle a). We just say

((λ (x) (and (inst x chair) (flying-vehicle x)))
  a)

Any such expression may be transformed into an expression with the same meaning (and truth value) by actually substituting the argument (here, a) for the λ-variable (here, x). In this case, we get

(and (inst a chair) (flying-vehicle a))

which does make the same statement about a. This inference rule we will call λ *reduction*. Since predicates are now individuals, we can quantify over them. For example, we can define equality with an axiom

(forall (x y) (iff (= x y)
           (forall (p) (iff (p x) (p y)))))

"Two objects are unequal if and only if they differ in some property." A logic in which one can quantify over all predicates is called a *higher-order logic*. Unfortunately, there are severe problems with all versions of the logic of descriptions, in either this version or the version of Section 6.5.2. Consider the property PP = (λ (x) (not (x x))). This is the property that any property has if it does not describe itself. PP is a property of properties, so it may be applied to itself

(PP PP)

iff

((λ (x) (not (x x)))
(λ (x) (not (x x))))

iff [via λ-reduction]
(not ((λ (x) (not (x x)))
(λ (x) (not (x x)))))

iff
(not (PP PP))

The unfortunate conclusion is that **(PP PP)** is true if and only if it is false. This sort of contradiction, from seemingly sound inference rules, is called a *paradox*. Paradoxes, like comets, are named after those who first sight them; this one is named after Bertrand Russell.

This paradox appears in all casual formulations of the logic of descriptions, from naive use of λ-expressions (Section 6.5.2) to set theory (Box 6.1), whether or not descriptions are identified with ordinary predicates. The discovery of paradoxes like this put a stop to untrammeled predication about descriptions. It was replaced by more cautious axiomatic theories, in which the right to identify properties with logical formulas was curtailed, making definitions like that of **PP** impossible. The extensional and intensional notions of property (corresponding to sets and logical formulas respectively) were pulled apart, and two sorts of theory sprang up, one about sets, considered as collections of objects; and one about predicates-as-objects. The first is called *axiomatic set theory*, the second, *higher-order logic*. The first has served as a foundational tool for mathematics; the second as a philosophical tool [Montague74], and, in the form of λ-expressions, as a vehicle for designing knowledge representations.

6.6 Complete Resolution (Optional)

For most purposes, what we have already said about theorem proving is sufficient. However, the algorithms we have presented are incomplete; that is, they will not always find proofs even when proofs exist. To ensure completeness, a more careful treatment of resolution is necessary. Also, a more thorough understanding of resolution will connect some seemingly disparate pieces of what we have presented, and shed light on the powers and limitations of deductive search techniques. One thing we should point out at the beginning is that none of the topics we cover in this section have anything to do with enhancing the *efficiency* of theorem proving. Making a theorem prover more nearly complete will almost always slow it down.

6.6.1 The General Resolution Rule

We introduced three different rules in Section 6.3: forward chaining, backward chaining, and conjunctive-goal handling. Somewhat surprisingly, all three of these can be seen as cases of resolution. In fact, resolution is the only rule you need, if you state it in a slightly more general form than we have so far.

One reason for the asymmetry between the forward and backward resolution rules was that one dealt with goals, and other with assertions. It turns out that goals may be thought of as a kind of assertion. We can view (Show: (inst block-21 prism)) as an attempt to prove (inst block-21 prism) by contradiction. We (pretend to) assert (not (inst block-21 prism)) into the database. We will assume that the following fact is available (we have given it in two forms, the usual if-then format and the version using or):

(if (inst ?x block) (inst ?x prism))
(or (not (inst ?x block)) (inst ?x prism))

Since the negated goal says that block-21 is not a prism, the disjunction requires that it not be a block either. More formally, we say that the negated goal *resolves* with the implication to give (not (inst block-21 block)). If (inst block-21 block) is in the database, then we have a contradiction, and the original goal is proved. Show: is, as far as logic is concerned, the same as not. It differs pragmatically in that we don't really assert it, but merely explore "consequences," i.e., subgoals, of it. For the duration of this section, we will ignore this difference. The negations of goals will be asserted along with everything else. We won't worry about who cleans up the debris after a proof attempt is finished.

The parallel between Show: and not extends to Skolemization. The goal (Show: (exists (y) (inst y prism))) gets Skolemized just the way (not (exists (y) (inst y prism))) would, to (Show: (inst ?y prism)). (Recall that the not flips the sense of the quantifier.) Hence the dual Skolemization rules we introduced in Section 6.3.3 are redundant.

The remaining asymmetry between the forward and backward chaining rules is due to our phrasing facts as implications. If we rewrite (if p q) as (or (not p) q), then the similarities of forward and backward chaining are summarized as follows

Chaining	From	And	Deduce
Forward	p'	(or (not p) q)	q'
Backward	(not q')	(or q (not p))	(not p')
Generalization	(not m')	(or m n)	n'

In the first case, $m = $ (not p), $n = q$. In the second, $m = q$, $n = $ (not p). The only difference is where the not is sitting.

One further generalization is to allow both inputs to the rule to be disjunctions. This gives us the rule

From (or n_1 (not m')) and (or m n_2)
infer (or n_1' n_2')

The previous examples reduce to this one, with $n_1 =$ false. So far, we have not put any constraints on the pieces of formula to be unified during resolution. However, in each case the pieces have been "literals." A *literal* is either an atomic formula or the negation of an atomic formula. It is not hard to see that any formula can be transformed into an equivalent conjunction of disjunctions of literals, when it is said to be in *conjunctive normal form*. To effect this transformation for any formula, first eliminate explicit quantifiers, then change all implications into disjunctions, then repeatedly apply the transformations of Figure 6.22. Disjunctions have the advantage over implications that they are symmetrical: all the disjuncts behave the same. This fact is usually emphasized by thinking of each disjunction as an unordered set of literals $\{q_1, \ldots, q_n\}$, called a *clause*. In most of our examples, clauses will be in one of three simple forms

1. A *unit clause* $\{p\}$, representing a simple assertion in the database.
2. A clause of the form $\{$(not p_1) , . . . , (not p_n), $q\}$, derived from an implication (if (and $p_1 \ldots p_n$) q). We will call these *implication clauses*.
3. A clause of the form $\{$(not g_1) , . . . , (not g_n)$\}$, derived from the goal (Show: (and $g_1, \ldots, g_n$)). We will call these *goal clauses*, and often write them in the form $\{$(Show: g_1) , . . . , (Show: g_n)$\}$.

Now the resolution rule, in its full generality, can be stated thus:

Suppose that C_1 and C_2 are clauses that have been
standardized apart (i.e., have no variables in common), where

$$C_1 = \{l_1, l_2, \ldots, l_a\} \bigcup \{p_1, \ldots, p_m\}$$

and

$$C_2 = \{(\text{not } k_1), \ldots, (\text{not } k_b)\} \bigcup \{q_1, \ldots, q_n\}$$

and θ is an MGU (most general unifier) of $\{l_1, \ldots, l_a, k_1, \ldots, k_b\}$.
Then from C_1 and C_2 infer $\{p_1\theta, \ldots, p_m\theta, q_1\theta, \ldots, q_n\theta\}$

(not (or $d_1 \ldots d_n$)) $\rightarrow$ (and (not d_1) . . . (not d_n))

(not (and $c_1 \ldots c_n$)) $\rightarrow$ (or (not c_1) . . . (not c_n))

(or $d_1 \ldots$ (and $c_1 \ldots c_m$) . . . d_n)
  $\rightarrow$ (and (or c_1 d_1 . . . d_n)
          . . .
        (or c_m d_1 . . . d_n))

Figure 6.22 Transformations to conjunctive normal form

The *l*s and *k*s are said to be the *literals resolved upon*. The resulting clause is said to be a *resolvent* of the other two. The clauses are unordered, so our placing of the resolved-upon literals at the front is purely for exposition; *any* subformula can be resolved upon. Another consequence of the set notation is that there are no duplicates in the output. If some $p_i\theta$ = some $q_j\theta$ then there is just one occurrence of this literal in the resolvent.

In the great majority of cases, $a = b = 1$, that is, there is just one formula resolved upon in each clause. Then we can state the rule more compactly, using our "prime" notation for unification in inference rules, as

From $\{l, p_1, \ldots , p_m\}$ and $\{(\text{not } l'), q_1, \ldots , q_n\}$
infer $\{p_1', \ldots , p_m', q_1', \ldots , q_m'\}$

The more general formulation is necessary in order to ensure completeness, but we will encounter no examples here.

The empty clause, $\{\}$, represents a contradiction, and a proof by contradiction may be thought of as an attempt to deduce the empty clause. Resolution is a *complete* rule of inference in the following sense: If a formula *g* follows from a set of formulas *S*, then there is a sequence of resolutions of clauses in *G* that terminates in the empty clause $\{\}$, where *G* is the clause form of $S \cup \{(\text{not } g)\}$. To make this concrete, we will show our block-and-prism example one more time, in clause form

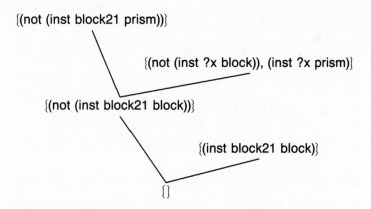

Here we have used the traditional notation, in which arcs are drawn from literals resolved upon to the resolvent.

It is instructive to watch how resolution handles conjunctive goals. Recall that a goal of the form (Show: *r'*) will get chained through (if (and *p q*) *r*) to generate the conjunctive subgoal (Show: (and *p' q'*)). This is to be handled by finding variable bindings that are answers to both (Show: *p'*) and (Show: *q'*). Resolution does this automatically. The implication becomes {(not *p*), (not *q*), *r*} The output of the resolution is {(Show: *p'*), (Show: *q'*)}. (Show: here means the same as not, but reminds us that we are dealing with goals.) The resolution rule will let us resolve this goal clause against {*p''*} to give {(Show: *q''*)}, or against {(not *s*), *p''*} to give {(Show: *q''*), (Show: *s'*)}. The first of these can be seen as solving *p'* and going on to *q'*; the second, as continuing to work on *p'* by moving to a subgoal. Either way, *q* gets transformed to *q'*, then *q''*, and so on until all the subgoals of *p* are handled. When *q* finally gets worked on, it will have been instantiated with variable bindings from the proof of *p*. If there is no proof of the instantiated *q*, the current line of proof will go nowhere, i.e., never lead to a contradiction. But other resolutions will generate alternative variable bindings that may produce a provable instance of *q*. For example, consider the goal (Show: (r ?x)), which meets with the implication clause {(not (p ?y ?z)), (not (q ?z))), (r ?y)} . Unification gives {y=?x} as variable bindings, so we have the subgoal {(Show: (p ?x ?z)), (Show: (q ?z))}. Say the database further contains

{(p d b)}   {(p a c)}
{(q c)}   {(q a)}

There are two ways to see what happens next. We can think of the process as finding the answer (p a c) to the first Show:, and the compatible (q c) to the second, so that {x=a} would be the answer to the original query. Or we can think of it as continuing to do resolutions using {(Show: (p ?x ?z)), (Show: (q ?z))}. This goal clause will resolve with {(p d b)} to give {(Show: (q b))}, which goes nowhere. It will also resolve with {(p a c)} to give {(Show: (q c))}, which succeeds.

If the database had not contained (p a c), but instead

{(not (s ?u ?v)), (p ?u ?v)}
{(s a c)}

then the first formula could have been used to generate {(Show: (s ?x ?y)), (Show: (q ?y))}. This would resolve with {(s a c)} to give {(Show: (q c))}, with the same ultimate answer as before.

As we set out to show, a series of resolutions automatically generates answers to one conjunctive goal, then tries them out on the others.

6.6.2 Search Algorithms for Resolution

The interpretation of clauses as conjunctive goals should look familiar to you. It is quite similar to our representation of partial solutions to a goal tree such as that of Figure 6.11. Have we rediscovered goal-tree searching in another form? Yes and no. The difference between goal-tree searching and unrestricted resolution is that the former allows resolutions only between partial solutions and assertions. Unrestricted resolution allows resolutions between partial solutions as well.

This restriction is the reason why goal-tree searching is incomplete. Consider this example:

(on block1 table)
(on block2 table)
(or (color block1 green) (color block2 green))

Backward chaining will not find any answer to the goal (Show: (exists (x) (and (on x table) (color x green))), "Show there is something green on the table." Skolemized, this is:

(or (Show: (on ?x table)) (Show: (color ?x green)))

However, it is possible to infer this with complete resolution. Figure 6.23 shows a derivation of the empty clause for this goal.

The key difference between this resolution proof and the backward chaining attempt is the step where {(color block2 green)} is resolved against {(Show: (color block2 green))}. Both of these clauses are derived from the original goal, and hence both would be partial solutions in the goal-tree version. (To get even this far we would have to write the disjunction in the form (← (color block1 green) (not (color block2 green))), and the partial solution would occur as the goal (Show: (not (color block2 green))).)

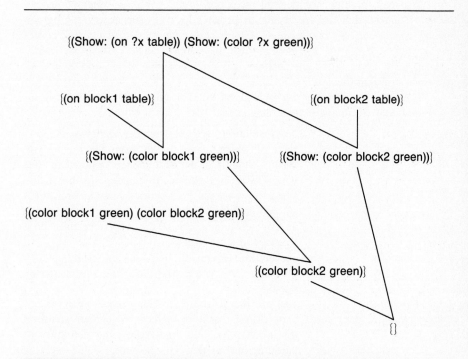

Figure 6.23 Resolution proof that something green is on the table

Full resolution requires a somewhat different control structure from backward chaining. Goals are treated the same as other assertions. All are asserted into the same database, and inferences are done repeatedly until {} is inferred (or some resource is exhausted). At that point, the database is full of garbage inferred from the negation of what we wanted to prove, all of which must be discarded before the next proof is attempted.

Resolution proofs do not always return tidy answers the way backward chaining does. In Figure 6.23, when the two partial solutions are resolved with each other, from that point on there is no definite answer; if you trace the variable bindings back, you will find that both {x=block1} and {x=block2} were generated along the way. We can interpret this outcome as a disjunctive answer: Either block1 or block2 is green and on the table.

Another consequence of the completeness of resolution is that it handles proving implications automatically. In Section 6.4 we mentioned a geometry theorem prover that proved theorems of the form (if p q) by asserting p and attempting to prove q. This seems correct, but backward chaining will not do it. In clause form, the negation of (if p q) is the clausal representation of p, plus the clausal representation of (not q), or (Show: q). Hence resolution does the right thing automatically.

The main problem for general resolution is that too many interactions can occur. Suppose that we are trying to prove g, a consequence of, say, group theory, represented by axiom set A. Simple resolution tells us to infer all consequences of $A \cup \{(\text{not } g)\}$, looking for the empty clause. But "all consequences" of $A \cup \{(\text{not } g)\}$ includes all consequences of A, and hence all theorems of group theory.

The name *resolution strategy* is given to a rule that restricts which resolutions are done. Here are some strategies that have been used:

Set-of-support	No resolutions are allowed between two clauses, both of which were drawn from the theory you started with (A in the example, as opposed to (not g)). This is like backward chaining, in that it distinguishes between goal clauses (derived from (not g)) and nongoal clauses.
Input resolution	In any resolution, one of the resolvents must be a member of $A \cup (\text{not } g)$.
Unit preference	Resolutions involving unit clauses (with just one element) are done first (or, in the extreme, exclusively).
Lock resolution	Just one literal from each clause is resolved upon.
Subsumption checking	Any clause that is subsumed by another clause is discarded. (We must generalize the definition of subsumption so that C_1 subsumes C_2 if there is some substitution θ such that $C_1\theta \subseteq C_2$.)

Some combinations of these strategies preserve completeness, some don't. Our goal-search scheme combines set-of-support, input resolution, and unit preference. This combination is obviously incomplete.

6.7 References and Further Reading

There are several books on elementary mathematical logic available. They go into more detail on the semantics of the predicate calculus. See [Mendelson64]. The clearest statement of the usefulness of logical analysis of representations appears in a series of papers by Patrick Hayes [Hayes77, Hayes84, Hayes84a].

Concerning the two domains we presented as examples of formal theories, the material on spatial relationships was taken from [McDermott84]. For more on conceptual dependency and its descendants, see [Schank75, Schank77] and [Cullingford78]. We noted that there were some problems with the analysis of **prevent** given in our formalization of CD. This was one of several places where we touched upon issues relating to time and possible events. Another place was in our brief discussion of counterfactual conditionals. For more on these topics see [Allen81, McDermott82].

There are many other examples of complete fact bases which we could have used in place of the two we chose. See, for example, Hayes's theory of liquids [Hayes84a], or McDermott's theory of temporal processes [McDermott82]. There are also many examples in AI of less formal approaches, which are careful enough to be close to the standards of rigor we advocate here. To mention just a handful, see Wilensky's theory of plan and goal interactions [Wilensky83], or Charniak's theory of painting [Charniak78], or Schank and Carbonell's theory of political transactions [Schank79], or Rieger's theory of processes [Rieger76].

Resolution was invented by Robinson [Robinson65]. The original form was what we defined as *complete resolution*. At about the same time researchers were looking into the procedural view of logic (e.g., forward vs. backward chaining). One of the early developments here was Planner [Hewitt71]. The two streams joined to form the goal-tree based resolution which is the primary form used in AI. For more on theorem proving and its application to AI, see [Nilsson80, Kowalski79], or [Chang73]. Logic programming is another offshoot of this work and many feel that it has special relevance to AI programming. Kowalski's book talks about this. The major programming language based on logic programming is Prolog; see [Warren77, Clocksin81].

As should have been made clear in these pages, actually getting a deductive retriever to do what you want, and in reasonable time, is not easy. For the basics of implementing a deductive retriever see [Charniak80]. For more on particular topics one might look at [Bledsoe78, Cox80] (on Skolemization), [Bruynooghe80, Pereira80, McDermott77] (on independent conjunctive goals), [Shapiro80] (on repeated goals), [Wos67, Plotkin72, Knuth70] (on equality), and [deKleer77] (on the use of **Show:** as a pseudo connective).

Theorem provers have been used for many purposes. The classic use is proving mathematical theorems. Resolution was invented by people interested in this problem, and resolution is still being applied to it [Wos83]. Some of the mathematical domains that have been tackled include: plane geometry [Gelernter59], algebra [Winker81], and properties of computer programs [Boyer79]. For a discussion of what human mathematicians might be doing, see [Michener78].

Deductive retrievers have also been used for tasks like these: ATN-style parsing [Pereira80a] (also see Exercise 6.30), control of a problem solver [Genesereth83], proposing plans of action [McDermott78], question answering/database access [Gallaire78], and finding explanations for faults in electronic circuits [McDermott82a].

Various extensions to first order logic have been proposed. For more on nonmonotonic logic see [Clark78, McDermott80, Reiter80]. For a logician's view of possible-world semantics see [Lewis73]. An AI application of possible worlds is given in [Moore80].

Exercises

6.1 Explain why "If *p*, then I'm a monkey's uncle" is a way of asserting that *p* is false.

6.2 In practice, programs using CD compensate for the absence of an **ungrasp** primitive by combining **grasp** and **not**. Explain why this is not the usual notion of negation. What sort of general "not-ish" operator is wanted?

6.3 Explain why our analysis of **prevent** (Section 6.2.2) makes it hard to express propositions like, "The South's winning the Civil War would have prevented the United States from becoming a world power."

6.4 If you don't like the concept of "nonactual" event, you might prefer to think of **prevent** as a relation between an event and an event *description*. Under this approach, we would write (**prevent ev1** (**do john22** . . .)) instead of (**and** (**event ev2** (**do john22** . . .)) (**prevent ev1 ev2**)). Explain why this approach would make it hard to say "**ev1** prevented **ev2** from preventing **ev3**." Would it be any easier under the scheme we have adopted?

6.5 Yet another idea is to make **prevent** be a primitive act: (**prevent** *desc*) would denote the action of preventing the event with the given description. This would allow preventing preventing. What about expressing "The change in temperature prevented John from skiing"?

6.6 Try representing the following story as a fact base: "Mary was hungry. She decided to go to McDonald's. When she got there, she saw that it had burned down."

6.7　In Section 6.2.3 we pointed out that many natural-language inputs can require quantifiers in their internal representation (as in "John did something . . ."). Does the vision system produce inputs that require quantifiers? Give an example or argue that quantifiers are unnecessary.

6.8　Try translating some of the shape descriptions of Chapter 3 into predicate calculus. Explain why quantifiers are necessary for rendering parametrized shape descriptions. Try describing the shape of a generic telephone.

6.9　Try writing axioms to define the effects of various primitive acts in terms of state changes, the way we did with **ptrans** in Section 6.2.3.

6.10　It seems plausible that any subevent of an **actual** event must be actual. Write an axiom to this effect. Can you think of some counterexamples? Can you think of some other such rules that deserve to be stated?

6.11　Formalize these axioms of CD theory: "If a story character kills a good character, then the killer is wicked." "If two characters are talking, then either they are using a telephone or they are close together." Make up some others. Why is it so hard to make up axioms relating goals, plans, and beliefs?

6.12　Express the following things in predicate calculus. For each, carefully explain the meaning of each vocabulary item you introduce.

　　a) Roses are red; violets are blue.
　　b) Every elephant has a trunk.
　　c) Every chicken hatched from an egg.
　　d) Anyone with two or more spouses is a bigamist.
　　e) Someone profited from the Great Depression.
　　f) Some language is spoken by everyone in this room.
　　g) Everyone in this room speaks some language.
　　h) The coat in the closet belongs to Sarah.
　　i) One of the coats in the closet belongs to Sarah.
　　j) For a spacecraft to fail, every copy of one of its systems must malfunction.
　　k) Fred did something to annoy Wilma.
　　l) Blondes have more fun.
　　m) If you push anything hard enough, it will fall over.
　　n) All men are created equal.
　　o) To make brownies, follow the directions on the package.
　　p) You always hurt the one you love.
　　q) Everybody loves somebody sometime.
　　r) An apple a day keeps the doctor away.

6.13 This exercise concerns varsubst, which computes *patθ* for a pattern *pat*
and a substitution *θ*.

    a) Write this function. In Lisp, the easiest way to represent substitu-
tions is as *association lists*, of the form ((*var val*) (*var val*) . . .).
You will need to pick some internal representation for ?*var*, such
that is-var tests whether something is of that form, and var-sym
takes such a thing and returns its symbol: (var-sym '?x) => x.

    b) Write a second version in which the variable values of *θ* are allowed
to contain some of the variables bound in *θ*. In this version,

        (varsubst '(p ?x (f ?z)) '((x (g ?y)) (z (f ?x))))

should return

        (p (g ?y) (f (f (g ?y))))

where the version of part (a) would return

        (p (g ?y) (f (f ?x)))

6.14 The substitutions found by our version of unify do not quite satisfy the
mathematical definition of substitution. With the arguments

        (p ?x (f ?x))   and (p (g ?y) ?z)

it will return {x=(g ?y), z=(f ?x)}. Technically, it should return {x=(g
?y), z=(f (g ?y))}. The difference is that the second version has all variables bound in the unifier substituted into the terms of the unifier; we will
call such a substitution "flat."

    a) How would var-unify have to be changed to return flat substitutions?

    b) Which version of varsubst (Exercise 6.13) is used on which sort of
substitution?

    c) Which kind of substitution costs more, at what times?

6.15 Write the function to check whether variable occurs in *patθ*, which is
called by var-unify (in Figure 6.7). Note that it should take three arguments. What difference does it make whether it must work with flat or
nonflat substitutions?

6.16 Write a function (standardize *p*) that replaces all the variables in *p* with
brand-new variables (for which you may want to use (gensym), described
in Chapter 4). For example, (standardize '(foo ?x ?y (f ?x))) might
return (foo ?g0058 ?g0059 (f ?g0058))).

6.17 We want to write a rule which says "A computer is fast if no one is
logged into it" in implicit-quantifier form. Someone produces

        (if (and (inst ?c computer) (not (logged-into ?x ?c)))
          (fast ?c))

    a) Explain why this is wrong. Give a case where it can infer that a
computer is fast incorrectly.

b) Produce a correct version.

6.18 Write a Lisp program to Skolemize formulas. It will be a recursive program that passes down two pieces of information: the parity of the number of nots surrounding the current piece of formula, and the universals that dominate it. It should keep a global table of Skolem terms, and be sure to introduce the same term for each occurrence of an existential variable.

6.19 Show that, from the database of Figure 6.9, all of these are deducible via backward chaining:

> (respect sally sally)
> (not (older sally sally))
> (respect fred oswald)
> (not (older oswald fred))

Even though Fred is an adult and Oswald is a child, we cannot deduce that Fred respects himself. What fact would we have to add to enable this deduction?

6.20 In the exercises for Chapter 5, we asked you to write a function gsearch to do arbitrary goal-tree search. To apply it to theorem proving, you must do three things

a) Choose a representation for the "partial objects" in the domain. Here they will be alists, representing substitutions. The other part of a partial solution is a list of choices ("or nodes"), which in this case are deductive goals.

b) Write an *extension function* that takes a goal and a set of variable bindings, and returns a new set of variable bindings, plus a (possibly empty) set of subgoals. The function must look through a database, which you can represent as a list of assertions.

c) Write an *estimation* function that estimates the difficulty of a choice (goal).

6.21 Try different estimation functions for the theorem prover you wrote in Exercise 6.20. Two that come to mind are

a) the size of each goal (as measured, say, by the total number of atoms)

b) 1000 — the number of assertions in the database that unify with each goal.

In case (b), we subtract from 1000 so that goals with fewer answers come out harder.

6.22 Suppose that g_1 and g_2 are sibling goals in a partial solution. Explain why if a complete solution can be obtained by working on g_1 first, the same solution can be obtained by working on g_2 first. Explain why this means that it is positively harmful to work on more than one goal from a given partial solution at the same time.

6.23 In the search of Figure 6.16 we used two criteria for what to do next

    a) Work on the partial solution with the fewest sibling goals.

    b) For a given set of siblings, work on the sibling that resolves with the fewest assertions.

Find a case in which these criteria will lead to an infinite search, even though a finite sequence of chainings will find an answer. Think of improved criteria.

6.24 Sketch the axioms for the predicate **chess-win** mentioned in Section 6.4. Consider the goal tree generated by the goal (Show: (chess-win *initial-board* white ?move)). What is the relationship between it and the game tree for chess?

6.25 For the example of Figure 6.16, verify that if the criteria for what to try next are replaced with

    a) Work on the most recently generated partial solution (''depth-first'')

    b) For a given set of siblings, work on the leftmost sibling (''left-to-right'')

then the search will never halt.

6.26 Verify that replacing the first axiom in Figure 6.15 with

    1   (← (above ?x ?z)
            (and (on ?y ?z) (above ?x ?y)))

will allow a theorem prover to find the correct answer to (Show: (above ?x table)) even given the search criteria of Exercise 6.25. How different is the theorem prover's behavior on the goal (Show: (above block4 ?z))? Is there an alternative axiom that would work better?

6.27 Suppose a database contains these assertions:

    (→ (on ?x ?y) (supports ?y ?x))
    (← (on ?x ?y)
       (and (above ?x ?y) (touching ?x ?y)))
    (above terminal3 table4)
    (touching terminal3 table4)

    a) Show that (supports table4 terminal3) is deducible from these facts.

    b) Explain why the query (Show: (supports table4 terminal3)) will not return yes.

What general principle does this result demonstrate?

6.28 In Section 6.4.2 we pointed out that (→ (and p q) r) could be stated as (→ p (→ q r)). What is the other way to state it? In what circumstances would which formulation be better?

6.29 Try the following goal on the **append** procedure given in Section 6.4.2:

>   (Show: (append ?x ?y [how about that]))

How many answers are there? What is the procedural interpretation of this result?

This is an example of how logic-programming procedures can be ambiguous as to which variables are inputs and which are outputs. In Section 6.4.2, we treated ?x and ?y as inputs, ?z as output; in this exercise, we were able to reverse the roles.

6.30 We said in Section 6.3.4 that backward chaining was a "universal goal-tree generator." That being the case, we ought to be able to express top-down, ATN-style parsing as a theorem-proving problem, and indeed we can. There are several ways of doing it. One is to introduce a predicate **parse**, where (parse *string struc rest*) means that *string* may be analyzed as consisting of prefix with structure *struc*, followed by the string **rest**. We will represent strings as lists of words; structures will be predicate-calculus terms. For brevity, we will represent (cons *a* (cons *b* . . . (cons *z* nil))) as [*a b* . . . *z*], as described in Section 6.2.4, but remember that (cons *a* [*b* . . . *z*]) unifies with it.

For instance, we would like to parse the sentence [the boy ran] into a structure like this:

>   (s (np the boy)
>   (vp ran))

We can accomplish parsing with rules like these:

>   (if (category ?w proper-noun)   ; *If the string begins with*
>   ; *a proper noun, then it may*
>   (parse (cons ?w ?r) (np ?w) ?r))   ; *be analyzed as beginning*
>   ; *with a one-word np.*

>   (if (and (category ?w1 det)   ; *If the string begins with a*
>   (category ?w2 noun)   ; *determiner, a noun, and a*
>   (parse ?b (pp ?pp) ?c))   ; *prepositional phrase, then*
>   (parse (cons ?w1 (cons ?w2 ?b))   ; *it may be analyzed as*
>   (np ?w1 ?w2 (pp ?pp))   ; *starting with a noun phrase*
>   ?c))   ; *made of these three things.*

Try adding more rules, then giving the top-level goal

>   (Show: (parse [the boy ran] ?s nil))

to your theorem prover. This is a request to find analyses ?s of the sentence with nothing left over.

6.31 Consider the inference rule:

$$\frac{(\text{if } r\ p'),\ (\text{if } p\ q)}{(\text{if } r'\ q')}$$

Show that this is a special case of resolution.

6.32 Explain why the transformations in Figure 6.22 are valid.

6.33 In Section 6.6, we showed that resolution is a generalization of backward chaining. Show that it is a generalization of forward chaining as well, by proving the following theorem:

> If $S\ \cup\ \{(\text{Show: } g)\}$ leads to the empty
> clause by a series of resolutions,
> then there is a series of resolutions leading from S
> to h, where h subsumes g.

6.34 Verify using resolution (Section 6.6) that if p and (not p) follow from premises S, then any conclusion does. This will make theorem provers significantly different from people only if such inconsistencies are routinely exploited by a theorem prover to prove arbitrary theorems. Explain why a practical theorem prover, given a theorem to prove from an inconsistent set, will usually not find a proof based solely on the inconsistency.

6.35 Implement the "negation as failure" idea by having your theorem prover (see Exercise 6.20) handle goals of the form (consistent p) as described in Section 6.5.1.

6.36 Show that Russell's paradox applies to the interpretation of λ-expressions as sets. That is, with PP defined as in Box 6.2 prove (iff (describes PP PP) (not (describes PP PP))).

6.37 We noted in Section 6.4.1 that repeated subgoals with variables in them must be treated specially. What we said was this: "If the [repeated] goal does have variables, then answers to the original occurrence must be fed back into the subgoal." To really understand what this means it is necessary to try an example. In particular, try the goal (above ?what bl-1) on the database of Figure 6.15, and try to find all possible bindings for ?what which will make this true. Assume that we use the choice criterion used in Figure 6.16, augmented by our rule for repeated subgoals. Note that one of the partial solutions generated from the initial goal will be generated by using 1 from Figure 6.15, and will have the following subgoals: (above ?what ?y) and (above ?y bl-1). The second of these is a repeat of the initial goal. Show how returning to the initial goal, finding the other solutions to it, and then substituting them into the repeated case does the right thing.

This chapter builds on Chapter 6. Chapters 9 and 10 depend upon the idea of schema from Section 7.2.3. Chapter 9 also uses the idea of hierarchical organization of time maps, developed in Section 7.4.3. Chapter 8 is complementary to Section 7.6 in describing a different approach to expert systems.

Memory Organization and Deduction

7.1 The Importance of Memory Organization

In Chapter 6, we focused on the abstract content of data in the "database" of a robot. This tactic enables us to concentrate on how to express a set of statements at all. But it means we have neglected questions about how these statements are to be accessed and used. One thing to emphasize is that in an actual implementation the requirements of *memory organization* end up dictating what data structures are actually found. It is fairly rare in practice to find data structures that are simple transcriptions of predicate-calculus formulas.

As an example, let's look at a particular memory structure, the *script*. Scripts were designed to help explain understanding of event sequences (or stories). A script is a stereotyped sequence of events, such as the events in getting your hair cut or going to a restaurant. To oversimplify, we can represent a script as a list of event descriptions, which contain *script variables*. For instance, getting your hair cut (at a beauty parlor) has script variables Beauty-Parlor, Receptionist, Beautician, Chair, Sink, . . . and a sequence of event descriptions, as in Figure 7.1. (Of course, each event description should be formalized, but we will neglect this.) The predicate-calculus representation of this sequence might be something like Figure 7.2.

A typical way the script might be used is to understand a simple story about someone getting a hair cut, like this one:

Frieda needed a haircut. When she got to the beauty parlor, she was sorry that Suzy, her favorite beautician, wasn't there. Frieda was even more dismayed when she saw her Mohawk haircut. She left no tip, and stalked out.

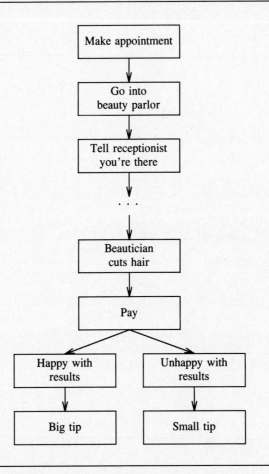

Figure 7.1 The beauty-parlor script

We will talk about story understanding in more detail later (Chapter 10), and here just give a sketch of what happens. The first sentence tells the computer that the beauty-parlor script might be relevant, and the second sentence confirms this. The machine then *matches* sentences with script elements, *binding* script variables as it goes. Because script-understandable stories are almost by definition boring, the machine should expect to skip most of the script events for any given story, and just assume them. Where the script branches, the machine must take the best-matching branch.

One way to implement script matching is to maintain two pointers, one into the story and one into the script. As the story pointer is advanced, so is the script pointer. At any stage, the few event descriptions just after the pointer in the script are "accessible" in a way that event descriptions from other scripts are not, even though, taken as abstract facts, they are all equally believed true.

```
(forall (ev)
   (if (inst ev haircut)
      (exists (cust bp recep h . . . ev1 ev2 ev3 . . .)
         (and (inst cust human)
              (inst bp beauty-parlor)
              (inst recep receptionist)
              . . .
              (sub-event ev1 ev)
              (event ev1 (do cust (Make appointment with bp)))
              (seq ev1 ev2)
              (sub-event ev2 ev)
              (event ev2 (do cust (Go into bp)))
              (seq ev2 ev3)
              . . .
              (sub-event ev14 ev)
              (event ev14 (do cust (Pay bp)))
              (overlap ev14 ev15)
              (state ev15 (satisfied cust h))
              (seq ev14 ev16)
              (event ev16 (do cust (Leave a tip)))
              (or (and (> h 0) (big-tip (tip ev16)))
                  (and (≤ h 0) (small-tip (tip ev16)))))))))
```

Figure 7.2 The beauty-parlor script in predicate calculus

Accessibility is just as important as content. It does no good to believe a fact if you fail to recognize when it's relevant. Hence an implementation of a knowledge structure will often sacrifice uniformity for the sake of efficiency. For example, an arrow between two event descriptions has content "This event is followed by that one." The content is not represented explicitly or, rather, it is represented by a special-purpose notation with just one predicate, "**arrow**." Furthermore, the content is not used in general-purpose deduction; instead, the story-matching algorithm just follows links. A link not only represents a fact, but also serves as an organizing device.

In this chapter, we will examine techniques for memory management. It will be obvious that these techniques involve careful combination of data structures with special-purpose inference algorithms. It is impossible to separate these two. However, we will structure the discussion so that it focuses more on data structures at the outset, and increasingly on programming techniques as the chapter progresses. Some of the later sections focus on special-purpose deductive techniques for areas such as spatial and temporal reasoning. These are of great interest to AI researchers because general-purpose methods do so badly on them, while people do rather well. Finally, in the last section, we will look at a technique of a different sort — rule-based programming — which is not specialized to any domain, but is of value in solving ill-specified problems of the sort AI is often concerned with.

7.2 Approaches to Memory Organization

7.2.1 Indexing Predicate-Calculus Assertions

The most straightforward approach to representing facts in memory is to maintain a database of (Skolemized) predicate-calculus facts, which are then manipulated by a theorem prover. As we suggested in Chapter 6, such a theorem prover would require that these two operations be cheap:

1. Adding and removing formulas
2. Finding all formulas that unify with a given formula, called the *fetch pattern*.

One example of (2) is found in backward chaining. Given a goal, G, the database *gatekeeper* needs to find all formulas of the form G' or $(\leftarrow G'\ S)$, where G' unifies with G. In the first case, G itself is the fetch pattern. The second case can be thought of as finding a formula that unifies with fetch pattern $(\leftarrow G\ ?v)$, where $?v$ is a variable that does not occur in G.

All schemes for making formula-finding cheap rely on the following idea. The fetch pattern is not made up entirely of variables. For instance, the fetch pattern (contains ?x a) has a constant contains as its first element, and a constant a as its third. Any matching formula in the database must not have a different constant in one of these positions. The matching formula (contains universe ?y) has contains as its first element, and no other constants in places the fetch pattern has constants. The formula (contains new-york empire-state-bldg) has a different constant as its third element, and does not unify. Therefore, formulas in the database must be stored in such a way that it is easy to retrieve, given a constant and a position, all the formulas that have that constant (or a variable) at that position. This is called *indexing* the formulas. (The phrase *secondary index* from database management refers to the same idea.) To accomplish a fetch, we derive several *keys* from the constants in the fetch pattern, and use them to look up formulas in the index.

The most straightforward way to do this is to attach to every constant a list of all the assertions it occurs in, organized by where in each assertion the constant occurs. That is, we associate with each symbol a structure of the form

    ((*pos N -formulas-*)
     (*pos N -formulas-*)
     . . .)

Each *pos* is a position, and each *N* is the number of formulas in which the constant occurs at that position. Following *N* are the actual formulas. Variables are treated as the symbol *var*. So, for instance, the database might have the lists shown in Figure 7.3 (and many others). We represent positions as tuples of integers. The empty tuple < > designates the entire formula, <1> its first element, <3 1> the third element of the first element, and so on.

```
contains:
    ((<1> 4 (contains new-york empire-state-bldg)
            (contains us new-york)
            (contains universe ?y)
            (contains us california))
     (<1 2> 1 (← (contains ?x ?y)
                 (and (contains ?x ?z)
                      (contains ?z ?y)))))

new-york:
    ((<2> 1 (contains new-york empire-state-bldg))
     (<3> 1 (contains us new-york))
     . . .)

*var*:
    ((<3> 1 (contains universe ?y))
     (<2 2> 2 (← (mortal ?x) (inst ?x human))
              (← (contains ?x ?y)
                 (and (contains ?x ?z)
                      (contains ?z ?y))))
     (<3 2> 1 (← (contains ?x ?y)
                 (and (contains ?x ?z)
                      (contains ?z ?y))))
     . . .)
```

Figure 7.3 Some buckets in an indexed database

Given a fetch pattern, the machine can find formulas to unify with it by walking through the pattern recursively, finding constants at particular positions, and getting the corresponding formula lists, called *buckets*, from the database. The algorithm is shown in Figure 7.4. A trace of the operation of index-fetch given the fetch pattern (contains universe (satellites jupiter)) is shown in Figure 7.5.

In this figure, => is used to indicate what a call returns. Most indexing methods, including this one, do not return just those formulas that are guaranteed to match the fetch pattern. For instance, if (p ?x ?x) is the fetch pattern, it will return all formulas beginning with p. Not all of these formulas will survive the unification that follows fetching.

While this algorithm is better than just keeping one big list, it is not very good. Intersection is not that cheap an operation, unless we have a way of marking the formulas, in which case the machine can intersect two lists by marking the formulas in one list, and collecting the marked formulas from the other. (See Exercise 7.10.) This algorithm takes time proportional to the sum of the lengths of the two lists, rather than the product, as the naive algorithm would. For formulas to be markable, they must be stored in a ''uniquified'' format; that is, for any formula p stored in the database there must be a list (p - *marks-etc*-) such that every occurrence of p must point to exactly this list in memory. If one such occurrence is marked (by making a recognizable alteration

Function: index-fetch
Arguments: pat — a pattern (and not a variable)
            pos — a position
            ; This function finds formulas in the database with
            ; patterns at position pos *that unify with* pat.
Algorithm:
    Get the bucket for *var* at pos, that is, the
        set of all formulas that have a variable here.
    If pat is an atom, combine the formulas in the *var*
        bucket with the bucket for pat at position pos.
    Otherwise, combine the *var* bucket with the
        formulas returned by calling list-index-fetch
        with arguments pat and pos.

Function: list-index-fetch
Arguments: pat — a nonatomic pattern (a list of terms)
            pos — a position
            ; This function finds formulas in the database with
            ; nonvariable patterns at position pos *that unify with* pat.
Local variables: result — a list of formulas to be returned.
Algorithm:
    result ← bucket for predicate or function
        of pat at position corresponding to first element
        below pos (that is, $<1\ m\ n\ ...>$, where
        pos is $<m\ n\ ...>$)
    If result is not empty,
        Loop through the remaining elements of pat, calling
            index-fetch on each nonvariable element,
            with pos extended to designate successively
            the second element, third element, etc. of the
            original pos (that is, $<2\ m\ n\ ...>$,
            $<3\ m\ n\ ...>$, etc.)
        Set result successively to its intersection with
            all the values returned by index-fetch
            (If it ever becomes empty, the algorithm can stop.)
    Return result

Figure 7.4 Algorithm for finding formulas in a database

to the mark field), then all occurrences are marked. (The *-etc-* are for other slots we will need for various purposes.)

The mark-and-test algorithm is faster than the naive algorithm, but it can still take a long time on large buckets. If one of the lists is much longer than the other, the time to intersect could become larger than the time to do a few unifications. Since the only purpose of the intersection is to avoid unifications, it might be more economical to just take the shortest list if it is only a few elements long. For instance, suppose that one list is of length 1, and the other is of length 100. Intersection will take 101 operations. The best possible advantage gained by doing the intersection over just taking the length-1 list is for this

index-fetch *Pattern:* (contains universe (satellites jupiter))
 Position: < >
Include bucket for *var* *at* < >
=> ()
list-index-fetch: (contains . . .) *at* < >
 Include bucket for contains *at* <1>
  => ((contains new-york empire-state-bldg)
   (contains us new-york)
   (contains universe ?y)
   (contains us california))

 index-fetch: universe *at* <2>
  => *Empty bucket for* *var* *at* <2>, *plus*
   ((contains universe ?y))

 At this point, result=((contains universe ?y))
  index-fetch: (satellites jupiter) *at* <3>
   Include bucket for '*var* *at* <3>
   => ((contains universe ?y))
   plus
   list-index-fetch: (satellites . . .) *at* <3>
    index-fetch satellites *at* <1 3>) => ()
    => ()
   => ((contains universe ?y))

 result *remains* ((contains universe ?y))
  => ((contains universe ?y))
=> ((contains universe ?y))

Figure 7.5 Trace of index-fetch

intersection to be null. That is, we can save at most one unification. If unification takes less than 100 times as long as marking or testing, we are better off doing the unification. (See Exercise 7.11.)

Another improvement treats the predicate position in a special way. Note that the predicate position is never a variable in a fetch pattern. (We never fetch something like (?p a b), because it is not allowed in first-order logic, and doesn't really take us very far toward higher-order logic. See Chapter 6.) Therefore, we can extend our index to three layers: constant, predicate, and position (instead of the current two, constant and position). A bucket would be retrieved by giving three values, one per layer. E.g., the bucket for new-york, contains, and <3> would hold all formulas of the form (contains x new-york).

The index structure attached to new-york would look something like Figure 7.6. At this point, we stop worrying about the speed of intersection, and start worrying about the speed of the linear search through the top-level table. If there are 100 predicates involving New York, then to access one of them will require a linear search down a list 100 long. It might be worthwhile to replace

```
new-york:
    ((contains (<2> ...)
             (<3> ...))
    (population (<2> 1 (population new-york 9000000))
             ...)
    (lives-in (<3> ...))
    (belongs-to (<2> ...))
    ...            ; and many, many more
    )
```

Figure 7.6 Three-layer index structure

the top-level list with a *hash table*, a data structure that will allow access to an element, given a predicate, in constant time (in the average case). (See Chapter 1).

One can refine such indexing schemes further. As the number of levels increases, we can generalize the idea to include an indefinite number. At this point, it is better to start talking about general discrimination trees. (The ones we talked about in Chapter 5 can be adapted to the present purpose, if care is taken with variables.)

7.2.2 Associative Networks

One can also build data structures representing facts in a more indirect way. We have already seen this idea implemented in scripts, where we used an arrow (in the machine, one or more pointers) to represent "this event is usually followed by that event." The advantages of doing this are that it saves space, and that it encourages the use of efficient special-purpose graph-search techniques to do inference. The phrase *associative network* is often used to describe representation systems based on graphs whose links correspond to predicates.

An important class of techniques of this kind might be called *associative analog* inference. We let the pointer structure of the associative network mirror the structure of a set of relationships we are trying to capture. For example, one could represent a city map as a graph whose nodes and arcs correspond to intersections and streets. Finding a path through the city is accomplished by finding a path through the graph. (We will say more about this idea in Section 7.5.)

Running a general-purpose theorem prover on the corresponding axioms would be less efficient, for these reasons

1. Following a pointer is intrinsically cheaper than doing the unification that even the shortest deduction requires.
2. The graph searcher can mark the graph as it goes, to avoid getting trapped in cycles or pursuing a path inferior to one it has already found. Theorem provers have both of these problems.

3. The graph searcher can take advantage of domain-dependent heuristics. In Section 7.5 we will suggest that a path be found at the region level first, and this path used to guide formation of the street-level path.

Advantages like these are to be had in most domains, but the price paid for speed is inflexibility. A graph searcher handles deductions involving a predicate (like connected-to in the spatial-map case), but only a small fraction of the possible deductions. The map can store (connected-to a b), but it cannot handle

```
(forall (x) (if (connected-to x a)
               (connected-to x b)))
```

"Everything connected to a is also connected to b," without extending its special-purpose machinery. (Such extensions are often practically impossible.)

In our opinion, the speed outweighs the inflexibility. Normally, 99% of the deductions needed do fall under some special case, and you may as well take advantage of this fact. Besides, the advantages of theorem provers in principle rarely translate into practice, because theorem provers often take a long time to arrive at an answer.

What exactly do "links" look like inside the computer? We have argued that the content of a link is equivalent to some assertion; the implementation can be surprisingly close as well. An assertion such as (contains a b) might be represented using three data structures:

1. The actual list (contains a b)
2. An indexing pointer to this list from a
3. An indexing pointer to the list from b

Where exactly these pointers go depends on which indexing scheme we implement. We can ignore all such issues here, and just think of the pointer as running directly from a or b.

Now suppose we wanted to use a "contains link" instead. We could just put a link from a with the contents "contains b." (For those who read Chapter 2, the easy way to do this in Lisp is to execute (putprop 'a 'b 'contains).) However, this is inadequate, for several reasons. One is the absence of a "back pointer," as discussed in Chapter 1. We have to be able to get from b to a as well as from a to b (to find out what contains b). Furthermore, a may be known to contain several things, so the entity attached to a with the label "contains" must be a list of things. The simplest way to go is to let this be a list of pairs. So to represent (contains a b), (contains a c), and (contains d a), we would set up the pointer structures shown in Figure 7.7. We will use the term *pointer pair* for a list of two elements, each of which points to it (through a couple of layers of indirection). The pointer from the first element will be taken as the "forward pointer"; the pointer from the second, as the "back pointer." This is the data structure that we will assume underlies what we draw as labeled arcs.

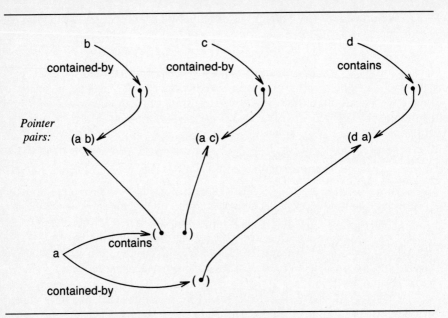

Figure 7.7 Data structures for implementing links

But this is virtually the same data structure that we were calling "assertions" before! The differences are subtle.

1. The pointers from **a** and **b** that we envisaged in Section 7.2.1 were filed under names like <2> and <3>; here we use **contains** and **contained-by**. However, once we went to the "three-level scheme" in which we used both the predicate and argument position, this difference is of no consequence. That is, the key <**contains**, <3>> that we used on the property list of **new-york** has exactly the same content as **contained-by**; both mean, "the second argument of a **contains** relationship."

2. In the new scheme, we avoid repeating the symbol **contains** over and over. However, this is a detail. We could have omitted the predicate in the "assertional scheme," recovering it from the key; and we could just as well include it in the "link" scheme (as most systems actually do). Similarly, since we might very well want to mark links, we would make sure to provide a mark field in them the way we did with "markable assertions" in Section 7.2.1.

3. The real difference is that we avoid doing backward chaining, or even unification, in the link version. That is, to find what **a** contains, we do not call a general-purpose backward chainer with goal (**Show:** (**contains a ?what**)) which looks first for an assertion to unify with this pattern, then checks for a rule (← (**contains a ?x**) . . .). Instead, we (a) get the

contains links, and (b) take the second element of each of them. This is
a lot faster.

Once again, the trade-off is the same: flexibility is sacrificed for efficiency.

In other cases, links can look somewhat different from assertions. Consider the equality predicate. (= a b) differs from (contains a b) in that it is
symmetric. It seems wasteful to store both this assertion and (= b a), since
they mean the same thing. Instead, we can point from each constant to a list of
all the things that are known to be equal to it. So (= a b), (= b c), and (= a
d) can be stored by having one central list (a b c d) that all four symbols point
to (under the ''='' indicator, presumably). Note that it is just as easy to
retrieve (= c a) from this data structure as to retrieve a fact that was explicitly
stored in it. The data structure is doing inferences from the transitivity and
symmetry of equality automatically.

Although we have made a good case for the equivalence of links and
assertions, it seems as though we are ignoring one big difference. A link is usually drawn as a labeled arc, which appears to limit it to representing a binary
relationship (a relationship between two entities). There is no such limitation on
assertions. However, any assertion involving predicates with more than two
arguments can always be translated into a set of ''binary assertions'' by what
should by now be a familiar transformation to you: Just turn

$$(p \; a_1 \; a_2 \ldots a_N)$$

into

(inst r p-relationship)
(arg1 r a_1)
(arg2 r a_2)
$\ldots$
(arg$N$ r a_N)

where r is a new constant denoting the ''relationship'' we are talking about.
This is what we called *slot-assertion notation* in Chapter 1. (In Chapter 6 we
talked about this translation for event notations.) Figure 7.8 gives an example.

What we have done is transform links into nodes, and pointers into links
(pointer pairs). In principle, we could do this transformation to all assertions,
so that everything we thought of as an assertion in predicate calculus becomes a
relationship node; while labeled, binary arcs (or pointer pairs, internally) are
reserved for joining such relationship nodes with their arguments.

This is elegant, but undermines much of the unique charm of associative
networks. The main advantage of such schemes is precisely that they admit of
different ad hoc representations of different links. We have seen three already:
labeled arcs (for binary predicates), equivalence classes (for symmetric and transitive predicates like equality), and explicit nodes in the network (for predicates
with more than two arguments). Each must be deciphered by a special-purpose
link traverser, but substantial efficiency can be gained by doing this. This is

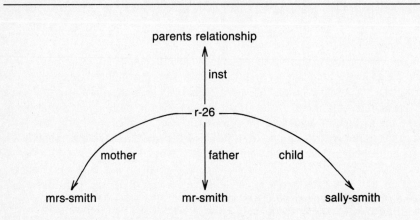

parents relationship

inst

r-26

mother   father   child

mrs-smith   mr-smith   sally-smith

Figure 7.8 Link representation of (parents mr-smith mrs-smith sally-smith)

why, in Figure 7.8, we have left the inst link as an ordinary labeled arc. As we will see in Section 7.2.3, treating inst links in a special way can pay off.

We will work up to this idea by way of an application of equality links. The general use of equality in performing inferences is quite difficult, because an equality can be used to rewrite a term at any level in a formula, and it is not always clear which terms to rewrite (or even which way). (See Chapter 6.) However, an important special case occurs when two constants are asserted equal. In this case, we can think of this assertion as an ''='' link between them, and then just have the retrieval algorithms treat them as the same object.

For example, suppose that in the process of reading a detective story, several facts are accumulated about Ackroyd, the butler (e.g., ''Ackroyd had lost heavily at the gambling tables,'' ''A grateful Lord Innings had left millions to his devoted servant Ackroyd''), and several quite distinct facts about the murderer (e.g., ''The murderer bludgeoned Lord Innings with a cricket bat''). Then we discover that Ackroyd and the murderer are the same: (= ackroyd murderer-97). Suppose we now inquire of our database where Ackroyd was on the night of the murder, having made the following changes to our usual retrieval techniques:

1. We alter index-fetch (Section 7.2.1) so that, in addition to finding (bucket pos pat) when pat is an atom, it finds (bucket pos e) for every atom asserted = to pat.
2. We alter unify (Chapter 6) so that, in addition to comparing two atoms for equality, it also checks to see if they have been asserted =.

The goal is (Show: (location ackroyd ?where night-103)), where night-103 is the night of the murder. Then index-fetch will include the bucket under <location, <2>> for murderer-97 as well as for ackroyd, and hence will find the assertion (location murderer-97 crime-scene night-103) in the database. The unifier, when it compares this with the query, will realize that the two terms ackroyd and murderer-97 are equal, and the unification will succeed. (See Exercise 7.14.) Furthermore, we also have the option of treating equality differently in other circumstances. In Section 7.2.3 we will see that this has its uses.

We have lapsed back into talking about assertions. But from now on, when we say "assertion," you may as well think "link," and vice versa. The similarity between the two ideas is so close that which to visualize in a given context hinges on slight differences of emphasis between content and indexing. We will try to pick the best on each occasion, but as a mental exercise try translating each occurrence into the other. To repeat, the key difference is whether the data structure is to be queried by uniform unification-based inference techniques, or something zippier and more specialized.

In the "butler did it" example, we assumed that location assertions were stored as assertions; it is reasonable to suppose that = assertions are stored as links. But what if location assertions were stored as links, too? This would simply mean that some alternative to unification was being used to process them. In that case, we could still make sure that ackroyd and murderer-97 were treated the same, but we would have to modify the special-purpose location handler to do it. Alas, one problem with special-purpose techniques is that they can interfere with one another. Every time we introduce a new technique, we must make sure that all the others interact correctly with it.

7.2.3 Property Inheritance

We introduced this chapter by talking about scripts, and it is time to return to that subject. The essential feature of a script is that it consists of a large conjunction of facts with free variables (as in the consequent of the implication of Figure 7.2). When the script is used, values are found for these free variables. The resulting conjunction of instantiated facts is a *script instance*, a particular story involving a beauty parlor.

From now on, we will usually use the word *schema* to mean a large set of facts with variables, since the idea has been applied in many contexts besides scripts. An example we have already seen are the *parametrized shape descriptions* of Chapter 3. The "abstract schema" is the predicate-calculus version. The "concrete schema" is the actual data structure implementation. The object you get when you plug values in the for the variables we will call a *schema instance*.

A key problem in memory organization is the efficient management of schemas and schema instances. A common approach is to join individuals to schemas describing them by another sort of associative link, the *property-inheritance* link. This is like an equality link, but asymmetric; the pointer is followed just one way. We will identify the meaning of this link with two predicates we have seen before: (inst *individual class*) and (isa *subclass superclass*). See Figure 7.9. The intention is that fifi and fido are to be inferred to be furry, friendly, and so forth. This is accomplished by having the retrieval

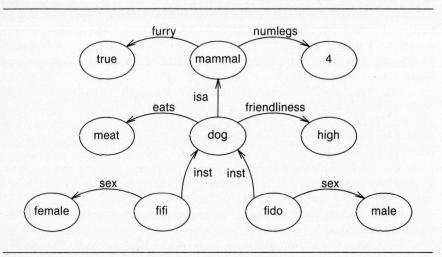

Figure 7.9 A simple property-inheritance hierarchy

system search up inst and isa links. For instance, if we ask it for fido's sex, it will just follow the sex pointer, and get male. If we ask whether fido is friendly, it will try the same thing, not find a friendliness pointer, follow the inst link, and find one. For furriness, two links would have to be searched.

This is quite efficient, and much more efficient than the obvious way to implement the corresponding inference in a theorem prover. The content of the complex surrounding dog is

> (forall (x) (if (inst x dog)
>   (and (friendliness x high)
>   (eats x meat))))

A theorem prover will have serious problems finding its way through a large database of such schemas. Suppose we had the goal (Show: (friendliness fido ?x)). Assuming that the if in each schema is interpreted as a backward-chaining rule, then many subgoals of the form (inst fido *class*) will be tried, all but one of which will eventually fail.

Note again that we have adopted a carefree attitude toward the exact translation of links to assertions. In particular, the dog and mammal nodes now behave differently with respect to links from the way fifi and fido behave; there is an implicit universal quantifier. A consequence is that, if we wish to record (say) (numerous dog) (i.e., "There are lots of dogs") we cannot simply hang a numerous link off dog. If we did, we could infer that fifi and fido were numerous, which is meaningless. To avoid problems like this, in a practical system we would split dog into two nodes, one as a place to hang properties of the class of dogs, and one as a place to hang properties of all dogs.

Another way to express this dichotomy is to represent implicitly quantified statements about dog, mammal, etc. using "pseudo-assertions" containing terms representing "typical" entities. For instance, since all stop signs are octagonal, we can add to the database an assertion (shape #typical-stop-sign octagonal). Contrast this with (numerous stop-sign), which refers correctly to the class stop-sign rather than the "pseudo-individual" #typical-stop-sign. The statements from Figure 7.9 would come out like this

(sex fido male)	(friendliness #typical-dog high)
(sex fifi female)	(eats #typical-dog meat)
(inst fido dog)	(isa dog mammal)
(inst fifi dog)	(furry #typical-mammal true)
	(numlegs #typical-mammal 4)

In general this technique allows you to represent schemas of the form

    (forall (x) (if (inst x *class*)
            (and (*p1* x *v1*)
                 (*p2* x *v2*)
                 . . .)))

as a set of pseudo-assertions

    (*p1* #typical-*class v1*)
    (*p2* #typical-*class v2*)

Now suppose the machine fetches (Show: (shape obj-104 ?what)), where obj-104 is known to be a stop sign, (inst obj-104 stop-sign). The query and the assertion differ in that the query has a constant *c* where the assertion has #typical-*s*, where *s* is a superclass of *c*. If the index-fetching programs (Section 7.2.1) are modified to search for #typical-*s* for every superclass *s* of every constant, then the query and the assertion will find each other after all. Thus the database will now look like Figure 7.10.

This idea requires the isa hierarchy to be represented twice, as explicit inst and isa statements in the predicate calculus, and implicitly as links forged within the indexing mechanism. The latter, less visible representation depends entirely on the former (and care must be taken that changes in inst and isa assertions are reflected inside the index).

The most interesting issue concerning associative networks containing inst and isa links is how to generalize the schemas at nonindividual nodes (like dog). It is rather limiting to insist that each schema be of the form

    (forall (x) (if (inst x *class*)
            (and (*pred1* x *val1*)
                 (*pred2* x *val2*)
                 . . .)))

Although any pattern of nested quantifiers is possible (see Chapter 6), a common one is to have a single existential inside a single universal, as shown in Figure 7.11. For example, the predicate-calculus version of the beauty-parlor script shown in Figure 7.2 has this form. There the existentially quantified variables

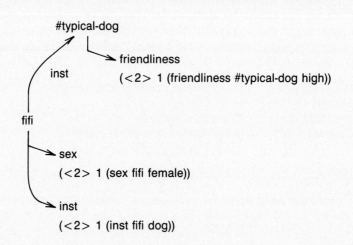

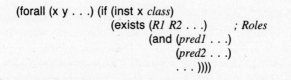

Figure 7.10　An indexing method for schemas

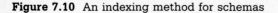

```
(forall (x y . . .) (if (inst x class)
                (exists (R1 R2 . . .)      ; Roles
                    (and (pred1 . . .)
                         (pred2 . . .)
                         . . . ))))
```

Figure 7.11　Typical schema pattern

are the beauty parlor, the actions which will take place, etc. We will call these the *roles* of the schema or script.

For that matter, even our **dog** schema is better represented in this new format. Just as the existence of a "beauty-parloring" event implies the existence of a beauty parlor, etc., the existence of a dog implies the existence of parts of the dog (the head, legs, etc.) plus such ancillary items as an owner and license. The resulting schema for dog would then look like this:

```
(forall (x) (if (inst x dog)
             (exists (head owner license  . . .)
                 (and (friendliness x high)
                      (own owner x)
                      (holder-of owner license)
                      (part-of head x)
                      . . .))))
```

When we Skolemize this formula it becomes:

```
(if (inst ?x dog) (and (friendliness ?x high)
                       (own (owner-of ?x) ?x)
                       (holder-of (owner-of ?x) (license-of ?x))
                       (part-of (head-of ?x) ?x))
                       . . .))))
```

The roles of the schema are now functions. Again turning these into #typical-dog assertions results in statements like

(holder-of (owner-of #typical-dog) (license-of #typical-dog))

Unfortunately, when we now try to index these assertions we run into trouble. The crucial step in Figure 7.10 was introducing #typical-dog and indexing statements about dogs there. But how should we index (owner-of #typical-dog)?

To see why this is a problem, we should remember that in a real example we will not be asking about (owner-of fido). Rather we will enquire about fred, who we know is Fido's owner. That is, we will have stored in the database facts like

(:= (owner-of fido) fred)
(:= (license-of fido) license-4)

Here the predicate := is meant to be like equality, except that it also tells us that the equality relation is meant to be used in a particular direction, with the Skolem function (owner-of fido) replaced by fred, and not vice versa. Nor should := be handled by the indexer like the equality scheme mentioned in Section 7.2.2. That algorithm required having the indexer, when searching for assertions involving a constant, to check all the other constants known to be equal to it. With := the indexer cannot check for all the things equal to an object, because an object could easily have hundreds or thousands of := statements about it, one for each role it played in a schema.

The following example will make the difficulty clearer. Given the information above about the relation of fred and license-4 to fido, the following query might come in:

(Show: (holder-of fred license-4))

This fact should follow from the other facts in the database. The basic index-fetching algorithm would look for rules with fred in the second position, and license-4 in the third, but there are no such rules. If we adapted the equality algorithm from Section 7.2.2, the indexer would have to look at every role that fred and license-4 might fill. Our schema indexer which we used for dogs will not work either. It allowed us to infer facts about fido from facts about dogs. But in the case at hand no dog is mentioned, so it does us no good.

There have been several proposals for handling this problem in the literature, but all have problems. One possibility is to not index such rules at all, at least not in the sense of indexing we have been considering. Rather, dog would point to all of the rules in its schema, and whenever the topic of dogs ''comes up,'' (say, in a conversation the machine is engaged in), the machine adds that schema to a list of currently active schemas. Then when a request is made, all currently active schemas are checked. Note that for this to be at all efficient the number of active schemas must be small because the time to retrieve a fact (or decide that it cannot be proved) will be proportional to the number of active schemas. If this number gets large, say in the hundreds, then requests could get time-consuming.

It is our best guess that the number of active schemas can get large. To take a trivial example, consider the sentence, "The lawyer took a cab to a restaurant near the university." The next line might require information about any of the four main nouns. Furthermore, each of these will have information spread around at different levels of the isa hierarchy. So information about **lawyer** might be found under the schema for **professional, wage-earner, person, mammal, animal**, etc. It is conceivable that this one sentence could involve a system in twenty or thirty active schemas.

Assuming that this is correct, a better way of retrieving information from such schemas is needed. We propose a method which is a modest extension of our last schema indexer. The idea is this: Skolem functions are not indexed literally but rather by the type of entity which could be a value for the function. Let us assume that as part of our schema we had the following

> (inst (owner-of #typical-dog) person)
> (inst (license-of #typical-dog) dog-license)

Then we could index (**owner-of #typical-dog**) under **person** and (**license-of #typical-dog**) under **dog-license**. That is, we would have a data structure like that in Figure 7.12, plus the assertions

> (inst fred person)
> (inst license-4 dog-license)

Now consider what happens when a request comes in to prove

> (holder-of fred license-4)

Under **holder-of** it will find some formulas about responsibility for things like

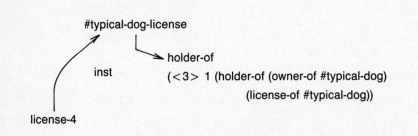

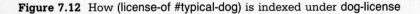

Figure 7.12 How (license-of #typical-dog) is indexed under **dog-license**

licenses. Under **fred** it will find nothing, but going up the isa hierarchy it will get to **person**, where the appropriate fact will be found, as will be the case when it goes up from **license-4** to **dog-license**. The net result is that to the user it appears as if we have a copy of the **dog** schema, but with values from the := statements substituted for the existential variables. This is sometimes called a *virtual copy*. Although we did not illustrate this in either Figure 7.12 or Figure 7.10 the inheritance does not stop after one **inst** link; one schema can be a virtual copy of another, via **isa** links.

We also mention this indexing method because it has properties that make it appealing in story comprehension. As we will discuss in Chapter 10, one problem we face in story comprehension is recognizing that an action performed is, in fact, expected by a schema. Thus we might know that Norman was **restauranting** and thereby have an instantiation of this schema. Suppose the comprehender then saw a sentence like "Norman asked the waitress for a menu." While we are not interested in the exact representation of this sentence, we are concerned with the fact that it will mention **waitress-22** and **menu-14** which will be instances of **waitress** and **menu** respectively. The formula we wish to find, however, will not mention these objects, but rather (**waitress-of ?restauranting**) and (**menu-of ?restauranting**). However, if these items are indexed under **waitress** and **menu** then the appropriate formula will be found.

There is one other aspect of the virtual-copy idea which is both a benefit and a problem. Note that in the previous example about the menu, the appropriate formula would be found even if we had not previously known that Norman was eating out. More generally put, this approach does not distinguish between scripts that have been instantiated (recently) and those which have not. This property can be useful, since the story might start out with the line about asking the waitress, and we would still want our system to retrieve the formula from the **restauranting** script and thus, presumably, create a new instance of the script. However, in other cases this same property may cause problems since it will not be very selective about the statements it retrieves. (See Exercise 7.29.)

As we have described them so far, virtual copies can have information not found in the schemas from which they are derived. If Frieda chewed gum while she waited at the beauty parlor, we could just add that event. It is equally important to be able to delete or modify the information. For instance, suppose we want to represent McDonald's as a virtual copy of the restaurant script. One place where it differs is in the sequence of events. At McDonald's, you pay before you eat. If we simply add in the appropriate "precedes" links, then we will introduce a cycle, since the old links are still "virtually" there. See Figure 7.13. There is no agreement how to "cancel" the information.

7.3 Data Dependencies

AI databases are not static. Assertions and links come and go, and the inferences they trigger must be kept up to date. In this section, we will briefly survey methods for making sure it all happens correctly.

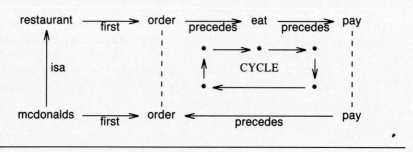
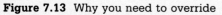

Figure 7.13 Why you need to override

Suppose that a program adds an assertion p to the database, and later adds $(\rightarrow p\ q)$. Now the inference of q occurs. Next suppose that p is erased. There is no longer any reason to believe the assertion q. The problem is for the database manager to notice this.

The solution is to attach to every assertion a record of how it got there. (By "assertion" in this discussion, we mean "assertion or link.") Such a record is called a *data-dependency note*, since it typically records the dependence of one assertion on some others. You may think of this as a proof, but the relationship may be weaker than the term "proof" implies.

We will draw data-dependency notes as shown in Figure 7.14. Assertions are drawn as squares or rectangles, linked by arrows to circles representing *justifications*. A justification joins a conjunction of *justifiers* to the supported

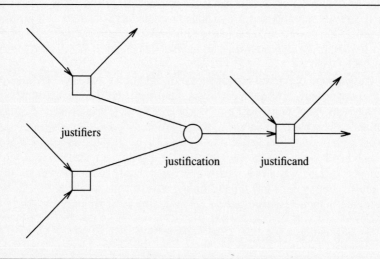

Figure 7.14 Schematic data-dependency note

assertion, known as the *justificand*. An assertion may have more than one
justification. Figure 7.15 shows an example of a data dependency.

Now, whenever an assertion is erased, we must erase everything for which
it was the sole support. This can be tricky. If an assertion is supported by
more than one justification, then all of them must be erased before it is. But
cycles in the dependency structure must not fool the system. In Figure 7.16, *A*

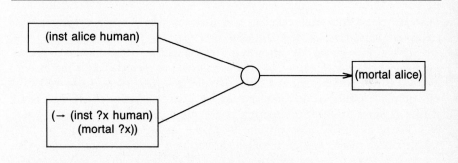

Figure 7.15 The data dependencies for (mortal alice)

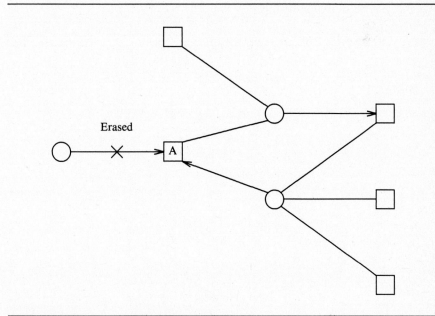

Figure 7.16 A circular data dependency

must be erased, even though it still has a justification, because that justification itself depends on *A*. *A* does not have *well-founded support*.

Actually, once data dependencies are in use, we cannot simply erase an assertion any longer. If it still has well-founded justifications, then this erasure is an error; if it does not, then it should have been erased already. Instead, the basic database operations are

- Add a new assertion and its initial justification
- Delete a justification (which may cause some assertions to be deleted)

We call the module that maintains and uses the data-dependency network the "Reason Maintenance System" (RMS).

What are drawn as arrows in the graphical representation of data-dependency notes in Figure 7.14 are implemented as pointers in the machine, of course. The representation is a little different from the pointer pairs we looked at before. A justification is implemented as a list of justifier assertions. Every assertion points to a list of its justifications. In addition, every assertion points to a list of its justificands, not directly to the justifications it occurs in. This simple device means that justifications do not have to point to justificands. See Figure 7.17. We have generalized the idea of back pointer to a "pointer cycle." Given any object in the triad *justifier-justification-justificand*, we can get to any other by following at most two pointers. The format of the assertions in Figure 7.17 is a further extension of the format we advocated earlier. Here we require assertions to be stored in the form

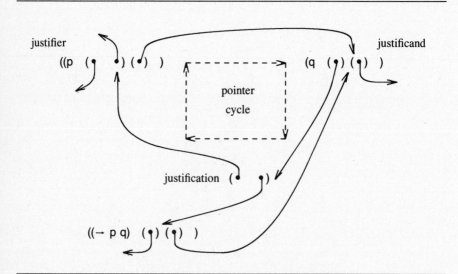

Figure 7.17 Internal pointer form of data-dependency notes

    (*formula pointers-to-justifications pointers-to-justificands*)

In practice, we would also need the mark field we described in Section 7.2.1.

    At the beginning of this section, we agreed to talk in terms of assertions, even though the ideas we have looked at apply to other data structures, such as links. But now that we have gotten down to pointer structures, an obstacle looms. In a practical system, different fact representations will be combined; one part of the program might use assertions and another links, for instance. Do we have to have several different RMSs and special conventions for links between them?

    A better idea is to provide a single abstract data type for the RMS to manipulate, called a "data-dependency node" or *ddnode*. The squares of Figure 7.14 correspond to ddnodes. From the RMSs point of view, there are two kinds of node:

1. ddnodes, which correspond to things the program "believes"
2. justifications, which record what supports what.

These are connected in pointer cycles as shown in Figure 7.17. Furthermore, the ddnodes point to the assertions or links, and vice versa. See Figure 7.18.

    From the point of view of the RMS, the object of the game is to label ddnodes properly. As the set of justifications changes, the proper labels change, and the RMS reassigns them. A ddnode is labeled "IN" if it has well-founded support; and "OUT" if it does not. A label of "OUT" does not mean that the assertion corresponding to that node is believed false; it is supposed instead to mean that the node is "not there," just as if it had never been asserted. To make the assertion false, there must be another node corresponding to its negation, which is "IN."

    The "OUT" label is a strange concept. We didn't need it before, because when something was not supposed to be there any more, it got erased. But the layer of abstraction between the RMS and the database has caused a problem: the RMS doesn't know how to erase things. Erasing involves operations like removing assertions from an index (or undoing back pointers from a link), and the details of how to do this vary between concrete representations of facts.

    The solution is to attach an "erasing" function to every ddnode, which knows how to erase it. Then the RMS can call this function for every ddnode that gets labeled OUT. This means that OUT labels hang around for only a small amount of time before the nodes they're attached to are erased completely. In other cases, we may want to cause things to be OUT temporarily, then bring them back IN. The usual case is for exploring hypothetical worlds. The machine temporarily makes some database changes, which cause new deductions and temporary erasures. It makes some inferences in this new database, then undoes the changes, relying on the data-dependency system to restore the database to its original state. Exercise 7.18 asks you to implement an RMS.

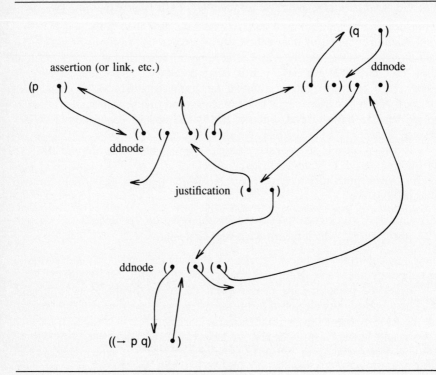

Figure 7.18 Pointer structures for ddnodes

7.4 **Reasoning Involving Time**

In Chapter 6, we talked about time in the abstract, through the concepts of "state" and "event." Practical programs have to worry about these concepts for two reasons. First, things change. A realistic database must keep track of what's true at various times, not just the present. We have already stumbled upon this issue several times, most recently in representing the location of Ackroyd the butler on the night of the murder in Section 7.2.2. We made up a predicate **location** with a wholly ad hoc time slot. We need a more uniform and efficient way of retrieving the true states of affairs at different times.

Second, the machine may have at its disposal ways of intervening in the world in order to achieve its goals. This will be our topic in Chapter 9. As a prerequisite to that topic, the machine must be able to reason about what will happen with and without intervention. For example, suppose you leave the water in the bathtub running for one hour. What will happen? What will be the volume of water in the tub at the end of that time?

We will use the term *projection* to cover both of these issues: the inference from what's true at one time to what's true at another; and the maintenance of and retrieval from a database of such inferences. (In Chapter 10 we will briefly look at "abductive projection," in which events are proposed as explanations for observed states of affairs.)

7.4.1 The Situation Calculus

A state is something that is true for a while, false for a while, and so on, like the state of John being in his house. An event is something that can happen, like John going to his house. Events are often the transitions between states:

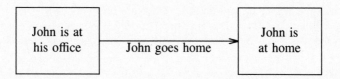

A durable approach to representing states and events is the *situation calculus*. A situation is a time interval over which no state (of interest) changes truth value. (It may be a single instant.) We can write (T *s p*) to mean that state *p* is true in situation *s*. (not (T *s p*)) means *p* is false in situation *s*.

The situation calculus talks about time in a somewhat different way from Chapter 6, where we introduced the idea of a "time token," an occasion on which a state is true or an event occurs. (These two subvarieties were called "state tokens" and "event tokens," respectively.) In the basic situation calculus, we speak only about situations and the transitions between them. Let (result *s e*) be the new situation that results if *e* occurs starting in the situation *s*. So we have facts like

        (T (result ?s (do john (go (home john))))
            (loc john (home john)))

"After John goes home, he is at home."

As we recommended in Chapter 6, let's look at the semantics of this formula carefully. The predicate T requires as arguments a situation and a state. So the term (result ?s (do john (go (home john)))) must denote a situation; in fact, it denotes the situation resulting from the event (do john (go (home john))) occurring in situation ?s. The second argument to T must be a state, and it is: (loc john (home john)). So the formula asserts that this state is true in the situation resulting from the event (do john (go (home john))) in situation ?s (an arbitrary situation). The formula states that *if* John goes home, *then* he will be home. To state that in a given situation a given event actually does occur, we use the predicate (occur *situation event*), as in (occur s-29 (do john (go (home john)))). States often give rise to events. An ice cube left outside will melt:

```
(if (and (inst ?x icecube)          ; If an ice cube ?x is
           (T ?s (outside ?x))        ; outside in ?x and
           (T ?s (> (amb-temp) 0)))   ; the temperature is above
      (occur ?s (melt ?x)))           ; 0, it will melt.
```

We can use rules like this to go from states to events to states. Suppose we have

```
(if (and (inst ?x icecube)          ; If an ice cube ?x is
           (T ?s (on ?x ?y)))         ; on ?y in situation ?s
      (T (result ?s (melt ?x))        ; then in the resulting
          (wet ?y)))                  ; situation ?y is wet.
```

"When an ice cube melts, it wets the surface it's on."

So if situation s-21 is one in which cube-32 is an ice cube on the picnic table table-41, we can infer that cube-32 will melt and that table-41 will get wet:

```
(occur s-21 (melt cube-32))
(T (result s-21 (melt cube-32))
    (wet table-41))
```

Such inferences can proceed in chains, so that we can pursue any causal sequence as far as we like. As promised, we will use the term *projection* for the process of making inferences about what a system will do, and keeping track of those inferences as more information is learned.

Projection is surprisingly difficult. Suppose that another ice cube, cube-33, is introduced in situation s-22 = (result s-21 (melt cube-32)). Can we deduce that cube-33 will melt as well? No, because we would need to infer

```
(T s-22 (> (amb-temp) 0))
```

and this does not follow from what we have postulated. We need to say explicitly

```
(if (and (inst ?x icecube)
           (T ?s (> (amb-temp) 0)))
      (T (result ?s (melt ?x))
          (> (amb-temp) 0)))
```

That is, the melting of an ice cube will not lower the ambient temperature.

This sort of axiom, which states that something will not change, is called a *frame axiom*. The need to infer explicitly that a state will not change across events is called the *frame problem*. It is a problem because almost all states fail to change during an event, and in practical systems there will be an enormous number of them, which it is impractical to deal with explicitly. (This large set forms a "frame" within which a small number of changes occur, hence the phrase. Unfortunately, the word "frame" has also been used as (more or less) a synonym of our term *schema*, which has led to much confusion about the exact meaning of the phrase "frame problem.") Although it is particularly acute for the situation calculus, the frame problem seems to surface in some guise in every formalism. In its most general form, it can be seen as the problem of inferring whether something is true at a given time. Different calculi refer to times in different ways, but they all have this problem.

The result notation has other problems, too. Its use encourages us to focus on transitions between discrete states, such as "frozen — melted." In real life, such transitions are realized smoothly: an ice cube shrinks in such a way that its solid volume passes through every point between 8 cc and 0 cc. This means that time slides through an infinite number of situations, each lasting an instant, between the initial situation (s-25, say), and the final one (result s-25 (melt cube-41)). Other notations are needed to talk about all these situations.

Suppose, for instance, that the ice cube is melting on a kitchen counter in which a live wire has been left carelessly dangling in a pile of salt. As soon as the water gets to the salt, electricity will flow and a fire may occur. Reasoning about when this will occur requires thinking about the continuous change; the situation (result s-25 (melt cube-41)) is not relevant.

The situation calculus is most useful when one can pretend that there is a single "next" situation (next s) after s, such that if e occurs in s, then (next s) = (result s e). There are certainly plenty of simple domains in which this assumption will work. Without it, we may find it hard to infer anything about (result s e), without knowing what else is going on in the world.

In many applications, a program only needs to think about the "current" situation. In that case, we can drop all explicit references to situations, and just keep in our database the facts true in the "current" one. (We put "current" in quotes because it usually is a representation of a hypothetical world, not the actual present moment the machine finds itself in.) Then, as events occur, the machine can model them as simple changes to the database. For instance, it can transform

    (frozen cube-30)
    (on cube-30 picnic-table-3)
    (> (amb-temp) 0)

into

    (melted cube-30)
    (> (amb-temp) 0)
    (wet picnic-table-3)

This is quite efficient, since most things in the database will be left untouched. There is no special mechanism needed to infer that something is still true after a change. On the other hand, there is some question whether this technique represents time at all. It does not distinguish, for instance, between erasing something because it is a mistake and erasing it because it ceased to be true.

When the technique is appropriate, we can describe any event in terms of an *addlist* and *deletelist*. A deletelist is a list of facts that become false when the event occurs; an addlist is a list of facts that become true. For example, the event (melt x) may be described as

DELETE: (frozen *x*)
ADD: (melted *x*)

Care must be taken when *data dependencies* are used in conjunction with addlists and deletelists. Consider the rule

(→ (and (melting ?x)
         (on ?x ?y))
     (wet ?y))

When ?x is through melting, we will remove it from the database; but then (wet ?y) will be removed, too. The rule should have been written to conclude that "?y *starts to be* wet"; it should also say how long it will stay wet (or what could make it stop being wet). However, as soon as we start talking about continuous, autonomous change, we have gotten beyond what addlists and deletelists can express.

7.4.2 Temporal System Analysis

If we cannot get away with representing just one situation (the "current" one), then we must find some way to implement a database in which many different situations are described. We cannot seriously expect to implement such a thing as an ordinary predicate-calculus database whose elements are of the form (T *situation state*), where the *situation* is expressed using result or something similar. Let's look again at the problem of retrieving where Ackroyd was on the night of the murder. Presumably this will be a query of the form (Show: (T *S* (loc Ackroyd ?where))), for some situation *S*. But *S* must be a term denoting some situation occurring that night, and these terms have no particular regular structure. A computer program trying to reason about the night of a murder might know of hundreds of events that took place that night. Its knowledge of Ackroyds location might be relative to most any of them. If its temporal retrieval system knows that on the night of the murder, starting at s-546 at 7:00 PM, the dog barked, Channel 5 showed a Three Stooges movie, and a light was turned on in the house, in that order, then it could try *S* equal to this:

(result (result (result s-546 (do dog5 (bark)))
                (movie-shown . . .))
        (do person (turn-on-light . . .)))

Unfortunately, the temporal database might have stored its knowledge of Ackroyd's location in terms of some other event sequence that occurred on the night of the murder, in which case the indexing mechanisms we have described previously will not retrieve anything. To state the problem quite generally, the database must contain formulas tagged in some way with the times at which they are true, and fetch patterns must mention times of interest, but these two descriptions of times will usually not be identical. Hence there must be an efficient way of comparing such time descriptors, and we must build into the retriever mechanisms for comparing the time periods over which stored states are true with the time period being asked about.

The most commonly accepted solution to this problem is to return to the use of time tokens as described in Section 6.2.2. Thus rather than telling the system facts like

(T *some-situation* (loc Ackroyd house-3))

we will instead be saying things like

(actual-state state-101 (loc Ackroyd house-3)).

This is not to say, however, that we have abandoned the use of situations. Rather a time token can now be understood as extending over one or more situations (possibly a infinite number). Thus it is still meaningful to ask if two things are true in the same situation:

(and (T ?sit (loc Ackroyd house-3))
     (T ?sit (on carpet-1 Lord-Innings)))

However, now such requests cannot be answered by looking for the statements directly in the database. Rather there will be special-purpose algorithms and data structures for answering such requests based upon what is known about time tokens and the situations they extend over. This section and the following one describe these algorithms and data structures.

Once there are good ways of retrieving facts true at given times, we must make sure that further inferences can be drawn. We cannot hope to make arbitrary inferences efficiently, so we must identify the important ones and build special-purpose inference algorithms for them. In a traditional predicate-calculus database, there is a simple model of the important inferences: backward and forward chaining. In earlier sections of this chapter we have identified further useful inference patterns, such as as property inheritance, for which there are good algorithms. What are some of the important patterns involving time?

One simple pattern is *overlap chaining*. If p is true over time period $T1$, and (if p q) is true over $T2$, then q is true during the intersection of $T1$ and $T2$, if they overlap. As with static resolution, we can visualize this inference being done at assertion time (as soon as both premise states appear) or at query time (when somebody asks about q).

However, there are forms of inference that do not fit this pattern. Consider these facts:

- If blood pressure is high for a long period of time, kidney damage will gradually occur.
- Kidney damage causes blood pressure to rise.

Suppose that knowing these facts, you were told that Fred had some problem that causes slightly elevated blood pressure for several years. From Fact (1), you could conclude that after a while Fred's kidneys would start to go. From Fact (2), you would conclude that Fred's blood pressure would get even higher.

But then you could use Fact (1) again, and so forth. This reasoning pattern exemplifies several issues:

- Often the conclusion of a temporal inference covers a different time period from the premises (usually later).
- Temporal facts often involve continuous-valued variables. These facts often state that something increases "more than it otherwise would"; or they constrain the rate of increase of a quantity without specifying the absolute amount.
- Loops in reasoning chains are more prevalent than in ordinary resolution. A naive implementation might go into an infinite loop, producing an infinite sequence of assertions about Fred's blood pressure and kidney damage, when what is wanted is a simple conclusion that the blood pressure will increase more than it otherwise would (and that Fred will have serious health problems).

Although it is clear that the situation calculus is an inadequate framework for dealing with inferences of these kinds, no clear alternative has emerged. One thing common to all approaches is to talk less about individual situations, and more about the time intervals over which things happen or remain true. However, there are two different directions in which researchers have gone starting from this basic idea. One group has focused more on the "database issues": how do you manage update of and retrieval from a long-term store of time tokens? The other has focused on "inference issues": how do you predict what will happen or explain what has happened? We call a program of the first kind a *time-map manager (TMM)*. We call a program of the second kind a *temporal-system analyzer (TSA)*. In the long run, what we need is a *projection manager*, which would take responsibility for analyzing systems, deducing their behavior, putting the resulting new time tokens into a time map, and helping to perform updates, notice inconsistencies, and so forth. But to date most systems have fallen into one category or the other.

In the rest of this section, we will present a hypothetical TSA. Such a system manipulates a system description giving the "laws of motion" of a system. Typically these laws relate a group of continuously varying quantities, as in these paradigms:

- "Quantity 1 is proportional to quantity 2."
- "A positive value for quantity $q1$ causes a change in quantity $q2$, other things being equal." (We say that quantity 1 *influences* quantity 2.)
- "After event or state c, then state s will become true (with delay d)."

An example of the first type of law is, "The volume of water in the tub is proportional to its depth." An example of the second type is, "Water flowing into a bathtub tends to increase the volume of water in the tub." (Note that the water flowing in tends to increase the volume, but other influences, such as water flowing down the drain, may offset the increase.) An example of the third type of law is, "After the alarm clock is set, it will go off (at the set time)." We will neglect this type for the time being, and focus on laws about proportionalities and influences.

It is important that a system description be *closed*, that is, that it list *all* of the causal interactions between pieces of the system. Without this assumption, we would never be able to conclude anything about what will happen, because there might be some unknown influence actually driving the system's behavior. With the assumption, it makes sense to "add up" all the known influences on each quantity, and see which way it will go. (See Exercise 7.5.)

Before attempting to formalize temporal-system analysis, we will work out our bathtub example in some detail. Suppose that the initial conditions are these

- The water is flowing in.
- No water is flowing out (the plug is in).
- The water is not overflowing.

From these facts, plus the law about the influence of water flow on water volume, we can deduce that the volume will increase. Eventually, it will reach the capacity of the tub. At this point, new "laws of motion" become active. A new quantity, the "overflow," comes into existence. This quantity has a negative influence on water volume, and its rate is proportional to the excess of water volume over capacity. Initially, because water volume is increasing, the overflow is increasing. But then eventually the overflow rate will equal the inflow rate, and the volume will stabilize, at some point larger than the capacity of the bathtub. The overall structure of the inference looks like this:

	Episode 1	Episode 2
Active processes	(fill-container tub-12)	(fill-container tub-12) (overflow tub-12)
Events	Water level increases	Water level stabilizes

This is an intuitively correct projection of the behavior of this system. Anyone can understand it, and most people could produce it for themselves with a little thought. Now we must formalize it.

The key concept is a sequence of state tokens of the form

(active-process *process*)

as in

(actual-state s-100 (active-process (fill-container tub-12)))

Our formal reasoning chain is much like the informal one given above. From initial conditions the TSA infers which processes are active at first; from there it infers states concerning influences and proportionalities; it adds up the influences to deduce which way quantities will change; it finds interesting thresholds whose crossing will cause a different set of processes to become active; and the algorithm is repeated. An interval over which a given set of processes is active is a *process episode*.

Within a given process episode, the TSA will keep track of formal versions of the laws we already mentioned:

(proportionality *quantity1 quantity2 sign*)
(influence *quantity1 quantity2 sign*)

as in

(actual-state s-106 (proportionality (water-depth tub-12)
                                  (water-volume tub-12)
                                  positive))

(actual-state s-101 (influence (flow-into tub-12)
                            (water-volume tub-12)
                            positive))

These states are not intended to imply that the laws relating various quantities are linear. The state (proportionality *q1 q2* positive) does not mean that there is a linear function relating *q1* and *q2*, but only a monotonic one. (A *monotonic function* is one which always moves in the same direction. If the sign is positive, the value will always increase, or at least not decrease. If the sign is negative, the value will never increase.) Furthermore, a quantity can be proportional to more than one other quantity. The intent is that if all but one input quantity is held constant, then the output is a function of the one varying input. The function is unknown, but is increasing if the *sign* is positive, decreasing if it is negative. For instance, the kinetic energy of a rocket is $mv^2/2$ so it is proportional to both *m* and *v*.

The influences and proportionalities are inferred from rules like this:

(forall (s cont) (if (T s (active-process (fill-container cont)))
               (and (T s (influence (flow-into cont)
                                 (water-volume cont)
                                 positive))
                    (T s (influence (flow-out-of cont)
                                 (water-volume cont)
                                 negative)))))

From this implication the TSA can infer a complete list of proportionalities and influences. It combines these with the given conditions:

(actual-state s-102 (positive (flow-into tub-12)))
          ; *The water is flowing in.*

(actual-state s-103 (= (flow-out-of tub-12) 0))
          ; *No water is flowing out (the plug is in).*

to derive state token s-105 (see Exercise 7.20):

(actual-state s-105 (increasing (water-volume tub-12)))
          ; *The volume is increasing.*
(same-time {s-100 s-101 s-102 s-103 s-105 s-106})

As the second formula says, all of these *state tokens* occupy the same interval, which consists of an infinite number of situations over which the volume in the tub increases.

To manage transitions between episodes, the TSA must keep track of thresholds at which **active-process**es change. It uses facts like this:

```
(forall (s cont)
    (if (T s (≥ (water-volume cont) (capacity cont))))
    (T s (active-process (overflow cont)))))
```

which states that an **overflow** process is active if and only if the capacity is exceeded. Actually, explicitly it says only the "if" half; but we once again invoke the idea that the description of the system is *closed*, so the TSA can infer that the only active processes are those that can be explicitly inferred to be active; and as soon as all known conditions implying the existence of a process cease, the TSA can infer that the process ceases. (See Exercise 7.5.) We use the term *quantity conditions* for the inequalities that determine which processes are active. For the bathtub example, the quantity condition

```
(≤ (water-volume cont) (capacity cont))
```

determines whether the overflow process is active or not. It is initially false, but the TSA can deduce from state token **s-105** that it is going to become true.

There are several problems with TSAs we have not addressed yet. The two most important ones are concerned with uncertainty and loops. The uncertainty problem arises because in general there are counteracting influences and alternative thresholds. Suppose that while the water is rushing into our bathtub the plug is pulled. The water level might rise or fall, depending on which influence is greater. Or consider a furnace, trying to raise the temperature of a room, while the oil level in its tank falls. There are two relevant thresholds: for the temperature, the thermostat's setting, and for the oil, zero gallons. Different things will happen depending on which is reached first.

The solution to the uncertainty problem adopted by most TSAs is to consider all possibilities, that is, to produce a tree of alternative histories of what will happen. Although this fits elegantly with the solution to the loop problem discussed below, it seems in many cases that the program should be able to use information about expected sizes of various influences and rates to rule most of the alternative histories out. In fact, this sort of inference is currently done by the humans programming the TSA, by just not telling it about "negligible" factors, such as evaporation from the bathtub. (A related problem is the inability of most TSAs to judge the magnitudes of quantities like the excess of water volume over capacity once the bathtub is overflowing. We humans know that the excess is very small, but nowhere in the TSA output does it say that.)

The other crucial issue is how the TSA notices and handles loops. Loops can occur within each process episode, and over several such episodes. At the within-episode level, they appear in the form of cycles among the influences. A quantity can influence itself (usually indirectly), either positively or negatively.

A *positive feedback* means that the quantity will increase or decrease dramatically. (See Exercise 7.6.)

A *negative feedback* occurs when a quantity influences itself negatively. In the simplest case, it means that an equilibrium will be reached. The overflowing bathtub may be analyzed this way:

$$\text{volume} \xrightarrow[\text{+proportional}]{} \text{outflow rate} \xrightarrow[\text{—influence}]{} \text{volume}$$

That is, the volume indirectly influences itself negatively. Hence it seems that we may conclude there is some volume at which the outflow exactly balances the inflow. (This is phrased somewhat differently from our previous analysis.) However, such inferences are not always correct. Consider a pendulum. Here the height of the pendulum influences the downward force on it, which influences its height; but the pendulum will oscillate, not drift gently downward. Most TSAs simply assume that oscillation will not occur at the continuous level. Instead, they take care of it at the interepisode level. That is, they will break the pendulum motion into episodes "move down," "move up," "move down," etc., and recognize that there is an oscillation there. We will look at this problem next.

Any system that projects by producing a series of episodes may find itself repeating one of them. (This is just as true of systems based on addlists and deletelists, described in Section 7.4.1.) The pitfall is that in pursuing a chain of the form, "First this will happen, then this, then that, . . ." the chain will go on forever. Of course, an outside agent can always step in and stop it when it has gone on too long, but that's not the point. If the TSA produces as its analysis of a flip-flop something like this:

It will go on
Then it will go off
Then on
Then off
On
Off on off on off . . .

it has failed to analyze it correctly. It should instead produce: "It will alternate between on and off forever."

If the closed system being analyzed is a finite-state machine (such as a flip-flop), all we have to do is keep a history of its state. As soon as a state repeats, we can stop (assuming there aren't too many). It may appear that a bathtub is not a finite-state machine, but process analysis allows us to view it as one. The current state can be described as

- The set of active processes
- The signs and directions of their quantities

For instance, a spring system will eventually repeat a state like "Spring stretch > 0, spring velocity < 0," and we detect oscillation. (Of course, this abstraction leaves something out. If the spring loses energy to friction, then the second time the state is seen, the velocity will be smaller than before. Hence, eventually the oscillation will die out. See Exercise 7.21.)

We can summarize all this with the algorithm of Figure 7.19. The result of this algorithm for an oil-burning furnace controlled by a thermostat is shown in Figure 7.20. Note that the TSA uses a graph to handle both problems — uncertainty and loops. Two arcs leaving a node means that the TSA can't tell which episode will occur next; an arc going back to an earlier node means that a repetition may occur. Hence Figure 7.20 may be read as,

> The furnace may come on and stay on until the oil runs out (because it is so cold outside that the furnace can stabilize the temperature only at a level below that required by the thermostat). Otherwise, the thermostat will cycle on and off zero or more times; either it will continue to do this forever, or during one of the on cycles the oil will run out and the thermostat will stay off forever.

(See Exercise 7.22.)

There are many open problems in temporal-system analysis. Let us return to our bathtub, which we left starting to overflow. If we ask, "What will happen next?" a person has no problem seeing that the water has to go *somewhere*. (A person would probably visualize some bathroom, but we will neglect that

---

Function: TSA
Arguments: A set of initial conditions.
          A database describing processes, especially
             influences and proportionalities.
          Quantity conditions.
Local Variables: G — A graph of process episodes.
           Q — A queue of unprojected episodes.
           E — The current episode.
Algorithm:
    E ← the initially active processes.
        (inferred from initial conditions plus database)
    Loop: Add up all influences on quantities in E. (Exercise 7.20)
        For each changing quantity, identify (from quantity
           conditions) the thresholds it will cross.
        The result is a set of successor episodes $E_1, \ldots, E_n$.
           (There will be just one if there is no uncertainty about
             net influences or which threshold is crossed next.)
        For each E_i, if it is not in G, add it to G and to Q.
        Add an arc from E to each E_i.
        Repeat while there is an episode in the queue Q.
           Remove an episode and E ← that episode.
        Return G

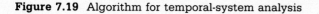

Figure 7.19 Algorithm for temporal-system analysis

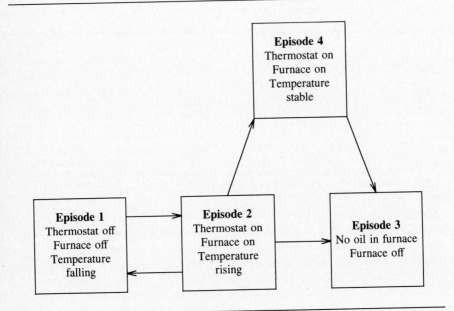

Figure 7.20 Process-episode graph for thermostat

detail.) It will flow down the sides of the tub, onto whatever surface is supporting the tub, and so forth. These inferences rely on facts about conservation of
mass, geometry, and intuitive physics, facts which are just not considered part
of temporal-system theory. For that matter, our initial models of the filling and
overflow processes should have been derived from facts about the geometry of
tubs.

One attempt to deal with some of these issues is the work of Hayes on formal theories of liquids [Hayes84a]. The goal of his theory is to find ways of
describing the geometry of situations without too many commitments to the
details of shapes. (Objects are described as entities like *laminas* (thin surfaces),
or *open containers*, without many more details.) The theory goes on to describe
events involving liquids (pourings, spreadings, etc.) in terms of the shapes of
those events, which must be congruent to the shapes of the conduits they occur
in. Although the shape of an event may be a hard concept to grasp, it is basically an event token restricted to a particular place. (Such a shaped event is
called a *history*.)

Finally, we have focused on a particular form of temporal inference,
involving influences and proportionalities among continuous-valued quantities.
We have omitted a large class of seemingly more straightforward inferences
based on rules of the form

> If *cause-event* happens, then a little while later
>   some other *effect-event* or *state* will happen.

Setting an alarm clock is an example. We will call these *causal-sequence rules*.

It is not easy to incorporate this sort of inference into the TSA framework. This may seem surprising, since process-episode graphs like that of Figure 7.20 may seem to express rules of this same form. ("If the thermostat goes off, then a little while later it will go on again.") The difficulty is integrating the effects predicted by a causal-sequence rule into an existing graph. Suppose, for instance, that as a result of some inference we added to our bathtub example the fact that in 15 minutes the plug will be pulled. Since the TSA has no idea how long it will take the bathtub to fill, it cannot know what difference this will make to its conclusions.

What this example brings out is that integrating multiple sources of information can be thought of as *revising* the projections made by a TSA. In this case, the program must modify its predictions in the light of a newly predicted event. Another case would be predicting the effects of two processes that proceed in isolation for a while and then come together. In both of these cases, we must think of the projection made by the TSA as a permanent database, which is revised to reflect new information. Managing such a database is the topic of the next section.

7.4.3 Time-Map Management

We use the term *time map* to refer to a permanent database of state and event tokens, managed by a *time-map manager* (TMM). The sorts of questions a TMM should be able to answer are exemplified by these

- Did you get married before or after you went to college?
- Are you planning to finish that program before the conference?
- What museums have you visited recently?
- Will the bathtub overflow before I get off the phone?

The temporal relations in a TMM are managed as an associative network. There is more than one way to arrange this network. We could let the nodes be time tokens, and the arcs be relations between them, as in Figure 7.21. Because the nodes represent time tokens, which in general occur over intervals of time, an arc label must be capable of capturing any relation between two time intervals (e.g., *I1 overlaps I2, I1 coincides with I2, I1 starts at the same time as I2 and ends before*, etc.)

A simpler idea is to let the nodes stand for situations and the arcs stand for intervals, some of which coincide with time tokens. The only situations that are explicitly represented are those that begin and end time tokens. The only relation that needs to be represented is *S1 is before or the same as S2*. The events of Figure 7.21 would, in this version, be represented as Figure 7.22. Here arrows are not labeled since a vertical arrow indicates "same time" while

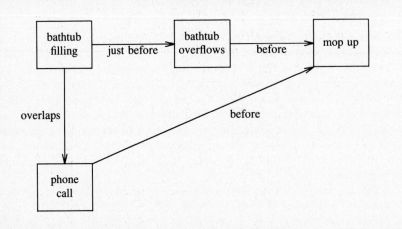

Figure 7.21 A time map

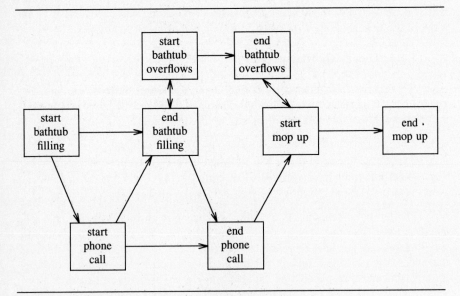

Figure 7.22 Another version of the same time map

one moving to the right indicates "before." We will call this a *point-based* time map, as opposed to the earlier *interval-based* version.

In either version, to answer questions about two time tokens, the TMM finds paths between them, and combine the relations on their arcs. For example, if the program is asked, "Did the phone call begin before the bathtub overflowed?" in the interval-based version shown in Figure 7.21, it would combine the "overlap" arc with the "just before" arc to conclude that the answer was yes. In the point-based version, Figure 7.22, it would find the answer immediately. The interval-based representation packs more meaning into a single arc, so that it can infer relationships the point-based representation must state explicitly. On the other hand, the interval-based representation needs more complex inference rules to handle a larger class of relationships among nodes.

In a realistic time map, there should be duration information attached to the intervals. Often the map records that two event sequences start at the same time, without explicitly recording the relationships among the events in each sequence, as in Figure 7.23. If there is a query about the relationship between two elements of the sequence, a durationless time map will not be able to answer it. If there are approximate durations stored (e.g., a phone call is expected to last "5 to 10 minutes," bathtub filling "10 to 20"), then by adding up durations of consecutive events we can arrive at an estimate of the time lapse between any two events or situations.

There are substantial problems in making time maps practical. First, we must cope with the inefficiency of searching large graphs. If the question is, "Did you learn to walk before you went to college?" the TMM may have to search a long time to find the correct path.

There are several techniques to allay this problem. One is to associate dates with some time tokens. Two dated time tokens can be compared immediately. So if you can find a path from "learn to walk" to "go to school first time (1955)," and if "go to college" is dated 1967, then search can stop [Kahn77]. A more general idea is to impose a hierarchy on the graph. That is, we treat large time tokens as organizing devices for short ones. An example is shown in Figure 7.24. Now, to find a path from one time token to another, we go up in the hierarchy until we find two comparable containers of the time tokens in question. In the example, we will find "childhood" and "youth."

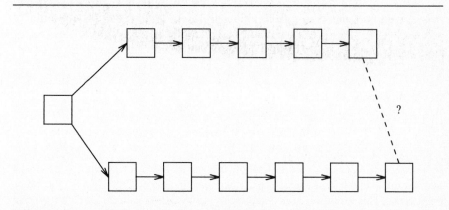

Figure 7.23 Two parallel sequences of events

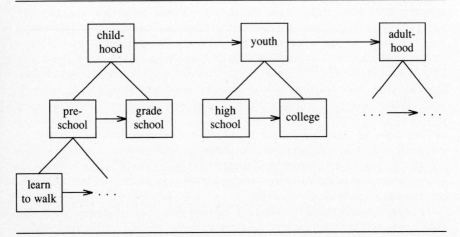

Figure 7.24 Hierarchical time map

Since everything contained in childhood is before everything contained in youth, we can conclude that learning to walk occurred before going to college. This use of hierarchy is not foolproof, but usually gives fast, reliable answers. Also, it is a natural organizing device, since short time tokens are naturally thought of as being parts of longer ones. (See Exercise 7.24.)

A second major problem is that being able to relate two given time tokens is not enough; we also need indexing mechanisms, so that one can *find* time tokens. Queries come in in the form of patterns rather than internal time token names. A typical query might mention "when you learned to walk," not tok-39. Of course, if we use ordinary syntactic indexing (as in Section 7.2.1), then an assertion (event tok-39 (acquire-ability self walking)) would be indexed so that it could be found easily given the fetch pattern (event ?tok (acquire-ability self walking)). This process takes us easily from patterns to time tokens.

Unfortunately, such a fetch pattern does not usually occur in isolation. Instead, it is usually part of a conjunctive goal. For instance, a query such as, "Did you visit any museums with your spouse before you were married?" would correspond to the goal:

> (Show: (and (event ?ev (museum-visit self ?museum))
>   (companion ?ev fred-13)   *; Assuming robot*
>   (before ?ev 1978)))   *; married Fred in 1978.*

If we are dealing with a cultured robot, the first conjunct could find a very large number of event tokens, which will then have to be filtered against the other conjuncts. This could be quite inefficient. (See Exercise 7.25 for more precise details.)

The solution is to specialize the index so that conjuncts describing event tokens are handled inside the index rather than by a conjunctive-goal mechanism. The retriever would take all the conjuncts at once, and use a discrimination tree to zero in on events satisfying them. For instance, the third conjunct might be handled by presorting all events matching the first conjunct by date.

At the beginning of Section 7.4.2, we discussed the problem of building a temporal database with associated inference engine analogous to the static version of Chapter 6. In that section we looked at inference issues, in this section at database issues. It would be nice to report that the two efforts were converging, but so far they have not. For instance, consider the process-episode graph of Figure 7.20. Can we put such a thing into our time maps? No, because the graph represents all the things that *might* happen; time maps are best at representing what *will* happen.

On the other side, there has been little work on inference in time maps. We mentioned *overlap chaining* at the beginning of Section 7.4.2, the inference from a state token p and an overlapping state token (if p q) to a state token for q during the intersection. No time map has actually done this inference. (See Exercise 7.26.)

A related issue is noticing potential contradictions, when p and (not p) may overlap. Possible contradictions often arise when new causal sequences are added to a time map. Suppose the time map records that the furniture in a given room is arranged in a certain way. As with other information, this will be a time token with a duration, presumably long enough to last over a period of years. If the robot decides to rearrange the furniture, then it will add to its time map a new set of state tokens concerning the new locations of various pieces of furniture. If initially there was a time token stating that the piano was adjacent to the couch, now there will be an overlapping time token stating that the two are not adjacent. See Figure 7.25. If the time map is allowed to stay in this condition, it will be contradictory. The solution is to alter the state token beginning earlier so that it ends when the other one begins. In other words, the stored duration for a time token is usually a default, which must be overridable when information about new events is acquired.

7.5 Spatial Reasoning

When we last looked at vision, in Chapter 3, we had pursued it to the point at which the vision module was manipulating descriptions of physical objects, including their positions and shapes. Although the main task we had in mind there was *recognition* of familiar objects, it is obviously important to *reason* about shape, position, and motion as well.

There is no one problem of spatial reasoning. Here are some interesting problem areas

1. *Route finding*: Consider the problem of getting to the nearest street. If you are like most people, you have a subjective impression of "seeing" the path to the nearest street. As we said in Chapter 3, it is hard to say

Contradiction

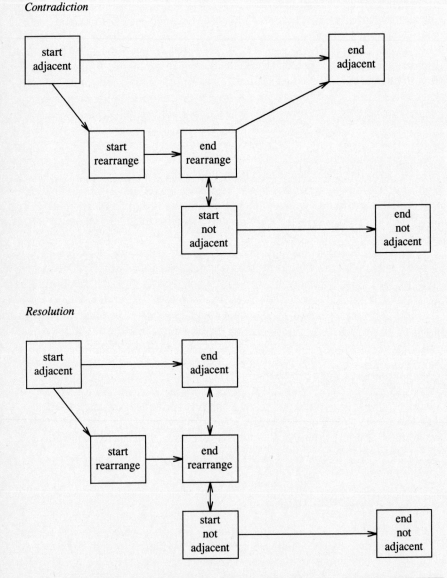

Figure 7.25 Resolving apparent contradiction in time map

exactly what this experience amounts to, but it shows that people are quite good at this task.

2. *"Naive physics" problems*: Consider trying to land a helicopter in a forest. How close can the helicopter get to the ground? What part of the

helicopter will hit what first? To answer these questions requires producing a representation of the approximate shapes of a typical helicopter and forest.

3. *Design*: Try to design an object to use to suspend a flashlight over a picnic table. This requires finding something to attach the flashlight to, that can be attached to something else, either the picnic table (in an arch configuration), or a tree overhead.

The first of these areas, *route finding*, has received the greatest attention, because it requires the least amount of worrying about motion. Everything may be assumed static except the position of the navigator, who is small compared to the areas to be traversed. (Of course, as vehicles are taken into account, this assumption becomes less valid.)

There are two basic approaches to route finding: the *path-oriented* and *shape-oriented* approaches. The path-oriented approach assumes that the world is organized into *places* and *paths*. Cities provide the best examples, where places correspond to buildings or intersections, and paths correspond to streets. Thinking of a route means finding a sequence of streets to take you from one place to another. If the machine knows where it is, and knows where it wants to go, all it is has to do is find a path through the graph of streets. However, such graphs can be rather large, and we must use some tricks to find a way through them.

The hierarchy idea works here as well as in time maps. It often happens that a localized group of places is tightly interconnected (that is, there are many routes among them that are known to the machine), while there are only a few known routes from this group to places outside the group. A city is an obvious example of such a group, but a neighborhood within a city might be one as well, if it was isolated from other neighborhoods by rivers or railroads, or if the ignorance of the machine kept the number of known connections to other neighborhoods low. Suppose that we assign every place to such a group, and think of each group as a new, higher-level place. The paths joining the higher-level places are the large thoroughfares at the lower level. So, to find a route from a building in one city to a building in another, the machine might do the following steps:

1. Find a route between the two cities. This will be a series of highways, possibly through other cities.

2. Drop down to the street level, and figure out how to maneuver within each city.

There are some interesting issues here. Suppose the high-level plan requires taking Interstate 66 to Fooville. To translate this back to the street level, the machine must keep a table of correspondences between different paths into Fooville and particular low-level places. For instance, it might record that the low-level place corresponding to the Interstate-66 entrance to Fooville is Exit 99, which coincides with the corner of Elm Street and Dutch Avenue. (We will study this idea of making plans at different levels of detail at greater length in Chapter 9.)

Once we have groups of places, there is no reason not to have groups of groups, and so on. Rooms are grouped into buildings, which are grouped into neighborhoods, which are grouped into cities, which are grouped into metropolises. The algorithm given above must be generalized to deal with this hierarchy, as shown in Figure 7.26.

There are cases where the path-oriented approach is inadequate. Consider planning to get from a room in a building on one side of a street to a room in a building on the other side of the street. It is plausible to suppose that the corridors of each building form a path network, but this idea breaks down when you come to the street itself. It is simply a large open space; you can cross it anywhere. We could store the street as two paths, one for going along it and one for going across it, but it is not clear what the places at each end of the cross-path are, or how they relate to the front door of the building. It looks as if we will need several cross paths.

```
Function: route-finder
Arguments: s — a starting point.
           d — a destination.
Local variables: Q — a queue of route-finding subproblems.
                 ps — an intermediate starting point.
                 pe — an intermediate destination.
Algorithm:
    Find the highest level of the map hierarchy in which
        s and d are in different places ps and pd.
        ; (E.g., these could be different cities, where s
        ; and d are offices in two different universities.)
    Initialize Q to nil
    Loop: Find the shortest path between ps and pd
          This will be a sequence of links and place nodes;
          Loop: For each place node n along the way,
                Add to Q the problem of going from
                    the place ps where the path enters
                    n to the place pd where the path
                    leaves n
          Endloop:
          While Q is not empty,
              Remove from Q the next subproblem, with new
                  values of ps and pd and repeat.
    Endloop:
    Put all the problem solutions together
```

Figure 7.26 Hierarchical route-finding algorithm

Evidently, paths work best when the space to be navigated consists of basically impassable matter (the city as a whole), with many long, thin conduits through it (the streets). When this assumption is not true, we start having to think more generally about representing the actual configurations of conduits and barriers. In particular, we need to store:

1. Information about the shapes of known objects
2. The approximate positions and orientations of objects
3. How objects are connected to each other

When the route-finding problem is thought of in this way, then two overall cases emerge: finding a route through a mainly empty region, and finding a route through a mainly full region. In the former case, the problem is to retrieve obstacles from the database, and plan to go around or through them. In the latter case, the problem is to retrieve conduits, and go along them.

In both cases, the key inference problem is to find all objects that fall into some spatially organized category, such as "Large barrier lying between building 1 and building 2," or "Street pointing toward Dutch Avenue." One possibility is to use a discrimination tree to sort objects by their position, orientation, and other properties. As with hierarchical street networks, the discrimination-tree idea produces plans that require further passes to fill in details. For instance, having found a large street to take, it must now figure out how to get to that street, and when to leave it to get to the actual destination. (There is a further problem in tighter spaces of actually maneuvering the robot to fit through the available spaces. We will talk a little about it in Chapter 9.)

The path-oriented and shape-oriented approaches suggest two different ways of finding routes through street networks. The former suggests thinking of the problem as a graph search. This has the advantage that it requires no information about the actual positions of objects in a more global frame of reference. The latter suggests thinking of the problem as retrieving a conduit with the required orientation and position, and hence it can zero in on good streets without searching through a graph. However, it does require information about where the origin and destination are in the city. It would not be hard to devise a hybrid algorithm that could take advantage of global information when it was available, and fall back on graph search when it wasn't. An interesting open problem is how paths are derived from more basic shape information.

7.6 Rule-Based Programming

Many of the techniques used to implement theorem provers have found their way into more practical programs, often called *rule-based* systems, or *expert* systems. These are programs for performing tasks requiring expertise but no great insight, such as prescribing antibiotics or configuring computers.

In some sense, any computer program is an "expert" at something. A payroll program is a sort of idiot accountant. We are more interested in domains where it is hard to break the job down into an algorithm once and for all. If you ask experts how they do a task like geological prospecting, they will tell you a few random things ("We look for evidence of ancient sandbars"), but cannot usually articulate everything they know. This is frustrating, but not too surprising; most experts are called on to do, not to teach.

However, this phenomenon makes it hard to capture their performance in a computer program. You cannot interrogate the experts, then go off and code up what they said. Instead, you must enter into a longer-term relationship, in which you keep coming back to them for criticism and extensions of the program, until it begins to solve a significant fraction of problems in the domain. A program of this kind must be open-ended; it is never finished, and must be easy to modify at all times. Furthermore, it should supply tools to make it easier to understand how it went wrong and how to change it.

Basing a program on *rules* helps. A rule is a piece of knowledge, one thing the program ought to know. It is called a rule because things to know often are of the form

> If < circumstances >
>   then < do action, or conclude something >

There are several different sorts of systems with rules that look like this. Some of them are essentially theorem provers. That is, they are trying to deduce things, using rules of the form "If p is true, then q is true." (In Chapter 8, we will look at systems with a slightly different form of rule, which attaches to its conclusions a measure of how strongly, or with what probability, they are believed.)

At the other end of the spectrum are *production systems*, or PSs. These are systems with the following components:

1. A *working memory* (WM): a set of data structures representing the current state of the system
2. A *production memory*: a set of rules of the form < working memory pattern > → < working memory changes >
3. A *rule interpreter*: which applies the production rules to the working memory

The production interpreter repeatedly looks for production rules whose left-hand sides match working memory. (Matching is like unification; see below.) On each cycle, it picks a rule, and does what its right-hand side dictates. For example, here is a PS to print out every active goal

> Rule 1: (goal (print-goals)) AND (goal ?x)
>   AND ABSENT (printed ?x)
>   → DO (print ?x) AND ADD (printed ?x)
>
> Rule 2: (goal (print-goals))
>   → ERASE (goal (print-goals))

Suppose the working memory contains the elements

(goal (find-oil))
(goal (stack-up-blocks))

and we add the element (goal (print-goals)). Then Rule 1 "fires," that is, its left-hand side matches working memory.

The left-hand side, or *condition*, of each production consists of a set of PRESENT patterns and ABSENT patterns. The left-hand side *matches* WM if there is an assignment of values to its variables such that each of the resulting instances of its PRESENT patterns is actually present in memory, and each instance of its ABSENT patterns is absent.

In our example, Rule 1 can be satisfied more than one way. One way is to take ?x = (find-oil), since (goal (find-oil)) is in WM, and (printed (find-oil)) is not. This firing causes (find-oil) to be printed, and (printed (find-oil)) to be added to WM. The actions of rules fall into two classes: input-output to the real world ("DO") and changes to WM ("ADD and ERASE").

On the next cycle, the rule is satisfied a different way, with ?x bound to a different goal. (The presence of (printed (find-oil)) prevents the rule from being triggered with ?x = (find-oil) again.) Eventually, all of the following are printed

(find-oil)
(print-goals)
(stack-up-blocks)

(not necessarily in this order). Then Rule 2 fires, and removes (goal (print-goals)) from WM.

An important issue in designing a PS is *conflict resolution*. On each cycle, more than one rule may be firable. We could adopt a policy of firing all applicable rules in synchrony, but this is rarely done. Instead, a *conflict-resolution strategy* is incorporated into the rule interpreter, which chooses the rule to fire when there is more than one.

You may have wondered, in our example, why Rule 2 didn't fire immediately, since its left-hand side matched at all times. It didn't fire because of a conflict-resolution strategy which specifies that, if two rules are firable, and the pattern of one is a superset of (i.e., is more specific than) the pattern of the other, then the more specific one fires. The more general one may eventually fire, as in our example, or the more specific ones may change things so that the general one never fires.

Conflict-resolution strategies usually consist of several "policies," of which "use most specific" would be one. In our example, Rule 1 adds (printed ?x) to WM, so that Rule 1 will not fire forever on the same data. This sort of thing gets to be a nuisance, so we can change the rule interpreter so that it never fires the same rule on the same data twice. Then we could have simplified Rule 1 to be

Rule 1: (goal (print-goals)) AND (goal ?x)
         → DO (print ?x)

Another element of a conflict-resolution strategy is to give priority to rules whose patterns have matched for the shortest time. That is, suppose we have three rules, such that initially Rules 1 and 2 are firable, and 3 is not. Suppose Rule 1 wins, and fires, and changes WM so that 3 is now firable. Then this strategy says to let 3 run instead of 2 (unless specificity or some other higher-priority consideration says the opposite). The intent is to focus attention; Rule 3 is evidently supposed to finish what Rule 1 started, so we let it do that before Rule 2 gets to go.

A good conflict-resolution strategy helps keep rules short and modular. When you add a new rule, if it is more specific than another one, it will automatically override. The person adding the rule doesn't even have to know that this occurred.

A PS interpreter is said to execute a *recognize-act* cycle. Finding an appropriate production is "recognition": the situation is classed as one in which this rule will make progress. Executing the right-hand side is "action." The hope is that the system will be able to react smoothly to a variety of situations.

A PS achieves sequential behavior without being sequenced. For instance, suppose it has two tasks, and two groups of rules are poised to run in order to carry them out. If group 1 wins (via conflict resolution), but its actions do not disturb the conditions required to trigger group 2, then group 2 will run when group 1 is finished. Nowhere do you have to say, "First do task 1, then task 2." If explicit sequencing is required, then the rules of group 2 must be amended so that their patterns include an element saying "Group 1 is finished"; and group 1 must be amended to add this element when it *is* finished. Too many modifications like this tend to spoil the modularity.

One of the most important issues in production-system design is efficiency. Although the programmer thinks in terms of all the rules being polled on each cycle, actually running a PS this way would cause it to run slower and slower as more rules were added. Instead, we must index the rules so that, as the WM changes, we can efficiently find rules that might now be ready to fire. A rule is brought a little closer to firing whenever an instance of one of its **PRESENT** patterns is added to WM, or an instance of one of its **ABSENT** patterns is removed.

7.7 References and Further Reading

While there is a lot of lore on indexing, little of it is published, since it often has a flavor of "hacking." We can point you to [Shapiro79a] which introduces the idea of indexing first by predicate, and then by the atoms in the formula. For a general reference on implementing indexing schemes see [Charniak80], especially Chapter 14. The standard reference on hash tables is [Knuth73].

An anthology of articles about associative networks is found in [Findler79]. Many associative-network researchers think of their formalisms as more than just indexes for predicate calculus. See [Bobrow77, Woods75] and [Brachman79] for the issues from their point of view.

What we have called *schemas* have come up in many guises in the literature. We noted the use of the term *scripts* as a special case of a schema. The classic work on scripts is [Schank77]. Minsky's idea of a *frame* [Minsky75] is quite similar to our schemas, as is Bobrow and Winograd's *unit* [Bobrow77]. That retrieval from scripts was a serious problem was first pointed out by Fahlman [Fahlman79] who coined the term *virtual copy*. Fahlman also proposes a parallel architecture scheme for solving the problem. The indexing method we give for retrieval from schema is taken from [Moore75] and [Charniak81a]. For more discussion of this issue see [Brachman79] and [Schank82].

Data dependencies as we have presented them were perfected by Doyle [Doyle79], who also coined the term *reason maintenance system*. Chapter 16 of [Charniak80] goes into some detail on the implementation of data-dependency systems. See [McDermott83a] for more recent results.

The classic works on the situation calculus are [McCarthy58] and [McCarthy69]. The latter paper also includes the first discussion of the frame problem. One of the inventors of the situation calculus, Pat Hayes, is now one of its strongest critics. His paper [Hayes84a] proposes an entirely different ontology based on space-time chunks (called "histories") rather than simple temporal intervals. A more traditional approach is presented in [Allen81, Allen84] and [McDermott82, Dean83]. Allen's approach is interval-based while McDermott and Dean's approach is point-based. [Kolodner83] discusses how retrieval from a hierarchical time map might be organized. We will say more about her program in Chapter 11.

Our use of the term *projection* is due to [Wilensky83] and subsumes what have been called *envisioning* and *envisionment* in [deKleer82]. Our hypothetical *temporal system analyzer* was based on work by [Hendrix73, Rieger76], [Forbus84, deKleer79], and [Kuipers82]. The latter three give specific algorithms. [Letovsky83] looks at the question of using information about expected sizes of influences to rule out most alternative histories. [Hayes84a] contains the first known proof that if you leave the bathtub plug in, and the water on, your floor will get wet.

Path-oriented approaches to spatial reasoning are described in [Kuipers78, Elliot82]. A more space-based approach is found in [McDermott84], which also introduces the use of discrimination networks for finding paths and other spatial objects. See [deKleer79] and [Forbus81] for preliminary studies in the use of spatial reasoning for naive physics. They restrict consideration to a point object and one-dimensional space in which to move.

The collection [Waterman78] has many articles about rule-based systems. [Davis82] describes two such systems in great detail. [Forgy79] describes an efficient technique for keeping track of how close each rule instance is to firing, and updating these records as working memory changes.

Exercises

7.1 In Figure 7.3, what would the database look like after removing the assertion (contains us new-york)? After adding (owns new-york (city-hall new-york))?

7.2 For each data-dependency diagram in Figure 7.27 decide whether it is a syntactically legal diagram and, if legal, whether it could actually occur in a real data-dependency system. Explain your answers.

7.3 Each of the following formulas is either basically fine, obviously false, or semantic nonsense. Decide which. Produce corrected versions of the wrong ones. (The English translations give the intent of the formula, not what it actually means.)

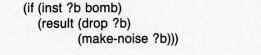

      (if (inst ?b bomb)   *; If you drop a bomb*
        (result (drop ?b)   *; it will make noise.*
           (make-noise ?b)))   *;*

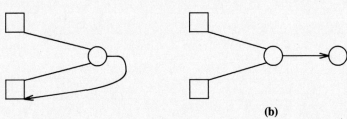

(a)

(b)

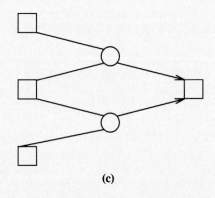

(c)

Figure 7.27 Possibly illegal data-dependency diagrams

```
(if (and (inst ?person person)          ; If a person
         (T (on ?person roof)           ; is on the roof and
            (do ?person (jump)))        ; jumps, the person
      (on ?person ground))              ; ends up on the ground.

(if (T ?s (own ?per1 ?obj))            ; If a person owns an
                                        ; object, then the
      (T (result ?s                     ; result of giving
           (give ?per1 ?obj ?per2))     ; it to person2 will be
         (own ?per2 ?obj)))             ; that person2 owns it.
```

7.4   Trace the workings of the route-finding algorithm in Figure 7.26 given the problem of getting from Brown to Yale and the graphs in Figure 7.28.

7.5   In Chapter 6, we talked about *nonmonotonic inference* patterns, such as an inference from facts about various income sources to a conclusion about total income. Point out some similar nonmonotonicities in temporal-system analysis (Section 7.4.2).

7.6   Suppose a population of mice is supplied with plenty of food and obstetrical care. What will happen? Express this problem in terms of temporal-system analysis. (Take the number of mice to be a continuous quantity.) What influences what? What are the thresholds?

7.7   Formally specify a process structure for a thermostat system which would have the behavior shown in Figure 7.20.

7.8   Implement **index-fetch** (from Figure 7.4). There are two subtasks worth mentioning:

    a) You must implement a function **bucket** that, given a symbol and a position, returns a list of all formulas with that symbol in that position. (Presumably it will look on the property list of the symbol.)

    b) You must implement positions. One way is to just implement the position $<m\ n\ ...>$ as the list $(m\ n\ ...)$. However, it will be harder to implement **bucket** efficiently using this representation, since it will have to use **equal** to test if two positions are the same. Another idea is to represent positions as symbols themselves, with names like **1-3-4**. (In some Lisp dialects, it is illegal for a symbol to start with a digit. But there is always some way to override such a rule. In many dialects, vertical bars can be used to delimit the names of symbols containing strange characters, so that the symbol **1-3-4** would be written **|1-3-4|**.) On the property list of each such symbol is placed a list of subpositions; **1-3-4** might have the list **1-1-3-4**, **2-1-3-4**, and so forth. The function **list-index-fetch** would generate positions successively by marching down this list. If the list of subpositions runs out before **pat** does, the list can be extended, so that it always has as many elements as the longest list

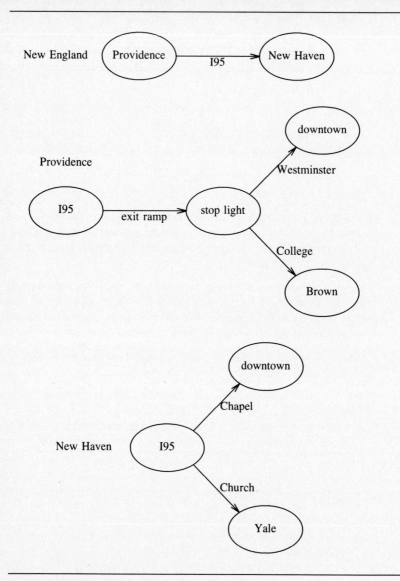

Figure 7.28 Example spatial networks

seen in this position. With this implementation, bucket can use assq to look for positions.

7.9   We have suggested storing index structures on the property lists of symbols. But numbers and strings can also occur in assertions. How can those be handled?

7.10 As explained in [Charniak80], Chapter 10, the most efficient way to intersect two lists $L1$ and $L2$ is to make sure that two elements to be treated as
duplicates of each other are eq, that is, are stored in exactly the same
location in memory. Then an alteration of one occurrence will also be an
alteration in the other. This is automatically true for lists of symbols; a
change to the property list of a symbol found in $L1$ will of course be
detectable when you encounter the same symbol in $L2$. Making a change
that someone else can detect later is called *marking* a data structure. The
intersection algorithm then marks every element of $L1$, and collects every
marked element of $L2$ (and, of course, cleans up the marks on $L1$ so they
don't interfere later). (See Exercise 2.16.) Revise the data structure used
by index-fetch (Section 7.2.1) so that it contains "markable formulas."
The simplest way to do this is to enlarge each formula to the format (*formula mark*). It is important to make sure that every occurrence of the formula in the database is a pointer to this exact list. Then you can mark a
formula by changing its cadr.

a) Implement a function to add a formula to the database if it is not
already there. If the formula must be added, then the same markable version must be pointed to from all the appropriate buckets.

b) Write a formula-list intersection function to be called by list-index-
fetch. It must set, test, and clear marks as explained above.

7.11 Write an improved list-index-fetch algorithm, which discards very long
buckets (instead of intersecting them with a). Test empirically how long a
list has to be before this becomes worthwhile.

7.12 In Section 7.2.1 we noted that it could be expensive to search through the
linear table on the property list of a symbol like new-york:

```
new-york:
    ((contains
        (<2> . . .)
           (<3> . . .))
     (population
         (<2> . . .))
    . . .
    ; This list could go on for quite a while.
     )
```

We recommended replacing this list with a hash table. Explain why it was
comparatively cheap to get to the new-york index in the first place. (*Hint*:
See Box 2.3.) Is there some way to avoid implementing hash tables yourself by using the Lisp symbol table ("oblist") again?

7.13 We left a gap in our description of the "three-level" indexing scheme in
Section 7.2.1, in that we did not specify what the predicate key was. For
instance, suppose the fetch pattern was (not (contains new-york (city-hall
sacramento))). What should the predicate slot be when the fetch key is

new-york? What about when it is sacramento? What about when we are fetching

    (← (not (contains new-york (city-hall sacramento)))
       ?sub)

There are two possible answers:

a) Add another layer of indexing, which is keyed off the "context" of the symbol being searched for. There are six possible contexts:

    $(p \ldots$ sym $\ldots)$
    (not $(p \ldots$ sym $\ldots))$
    (← $(p \ldots$ sym $\ldots) \ldots)$
    (← (not $(p \ldots$ sym $\ldots)) \ldots)$
    (→ $(p \ldots$ sym $\ldots) \ldots)$
    (→ (not $(p \ldots$ sym $\ldots)) \ldots)$

For ordinary deductive retrieval, these are the only six possibilities. In each case, the appropriate predicate key for the indicated occurrence of *sym* is *p*.

If the symbol occurs below the top level (as sacramento does in the example), then just take the nearest enclosing predicate (here, contains).

b) Adopt a more uniform scheme in which all subexpressions of a formula are treated the same way. That is, a nonatomic subterm like (city-hall sacramento) is turned into a unique machine address by doing an index-fetch, and then this address is used as the key to combine with contains at the higher level. If the subterm contains variables, several addresses will be found, all of which must be tried at the higher level.

Implement one or both of these schemes.

7.14 Implement the equality-link scheme described in Section 7.2.2, by making the suggested changes to index-fetch and unify.

7.15 Write a program (find-containers x) to find objects containing x by following links, as in Section 7.2.2. Write two versions of the function, one for the pointer structure of Figure 7.7, and one for a pointer structure like that of Figure 7.8.

With that under your belt, write a more general function (link-trace x label direction) to find all objects joined to x by a relation label in the given direction. For the binary link representation of Figure 7.7, direction is either forward or backward. So find-containers could be simulated by calling (link-trace x 'contains 'backward).

For the more general representation, we will call the function rel-trace, and it will have to have two direction parameters: the argument position of x, and the argument position of the desired result. So find-containers could be simulated by calling (rel-trace *x* 'contains-relationship 'container 'containee). To find all of Sally Smith's mothers, we would call (rel-trace 'sally-smith 'parent-relationship 'child 'mother).

7.16 Implement the inst-isa hierarchy described in Section 7.2.3. (You may find the results of the isa exercises at the end of Chapter 2 useful.)

7.17 In the discussion of property inheritance we translated an associative network about dogs and animals into statements about "typical dogs," etc. While we looked at the issue of indexing such statements, we did not point out related issues that arise when one tries to unify such statements. Discuss what the unifier should do in the following cases

   a) (unify '(pretty #typical-flower) '(pretty flower-14)) where (inst flower-14 flower)
   b) (unify '(pretty #typical-flower) '(pretty ?what))
   c) (unify '(love #typical-animal #typical-child) '(love ?x ?x)) where (isa child animal).
   d) (unify '(holder-of (owner fido) (license-of fifi)) '(holder-of (owner-of #typical-dog) (license-of #typical-dog))) where fido and fifi are dogs.

7.18 Implement a data-dependency scheme as described in Section 7.3. To do this, you must

   a) Augment the formula representation to contain a slot for a ddnode.
   b) Implement ddnodes.
   c) Augment the assertion adder of Exercise 7.10 to take a justification argument.
   d) Write a routine to erase justifications, and propagate the erasure if need be.

The last item is the most interesting, since it must be careful not to be fooled by loops in the data-dependency network.

7.19 In Section 7.2.2 we talked about recording equalities by pointing from a term to a list of everything known to be equal to it. Unfortunately, this idea makes it hard to erase an equality. Devise a scheme (using data dependencies) without this problem.

7.20 In Figure 7.19 we gave an algorithm for performing temporal-system analysis. A crucial subroutine of this algorithm is the one that adds up the influences during each episode in order to predict which way quantities will change. Describe how this subroutine would work. It must take

   • Initial conditions (the signs of some of the quantities and how they are changing when the episode begins)
   • Facts about proportionalities and influences

and produce an account of what each quantity will do (increase, decrease, or remain constant). The algorithm should trace effects from known quantities to unknown ones, through proportionality and influence statements. Because of the possibility of ambiguity, the output will be a set of alternative predictions. For instance, if Q is influenced positively by $Q1$ and negatively by $Q2$, both of which are positive, then there is no way to tell which way Q will go.

7.21 TSAs tend to have two levels of structure: a low-level continuous structure, described in terms of influences; and high-level discrete structure, described in terms of transitions between low-level ones. Their overall output is therefore expressed in terms of transitions between process episodes. Why do we find just two levels, with the discrete occurring over a longer time span than the continuous? It is easy to think of counterexamples. A string of discrete interactions can often be summarized as a continuous process over a long time span. The growth of the mouse population of Exercise 7.6 is such a continuous abstraction of a series of discrete events. In the case of an oscillating spring, we have at least three levels:

a) *Continuous*: Process episodes during which velocity and acceleration have fixed signs.

b) *Discrete*: A cycle of such process episodes.

c) *Continuous*: Gradual decay of the energy in the spring due to damping.

How might you generalize the algorithm of Figure 7.19 to handle multiple levels like this?

7.22 In our exegesis of Figure 7.20, we were careful to leave open the possibility that the thermostat could loop forever, because there is nothing in the analysis to indicate that sooner or later the oil will run out. Justify our caution by giving an example of a system with a similar analysis in which it is possible for the loop to go on forever.

7.23 In Section 7.4.3 we discussed two different versions of a time map, exemplified by Figure 7.21 and Figure 7.22.

a) Specify in more detail the algorithms for inferring the relations between any two time tokens or situations by finding paths between them and putting the arc labels together. In the case of the "time-tokens-as-nodes" version, this exercise requires you to enumerate all the possible relations between two time tokens (*hint*: enumerate all the possible relations among their endpoints); and what you can infer from two such relations. Note that in general the result will be a *disjunction* of relations. For instance, let us use the term *I1* overlaps *I2* to mean that *I1* starts before *I2* and ends during *I2*. If *I1* overlaps *I2* and *I2* overlaps *I3*, what is the relation between *I1* and *I3*? *I1* might end before *I3*, end just when *I3* begins, or end during

I3. Hence *I1 precedes*, *just precedes*, or *occurs before I3*. Because of this phenomenon, in general the arcs of such a time map must be labeled with a disjunction of relations.

b) Suppose that the intervals in a time map are labeled with their approximate duration in minutes. (E.g., the label **5,6** means the interval lasts for between 5 and 6 minutes.) How could each of the algorithms make use of this information?

7.24 Figure 7.24 shows a hierarchically organized time map. Explain why this is easier to achieve in an interval-based representation (as in Figure 7.21) than in a point-based one (as in Figure 7.22).

7.25 In Chapter 6, we described the idea of *procedural attachment*, where a deductive goal is handled by calling a special-purpose procedure when it is appropriate. Time maps are a good application of this idea.

a) The first step is to make sure that whenever a temporal relation is asserted, it is stored in the time map. If we assume a point-based representation for simplicity, then we want to arrange things so that whenever

> (before *situation1 situation2*)

is asserted, the corresponding arc is added to the time map. Add this feature to your favorite deductive database.

The association of time tokens with boundary situations will be made using the ordinary database, using assertions like these

> (event-bounds *name pattern begin-sit end-sit*)
> (state-bounds *name pattern begin-sit end-sit*)

as in

> (event-bounds ev-41
>   (do jack (atrans kite-23 janet))
>   sit-303 sit-305)

b) During backward chaining, there must be special-purpose procedures for handling goals involving the **before** predicate, exemplified by these patterns:

> (before s-303 s-305)
> (before ?s s-305)
> (before s-303 ?s)

Add a **before** handler to your deductive retriever. Note that it may use different algorithms for the three cases above. For instance, it might search from both bounding situations when both are specified, but it obviously can't use this algorithm when only one is specified.

c) Explain how the system would handle this query:

```
(Show: (and (state-bounds ?stok
                         (married robot ?x)
                         ?sb ?se)
            (event-bounds ?etok
                          (museum-visit robot
                           ?museum)
                          ?eb ?ee)
            (before ?ee ?sb)))
```

How would the behavior differ if the conjuncts were reordered?

7.26 At the beginning of Section 7.4.2, we discussed "overlap chaining," the inference that q' is true over the intersection of two intervals in which p is true and (if p' q) is true. (Note that this is a different sense of "overlap" from that of Exercise 7.23.) What are some of the problems in actually implementing this in a time map?

7.27 Design and implement the database for the hierarchical path-oriented route finder described in Figure 7.26. It will presumably consist of a set of nodes representing places and paths, joined by links of various types. An important set of links concerns different levels of abstraction. Places must be joined to "superplaces" containing them and "subplaces" they contain. For a high-level place, every path coming into it must point to the subplace corresponding to it. (E.g., the connection between a highway and a city must point to the intersection where this highway comes into the city.)

7.28 Indexing mechanisms like those of Section 7.2.1 can be used to implement production systems (Section 7.6) efficiently. The key idea is to check after every change to the working memory for rules that may now be firable. Explain how to index rules so that this check can occur.

7.29 In our discussion of the isa hierarchy in Chapter 6, we noted briefly that we would assume that an object was only an **inst** of one class, and each class only had an **isa** relation with one superclass. To make this semiplausible, we noted that we would represent facts like "Rudolf is a letter-carrier" by

(profession rudolf-2 letter-carrier)

The reason the predicates **inst** and **isa** are of such importance, however, is that in our discussion of property inheritance, we have developed special purpose deductive machinery to make property inheritance via *isa* links very efficient. Thus if we do not store Rudolf's profession using an **isa** relation, it would seem that we will have no built-in way to derive, say,

(wear rudolf-2 ?what)

and come out with the answer "uniform." One possible solution to this problem is to formalize the notion of profession in a quite different way. We will introduce a **postofficing** schema, which will specify how letters get delivered. It might look like this:

```
(if (do ?postoff (postofficing))
    (and (inst (letter-carrier ?postoff)    ; Only humans deliver mail.
               human)                        ;
         (inst (lets-of ?postoff)            ; The letter role is filled
               letters)                      ; by letters,
         (inst (unif-of ?postoff)            ; the uniform
               uniform)                      ; role by a uniform, etc.
         . . .                                ;
         (wear (letter-carrier ?postoff)     ; THIS IS THE
               (unif-of ?postoff))           ; CRUCIAL LINE.
         . . .))
```

Thus now **letter-carrier** is a role in the **postofficing** schema. We will then represent the fact about Rudolf's profession as (more or less):

(: = (letter-carrier postoffice-5) rudolf-2)

Given the above facts about Rudolf and letter carriers, and given a request to show what Rudolf wears, will the schema indexing method suggested in this chapter find the necessary fact? Either way, briefly explain why. If the answer is no, improve the mechanism so that it will work. If the answer is yes, comment on how good the indexing method is in preventing useless calls on the rule.

8

Abduction, Uncertainty and Expert Systems

8.1 What Is Abduction?

Chapter 1 stated that abduction is the generation of explanations for what we see around us. Thus we noted that it could be thought of as having the following form:

```
(if a b)
b
-------
a
```

For example, when people are drunk they do not walk straight. If Jack cannot walk straight, we might guess that he is drunk.

```
(if (drunk ?person) (not (walk-straight ?person)))

(not (walk-straight Jack))
----------------------------------------------------
(drunk Jack)
```

Thus abduction tells us that one hypothetical explanation for Jack's inability to walk straight is that he is drunk. Naturally, this is only a guess, for it may be that Jack just got off a roller coaster and is still dizzy from the experience. Thus abduction is only *plausible inference*.

8.1.1 Abduction and Causation

Not all inferences of the form ''(if *a b*) and *b*, therefore *a*'' can be thought of as generating an explanation, and therefore, not all are considered abduction. For example:

```
(if (in ?patient ward5)          ; All patients in ward 5
    (have ?patient cancer))      ; have cancer.


(have Eliza cancer)              ; Eliza has cancer, so
----------------------------     ; hypothesize as the reason
(in Eliza ward5)                 ; that she is in ward 5.
```

In this example, starting from reasonable statements we generate the unreasonable explanation that Eliza has cancer *because* she is in ward 5.

The problem is that our notion of "explanation" seems to have a lot to do with causality. In the first example we understand that people cannot walk straight *because* they are drunk. In the second example, however, we do not normally construe the statement that everyone in ward 5 has cancer as causal. Note however, that if it were causal, and that indeed they got cancer because they were in ward 5 (say the air was filtered through a particularly virulent form of asbestos) then we *would* interpret the proposed answer as a reasonable explanation.

The point is that causality and logical implication are not the same notions. They are close however, and logicians have tried for some time to reduce causality to implication, if only because causality has proved to be a difficult notion to pin down, while implication is well understood. Success in this enterprise would probably also mean that we could define abduction in strictly logical terms. But success has not been forthcoming, and most doubt that it can be done. Rather we will assume that causality is a primitive notion, not reducible to simpler concepts, and that abduction must really look something like

```
(cause ?x ?y)          ; ?x causes ?y
?y                     ; and ?y is true
----------------------  ; so hypothesize
?x                     ; ?x as explanation.
```

With this said and done, however, we will feel free to play loose with the distinction, and often substitute implication where causality is really called for.

8.1.2 Abduction and Evidence

Like deduction, abduction requires that we find pertinent facts and apply them to infer a new fact. However, abduction requires something else. Unlike deduction, we can get more than one answer in abductive reasoning. So, if your dog walks into the house wet, we might assume that she was caught in a sudden shower. But then again, she might have been sprinkled by a neighbor's lawn sprinkler. The extra required step is deciding which of the answers is the best one, and it is this that we will concentrate on in this chapter.

Unfortunately, there is no foolproof way to decide between alternatives. We might look outside to see if the sidewalks are wet and, if so, that would tend to suggest that it was a shower, but then again, it might have been the lawn sprinkler which hit both the dog and the sidewalks. The best we can do is to find one hypothesis more and more likely, or probable. To make decisions of this sort in the face of uncertainty we must weigh evidence. To do this we must know (a) how strongly a fact weighs for or against a conclusion, and (b) how to combine pieces of evidence into a final conclusion. We will see that statistics and probability theory offer well-understood ways of doing these things.

There are many areas within AI where abduction, or the weighing of evidence, comes up. Since the problem is particularly severe in medical diagnosis, we will take medical diagnosis as the illustrative domain for most of our discussion. (It is an acute problem in medicine because the limits on doctors' ability to explore and find out what is going on often means that they cannot be sure of the diagnosis. Your authors, knowing even less, have felt free to make up examples as needed. None of these medical ''facts'' should be taken seriously.)

But we should emphasize that medical diagnosis is hardly the only topic we could have chosen. For one thing, medical diagnosis is one kind of repair problem. Repairing something (say, a piece of equipment) has two phases: in the first we find the problem, and the second we modify the object so that the problem goes away. The first of these is an abduction task, since we find the problem by generating a causal explanation for the funny behavior we observe. Program debugging also fits this mold.

Perhaps less obviously, many of the input-handling problems discussed in earlier chapters can be viewed as abduction. As we noted in Chapter 3, vision can be viewed as a problem of finding an explanation for the array of light intensities picked up by a TV camera. Such an explanation would presumably be in terms of a set of physical objects in front of the camera, lit from certain directions. However, a quick review of Chapter 3 will show that we spent little time on the weighing of evidence — a topic which will dominate the present chapter. It is not that this problem has been solved for vision. Rather, before one can weigh evidence one must have it, and our concerns in Chapter 3 were to develop the evidence in the first place: from stereo vision, or texture, or line labels. (Interestingly enough, the last few years have seen several researchers introduce into vision probabilistic methods such as the ones we will be studying in this chapter. These are still quite new however, and as yet unproven.)

8.1.3 Expert Systems

There is one other theme which will wind its way through this chapter — expert systems. As we noted in Chapter 7, an expert system is a rule-based AI application program for doing a task which requires expertise. There is no necessary connection between abduction and expert systems. Some expert systems, like *Xcon*, a program which configures computers (see Chapter 1) are better classified as problem-solving programs. Nevertheless, most expert systems have performed abductive tasks, such as medical diagnosis. Conversely, most of the standard examples of programs which do abductive reasoning under uncertainty are expert systems — all of the examples we use in this chapter are.

Thus this chapter can also be viewed as a brief guide to some of the classic expert systems.

Box 8.1

Expert Systems and Applied AI

Naturally, people in AI have been working on expert system-like problems for quite a while, but the first person to recognize them as a natural class, and one that cried out for automation, was Edward Feigenbaum of Stanford University. The first such program that Feigenbaum and his group worked on was called *Heuristic Dendral*. This program establishes the structure of a molecule given (a) its atomic formula (e.g., H_2O for water) and (b) its *mass spectrogram*. A *mass spectrograph* is a machine that bombards an unknown sample (in gaseous form) with electrons. This has the effect of breaking its molecules into pieces, most of which will have a net electric charge. By putting the pieces through a magnetic field it is possible to get an estimate of the masses of these particles. This is the output of the mass spectrograph, and it is called a mass spectrogram. One will not get all possible masses, since molecules are more likely to break in some places than others. By knowing these rules, and by knowing the masses, it is possible to guess how the atoms of a single molecule of the unknown substance are put together. This is what Heuristic Dendral does. Subsequent to Heuristic Dendral, the Stanford group worked on several other programs, one of which, Mycin, we look at in this chapter.

For many problems like medicine, mineral exploration, and so on, the expertise needed is in short supply and is expensive. If these tasks could be automated completely, or even if the expert could be given significant aid, the economic benefits would be large. This has naturally attracted the attention of many companies. So today, for the first time, one finds a steadily growing number of companies creating AI groups to apply expert system technology to problems in their area. One also finds many new companies being created to sell such programs to other companies.

One must, of course, be careful in the selection of the problem to be automated. Our ability to write programs to do these tasks is still quite primitive, and unless the problem is carefully circumscribed, it will probably fall outside the range we can handle today. However, there are many people betting that even with the limitations of current technology, there are a lot of problems out there that can be solved. Some of the problems that people are attacking are diagnosis of machine malfunctions, helping computer salespeople, analyzing oil-drilling information, and providing financial planning advice.

8.2 Statistics in Abduction

Earlier we said that abduction is only "plausible inference." We could have equally well said that it is "probable inference." If we know the *probability* of alternative answers, then the best guess is the most probable.

There is, of course, a mathematical basis for such judgments, namely statistics and probability theory. Indeed, the statisticians could claim to have already "solved" the "make the best guess" problem, were it not that their answer depends on unavailable information. So we cannot adopt their solution wholesale, but instead must look for places where simplifying assumptions can be made. Nevertheless, it behooves us to start with these well-known mathematical techniques so we can see how far they will take us and, conversely, where and why heuristic methods must take over.

8.2.1 Basic Definitions

Suppose you are a doctor, and you want to decide what a patient of yours is suffering from — a typical abduction problem. One way to look at this is to ask, of all the people in the world who have, or have had, the exact same symptoms as this patient, what *they* were suffering from. If you had a large body of such people, and you knew all the numbers, the diagnosis most likely to be correct for the current patient would be that disease that was most common in the group of people who had exactly the same set of symptoms. (This is assuming, for the moment, that we must restrict ourselves to the information given, and may not propose other tests to try.)

To simplify this somewhat, suppose we consider a case about which we know exactly one fact, that the patient's skin is too yellow. We might ask, what are the possible things the patient might be suffering from, and what is the likelihood of each. In statistics this is called a *conditional probability* and is written:

$$P(disease|symptom)$$

This is read as "the probability of disease given symptom." So, for example, if we knew that of all people who had overly yellow skin, 19% had "pickled liver" (our nontechnical term for damage to the liver from overconsumption of alcohol), we would have:

$$P(\text{pickled-liver} \mid \text{yellow-skin}) = 0.19$$

A conditional probability is to be distinguished from an *unconditional probability*, written:

$$P(disease)$$

This is the probability of the disease before any symptoms have been seen. Unconditional probabilities are also called *prior probabilities* because they are the probability of something *prior* to any evidence. In a similar fashion, conditional probabilities are called *posterior probabilities*.

Because the notion of conditional probability is so important, let us define it more rigorously. To do this, suppose we had a "snapshot" of everyone in the entire world at this very second, and all of them were labeled with the diseases and symptoms they had. We will call the set of people captured in this snapshot **People**. This set can be broken up into subsets corresponding to people with no diseases, people with colds, people with pickled liver, etc. Naturally, these subsets will overlap. There will be people with, say, both colds and pickled livers. This gives us the situation in Figure 8.1(a). Here we see the set of all those who have pickled liver, (call this set **Pickled-Liver**), while Figure 8.1(b) schematically shows the relation of this set to the set of all those who have yellow skin (called **Yellow-Skin**). Typically we will be interested in the size of these sets, in which case we will surround the set name with "| |." With these definitions we can define the following concepts

$$P(\text{pickled liver}) = \frac{|\text{Pickled} - \text{Liver}|}{|\text{People}|}$$

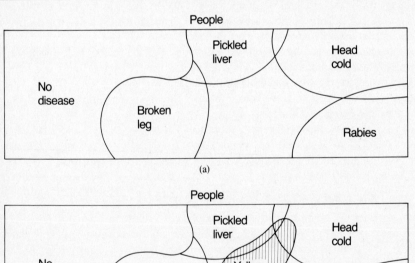

(a)

(b)

Figure 8.1 Diseases and symptoms

$$P(\text{pickled liver}|\text{yellow skin}) = \frac{|\text{Pickled} - \text{Liver} \cap \text{Yellow} - \text{Skin}|}{|\text{Yellow} - \text{Skin}|}$$

$$P(\text{yellow skin}|\text{pickled liver}) = \frac{|\text{Yellow} - \text{Skin} \cap \text{Pickled} - \text{Liver}|}{|\text{Pickled} - \text{Liver}|}$$

In the general case where the patient has not one symptom but n of them, then for each disease d_i we want to know:

$$P(d_i|s_1 \& s_2 \& \ldots \& s_n) = \frac{|d \cap s_1 \cap s_2 \ldots \cap s_n|}{|s_1 \cap s_2 \ldots \cap s_n|}$$

If we want to calculate conditional probabilities, these equations are rarely of any use since we hardly ever have the necessary sets to work with. (In particular, our notion of a "snapshot" of everyone at this second, appropriately labeled, is an obvious fiction.) However, these things do serve to define the concept of conditional probability. One way to interpret this definition is to see the *prior probability* of pickled liver in the following light

$$P(\text{pickled liver}) = P(\text{pickled liver}|\text{people})$$

$$= \frac{|\text{Pickled} - \text{Liver} \cap \text{People}|}{|\text{People}|}$$

$$= \frac{|\text{Pickled} - \text{Liver}|}{|\text{People}|}$$

This last equation is true because all instances of people with pickled livers are instances of people, and therefore the intersection removes nobody.

The reason this is a useful way to look at things is that we can now understand conditional probability of a given b as a prior probability, but where we have changed our focus from all people to simply those people with condition b.

Some of the information we will receive will be of a negative sort: the patient does not have yellow skin or there is no elevated blood pressure. This sort of information is easily incorporated because probabilities of negative facts are related in a trivially simple way to their positive counterparts.

$$P(\text{not } s) = 1 - P(s)$$

$$P(\text{not } s|d) = 1 - P(s|d)$$

(The proofs are left as an exercise.)

It is important to remember that when we write things like "pickled liver," and "yellow skin," our system will really be manipulating predicate-calculus statements, or their equivalent. So "pickled liver" might become something like this

(condition-of (liver-of ?patient) pickled)

We might then represent the conditional probabilities as facts about causal relations. That between pickled liver and yellow skin might be

```
(cause (condition-of (liver-of ?patient) pickled)
       (color-of (skin-of ?patient) yellow))
```

Depending on what statistical information our system needed, we could then add extra arguments indicating the statistical relations between the two:

```
(cause (condition-of (liver-of ?patient) pickled)   ; disease
       (color-of (skin-of ?patient) yellow)         ; symptom
       .50                                          ; P(symptom | disease)
       .01)                                         ; P(disease | symptom)
```

However, as long as we are just worried about statistics, we can ignore these fine points of predicate calculus representation.

8.2.2 Bayes's Theorem

We can't use the definition for the conditional probability of pickled liver given yellow skin directly because we never know facts like "of the i people with yellow skin, j had pickled liver." Indeed, almost all of the numbers we need are typically unavailable. However, one thing that most doctors know, if only informally, is how many of the patients with a given disease show a particular symptom. That is, a doctor will know that, say, "virtually all" of the pickled liver patients show yellow skin, while "the majority" have blood in the urine, but "hardly any" have puffy eyelids. That is, doctors tend to know, in a crude sort of way:

P(puffy eyelids|pickled liver) $\approx 1\%$
P(bloody urine|pickled liver) $\approx 60\%$
P(yellow skin|pickled liver) $\approx 90\%$

We mention this because there is a famous theorem of probability that says that if you know such figures, as well as the likelihood of the disease and the symptom, then you can figure out the conditional probability of the disease given the symptom. This theorem is called *Bayes's theorem*.

$$P(d|s) = \frac{P(d)P(s|d)}{P(s)}$$

While this may look mysterious, it is very easy to prove. Just substitute in the definitions for each probability, and we get this:

$$\frac{|d \cap s|}{|s|} = \frac{|d|}{|\text{People}|} \times \frac{\frac{|s \cap d|}{|d|}}{\frac{|s|}{|\text{People}|}}$$

If we multiply out the right-hand side, while recognizing that $|d \cap s| = |s \cap d|$, we end up with the left-hand side. The point of Bayes's theorem is that the numbers on the right-hand side are easily available, at least by comparison to the quantity on the left-hand side. Furthermore, for the simple case of the conditional probabilities for a single disease given a single symptom not all that many numbers are needed. So, if we have m diseases and n symptoms, then we will need about $n \times m$ numbers.

$$(mn \quad conditional \; probabilities) + (m \quad disease \; probabilities)$$
$$+ (n \quad symptom \; probabilities) = mn + m + n \approx mn$$

This last approximation is reasonable, since in a realistic diagnosis system we could have several hundred diseases, and several thousand symptoms, so,

$m = 500$
$n = 3000$
$mn + m + n = 1,503,500$
$mn = 1,500,000$

Now 1,500,000 such numbers is not insignificant, but a lot of these diseases and symptoms will be unrelated to each other. In such cases it should not be necessary to store any numbers. For example, we might just assume that in such cases the conditional probability is 0 (the conditional probability of yellow skin, given a detached cornea, an eye problem, is very close to zero). If, say, nine out of ten are zero, then in a realistic system we might make do with, say, 150,000 numbers. This is not small, but hardly a major problem for modern-day machines. (The assumption that the remainder are zero is not quite right, as we will see later, but a similar assumption will work fine.)

8.2.3 The Problem of Multiple Symptoms

So far we have considered only a single symptom. What we really want is the conditional probability given several symptoms. We can get Bayes's theorem for two symptoms by uniformly replacing s in the one-symptom version by $s_i \& s_j$.

$$P(d|s_i \& s_j) = \frac{P(d)P(s_i \& s_j|d)}{P(s_i \& s_j)}$$

Now things look less promising. Before we only needed mn numbers. Now we will need much more. For every pair of symptoms i and j we will need to know $P(s_i \& s_j|d)$ and $P(s_i \& s_j)$. The number of such pairs is $n \times (n-1) \approx n^2$. Using the n^2 approximation, and putting it into our previous formula for how many numbers we need to have in order to compute the conditional probabilities, we will have:

$$(mn^2 \; conditional \; probabilities) + (m \; disease \; probabilities)$$
$$+ (n^2 \; symptom \; probabilities) = mn^2 + m + n^2 \approx mn^2$$

Again, using our previous numbers, for m and n we are up to

$500 \times 3000^2 = 4,500,000,000$.

Even if we use our earlier assumption that most symptoms will have a zero conditional probability given most diseases, we will still have a lot of numbers. In these new circumstances the earlier assumption that one-tenth are nonzero becomes one in a hundred, but this still gives us

$$500 \times \frac{3000^2}{100} = 45,000,000$$

Now we are getting up to really large numbers. *And this is for only two symptoms.* Really we will have, say, forty or fifty symptoms that enter into a simple case. When discussing such large numbers, it hardly even makes sense to ask about the number of patients who suffered from exactly the same set of symptoms, *since in all likelihood there never was a patient in the previous history of the universe with the exact same symptoms.* Not only can we not store the statistics, there is no way we could ever get them in the first place.

Fortunately, there are assumptions we can make that are not always valid but that drastically simplify the situation when they are. They are called *statistical independence* assumptions. One such assumption is the statistical independence of two symptoms. This means that the probability of seeing one given the other is exactly the same as the general probability of seeing the first. So, if we are looking at some bacteria, we might classify them according to their appearance, and according to whether they grow better with or without oxygen. If the percentage of round bacteria that grow with oxygen is the same as the percentage of all bacteria that grow with oxygen, then roundness and growing with oxygen are independent attributes. We could make use of this fact when using such figures to decide what bacterium is causing a disease, given the laboratory tests.

More formally, the independence of two symptoms is defined thus

$$P(s_i|s_j) = P(s_i).$$

Given statistical independence of the two symptoms, one of the numbers we need can be computed using much more easily obtained numbers from the following equation

$$P(s_i \& s_j) = P(s_i)P(s_j).$$

(That this follows is left as an exercise.)

The idea that two things are statistically independent of each other has another important use. Earlier we noted that most diseases will be unrelated to most symptoms, and suggested that in such cases we would not have to store an explicit value for $P(d_m|s_j)$, thereby cutting down tremendously on the number of statistical parameters we would need to keep around. However, we suggested that in such cases we would assume that the values of these posterior probabilities would be 0, but then added that this was incorrect. We can now correct things. Saying that a disease is "unrelated" to a symptom is really an informal way of saying that the disease is statistically independent of the symptom.

$$P(d_m|s_j) = P(d_m)$$

This equation not only defines independence, but it also tells us what we should assume when we are missing a posterior probability. We should assume that the probability of seeing the disease after seeing the symptom is exactly the same as before we saw it, namely, the *prior probability* of the disease.

Yet another assumption that we might make is that the two symptoms are not only independent among people at large but also in the subset of people suffering from the disease d.

$$P(s_i|s_j \& d) = P(s_i|d)$$

This allows us to make the following reduction

$$P(s_i \& s_j|d) = P(s_i|d)P(s_j|d).$$

By using these two independence assumptions in Bayes's theorem we get

$$P(d|s_i \& s_j) = \frac{P(d)P(s_i|d)P(s_j|d)}{P(s_i)P(s_j)}.$$

This may not look any simpler, but the numbers it requires are exactly the same numbers we needed in the case of only one symptom. Thus given certain very strong assumptions that our symptoms are really measuring different things, we can eliminate the need for astronomically large amounts of statistical information to compute conditional probabilities for diseases given symptoms.

It is instructive to rewrite the previous equation as

$$P(d|s_i \& s_j) = P(d) \left[\frac{P(s_i|d)}{P(s_i)} \right] \left[\frac{P(s_j|d)}{P(s_j)} \right]$$

$$= P(d)I(d|s_i)I(d|s_j).$$

Here we used the following definition

$$I(d|s) \equiv \frac{P(s|d)}{P(s)}.$$

This is useful because it suggests how to modify previous probability estimates each time we get in a new symptom. We start out giving every disease a probability corresponding to how common it is in the universe of all people in our snapshot (its *prior probability*). Then to take a new symptom s_j into account, we multiply the previous probability of disease d_i by $I(d_i|s_j)$ to get the revised probability in the light of the newest information.

As we will see throughout this chapter, we virtually always modify probabilities by multiplying them by some factor. Because of this, and because probabilities vary over such a wide range (the prior probability of a cough is $\approx 2^{-2}$, but that of some rare disease might be $\approx 2^{-30}$) it makes sense to use the logarithms of probabilities rather than the probabilities themselves.

$$\log(P(d|s_i \& s_j)) = \log(P(d)) + \log(I(d|s_i)) + \log(I(d|s_j))$$

$$LP(d|s_i \& s_j) = LP(d) + LI(d|s_i) + LI(d|s_j)$$

We will call this last version the *logarithm combination rule*. If we use this rule instead of keeping around the various conditional probabilities, we really need to know the logarithm of the I factors, and we modify our belief in a disease by adding in this factor. Thus our causal statements connecting symptoms with diseases might look something like this

(cause (condition-of (liver-of ?patient) pickled)   ; *disease*
       (color-of (skin-of ?patient) yellow)   ; *symptom*
       2)   ; *log(I(disease|symptom))*

Let us consider how this works for a concrete example. Suppose we have a patient who comes in, and for some reason we want to decide if his problem is pickled liver or iron-poor blood. We will also assume the "facts" shown in Figure 8.2. (Any resemblance between the information in Figure 8.2 and reality is purely coincidental.) Figure 8.3 summarizes what happens to our beliefs in pickled liver and iron-poor blood as explanations of the symptoms. Initially we do not believe in either very much, but since iron-poor blood is more common, we believe in it more. When we see yellow skin, both are supported, but iron-poor blood more so, because its *LI* is higher (+9 *vs* +7). Finally, seeing bloodshot eyes raises our belief in pickled liver, but not iron-poor blood, and at

---

P(pickled liver)$=2^{-17}$
;   ==>   *LP(pickled liver)*$=-17$

P(iron−poor blood)$=2^{-13}$
;   ==>   *LP(iron−poor blood)*$=-13$
; *Iron-poor blood is ten times more common than pickled liver, and*
; *thus the average patient is more likely to have iron-poor blood.*

P(yellow skin)$=2^{-10}$
;   ==> *LP(yellow skin)*$=-10$

P(yellow skin|pickled liver)$=2^{-3}$
;   ==> *LI(pickled liver|yellow skin)*$=+7$
; *If we see yellow skin, the patient is 100 times more likely to*
; *have pickled liver than if we had no information about skin color.*

P(yellow skin|iron−poor blood)$=2^{-1}$
;   ==> *LI(iron−poor blood|yellow skin)*$=+9$
; *Yellow skin makes a diagnosis of iron-poor blood 500 times*
; *more likely.*

P(bloodshot eyes)$=2^{-6}$
;   ==> *LP(bloodshot eyes)*$=-6$

P(bloodshot eyes|pickled liver)$=2^{-1}$
;   ==> *LI(pickled liver | bloodshot eyes)*$=+5$

P(bloodshot eyes|iron−poor blood)$=2^{-6}$
;   ==> *LI(iron−poor blood | bloodshot eyes)*$=0$

Figure 8.2 Some facts for a medical diagnosis program

Disease	Initial value	After yellow skin	After blood-shot eyes
Pickled liver	-17	-10	-5
Iron-poor blood	-13	-4	-4

Figure 8.3 Change in probabilities with evidence

the end they end up nearly the same, with *LP*s of -5 and -4, which means that (according to our statistics), about one patient in 16 with these two symptoms has iron-poor blood, and one in 32 has pickled liver.

We should emphasize that to use Bayesian statistics the way we have, one must make very strong assumptions about the independence of symptoms, and the independence of symptoms given diseases. There is debate as to how debilitating such assumptions really are and, therefore, many of the programs we will be looking at in this chapter do not use the clean Bayesian mechanism we have just presented, adopting instead more heuristic methods of combining evidence. However, from our introductory point of view, these differences are minor, and we will simply ignore them.

8.3 The Mycin Program for Infectious Diseases

So far, our discussion of medical diagnosis has been quite theoretical, insofar as we have looked only at the mathematical basis for combining evidence using Bayesian statistics. Now let us look at some actual medical diagnosis programs.

One of the best known such programs is Mycin. The Mycin program is designed to diagnose, and then prescribe treatment for, an infectious disease (in particular, a bacterial infection of the blood). An infectious disease is one caused by an organism that can spread to another person (as opposed to, say, a heart attack). The problem is to first decide what bacterium is causing the disease (or what are the most likely possibilities) and second, based upon that decision, decide what antibiotic to give the patient to kill the bug off. Of these, we will concentrate on the first, since that is the abductive part of the task. The information we have to go on includes the obvious things (where the infection is, the patient's age, sex, history), plus more specialized things derived from laboratory tests. To perform these tests we take a *culture*, which is done by placing a small amount of material from the infected site on a sterile medium that will allow any bacteria found there to grow. If anything does grow, it tends to suggest that there is an infection, and the properties of the organism are important to the determination of the problem. Some of the relevant properties are

- What is the shape of the microorganism? They come in three varieties: *bacillus* (rod), *coccus* (sphere), and *spirillum* (spiral).

- Does the organism grow in the presence of air (is it aerobic) or without it (is it anaerobic)?
- How does the organism react to staining techniques? A particularly common stain is the *gram stain*. This is a chemical process that causes organisms to take on one of two possible colors. Depending on the result we speak of the organism being *gram positive* or *gram negative*.

An abbreviated sample of a Mycin dialogue with a physician is given in Figure 8.4. The physician's responses are the words written in all capital letters following the prompt sign **. The first three requests in Figure 8.4 are general background gathering, and are essentially canned output. Starting with question (4), the output is driven by rules that attempt to discover what the problem is.

A typical Mycin rule looks something like this:

---

(1) Patient's name: (first-last)
**FRED SMITH
(2) Sex:
**MALE
(3) Age:
**55
(4) Have you been able to obtain positive cultures from a site
at which Fred Smith has an infection?
**YES
-----------------infection-1-----------------
(5) What is the infection?
**PRIMARY-BACTEREMIA
The most recent positive culture associated with the
primary-bacteremia (infection-1) will be referred to as:
--------------------culture-1--------------------
(6) From what site was the specimen for culture-1 taken?
**BLOOD
The first significant organism from this blood culture
(culture-1) will be referred to as:
--------------------organism-1--------------------
(7) Enter the identity of organism-1
**UNKNOWN
(8) Is organism-1 a rod or coccus (etc.)
**ROD
(9) The gram stain of organism-1:
**GRAMNEG
. . .

Figure 8.4 A Mycin dialogue

If: 1) The gram stain of the organism is negative
    2) the morphology (shape) is rod
    3) The aerobicity is anaerobic
Then: The organism is bacteroides.

```
(← (is ?x bacteroides)
   (and (morphology ?x rod)
        (gram-stain ?x neg)
        (aerobicity ?x anaerobic)))
```

Here we have first given an informal version, and then a more formal version using our deductive notation from Chapter 6. This rule is somewhat odd, in that really the logical implication should go the other way. That is, *if* something is bacteroides, *then* it will have a rod morphology, and so on. Mycin writes this in reverse because it uses backward chaining to find suggestions as to the bacterium type. In the example above, when Mycin gets to the point of determining the identity of **organism-1** the process would start with the request:

```
(Show: (is organism-1 ?what))
```

One rule which will answer this would simply say "Find out if the doctor knows." This would generate question (7) in Figure 8.4. However, in that example, the doctor does not know, so rules like the previous one for bacteroides go into action. This, in what should now be a familiar backward-chaining fashion, calls rules for determining if the organism is a rod, anaerobic, and so forth. These generate further questions such as (8) and (9).

As written, these rules do not use any probability information. However, Mycin cannot deduce that the bacteria is bacteroides on the basis of the information tested by the rule — it might still be several other things. Thus the Mycin rules must deal in probabilities and the combination of evidence. From our previous discussion of combining conditional probabilities, we would need an *LI* factor added to the rules. That is, if the rule above applies, then we add the *LI* factor to the logarithm of the current probability of bacteroides. Including such a factor would give us:

```
(← (is ?x bacteroides)  LI = 3
   (and (morphology ?x rod)
        (gram-stain ?x neg)
        (aerobicity ?x anaerobic)))
```

The particular *LI* we used here, 3, is bogus, since first, we just made it up, and second, Mycin does not take a strictly Bayesian approach. Thus in Mycin one finds not probabilities and *LI*s but *certainty factors*. As we noted earlier, however, from our beginning perspective, the differences are minor, so we will just pretend that Mycin is a Bayesian program. Figure 8.5 gives other Mycin rules, with similar Bayesian modifications.

It is important to compare these rules to those we created in our discussion of pickled liver and Bayesian statistics. There we had a rule like:

```
(← (is ?x streptococcus-group-a) LI = 3    ; There is suggestive evidence that
                                            ; the infection is group-a
                                            ; streptococcus
     (and (sterile (site ?x))               ; if the site of the infection
                                            ; is normally sterile,
         (is ?x streptococcus)              ; and it is streptococcus,
         (portal ?x throat)))               ; and it entered the body through
                                            ; the throat.


 (← (is ?x neisseria) LI = 5                ; There is strongly suggestive
                                            ; evidence that the organism is
                                            ; neisseria
     (and (gram-stain ?x neg)               ; if the organism is gram negative,
         (morphology ?x coccus)))           ; and its shape is spherical.


 (← (contaminant ?x) LI = 5                 ; There is strongly suggestive
                                            ; evidence that the organism is
                                            ; a contaminant in the culture
     (and (sterile (site ?x))               ; if the organism comes from a
                                            ; normally sterile site
         (or (is ?x bacillus-subtilis)      ; and it is either bacillus
             (is ?x diphtheriae)))          ; subtilis, or diphtheriae.
```

Figure 8.5 Mycin rules

```
(cause (condition-of (liver-of ?patient) pickled)   ; disease
       (color-of (skin-of ?patient) yellow)          ; symptom
       3)                                             ; log(L(disease|symptom))
```

There are many differences, but the most important is that while this latter rule relates only one symptom to the disease, Mycin rules relate conjunctions of symptoms to diseases, and the corresponding *LI* factors are for these conjunctions.

8.4 Search Considerations in Abduction

8.4.1 Search Strategy in Mycin

As suggested above, the basic way in which Mycin works is reasonably simple. Essentially, the system requests that the theorem prover prove the theorem that there exists a diagnosis, and the theorem prover will start using the rules above to produce as many diagnoses as it can, each with an associated probability.

One consequence of this technique is that it gives us a way of automatically requesting further information when it is needed, something not explicitly covered in the Bayesian analysis we presented. Mycin asks questions in the course of applying a rule when it does not know the truth value of a formula in the rule (providing there is an indicator saying that this is something a physician might know).

One problem with this approach to information requests is that unless constrained in some way the system will try to use rules in any haphazard fashion. If Mycin were left to itself, this would hardly matter. But participating physicians tend to get upset when forced to answer questions that seem to wander all over the place. A common occurrence is that a rule, such as the one we saw for bacteroides, will have a subformula like this:

(morphology ?x rod)

As we have described it so far, this would lead to a question like "Is the morphology of the bacterium rod?" which expects a yes or no response. If the answer is no there will be other questions, possibly much later, asking about the other morphologies.

To prevent this, Mycin departs slightly from the standard depth-first backward-chaining search pattern by replacing such requests by generalizations, e.g. "What is the morphology of the bacterium?" In this way the focus of the interaction is maintained.

8.4.2 Bottom-Up Abduction

There is one major difficulty with the model presented in the last section. When we request that the system find a diagnosis, it will attempt to do so by finding any rule of the form

disease => symptom

and then look to see if the symptom is there. While this is fine for limited domains, it could get out of hand in a program designed to replace, say, a general practitioner. So, if our patient has an infectious disease, when we ask the system for a diagnosis, it will dredge up rules like this:

(← (heart-attack ?x) (funny-electrocardiogram-signals ?x))

It would try this even if we had said nothing about chest pain, or anything else that might remotely suggest heart attacks.

The problem is that our system is working too top-down. We want it to use what it already knows to suggest lines of thought, which would then suggest rules to try out. That is, we want a more bottom-up strategy. To put this another way, when examining a patient, a doctor does not immediately start working toward a diagnosis, but rather will first do some basic fact-finding by simply asking, "What's wrong?" The answer gives a first cut at possible causes, which can then be investigated.

To see how this might work, let us return to our Bayesian analysis of medical diagnosis. We will again use what we earlier called the *logarithm combination rule*.

$$LP(d|s_i \& s_j) = LP(d) + LI(d|s_i) + LI(d|s_j)$$

If we want to use the approach, but now from a bottom-up point of view, we get the algorithm in Figure 8.6. In this algorithm we have used $Lcur(d_i)$ to indicate the current belief in d_i. It is an abbreviation for the logarithm of the posterior probability of d_i given all of the evidence provided to date.

As we have already noted, a given symptom will say nothing about most diseases. We already said that in these cases the disease and symptom are independent.

$$P(d_i|s_j) = P(d_i)$$

From this it follows that

$$LI(d_i|s_j) \equiv \log\left[\frac{P(s_j|d_i)}{P(s_j)}\right] = \log\left[\frac{P(s_j)}{P(s_j)}\right] = \log(1) = 0$$

Thus as one might expect, if a symptom says nothing one way or the other about a disease, it will not affect the belief in the disease. Since a given symptom will have no affect on most diseases, it would be worthwhile to prestore a list of those diseases it does affect, and look only at them, rather than working through the list of all diseases.

Function: bayesian   ; *Assume the set of diseases*
Arguments: s_i — a set of symptoms   ; *and probabilities are*
                                                      ; *available to the program.*

Algorithm:
    Loop: For each d_i set   ; *Initialize current log of*
                $Lcur(d_i) = LP(d_i)$; *probability for*
    Endloop: ; *each disease.*

    Loop: Reading in symptom s_j ; *Main body, read in*
                until no more left   ; *symptoms and for each*
                Loop: For each disease d_i ; *one update the probability .*
                        $Lcur(d_i) = Lcur(d_i) + LI(d_i|s_j)$; *of each disease.*
                Endloop:
    Endloop:
    List top N diseases by Lcur.   ; *Output results.*

Figure 8.6 A bottom-up Bayesian algorithm

8.4.3 Search in Caduceus

There are several medical diagnosis programs that work like the algorithm in Figure 8.6. The one we will concentrate on is the *Internist/Caduceus* program. (The program is best known as "Internist," but due to naming conflicts changed to "Caduceus.") This program diagnoses internal diseases — that is, diseases of the internal organs, like heart, lungs, and liver, as opposed to problems of the eyes, bones, etc. Like Mycin, Caduceus is not strictly Bayesian either, but again, the differences are small, and we will ignore this complication.

As suggested by our bottom-up Bayesian algorithm, Caduceus initially expects the user to feed it a set of signs and symptoms to start it off. As each is entered, the program modifies the probability of all diseases with which the symptom is associated. This will produce a list of suggested diseases, ranked in order of how well they account for the input. If there are gaps in the input record, as there always will be (e.g., tests that would give information, but which have not been performed), Caduceus will use the highly ranked diseases to suggest which information ought to be gathered in order to clinch the diagnosis. Eventually it will get to a point where the cost of doing a test is more than the benefit in an improved diagnosis. At that point the program will stop. This technique is, of course, quite bottom-up, and as such does not suffer from the problems of our earlier top-down approach. However, where Caduceus really excels is in its handling of multiple diseases, so let us now turn to the issues raised in this regard.

8.5 Multiple Diseases

If we take our bottom-up Bayesian algorithm, what happens when a patient has more than one disease? We can no longer run our program as before if only because in situations where there is more than one disease, picking the most probable is no longer enough.

8.5.1 Multiple Diseases According to Bayes

There are several ways to handle the problem of multiple diseases within the strict Bayesian approach. We will consider just one of them. For the two-disease case the trick is to enter into our list of diseases "new" diseases that are really pairs of old diseases. That is, we will now have a disease of "glaucoma and rabies" or "pickled liver and heart valve problem," etc. Now when we get a new finding we update not only our old "standard" diseases, but these new "pair" diseases as well. Should it be a "pair" disease which comes out with the highest conditional probability given the totality of symptoms we conclude that the patient has two diseases, and not one.

To take a specific example, if a patient walks in with both heart murmur and pickled liver symptoms, what will happen? Typically, any symptom which had a nonzero likelihood given our first disease, pickled liver, will have a similar likelihood given the combination of pickled liver and heart murmur. Thus all of the symptoms that cause us to postulate pickled liver will also cause us to postulate the combination. However, because the initial probability of having both a heart murmur and pickled liver is much, much less that the likelihood of just the latter, if we were to stop after just seeing our pickled liver symptoms, the combination would not rank very high. But should we then see heart murmur symptoms, suddenly the combination will start looking very good indeed.

This simple change makes our algorithm valid again, but at a price. Our bottom-up Bayesian algorithm takes time proportional to the number of diseases it must consider (or to use the standard terminology, it is *linear* in the number of diseases it considers). To be able to handle all possible pairs of diseases, all such pairs must be included in the disease roster. Therefore, the running time of our algorithm will no longer be linear in the number of diseases, but will rather go up as the square of this number. So, if, as before, it knew of 500 diseases, it will now have 250,000. Plus, if we want to handle trios of diseases, then we will have an n^3 algorithm or, in this case 125,000,000 possibilities. Nor, of course, can we limit ourselves to trios of diseases. Combinatorial explosion strikes again.

Perhaps you may not be all that convinced that our program needs to handle this sort of thing. Most people go to a doctor when they have a particular, and single, problem, rather than waiting for everything to hit them. However, there are many symptoms which typically, but not always, are associated with "benign" diseases like colds. A cough may be an important clinical symptom, but then again, it may be that our patient simply had a cold. Even the most careful patient may have a cold at the time when he suddenly develops symptoms of a more serious complaint — one which takes him to see a doctor. But the doctor will see symptoms from two different diseases, whether they are benign or not, and somehow their causes must be untangled.

More importantly, the assumption that one goes to the doctor at the first hint of a serious problem is not always a good one. While it may hold true for the readers of this book, most of whom grew up in a socioeconomic bracket that takes good and prompt health care for granted, it does not hold true for other people who are less fortunate. In inner-city hospitals in the United States, quite a few people come in with multiple diseases, simply because they did not come in when they had symptoms of only one. Furthermore, it is these cases on which doctors want assistance, because it is these that are the most confusing.

8.5.2 Heuristic Techniques

We thus have a problem that must be faced, and an unpromising statistical "solution." It is at this point that our fidelity to Bayes's theorem must come to an end. However, it is not necessary to abandon the statistical approach entirely. Rather we will now add other, heuristic, techniques.

To see what we can do, let us abandon the approach of creating pair and triplet "diseases," and just stick with our single diseases. It is important to remember, however, that when we set things up in terms of our initial definitions, the fact that a person had disease X was not meant to exclude the possibility that he also had disease Y. As Figure 8.6 shows, there are overlaps between diseases. Naturally, our statistics should reflect the possibility of overlap. So, suppose a person comes in with multiple diseases, and we start feeding the symptoms into our algorithm. If we have no multiple disease entries, then at the end we should have a list of possible (single) diseases, but with more than one having a high probability.

To make this clearer, suppose our patient comes in with pickled liver, as before, but now also has, say, a heart valve problem. Initially the doctor will be told about the pickled liver symptoms, and only later will the doctor, when doing a routine examination, listen to the patient's heart and hear some suspicious sounds (a *heart murmur*). How will our medical diagnosis program react to this? Well, by the time the doctor hears the murmur, pickled liver will have a high current probability. But what will have happened to all of the other diseases (and in particular the valve problem) in the meanwhile? Some of them will now have a very low probability. These will be those whose symptoms are logically incompatible with the symptoms we have seen. So, a finding that a patient had, say, an excess of white blood cells would rule out a finding of too few white blood cells, and thus any disease that would cause the latter would be downgraded in probability by finding the former. Similarly, if we are told that our patient does not smoke, the probability of lung cancer would have gone down as well. But what about diseases that are unrelated in any way to the pickled liver symptoms, such as the valve problem? As we have already seen, nothing will happen to them at all; their probability will neither go up nor go down. We saw this when, in our initial discussion of our bottom-up Bayesian algorithm, we noted that if a disease is independent of a symptom, then $LI(d_m|s_j)=0$. Since this number is added into our current belief to get the revised belief, nothing will happen.

If we now go back to our hypothetical patient with a valve problem and a pickled liver, we see that as we get pickled liver symptoms, the probability of a valve problem will be unchanged. It will remain at its prior probability while that of pickled liver goes up. Then, when we start getting valve problem symptoms, the reverse will take place. Pickled liver will remain stationary, and valve problem will go up.

This seems to suggest that we handle multiple diseases using our old algorithm without change. But this is not quite true. Consider what we have after we are all done feeding in symptoms. We will have a list of diseases, each with an associated conditional probability given the symptoms we have seen so far. But what do we do with this list? Obviously we cannot just take the highest ranking candidate, because the patient may have more than one disease. Nor can we take all candidates over a certain threshold. If there are several different liver problems, each of which is pretty much consistent with the liver symptoms, the patient might be diagnosed as having all of them. One solution to this problem is seen in the Caduceus system.

8.6 Caduceus

Earlier we mentioned that the Caduceus program operated more or less by the bottom-up Bayesian scheme. It also has embedded in it a heuristic solution to the multiple-disease problem. In general, it tries to break up the list of diseases into a series of distinct groups. Each group has a set of disease diagnoses that account for roughly the same set of symptoms (see Figure 8.7). Within each of these groups it decides which is the best fit, using the rules above for the one-disease case. Once it makes such a decision it removes all of the symptoms that have been accounted for, and recomputes the conditional probability for the remaining hypotheses, each now trying to account for a new set of symptoms. It repeats the process until all symptoms have been accounted for.

More precisely, it does the following

1 Collects symptoms.
2 Applies the rules for the one-disease case to get an ordered list of diseases.
3 Creates a set consisting of the topmost disease from (2), plus any other disease that accounts for no more symptoms than the topmost. This has the effect of ignoring the symptoms that are not covered by the topmost disease.

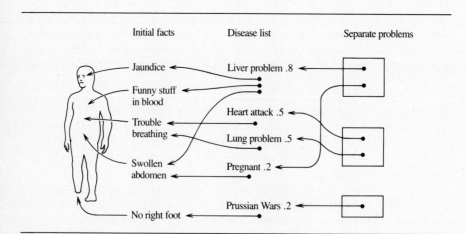

Figure 8.7 Multiple disease diagnosis

4   Until the topmost of this set is sufficiently higher than the next best, it keeps applying more tests to make the decision.

5   Having made the decision, it removes from consideration all of the losing diseases, and all of the symptoms that are now accounted for by the winner.

6   Repeats, starting at (2), if there are more diseases and symptoms to consider.

An example of its behavior is shown in Figure 8.8 and Figure 8.9.

This scheme has the advantage that it is a reasonably clear extension of the single disease case, and typically works well. However, there are situations in which it will start off in a direction that the doctor using the program finds queer. This occurs when the patient has, say, both a liver and a lung problem. The program will initially not recognize this, but will rather rank all diseases by how well they fit the totality of symptoms. Thus any liver disease that also produces some symptoms typical of lung problems will be ranked higher than all other liver diseases, simply because it accounts for more of the symptoms.

(doctor)
Caduceus consultation Sumex-Aim Version   *; Sumex-Aim is a group of*
                                               ; researchers in AI medicine who
                                               ; share computational resources.

Please enter findings   *; The prompt is a "*."*
* Age 26 to 55   *; This was entered by the*
* Leg weakness   *; physician.*
* Creatinine blood increased   *; There is a fixed vocabulary of*
* Alcoholism chronic   *; symptoms which must be followed.*
* Exposure to rabbits   *;*

  . . .   *; Skipping over a lot of symptoms.*
* go   *; This tells Caduceus to take over.*
Disregarding: *; Caduceus makes up its list of*
  Exposure to rabbits   *; diseases. The symptoms not*
  Leg weakness   *; mentioned by the topmost are*
  Creatinine blood increased   *; temporarily disregarded.*
  . . .   *; Skipping over a lot.*
Considering: *; These are the symptoms that are*
  Age 26 to 55   *; covered by the topmost disease.*
  . . .   *;*
Ruleout: *; Ruleout indicates that the pro-*
  Hepatitis chronic   *; gram is considering the following*
  Alcoholic hepatitis   *; diseases, no one of which is*
  Hepatic tuberculosis   *; clearly right. They are all*
  Hepatitis viral   *; various liver problems.*
  . . .   *;*

Figure 8.8 Trace of Caduceus — Part 1

Please enter Findings of jaundice
* go
. . .
Please enter Findings of pain abdomen
* go
Abdomen pain generalized ?
* no
Abdomen pain right upper quadrant ?
* no
. . .

Disregarding:
  jaundice
  . . .
Considering:
  Age 26 to 55
  Exposure to rabbits
  . . .
Discriminate:
  Leptospirosis systemic
  . . .

. . .
Leptospira agglutination positive ?
* Yes
  . . .
Conclude: leptospirosis systemic
Disregarding:
  . . .
Considering:
  Alcoholism chronic
  . . .
Ruleout:
  Micronodal cirrhosis
  Hepatic leptospirosis
  . . .
Conclude:
  Hepatic leptospirosis
  . . .

; On the basis of the diseases it
; is considering, Caduceus asks for
; further information. If the
; user has information it can be
; typed in. Typing "go" tells Caduceus
; to ask specific questions.
; The lack of abdominal pain makes
; the currently considered liver
; problems quite unlikely,
; so Caduceus now recomputes its
; beliefs in the various diseases
; and comes up with a new top candi-
; date, which causes different
; symptoms to be disregarded, and
; others now to be considered.
; The last time exposure to rabbits
; was disregarded. Now the top
; candidate explains it.
; Discriminate (as opposed to
; Ruleout) indicates that between
; 2 and 4 diseases are considered.
; Caduceus asks several questions,
; of which this is the crucial one
; since it clinches leptospirosis
; systemic.
;
; Now Caduceus returns to the
; problem of explaining the liver
; symptoms which it gave up on
; earlier. Now there is a new top
; candidate plus the possibility
; of liver complications from the
; already diagnosed leptospirosis
;
;
; And after two more pages of
; questions, this is concluded.
; There were still other problems
; but Caduceus could come to
; no further conclusions.

Figure 8.9 Trace of Caduceus — Part 2

Doctors, on the other hand, automatically discount this kind of illusory explanatory power. They know, for reasons which are, as of yet, unavailable to the program, that they will have to postulate both diseases anyway. Thus there is no reason to credit the liver disease for "accounting" for a symptom that will eventually be covered by the lung problem anyway. Eventually the program realizes that the liver disease is the wrong one, but in the meanwhile a lot of time can be wasted on this red herring.

Currently work is in progress on making Caduceus act more like physicians in this regard. The doctor makes a global assessment of the problem before trying to pin down the details. The global assessment is quite sketchy. It will consist only of the guess that there is a certain number of distinct problems, along with a partitioning of symptoms among the problems. Then the doctor attacks each problem in turn, allowing only symptoms assigned to that problem to count toward a winner. Of course, it is possible that the initial assessment is wrong, in which case the program will presumably be alerted by the fact that none of the alternatives of the disease set are working out very well as an answer. This suggests that the program could use a backtracking control structure, and hence in such situations it would return to the initial assessment procedure to report that a decision it made concerning the number and kinds of problems seems to be wrong.

Of course, we still must specify how the initial global assessment is made. A reasonable technique is a generalization of one often used in medicine. If a particular symptom is only consistent with one disease, then the symptom is said to be *pathognomonic*. Needless to say, such symptoms are few and far between, or else medical diagnosis would be much simpler than it is. However, there are symptoms that, while not predicting a particular disease, do fairly well at predicting a class of diseases. So, for example, the finding of jaundice almost always indicates that the person has a liver problem. The program would not know which liver problem, but a general classification would be sufficient for doing its global assessment. Thus, to make its initial classification, it would look for those symptoms that are pathognomonic to a class of problems, and then postulate that class as one of a set of diseases for which it must make a disease decision.

8.7 Bayesian Inference Networks

The model of diagnosis we have dealt with to this point is a very simple one. The physician observes symptoms, these directly suggest diseases, and the problem is to weigh the evidence provided by the symptoms to decide which diseases are present. As such, the model looks like that in Figure 8.10. Each disease d is directly connected to some subset of all of the symptoms s.

Many situations require more complicated reasoning, however. Consider a patient who might have arteriosclerosis. (Arteriosclerosis is hardening of the arteries, a common ailment of the old.) Such a patient will sometimes show symptoms involving the lungs. A doctor will explain these happenings by saying that arteriosclerosis can cause heart complications by making it difficult for the heart to pump blood. In particular, it can cause one of two *pathological states* called *right heart syndrome* and *left heart syndrome*, depending on which

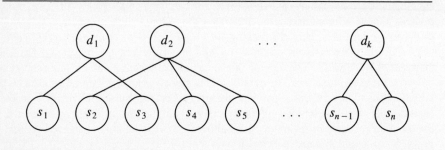

Figure 8.10 Simple diagnosis

side of the heart is affected. In the left heart syndrome, blood backs up into the lungs, so we see various lung symptoms.

In this example we see not only symptoms (the lung symptoms) and diseases (arteriosclerosis), but also intermediaries between the two (left and right heart syndromes). In medicine, these intermediaries are called *pathological states*. While in theory it is possible to do without them, that physicians consistently use them suggests that our programs should as well. If several different diseases can lead to problems with the workings of the left heart, then one will see the symptoms associated with left heart syndrome in all of them.

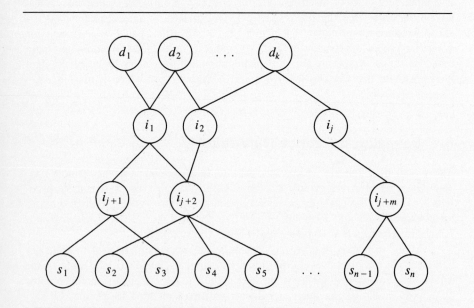

Figure 8.11 A Bayesian network

Rather than having to connect the symptoms to each of the diseases, by using pathological states, one may connect the symptoms to the pathological state, and then simply connect the single state to each of the diseases. By introducing such intermediaries, the connections between diseases and symptoms now look like those shown in Figure 8.11. There the i_js are the intermediaries.

To some degree, both of the programs we have considered do this, Mycin more so than Caduceus, but probably the program that best typifies this kind of reasoning is *Prospector*, a program that predicts the location of ore deposits. Prospector has what it calls "models" of situations in which ore deposits occur.

```
--------------------START-----------------------
In using PROSPECTOR, you will be asked questions
or you may volunteer information about a partic-
ular mineral prospect. The program will use your
information and the rules it contains to draw
conclusions about possible ore deposits on the
prospect.  Indicate your answers as follows:
  2 - Virtually certainly present
  1 - Probably present
  0 - No opinion one way or the other
 -1 - Probably absent
 -2 - Virtually certainly absent
-------Program Execution is now starting----------
Do you want to volunteer any evidence? YES
A Space name of evidence: SPACE-25L
   New likelihood of (Widespread Igneous Rocks): 2

B Space name of evidence: NIL


Proceeding to establish the likelihood of (Massive
   Sulfide Deposit):
1 Do you have anything to say about (Volcanic
   province and major fault zone)? 1
2 Do you have anything to say about
   (Mineralization)? 0
   ...
6 Do you have anything to say about (Rhyolite
   or Dacite plug)? YES
6a Have you anything to say about ...
   ...
In summary, the following have been observed:
The most likely deposit type is (Massive Sulfide
Deposit)  Its current probability is 0.01465.
```

; This material is printed
; out at the start of the
; session to orient the
; user. Since users will
; seldom be certain of con-
; clusions, they are asked
; for probability informa-
; tion an abbreviated form
; using numbers from 2 to
; −2 rather than probabil-
; ities from 1 to 0.
; Users may volunteer info,
; but they must know that
; SPACE-25L is the internal
; name for Widespread Igne-
; ous Rocks. Prospector
; provides a translation.
; The info is certain,
; and there is no more.
; Now Prospector starts
; requesting information.
; As number comes in, it
; is propagated through
; the network (except that
; 0 means "don't know").
; Answering with a YES
; tells Prospector to
; ask more detailed ques-
; tions on the topic.
;
; The conclusions are
; stated.

Figure 8.12 A trace of Prospector output

If the information input by the user matches one of its models, that would be taken as evidence in favor of ore being present. This problem is logically the same as that of the doctor trying to decide if a patient has a particular disease. Furthermore, like physicians, geologists are quite constrained in the information they can gather about a situation, so they too must deal in probabilities. Figure 8.12 gives a much edited transcript of a Prospector session. While it may not come through in our edited transcript, talking to Prospector is much like talking to Mycin. And indeed the similarly is more than skin deep since Prospector was modeled after Mycin. However, Prospector differs from the earlier program in several respects. First, as the transcript indicates, it allows the user to volunteer information, making it more like Caduceus in this regard. Second, Prospector explicitly uses a Bayesian approach to probabilities. Finally, Prospector makes more use of intermediate states.

Indeed, if one looks "inside" the program, one finds large networks through which probabilities percolate, starting with the bottom input nodes and working up to the topmost conclusions. Figure 8.13 shows a small part of a Prospector network. (Although Prospector is Bayesian, the formulation of Bayes's law that it uses is slightly different from the one used in this chapter. Thus the numbers in Figure 8.13 are only approximations to those used in the actual program.) While we will not go into exactly how such probabilities are to be propagated, a rule that works well in some cases (it requires more independence assumptions) is this

$$P(d_m|s_j) = P(d_m|i_n)P(i_n|s_j)$$

Here we have an intermediary i_n that relates the disease d_m and the symptom s_j (in geological terms it relates the hypothesis d_m to the evidence s_j). To see the import of this rule, consider the special case when the observation of s_j guarantees that the intermediary i_n is also present $P(i_n|s_j) = 1$. If this is the case then $P(d_m|s_j)$ will be exactly equal to $P(d_m|i_n)$. Then, to the degree s_j does not predict i_n, we lower the probability d_m. We could rewrite the equation above as follows:

$$P(d_m|s_j) = P(d_m)I(d_m|i_n)P(i_n|s_j)$$

Here we have made the substitution of $P(d_m)I(d_m|i_n)$ for $P(d_m|i_n)$. This says that we calculate the new probability of d_m on the basis of i_n as if we were sure of i_n, but then discount it by the probability of i_n. In the exercises we will refer to this last equation as the *probability propagation equation*.

8.8 Still More Complicated Cases

There are still more complicated situations that one may want to handle. For example, in the Bayesian networks of the previous section, we only considered how probabilities are propagated from bottom to top. While this is the most important thing we want from them, sometimes we need other kinds of probability propagation. For example, suppose we suspect that a person has a certain

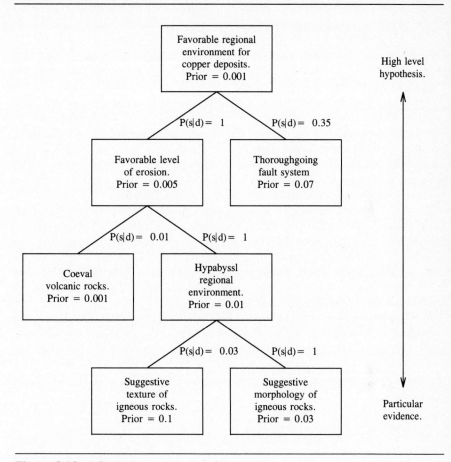

Figure 8.13 A Bayesian network in Prospector

disease (or a certain pathological state), and we also know that people with this disease often have heart attacks at a later point in the illness. It naturally would be prudent to get the patient to a hospital, and perhaps to an intensive care ward, to guard against such an eventuality. Note that this requires first propagating probabilities up to the disease and then down again to certain symptoms of the disease to recognize that they are likely. Systems like Prospector do not handle such cases.

Another example where more complicated propagation is required is where the presence of one disease makes the presence of a second more or less likely. Actually we saw this in the Caduceus transcript, where the presence of the first diagnosed disease suggested that the liver problem might be one that normally appears as a complication of the first disease. As this suggests, Caduceus handles such cases to a limited degree, but not in a completely general fashion. So research is continuing on these and related problems.

8.9 References and Further Reading

The most painless way to learn about Bayesian statistics is to take a course in the mathematical theory of statistics and probability. There are also countless textbooks on the subject.

As for the particular programs mentioned in this section, all are well documented in the literature. The Mycin program is the work of Shortliffe, Davis, and Buchanan. The most detailed description is in [Shortliffe76]. Particular emphasis on the rule format is given in [Davis77]. See [Shortliffe75] for a description of the evidence weighing mechanism used in Mycin, along with a discussion of why the program does not use the Bayesian methods presented here. For a counterargument on this point, see [Charniak83a].

The Caduceus program is a joint effort of a computer scientist (Pople) and a physician (Myers). The basic program is described in [Pople75] and [Pople77]. For a description of the revised version of the program, see [Pople82]. A particularly interesting article is [Miller82], which describes a test of Caduceus in which both it and physicians were given difficult cases from the medical literature. While the physicians clearly did better than the program, the difference was not as great as one might expect.

The Prospector program is primarily the work of Duda and Hart. The program is described in [Duda80] and [Duda78]. The Bayesian methods used by the program are described in [Duda76]. A case in which the program was used on a site that had yet to be explored is described in [Campbell82]. As it turned out, the program correctly predicted the presence of a significant mineral deposit.

For more on the problem of updating probabilities in a Bayesian network, the reader might consult [Pearl82].

Exercises

8.1   The independence of s_i from s_j is defined as $P(s_i|s_j)=P(s_i)$. Prove that from this it follows that $P(s_j|s_i)=P(s_j)$. That is, if s_i is independent of s_j, then s_j is independent of s_i.

8.2   Prove that given the definition of statistical independence of s_i and s_j, it follows that $P(s_i \& s_j)=P(s_i)P(s_j)$

8.3   Use elementary set theory and the definitions of the probability statements in terms of sets to prove the following two propositions.
   a) $P(not\ x)=1-P(x)$
   b) $P(not\ x|d)=1-P(x|d)$

8.4   Suppose a certain disease D has two symptoms associated with it, each one sufficient to absolutely confirm the disease. Assume that you have a system which uses the *logarithm combination rule* version of Bayes's theorem to find posterior probabilities. Characterize the posterior probability of D

after seeing both of the symptoms. Explain why this result occurred. *Hint*: It has to do with the assumptions that went into the logarithm combination rule.

8.5   Consider a program that operates according to the bottom-up Bayesian algorithm of Figure 8.6. How many numbers must such a scheme keep around permanently if there are 500 diseases and 3000 symptoms? How many if we make the assumption that only one out of ten of the $P(s_j|d_i)$ differ from $P(s_j)$, and we only store those that differ?

8.6   Is it possible to compute $P(d|not\ s)$ if you are given $P(d)$, $P(s|d)$ and the $P(s)$? (You are not allowed to make any further assumptions about the data.) If so, how? If not, why not?

8.7   Given the mythical data on the relations between certain symptoms and diseases shown in Figure 8.14, what are the following probabilities (you may assume the usual independence assumptions):

   a) P(drunk | throwing up)
   b) P(drunk | throwing up & female)
   c) P(pregnant | throwing up & female)
   d) P(pregnant | throwing up & female & yellow skin)
   e) P(pregnant | throwing up & not female)
   f) P(drunk | throwing up & not female & not age 0-to-10)

8.8   Write a Lisp program that will do simple medical diagnosis based upon the bottom-up Bayesian algorithm of Figure 8.6. Incorporate the default assumptions concerning missing $P(d|s)$, as well as the point made in the text concerning the precomputation of which diseases will have their probabilities altered by the observation of a particular symptom, and associate this information with the symptom (presumably on a property list). To simplify things, do not represent the facts about the world as predicate calculus assertions, but rather as atoms, like yellow-skin. Use the data provided in Figure 8.14. Show the probabilities associated with the various diseases given the following sets of symptoms

   a) throwing up
   b) throwing up, female
   c) yellow skin, enlarged stomach
   d) yellow skin, enlarged stomach, age 0-to-10

8.9   Discuss how we could extend our bottom-up Bayesian algorithm to properly handle situations where a finding contradicts what we would expect for a particular disease. How will this extension affect the number of statistical parameters needed by our system? How does it interact with our decision to use the logarithm of probabilities, and not the probabilities themselves?

; Diseases

$P(\text{pickled liver}) = 2^{-17}$
$P(\text{iron-poor blood}) = 2^{-13}$
$P(\text{pregnant}) = 2^{-11}$
$P(\text{drunk}) = 2^{-8}$

; Symptoms

$P(\text{yellow skin}) = 2^{-10}$
$P(\text{throwing up}) = 2^{-7}$
$P(\text{enlarged stomach}) = 2^{-10}$
$P(\text{male}) = 2^{-1}$
$P(\text{female}) = 2^{-1}$
$P(\text{age 0-to-10}) = 2^{-2}$
$P(\text{bloodshot eyes}) = 2^{-6}$

; Posterior Probabilities

$P(\text{yellow skin}|\text{pickled liver}) = 2^{-3}$
$P(\text{yellow skin}|\text{iron-poor blood}) = 2^{-1}$
$P(\text{bloodshot eyes} \mid \text{pickled liver}) = 2^{-1}$
$P(\text{bloodshot eyes} \mid \text{iron-poor blood}) = 2^{-6}$
$P(\text{throwing up} \mid \text{drunk}) = 2^{-2}$
$P(\text{throwing up} \mid \text{pregnant}) = 2^{-1}$
$P(\text{enlarged stomach}|\text{pregnant}) = 2^{-1}$
$P(\text{enlarged stomach}|\text{pickled liver}) = 2^{-8}$
$P(\text{female}|\text{pregnant}) = 1 \text{ (or } 2^{0})$
$P(\text{female}|\text{drunk}) = 2^{-4}$
$P(\text{female}|\text{iron-poor blood}) = 2^{-.5}$
$P(\text{age 0-to-10}|\text{pregnant}) = 2^{-30}$
$P(\text{age 0-to-10}|\text{drunk}) = 2^{-15}$

Figure 8.14 Data for a diagnosis program

8.10 Extend the program described in Exercise 8.8 to handle negative findings, as discussed in Exercise 8.9. Apply the program to the following sets of findings.

    a) throwing up, not female, not age 0-to-10
    b) enlarged stomach, not female,   bloodshot eyes
    c) not yellow skin, not age 0-to-10, not throwing up

8.11 Given the data in Figure 8.13, use the probability propagation equation to determine the effect of discovering coeval volcanic rocks on the probability of favorable regional environment.

9

This chapter pursues the subject of temporal reasoning developed in Section 7.4. Section 9.3.4 depends on the discussion of GPS in Section 5.7. Section 9.3.6 uses the Bayesian statistics developed in Chapter 8.

Managing Plans of Action

9.1 Introduction

This chapter is about robots — intelligent computers that act in the world. Robots actually exist, but are so far not very intelligent. The goal of robotics is to increase the dexterity and autonomy of these creatures. Part of this goal will be served by providing better sensors and effectors. We talked about one important sense in Chapter 3, and will talk about effectors at the end of this chapter. But our primary topic is what happens in between, where plans of action are generated and carried out.

Generating a plan can be thought of as programming oneself. Think back to some time when you had to get several things done on a tight schedule. You made a fairly detailed list, and then executed it. But there are several differences between programming and planning. The major difference is that a program is designed to be executed many times, each time on a different set of data; while a typical plan is executed just once. (You probably never used your chore list again.) Most programs live in a tightly controlled ''environment,'' namely, the inside of a computer. One can anticipate every effect of executing X := X+1. Plans are executed in a world full of surprises. Executing ''Go around the corner'' may possibly have as side effect ''Get hit by a truck.''

A plan must specify its expected results at each stage. If a departure is detected, the robot must be able to *replan*. An alternative would be to provide a large conditional mentioning everything that could go wrong, plus what to do in that case. But most of the arms of this conditional would never be used.

Finding a plan that probably will work is a special case of reasoning about time. In Chapter 7, we talked about *projection*, the process of predicting what a system will do. When the robot's own actions are included, the same sorts of reasoning are involved, except that the robot is ''free'' to do whatever it thinks

necessary to accomplish its goals. If its temporal modeling shows that something bad is going to happen, it can change its plans to eliminate that possibility.
Conceptually, therefore, the planning problem can be solved by a loop like the
inner loop of Figure 9.1

Several ideas from temporal reasoning carry over to the planning domain.
We assume that there is a *time map* in which past and future events are stored.
Some of these events are actions the machine performed or plans to perform.
For each such event, there is stored the fact that it is intentional, not accidental.
We will use the term *task* for the intention to perform an action. A robot will at
any time have several tasks, ranging from the intention to pick up a tool to the
intention to prevent its opponent from taking its queen. Because, as explained
in Chapters 6 and 7, events have hierarchical structure, so do tasks. A task to
go to a workstation might have several *subtasks*. See Figure 9.2. The structure
of subtasks of a task constitutes a *plan* for carrying it out. The phrases *task network* and *procedural network* are often used to mean the part of the time map
recording only the set of tasks and the temporal relations between them.
Indeed, for many planners, this is the only time map that is maintained.

At the bottom of the hierarchy are found *primitive tasks*, whose actions
require no planning to be carried out. Which actions count as primitive depends
on the available hardware and how fine-grained the analysis needs to be. A
robot with a welding attachment might treat welding a joint as a primitive
action; whereas a robot with no such special hardware might break it down into
actions such as "Grasp blowtorch," "Move blowtorch to work," "Ignite
blowtorch," etc.

The planner is started with a task, which it must *reduce* to primitive
actions. In a real system, execution would be interleaved with planning, but for
the time being we will neglect this. Hence the goal is just to produce a task network whose leaves are all primitives. Task networks are a kind of time map, so
in a way what we want the planner to do is start with a sketchy time map (a

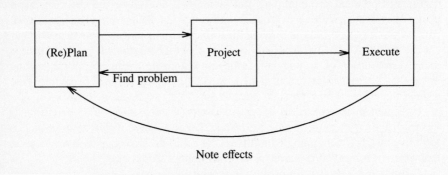

Note effects

Figure 9.1 The abstract planning loop

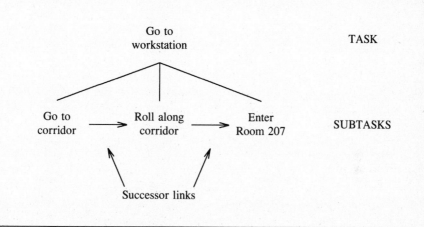

Figure 9.2 Task and subtasks

single task), and flesh it out by making choices about what to do and in what order to do it.

The machine is not told what its plans are; it must think them up. We will decompose this into two problems: *plan generation* and *planning decisions*. We can think of plan generation as a deductive problem: Given a task and the current situation, find a way to do that task. There is unlikely to be a general solution to the problem of plan generation. To pick up a tool, the machine must plan a collision-free trajectory for its arm. To prevent its opponent from taking its queen, it must find some clever chess move. (See Section 9.5.) Each class of plan-generation problems is a research area in itself. From the planner's point of view, the modules that propose plans are "black boxes"; we will use the term *plan generators* for them.

We can say more about the *planning decisions* which need to be made. Consider the example in Figure 9.3. The machine starts with two tasks — "Sand board" and "Spray-paint self." Wherever these tasks came from, it does not matter what order they are done in. However, finding plans for them quickly reveals interactions that will force some sequencing. There are two plans for Task 1. Each will require the sander to be held in one hand, but Plan 2 has the board in a vise, while Plan 1 has it in the robot's other hand. Each of these plans interacts with the plan for Task 2, which is, "Pick up the spray painter and blast away." This plan cannot be executed unless one hand is free. Here are the possible plans that fit this constraint:

1. Paint self, then sand board (using either plan).
2. Set up vise, then sand board and paint self simultaneously.
3. Sand board using both hands, then paint self.

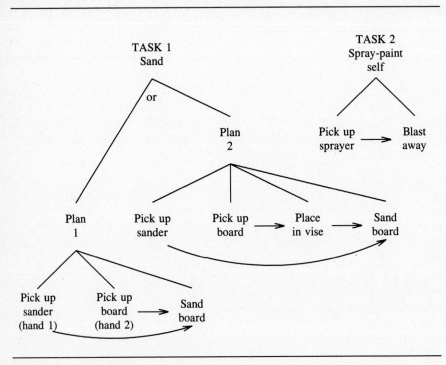

Figure 9.3 Coordinating two hands

We can distinguish between two varieties of planning decisions: *plan selection* and *plan coordination*. The former is deciding between candidate plans for a particular task (in the example, whether to use a vise or not). The latter is deciding between alternative sequences of executing multiple plans (whether to paint first or sand first). Both sorts of decision are based on expectations about the plan as a whole. The machine is trying to accomplish two global goals:

1. *Avoid plan failure*: A plan fails if it does not carry out its task. One way a plan can fail is for another plan to interfere with it. For instance, if the example of Figure 9.3 were changed so that Task 2 was "Paint the sander," then both plans would fail if executing Task 2 preceded executing Task 1, because using the wet sander would ruin the paint job and make sanding erratic.

2. *Minimize resource consumption*: Some plans cost more than others. In the example, if time is to be minimized, then the best sequence is to set up the vise and then finish both tasks in parallel.

Plan decision is a less domain-specific problem than plan generation. Each plan generator must provide predictions of the effects and resource consumption of the plans it produces. In addition, there must be domain-specific rules of the sort discussed in Chapter 7 for projecting the effects of events. Beyond this, it is up to the planner to pick the best version of the future.

Let's put this another way. Every situation and set of tasks encountered by the machine is unique. Its only hope for dealing with each new situation is to break it down into familiar elements, generate plans for them, then select and combine these fragments into an overall plan. This approach is not guaranteed to produce an optimal plan, but there is apparently no alternative. (A planner may on occasion create and debug new plans; we will talk about this topic in Chapter 11.)

An important class of plan failures are *protection violations*. A state is *protected* during an interval if it is required to be true throughout that interval in order for a task to succeed. For instance, during a telephone conversation, the state that ''There is a connection between this phone and that one'' is protected. A protection is *violated* if the state becomes false during that interval. Sometimes one of the machine's plans will violate a protection created by another. For instance, in the example of Figure 9.3, the planner is not allowed to pick up the board and then set it down before sanding it. We can express this as a protection of ''Board in hand 1,'' which could be violated by the plan for ''Spray-paint self'' if the board were set down so that the paint sprayer could be picked up.

The design of a complete planner would have to address the following issues:

1. What is the correct notation for plans?
2. How are time maps produced and maintained?
3. How can problems (such as protection violations) be anticipated and corrected?
4. How do you manage the search through the space of possible plans?
5. How are plans translated into actual action in the world?
6. How do you monitor the progress of a plan?
7. How do you replan when things go wrong?

Some of these questions have more complete answers at the present than others. The hardest to answer is number 6, ''How do you monitor the progress of a plan?'' This process is called *execution monitoring*, and requires expending resources to detect whether things are going as expected. For example, a robot might start a vat of chemicals reacting, then go to another room to do something else. To verify that the reaction is proceeding as planned, it will have to budget time to come back in the room and observe it. Little is known about how to manage such ''validation plans.''

9.2 A Basic Plan Interpreter

We suggested that plan generators varied from domain to domain, but that they always produced plans in a standard notation. A convenient way to view this situation is to treat plan generation as a deductive-retrieval problem. That is, the planner will find ways to execute tasks by looking for answers to the deductive problem:

(to-do *task action* ?way)

that is, "Find a ?way to do the *task*, whose action is *action*." Here ?way is itself an action. For instance, a robot working in a nuclear power plant might know that (to-do ?task (disable-reactor) (reset switch101)). Hence the goal (to-do task73 (disable-reactor) ?way) will find ?way = (reset switch101) as an answer. In practice, the deductive retriever can call special-purpose inference routines via *procedural attachment*, as explained in Section 6.4.2, in order to perform domain-specific inferences. However, we will ignore that here, and focus on the plans. We will often use the term *plan library* when we are assuming a rather shallow deductive scheme for finding plans.

One important observation is that we have posed plan generation as a "timeless" deductive problem. An assertion of the form $(\leftarrow$ (to-do $t\ a\ b$) $p)$ is intended to mean that if p is true *now*, then b is a way to do task t with action a. Strictly speaking, since ways to do things can come and go over time, all such rules should be "temporalized," using the notational devices of Chapters 6 and 7. Adopting the simpler convention means sneaking in an assumption that the legality of a plan depends only on the state of the world at the time it is adopted.

In order to present the fundamentals of plan notation, we will use a "toy" example domain, the so-called *blocks world*. This world consists of a set of labeled cubical blocks, plus a table. The only primitive action is to move a block to the table or to the top of another block. A block can be moved only if it is "clear," that is, has no blocks on top of it. It can be moved only to a place with enough space; the table always has space, but if the destination is another block, the destination must be clear. A typical task might be to get block a on block b, starting from the situation shown in Figure 9.4. The proper sequence of actions, or *plan*, is to put d on the table, then put c on the table,

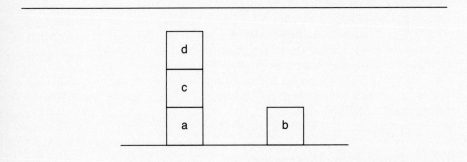

Figure 9.4 Blocks-world situation

then put **a** on **b**. To find this plan, we use the fact shown in Figure 9.5. This
rule says that to bring it about (**achieve**) that (**on ?x ?y**), a plan with three steps
suffices. Step **clearit** is to make sure **?x** is clear. Step **findspace** is to find
space for **?x** on **?y**. Step **doit** is to do the move. The two **order** clauses
impose a partial order on these steps: **clearit** and **findspace** must precede **doit**.
The two **protect** clauses set up two protections. They last from the end of their
respective preparatory steps to the beginning of the **doit** step.

The general form of a **plan** action is shown in Figure 9.6. In this figure,
the *init* and *fin* fields of a **protect** clause are terms of the form (**begin** *task*) or
(**end** *task*), which denote the times at which some arbitrary *task* begins or ends
execution, or just the term **now**, which denotes the time when the plan is constructed (as opposed to executed).

The **objects** are objects to use in carrying out the plan. For example, a
plan to drive a nail might mention the need for a hammer:

```
(to-do ?tsk (achieve (on ?x ?y))
    (plan
        steps: clearit (achieve (clear ?x))
               findspace (achieve (space-for ?x ?y))
               doit (move ?x ?y)
        order: (seq clearit doit)
               (seq findspace doit)
        protect: (clear ?x) (end clearit) (begin doit)
                 (space-for ?x ?y) (end findspace) (begin doit)
    ))
```

Figure 9.5 How to get one block on another

```
(plan
    objects: name1 formula1
             name2 formula2
             . . .

    steps: name1 act1
           name2 act2
           . . .
    order: (seq name name )
           (overlap name name )
    protect:
             state1 init1 fin1
             state2 init2 fin2

            . . . )
```

Figure 9.6 General form of a **plan** action

```
(plan-for: (drive-nail ?nail ?wood)
 objects: hamm (inst hamm hammer)
    . . .
 steps: hit-repeatedly
        (repeat-until (hit hamm ?nail) (flush ?nail ?wood)))
```

Here we have introduced the abbreviation (plan-for: *a* . . .), which is short for (= *a* (plan . . .)). We will use the term *plan schema* for an assertion of this form. We will neglect the objects slot of plan schemas until Section 9.3.2.

Getting back to our blocks-world example, the planner, when it decides to use a plan schema, must build a plan as it dictates. The result, in the situation of Figure 9.4, is to add to the *task network* the tasks shown in Figure 9.7. The two tasks (achieve (clear a)) and (achieve (space-for a b)), are ready to be worked on. The main task, (move a b), cannot be worked on until the first two are finished, as indicated by the arrows ("successor links") between them. (These come from the order clauses of plan schemas.) The task network explicitly indicates what states will be true after each step and will need to be protected for a while.

It is important to remember that a task network is just a special case of, or piece of, a "time map." It is a prediction about what is going to happen. In this example, it is a way for the machine to record that:

I am going to get a on b.
I will do this by doing three things:

    . . .

and so on

The reason to keep track of these things is the same as for any other application

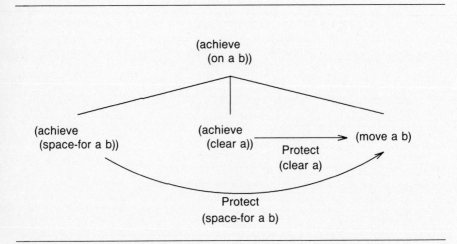

Figure 9.7 A task network

of time maps: to notice interesting or dangerous overlaps of states and events. We will talk more about this in the next section.

Not all **to-do** statements involve plan schemas. To handle the newly created subtasks, we will need rules like those shown in Figure 9.8, which mention the actions **(no-op)** and **(achieve** *p***)**, but not **plan**. The general form of **to-do** is **(to-do** *t a1 a2***)**, where *t* is a task and *a1* and *a2* are actions. To be consistent, we must assume that **(plan** . . . **)** is a term denoting an action, in particular the compound action performed whenever the three subactions are done in the required order without the protected states ceasing to be true too early. (The term **(plan steps:** . . . **)** doesn't look like other predicate-calculus terms we have seen, which are of the form *(function -arguments-)*. Its syntax has been "sugared" for readability. Box 9.1 talks about how to desugar it.)

The ideas of *task reduction*, *planning*, and *execution* are sufficient to design a simple plan manager. Figure 9.9 sketches one way of building it. If we apply this algorithm to an initial task network, it gradually extends the network downward (through *task reduction*) and to the right (as tasks are *executed*). Completing the task network of Figure 9.7 gives the network shown in Figure 9.10. If you read off the **move**s in the order permitted by successor links, neglecting **no-op**s, you obtain the sequence **(move d table)**, **(move c table)**, **(move a b)**, as desired. Exercise 9.12 asks you to implement this basic planning interpreter.

      (← **(to-do ?tsk (achieve ?p) (no-op)) ?p)**
          ; If **?p** *is already true, you can achieve it by*
          ; doing nothing.

      (space-for ?x table)
          ; There is always space for anything on the table.

      (← **(to-do ?tsk (achieve (space-for ?x ?y))**
                      (achieve (clear ?y)))
        (is ?y block))
          ; To find space for one block on another,
          ; clear the target block.

      (← **(to-do ?tsk (achieve (clear ?x))**
                      (achieve (on ?y table)))
        (on ?y ?x))
          ; To clear a block, put the thing on it on the table.

      (← **(clear ?x) (consistent (not (on ?y ?x))))**
          ; If you know of nothing on a block,
          ; then it is clear. (See Chapter 6 for
          ; the definition of **consistent***.)*

Figure 9.8 Blocks-world axioms for planning

Loop: Select a task that is ready to execute
      (all predecessors are executed).
      If it is primitive, then execute it.
      Else find a ?way such that
      (to-do *task task-action* ?way).
      If ?way is a plan,
          then create subtasks as it dictates.
          Else create one subtask with action ?way.
Endloop

Figure 9.9 A simple plan manager

An action like (plan . . .) is called a *macro-action* because it instructs the planner to create several subtasks organized in a certain way. The set of macro-actions that the planner knows about define a sort of "self-programming language." We can put whatever constructs we like into this language. For instance, we might want a simpler version of plan called seq: (seq a_1. . .a_n) is the action consisting of doing a_1 through a_n in that order.

A more interesting example is (repeat-until *act state*), which is done whenever the given *act* is repeated until the *state* becomes true. It is clear from the start that this will not give rise to a definite set of subtasks the way plan does; it will give rise to a sequence of subtasks with action *act*, but the length of the sequence will not in general be known before it is executed.

In conventional programming languages, the "test" part of a repeat construct causes no special problems. It is simply another expression to be evaluated, whose answer is interpreted as a "yes" or "no" (meaning, "yes, continue looping," or "no, stop"). Testing the *state* appearing in a repeat-until may itself be a problem requiring a complex plan. For instance, a robot may have to hit a nail with a hammer until the nail head is flush with the wood. Testing this may require moving the hammer out of the way, moving a camera into position, and examining the resulting scene for a protruding nail. This process may (with today's robots) be so expensive that it is more cost effective to hit the nail a few times between tests.

The example illustrates another point. In a conventional programming language, executing a construct like (repeat-until *act state*) causes precisely this pattern of behavior:

act - *test* - *act* - *test* - . . .

and no other. If you want *test* - *act* - *test* - *act* - . . ., for instance, you must use a different construct. In planning, we often want to be able to make commitments in small doses. For instance, in the task network of Figure 9.7, the plan schema has given rise to two unordered tasks, (achieve (clear a)) and (achieve (space-for a b)). It may be impossible to execute both of these tasks at once (if the robot has just one arm), but even so we don't want the machine

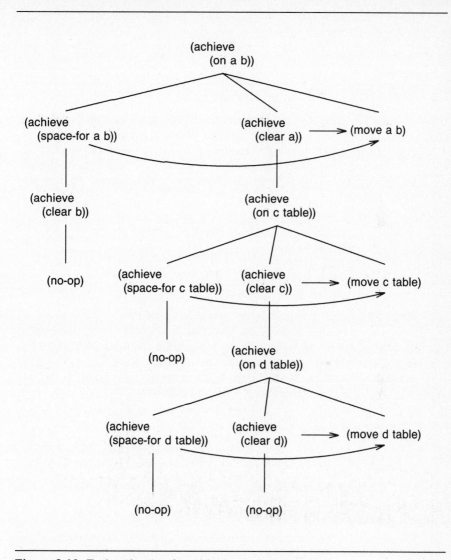

Figure 9.10 Task reduction for a blocks-world example

to commit itself to one order or the other this early. Other considerations may suggest an order later.

Similarly, in the **repeat-until** construct, we do not want to commit the machine at this stage to a rigid act-test cycle. It may be more cost effective to hit a nail a few extra times rather than test after every hit. It is revealing that it is often difficult for computer novices to understand the rigid act-test cycles of programming languages [Soloway82], possibly because humans are more like the planners we are sketching here.

Box 9.1.

Plans in the Future and in the Past

As we said, the syntax of plan violates predicate-calculus conventions. In this box, we examine whether syntax is the only issue involved, by providing a legal predicate-calculus version of the plan construct.

One version would have plan be a function of three lists (neglecting the objects slot), and refer to their elements with numbers. The on plan would become

```
(plan [(achieve (clear ?x)),
       (achieve (space-for ?x ?y)),
       (move ?x ?y)]
      [[1 3], [2 3]]
      [[(clear ?x) e 1 b 3],
       [(space-for ?x ?y) e 2 b 3])
```

which uses the list notation we developed in Chapter 6.

This is enough to prove the point, but looks rather ugly. It seems as if there ought to be some way to replace the numbers with variables. Indeed there is, by using λ-expressions. For the objects slot of a plan expression, we can use the some-act construct developed in Section 6.5.2. That is, we will interpret a term of the form

```
(plan . . .
    objects: name formula
         . . . )
```

as though it were

```
(some-act (name) formula
    (plan . . .
         . . . ))
```

Recall that (some-act (-vars-) formula act) meant the action done whenever act was done to objects satisfying the formula. That captures the intended meaning here nicely.

We will have to work harder to "desugar" the other slots. We will use a very general operator, (act-so-that d). This term describes an action that is executed by an agent a any time an event e_0 occurs that consists of a sequence of subevents $e_1, e_2, \ldots, e_n$, such that (describes d a e_0 e_1 $e_2, \ldots, e_n$). For instance, Figure 9.11 describes the action of going to hell in a handbasket. (Here the subevent equals the entire event.)

Now we can analyze plan as just a special case of act-so-that. Figure 9.12 shows the transformation from plan to act-so-that. If the plan had objects: as well, the desugaring would take us from

```
(act-so-that
    (λ (a m e)                        ; a = agent of action
      (exists (h)                     ; m = entire action
        (and (= m e)                  ; e = subevent
             (event e (do a (ptrans a hell)))
             (vehicle e h)
             (inst h handbasket))  )))
```

Figure 9.11 Going to hell in a handbasket

Plan format:

```
(plan
    steps: clearit (achieve (clear ?x))
           findspace (achieve (space-for ?x ?y))
           doit (move ?x ?y)
    order: (seq clearit doit)
           (seq findspace doit)
    protect: (clear ?d) (end clearit) (begin doit)
             (space-for ?x ?y) (end findspace) (begin doit))
```

Desugared version:

```
(act-so-that
    (λ (a e clearit findspace doit)
      (and (event clearit (do a (achieve (clear ?x))))
           (event findspace (do a (achieve (space-for ?x ?y))))
           (event doit (do a (move ?x ?y)))
           (seq clearit doit)
           (seq findspace doit)
           (true-between (clear ?d) (end clearit) (begin doit))
           (true-between (space-for ?x ?y)
                         (end findspace) (begin doit))
           (true-between (on ?x ?y) (end doit) (end e)))))
```

Figure 9.12 Analyzing plan in terms of act-so-that

```
(plan . . .
    objects: name formula
    steps: . . . )
```

to

```
(some-act (name) formula
    (act-so-that . . . ))
```

In Chapter 10, we will need axioms to the effect that, if someone carries out a plan, then there is actually a sequence of events corresponding to his carrying out every step of the plan. Here is a schematic version of such an axiom for a particular blocks-world plan:

```
(forall (e a)
   (if (event e (do a (plan . . .)))
      (exists (clearit findspace doit)
         (and (sub-event clearit e)
            . . .
            (event clearit (do a (clear . . . )))
            . . .
            (seq clearit doit)
            . . . ))))
```

Given our analysis of plan: we can write a general version of this "bridge axiom," shown in Figure 9.13. In English, the schema says that if e is an event in which a does an act-so-that with n event variables, then there are n subevents of e, as described in the act-so-that. For technical reasons (described in Box 6.1), this is actually an axiom schema; that is, you get one axiom out of it for each n by producing a version with one subevent variable, two, three, and so on.

Before going on, we might ask, if plan is a special case of act-so-that, why not use act-so-that instead? In fact, the Nasl problem solver of [McDermott78] and [Charniak83b] did work something like this. It would take a first-order description of what the task network would look like if a plan were adopted, and make the task network look like that. The λ-expression argument to act-so-that is just such a description. However, there is no way to carry out this transformation in general. (Proving this would take us into metamathematics. For those who know some mathematical logic, the proof hinges on the idea that if you could decide exactly what an arbitrary first-order description said about a task network, then you could decide whether an arbitrary first-order theory was consistent.) So, in practice, Nasl was given plan descriptions restricted to

```
(forall (a x e)
   (if (event e (do a (act-so-that
                         (λ (v_a v_0 v_1 v_2 . . . v_n)
                            p))))
      (exists (e_1 e_2 . . . e_n)
         (and (sub-event e_1 e)
              (sub-event e_2 e)
              . . .
              (sub-event e_n e)
              (describes
                 (λ (v_a v_0 v_1 v_2 . . . v_n)
                    p)
                 a e e_1 e_2 . . . e_n)))))
```

Figure 9.13 Axiom schema relating plans and events

essentially the special case embodied in plan. Since here we are treating the planning language as a sort of programming language, we have tried to confine our treatment to guaranteeably executable constructs.

9.3 Planning Decisions

In the last section, we emphasized an important difference between plans and programs — postponement of commitment. In designing a task network, the machine should make one decision at a time. If, for instance, the order of steps in a plan makes no difference to that plan, the planner should leave open the option of doing them in any order. Other considerations may force an ordering later.

This strategy makes the problem of *planning decisions* urgent, because it gives the planner so many decisions to make. From the most sweeping vantage point, planning decisions involve weighing alternative courses of events, judging their probability and utility. As such, they rely heavily on the ability to reason about time, which, as we saw in Chapter 7, is not well understood. Consequently, in order to simplify, most planners have made the following drastic assumptions:

- Nothing happens unless the robot makes it happen. (Picture an inert stack of blocks waiting for the robot to move it.)
- The effects of the robot's actions are predictable and instantaneous, and can be modeled in terms of finite "addlists and deletelists." (Chapter 7)
- Just one primitive action can be taken at a time.

The consequence of these assumptions is that nothing has to be modeled except the actions of the robot. A complete time map consists of a model of the initial situation, plus a record of the sequence of robot actions. (No record of how long these actions took, or the lengths of the gaps between them, is required.)

The current main line of research into planning derives from Sacerdoti's Noah program [Sacerdoti75]. Two offspring of Noah, Nonlin [Tate77] and Deviser [Vere83] fix bugs in Noah and extend it. All of these programs, because of their focus on static states of the universe, can limit themselves to a restricted class of actions and plan schemas. They all assume that the only nonprimitive action is (achieve p), "Bring it about that p is true." Deviser relaxes some of these restrictions, as we will see in Section 9.3.3. In what follows, we will talk about a hypothetical planner based mainly on Tate's Nonlin.

9.3.1 Anticipating Protection Violations

Earlier we distinguished between two main kinds of planning decisions: plan selection and plan coordination. Plan coordination is deciding on a sequence of execution for the plan. Given the restrictions we have just imposed upon the problem solver, the problem of plan coordination basically reduces to the problem of avoiding protection violations. That is, if there is only one agent in a deterministic universe, the only thing which might affect the results of a plan is how it interacts with other parts of the plan.

In Exercise 9.14 we suggest that a planner should detect protection violations as they occur. An alternative is to *anticipate* protection violations. To carry out this bit of "plan coordination," it will have to maintain data structures that record the intervals over which things must be protected. Because the only events that occur are the planner's own actions, intervals will be delimited by tasks. More precisely, since tasks can last for a while, we will use the endpoints of tasks to delimit intervals. Each task has two endpoints, (**begin** *task*) and (**end** *task*). An interval is then a pair of endpoints $<P_1, P_2>$, usually of different tasks. (We will allow one exception to this. The time of planning is also defined, and is denoted by the symbol **now**. Thus one might have an interval $<$**now**, (**end task-12**)$>$ which denotes the interval of time from the time of planning to the end of **task-12**.)

A *protection interval* is a triple $<F, P_1 P_2>$ consisting of a state F, and an interval $<P_1, P_2>$ over which it must be true. Anticipating protection violations requires making sure that no task T_i causing (**not** F) occurs during $<P_1, P_2>$.

For example, take the classic problems that arise when the robot attempts to bring about the conjunction of two states.

```
(to-do ?task (achieve (and ?p ?q))
      (plan
        steps: ach1 (achieve ?p)
               ach2 (achieve ?q)
        protect: ?p (end ach1) (end ?task)
                 ?q (end ach2) (end ?task)))
```

The schema for achieving a conjunction (shown graphically in Figure 9.14), says to achieve each conjunct and, of course, to protect it until the other is achieved. There are other ways of achieving a conjunction; if you want to delete all the files in a directory, you will usually not delete each one individually. But this is a general schema that is often worth considering.

Now take the problem of getting **a** on **b** and **b** on **c** starting from the situation shown in Figure 9.15. The general schema suggests reducing the conjunctive task to the network shown in that figure. The planner now uses the blocks-world schemas to reduce each task further, producing the network shown in Figure 9.16. The plan is unordered at the first level because the general schema is independent of which order is best to achieve the two conjuncts. But at the second level a possible interaction appears. The step 2.2 (**achieve (clear b)**) brings it about that **b** is clear. This state is then protected until the step (**move b c**). (We didn't make it explicit in the diagram, but the protection is there.) The step 1.3, (**move a b**), will make **b** nonclear. But steps 1.3 and 2.2 are unordered in the task network. There is no sequence of arrows joining them (or their supertasks).

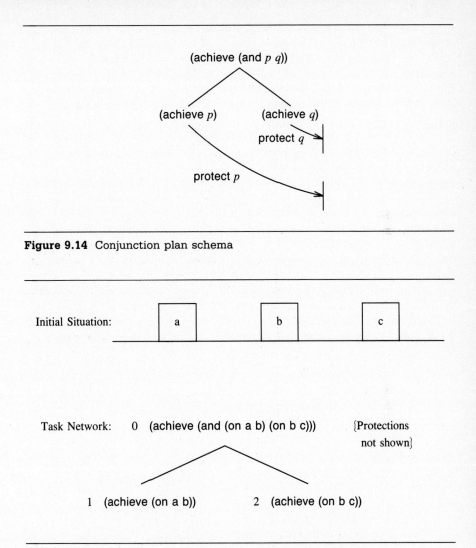

Figure 9.14 Conjunction plan schema

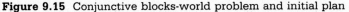

Initial Situation:

Task Network: 0 (achieve (and (on a b) (on b c)))   {Protections
                                                            not shown}

1 (achieve (on a b))   2 (achieve (on b c))

Figure 9.15 Conjunctive blocks-world problem and initial plan

As we have already discussed, the significance of such a partial ordering on plan steps is that it allows more than one legal execution sequence. For instance, steps 1.1, 1.2, and 1.3 may be executed in the order 1.1→1.2→1.3 or 1.2→1.1→1.3. Actually, there are many more possibilities, because 1.1 and 1.2 could be interleaved if they were reduced to complex task networks themselves. To see this, consider tasks 1 and 2. Since they are unordered, 1 could precede 2, or 2 could precede 1, or we could have a sequence like this:

2.1 → 2.2 → 1.2 → 1.1 → 1.3 → 2.3

In this case the execution of tasks 1 and 2 would overlap. (So assumption (c), above, that just one primitive action can be taken at a time, does not extend to nonprimitives.)

This last sequence would be unfortunate, since it would cause a protection violation. As we said, step 1.3 will fall in the protection interval <(clear b), (end 2.2), (begin 2.3)>, and hence the protected state (clear b) will be violated. The planner must make sure that this sequence does not happen.

There are in general two remedies when it is discovered that an interfering task may fall in a protection interval: the planner can put the interfering task before the interval or after it. In the present example, only one of these strategies works. Suppose it tries to put task 1.3 before task 2.2. There is another protection interval, <(on a b), (end 1.3), (end 0)>, which would then be violated by task 2.2. Hence, in this example, the only remedy is to put 1.3 after the protection interval, that is, after 2.3. In other examples, both options are open, and the planner will not be able to tell which (if either) will lead to a viable plan. It must be prepared to make a tentative choice; because there are many such choices, it must be prepared to *search* through the space of possible plans.

In yet other examples, neither option is open, and the plan is bound to fail. For instance, consider the classic problem of swapping two variables' contents. There are two tasks: Get X_1 into V2 given that it's initially in V1; and get X_2 into V1 given that it's initially in V2. The simplest plan for getting X_1

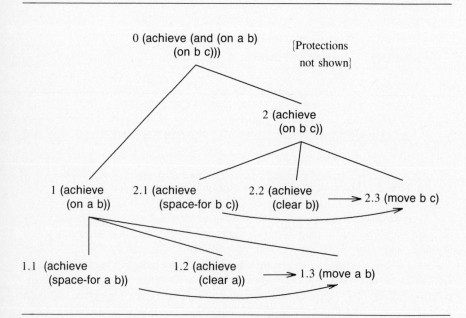

Figure 9.16 Task network after further reduction

from V_i to V_j is

$$(:= V_j \; V_i)$$

But using this plan twice gives two irreconcilable protection intervals. See Figure 9.17. Task 1.1 deletes (val V2 X_2) and task 2.1 deletes (val V1 X_1). Hence there is no ordering that maintains the integrity of the protection intervals. An entirely different plan must be found. (Sharp-eyed readers may note that these tasks "delete" a state in the sense that they make its truth value unknown, not in the sense that they make a truth value false, as in most of our examples. We will neglect this subtlety.)

Discovering possible protection violations is basically straightforward. The planner keeps track of its time map by maintaining in a predicate-calculus database assertions of the form

(taft *task state*)
   ; *state is true immediately after task.*

(protect *state* (end *task1*) (begin *task2*))
   ; *state is protected over the indicated interval.*

Then whenever a new effect or protection is set up, the planner can look in the database for possible conflicts. When it adds (taft *task state*), for instance, it must look for (protect (not *state*) . . .). If a protection interval and interfering task are found such that the task is not ordered with respect to the interval, then an ordering must be imposed (if possible).

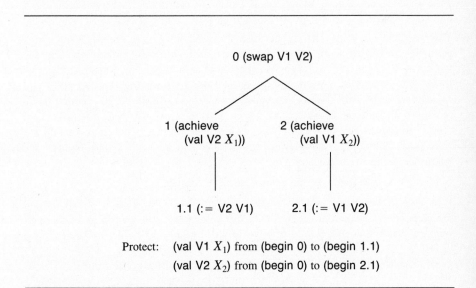

0 (swap V1 V2)

1 (achieve
   (val V2 X_1))

2 (achieve
   (val V1 X_2))

1.1 (:= V2 V1)

2.1 (:= V1 V2)

Protect: (val V1 X_1) from (begin 0) to (begin 1.1)

            (val V2 X_2) from (begin 0) to (begin 2.1)

Figure 9.17 Swapping two variables

Matters become surprisingly complex when we consider the problem of setting up the taft assertions in the first place. (This is just a way of doing temporal *projection* in the sense of Chapter 7.) The taft assertions depend in general on the state of the world when the task is performed, and this state depends in turn on the ordering of tasks, which is only partially known. For example, consider the simple action (move *x y*), ''Move block *x* to the top of block *y*.'' One effect of this action is that the block where *x* originally was now has nothing on it. But which block this is will depend on how the move action is ordered with respect to other planned actions.

The first assumption we will make is that there is no uncertainty about the state of the world before any tasks are executed. If *q* is an atomic formula with no free variables, then it is assumed that its current truth value (before any execution) is known to the planner. The way this assumption is usually implemented is to stipulate that if *q* cannot be proven true, it will be assumed false. This is called the *closed-world assumption*. (Compare Chapter 7.) For instance, if (on a b) is not explicitly known, (not (on a b)) will be assumed to be true. We will assume that initially every block is asserted to be on exactly one thing.

To deal with uncertainty due to task ordering, we need an algorithm that will proceed through the task network, figuring out the effects of each action. If task 1 definitely precedes task 2, then task 1's effects should be calculated first. Our algorithm will make the following basic assumption:

> If *p* has a given truth value after all known tasks that must precede task *T*, it will have that value when *T* is executed.

This assumption is too strong because *T* might have two predecessors which result in conflicting truth values, but let us start with this assumption, and see where it gets us. We will suppose that there is a predicate (has-effect *action state*) that is true at a particular point in time if executing that action would cause *state* to be true. What the planner must do is use the ''basic assumption'' to create a database of assertions about what is true just *before* a task, then apply has-effect rules to decide what is true just *after* it. The second group are expressed using the taft predicate described above, while the former are expressed using the predicate

(tbef *task state*)   ; *state is true just before task.*

We will use the name *Pre(T)* for the set of all tbef assertions for a task *T*, and the name *Post(T)* for the set of all its taft assertions. We can think of these as little databases that model what the world will be like just before and just after a task *T*.

Armed with this terminology, we can describe the algorithm thus:

1. Assemble *Pre(T)* by combining *Post(P)* for all immediate predecessors *P* of *T*.

2. Answer the query

(Show: (has-effect *action* ?effect))

in *Pre(T)*, where *action* is the action of *T*.
3. Assemble *Post(T)* by asserting (taft *T* ?effect) for each ?effect.

(See Exercises 9.17 through 9.20.)

Many things do not change as a result of an action's being executed. Hence the following convention will save a lot of computation: If there is no explicit taft or tbef statement concerning a state q, then its truth value will be assumed not to have changed since the initial situation.

Now let us relax the basic assumption. T may have two predecessors, tasks P_1 and P_2, unordered with respect to each other, such that one has effect q and the other (not q), and q may be relevant to some effect of T. When this case arises, it will be indeterminate whether q is true or false just before T. In the context of general time maps (Chapter 7), this indeterminacy is a more serious problem than it is here where every event is under the planner's control. The planner can simply choose an ordering that makes q come to have a determinate truth value. Before it can do this, however, it must be able to detect when q is both relevant and indeterminate. The latter requires that, in assembling the database *Pre(T)*, any state that is added by one task and removed by an unordered task be explicitly marked "indeterminate" (Exercise 9.20).

Even after all this work, the most perverse cases are still not handled. The problem is that, after the effects of T have been computed, a new task may be discovered that could alter *Pre(T)*. For example, after planning to take a plane to some destination you might then insert a planned taxi ride to get you to the airport. This would, among other things, change how much money you had in *Pre(fly plane)*. Hence the planner must record explicitly its belief in the relevant parts of *Pre(T)*. For instance, suppose that it bases its model of the effects of T on the truth of q just before T. Then it must set up a *projection-assumption interval* $<q, C, T>$, where C is the task that caused q to become true. The meaning of a projection-assumption interval is similar to the meaning of a protection interval: no task that asserts (not q) is allowed to fall in that interval. However, the reason for monitoring q is different. In the case of a protection interval, a violation means that some plan is in danger of failing. In the case of a projection-assumption interval, it means that some conclusion about what's going to happen is in danger of being wrong. Hence, when a projection-assumption-interval violation is discovered, there are three possible remedies: put the violator before the interval, put it after, or recompute the effects of the violated task.

As an example, suppose the planner has the task (move a b). As discussed above, the effects of this action depend on the current state. The planner's knowledge of that dependency is reflected in the axioms of Figure 9.18. Suppose that initially (on a d) is known to be true, and the planner has two tasks, *T1* with action (move a b), and *T2* with action (move a c). (The first might have arisen as a subtask of (achieve (on a b)), and the second as a

---

(has-effect (move ?x ?y) (on ?x ?y))
  ; *Moving ?x to ?y always leaves ?x on ?y.*

(← (has-effect (move ?x ?y) (not (on ?x ?z)))
    (and (on ?x ?z)
         (not (= ?y ?z))))
  ; *If ?x is moved from ?z to ?y,*
  ; *it is not on ?z anymore.*

(← (has-effect (move ?x ?y) (clear ?z))
    (and (on ?x ?z)
         (inst ?z block)
         (not (= ?y ?z))))
  ; *If ?x is moved from block ?z to ?y,*
  ; *then ?z becomes clear.*

Figure 9.18 More blocks-world axioms for planning

subtask of (achieve (clear d)).) If *T1* and *T2* are unordered with respect to one another, the planner may find itself projecting the effects of *T1* before it has thought about *T2* at all. As far as it can tell, a will still be on d when *T1* is executed, so it produces these three things (among others):

- An assertion (tbef *T1* (on a d))
- Assertions (taft *T1* (clear d)) and (taft *T1* (not (on a d)))
- A projection-assumption interval <(on a d), now, (begin *T1*)>; that is, a record that the predicted effects depend on (on a d) being true from now until (begin *T1*). Note the use of now to denote the current situation, that is, during planning and before any execution. See Exercise 9.17.

Later, the planner tries to project *T2*, with action (move a c). Assuming *T1* and *T2* are not ordered with respect to each other, *T2*'s effects are indeterminate. If *T1* occurs before *T2*, then *T2* will clear b. Otherwise, it will clear d. Our assumption is that indeterminacy in projecting tasks is intolerable, so the planner must make a choice:

1. It can order *T1* → *T2*: In which case *T2* will have as effects (taft *T2* (clear b)) and (taft *T2* (not (on a b))).
2. It can order *T2* → *T1*: In which case *T2* will have as effect (taft *T2* (clear d)) and (taft *T2* (not (on a d))). Furthermore, *T2* now falls in the middle of the projection-assumption interval set up for *T1*, and it wipes out the assumed state (on a d). (See Figure 9.19.) Hence the effects of *T1* will have to be recomputed. This time they will turn out to be (taft *T1* (clear c)) and (taft *T1* (not (on a c))).

As before, when we say "It must make a choice," we imply the existence of backtracking machinery. One choice is taken, and the other is saved in case this one doesn't work out.

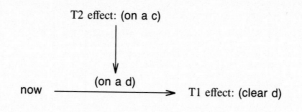

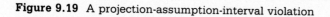

Figure 9.19 A projection-assumption-interval violation

There is one other use for the concept of assumption intervals. The planner must use **to-do** rules to decide how to reduce nonprimitive tasks. These rules resemble **has-effect** rules in that they depend on what's true just before a task is executed. Exactly the same issues arise. We must compute *Pre(T)*, eliminating known indeterminacies by choosing orderings of predecessors. To deal with indeterminacies that arise later, assumption intervals must be set up for every state that was used. We will call these *reduction-assumption intervals*. If the planner discovers a violation of such an interval, it must throw away the plan for it, and replan.

As an example of this phenomenon, consider Figure 9.20, which shows the "creative destruction" problem. Suppose the planner first works on the task **(achieve (on c a))**. Since this state is already true, the best plan for it is just **(no-op)**. But then when the planner gets to task 2.1.1, it discovers an action which may violate the assumption that **(on c a)** is true just before task 1. This fact was not protected; it isn't as if **(no-op)** would fail if the fact were false, since **(no-op)** never fails. Instead, the assumption that was violated was the assumption that **(no-op)** *is an adequate means of getting* c *on* a. Of course, there *is* a potential protection violation; task 2.1.1 can violate the effect **(on c a)** of task 1. But this violation can be eliminated by reordering; in fact, this reordering forces the reduction-assumption violation to occur, and means that task 1 must be re-reduced. (See Exercise 9.1.)

In total, we have three types of interval. If a potential violation is discovered, the offender can in principle be moved outside the interval (other constraints allowing). In the case where it must land in the interval, each type requires a different approach, as tabulated in Figure 9.21. We will use the term *assumption interval* to mean any of these three kinds.

We should point out that in the case of projection-assumption and reduction-assumption intervals, the recomputation does not stop with the immediately affected task. In general, recomputing the effects or plan for an action will change the effects and plan for all its successors, so they must all be recomputed.

To summarize, the complete planning algorithm is shown in Figure 9.22. Starting from a single task, it elaborates a plan for carrying out that task. When

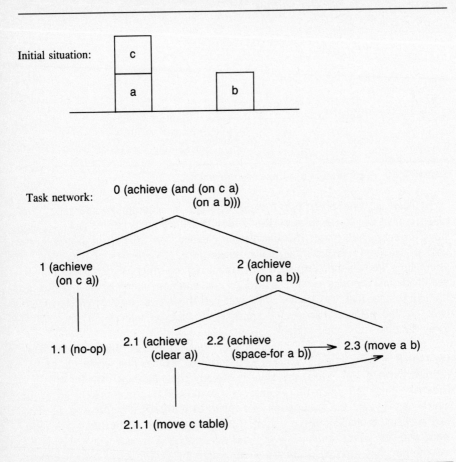

Initial situation:

Task network:

Figure 9.20 "Creative destruction" problem and plan

the algorithm halts, the task network will have been completely reduced to primitives, in a way that guarantees there will be no protection violations.

This algorithm is complex enough to deserve one more example. Consider the problem, shown in Figure 9.23, of performing the task (achieve (and (above a c) (above b d))). Switching from "on" to "above" makes it harder to anticipate bugs. To get *X* above *Y*, it suffices to put *X* on the topmost block above *Y*. As before, there are two subtasks, (achieve (above a c)) and (achieve (above b d)). But reducing them is now trickier than before because the steps depend on the order of the tasks. If (achieve (above b d)) is done first, then (achieve (above a c)) requires putting a on c. But if (achieve (above a c)) is done first, then a will be put on b, and we will get a protection violation. To foresee this, the machine has to know the order of the tasks, but it won't know the order until it has noted protection violations.

INTERVAL TYPE	CONSEQUENCES OF VIOLATION
Protection interval	The plan must fail in this case, so it is strictly forbidden.
Projection-assumption interval	Recompute the effects of the task at the end of the interval.
Reduction-assumption interval	Throw away the plan for the task at the end of the interval, and find a new one.

Figure 9.21 Handling assumption violations

Loop: While some nonprimitive task unreduced,
       Pick a nonprimitive task.
       Call plan generators to find a way to reduce it
         (enforcing orderings and setting up reduction-
           assumption intervals to eliminate indeterminacy).
       For each new subtask, project its effects (again
         eliminating indeterminacy). Find potential
         assumption-interval violations, and choose ways
         to deal with them.
       Set up protection intervals from plan schema, and
         for each one, find potential protection
         violations, and choose ways to deal with them.
Endloop:

Figure 9.22 Planning algorithm for anticipating protection violations

Let's see how our algorithm would handle this case. First, we define **above** as shown in Figure 9.24. Using these axioms, the planner, after initial maneuvering, has two tasks:

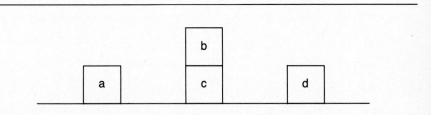

Figure 9.23 Put a above c and b above d

$T1$ = (achieve (above a c))
$T2$ = (achieve (above b d))

We will ignore the effect-computation phase, and focus on the task-reduction phase. Suppose it works on $T1$ first. Then it does a to-do query, and reduces $T1$ to (achieve (on a b)). However, it notes that this plan depends on reduction-assumption intervals

<(on b c), now, (begin t1)>
<(clear b), now, (begin t1)>

Next the planner works on $T2$, which gets reduced without difficulty to (achieve (on b d)) (and reduction-assumption intervals are created supporting this). However, as soon as it predicts the effects of this new subtask, it realizes that the first reduction-assumption interval is in danger of being violated. To avoid the violation, it places the action (achieve (on b d)) after $T1$. However, eventually this choice will result in a violation of the protected fact (above a c), because block a must be moved to clear b. When this problem is discovered, the planner will backtrack, and try putting (achieve (on b d)) somewhere else. It can't be put before the interval <now, (begin t1)> (because nothing can be planned for before now), so the planner is forced to put it in the interval. Hence it is forced to recompute the reduction of (achieve (above a c)). The upshot is that it decides to put a on c after putting b on d, the correct maneuver.

The use of backtracking by this algorithm is a mixed blessing. On the one hand, it "solves" the problem of making planning decisions. Any decision at all can be made correctly by repeatedly guessing and backtracking until the right guess is stumbled on. For instance, the problem of *plan selection* can be mixed in with all the other choices we have described. On the other hand, backtracking alone does not address the problem of choosing among feasible plans; it merely rules out completely infeasible ones. We will say more about search at the end of Section 9.3.4.

Tate's Nonlin planner used backtracking. The earlier Noah program did not. Where a choice was necessary, it picked one alternative and discarded the others. Here is a list of some choice situations and how they are avoided:

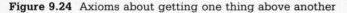

    (← (to-do ?tsk (achieve (above ?x ?y))   ; *To get ?x above ?y*
                   (achieve (on ?x ?z)))   ; *put it on ?z, the*
         (topmost ?z ?y))   ; *topmost block above ?y.*

    (← (topmost ?x ?x) (clear ?x))   ; *Define topmost above ?x*
    (← (topmost ?x ?y)   ; *as the first clear block*
         (and (on ?z ?y) (topmost ?x ?z)))   ; *in the stack ?x supports.*

Figure 9.24 Axioms about getting one thing above another

- Choice of plan: Noah assumes that there is exactly one plan known for any task. (Exception: if (no-op) will do as a plan, it will take that.)
- Projection assumptions: Noah assumes that the effects of a task never depend on whether an unordered task comes before or after it.
- Protection violations: Noah always puts an interfering task *after* the protection interval, never before it.

With restrictions like these, care must be taken in writing has-effect and to-do axioms or erroneous plans will result. The restrictions were ameliorated somewhat by the fact that Noah always reduced tasks breadth-first, so it was easier for the rule writer to anticipate and avoid timing errors.

9.3.2 Choosing Objects to Use

Not all interactions among plan steps are harmful. In some cases, the planner can notice that doing things in a particular order will save some wasted effort. One such fortuitous interaction is already handled by the algorithm of Section 9.3.1. Suppose that (no-op) is a legal plan for a certain task, given certain preconditions. Then the planning algorithm could find task orderings that would make those preconditions true. In particular, if a condition C is already achieved at one point in a task network, then a task with action (achieve C) can be accomplished by doing (no-op) if this task is placed in the network at some point where C is still true.

A related planning strategy is to *merge* tasks with similar actions. To be specific, we must bring back the neglected objects slot of plan schemas (Section 9.2). This slot specifies certain auxiliary objects to use in carrying out a plan. It doesn't name the objects, but just describes them. For instance, here is a plan for clearing a block:

```
(to-do ?tsk (achieve (clear ?x))
    (plan
        objects: surface (space-for ?x surface)
        steps: move-to-surface (achieve (on ?x surface)))))
```

This contrasts with the rule we gave in Section 9.2, which recommended always putting ?x on the table. The advantage of allowing anonymous objects (like surface in the example) is that the reasons to use a particular object may emerge only as the task network is elaborated. For instance, suppose the planner had the goal

```
(achieve (and (on a b) (on d c)))
```

where d is initially on a. It will wind up with the following two tasks (among many others):

```
(achieve (on d surface))
(achieve (on d c))
```

where *surface* refers to an anonymous surface. The first task is to clear a; the second comes from the original conjunction.

These two tasks can be merged, that is, treated as the same task, provided that c can be guaranteed to have space for d at the key moment. (See Exercise 9.22.) In this case, this condition happens to be needed anyway whenever (on d c) is made true, but in general it might not. For example, the planner might have a task to put d on something above c. To identify this task with a task to put d on e, the planner must be able to verify that e is above c just before the task resulting from the merge. But this is just another application of the algorithm we developed in Section 9.3.1 and Exercises 9.17 and 9.20.

If a task is never merged, and its anonymous objects never identified, then arbitrary objects with the required properties are chosen just prior to execution.

9.3.3 Temporally Restricted Goals

Deviser [Vere83] is an extension of Nonlin which gets beyond goals of the form (achieve *p*). It allows goals of the general form "Make *p* true, starting after time t_1 but no later than time t_2, and keep it true for duration *d*." (Times are specified as absolute dates.) This is useful when a planner has to interact with definitely scheduled events. For example, to plan to take a picture of the moon when it rises at 3:00 o'clock tomorrow morning, you could tell your robot to plan to have the camera pointed at the moon at 2:55 for a duration of ten minutes, and the shutter open at 3:00, for a duration of 0.1 second. The time during which the goal must start to be true is called its *window*.

Deviser adds to its plan schemas a **duration** slot, which says how long the plan will take. For example, we could modify our **achieve-on** schema to include a duration thus:

```
(to-do (achieve (on ?x ?y))
       (plan steps: . . .

              . . .
            duration: (/ (dist ?x ?y) robot-speed)
            . . .))
```

Note that the duration can depend upon the bound variables of the plan. In this case, the expected duration is the current distance between ?x and ?y divided by the robot's speed. (The object ?x will have to be carried from its present location to that of ?y.)

The top task given to Deviser has a window and duration associated with it. Whenever it is expanded using a to-do, windows and durations must be assigned to its subtasks. There is only one duration associated with a plan schema and plan schemas are restricted to being of the form

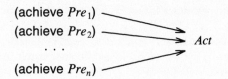

that is, a set of unordered preconditions, followed by a single primitive action *Act*. The duration of the schema really refers to the duration of this step. (The other steps will have durations determined by the schemas used to reduce them.) It is assumed that all the preconditions are to be protected until the end of *Act*.

Now the problem can be thought of as "propagating" window constraints from supertasks to subtasks. But there is no point in singling this situation out. Whenever two tasks are ordered, a constraint on the start time of one can influence the start time of the other. Vere presents a general algorithm for propagating the effects of such constraints. It is possible for Deviser to realize that the current set of constraints is inconsistent; as in Nonlin, such inconsistency causes backtracking.

Deviser allows external events not under the robot's control, that the robot must take into account. There are two kinds of event: scheduled and unscheduled. A scheduled event is one that has a definite time of occurrence. Deviser will order goals with respect to it just as it would any other activity, looking for good and bad interactions.

An unscheduled event is represented just like a plan schema, except that it is interpreted as meaning that the *Act* will occur automatically whenever the preconditions are satisfied. Figuring out when an unscheduled event is going to occur requires some new machinery. Whenever an **effect** assertion is produced, the planner must see if that completes a set of preconditions for an event schema. As before, making this decision may require ordering previously unordered tasks. However, reordering is now constrained by the windows attached to goals. The planner can often deduce the order of tasks from their global dates rather than requiring explicit chains of successor links.

It might appear that because some interactions are due to events not under the planner's control, ambiguous situations can arise. In Section 9.3.1, ambiguities could always be eliminated by forcing an order among tasks with situation-dependent effects (such as (move a b) and (move a c)). Picture the analogous situation in which the two events were not under the planner's control; there would be no way to tell which event occurred first. Such ambiguities are avoided by stipulating that events always occur as soon as their preconditions are satisfied. Hence they can be reordered by reordering the tasks that bring about those preconditions.

9.3.4 Planning by Searching through Situations

Our Nonlin-style planner *backtracks* when it runs into trouble. As explained in Chapter 5, backtracking is just another name for depth-first search. What is the search space in this case?

Recall that search requires the existence of a set of *operators* that transform *states*, a search problem being to discover a sequence of operators that transforms an *initial state* into a *goal state* (one satisfying a *goal-state description*). The space searched by our planner is the space of "partial plans," or task networks. Operators reduce tasks to subtasks, and impose orderings on hitherto unordered tasks. A goal state is a plan that is guaranteed to work without any protection violations.

A rather different use of search, and historically prior to Nonlin, is to search through world situations rather than through the space of alternative task networks. Under our stringent assumptions about time, we can think of planning as a search through possible states of the world. We can take the initial world model as the initial state; we can take primitive acts (described by addlists and deletelists) as operators; and the state of affairs to be made true (achieved) in the final world model as the goal description.

One planner that does this is called Strips [Fikes71]. It is an elegant adaptation of GPS (see Chapter 5) to planning. (The concepts of addlist and deletelist originated with the Strips group.) Strips represents world models as finite sets of variable-free atomic formulas, like {(in robot room3), (on block-1 block-2), . . . }. A state description is a conjunction of literals, whose variables are interpreted existentially. We will represent such conjunctions as finite sets of literals. For example, the goal $G=$ {(on block-1 ?y), (color ?y red)} means "Put block-1 on something red." Note that a symbol like on is now being treated as a predicate rather than a function that denotes a state of affairs. We can drop the distinction because Strips makes no explicit mention of time. (This is just as well, since otherwise our use of the word "state" for two different purposes would be even more confusing than it is. For the rest of this section, "state" will mean "state in the search space," and not "state of affairs.")

A goal conjunction G is matched against a state S. The result is, as for GPS, a set of differences, defined as follows. A *maximal match substitution* is a substitution θ such that for all other substitutions θ', $|G\theta - S| \leq |G\theta' - S|$. Here we use the notation $G\theta$ (introduced in Chapter 6) to mean the formula obtained by substituting the variable values specified by θ into G. A maximal match substitution is then one that minimizes the conjuncts of $G\theta$ not found in S. A *difference* between G and S is a formula p such that for some maximal match substitution θ, $p \in G\theta$-S. $G\theta$-S is said to be the *difference set* for θ. G matches S exactly, that is, there are no differences, iff $G\theta \subseteq S$ for some θ.

Suppose that S = {(on block-1 block-2), (color block-2 green), (color block-3 red)}. Then there are two maximal match substitutions for $G=$ {(on block-1 ?y), (color ?y red)}:

1. {y = block-2}, with difference set {(color block-2 red)}
2. {y = block-3}, with difference set {(on block-2 block-3)}

As with GPS, the search process aims at reducing differences. In this example, eliminating difference set 1 corresponds to coloring block-2 red; set 2, to putting block-1 on block-3. Either of these would bring it about that block-1 was on something red. To reduce these differences, Strips needs operators.

In Strips, operators are represented in terms of addlists, deletelists, and preconditions. A typical example might be the operator (move ?x ?y).

(move ?x ?y):   *; Move ?x from ?z to ?y*
   Precondition: (clear ?x), (clear ?y)
   Transformation: Delete: (clear ?y), (on ?x ?z)
                Add: (on ?x ?y)

which may be read as, "To apply move to ?x and ?y, make sure ?x and ?y are both clear, then delete the fact that ?y is clear, delete any current fact about the location of ?x, and add the fact that ?x is on ?y."

Contrast this with the original GPS operators. Two major changes are that (a) transformations are not black boxes, being always represented as add and deletelists; (b) there is no need for a separate operator-difference table; since differences are always missing propositions, the addlists always suffice to describe all differences reduced by the operator.

Unfortunately, the schema we gave for move will not work as shown. It does not specify the correct outcome in case ?y is the table, or in case ?z is not. We must supply different versions for each of these cases, distinguished by different facts that are true before the operator is applied. For instance, here is the version for when ?y is the table and ?z is a block:

(move ?x table):   *; Move ?x from ?z to the table*
   Filter: (on ?x ?z), (inst ?z block)
   Precondition: (clear ?x)
   Transformation: Delete: (on ?x ?z)
                Add: (on ?x table), (clear ?z)

Each operator schema gives rise to a large number of different operators, obtained by plugging in different variable values. (The original GPS allowed only a finite number of operators.) However, we can conceal this multitude inside the algorithm that implements the operator-difference table in GPS. The only requirement is that this function return a finite set of operator instances, as indeed it will. Given a difference, the function must find all operators that contain an addlist element that unifies with the difference. The results of the unification can be substituted into the operator to yield operator instances. For each such operator, instances are collected whose filters match the current state exactly. This procedure finds all relevant operators, and it finds only a finite number.

For example, given the difference (clear block-2), we can unify this with (clear ?z) in the addlist for the version of move given above, generating the operator instance

(move ?x table):   *; Move ?x from block-2 to table*
    Filter: (on ?x block-2), (inst block-2 block)
    Precondition: (clear ?x)
    Transformation: Delete: (on ?x block2)
                        Add: (on ?x table), (clear block-2)

If the filter is satisfied, then, as in all applications of GPS, the precondition becomes a *subgoal description*, which is matched against the current state, generating new differences. The eventual result is to produce an operator-difference tree like that of Figure 5.41. The "Filter" and "Precondition" slots of an operator schema are very similar. The only difference is that differences between the precondition and the current state will cause Strips to set up a subgoal, whereas differences between the filter and the current state will cause this operator to be ignored. It is usually obvious what conditions belong in which category. For instance, suppose we had a special operator for getting a block to the table when the block was glued to the wall. If we made "?x is glued to the wall" a precondition, then Strips would think about how to glue ?x to the wall if it weren't there already! Clearly, such a condition should be made part of the filter instead.

Both the filter and the addlist may supply multiple maximal match substitutions. For instance, here is another schema for **move**:

(move ?x ?y):   *; Move ?x from block ?z to block ?y*
    Filter: (on ?x ?z), (inst ?z block), (inst ?y block)
    Precondition: (clear ?x), (clear ?y)
    Transformation: Delete: (on ?x ?z), (clear ?y)
                        Add: (on ?x ?y), (clear ?z)

Suppose that we have the situation

{(inst block-3 block), (on block-1 block-2), (inst block-4 block),
 (clear block-1), (clear block-3), (clear block-4)}

and the goal {(clear block-2)}. There are three different operator-schema instances that apply:

1   (move block-1 table)   ; *Using the first schema.*
2   (move block-1 block-3)   ; *Using the second.*
3   (move block-1 block-4)   ; *Using a different instance of the second.*

Since there may be other goals later, we have to try all three.

Exercise 9.34 asks you to write a third schema defining **move**. Given all these schemas, Strips can solve the "creative destruction" problem given earlier. The result is shown in Figure 9.25.

We have gone on about Strips at such great length, not because it is the best way to generate plans, but because it is the most elegant version of GPS. It contains fewer black boxes and hence requires the problem poser to write less. Once you have defined the operators (in the simple, uniform addlist-deletelist notation), you are done.

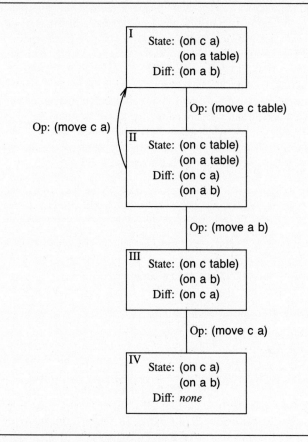

I State: (on c a)
 (on a table)
 Diff: (on a b)

Op: (move c table)

Op: (move c a)

II State: (on c table)
 (on a table)
 Diff: (on c a)
 (on a b)

Op: (move a b)

III State: (on c table)
 (on a b)
 Diff: (on c a)

Op: (move c a)

IV State: (on c a)
 (on a b)
 Diff: *none*

Figure 9.25 Creative destructions by Strips

Historically, robot planning and search through a space of temporal situations have been so thoroughly intertwined that one phrase, "problem solving," has been used for both. This situation is now changing, as it is realized that planning is a form of reasoning about space and time, on which the operator/state analogy poses too many restrictions. This is not to say that search is not important in robot planning, but it is search through the space of plans, not through the space of situations.

Noah and its descendants are interesting just because they show that this shift can reduce the amount of search required. Consider the problem of interacting goals, where one action undoes something accomplished by another. In Strips, this is noted by the fact that the resulting state is further from the goal than its ancestor; this can cause Strips to switch attention to a different part of the search tree. Noah avoids ever generating the faulty path, because it detects the potential problem, and alters the plan to avoid it.

As another example, consider how Strips generates all possible instances of each operator. We saw before that to clear block-2, Strips considered both putting block-1 on block-3 and putting it on block-4. Each operator would give rise to a different sequence of states in the search space. Noah instead just notes the plan step, "Put block-1 *somewhere*." (Section 9.3.2) Later, if there is a step to put block-1 on block-3, Noah will merge these two steps (ordering constraints permitting). That is, if there is an independent reason to put block-1 on block-3, Noah realizes that block-3 is the preferred destination.

Nonlin puts search back in, since Tate recognized that in many places where Noah makes a change to the plan there are alternatives that cannot be rejected. However, he ([Tate77], p. 889) makes the point that

> As in Noah, we expect that the first choice taken should lead to a solution . . . . Indeed, if failure occurs with the first plan being considered, our experience is that backtracking can lead to long searches since many consequent ordering choices may have been made because of an inappropriate choice early in the generation of the plan.

That is, so far no one has found the right search space.

9.3.5 Shallow Reasoning about Plans

The most impressive thing about many of the planning algorithms we have looked at is the ratio of their complexity to the complexity of the plans they manipulate. We restricted our plans down to loop-free sequences of achieve tasks, and even so had to go to incredible lengths to make sure that all harmful interactions were anticipated. If we attempted to broaden the class of plans that could be generated, the situation would get even worse. Furthermore, all of these inferences are cost effective only if the machine has an accurate model of the world, including the effects of its actions. As we will see in Section 9.4, such accuracy is rare in the real world.

An alternative paradigm for this area is to allow plans to be more complex, perforce making reasoning about them less airtight. For instance, we can allow constructs like the repeat-until mentioned in Section 9.2. Other similar borrowings from programming languages, such as if-then, also suggest themselves.

Many actions do not have effects of the sort assumed by Noah-class planners. Here are some examples:

- Roll a die (the effect is unpredictable).
- Look in a box (you will know what's in the box, but you can't say what it is at planning time).
- Run around the block (virtually the same as (no-op) in terms of effects).

There is a whole class of actions which are "executed" solely by constraining the execution of other actions. For instance, "Stay away from open flames" might well be part of a plan (for instance, if a robot has to transport gasoline through a factory). To carry this instruction out, the machine has to come up with a plan for carrying out its other instructions, such that this plan keeps the robot away from open flames. Such "parasitic" actions are called *policies*.

As we start adding such complexities to plans, they get harder to reason about. We can hope that the methods described in Section 9.3.1 are still appropriate, but they won't be foolproof. Furthermore, it is easy to supplant them with more ad hoc methods. For example, in the Nasl problem solver of [McDermott78], the problem of plan choice was dealt with by providing a *choice protocol*. Whenever the machine was faced with a choice among possible plans, it entered a special deductive scenario, in which it asserted which plans were possible options, then attempted to deduce which were "ruled out" or "ruled in." The program was applied to designing electronic circuits. Each plan step filled in part of the design. A typical choice rule would say something like: "If an amplifier is supposed to draw little power, use CMOS FETs." A similar paradigm has been used by the Molgen project [Friedland84]. This is a program that plans molecular-genetics experiments. In deciding what plan to use for a task such as "Isolate the bacteria containing plasmid 104," it uses rules such as "If the environment must not become saline, don't use any plan involving adding a salt solution."

Contrast this approach with that used by Nonlin and Strips. Each of these, in a different way, chose among alternative plans by trying them out, that is, by projecting each, and picking the first one that worked. The "choice rule" approach applies to domains where simulation of this kind is too difficult or uncertain. Instead of having to "visualize" exactly what will go wrong with a plan, the planner is allowed to do specific inferences to decide which way to go.

9.3.6 Decision Theory

If we decide to implement choice rules, what form should they take? Both Nasl and Molgen use "rule-in-rule-out" form, where the rules cause alternatives to be discarded or strongly favored. An alternative would be to view choice as a diagnostic problem, like the ones Mycin solves. The rules could use "certainty factors," which when combined would give an overall vote that would select a winning plan.

In Chapter 8, we looked at the mathematical theory underlying diagnostic programs like Mycin. As it happens, there is an extension, known as *decision theory*, which talks about choosing the best course of action. It is based on the assignment of probabilities and payoffs to all the possible outcomes of each decision. For instance, suppose we have a patient whom we have diagnosed (using the methods of Chapter 8) to be suffering from "enlarged thymus" with probability 0.75. Suppose there are two courses of action open to us: operate to remove the thymus (option OP), or do nothing (option NO-OP). The operation has four possible outcomes:

1. If the diagnosis is correct, and there áre no complications, the patient is cured, having spent money for the operation.
2. If the diagnosis is correct, and there are complications, then the patient is just as bad off as before, but is out the cost of the operation.
3. If the diagnosis is incorrect, and there are no complications, then once again the only cost is the cost of the operation.
4. If the diagnosis is incorrect, and there are complications, then the patient is even worse off than before.

We also need an estimate of the probability of complications. Let's say it's 0.15, and let's also stipulate that the occurrence of complications and the correctness of the diagnosis are independent, so that the probabilities may be multiplied to arrive at the probabilities of the four outcomes. See Figure 9.26. In order to compare these outcomes, we need to assign a numerical "payoff" to each of them. Some of the components, such as the cost of the operation, have obvious units they can be measured in. Others seem more intangible. Nonetheless, it is assumed that there is a scale of *utility* on which all outcomes can be ranked. This scale will vary from person to person, but we must assume that a given decision maker has such a scale. In the present case, suppose we rate outcomes as shown in Figure 9.26. (We have omitted the cost of the operation; it will reappear shortly.)

Given these data, we must rate the "overall goodness" of the option "Operate to remove thymus." We assume that this is just the *expected utility* of this option, arrived at by weighting each utility by its probability:

Expected utility =
       (probability of outcome 1) × (utility of outcome 1)
    + (probability of outcome 2) × (utility of outcome 2)
    + (probability of outcome 3) × (utility of outcome 3)
    + (probability of outcome 4) × (utility of outcome 4)
    = 600.

The expected utility is just the average utility you would get over repeated experiences of this kind. Picture the surgeon being presented with exactly this case several times in succession, and average the utilities of the outcomes. (See Exercise 9.7.)

	Outcome	Probability	Utility
1	Enlarged thymus, no complications:	0.64	1000
2	Enlarged thymus, complications:	0.11	0
3	Ordinary thymus, no complications:	0.21	0
4	Ordinary thymus, complications:	0.04	−1000

Figure 9.26 Probabilities and utilities of outcomes of operation

We can do a similar analysis for the "do nothing" choice. If the diagnosis is correct, and nothing is done, let us suppose the consequences of untreated enlarged thymus amount to -1000 "utility points." If the diagnosis is incorrect, then, to make a long story short, let us suppose that the real problem is less severe, so that the expected utility in this case is -100. We can now summarize the options in what is called a *decision tree*. See Figure 9.27. At the root of this tree is the decision. One branch, "operate," has a cost of 100, which is written as a utility of -100. The other, "do nothing," has an expected utility of -775. To arrive at the expected utility of the first decision, we add the -100 to the expected utility 600, arriving at a net of 500. Since this is preferable to the other branch, the operation is a good idea.

In this case, only the first branch of the tree corresponded to an action by the decision maker. But the theory can also encompass sequences of actions, in which future decisions must be anticipated. Often these actions can be expected to produce more information, and hence to change the outcome of various decisions. For instance, suppose that the doctor in this case knows of a diagnostic test that has not yet been performed. It costs 10 utility points, and reports on whether the patient really has enlarged thymus. In particular, if the patient really suffers from this condition, the test reports yes with probability 0.9. If he does not, it reports no with probability 0.75. Note that the test, like most tests in real life, is not perfectly reliable.

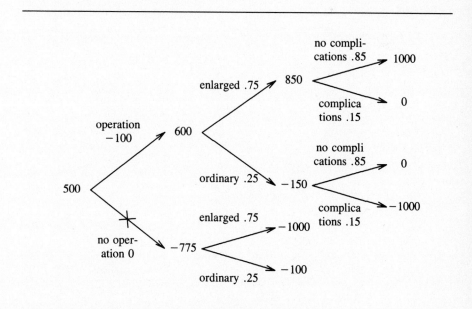

Figure 9.27 Decision tree for thymus operation

We now have a more interesting decision tree, describing the results of these options:

- Do nothing.
- Run the test; then decide what to do.
- Do the operation without the test.

The tree is shown in Figure 9.28. In this tree, we have simplified a bit by

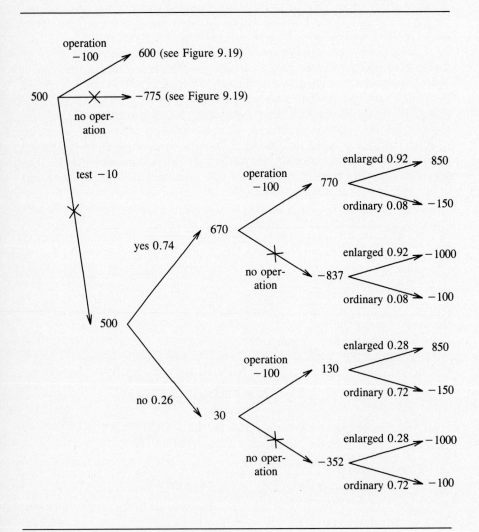

Figure 9.28 Complex decision tree

collapsing the "complications" option into the utilities of correct and incorrect diagnoses. Since 85% of the time the operation has no complications, the expected utility of the operation, given a correct diagnosis, is

$$0.85 \times 1000 + 0.15 \times 0 = 850$$

Similarly, the expected utility of the operation when the diagnosis proves to be incorrect is -150.

The other numbers in the tree are more interesting. We have three options at the outset, op, no-op, and test. If the test is done, then it may yield the answers yes and no. The probability of a yes answer is computed thus:

$$P(y) = P(y|e)P(e) + P(y|r)P(r) = 0.9 \times 0.75 + 0.25 \times 0.25 = 0.74$$

where e and r represent the thymus being enlarged or ordinary, respectively. Similarly, the probability of the test saying no is 0.26.

Suppose the test reports yes. We will be faced with the decision to operate or not to operate as before. However, the expected utilities have changed. The probabilities of the branches labeled "correct" and "incorrect" must be changed to take the new evidence into account. In other words, the numbers put there must be $P(e|y)$ and $P(r|y)$, rather than the *a priori* probabilities $P(e)$ and $P(r)$ we had there before. These probabilities are easy to compute, using Bayes's Theorem:

$$P(e|y) = \frac{P(y|e)P(e)}{P(y)}$$

and similarly for $P(r|y)$. The results are as shown in Figure 9.28. Not surprisingly, the probability that the previous diagnosis is correct goes up if the test result is yes, and goes down if it is no.

Now we assign expected utilities to every node of the tree, using the same rules as before. At *decision nodes*, we compute the expected utility for each possible action, and subtract the cost of performing that action. The utility at the decision node is then the maximum of the utilities of each action, and the chosen action is the one with that maximum net utility. At *outcome nodes*, we take the weighted average of the utilities of each outcome, using the probabilities of the outcomes as weights. For instance, the utility of the node where we decide to operate after the test yields a no outcome is

$$0.28 \times 850 + 0.72 \times -150 = 130.$$

These rules are applied repeatedly until a value for the entire tree, and hence a chosen action, is arrived at. (The rejected options have Xs drawn across them to indicate that they are nonoptimal.) Note that in this case the best action is still to do the operation; the test does not give us enough information beyond what we already know, given the small risk of complications and the danger of doing nothing. Hence there is no reason to do the test at all. (See Exercise 9.8.)

One might think that an elegant theory of this kind would have been assimilated into robot planners, but this has so far not been the case. The issues addressed by the two approaches are complementary. Planning research has focused on how plans are *constructed*; decision theory has focused on how they are *evaluated*. Decision theory is oriented around giving advice to human planners, who need no advice on coming up with options (quite the contrary), but do need advice on issues such as whether to continue testing or act on available information. Planning theory takes no account of probabilities at all; in fact, our assumption that action outcomes are completely predictable is inconsistent with the idea of keeping track of multiple outcomes.

We will see a similar split between Chapters 8 and 10. Chapter 10 will explore abductive processes where the problem is not to choose among given hypotheses but rather to construct them in the first place. Presumably in the long run decision theory will be integrated with both planners and understanders. Before that happens, other problems, such as how probability and utility estimates are arrived at in realistic circumstances, will have to be solved.

9.4 Execution Monitoring and Replanning

So far we have talked about creating plans. This is a fairly pointless activity unless the machine has means of carrying the plans out. As soon as we introduce them, the problem of "feedback" arises. There are few planning domains where the planner can be 100% sure that the primitives it executes have the desired effect. There are several sources of error:

- Limb movements are never precise, because of limitations of physical motors and gears. (See Section 9.5.1.)
- The machine's model of the world is often wrong.
- Some actions involve random processes, or depend on facts the machine is ignorant of.

The only remedy for such errors is for the planner to watch its own actions, and check the results. This process is called *execution monitoring*. There is as yet no general theory of execution monitoring. Such a theory would spell out the optimal pattern of resource expenditure to test the effects of action. At any time, the planner has a set of states it expects to be true. It can decide to spend some resources testing some of them. Whether to spend them depends on factors like these:

- The probability that a given state's truth value is accurately known
- The expense of a given plan for testing a state
- The accuracy of such a plan

Note that execution monitoring requires further planning, and that these plans may also require execution monitoring. A plan to bake a cake may require checking the cake every now and then to see if it's done. This plan will require planning a trip to the kitchen, which will require the robot to look at the scene as it rolls toward the kitchen. Fortunately, such recursions usually bottom out with actions that "monitor themselves." An action such as "Look for the kitchen door" is self-monitoring because if it fails, the robot will know it.

Because there is no general theory, it is reasonable to expect practical robot plans to contain ad hoc execution-monitoring advice. That is, between steps that actually accomplish parts of the plan, there are steps whose only function is to check on progress. We often find such steps in recipes and repair manuals: "Open the gazorn cover. You will see a blue frammis . . . ." If you don't see a blue frammis, you know you have done something wrong. Explicit execution-monitoring steps like these are found in the directions people give for getting to places [Riesbeck80].

As we have said, planning and execution are normally interleaved. The reason is simple: there is no point in planning out every task before executing any of them, because events can occur while executing the first tasks that will make the plans for the later tasks wrong. Of course, not planning ahead at all can be just as foolish. Just as for execution monitoring, there is no general theory about when to reduce a task in advance, and when to wait until it is closer to execution. One idea is to let the plan generators return "Insufficient information," meaning, "Call me again when this task is nearer to execution."

The machinery for interleaving planning and execution is straightforward. Execution can proceed as soon as a single primitive task is ready for execution (i.e., has no unexecuted predecessors). After every primitive is executed, the world model is updated to reflect the new situation. There are two kinds of update. If the plan is completely correct, then the machine just makes $Post(T)$ be the new database. On the other hand, the execution of a "monitoring" step is likely to disabuse the planner of some belief, in which case we must actually change $Post(T)$. Such a change has the same kind of effect as we described in Section 9.3.1: it may reveal that the effects or reduction of subsequent tasks are wrong.

There is a large problem that we will have little to say about here: explaining unexpected results. Suppose that a robot rounds a corner and fails to see what it expects. There are several possible explanations, including

1. The robot is lost (it is not where it thinks it is).
2. The robot's "internal map" is wrong.
3. Something has changed since the last time the robot was here.
4. The vision system is malfunctioning.

Generating and choosing among the proper explanations is just the abduction problem, which we examine in Chapters 8 and 10. Here we will simply point out that choosing among competing explanations may involve some testing, and hence some planning and execution.

When the expectation failure has been explained, some tasks will be classified as *failed* and some as *failing*. A task has failed if it can no longer be executed properly. Most failed tasks are in the past. A task is failing if its plan needs to be corrected to avoid having it fail. For example, the plan for the task "Go to the store" in Figure 9.29 has as subtask "Start the car," which has as

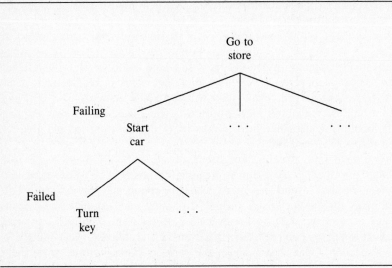

Figure 9.29 A snag in going to the store

subtask "Turn the key in the ignition." The expected result of the bottom task is "Engine starts." If no engine roar is heard, then the planner can assign blame to the last task. The task has failed because its desired effect did not occur.

At this point, "Start the car" is *failing*. Unless something new is tried, it will fail. In this case, the machine should realize that "Turn the key" just fails now and then, so it can produce the same plan all over again. If it fails a second or third time, then the supertask "Start the car" has failed, and attention shifts to a yet higher level, "Go to the store," which is now classed as failing. A new plan must be found, so all the components of the old plan are *abandoned*, including the failed "Start the car" and the steps that were planned after that. If no new plan can be found, then "Go to the store" has failed. As before, you abandon it and try to figure out another way of doing what you would have done at the store. We summarize this with the program sketch of Figure 9.30. This scheme embodies an assumption that the machine should abandon as little of the plan as possible. There is no reason in principle why it should not abandon its entire plan and start again, but it seems intuitively reasonable to try to avoid this.

Unpleasant surprises are all too common, but pleasant surprises are not that rare either. (For instance, you get in the car to go to the store to buy a flashlight to replace one you lost, and discover the lost flashlight in the car.) Indeed, the flux of experience so often alters our plans in one way or another that some have argued that the picture of planning as systematic generation of plans is misleading [Hayes-Roth79], and the algorithm should be redesigned to take advantage of *opportunism*. Certainly if we were capable of designing robots as independent and perceptive as we are, then task networks would become large, permanent data structures, most of whose contents were tasks

·Repair failing-task
    If there is an alternative way to do it,
      then plan to do that.
    Else Flush failing-task

Flush failed-task
    Mark it and its subtasks "abandoned."
    If there is a way to redo it
      then plan to do that.
    Else if it has a supertask
      then Repair its supertask.
    Else the robot's entire life has been a failure.

Figure 9.30 Schematic algorithm for plan repair

waiting for good opportunities to be executed. (For instance, a human often forms a task of the form, "Read such-and-such a book"; rather than plan it immediately, the task tends to be thought about only when the planner wanders past a library or bookstore.) Indexing such mainly dormant tasks so that they are thought about only when it is productive to do so is an interesting problem. However, in the current poor state of robot sensors and effectors (see Section 9.5.1), thinking about such issues tends to be pointless. Sensing anything at all is so expensive and unreliable that each glance at the world must itself be planned carefully; the odds that something completely unexpected will turn up and be recognized by the robot as an opportunity are negligible. (But see Section 9.5.2.)

9.5 Domains of Application

Now that we have surveyed plan-management techniques, we will look at two domains in greater detail: robot planning and game playing. What we will discover is that the general techniques are only a fraction of what is needed in each of these areas.

9.5.1 Robot Motion Planning

Moving our muscles to pick something up and move it around seems effortless to us, but then so does looking at something. In fact, a lot of computation is necessary for each of these skills. There is a whole level of planning here that cannot be handled by the general methods we have discussed so far. Here is what is typically required for the robot to pick up a block X

1. It must find X, the block to be moved. If it knows roughly where X is, it must point its camera in that direction, and analyze the image until it finds

a block matching X's description. We talked about this process in Chapter 3, and will not talk about it further here.

2. It must move its hand to X's location. A hand is a physical object, so it is governed by Newton's laws. To get it to go somewhere, we have to give it a series of shoves, and we have to make sure that it stops in the right place. The hand is not floating in the air, to be moved telepathically, but is connected to a *base* via a series of *joints*, which can only move in certain ways. The base may or may not be mobile.

3. It must grasp X. Assuming the hand is correctly positioned to do this, it must close the hand until it makes contact. For the robot to be able to tell that contact has been made, *force sensors* are required in the hand, which tell how much force is being exerted on it. (Empty air exerts no force.)

4. It must move X to its new destination. As before, this requires figuring out a series of joint movements, and a series of motor impulses to make those movements happen. Also, if the object is bulky or is heading for an awkward place, the robot must find a path for it to take that does not cause it to bang into anything. It must place X in its new position by lowering it gently until it senses contact.

5. Throughout all these steps, the TV camera and force sensors must be used to verify that what is happening is within allowed tolerances. For instance, if the force sensors suddenly register nothing, that means the robot has dropped the object it was carrying.

9.5.1.1 Robot Kinematics. Suppose for the time being that our robot has a stationary base, and an arm extending from it. The arm will have several *joints*, at each of which a limited amount of motion is allowed. Usually a joint allows a rotation around one axis. (Some joints can extend and retract instead of rotate.)

Suppose an arm has just one joint. Then its tip could reach any point in a circle, as in Figure 9.31. This might be sufficient. For instance, one conveyor belt might pass under one point in the circle, another under a different point,

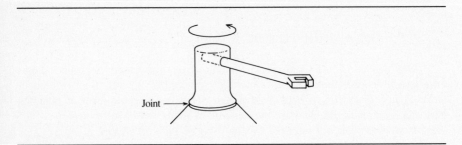

Joint

Figure 9.31 One joint

and the arm's job might be to pick things off one belt and transfer them to the other.

In general, though, we will need more joints. How many? Consider this argument: A circle is a space of one dimension. That is, one real-valued coordinate is necessary and sufficient to specify any point on the circle. One joint is necessary to access any point in a circle.

Now say we want to access every point on a hemisphere of points at a distance R from the robot. This is a space of dimension two; it takes two coordinates (e.g., two angles) to specify a point. It also takes two joints, not surprisingly. A possible arrangement is given in Figure 9.32.

So how many joints does it take to access every point in a *volume* surrounding the robot? Three. Several arrangements are possible. For example, we could add a retractile joint to the gizmo in the figure. Or we could add another rotator. Each arrangement gives us a somewhat different accessible volume.

There is another complication. The arm will often be manipulating a tool of some kind. In general its orientation in space takes three parameters to describe. (To convince yourself of this, visualize a camera. We need two parameters to describe the direction it is pointing, and one to describe its orientation around that axis. For example, while taking a picture of a skier coming down a slope that faces west, the first two parameters might have values 0 (east) and 45° (up the slope), and the third 90° (camera rotated to "portrait" mode).)

The term *degree of freedom* is used to include coordinates and orientation parameters. Since we want to be able to hold our tool at an arbitrary orientation and point within some volume, it has six degrees of freedom, and hence we will need six joints. (Assuming each allows one degree of freedom; some, like ball-and-socket joints, allow more.)

Any position or motion of the robot must be analyzed in terms of joints. The analysis can become complex. To begin with, we must be able to compute, from a desired position and orientation of the hand, joint positions that

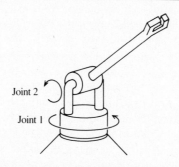

Figure 9.32 Two joints

correspond to it. This is part of *kinematic analysis*. The mathematical tools required go beyond what we can show in this book, but a simple example will demonstrate. Suppose that in Figure 9.32 we equip the hand with another degree of freedom, by allowing the arm to extend and retract. Now suppose we wish to place the hand at point $<x, y, z>$. The joints' positions are defined by three different variables, θ, the angular position of the first joint; ϕ, the angular position of the second joint, and r, the length it is extended to. The problem of the robot is to figure out values for these parameters that put the hand at $<x,y,z>$.

Fortunately, in this case, this is the familiar problem of translating from Cartesian to spherical coordinates, with solution

$$\theta=arctan(\frac{y}{x}) \quad \phi=arcsin(\frac{z}{r}) \quad r=\sqrt{(x^2+y^2+z^2)}$$

In case this is unintelligible to you, relax. We just want to make the point that coordinate transformations are an important part of reasoning about jointed systems ("linkages"). As these systems become complex, you must switch to a uniform language for talking about such transformations, the language of *linear algebra*.

Once you have solved for the joint values at the initial position of the arm and desired position, you have to figure out how to get from one to the other. The simplest way is to crank every joint at once. We will represent joint coordinates schematically: q_i is the ith coordinate (e.g., θ or r). If there are N joint coordinates, then we will have N pairs $q_{i\ Initial}$ and $q_{i\ Final}$. Suppose that we decide to take time T to get from the initial to the final position. Then we crank joint i at the speed

$$\frac{q_{i\ Final} - q_{i\ Initial}}{T}$$

We will call this method *uniform* motion. (We have neglected time to accelerate and decelerate. The issue of the force necessary to realize desired motions is too complex to examine here.)

The only problem with uniform motion is that it can produce weird trajectories for the hand to follow. All parameters are treated the same, even though some correspond to angles, some to distances. An observer would see the arm curl around confusingly, and eventually arrive at the right place, as all the parameters settle to their correct values at once. This doesn't really matter, unless there are obstacles to be avoided (such as the observer!).

In many cases, straight-line motion is preferred. But getting the hand to move in a straight line means picking more complicated time functions for the individual joints. For example, in our three-jointed robot, to go from point A to point B in Figure 9.33, the uniform method would cause the arm to be spun around (as θ goes from 0 to 90, ϕ stays 0, and r stays at its max). The straight-line method would cause θ to change as before, but would require r to retract and then extend again. (In this case, uniform motion actually looks simpler, but that won't be true for more complex examples.)

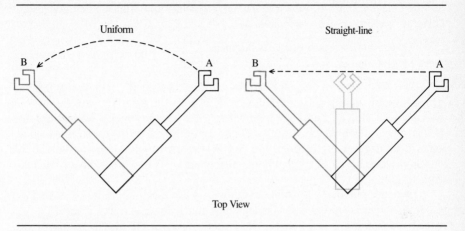

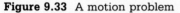

Figure 9.33 A motion problem

9.5.1.2 The Need for Feedback. Whatever the abstract solution, actually getting a mechanical device to carry it out is tricky. It is not sufficient to build an arm and tell it to move. Even the best arm will move in a slightly different way from the way it was told. The only way to compensate for the presence of *noise* of this sort is to provide *feedback* control. The robot arm must be provided with sensors that compare the actual movement with the intended movement. Then, under hardware or software control, one can correct the errors that are detected. See Figure 9.34.

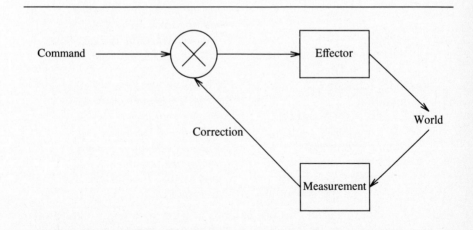

Figure 9.34 Typical feedback loop

We have looked at one kind of robot motion, motion through empty space. There are two other sorts of interest:

- Motion until some obstacle is bumped
- Motion along a surface or through a conduit

The first type is exemplified by closing the hand until something is grasped, or by setting something down. It is called a *guarded move* because it must proceed slowly, checking for bumps. The second type is exemplified by putting a peg in a hole, or closing a door. Here the motion is constrained along some of its degrees of freedom; the peg must pull straight along the hole axis, the door must be closed by pulling tangentially. These are called *compliant motion*.

For both guarded and compliant moves, we need *force feedback* as well as *position feedback*. A force sensor tells how much force is being exerted on the robot by something it is touching. In a guarded move, the goal is to stop when this becomes positive. In compliant motion, the goal is to maintain some amount of force on an object, using a feedback loop; if the force gets out of line, a correction is applied.

It may sound like programming robots is incredibly tedious. At the lowest level, it is. One goal of robotics researchers is to conceal this level from the average "robot programmer," and let the programmer suggest high-level actions (e.g., one of the three sorts of motion), which the software will turn into detailed commands to joint motors, feedback loops, etc. Here is an example of a program, written in the Lisp-like robot-assembly language Lama [Lozano-Perez77], for dropping a peg into a hole:

```
(strategy drop-into (peg hole)
   (rotate : (change r by 0.1)     ; The first step is called rotate
                                    ; r is the angle the peg makes
                                    ; with the work area. Rotation
                                    ; may stop when the peg and hole
      such-that                     ; have approximately parallel axes.
         (almost (aligned peg hole)
            0.1))
   (shift : (change y)             ; y is the height above the work area
      such-that                     ; so this command says to lower
         (left-of (peg center)      ; the peg until it is
            (hole center)))         ; to the left of the hole.
   (landing : (change x)           ; Similarly, changing x means
      such-that                     ; moving the peg sideways
         (contact (peg front)       ; until the peg is hovering
            (hole front))))         ; over the hole.
```

Each step specifies its action not just in terms of what to do (e.g., (change y)), but also in terms of desired effect (e.g., (left-of (peg center) (hole center))). It is up to the compiler to produce code for bringing this effect about, and monitoring whether it has been achieved.

As more and more decisions are left to the compiler, which must integrate them with decisions made for other, concurrent tasks, the compiler comes to resemble a planner, and the programs become plan schemas. The ultimate goal is to describe only the final desired result to the system, and have it produce the entire plan.

9.5.1.3 Finding Routes through Cluttered Work Areas. The last topic we will look at in this section is the problem of movement through a cluttered area. The problem is to find a path that does not intersect any of the clutter. Our examples will be two-dimensional, with polygonal obstacles instead of solids; furthermore, we will shift viewpoint slightly, and assume a convex mobile robot of constant shape, rather than a flexible arm. (These are not trivial restrictions.)

All of these algorithms treat the problem as one of search. But this is a textbook example of the phenomenon we described in Chapter 5, that discovering the space is most of the problem. The algorithms take a cluttered space and from it extract *path segments*. The complete path is then strung together out of several segments. The classic way to do this is to draw arcs between vertices of the obstacles that can "see" each other, that is, such that a line can be drawn joining them that does not pass through any other obstacle. We form a graph consisting of these arcs plus the sides of all the obstacles; we include the robot

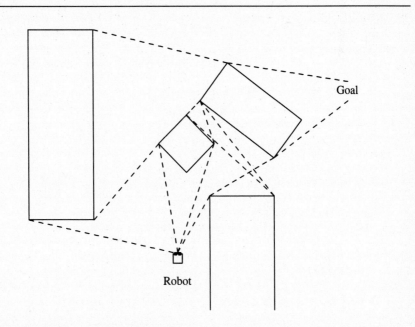

Figure 9.35 An obstacle course

and its destination as vertices. See Figure 9.35. If the robot is very small (essentially a point) compared to the obstacles, the shortest path from current location to the end must be a subset of this graph. (Following the arcs corresponding to walls means that the robot must "hug" the wall.)

If the robot is not a point, then we must modify our approach. There are two ways to do this. If the robot is fairly compact, we can pretend it is spherical. Then we can take each obstacle, and replace it with a bigger obstacle, obtained by expanding each boundary by the radius of the robot. In this artificial space, we can now pretend the robot is a point again. See Figure 9.36.

If the robot is elongated or oddly shaped, this procedure will still work (if we take the maximum radius), but some paths will be missed where the robot could squeeze through by turning in the right direction.

An alternative solution searches the space in a somewhat different way. Rather than create paths that hug the obstacles (which are tricky to follow anyway), this algorithm finds obstacles that "face" each other, and generates a path segment that corresponds to passing between them. This path segment is not a line, but a generalized cylinder (see Section 3.5.4), bounded by the facing obstacles. Since the obstacles are polyhedral, their faces are planar (linear in two

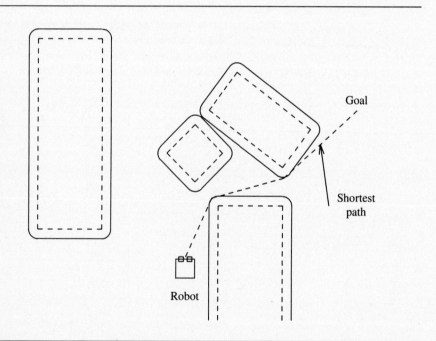

Figure 9.36 Growing the obstacles

dimensions), so the path segment is either an ordinary cylinder, or it tapers in one direction. See Figure 9.37.

Now we do an ordinary search through the path segments. If two segments meet, then we can compose them into a path, but we have to be careful about robot orientation. The legal orientations for the robot on one path have to overlap the legal orientation on the other. If the legal orientations are compatible at all points where path segments are sutured together, then an overall path can be constructed, which will require the robot to twist and turn as it progresses.

9.5.2 Game Playing

In Chapter 5, we talked about game trees, but mentioned that it was unlikely that game trees were the best framework for finding good moves in games. Humans make plans against their opponents in games, and it is reasonable to expect that good computer programs will do the same. But very few programs have been written that work this way. An exception is Paradise [Wilkins80], which made plans for the game of chess. Paradise makes a plan that consists of an initial move, plus ideas on what do to in the event of various opponent replies. So, unlike many game-playing programs (see Chapter 5), it can actually continue to pursue its plan after the opponent has responded.

Planning in games is rather different from the kinds we have examined before. The most obvious difference is that there is an opponent to worry about. Plans cannot be sequences of things to do, but must include conditionals that react to the various options open to the opponent. Another difference is that

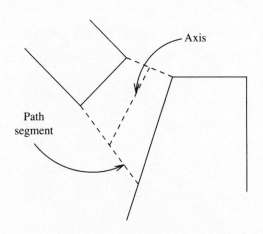

Figure 9.37 The structure of a path segment

tasks come and go as the game progresses. Although one can consider there to be an overall goal, "Win the game," normally the player will become aware of shorter-term opportunities that can be exploited, without caring exactly how they will lead to a win.

On the positive side, many games have the advantage that events are "crisper." In a game like chess, the machine's sensors are perfectly reliable, and the current state of a game is always known in its entirety (except for the opponent's intentions!). Such a game is one of *perfect information*. In a game like poker [Waterman70], not everything is known (the opponents' cards are concealed), but even here at least time is quantized nicely. Players do not act chaotically, but take turns in a rule-governed way. These advantages have traditionally made games attractive domains for AI research.

Because game playing requires seizing opportunities, the first thing a game-playing program must do is analyze the current situation and come up with interesting and feasible tasks. This process is called *task noticing* (compare [Wilensky83]). For instance, Paradise will find apparent opportunities to attack, fork, skewer, check, or in some other way wreak havoc on its opponent. (If you do not know much about chess, rest assured that these are fiendish things to do. Forking, for instance, means attacking two pieces at once, so that the opponent can only save one of them. Paradise did not play a full game of chess, but was designed to work only in situations where a clever plan existed that would cause overwhelming damage to the opponent. Hence it was a little "overconfident" in its search for such a plan; it always "knew" one could be found!)

An apparent opportunity does not always pan out. To check for this, Paradise would simulate its plans for several ply, fixing bugs and verifying that the opponent had no valid response.

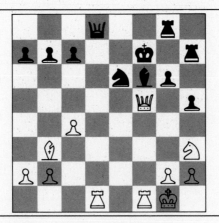

Figure 9.38 Chess problem solved by Paradise

For those who know some chess, it is instructive to see how Paradise planned its way through a position. Consider Figure 9.38. The task noticer would look for ways to execute the task **(threaten)**, and see that moving its rook to Q7 could threaten the black king. Hence it proposes the subtask **(safemove rook Q7)**. (The action **safemove** means "move without fear of the piece being immediately taken.") Unfortunately, Q7 is under attack by the black queen, and the protection the white queen might offer is blocked by the black knight. Hence the program generates a subtask, **(decoy black-knight)**, and finally generates the primitive action **(move white-knight N5)** as a plan for this task. (See Figure 9.39.) After further elaboration, the final plan (not shown in the figure) may be summarized (in English) like this ([Wilkins80], p. 175):

> Play N-N5. If black captures the knight with his knight, attempt to safely move the rook on Q1 to Q7. Then, if black moves his king anywhere try to safely capture the black rook on R7, and if black moves any piece other than his king, try to safely capture the king with the rook.

One reason why so few chess programs have made plans is that brute force works too well for this game. The best chess programs to date have been written in machine language, or even used special hardware, in order to achieve maximum speed in examining board positions.

A better game to use as a domain for planning would be one that involved some amount of gambling, because then it would be impossible to apply game-tree search methods. One such game is Risk^{TM}, manufactured by Parker Brothers. In this section, we will use Risk as an extended example. As far as we know, no one has written a planning program for this domain.

The object of Risk is to take over the world, represented as a set of countries, grouped into continents. This is done by simulated military battles

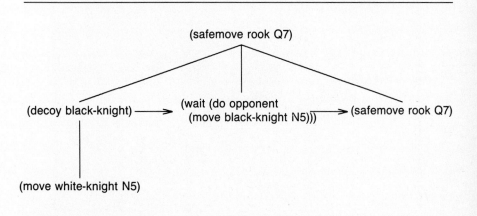

Figure 9.39 Task network for chess problem

between sets of "armies," which attack from one country to an adjacent country. Each player has a stock of armies (small plastic or wooden markers). Other equipment required are five dice, and a set of "Risk cards." There are 44 of these, one for each of the 42 countries, plus two jokers. Each joker has a picture of a soldier, a horseman, and a cannon. Each of the 42 regular cards has one of these symbols, in addition to the picture of a country. The symbols are important in making up "sets" of cards.

Initially the 42 regular cards are shuffled, and dealt out to the players. Each player gets to put an army on each country whose card he is dealt. Then the cards are all shuffled together again for a later draw, and play commences. Play consists of a series of moves, in which each player gets to attack in turn. During a move, a player draws a certain number of armies, and uses them to attack other players; the role played by the other players is almost completely passive.

Throughout the game, however, players can make alliances, usually guarantees not to attack each other for one or two moves. These arrangements are informal, and may be broken (at the risk of ruining one's reputation for reliability). Bargaining over alliances gives players something to do during someone else's move.

Figure 9.40 The Risk board

The number of armies drawn on each move depends on several things. As a player you get a basic allowance of max(3, $n/3$) armies if you occupy n countries at the beginning of your turn. In addition, you get extra armies if you own all the countries in a continent. The continent of Australia is worth two such extra armies; Asia, 7; Europe, 5; North America, 5; South America, 2; and Africa, 3. A continent is worth more the larger and harder to defend it is. Players do not usually succeed in keeping the big continents long enough to collect on them.

The most important source of armies is sets of cards. On every turn, if you take a country, you get to draw a card from the pile. A *set* of cards is defined as three cards with the same symbol (soldier, horseman, cannon), or three cards with three different symbols. A joker and any two cards make a set. You may turn in a set at the beginning of your turn; if you have five cards, you are obliged to turn one in. You get two armies for each country you own that appears on a card in the set; these two must be placed on that country. More important, you get a lump of armies you can put down on any of your countries. The size of these lumps grows throughout the game. The first set is worth 4 armies, the second 6, the third 8, then 10, 12, 15, 20, and from then up by fives.

There are two sources of cards: the one you get after every turn for taking a country in that turn; and the cards belonging to players you wipe out. If these cards form a set, you can immediately, in mid-turn, cash them in for more armies, and keep attacking.

The fact that the number of armies awarded for a set of cards gets very large makes the game somewhat trivial after a while. By the time the cash value of a set of cards gets to forty or fifty, it is usually possible to wipe a player out, then use that player's cards to get an even bigger pile, and wipe someone else out, and so forth. This phenomenon tends to make players take chances as soon as possible, making the game exciting, but ensures its inferiority to chess as an intellectual pastime.

So much for the overall course of the game. The tactical phase of Risk involves a player plunking down armies on already-occupied countries, and attacking new ones. Here is how this works: A player attacks from one country A into a neighboring country D (occupied by a different player) by rolling dice. You can roll one die if you have two armies in A; two dice if you have three; and three dice if you have four or more. (You cannot attack at all if you have only one.) The number of dice the defender can roll is also based upon possession of armies; one die for one army, two for more than one. The outcome of the battle depends upon the following algorithm: The highest attacking die is compared with the highest defending die; if each player rolled more than one die, then the next highest are also compared. The defender wins ties. So, if the attacker rolls 6-5-2, and the defender rolls 5-5, then the attacker wins the 6-5 battle, and the defender wins the 5-5 battle. The loser must remove one army (so each player would lose one army in this example). After each battle, it is up to the attacker to keep rolling or break it off.

If you succeed in wiping out all the armies in country D, then you must move some of your armies from A to D. You must move as many armies as you rolled dice, but you may move as many as you like, provided you leave A occupied. Quite often, you will move all but one army into D, and continue attacking the next country from there.

When you are done attacking, two further events occur. First, you get a "free move," moving as many armies as you like across one border between countries you occupy (but leaving at least one behind). Second, if you took any countries at all, you draw one card.

The smallest unit of Risk planning is the attempt to attack a specified group of countries, starting from currently occupied territory. Sometimes you just want to attack as far as you can, but usually you have a definite goal in mind, such as taking possession of a complete continent. You pick such a goal based on your estimate of how likely you are to achieve it, and the penalties for trying and failing compared to not trying. (For example if you don't wipe out a weak player, and someone else does, you will be in bad trouble.)

Given an objective, the player will often plan a *Risk tour* for achieving it. A Risk tour is a plan to move a mass of armies through a specific sequence of enemy-held countries. One constraint on the choice of tour is that at the end the surviving armies be located near the border of the attacker's territory, for later attack or defense. A tour sometimes involves two or more country-attack sequences, or even a "split," where because of the connectivity of the enemy holdings, the mass of armies must be divided, each submass being sent along a different route.

Figure 9.41 shows a plan for taking Australia (starting in Eastern Australia). This plan is generated by a plan generator, the *Risk tour generator* to be exact, that produces a plan for taking a set of countries that attempts to satisfy two constraints:

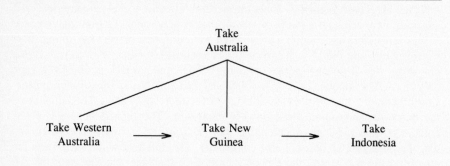

Figure 9.41 Plan for taking Australia

- The path taken must be legal.
- It should leave armies in border areas, where they can attack or defend against other players' armies more easily.

Each subtask may be further reduced to dice throws, but not in so tidy a way. Obviously, you do not know how many throws will be necessary to take New Guinea. You don't care exactly how many are necessary, so long as the number of armies left is sufficient to carry out the rest of the plan. We will label the first step of the plan with a statement to the effect that "at least nine armies must be left after this step." (The precise number of armies needed depends on the number of defenders in each country.) This is an example of a protection. So the representation of the plan above must include this information:

Number	Step	Protect
1:	Take Eastern Australia	Have nine armies left
2:	Take New Guinea	Have five armies left
3:	Take Indonesia	

If a protection violation occurs, then the plan has failed, and the Risk player must replan. The plan is made only when there are sufficient resources to carry it out, so a protection violation is a fairly rare event, due to unlucky dice.

Risk tours occur as plans for long-range goals like these:

- Take one country to earn a card.
- Take and hold a continent.
- Take a continent away from another player.
- Wipe out another player.

As in chess, tasks like these come and go as the game progresses, and there must be a task noticer to find them. Tasks must have different priorities. Eventually, holding card combinations becomes more important than anything else, so getting at least one card per turn is vital. On every turn, a player must take at least one country to get any cards, so this will be a recurring high-priority goal. On the other hand, it is usually not difficult to take at least one country. In fact, this goal will be attained by almost any series of actions, in particular, by a Risk tour. On a given turn, a player must plan a series of actions that will probably achieve as many of the high-priority goals as possible.

For example, suppose a player has three new armies to plunk down, and currently holds South America. Opponents control North America and Africa, or threaten to. The player's goals include

g1) Hold South America
g2) Take part of North America
g3) Take part of Africa
g4) Take at least one country

One possible plan, summarized informally in English, would be

> Make an alliance with the player holding North America (e.g., agree not to attack each other for two turns). Then put all three armies on Brazil, and take North Africa. Then move survivors back to Brazil, and take your card.

This plan, if it works, will satisfy goals g1, g3, and g4. It will not satisfy g2. Goal g2 will have to await another opportunity, or go unfulfilled.

Because the machine is noticing when tasks are appropriate, instead of being fed one task at a time by a human, it can easily dream up more tasks than can actually be accomplished. Hence the paradigm of producing independent plans for each task, then coordinating, may produce a hopelessly ambitious swarm of plans, which simply cannot be coordinated. There are two ways to cope with this situation:

1. You can postpone or forgo lower-priority tasks. In many cases, a task becomes impossible if forgone too long, and is said to have *failed*. This is the inevitable fate of many tasks.
2. More pleasantly, you can often *edit* a plan for one task so that is achieves another as well. For example, suppose the goal noticer creates a task "Spoil continent" for every whole continent gained by any other player. The plan generator for such a task would create a plan to march from the nearest fortified country of yours to the continent in question. This plan might well conflict with a higher-priority plan for capturing a neighboring continent. But often this plan can be edited, by inserting a sidetrip into it, which accomplishes the same damage.

As we said at the beginning of the chapter, each task will have a *plan generator*, a special-purpose program for proposing plans to achieve that one goal in the current situation. In the Risk domain, plan generators usually call the tour finder. Plan generators often find more than one possible plan. This raises once again the crucial problem of *plan selection*. Obviously, it speaks in favor of a plan that it can be easily edited to accomplish other high-priority tasks, or that it does not conflict with them at all.

These considerations suggest the following sort of planning algorithm: Produce some candidate plans for the hardest, highest-priority task. Then, for each remaining task in order of decreasing priority, look for plan edits that will achieve it. If you don't find one, call the plan generator for the task, and resolve conflicts between it and the candidate plans by editing. (See Exercise 9.31.)

9.6 References and Further Reading

Historically, the earliest planners were of the Strips variety, in that they searched through a space of situations, rather than plans. See [Ernst69] for this earlier "problem solving" tradition, from which Strips sprang. The treatment of [Nilsson80] covers some of the same material as this chapter, in a quite different way. It describes a Noah-style planner as an outgrowth of a Strips-style planner, which is historically accurate. The switch occurred in the mid 1970s with the work of [Sacerdoti75] and [Sussman75]. A lot of the current terminology stems from this period, such as *creative destruction* (Sacerdoti) and *protection violation* (Sussman). The planner we presented is closest to that of [Tate77].

Subsequent work has adopted the planning space view; see [McDermott78, Charniak83b, Miller83]. An interactive planner that closely resembles the planners we talk about here is presented in [Wilkins84].

See [Allen83] for a problem solver based on constraints applied to time maps. Stefik [Stefik80] expands on the idea of constraints, generating along with the plan a set of constraints on the uninstantiated objects in it. When necessary, domain-dependent methods were used to find objects satisfying the constraints. The notion of *policies* is defined in [McDermott78]. For the definitive blocks world program see [Fahlman74].

Consult [Raiffa68] for a more detailed explanation of decision theory. As we noted, little has been done on combining decision theory and planning. For an exception see the proposal of [Feldman77].

As yet there are few accessible works on robotics. See [Paul81] for a somewhat theoretical description of kinematics, dynamics, and programming. For more information on particular topics the reader might look at [Taylor79] (on straight line motion), [Mason81] (on guarded moves), and [Summers82, Paul77, Finkel75] (on robot control languages). Our discussion of route finding is a composite of [Thompson77, Udupa77, Lozano-Perez81] and [Brooks82].

Exercises

9.1 Finish the example of Figure 9.20. Show that after the reduction-assumption violation is taken care of, the resulting plan has a potential protection violation. Explain how it would be handled.

9.2 All of the examples we examined in Section 9.3.1 that if a nonprimitive task had an effect p, then some one subtask was responsible. (For example, (achieve (on a b)) has (on a b) as an effect, and this is due to the action of the subtask (move a b).)

a) Show that, given this assumption, it is unnecessary and even misguided to find cases where a nonprimitive task causes a protection violation.

b) Give example of tasks that do *not* have this property.

9.3 The robot workspace shown in Figure 9.42 features an arm that can reach down, grasp an object, and carry it someplace. More precisely, there are three actions:

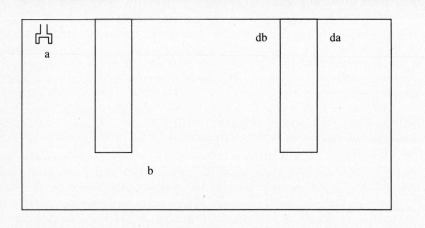

Figure 9.42 Robot errand problem

(**grasp** *object*) succeeds if hand is over object and is empty.
(**ungrasp**) always succeeds, and causes anything in hand to be deposited on floor.
(**move** *loc*) where loc is reachable via a straight-line motion without colliding with anything.

a) Show separate plans (*not* plan schemas) for the actions

(achieve (at a da))
(achieve (at b db))

starting in the state shown in the diagram. Be sure to describe any protections and other assumptions that pop up. You do not have to sketch the plan generator in any great detail, but you may find it necessary to say something about it in order to be specific about assumptions.

b) Explain how the planner of Section 9.3.1 would put these two plans together if required to carry out both actions. (Note that we assumed all actions were instantaneous in Section 9.3.1.)

c) Explain why the planner cannot find a plan like this:

Grasp a; Move south; Move east to near b: Ungrasp;
Grasp b; Move northeast to db; Ungrasp; Move southwest to near a;
Grasp a; Move east; Move north to da; Ungrasp;

(Note: This format is too sketchy as an answer to Question 1.)

d) Suggest a planning algorithm that is able to splice in "side trips" this way. What further annotations will plans need for this algorithm to work?

9.4   Suppose we gave the planner of Section 9.3.1 the conjunctive subgoal:

> (and (achieve (own robot hammer))
>   (achieve (own robot nails)))

To achieve owning either of these things there is a plan consisting of three substeps, achieving (at robot store), buying the object, and achieving (at robot home). Naturally the state achieved by the first step is protected until the start of the second step. We will assume that buying something is a primitive action, and that achieving at someplace can be done by a (no-op) if the planner is already there, or by the primitive action ptrans (Chapter 6) otherwise. Will the planner necessarily produce a plan that avoids going to the store twice? Explain your answer.

9.5   Suppose that in projecting a task the planner of Section 9.3.1 discovers that *two* predecessor tasks assert a state that the projection depends on. It could then either set up two projection-assumption intervals, or just one. Explain why choosing one at random would suffice (that is, would never cause trouble later).

9.6   Prove that the operator-difference tree produced by Strips as described in Section 9.3.4 will always be finite.

9.7   Show that the expected utility formula discussed in Section 9.3.6 makes sense. Assume that a decision maker is confronted with a long sequence of identical decisions (same probabilities and utilities each time), and show that the average utility is as predicted.

9.8   In the problem diagrammed in Figure 9.28, how high would the probability $P(y \mid e)$ have to be before performing the diagnostic test would be worthwhile? Recall that as presented this probability is 0.9.

9.9   In Chapter 7, we talked about finding routes through cities. In Section 9.5.1.3, we talked about finding routes through cluttered work areas. How can the two algorithms be combined? Is there a more general algorithm that subsumes both of them?

9.10 If you ever had to fix a plumbing leak, you probably had to put your arm in some strange positions in order to get your hand to where you needed it. Show that a arm with six degrees of freedom is not, in general, enough to ensure that your hand will get to the desired spot in the desired orientation. Why does this not contradict what we said in the text about the need for six degrees of freedom?

9.11 From the axiom schema of Figure 9.13 and the assertion of Figure 9.43, show that Jack actually goes to hell.

9.12 Implement the basic blocks-world planner described in Section 9.2. You will require a representation of the task network. You can use an associative-analog data structure, where task links are represented as

```
(event e33
  (do jack
    (act-so-that
      (λ (a m e)
        (exists (h)
          (and (= m e)
               (event e (do a (ptrans a hell)))
               (vehicle e h)
               (is h handbasket)) )))))
```

Figure 9.43 What Jack did

pointers; or if you have access to a good deductive retriever, you can use assertions about tasks in a database.

The planner must distinguish between "ready" and "blocked" tasks. A task is *blocked* if some predecessor is not finished; otherwise, it is *ready*. For now, plan only the ready tasks. The output of this simple planner will be a task network such that every ready task is primitive.

In doing this exercise, you will have to class actions into three groups:

1. Primitives: which can be executed without further ado (by Lisp functions outside the planner; see Exercise 9.13).
2. Problems: which need reduction by looking in a "plan library" (that is, doing a deduction of (to-do *task problem* ?way)).
3. Macro-actions: such as (plan . . .), that is, complex actions built up out of simpler ones. Each macro-action must have a special handler inside the planner that knows how to set up the required subtasks, using the steps and order fields of a plan schema. (We will neglect the protect fields until Exercise 9.14.)

The resulting planner is slightly more general than that of Figure 9.9:

```
Loop: While some task is ready
        Pick a ready task.
        Case on task type:
            Primitive: Do it.
            Problematic: Find a way to-do it, and
                            reduce it to a single subtask.
            Macro: Reduce it to zero or more subtasks
                    in a special way.
Endloop:
```

There may be more than one plan generated for a problematic task. For instance, suppose we gave the planner the problem to (achieve (on d c)) in Figure 9.4. Since this is already true, we will get two answers back from the plan library, (no-op) and a complicated plan. Make sure that your planner chooses (no-op) over any other action.

9.13 Supply the planner with an execution module. Implement primitive actions by Lisp functions that print out English instructions to a human agent. After each action is executed, its successors becomes "ready," and are reduced to primitives in their turn. If a task has no successors, then we must check to see if its supertask is now finished. If the supertask is a **plan**, it will be finished, and its successors will become ready, when all its subtasks are finished.

9.14 The planner implemented in Exercises 9.12 and 9.13 makes no use of the **protect** notes in plan schemas. Suppose that in the midst of executing the plan for getting **a** on **b**, some mischievous robot comes along and puts **c** back on **a** just before the move. Then presumably some arm malfunction will occur, and the plan will fail. (The mischievous robot may be the machine itself if it has other plans interfering with this one.) It would be nice to anticipate and avoid the problem (Section 9.3.1), but we should at least be able to detect when it occurs.

Change your representation of task networks so that they record protected states, and the time intervals over which the protections last. Change the **plan** macro-action handler so that it sets up these records. Then the execution module should inquire after every action about the status of each protected state. If a protection violation is detected, then the plan containing the protection should be marked as "failing." (Section 9.4.) See Exercise 9.24.

Because your planner has no senses of its own, it must inquire about a protected state by asking a human.

9.15 Add the macro-action **repeat-until** to your problem solver. The action (**repeat-until** a p), as explained in Section 9.2, means to execute a until p becomes true. Hence a **repeat-until** task will have two subtasks, one to do a and one to test p. The situation here is a little different from the one we presuppose in most of the examples in this chapter. Usually we assume that if all the subtasks are done, the supertask is done. Here, if the p-test task finds that p is true, then the a task must be *abandoned*. If the a task finishes, a new one must be started.

To cause these events to happen, you must augment your task representation with a *finish function*, which tells the problem solver what to do when the task finishes. The p-test finish function must abandon the a task, while the a finish function must create a new subtask. These finish functions are attached to the subtask by the special-purpose handler for tasks with macro-action (**repeat-until** a p).

9.16 The purpose of this and the following exercises is to build a planner as described in Section 9.3.1. We will start with a nonbacktracking version (like Noah), and work up to something more like Nonlin. (See Exercise 9.20.) The first step is to write some utilities for searching hierarchical time maps, which is what task networks are.

a) Write functions

first-ends-before-second-begins
first-ends-before-second-ends
first-begins-before-second-ends
first-begins-before-second-begins

for testing relationships between tasks. Each takes two task arguments, and tests whether the indicated relationship holds. For example, (first-ends-before-second-begins *t1* *t2*) is true if there is a
chain of one or more successor links from a supertask of *t1* to a
supertask of *t2*, counting *t1* and *t2* as supertasks of themselves.

b) Write functions (im-preds *t*) and (potential-im-preds *t*) for finding
tasks that definitely come immediately before *t*, or might come
immediately before *t*, respectively. A "potential predecessor" of *t*
is a task that either is an immediate predecessor, or is not ordered at
all with respect to *t*.

9.17 Design the module that constructs, for all tasks *T*, the databases *Pre(T)*
and *Post(T)* describing the world just before and just after task *T*. We
don't actually need to build a new database. Instead, we introduce the
predicate (tbef *task state adders*), true if *state* is true immediately before
task, just as we let (taft *task state adders*) be true if *state* is true just after
task. Note that in these exercises we have added a new *adders* argument
to tbef and taft. This is a list of the tasks that actually caused the state to
be true at this point. This list is necessary for setting up protection intervals.

The algorithm must sweep through the task network, processing the prede-
cessors of a task before the task itself. Hence when it is time to compute
Pre(T), *Post(P)* will have been computed for every immediate predecessor
P of *T*.

If predecessors never disagree, then *Pre(T)* will be the union of all the
Post(P)'s. That is, (tbef *T q a*) if (taft *P q a*) for some *P*. In this exercise, we will assume that predecessors never disagree. (But see Exercise
9.20.)

Once *Pre(T)* is computed, we can easily produce *Post(T)* for use in computing the effects of *T*'s successors. We just use statements of the form

(← (has-effect *T* . . .)
    (and q_1. . .q_n))

If q_i is true in *Pre(T)*, then the indicated effect (in the form of a taft statement) can be added to *Post(T)*. In determining if q_i is true in *Pre(T)*,
one of the following three cases applies:

1. There is an explicit statement of the form (tbef *T q_i a*) or (tbef *T*
(not q_i) *a*).

2. There is no **tbef** statement, and q_i is found in the database, which represents the initial situation. The proposition q_i is assumed to still be true.

3. Neither of the previous two cases applies, so q_i is assumed still false (the *closed-world assumption*).

Finally, if (**taft** q_i a), and no **has-effect** statement modifies the truth value of q_i, then we just carry it over and assert (**taft** T q_i a).

9.18 In practice, it is asking too much to insist on finding (**tbef** T (**not** q_i) a) in the database. Modify your code so that it uses the **contradicts** predicate, exemplified by these axioms:

(**contradicts** (**on** ?x ?y) (**on** ?x ?z) (**not** (= ?y ?z)))
 ; *?x cannot be on two things at once,*

(**contradicts** ?p (**not** ?p) (**always**))
 ; *?p always contradicts (not ?p).*

That is, (**contradicts** p q *cond*) states that p and q cannot be true at the same time, if *cond* is true. (**always**) should be asserted as an axiom.

9.19 The next step is to write the module that looks for conflicts among tasks. Whenever a plan schema is used, statements of the form (**protect** *state* ...) should be added to the global database. Every time a **protect** or **taft** statement is asserted, the program should look for a potential protection-interval violation, when all of the following are true:

- The database contains (**taft** T_0 p a).
- The database contains (**protect** q P_1 P_2).
- It can shown that (**and** (**contradicts** p q ?cond) ?cond).
- T_0 may fall in the interval $<P_1, P_2>$.

The program should then try to add *successor links* to ensure that T_0 comes before or after that interval, when the coast is clear.

9.20 In this exercise, we will start to deal with the perverse cases discussed in Section 9.3.1. The goal is to revise the task-effect projector so that it can react gracefully to surprises about the effects of tasks.

The first revision is that the **tbef** computer must deal with indeterminacies due to uncertainty about task order. For each potential predecessor P (see Exercise 9.16), the program may or may not have produced *Post(P)*. (It is reasonable to assume that known predecessors have already been run through this algorithm, but two tasks can be potential predecessors of each other.) The algorithm must simply ignore potential predecessors for which *Post(P)* is not available, and catch potential interactions with them later.

We must change the *Pre(T)* algorithm developed in Exercise 9.17 to handle the case where two predecessors of T disagree. In this case, the machine must assert (**tbef?** T q *adders deleters*). This assertion says that

q is either true or false just before T, being added by the tasks *adders* and deleted by the tasks *deleters*, whose order is unknown so far. We will also need an analogous taft?. Such indeterminacies will be unimportant if q is irrelevant to the effects of T. However, if it is decided that they are relevant, then some task ordering must be picked in order to eliminate the indeterminacy. Hence there are two steps: noting indeterminacies in *Pre(T)*, and deciding they are relevant. The basic algorithm for noting the status of q just before T is shown in Figure 9.44.

Once *Pre(T)* is computed, the machine must produce *Post(T)* just as in Exercise 9.17, using has-effect statements. The deductive retriever that tests the antecedents of has-effect rules must notice when the outcome

---

Collect five lists:
> definite yes: All immediate predecessor tasks such that
>> q is true after them.
> definite no: All immediate predecessors such that something
>> contradicting q is true after them.
> definite maybe: All immediate predecessors such that
>> (taft? *pred q . . .*) is true.
> potential yes: Potential immediate predecessors such that
>> q is true after them.
> potential no: Potential immediate predecessors such that
>> q is false after them.

(We can neglect potential maybes, since they will have predecessors that are the real source of indeterminacy.)

If the "definite-yes," "definite-no," and "definite-maybe"
> lists are all empty, then check whether q is true or false now.
>> If it is true, then add the pseudo-task now
>>> to the definite-yes list.
>> Else add now to the definite-no list.

If the definite-yes list is nonempty,
> and all the "no" and "maybe" lists are empty,
then q is definitely true before T, so assert (tbef T q *adders*),
> where the adders of q are the union of all the adders
> from taft assertions (plus [now] if q is true now).

Similarly, if the definite-no list is nonempty,
> and all the "yes" and "maybe" lists are empty,
then q is definitely false before T.

Otherwise, add a (tbef? T q *adders deleters*) assertion
> to the database. As before, the *adders* and *deleters* are
> obtained by collecting all of the adders and deleters from taft
> and taft? assertions.

Figure 9.44 Algorithm for determining *Pre(T)*

depends on an indeterminate state, and must propose orderings to set the truth value one way or the other. That is, if the outcome of a **has-effect** rule depends on an assertion (**tbef** *T q adders deleters*), then it must choose one of the adders or deleters, and set up an *assumption interval* between it and *T*.

If the task picked is an adder, then every deleter must be put outside the interval; if it is a deleter, then every adder must be put outside the interval. This will be accomplished in Exercise 9.21.

9.21 Implement the algorithm shown in Figure 9.22. There are two circumstances when possible assumption violations must be checked:

1. Whenever an assumption interval is set up, the planner must look for possible violators and deal with them.
2. Whenever a task is projected, the planner must look for assumption intervals this task may violate, and deal with the potential violations.

Extra credit: implement backtracking.

9.22 Write the module that merges tasks with similar actions. (Section 9.3.2.) This requires altering the plan-schema expander to handle the **objects** slot of a plan schema. The way to do this is to create some "anonymous" constants representing the objects, and associate with each of them (on their property lists, perhaps) their desired properties. Then to merge two tasks, their actions must "match" in the sense that they differ only in slots where one or both have anonymous constants. For instance, the two actions

    (**putbetween** a *anon1 anon2*)
    (**putbetween** a b *anon3*)

match, with *anon1* identified with b, and *anon2* and *anon3* identified with each other. For the match to be valid, all the properties of the anonymous objects involved must be consistent. In the example, b must have all the properties of *anon1*, and *anon2*'s and *anon3*'s properties must be consistent. (Note that this is what the matcher for the story comprehension system from Chapter 10 must do as well.)

Once the identification is made, one of the anonymous objects involved can be discarded. For instance, *anon1* can be replaced by b everywhere in the task network, and *anon3* can be replaced by *anon2*. (The list of properties for *anon2*'s must be augmented with the properties of *anon3*.)

9.23 The planner designed in Exercises 9.16 to 9.21 goes to incredible lengths to avoid protection violations. Explain why all of this effort hinges on the assumptions made about time at the beginning of Section 9.3. That is, for each assumption, explain how relaxing it could make possible a protection violation that wouldn't be caught by the methods we have discussed.

9.24 As pointed out in the last exercise, the planner designed in Exercise 9.16 to 9.21 is very sensitive to assumptions about time. As an alternative, design an execution-monitoring strategy that waits until a protection violation has occurred, and then attempts to reverse it. For example, one strategy is to redo the violated task. Consider how this strategy would work on the blocks-world example of Figure 9.16. If the problem solver did not notice the looming protection violation, and put a on b first, then it would detect a violation as soon as a was moved to the table. At that point, it could create a task to put a back on b. When would this task be allowed to run? What is the general rule for when a task can be redone?

9.25 Implement the algorithm for finding maximal match substitutions, defined in Section 9.3.4. (If you need a hint, we will supply an outline of essentially this algorithm in Chapter 11.)

9.26 GPS needs another algorithm for comparing two states, in order to build a discrimination tree and avoid working on the same state twice. Explain why it is different from the algorithm of Exercise 9.25. Design it.

9.27 Implement Strips. Can it be written so that it calls the GPS function written in Exercise 5.23?

9.28 Write a program to make plans for the game of tic-tac-toe. This game is guaranteed to be at least a draw for the player who moves first, so it should be possible to find some pretty good plans at the beginning of the game. What's involved if the problem is to make a plan starting from an arbitrary position?

9.29 Write a program to manage a Risk game (Section 9.5.2). It will not take part, but will just keep track of who owns what, whose turn it is to move, how many cards each player holds, etc. If the program is well designed, no other board should be necessary.

9.30 Write a program that finds a Risk tour, starting in a given country, that will take every country in a specified set *C*. The program should take a preferred set of "stopping points," and should try to return a tour that ends in one of them. You may assume any representation you like of the adjacency relationship for countries. *Hint*: This is a search problem, in which the states are *partial paths* through the map. A partial path has a good score if it doesn't bypass a country in the set *C*, and if it doesn't lead out of a preferred stopping point to a nonpreferred stopping point.

9.31 Write a program to produce the best composite plan for a set of Risk goals, by editing higher-priority plans to achieve lower-priority goals as side effects. One way to do this editing is to call a deductive retriever with the query (edit *existing-plan new-goal* ?newplan). Sketch some example rules that conclude this for the Risk world.

9.32 In Section 9.3.4 we described two Strips-style schemas for the operator **move**. Which one was missing? Describe it.

9.33 In Section 9.3.4 we differentiated between the "Filter" and "Precondition" of an operator. The latter is to be achieved if false, the former not. How was this distinction made in the hierarchical planners discussed earlier?

9.34 Explain in detail the derivation of the search space shown in Figure 9.25. You will need to introduce one more version of the **move** operator schema.

10

Language Comprehension

10.1 Story Comprehension as Abduction

Our discussion of language in Chapter 4 was in many respects incomplete. For one thing, we took the process only to the stage of translation into internal representation. Intuitively, much more seems to be going on when we hear a sentence, and even many questions about translating into internal representation were left unresolved. As we noted at the time, questions of noun-phrase reference or word-sense disambiguation can be handled only by more complicated processes — processes which involve our knowledge of the world around us. The discussion of what these might be was put off. It is now time to fulfill, as well as our knowledge permits us, the promises made at the time.

Our overall topic is understanding language, and "understanding" is a concept that is hard to define. It seems at first that whether one understands or not is a matter of whether one has a certain subjective experience, and it is hard to see how to get a computer to have such a thing. But we will assume that the experience is secondary and that the principal component of understanding is the *extraction of as many correct and useful inferences as possible* from an utterance or text. At present, it is hard to be rigorous about what "correct" and "useful" mean.

For example, consider the following simple story

Fred went to the supermarket. He found the milk on the shelf. He gave the checkout clerk some money and left.

Suppose we were asked why Fred gave the checkout clerk some money. A reasonable answer would be, "He was buying the milk." But note that the story never actually said this; we inferred it. In fact, this is just another example of

an *abductive inference*, because we are inferring the causal reasons behind
Fred's behavior, just as in Chapter 8 we were trying to find the causal reasons
for the signs and symptoms shown by a medical patient. In this chapter, we
will assume that understanding language is this kind of abductive process, a
search for the best overall explanation for the actions of characters in stories,
and speakers in conversations. (Our "stories" will rarely be more than three
sentences long, and will almost always be mundane reports of events, as in a
newspaper, rather than anything resembling literature.)

Although the ability to answer questions is good "behavioral" evidence
that an understander has made the proper abductive inferences, the ability to
make proper abductive inferences is not sufficient in itself to answer questions.
One must also be able, at the very least, to phrase the answer in English. In addition, question answering requires figuring out what answer is appropriate. For
instance, the question "Why did Fred give the clerk money?" has many possible correct answers: "The clerk asked for the money," "Fred was paying for
the milk," "He wanted to take the milk home," "He wanted the milk," etc.
Which one is appropriate depends in large part on the context of the question
(see [Lehnert78]). Thus our ability to answer the questions depends on an abductive ability to have the right information at hand, and a question-answering
ability to select from that information a subset which appropriately answers the
question. In this chapter we will look only at the first of these.

This is our third look at abduction. In Chapter 3 we studied vision, which
may be thought of as the inference of a scene from the image it produced. In
Chapter 8 we studied medical diagnosis, the inference of a disease from the
symptoms it produces. Here the range of explanatory hypotheses is in principle
much broader, because a natural-language input could be about almost anything.
To narrow our focus, we will assume that an abductive hypothesis is primarily
an instance of a *schema* of the sort we discussed in Chapter 7. In the story
above, the schema might be one about shopping at the supermarket. To narrow
the focus even further, we will restrict consideration to *plan schemas* (Chapter
9). Selecting and instantiating such a schema is equivalent to an abductive inference about the goals and plans of the planner in question. For instance, to
understand this story,

> Fred needed money for heroin desperately. He bought a gun.

the reader must infer that Fred is planning an armed robbery. Our theory proposes that understanding this text is a matter of instantiating the "armed robbery" plan schema. We will use the term *motivation analysis* for this kind of
abduction.

Even within this framework, other sorts of abductive inference will be
necessary. Consider these two stories:

> Sally needed some money. She went to ask her mother for some.

> Sally needed some money. She wrote a proposal to the National Science
> Foundation.

In the first example the reader infers that Sally is a child asking for a small amount of money; in the second, that she is a researcher asking for a large amount. These assumptions are made because they explain why the plans involved ("ask mother" vs. "ask National Science Foundation") make sense. We will use the term *auxiliary assumption* for an inference that is required for a schema to be applicable to a story.

A background question for this chapter is whether there is a "unified theory" of abduction that would link vision, medical diagnosis, and language comprehension. We have no answer, but we do have an excuse for the apparent divergences. The problem that hits one first in medical diagnosis is that of hypothesis evaluation — deciding which disease the patient has. In story comprehension one rarely deals with anything less than obvious choices. On the other hand, story comprehension forces one to worry about a much broader range of abductive hypotheses. In our stories about Sally's asking for money, one must not only guess that money borrowing is taking place, but also who is playing which role in the schema, and how old Sally is. However, eventually both story comprehension and medical diagnosis will have to consider each other's problems, and we may yet see a convergence of methods.

10.2 Determining Motivation

10.2.1 Motivation Analysis = Plan Synthesis in Reverse

A major idea of this chapter is that we recognize the intentions of others by attributing to them the same planning abilities that we have. When we see another person doing something, we ask "Given this action, what task could it be in the service of?" Thus determining motivation can be thought of as the inverse of the planning problem, "Given a task, what action is appropriate to carry it out?" Planners have tasks they wish to perform, and their actions are typically in the service of these tasks. Now, however, rather than knowing a high-level task, and having to reduce it to low-level actions that can be performed directly, we see or hear the low-level actions (turning the faucet), and we wish to infer the high-level goals (taking a bath).

There are two basic ways to go from an observed action A to a higher-level explanatory goal G. The first is for A to be a way of doing G. For instance, A could be "commit armed robbery," and G could be "get some money." The second is for A to be a step in doing G. For instance, A could be "buy a gun," and G could be "commit armed robbery." Note that the A of the first example is the same as the G of the second; the same fact can serve as the item to be explained or as the explanation. Indeed, we expect this to happen. Explanation is an iterative process. Once an explanation is found for the input, the machine must turn around and find a deeper explanation for the explanation. So it might well proceed from an observation of buying a gun to an inference that the buyer is carrying out an armed robbery, to an inference that he is trying to get some money. The process stops when no deeper explanation can be found.

Let us switch to a less violent example, the plan for lighting a cigarette, shown in Figure 10.1. There are many problems with this formalization. For one thing, actions such as **set-fire-to** must be taken with a grain of salt. It may well be the case that this will be broken down into more primitive actions, or, perhaps, expressed as achieving the state of "on fire." Also, our representation is neutral between using a match and, say, a blow torch. To some degree this is good, because in the absence of the former, a clever (and desperate) person might resort to the latter. Nevertheless, a really good analysis would note that most any flammable object could be used, but matches are the method of choice. However, we will ignore such defects in our formalization.

When presented with the task of smoking a cigarette, a problem solver such as those discussed in Chapter 9 would proceed to solve the problem by re-trieving such plan schemas, and putting them together. As discussed in Chapter 9, the planner (i.e., the smoker) will have plan choices along the way, such as how to light up. In Chapter 9, our focus was on how to make those choices. Fortunately, that has now become someone else's problem; our problem is to infer which choices were made. We can think of the set of all plan selections as giving rise to a goal tree of the sort we examined in Chapter 5. (See Figure 10.2.) In terms of the constructs we developed in Chapter 9, the "and nodes" correspond to plans, broken down into steps all of which must be executed. When such a plan is executed, we will typically find the following pattern:

```
[plan-for: cigarette-lighting

    objects: fire (inst fire flammable-object)      ; The fire source
                                                    ; should be flammable.
             cig (inst cig cigarette)               ; The thing to be lit
                                                    ; is a cigarette.
    steps: set-fire-task (set-fire-to fire)         ; The substeps
                                                    ; involved include
           touch-task (touch fire cig)              ; lighting the fire,
                                                    ; touching it to the
           inhale-task (inhale-through cig)         ; cigarette, and
                                                    ; inhaling.
    timing: (seq set-fire-task touch-task)          ; First we light the
                                                    ; fire, then we touch
            (overlap touch-task inhale-task)]       ; it to the cigarette,
                                                    ; while inhaling.
```

Figure 10.1 A plan schema for lighting a cigarette

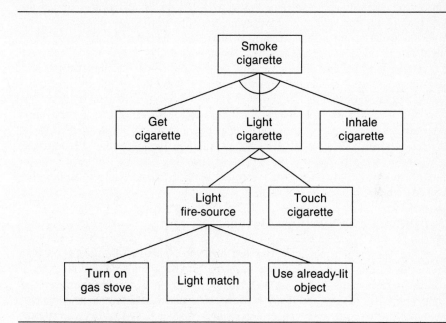

Figure 10.2 Goal tree for smoking a cigarette

    (and (event *s A*)   *; A is a step*
         (event *p G*)   *; G is a plan*
         (sub-event *s p*))   *; A is part of G*

Since this pattern is so useful, we will abbreviate it as (plan-step *G A*); that is, the planner's executing *G* explains the execution of *A*.

The other pattern of explanation corresponds to the "or nodes" of Figure 10.2. Below each such node is a set of alternative ways of doing the action at that node. Each corresponds to a different to-do statement, such as:

    (← (to-do ?tsk (set-fire-to ?fire-source)   *; One way to set fire to*
                   (match-light ?fire-source));   *something is to use the*
                                                   ; plan for lighting a match
       (inst ?fire-source match))   *; if the thing is a match.*

While a planner would start at the top of the goal tree and work its way down, a motivation analyzer would do just the opposite: it would start at the bottom (from an observable action) and work its way up the tree. So if it sees a person touching a cigarette to the flame on a gas stove, it should infer that the person is trying to light the cigarette. Similarly, if it knows that a person is trying to light a cigarette, the person presumably intends to smoke it. At each step it is looking for a goal action *G* such that the given action *A* is either one way of accomplishing *G* (using a match is one way of getting fire) or is a step of the plan for doing *G* (touching the cigarette to the fire is a plan-step of lighting it). These two possibilities correspond respectively to the **or** and **and** nodes of the goal tree. Thus one step at a time it works its way up the plan-schema tree, until it gets to an action that it believes is often done for its own sake (smoking a cigarette), or one that has already been mentioned in the story. We will assume that this is done for each line of a story as the line comes in, and that the process finishes before subsequent lines are read. More formally, the process is that shown in Figure 10.3.

At this point, we have not been careful about describing how the abduction algorithm makes use of the formal plan representation. You may also be wondering about exactly what auxiliary assumptions the algorithm is required or permitted to make. We will fill in those gaps (for readers who worry about them) in Section 10.4. However, there are several crucial issues to discuss before descending to that level of detail.

10.2.2 Deciding Between Motivations

The motivation analyzer doesn't have the planner's problem of plan choice, but it does have the inverse problem, choosing among alternative explanations for an action, that is, in the terms of Figure 10.3, among alternative *G*s for a given *A*. (There are many reasons why someone might light a match.) Fortunately, there are some general rules that will account for many situations. The simplest is to *choose motivations that have been postulated for independent reasons*. This is a specific instance of the general rule known as *Occam's Razor*, which we encountered in our discussion of medical diagnosis in Chapter 8. If the machine already believes that Jack wants to light a cigarette, it should have little trouble deciding why Jack lit a match. The algorithm of Figure 10.3 is already biased in favor of Occam's Razor in that finding a previously postulated action is one way in which the loop is terminated. The other way is finding

---

A ← action mentioned by story

Loop: If A has already been mentioned, or
     if it is done for its own sake, exit loop.

     Find an action G such that either
          (to-do ?tsk G A) or
          (plan-step G A)
     making whatever auxiliary assumptions are necessary.

     If there is no such G, exit loop.
     Assert G.
     A ← G
Endloop:

Figure 10.3 Motivation recognition algorithm — version 1

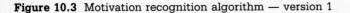

an action which is done for its own sake (such as eating). Given a choice among explanations of an action, the machine should prefer one that will cause the algorithm to halt on the next iteration, that is, an explanation that is already postulated or done for its own sake.

A slightly more complicated, yet still very general, rule would be *choose the possibility which uses the most specific characteristics of the input.* So if we see Fran picking up a newspaper, we might assume that she wants to read it, or we might assume that she wants to swat a fly. The option of reading uses the fact that newspapers are one form of reading material, while the option of swatting a fly only makes use of the fact that newspapers are physical objects, suggesting that the former is a better guess.

This last example could also be explained by a rule like *if we have several possibilities, and one requires the creation of a new object and the others do not, then restrict consideration to the ones which do not (unless overruled by the previous rule).* The "swatting" explanation assumes the existence of a fly, and if we do not know of one, then the "reading" explanation would be the better guess. (But see Exercise 10.2.) Adding these rules to our algorithm of the previous section gives us the revised version shown in Figure 10.4.

Unfortunately, this version of the algorithm is too optimistic about the grounds for choosing among explanations. Often we can reduce an action to an already postulated one, but only after going through many layers of intermediate

---

A ← action mentioned by story

Loop: If A has already been mentioned, or
     if it is done for its own sake, exit loop.

Find an action G such that either
    (to-do ?tsk G A) or
    (plan-step G A)
making whatever auxiliary assumptions are necessary.

If there is no such G, exit loop.

If we find more than one G, pick the one which
satisfies the most important constraint (in order):
  i) The G which already exists
  ii) The G which is done for its own sake
  iii) The G which makes most specific
     use of the objects in A.
  iv) The G which requires the fewest
     new objects

Assert G
A ← G
Endloop:

Figure 10.4 Motivation recognition algorithm - version 2

actions where we have no basis for making a choice. To take a new example, suppose we are told that Jack wants to commit suicide. If we then see him buying some rope, we know why. But look at this from the point of view of reconstructing the plan-schema tree. When the algorithm looks at why a person might get a rope, it will find many possibilities, from jumping rope, to hanging out the laundry, to hanging another person. At this point none of the possibilities looks any better than any of the others. To the human reader, "hanging a person" looks better, but remember that the input was not this, but rather "commit suicide." Our current algorithm of "find a goal task, assume it, repeat" will have no knowledge that hanging is any more plausible than the other uses of rope. Suppose, however, that we modify our algorithm so that it goes an extra step, and looks to see why a person might hang out the laundry, etc. A person might hang out the laundry in order to dry clothes. By doing this successively for several levels of postulated actions, eventually it will find "commit suicide" (through "hanging") and the rule of Occam's Razor will apply. As Figure 10.5 shows, we have a search on our hands, through the space of alternative goals that would explain the action "get rope." (In order to retain the convention that high-level actions are placed above lower-level ones, we have had to reverse our convention for depicting search spaces; here the initial state is at the bottom.)

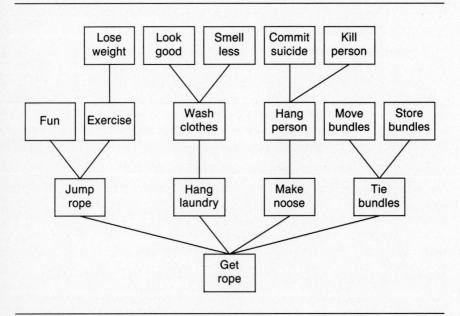

Figure 10.5 Reasons for getting a rope

Given that we have the situation shown in Figure 10.5, there are two problems to be addressed, one comparatively minor, the other very important. The minor one has to do with what would happen if we reversed the lines of our story. That is, suppose we had

Jack got a rope. He wanted to commit suicide.

We have been assuming that our abduction process goes to work when the line comes in, and finishes before further lines are read. Thus when it starts looking for reasons for getting a rope, it will not find anything that can be confirmed. What should it do in such cases? One option is to do nothing, and just go on to the next line. This is plausible, but our algorithm, when applied to the second line of the story, will not connect it up with the first line. The problem is that the algorithm "looks up" the tree, but not "down." The program would look for a reason why Jack wanted to commit suicide.

One way to solve this problem is to process the first line of the story differently. Rather than simply giving up when it finds nothing, the algorithm could instead remember what possibilities were considered. Thus when confronted with the first line of the story, "Jack got a rope," it would remember the various higher-level goals considered but, rather than accepting these things as reasons why Jack did it, it would mark them as "potential" reasons. Then when it got "He wanted to commit suicide," it should already be marked as a "potential reason" for getting the rope and so the algorithm would convert it to a "real" reason and remove the alternatives.

But these difficulties are minor compared to the real problems involved in multiple explanations. If each action has many possible explanations, and each of these, in turn, has many explanations, then the space of explanations to be searched will be quite large, and looking for an already established goal will be very expensive. There is currently debate in AI circles about how large this space actually is, and if it is large, whether there are any ways to effectively prune the search space in order to make the search more efficient.

One way to enhance efficiency might be to reverse the search order, and go from proposed explanations down to facts to be explained. However, as Figure 10.6 suggests, the search from high level to low is likely to be as bushy as from low to high.

The underlying notation in these two figures is our predicate-calculus plan schemas, but it is no accident that we have switched to an associative-network notation in which many details are suppressed. This notation emphasizes that a short path of **to-do** and **plan-step** links between two nodes is likely to correspond to an explanation of one in terms of the other. Finding such a path is a memory-search problem. One trick for speeding up such a search is to run it from both nodes simultaneously. One process searches out from "commit suicide," while the other is searching out from "get rope." These processes are following pointers, as in Chapter 7, but with a difference. Each time one touches a node, it marks the node in some way. When one of the processes comes upon a node marked by the other, a complete path has been found. (It can be assembled by having each mark contain a pointer back toward the node

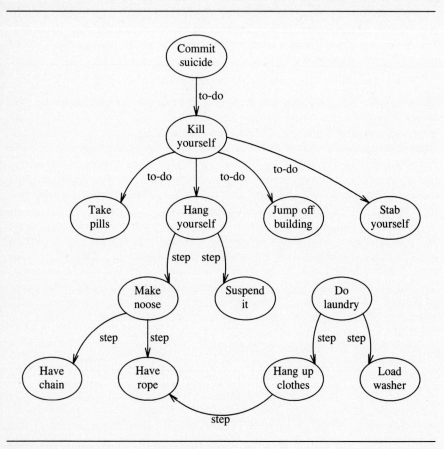

Figure 10.6 Ways of committing suicide

its process came from. These pointers can be traced back to the node the process started with, rather like Hansel and Gretel.) This kind of algorithm is called *marker passing*, or (among psychologists) *spreading activation*.

We can think of marker passing as an efficient but dumb preprocessor that finds candidate explanation paths to be thought about more carefully by the abduction algorithm. It is efficient because it neglects all questions of getting variable bindings right, or of what auxiliary assumptions might be required. If the search space through a knowledge base is quite large, then this stupidity could be a great asset because it might make it possible to implement marker-passing algorithms on simple parallel hardware. One way to build this hardware is to have one processor per memory node, and have them pass markers by literally sending each other messages. Since each processor could send and receive messages independently of what other processors were doing, the time to find a path would depend only on the length of the path. The number of paths would be irrelevant. Needless to say, many researchers are pursuing hardware designs of this type with great energy. (There are many problems with getting the scheme to work. One is to figure out how to make the processors cheap enough so that the parallel computer could contain a million of them. Another is how to manage all the required connections among them.) Even if parallel hardware is unavailable, the efficiency of marker passing may make it worthwhile, especially if the database to be searched is big but not enormous.

We can then imagine modifying the algorithm of Figure 10.4 to take marker passing into account. Whenever the algorithm finds more than one possible explanation it will look to see if any of the explanations is on a marked path to nodes marked earlier in the story. If this path "makes sense" then that alternative will be selected as the explanation. So in the "suicide — rope" example "Getting a rope" would find many reasons, but only "Make a noose" would be on a path found by the marker passer.

While this is a nice solution to the problem, it must be stressed that marker passing has many problems which must be solved if it is to be used here. The most obvious problem with marker passing is that if there is no restriction on how markers propagate, the system will end up marking the entire memory because every concept is eventually reachable from every other one. The standard solution is to place limits on how far markers can propagate, and hope that the connections one wants will always be the close ones. But it takes a lot of faith to believe that this hope will always be fulfilled.

At first glance it might seem obvious what restrictions are necessary to achieve efficiency. Since all we are interested in are **to-do** and **plan-step** links, those might seem to be the only ones markers must propagate across. But suppose that in our story about poor Jack we had used the word "jump rope" instead of "rope." Then in order to find the connection the machine would have to mark from the jump rope node through an **isa** link to the rope node. But if we allow unrestricted marking up and down **isa** links, then the entire memory would be marked quickly. In many cases the connections found would be useless. For example, suppose **rope** and **suicide** are four nodes apart. If the next line of the story is, say, "Then Jack got a chair," how far would **chair** be from **rope**? It is not too hard to imagine that a marker passer would find a four-link connection between the two — intersecting at **man-made-object** perhaps — instead of what could be a slightly longer connection between **chair** and **hanging**.

Also note that we suggested passing markers from **rope** and **suicide** and looking for the intersection. If one uses a breadth-first search, and interleaves searching from the two nodes, one will always find the shortest path first. But this is not a realistic model in story comprehension. When the system sees **rope**, how can it know to look for connections between it and **suicide**, as opposed to it and **jack-33**, or any other node which would have appeared in the story? It can't. Thus it seems more reasonable to assume that the marker passer passes markers from each node as it is encountered in the story. If it intersects with markers which had been laid down previously, then there is a potential path. Note that this scheme still guarantees that the shortest path between two nodes is found first. Also, this marker passing regime raises new questions about how long markers persist in memory.

Once we view markers as persisting in memory, it is possible to use them to solve a problem which arose earlier. This is the problem of what to do when the subevent is mentioned first, as in

John got a rope. He wanted to commit suicide.

Previously we suggested that when "John got a rope" failed to find an explanation it would leave around "potential explanations" of which "commit suicide" would be one. But now rather than leaving around "potential explanations" it can leave around marks. Then we will recast the motivation analysis algorithm so that it simply asks the marker passer for paths it found, and looks to see if they are of the proper type. (Roughly speaking a proper path would consist of **to-do** and **plan-step** links, but as we noted earlier, it is slightly more complicated than this.) So looking at the "suicide" example again, when the algorithm marks from **suicide** it will find the marks left from **rope**. The resulting path will be returned, and the explanation processed. This version of the algorithm has the nice property, therefore, that it treats the two versions of the suicide example in a completely uniform way, rather than requiring special processing for one of them. The new algorithm is shown in Figure 10.7.

Note that this algorithm no longer does any fetching of **to-do** or **plan-step** statements from the database. This greatly simplifies it, but it means that the algorithm places great reliance on the marker passer working properly. As we have seen, there are reasons to question if marker passing can stand up to these demands. Finding answers to these questions is obviously important.

10.2.3 When to Stop

An important issue in abductive comprehension is what needs to be explained. Our plan-based algorithm is content to stop at a schema, like eating, that people "just do." Similarly, the sentence "It was raining" requires no explanation; it's not unusual for rain to fall. Hence states must be classed as "normal" or "nonnormal," and explanations must be sought only for the nonnormal ones.

Pass markers starting from the entities mentioned in A.

Loop: Look at each path returned from the marker passer.
    If it is a valid path to an action which has not
    already been explained, create the actions required
    by the path (along with the connecting subtask
    statements).
Endloop:

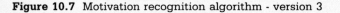

Figure 10.7 Motivation recognition algorithm - version 3

An extreme case of normality is a fact that is already known to the machine. Such a fact will require no explanation because it will have been explained already, when first acquired.

An intermediate case is a fact that is true by default. The sentence "Fred's bicycle had two wheels" requires no explanation, since bicycles have two wheels by default. It is true that the sentence sounds a little odd, but that's because the reader may want an explanation about why the speaker bothered to say it. (See Section 10.5.) The usual case is for a sentence to be explicit about *violated* defaults, as in "Fred's bicycle had only one wheel; the other had been stolen." Such violations do require explanation, here provided by the second clause.

We talked about defaults in Section 6.5.1. The main thing to remember about that discussion is that formalizing defaults requires *nonmonotonic* reasoning. What is believed true based on a default can be revised if new information comes in which upsets the default.

10.3 Generalizing the Model

So far we have restricted our abduction process to the information contained in the simple plan schemas used in Chapter 9. We have treated comprehension solely as the problem of selecting the proper schema. In this section we will sketch (but only sketch) how our algorithm might be extended to discover more complex hypotheses.

10.3.1 Abductive Projection

To keep our discussion focused, we have only considered abductive hypotheses about people's motivations. There is one other large class of hypotheses which does deserve mention — hypotheses about inanimate causality.

In Chapter 7 we looked at the projection problem — trying to determine the future state of a system based upon the current state and the causal relations involved. In story comprehension we are often faced with the inverse problem, determining a previous state and causal history given a resulting state. For example:

> Norma left some ice cubes in a bowl. Her mother was upset when she found that her antique earthen bowl was wet.

Here the problem is to deduce that the process of ice cubes melting was responsible for the wetness. While it is hard to tell from the artificially short examples we use, it is unlikely that in a more realistic setting a reader would have read the first line and started a projective simulation in order to determine the consequences of Norma's actions. Too many things like this get mentioned in stories to make such simulation feasible. Rather we read along and figure things out when some future event needs explanation. To take another example, if Joan drives to the store, it seems unwarranted to deduce the wear on the tires, the consumption of gas and oil, the motion of the pistons, etc. If she runs out of gas, we can figure out the cause later. This is not to say that we *never* use straightforward projection in the course of story comprehension. If an action is somewhat unusual we do seem to predict its consequences. For example "Jack put an ice cube on the rug" would probably lead us to think that at some later time the rug would be wet. But in the course of normal actions leading to normal states, it seems unlikely that we go to so much trouble.

We started with the example about ice cubes because it was one which we used in our discussion of projection in Section 7.4. There we had the following rules:

```
(if (and (inst ?x icecube)        ; If an ice cube ?x is
         (T ?s (outside ?x))      ; outside in ?x and
         (T ?s (> (ambtemp) 0)))  ; the temperature is above
    (occur ?s (melt ?x)))         ; 0, it will melt.

(if (and (inst ?x icecube)        ; If an ice cube ?x is
         (T ?s (on ?x ?y)))       ; on ?y in situation ?s
    (T (result ?s (melt ?x))      ; then in the resulting
       (wet ?y)))                 ; situation ?y is wet.
```

The behavior of a causal explanation program will be similar to the motivation analysis program already outlined. When the bowl is found to be wet, rules which lead to this conclusion will be investigated, just as plans which contain a certain action are investigated when that action is performed. In the case at land, the melt → wet rule will be found, and its preconditions (?x is an ice cube, and is on the bowl's surface) are found to be satisfied, so it is an obvious candidate. Assuming this path is investigated further, the system would then want to explain why the ice cube melted, in which case the first of the two rules just mentioned would do the job. Of course, there would be other rules which would explain wetness — the bowl was rained upon, put under a sprinkler, etc. In the general case we will have the same problem we saw in motivation analysis, where there were many possible explanations leading to a possibly large search. We would expect marker passing to be just as useful in managing it.

One particularly complex area of projection is understanding characters' emotions. At first glance it may be surprising that something so obviously human as emotion be linked to projection, which we use for inanimate causality. However, the connection is reasonably tight. While the *content* of a rule governing emotion has to do with peoples actions, the *logic* of the rule seems closer to standard cause and effect. If someone does something nice for you, you simply start to feel grateful. One does not *plan* to to feel angry, or *decide* to feel grateful.

Understanding emotion in stories has two parts, recognizing what emotions the characters experience, and using that knowledge to understand their further actions. We will concentrate on the first of these. Consider this story:

> Richard hadn't heard from his old roommate Paul for years. Paul had lent Richard money which was never paid back, but now Richard had no idea where to find his old friend. When a letter finally arrived from San Francisco, Richard was anxious to find out how Paul was.
>
> Unfortunately, the news was not good. Paul's wife Sara wanted a divorce. Not knowing who to turn to, Paul was hoping for a favor from the only lawyer he knew. Paul gave his home phone number in case Richard felt he could help.

One program which can handle such stories to a limited degree is the Boris system [Dyer83]. To give some idea of the complexities involved here, just consider understanding how Richard felt in receiving the letter. Most people report that Richard was "happy" to receive the letter. However, the theory of emotions initially used in BORIS predicted that if people do something which you like, then that will cause you to either like them, or feel grateful to them. This makes sense, but it cannot be the complete story since it does not work here. Richard was glad to get the letter, but its receipt did not make Richard grateful to Paul. This is important since if Richard goes on to help Paul, we do not want the system to think that this was because he was grateful to Paul for having sent the letter.

At the very least, we should modify the rule so that it states that the person who benefits from the action will only feel grateful if the person who does the action did it with the intent that it make the other person happy.

Recip will feel gratitude to *doer* if and only if:

1) *doer* performed an action *act* which made *recip* happy, and
2) *doer* intended that *act* have this effect.

Since in this case Paul did not send the letter for the purpose of pleasing Richard, there is no reason for Richard to feel grateful. Unfortunately this is still not sufficient. We leave it as an exercise to the reader to make up examples which show that the new rule gives neither necessary nor sufficient conditions for a feeling of gratitude.

10.3.2 Understanding Obstacles to Plans

Our treatment of motivation analysis has focused on recognizing plans and matching them to subsequent inputs. According to this model, the ideal case occurs when a series of inputs describes a character carrying out a plan without a hitch. Unfortunately, most event sequences — certainly most real stories — do not fit this case. Consider this story

> Fred was hungry. He went to ask his mother for a quarter to buy ice cream, but he couldn't find her. So he went to get an apple from the refrigerator. But the refrigerator was practically empty. To take his mind off his growling stomach, he went out to play.

This is a story about planning, all right, but not one in which instantiating one schema leads to a happy ending. Fred has a choice of plans ("eat ice cream," "eat something from refrigerator"). He chooses the first, and its first step involves a subtask of getting some money. Since Fred is a child (an auxiliary abductive assumption), asking mother is a good plan. Unfortunately, this plan fails because its step, "Be near mother," is unfeasible. So Fred switches to a different plan. It fails as well, and so the task "Assuage hunger" is abandoned.

The phenomena exhibited here, plan selection, execution monitoring, replanning, and task abandonment, are not new to us; we studied them in Chapter 9. It is hardly surprising to find them in stories about planners. If a machine is to understand any but the dullest stories, it will have to expect them as well.

Fortunately, the understander does not have to duplicate the planner's reasoning in all its details. No one has trouble understanding the sentence, "John's house needed painting, so he started calling painters." John may have gone through careful reasoning to decide whether to paint it himself or hire someone, but all the understander has to realize is that he picked the "hire someone" plan, and this choice is perfectly reasonable. The understander doesn't have even to enumerate the other choices. It probably did not occur to you that John might have persuaded his wife to paint the house, yet you would have no trouble understanding a story in which John started trying to persuade his wife to undertake this project.

Hence our model, which does not explicitly reason about plan selection, seems quite reasonable. Once it has found some plan that accounts for a character's actions, it normally does not need to explain why other plans were not chosen.

The algorithm does need modification to handle execution monitoring, during which a character can encounter obstacles to his plan. Fortunately, we can neglect all questions about sensory input; the text must mention all obstacles, explicitly or implicitly.

The most explicit case is that in which the text spells out a task failure. Our story about Fred says explicitly that he couldn't find his mother, and hence spells out his inability to carry out a crucial step of the "ask mother" plan. Our algorithm can be modified easily to handle this case. An input of the form, "X couldn't do A" is handled by first processing it as if it had been "X did do A." The higher-level action G found will serve as an explanation for why X *wanted to* do A. When a subsequent input is explained in terms of a competing plan G', the understander can mark G as having *failed*. (The algorithm cannot tell exactly which schemas to abandon until subsequent input tell it what the planner did. In our story, Fred persists in seeking money after his initial failure, but eventually gives it up.)

Now for the implicit cases. Often stories do not explicitly state which plan step fails, but provide enough information to make it obvious that some step will fail. Human readers seem to prefer such indirection, because it provides information about why the failure occurred, but it is hard to get a machine to make the connection. One clue is the use of the word "but." Any sentence that begins "*X* wanted to do *A*, but . . ." strongly indicates that a snag is coming. Unfortunately, we still need an algorithm to make the connection.

Let's look at another example

Jack walked into a restaurant and sat down at a table. He picked up a menu. It was in Chinese.

We instantly infer that his plan is in trouble because we decide that Jack can't read Chinese. Why should this inference be made at this point?

To answer this question we must examine the pattern of omissions in stories. The plan for reading a menu must explicitly state that the planner must be looking at it. But it is not necessary to mention this event in the story because the reader will infer that it happened anyway. Most story characters can look at a menu so easily that it is almost redundant to mention their success in executing this act. But suppose the story was

Jane walked into a restaurant. She had been blind since the accident a year before.

Suddenly reading a menu (and many other tasks) have become interesting challenges for our story character.

We will capture these facts about interesting and trivial tasks by introducing the predicate (prereq *action state*) as in

```
(prereq (look-at ?agent ?x)        ; To look at something
        (not (blind ?agent)))      ; you must be sighted.
```

If the prerequisite state is unsatisfied, then the agent will fail at the action event. (Sometimes the agent can do something to satisfy the prerequisite; see Exercise 10.9.) If an action is primitive, and there are no unsatisfied prerequisites, the machine can assume it is trivial.

We combine this analysis with a belief that sightedness is a default, as explained in Section 10.2.3, and deduce that initially Jane has no unsatisfied prerequisites. When the fact about her blindness comes in, all these deductions are reversed. Similarly, the Chinese-menu example is handled by a fact like this:

```
(← (prereq (read ?agent ?document)        ; A prerequisite of
           (know-language ?agent ?language)) ; reading something is
   (expressed-in ?document ?language))    ; knowing the language
                                          ; it is expressed in.
```

To begin with, somehow the fact that someone named Jack is going into a restaurant must cause the machine to infer that the restaurant is in an English-speaking country, and Jack is a native speaker of English. From these facts, two defaults follow, that the menu is in English and that Jack knows English. Together these cause Jack's reading the menu to be classed as trivial. The first default is upset by line 3 of the story, causing an unsatisfied prerequisite to appear, supported by a third default, that Jack does not know Chinese. Note that a fourth line, "Fortunately, he spoke fluent Chinese," would reverse this default and eliminate the unsatisfied prerequisite again.

Another fairly easy story-understanding problem is exemplified by Norma's difficulties in the following story

> Norma was developing a roll of pictures of her trip to El Salvador for *Newsweek*. Halfway through the job, her editor walked into the darkroom, letting the sun shine in. Norma growled an unprintable greeting.

The understander must recognize that a protection violation has occurred. This seems simple enough. Whenever it infers that a plan is being followed, all of its protections must be noted. Any event that causes the negation of a protection will cause the plan to fail.

Unfortunately, all these ideas lumped together make only a fragment of a complete theory of implicit plan-failure descriptions. See Exercise 10.10 for an example that goes beyond this fragment.

To summarize this section, inferring an explanatory plan is not just a matter of instantiating a schema. Once a plan is inferred, it must be "tracked" in parallel with the decisions of the planner. Protections must be filed and violations noted. The steps of the plan must be analyzed for interesting prerequisites. An impossible prerequisite, failed subtask, or violated protection must cause the plan to be noted as failing. Subsequent inputs may cause a new schema to be instantiated for some supertask, in which case the old ones must be tagged as abandoned.

10.3.3 Subsumption Goals and repeat-until

With the revisions of the previous section, we can view the motivation analysis algorithm as an alternate interpreter for the plan schemas of Chapter 9. In that chapter, we mentioned that many extensions to the plan schema notation would be useful. One of them was actions of the form

(repeat-until *action state*)

The idea here is that *action* is repeated over and over again until *state* is true. For example, we repeat the action of "hit the nail with the hammer" until "nail flush with wood" is true.

Viewed from the point of view of motivation analysis, the major difference between an action embedded in a repeat-until and a simple sub-event is that the former can happen many times in the story without the need to postulate different superior events. That is, if we saw a nail hit by a hammer a second time, we would not say that there were two "drive nail" events. There are, however, complications. One such is the notion of a *subsumption goal*. A *subsumption goal* is one which is done in order to handle a recurring problem. For example, one seldom buys a car in order to solve a particular problem (like going out for dinner one evening). Rather one buys it to solve a host of transportation problems, like having to get to work every day. That is, the goal of getting a car *subsumes* many particular problems. One way that such goals arise is to help with a task within the scope of a repeat-until action.

(repeat-until *"Get to work at 8:30 AM, Monday to Friday"*
            "You lose the job")

But while **repeat-until** is probably the most common way that subsumption goals arise, it is not necessarily the only way. Essentially subsumption goals can be thought of as goals which have migrated up out of the plans from which they initially arose. So having a means of transportation migrated out of the "get to work" goal, to a higher level. This is worth while only if the goal will occur several times. Thus, in principle, if we had several unrelated actions, all of which had a common subevent, this too could be migrated upward. (If you agreed to be in charge of the local Boy Scout scrap paper collection, were going to move to another house after that, and wanted to buy several large pieces of machinery for your business, you might buy a truck first.)

It is reasonably simple to imagine how to extend our basic algorithm to handle subsumption goals. The algorithm looks for supergoals in the usual fashion. For "owning a car" it will find "getting some place" which in turn matches "get to work at 8:30." Thus far it is our usual algorithm. The extension is to put in a special-case check to see if the supergoal occurs several times. As we have noted, this will most frequently be the case when the supergoal is embedded in a **repeat-until**. If the supergoal does occur several times, then the original goal ("buy a car") is classified as a subsumption goal.

10.4 Details of Motivation Analysis (Optional)

In the last section we saw that our algorithm needs some extension in "breadth." In this section we will show that it needs more "depth" as well. In fact, we are going to dispense with all the enhancements of Section 10.3, and go back to the problem of instantiating a single schema to account for an observed series of actions. The technical details of this problem are surprisingly intricate. Recall that there are two basic ways of explaining an action A. The machine can find a G such that G is a way **to-do** A; or it can find a G such that G has A as a **plan-step**. While the two cases might seem symmetrical (and we encouraged thinking of them this way for simplicity), in fact the **plan-step** case is more complex. In this section we will show that there are two aspects of this case that require special handling: (a) How does the machine find plans that A might be a step of? (b) How does the machine decide that A actually matches some step of a proposed plan? We will postpone the first question until we have answered the second.

10.4.1 Abductive Matching

The problem we address in this section is, given a possible motivating plan G for the action A, determine if A actually matches some step of G. As we will show, straight unification will not do what we want.

Let us start with a small section of our original plan for lighting a cigarette.

```
[plan-for: cigarette-lighting
     objects: fire (inst fire flammable-object)    ; The fire source
                                                   ; should be flammable.
             cig (inst cig cigarette)              ; The thing to be lit
                                                   ; is a cigarette.
       steps: set-fire-task (set-fire-to fire)     ; The substeps
             . . . ]                               ; involved include
                                                   ; lighting the fire.
```

When we introduced this notation in Chapter 9, we noted that if the plan actually took place, then one would be entitled to assert the existence of the objects required by the plan, as well as the subevents needed to carry the plan through to completion. This would give us something like what is shown in Figure 10.8. There we first give a standard predicate calculus version, followed by the same thing in implicit-quantifier form. Naturally, in the implicit-quantifier version we have replaced the existential variables (which we called "roles" in Chapter 7) such as fire or set-fire-task, with Skolem functions like fire-source-of, which specifies the fire source as a function of the particular act of cigarette lighting. For example, if we are talking of a particular act, say cigarette-lighting-93, then the associated fire source would be

```
(fire-source-of cigarette-lighting-93)
```

So far this is just notation, but it suggests viewing the search for a plan-step explanation of an input as the search for a particular plan schema to instantiate, thus generating descriptions of all its steps. In particular, suppose the machine is given the input "Jake lit his cigarette lighter," which we will assume is represented thus:

```
(actual-event lighter-lighting-104
         (do jake-5 (set-fire-to lighter-113)))
```

If the system assumes that Jake is lighting a cigarette, that would generate the substep of lighting some flammable object. This in turn ought to match the input, thereby providing an explanation. More formally, assuming

```
(actual-event cigarette-lighting-93
         (do jake-5 (cigarette-lighting)))
```

will generate

```
(actual-event (set-fire-task light-cigarette-93)
         (do jake-5
              (set-fire-to (fire-source-of light-cigarette-93))))
```

This is supposed to explain our original input.

```
(actual-event lighter-lighting-104
         (do jake-5 (set-fire-to lighter-113)))
```

```
(forall (light-cigarette agent)
    (→ (actual-event light-cigarette
                  (do agent (cigarette-lighting)))   ; Lighting a cigarette
        (exists                                        ; involves the following:
            (fire cig set-fire-task touch-task         ; There will be a source
                            inhale-task)               ; of fire, plus various
                                                       ; subevents.
            (inst fire flammable-object)               ; The source of fire
                                                       ; must be flammable.
            (actual-event set-fire-task                ; First the agent sets
                (do agent                              ; fire to the fire
                    (set-fire-to fire)))               ; source.
                                                       ; This is a subaction
            (sub-event light-cigarette set-fire-task)  ; of the main light
                                                       ; cigarette task.
                . . . )))                              ;


    (→ (actual-event ?light-cigarette                  ; Lighting a cigarette
                  (do ?agent (cigarette-lighting)))    ; involves the following:
        (and                                           ;
            (inst (fire-source-of ?light-cigarette)    ; fire-source-of is a
                  flammable-object)                    ; Skolem function which
                                                       ; names the fire source.
            (actual-event (set-fire-task ?light-cigarette)  ; First the agent sets
                (do ?agent                             ; fire to the fire
                    (set-fire-to                       ; source.
                        (fire-source-of ?light-cigarette))))  ;
                                                       ;
            (sub-event ?light-cigarette                ; It is a subaction of
                  (set-fire-task ?light-cigarette))    ; lighting a cigarette.
                . . . ))
```

Figure 10.8 Cigarette lighting before and after Skolemization

While the the input and the generated explanation are similar, and we want them
to match, they will not, in fact, unify. The problems arise with the following
two submatches

(set-fire-task light-cigarette-93)   (fire-source-of light-cigarette-93)

lighter-lighting-104   lighter-113

At a purely syntactic level, these obviously do not match. Conceptually, the
first pair should match if and only if the system believes that the instance of
lighter lighting, lighter-lighting-104, was done as the set-fire-step in cigarette
lighting. If the system believes it was done for some other reason then it should
not make the match. Similarly, if it believes that lighter-113 is intended as the
source of fire for lighting the cigarette, then the second match should go
through.

To make this more concrete, suppose that for some reason the system already knew that the fire source used in this particular act of cigarette lighting was lighter-113. Such a fact might be recorded in the database as this:

(: = (fire-source-of light-cigarette-93) lighter-113)

The use of : = is the same as in Chapter 7, and is intended to indicate that the right-hand side should be substituted in for the left-hand side. Now if the system has the necessary : = statements, it will be possible to match the incoming statement from the story to the one found in the database. But in general it will not have such statements. The reason is simple. If it already knows that, say, lighter-lighting-104 was the set-fire-task of light-cigarette-93, then it already knows why the agent is doing the action. That is, it already knows the superact, it is light-cigarette-93. Our problem in this chapter is to discover such facts. Thus while replacing Skolem functions by their standard names is a good idea, in the case at hand there is no : = statement to use. Instead, the matcher will have to respond to this requested match with something like "I can make the above match if you grant me the following assumptions":

(: = (fire-source-of light-cigarette-93) lighter-113)
(: = (set-fire-task light-cigarette-93) lighter-lighting-104)

These are the two equality statements, that, if present, would have allowed the match to go through.

Hence the algorithm should feel free to assume them. After all, abduction is finding the best set of assumptions to make, and these seem pretty good. In fact, we will have made three assumptions to get this far, these two plus the original assumption that a cigarette lighting was occurring. We can now see that what we casually labeled as finding a G that had A as a plan-step is just this process of inferring a schema instance plus a series of : = assertions relating objects in the story to roles of the schema. Making such an assertion we will call *filling a role* of the schema instance. The object involved is said to *fill* the role.

We cannot allow the machine to be too casual about making explanatory assumptions. But these seem quite reasonable. For one thing, we allow this kind of equality positing only when it involves a Skolem term that has not already been identified. (Otherwise, almost any unification could be gotten to succeed by assuming enough weird equalities.) That is, we do not allow non-Skolem terms to be assumed equal this way, and we do not allow a role to be filled this way twice.

There is another constraint on such equality assumptions, namely, that they be consistent with what is already known. When the machine is considering filling a role, the proposed filler must be compatible with what the plan schema requires for this role. In particular it should be the right kind of object. For example, we should only try to fill the fire-source role with things that are flammable-objects. Suppose we had "Moe was going to light a cigarette. He hit it with a hammer." Assume for the sake of argument that the second line would imply that Moe brought the hammer into contact with the cigarette.

Since the hammer is not a flammable object, the algorithm would not consider the match, and thus would *not* assume the fact:

(: = (fire-source cigarette-lighting-222) hammer-95)

There is one further complication in the matching process, although not a serious one. It is possible that in the course of doing one such abductive match it will be necessary to do others, with the first match going through only if the others do. In the example we have been considering, we have concentrated on the match between lighter-113 and (fire-source cigarette-lighting-122). Suppose that prior to establishing this match the machine had first tried to establish the other equality, namely,

(: = (set-fire-task light-cigarette-93) lighter-lighting-104)

According to the rules we have set up, this match will go through only if the object in question, lighter-lighting-104, is of the appropriate type to fill the role we wish to assign it, namely, set-fire-task. This is equivalent to asking if the two actions match up:

(do jake-5 (set-fire-to (fire-source-of light-cigarette-93))))

(do jake-5 (set-fire-to lighter-113)))

If the system did this first, in the course of so doing it would have established that lighter-113 could fill a fire-source-of role.

Our account of abductive matching has provided us with a theory about one source of auxiliary assumptions, equalities that specify role fillers. This seems like a good place to mention another source of auxiliary assumptions. In our technical discussion, we have assumed that the algorithm must deductively retrieve statements of the form (to-do . . .). Suppose that the database contains a fact of the form

$(\leftarrow$ (to-do ?tsk G A)
  $P)$

If P can be deduced, then there is no problem. If it can't be, then it may be worthwhile for the understander to just assume it true (if not already known false). For instance, in Section 10.1 we gave an example story about Sally asking her mother for money. Suppose the database contained the fact

$(\leftarrow$ (to-do ?tsk ?agent (get-money ?amt)	; *Asking mom is a good*
(ask-mom ?agent ?amt))	; *idea*
(and (age ?agent child)	; *if you are a child,*
(not (orphan ?agent))	; *not an orphan,*
(< ?amt $1)))	; *and the amount is small.*

(Here we have added an extra argument to to-do, to handle multiple agents.) The action ask-mom is described as a plan schema elsewhere. Since this schema would explain Sally's actions, it seems reasonable to assume she is a child, and the amount of money is small. Note that the algorithm does not assume she is a nonorphan in the same way; instead, that is a default for the average child in a story.

What we are suggesting is building a special *abductive retriever* for use by the story understander. Given a subgoal that is not satisfied, but not known to be false, it just goes ahead and assumes it true as an auxiliary assumption. Something of this sort should be assumed for retrievals of to-do and plan-step to explain actions.

10.4.2 Finding Possible Motivations

In the last section we explained how, once a plan schema had been proposed, its steps could be matched against inputs. The other problem we promised to solve is proposing possible plans G that an input action A might be a step of. Consider

Fred went to the supermarket
Bill picked up a cigarette.
Mary opened the milk carton.

Given sentences like these our system must come up with suggestions like supermarket-shopping or cigarette-smoking or drinking.

Making these connections requires indexing the appropriate plan schemas so that the lines above key into them. We have already looked at the issue of indexing such schemas. The beginning of Chapter 7 pointed out that a possible way of indexing them would be to have a pointer into the schema, indicating how far along in the plan the actor in the story had reached. As the story progressed, the pointer would be moved farther and farther along.

While this is a plausible indexing scheme, it has one major limitation. It works only if the system already knows what plan schema is in force, so that all it need do is match the new action against the subsequent subevents of the plan. However, in cases where we are introducing a new plan, such as the sentences above, this indexing method will not work.

One standard solution to this problem is to provide a new data structure that indexes plan schemas by the ways in which they may be introduced. If a schema can be introduced in only a small number of ways, this would seem to be the right thing to do. However, it is by no means clear that schemas have such limited accessibility. Rather it would seem that most, if not all, of the information in a schema provides access to it. For example, consider the restaurant-dining schema, and what can bring it to mind.

Norman went to a restaurant.
Norman picked up a menu.
Norman ordered a steak.
Norman paid for the meal.

All of these suggest restaurants. Of course, there are sentences from restaurant stories which do not in themselves suggest eating in a restaurant.

Norman sat down at a table.
Norman asked for a glass of water.
Norman ate his steak.
Norman paid the bill.

But this could be simply because the actions are indexed under more than one possibility, and no decision could be made. Some support for this is given by the fact that often two such sentences are sufficient, whereas neither by itself will do.

Norman ate his steak and paid the bill.
Norman sat down at a table and asked for a glass of water.

These are further examples of the kind of thing we worried about earlier in our discussion of what to do when there is more than one possible motivation.

Furthermore, the to-do statements associated with a plan schema also can bring it to mind. For example:

> (← (to-do (achieve ?agent (know ?agent ?fact)) ; *To learn a fact,*
> (read ?book)) ; *read a book which*
> (contained-in ?fact ?book)) ; *contains the fact.*

This rule would tell us about the motivation of someone reading a book. Thus it seems reasonable to assume as a first approximation that all of the information in a schema can serve to bring it to mind.

If this is indeed the case, then one would like an indexing mechanism which will allow an action to be seen as part of a plan schema whether or not the plan schema has been instantiated in the story. A mechanism which has this property was suggested in Section 7.2.3. Basically this mechanism indexed all the statements in a schema separately, as if they were independent predicate calculus statements. However, the variables and roles in the schemas needed special treatment. First, the variable referring to the object which is an instance of the schema (the particular lion in a lion schema, a particular instance of grocery shopping in a grocery-shopping schema) is replaced by the pseudo-object #typical-*object* (for example, #typical-lion or #typical-grocery-shopping). In

---

> (inst (fire-source-of #typical-cig-light) ; *The fire-source-of is a*
> flammable-object) ; *flammable object.*
>
> (actual-event (set-fire-task #typical-cig-light) ; *First the agent sets*
> (do ?agent ; *fire to the fire*
> (set-fire-to ; *source.*
> (fire-source-of #typical-cig-light)))) ;
>
> (sub-event #typical-cig-light ; *It is a subaction of*
> (set-fire-task #typical-cig-light)) ; *lighting a cigarette.*

Figure 10.9 Cigarette lighting as #typical-cig-light

Figure 10.9 we have taken the version of cigarette lighting in Figure 10.8 and applied the necessary transformations.

The indexer must also handle the roles in the schema in a special way. If a role must be filled by an instance of *object*, then references to that role will be indexed under #typical-*object*. So in our schema for lighting a cigarette, the cig role must be filled by a cigarette, so any place in a formula where (cig #typical-cig-light) appears will be indexed under #typical-cigarette. In Figure 10.10 we see what a small part of a database index which included our light-cigarette schema would look like.

Such a data structure is called a *virtual copy* of a schema. Our original reason for introducing this idea was to extend the quantificational power of associative networks while retaining their indexing efficiency. As we pointed out briefly in Chapter 7, this indexing mechanism has the nice feature that an event from a nonactive schema will be found as a possible explanation for an incoming action. For example, suppose our story included the line "Susan brought her lighter to her cigarette." Furthermore assume that this is represented in a fashion corresponding to the representation in the schema.

```
(actual-event touch-84 (do susan-2
                          (touch lighter-11 cigarette-9)))
(inst lighter-11 cigarette-lighter)
(inst cigarette-9 cigarette)
```

The indexing mechanism from Chapter 7 will look under event, do, etc., which

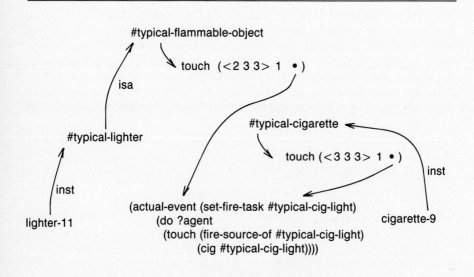

Figure 10.10 Indexing part of the light-cigarette schema

will point to too many assertions to be worth rummaging through. Things are more interesting when it looks under lighter-11 and cigarette-9. As shown in Figure 10.10, in the course of going up the isa hierarchy from these objects it will find this fact:

```
(actual-event (touch-task #typical-cig-light)
        (do ?agent (touch (fire-source-of #typical-cig-light)
                (cig #typical-cig-light))))
```

This is, of course, what we want found.

This section has been technically intricate, so let us summarize the algorithm. Given an input action A, the machine is to ask the database if it has seen it before. If A is literally present, then explanation stops. If A matches an item in a virtual copy of a schema, as just described, then the corresponding schema instance is proposed as an abductive assumption. To verify that this assumption explains the input, the machine must instantiate the schema and match the input against promising subevents of it. As explained in Section 10.4.1, making such a match work may require further abductive assumptions, which fill roles in the schema.

Note by the way that if our algorithm is to use a marker passing scheme as suggested in Section 10.3, the marker passer will be using the virtual-copy database we have just described. It may not be obvious how these two can coexist. As has been often the case in this chapter, this is an area that requires extensive research. A good place to start, however, would be to model the process after associative networks. As with our typical translations into associative network notation, one can imagine that the terms are nodes and the predicates links. Thus if sue-25 picked up cigarette-81, marking from cigarette-81 would pass marks to sue-25. To introduce the virtual-copy aspect of this, we can expand on our idea by considering #typical-cigarette a pseudo-object, denoting a typical cigarette. Thus it is a term and will have marks passed to it. So starting from cigarette-81 marks would also be passed (via an isa link) to #typical-cigarette. On this node there would be statements about what happens during light-cigarette, and thus that schema (and the things to which it connects) would be marked as well.

10.5 Speech Acts and Conversation

While the last sections were concerned with understanding the motivations for actions in general, one very important class of action was not covered, or at least not explicitly. These are the actions that simply involve "saying things." This class of action has received particular attention within the philosophical community over the last thirty years or so, where such actions have been labeled *performative sentences* or, alternatively, *speech acts*. (Strictly speaking, the term "speech acts" includes things other than performative sentences, but we will not insist on the distinction.) Many sentences can be thought of as either true or false, in the sense that they correctly or incorrectly describe some fact about the world (e.g., "Fran knows the Pledge of Allegiance"). But many sentences do not fit this mold. For example:

> I bet you ten dollars that we get the grant.
> I christen this boat the *Andrea Doria*.

Such sentences are best understood as performing some action, such as betting, or christening. At first glance this may seem odd, since more common actions, such as hitting a baseball, cause movement in the world, while here there is none. But if we are not to allow actions such as christening, it is hard to explain what all of those people gathered around that boat think they are doing. Once we do allow such things to count as actions, it is reasonable to suppose that simply "saying something" can accomplish them. Thus the sentences above count not as descriptions but as actions — as "speech acts."

These examples are striking because they are very different from the more typical day-to-day uses of language. But once we recognize that we are performing actions when saying such sentences, we can recognize the actions involved in more commonplace examples as well. So when we say "From which gate does the 5 P.M. flight to LA depart?" or "Put the block on the table!" we are not making true or false statements, but rather performing the actions of *asking* and *commanding*. Indeed, we can even ask if our normal declarative sentences should simply be seen as such, or rather as performing the action of *informing*. As we shall see, there is a certain plausibility to this latter view.

Having recognized that certain sentences perform actions, philosophers have divided the actions into several different parts. One, called the *locutionary act*, is the process of making sounds (or putting some marks on paper) that obey the syntax and semantics of a language. As such, locutionary acts are what we studied in Chapter 4. We mention them here only to differentiate them from those that follow. Another action, the *illocutionary act*, can roughly be thought of as the intent of the sentence. These are the actions we have discussed in the preceding paragraphs: asking, commanding, christening, betting, apologizing, etc. These are referred to as the *illocutionary force* of a particular sentence. Last, there is the so-called *perlocutionary act*. This is the desired action I hope to accomplish by saying what I say. So the illocutionary act of apologizing has the goal that you forgive me. Your action of forgiving me is the perlocutionary act. Similarly, if I command (an illocutionary act), I hope I will get you to "do what I say" (a perlocutionary act), while if I inform, I hope you will come to believe. So in saying something, one does not oneself perform the perlocutionary act. Rather, one hopes to persuade the listener to do it.

Box 10.1

How Philosophy Came to Language

Most of us grow up with the idea that philosophy is concerned with questions like "How can one distinguish good from bad?" or "What is the meaning of life?" To someone with such preconceptions it may seem odd to have philosophers looking into the details of how we use language. Yet at several points in this book we have come across ideas borrowed from philosophy. In Chapter 4 we noted the distinction between the "sense" and "reference" of noun phrases, a distinction made by the philosopher Frege, and the notion of speech acts from this chapter has philosophical origins as well. Furthermore, although we did not mention it, Russell and Whitehead, whose book *Principia Mathematica* [Whitehead25] perfected the predicate calculus, were interested in it for reasons that were as much philosophical as mathematical. We might ask, how did philosophers get into the language game?

Another conception we have about philosophers is that they tend to say outrageous things like: "There are no material objects" or, from Heidegger, "Does the Nothing exist only because the Not, i.e., the Negation, exists?" While this has gained some philosophers a certain notoriety, it has led to widespread disagreement in the field, which in turn has led to a widespread feeling among philosophers that since nobody can agree with anybody else, they must be doing something wrong.

The reaction to this, at least among English-speaking philosophers, has been a turn to *linguistic philosophy*. Philosophers of this stripe believe that philosophical problems can be solved (or shown to be false problems) by careful attention to the language in which they are stated. So philosophy, unlike science, does not attempt to discover facts about the world, but rather, at best, can only clarify concepts. For example, a classic muddle is the "proof" of the existence of God, which goes,

God is perfect; perfection requires existence; therefore, God exists.

If we try to translate this into the first-order predicate calculus, we find we cannot. The statement "perfection requires existence" simply has no translation. About the closest we could come is:

(forall (x) (if (perfect x) (exists (x))))

but this is simply syntactic fruit salad according to the rules of the formalism. Existence is not a predicate like "perfect" in predicate calculus, and therefore it cannot be used like this. To Russell and Whitehead, that the proof could not be stated in their logic was a plus. The attempted translation made obvious what we intuitively knew all along, that the reasoning is gibberish. The same is true for the earlier quote from Heidegger, "Does the Nothing exist only because the Not, i.e., the Negation, exists?"

However, linguistic philosophers are not themselves a united bunch. They have tended to split into two groups. One, of which Russell is the most eminent member, has been called the *ideal language philosophers* because of their attempt to create an ideal language in which it would be impossible to state the philosophic absurdities of yesteryear. The other group, the *ordinary language philosophers*, have claimed that ordinary language, if used with care, is already an "ideal language." To understand why one might say that, consider again our first philosophic oddity

"There are no material objects." Unlike the Heidegger quote, we can state this in logic.

```
(not (material-object ?x))
```

As usual the ?x is universally quantified so this states, in effect, "everything is not a material object." Nevertheless, from the standpoint of ordinary English the statement is an odd one because we all know that all sorts of material objects exist, the book you are holding being a prime example. This, the ordinary language philosophers would say, is simply because the philosopher who made the claim was not using words as they are intended to be used. He is not using them according to the rules of the "language game," to use a phrase of Ludwig Wittgenstein [Wittgenstein53].

From this perspective, the work in speech acts can be seen as an attack on the ideal language philosophers from an ordinary language philosopher. The predicate calculus is intended to express true statements about the world. But if, as speech act theory would have it, we are not in the business of making true statements (or at least only incidentally so), and instead are making speech acts like inform, request, etc., then so much the worse for our "ideal" predicate calculus.

We in AI tend to mix all of this up by, for example, formalizing performative sentences in the predicate calculus. But the philosophers' concerns are not ours. We are looking for tools to use, and if the designer had some other idea in mind, it hardly matters to us.

10.5.1 Speech Acts in Problem Solving

To this point, our discussion has been in the abstract — without particular reference to AI. However, the connection is not hard to find. As with any action, speech acts are performed in the service of some goals (the perlocutionary acts, in the terminology introduced above). As such, the production of speech acts should be governed by our problem-solving faculties.

Suppose, to take a simple example, that some agent *A* wants another person *P* to perform some action, *ACT*. One way to accomplish this task is to simply request that *P* do it. We can express some needed knowledge in our problem-solving terminology:

```
(prereq (request ?A ?P ?ACT)      ; To successfully request someone
        (can (do ?P ?ACT)))       ; to do something, the listener has
                                  ; to be capable of doing it.

(effect (request ?A ?P ?ACT)      ; The immediate result of a request
        (do ?P ?ACT))             ; is that the person does what was
                                  ; requested.
```

This formalization is too simple, and the statement that all you have to do is request and the listener "jumps to it" is rather optimistic, but with such rules, or more sophisticated variants, we can see how a particular speech act, request, could come up in the course of elaborating a plan. So, if Jill wants Bill to leave the room, she might use these rules to decide that she should do this:

(request jill-2 bill-4 (do bill-4 (leave bill-4 room-7)))

prereq: (can (do bill-4 (leave bill-4 room-7)))

effect: (do bill-4 (leave bill-4 room-7))

She would then see that if this is to be a meaningful request, Bill must be capable of it, and so forth.

Similarly, a first approximation of the speech act **inform** might be this

(effect (inform ?A ?P ?FACT)	; *If A tells P a fact*
(know ?P ?FACT))	; *then P will know that fact.*
(prereq (inform ?A ?P ?FACT)	; *A prerequisite of informing*
?FACT)	; *someone of a fact is that*
	; *it be true.*

One particularly interesting kind of **inform** is informing someone that you want him to do something. This is interesting because "informing someone that you want him to do something" is quite close to "requesting someone to do something." So if we modify the earlier example of Jill's **request** that Bill leave, and change it so that Jill now **informs** Bill that Jill would like him to leave, we will get this

(inform jill-2 bill-4	; *Jill informs Bill*
(want jill-2	; *that she wants*
(leave bill-4 room-7)))	; *Bill to leave the room.*
prereq: (want jill-2	; *Jill must want*
(leave bill-4 room-7))	; *Bill to leave the room.*
effect: (know bill-4	; *Now Bill knows*
(want jill-2	; *that Jill wants*
(leave bill-4 room-7))	; *him to leave.*

While requesting that someone do something and telling him that you want him to do it are identical, or at least very close, in our formalization they look quite different. For example, in the first case the effect is that Bill leaves the room, while in the second, Bill does nothing but he is aware that Jill wants him to leave. If anything, the second seems more reasonable (people do not always comply when you ask them to do something), and hence we should consider changing our formalization of **request** so that it produces results more like that of **inform**. We can do this as follows:

(prereq (request ?A ?P ?ACT)	; *For a request to someone*
(can (do ?P ?ACT)))	; *to do something to be successful,*
	; *the person given the request must*
	; *be capable of doing it.*

```
(effect (request ?A ?P ?ACT)        ; The immediate result of a request
       (know ?P                      ; is that the person knows that the
            (want ?A (do ?P ?ACT)))) ; requester wants him or her
                                     ; to do the act.
```

(By the way, throughout this section we will need the predicate **know** to represent an individual's knowledge of the world. This is a tremendously difficult predicate to formalize and we will make no attempt to even be consistent in our usage, much less accurate.)

There are other changes we could make to bring the concepts of **request** and **inform - want** still closer together. However, the purpose of this section is to show how speech acts can be viewed from a problem-solving perspective, and we have done that.

10.5.2 The Recognition of Speech Acts

Once we place speech acts in the domain of problem-solving actions, the recognition of speech acts should be like the recognition of any other problem-solving action. Thus if Steve asks "The train to London leaves from which track?" we can use our rules to decide that he has the goal of knowing this fact. From that, in turn, we might conclude that he intends to take that train, and from that we might guess that he wants to be in London. That our train of abduction starts from a speech act rather than an act of the more muscular variety matters not at all. This example is illustrated in Figure 10.11. One complexity introduced in this example is the problem of formally representing a question. Up until now all of our speech acts have been statements, and thus reasonably straightforward within the predicate calculus. Representing questions and commands is not so obvious. We have simply made up a notation to use in Figure 10.11 without giving it a lot of thought.

Except for the problem of representing questions, Figure 10.11 shows a straightforward application of our previous analysis to the domain of speech acts. There are, however, more complicated situations. Consider sentences like:

Can you reach the salt?
Can you pass me the salt?
Could I have the salt?

All of these have the form of questions, but considered as speech acts they are really requests to the listener to pass the salt. Because the superficial form of the speech act is different from the intended speech act, such utterances are called *indirect speech acts*. Can our abduction machinery account for indirect speech acts as well?

The best current answer seems to be "almost." Some cases are particularly easy. For example, in our earlier discussion we noted that informing people that you would like them to do something is similar to requesting them to do it. This can be considered an indirect speech act, since we are using an **inform** to carry the illocutionary force of a **request**. If we could be successful in having

---

(ask steve-1 porter (which (x) (leave-from train-to-london-4 x)))

and

(if (know ?p2 fact)
   (result (ask ?p1 ?p2 ?fact) (know ?p1 ?fact)))

allows us to conclude that

(achieve steve-1
   (know steve-1 (which (x) (leave-from train-to-london-4 x))))

is a task of Steve's.

If we then use this fact in our process, we can use

(plan-for: take-train
    steps: (know agent (which (x) (leave-from train x)))
           (be-at agent (the (x) (leave-from train x)))
           (get-on agent train)
           . . .)

to infer

(do steve-1 (take-train train-to-london-4))

We might then go on and infer Steve wants to be in London, but the
process is exactly the same.

Figure 10.11 Deciding on the goals of a question

the effects both come out the same, then we have successfully handled one instance of an indirect speech act.

However, the examples in which a request is disguised as a question are
more difficult. Consider first the example, "Can you reach the salt?" Suppose
we strip this of the fact that it is a question, and pretend that we are simply told
the fact "You (Alice) can reach the salt," or, to make it a real action, "Alice
reached the salt." If we simply used our previously described algorithm on such
a fact, we could find many possible reasons why this fact would be of possible
interest: "Alice will salt her food," "Alice will give someone the salt," "Alice
will throw the salt at someone," and so on. In fact, however, it would probably decide on the first of these, as opposed to, say, the second, because the
first makes the most specific use of the fact that we are dealing with salt, and it
would not need to figure out which person would get the salt, much less why
that person in turn would want the salt.

Since this is not the normal interpretation of the question, it must be the
speaker's asking Alice this question that gives us the proper interpretation. But
neither can it simply be knowledge of **ask**. While we have not defined the action completely, in Figure 10.11 we noted that the result of an **ask** is that the

asker knows the answer (or some such). Why would the speaker want to know
whether Alice could reach the salt?

There are several possible responses. Most start out with the observation
that Alice's reaching the salt is required for Alice passing it. We can then go in
one of several ways. The first is to say that asking about Alice's ability is a
reasonable problem-solving response to the task of getting the salt. That is,
since asking Alice to pass the salt would be pointless if Alice could not reach it,
then we first find out if she can. If we had such a rule, then our motivation
analysis program would find that a good reason for asking if a person can do X
is that you want that person to do X, and from there we can clearly go on to a
complete analysis.

There are, however, many problems with this. People will ask questions
like this even when they know the answers. Furthermore, if it were true that
people ask these questions for legitimate problem-solving reasons, then why is it
considered "silly" to answer them in a literal fashion? If you are asked "Can
you pass the salt?" a response of yes is not considered appropriate. Thus it
seems unlikely that the question itself has problem-solving significance.

There are two alternative theories. Perhaps the simplest is that the use of
a question in such indirect speech acts is a pure formality. So, for example, if
we say "Pass the salt, please," the "please" does not in itself have problem-
solving content, but rather is a polite convention in language. The general idea
would be to claim that questions serving as requests are basically the same sort
of thing. It is more polite to say "Can you pass me the salt?" than "Pass me
the salt." If this is correct, and the question format is simply a convention of
language (or perhaps just of English), then the understanding of such phenomena
should take place during the analysis of the linguistic input, and not here in
motivation analysis. As such, this topic would have been more appropriate in
Chapter 4 in which we discussed parsing English.

An alternative theory starts from what has been called *conversational implicature*. The idea is that people talking to one another tacitly agree to obey
certain conventions, called *conversational postulates*. These are reasonably simple, such as "be relevant," "be helpful," and "be complete." This latter rule
would be assumed in our understanding of a sentence like "Norma has four
children." Upon hearing this we would normally, and reasonably, assume that
Norma has *exactly* four children. Strictly speaking, this sentence is compatible
with Norma having five children as well, since obviously if she has five, then
she also has four. Nevertheless, no one would interpret the sentence in this
latter fashion. The explanation, according to the conversational implicature
theory, is that we assume the rule of "be complete," and this would require
saying "five" if that is how many children Norma has.

In a somewhat analogous fashion, the rule of "be relevant" would apply
in our examples of indirect speech acts, such as "Can you reach the salt?" Let
us assume that the salt is in plain view, and quite near the listener. The reasoning would then go as follows: the speaker cannot be interested in knowing if I
could reach the salt, since it is obvious to everyone present that I can. For the

speaker to ask that question would be to "disobey" the rule of relevance. Hence that must not be the literal intent of the question.

Support is offered for this analysis by the observation that were the salt not in plain view, then the question "Can you reach the salt?" could be answered yes or no, although if yes, passing the salt would still be polite.

Both analyses, that in terms of "polite conventions" and that in terms of "conversational implicature," have something to recommend them, and we suspect that elements of both come into play in many examples. But they both leave something out. How does the listener decide what action is being requested, once an answer to the literal question has been ruled out as inappropriate? For any single example, it is relatively easy to think of clues which could be used. As we have already noted, reaching the salt would be a subaction of passing it. Thus for this example a possible rule is *a question about the ability to do a subaction of an action* A *is really a request to do* A.

The problem is that there are a wide variety of such examples. An extreme example is one in which you are sitting on a doorstep, and a neighbor comes along carrying a large box. The neighbor says "Door please." Here we have no subaction, indeed, no sentence. Yet clearly we have a request to open the door. It would seem that we simply look for some activity associated with doors that would be useful to the speaker. One way we might find such an action would be to use something akin to the spreading activation or marker passing ideas mentioned earlier. However, this is no more than an observation. How such problems are to be handled is still to be worked out.

There are other complexities within speech act analysis as well. When a person makes a statement S, we must both analyze the intent of the act of saying S, and then look internally to S to see if things within it require analysis. So far in this section the examples we have considered have finessed this problem. For example, the reasons why someone says "I want the salt" (e.g., so you will pass it, so it can be used) are a superset of the reasons why the speaker wants it (so it can be used). This simplification made it necessary only to analyze the motivation behind the utterance. But this is not always the case. For example, if Fred says "Bill hit me," we might want to know both why he said that, and why Bill hit him. How we synchronize these two explanatory processes has yet to be investigated.

10.5.3 Conversations

We introduced speech acts as a special case of actions in general, and the recognition of speech acts as, more or less, a special case of motivation analysis. It is also the case, however, that speech acts were our first brush with the idea of conversations and their structure. Admittedly, asking someone to do something is not much as conversations go, but it is a start. In this section we will look at more complicated examples.

Typically, when we think of conversations, we think of deep conversations, between friends or relations, about subjects of significance to them.

These, however, are pretty difficult terrain, so let us start with one closer to the kinds of things we were concerned with in speech acts.

S1: Could you mail a letter for me?
S2: Sure.
S1: It is on the mantel. If it does not reach LA by the
     day after tomorrow, I will have to pay a fee.

Here S1's first line is, in fact, a speech act of the normal request variety. S1's subsequent statements are informs, but they are not completely separate actions. Rather they fill in detail about the original desired action. S2 must recognize this, or else, for example, the last line will not be seen as a statement that the letter must be mailed soon. While there are many complications (the last sentence is a very difficult one indeed), the basic idea is to recognize that in any plan for mailing a letter, the person doing the action must know certain facts, such as the location of the letter to be mailed. The plan might state this requirement explicitly, although given the ubiquity of such requirements, it would be better to have it inferred. Either way, S1's second sentence should be viewed as an inform so that the goal is that S2 know the fact. Thus S1's action has a result that matches something in S2's plan for letter mailing, namely,

(know S2 (location letter-1))

But the example about mailing a letter is a relatively easy conversation to understand, if only because it deals with a single topic. Real conversations are seldom like that. Consider the following (made up) example, of two people discussing how to write a Lisp program:

1 S1: I think we should use a global variable here.
2 S2: I am not so sure.
3   Like, I tried that in the telephone-operator assignment.
4   It resulted in a terrible bug.
5 S1: Oh, by the way, you got a phone call from Fran.
6 S2: Did she say what she wanted?
7 S1: No, but she said it was nothing important.
8 S2: OK, I will call her later.
9   At any rate, it took me three days to find it.

In this artificially compressed example, lines 1 and 2 are on a particular topic. Lines 3 and 4 are on the same topic, but are separate, dealing as they do with a particular example of the issue. Lines 5 through 8 are clearly distinct, while 9 returns to where the conversation had left off on line 4.

The idea that conversations have such structure is supported by the use of phases like "OK," "at any rate," and "by the way." It is difficult to assign them any "meaning" in the traditional sense. Rather they seem to be conversational markers, indicating boundaries between different sections of the conversation. "By the way" says that what is coming will have no direct relation to what came before while "like" flags an example (although not in the dialect that uses expressions such as "like, wow!"). "OK" seems to dismiss the topic of the telephone conversation, and this is reinforced by the "at any rate," which signals a return to a previous topic. Of course, this example is idealized in that it is rare for *every* conversational shift to be signaled in this way, but people's use of such key phrases is too consistent to be accidental. The net result is a model of conversation which has a general tree-structure format, as shown in Figure 10.12.

But one is still entitled to ask: If there is this structure to conversations, how should it be manifested in our representation of what is going on? And this question is in turn bound up with a second question: What effect does the recognition of this structure have on further processing of the conversation. Or in other words, why bother?

As is frequently the case, it will be easier to start with this second question and then, having some notion of what we might expect to gain from the recognition of such structure, suggest an implementation that provides the benefits outlined. However, since the benefits will be primarily in the domain of referent determination, we will have to take up that topic first.

10.6 Disambiguation of Language

So far in this chapter, we have concentrated on the problems of constructing "explanations" for what we read in a story, or what we hear in a conversation. Now we will turn to a problem that we have put off several times — how our understanding of what we read or hear enters into the process of translating between natural language and internal representation. In particular we will look

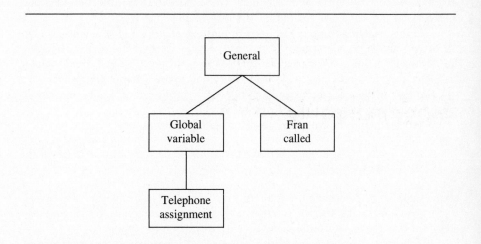

Figure 10.12 The structure of a conversation

at two aspects of this, referential disambiguation and word sense disambiguation.

10.6.1 Referential Ambiguity and Context

In this section we will be concerned with the use of context in determining noun-phrase reference. Before we start, however, it is useful to remind ourselves of the discussion of noun-phrase reference in Chapter 4. There we took a noun phrase "the red block" and produced a description

```
(and (inst ?x block)
      (color ?x red))
```

We then suggested that the word "the" added on a command to find the appropriate item in the database, like this

```
(retrieve-val '?x '(and (inst ?x block)
                          (color ?x red)))
```

We assumed that retrieve-val would find only one possible item in the database.

As we have already noted, however, noun phrases can, in general, refer to any one of a number of individuals. This is most evident in the case of pronouns, but it can occur with full noun phrases as well. Consider this example:

> It was Jack's birthday. Janet and Penny went to the store. They were going to buy presents. "I will get Jack a top," said Janet. "Don't do that," said Penny. "Jack already has a top. He will make you take (it/the top) back."

Both the pronoun and the full noun phrase produce pretty much the same dilemma to a reference determination routine. There are two tops mentioned, and the correct one is not the last mentioned, but the previous one.

In this example in particular, and in most such cases, the ambiguity can be resolved only by "understanding" the text. There are exceptions; for example, in "Russell hit him," syntax alone dictates that "Russell" and "him" cannot refer to the same individual. Nevertheless, context plays the predominant role. As one case of how context is brought to bear, we will examine how motivation analysis can help in resolving references.

To take a specific example, consider the following story.

> Jack was shopping at the supermarket. He picked up some milk from the shelf. He paid for it and left.

Here we want to determine the referent for "it" in the last sentence. However, before we look at the specific problem of noun-phrase reference, let us consider how our process of motivation analysis will operate on the example.

The first line will establish that Jack is engaged in an instance of supermarket-shopping, say supermarket-shopping-77. Assuming that we know that the usual reason for doing this is to obtain possession of one or more things, then our procedure would assert this as well, but this is not important for our current purposes. More important is what happens at the next line, when it tries to establish why Jack picked up the milk. Presumably one fact it knows about shopping is that it is necessary to physically obtain the item to be purchased. That is, part of the **supermarket-shopping** schema will look something like Figure 10.13. (There are a lot of problems with this, including the assumption that only one item is to be purchased. Obviously this is simplistic, but to assume otherwise would just introduce distracting complications.) We get from the story that Jack picked up **milk-4**, an instance of milk, and the algorithm finds **pick-up-task** when it looks for reasons why Jack performed this activity. The next step of the process is to make sure that it can abductively match the two. (See Section 10.4.1.) It will be trying to match these:

(do jack-2 (pick-up (bought-item supermarket-shopping-77))
(do jack-2 (pick-up milk-4)

where **bought-item** is the Skolem function corresponding to the **bought** role. Clearly the match can be made to work, provided the machine can make this role-filling assumption

(:= (bought-item supermarket-shopping-77) milk-4)

(Again, := indicates that the right-hand side should be substituted for the left-hand side.) This fact will be entered into the database of facts about the story.

When the next line comes in, the processing is essentially identical, but there is a pronoun to deal with. The idea we wish to exploit is that resolving the pronoun reference amounts to making another abductive equality assumption. In this case, if we assume that "it" refers to **milk-4** then it will be much easier to construct a reason for Jack's action than it would otherwise. In particular, with that binding it can match the **pay-task** of the supermarket shopping schema.

[plan-for: supermarket-shopping	
objects: agent (inst ?agent person)	*; The agent should be a* *; person.*
store (inst ?store supermarket)	*; The shopping takes place at* *; a supermarket.*
bought (inst ?bought food)	*; The thing to be bought is* *; food.*
steps: pickup-task (pick-up ?bought)	*; The agent picks up the food,*
pay-task (pay-for ?bought)	*; and should pay for it.*
. . .	*; Lots more we have left out.*
timing: (seq ?pick-up-task ?pay-task)]	*; Get the food and then pay.*

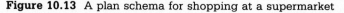

Figure 10.13 A plan schema for shopping at a supermarket

These equality assumptions are quite similar to the role-filling assumptions we looked at before. One approach to managing them is to use much the same machinery as for filling roles. This means leaving the pronoun initially unresolved, allowing later processing to make a decision. An alternative is to make a guess as to the correct referent, but be prepared to back up if the guess proves untenable. We will come back to this alternative later.

If we want to leave the pronoun initially unresolved, a good starting point is to note that the predicate calculus offers a standard way of doing it. In the case at hand, we could represent the meaning of the last sentence in the supermarket story this way

```
(exists (it)                        ; There is something such that
   (do jack-2 (pay-for it)))        ; Jack paid for it.
```

Here we have used an existential quantifier to express the fact that there is something which fits the bill, while at the same time making no claims about what sort of thing this something is. When we convert this to implicit-quantifier form the existentially quantified variable becomes a function of zero arguments — in other words, a constant.

```
(do jack-2 (pay-for it-47))         ; it-47 is a Skolem constant.
```

Now consider what will happen when the normal motivation analysis machinery goes to work. It will first look for possible motivations. One it will find will be this

```
(do jack-2 (pay-for milk-4))
```

This is the action from the supermarket plan schema, but with milk-4 substituted in as the filler of the bought-item role and jack-2 substituted in as the agent. In the course of trying to match the two statements, everything will trivially match except it-47 and milk-4. Those who read the optional section on abductive matching (Section 10.4.1) will remember that we said that we would allow our unification matcher to unify a Skolem function against a real object providing that doing so did not contradict anything it already believed. This is just a special case of the same situation, in which the Skolem function involved is a function of no variables. Since nothing is inconsistent with this binding, it will be made, and the following statement added to the database

```
(:= it-47 milk-4)
```

The same technique handles definite descriptions. In Chapter 4, we had the machine use the noun phrase to construct a description of the referent, and we assumed that the word "the" told it to tack on the function retrieve-val to find the referent. We will now change what "the" does. In the new version, "the" says to replace the variable by a Skolem constant and assert the description. So for the noun phrase "the red block," the system would assert

```
(inst skolem-22 block)
(color skolem-22 red)
```

Typically the system will find that **skolem-22** is equal to some already existing object, in which case it can be uniformly replaced by that object.

This algorithm has two nice side effects worth pointing out. First, it can handle examples in which later descriptions of an object include new information. For example

> Henry was flying a kite. Suddenly the wind started to blow very hard and the string broke. Henry shouted, ''My new kite is flying away.''

Here the last sentence describes the kite as being new, and belonging to Henry, neither of which was mentioned earlier. If the system used the methods of Chapter 4 no possible referent would be found, because it would know of nothing which had all of the required properties. In this revised version, there is no problem. The Skolem constant is created, and presumably abductive projection will suggest that it can make sense of the line provided that the new kite is the one being flown. Since at this point all that is required to make the identification is the lack of conflicting information, the referent will be found.

A second nice side effect is the way the algorithm handles examples in which the noun phrase refers to an object mentioned only implicitly in the text. In the kite example, the second line referred to ''the string.'' No string had been mentioned in the text, but human readers had no trouble with the sentence. This is a reasonably common occurrence:

> I bought a used car. *The horn* stopped working after two days.
> I finished writing a book, but I still have to write *the dedication*.
> I went to a concert last night. *The intermission* lasted forty-five minutes.

It is interesting to note that, given our analysis of schemas and the Skolem-constant method of noun-phrase reference, this phenomenon reduces to the case where the referent is explicitly provided. We have already noted that our schemas assert the existence of collateral objects, as when the beauty-parlor schema asserts the existence of a hair dresser. If we assumed that mentioning a kite causes the **kite** schema to be filled in and explicitly put into the database, then once the kite is mentioned there actually will be an object in the database for ''the string'' to refer to. Of course, as we have already noted, in practice we do not want to have to explicitly put everything we know about kites into the database every time one is mentioned, but instead want our schemas to act as virtual copies.

We initially said that there were two methods for integrating contextual information into the referent-determination process. While the Skolem-constant method is simplicity itself, and is probably the method of choice, it does lose track of one important bit of information. A standard rule for noun-phrase reference is that a noun phrase refers to the last-mentioned object of the appropriate type. That is, a noun phrase like ''the red ball'' refers to the last red ball mentioned, while a noun phrase like ''it'' generally refers to the last mentioned inanimate object. While this rule does not always work, it is correct about 90% of the time. Furthermore, there will be cases where locality of reference plays the deciding role. For example

> "I bought a new car yesterday," said Sue. "Oh," said Bill, "What color is the car?"

Here the "the car" obviously refers to the one Sue bought, but it would be difficult at best to attribute this decision to motivation analysis, abductive projection, or the like. This suggests extending our reference-resolution method to include a "last mentioned" rule for the cases where no suggested referent is found during motivation analysis. That is, if no referent is found during motivation analysis, the last-mentioned possible referent is assumed.

Nevertheless, the "last-mentioned object" rule is *so* good that it seems unfortunate to relegate it to a "if all else fails" position. This suggests a second method of applying our motivation analysis information. Rather than putting in a Skolem constant, this method will simply put in the last-mentioned object. In the supermarket example, the program would guess initially that the "it" that Jack paid for is shelf-1. It will then apply the normal methods to look for motivation. Needless to say, in this example it will not be very successful. On the other hand, it will not be completely unsuccessful. It can create *some* motivation. For example, it could make the assumption that the supermarket sold home-improvement materials, such as shelves. We could imagine an algorithm which tried to avoid making too many such added hypotheses by trying an earlier referent.

This scheme would resemble the one we discussed in Chapter 4 which would enable ATNs to handle semantic preferences. The ATNs kept several alternative hypotheses around, ranked according to semantic reasonableness. Whenever it had to choose a path to follow, it always chose the one ranked highest. For pronoun problems there will always be several alternative hypotheses. Initially they will be ranked according to the order of the possible referents. The first might have a score of 0, the second −2 the third −4, etc. Then each time our motivation analysis has to postulate a new object or action, it will subtract 1 from the score of that alternative. If that brought the alternative lower than any of the competition, it would be put back on the agenda, and another possibility would be tried until it too required too many hypotheses, or until one succeeded.

Implementing this method would require a different modification to the noun-phrase scheme presented in Chapter 4. The basic idea is to replace retrieve-val by a function which returns the last mentioned, but which can be made to return more possibilities later if the first one requires making too many assumptions.

Note that in most normal conversations we start out with relatively complete descriptions of the objects we wish to talk about (such as "the dog I saw at your house yesterday") and subsequently abbreviate to shorter phrases (like "the dog"). The "guess and back up" method fits nicely here since the last-mentioned dog will virtually always be the right one. On the other hand, the

Skolem constant method looks very good in cases where we have several pronouns (for example, ''He told him that he had it''). Having to try various combinations of the possible referents until the right one is found looks discouraging. The Skolem constant method is seductive because it offers the hope of getting things right without the search. Perhaps someone will discover a method which combines the best features of both.

10.6.2 Conversation and Reference

In the previous discussion we characterized one method as starting with the most recent possible referent and working backwards. There is reason to believe, however, that this is not exactly the ordering method the referent-determination method should use. While it is not possible to show such examples in a short space, it is quite easy to have a pronoun refer to an object which was mentioned a page or two back, and not since. This can occur, for example, when we have two characters engaged in a conversation about, say, a lost object. Suppose the conversation must be terminated for some reason. When the characters resume the conversation, it is possible for them to start out with a phrase like ''So, did you find it?'' Taking the possible referents in reverse chronological order would at best result in an incredible waste of time, and at worst result in a wrong choice of referent. The problem is that no account is taken of the structure of conversations.

Once we have recognized that conversational structure can play a role in reference determination, it is possible to recognize more subtle examples. Consider again the sample conversation we used earlier.

1	S1:	I think we should use a global variable here.
2	S2:	I am not so sure.
3		Like, I tried that in the telephone operator assignment.
4		It resulted in a terrible bug.
5	S1:	Oh, by the way, you got a phone call from Fran.
6	S2:	Did she say what she wanted?
7	S1:	No, but she said it was nothing important.
8	S2:	OK, I will call her later.
9		At any rate, it took me three days to find it.

In the last line, an algorithm that took no account of conversational structure might try the previously mentioned phone call as the referent of final ''it'' in the sentence.

In our earlier discussion of the structure of conversations, we put off the question of how such structure is to be represented until we had a better idea of what we hoped to gain from our knowledge of the structure. We can now answer the question of benefits, at least in part. We want our knowledge of structure to fix these reference problems. We do not want to consider referents if they are not plausibly part of the conversation we are currently in, and more specifically, if they are not part of the same section of the conversation. But getting this behavior is not easy. Assuming that one can track the structure of the conversation, it is still necessary to put in the rules restricting pronoun reference. This can be done easily enough, but the result is quite ad hoc in that one must introduce at least two new data structures: the structure of the conversation (presumably a tree structure like that in Figure 10.12) and for each subconversation, the set of objects that are mentioned in that section. These are used only for referent determination. While this is what current theories would have us do, it is an unsatisfactory scheme. Somehow it seems unlikely that the mind has developed whole new structures simply to track conversations and use that information to determine referents. A much more likely possibility is that the work on conversation is actually telling us something about memory organization in general. That is to say, if we really understood what was going on, we would replace the ideas of Chapter 7 with some new ones which automatically predicted the structure of conversations, and which would automatically make noun-phrase-referent determination sensitive to this structure. Unfortunately, nobody has the necessary ideas.

10.6.3 Word Sense Disambiguation

Now let us turn to the other unexamined ambiguity problem, word sense disambiguation. There are two influences on the choice of word sense in a sentence. On one hand, there are the logical constraints of the story and the immediate sentence, and on the other there are the "associative" connections between the word senses and the context.

The programmer was near the terminal.
The plane was near the terminal.

The porter studied the case.
The lawyer studied the case.

These are examples where associated connections seem to be the dominant force in our decision as to the correct word sense. There is certainly nothing absurd in saying that a lawyer studied a piece of baggage, or that a programmer was near an airplane terminal, yet these are not the interpretations we normally assume in the absence of other context. In other examples, however, the logic of the situation dictates one meaning or another.

The woman was in the terminal.
The case was over in two weeks.

The association-type examples presumably have little or nothing to do with the motivation analysis we have been studying. Motivation analysis assumes goal directed behavior. The associations can have nothing to do with either goals or behavior. However, there are several related ideas which might do the job. One is the *scriptal lexicon*. As you may remember, *scripts* are a form of schema that deal with stereotyped activities. Scriptal lexicons are dictionaries associated with particular scripts (schemas), specifying the words which correspond to concepts explicated by that schema. So, for example, the schema for **poker** will have in its lexicon the word "call," with a pointer to the part of the poker schema corresponding to calling a bet. The schema for, say, square dancing would also have "call," but a quite different definition. There might be a standard dictionary with the most common senses, but the specialized ones would be in the individual schemas. Thus when a new word comes in, the word sense disambiguation procedure would first look for definitions in each active schema and, if it finds one, then that will be the first sense to try. If none of them say anything useful, it would then try the standard lexicon. So if we were talking about people playing poker on a train, and the procedure were trying to disambiguate the word "call," it would have a situation like than in Figure 10.14. Note that the scriptal lexicon theory has the property that irrelevant senses of the word are never even seen. There is some controversy in psychological circles as to whether or not people have this property. While introspectively we certainly are not aware of the unselected senses, there is some evidence that immediately after a word is heard we unconsciously access all possible meanings. From a purely AI point of view, the attractiveness of the scriptal lexicon theory will depend on how well we can associate word meanings with particular schemas, and how many schemas are active at any one time. If the number is large, say fifty or sixty, we would have the unattractive alternative of looking through all those lexicons, rather than one combined lexicon. Admittedly, the "stories" we have looked at would not require so many active schemas, but as our quote marks around "stories" suggest, we have been dealing with rather simple examples. Consider again an earlier example used to illustrate the problems of understanding emotion

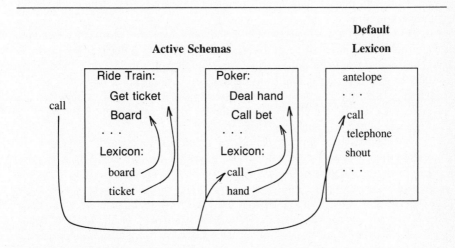

Figure 10.14 The scriptal lexicon

> Richard hadn't heard from his old roommate Paul for years. Paul had lent Richard money which was never paid back, but now Richard had no idea where to find his old friend. When a letter finally arrived from San Francisco, Richard was anxious to find out how Paul was.

> Unfortunately, the news was not good. Paul's wife Sara wanted a divorce. Not knowing who to turn to, Paul was hoping for a favor from the only lawyer he knew. Paul gave his home phone number in case Richard felt he could help.

Even in the few lines presented here we find the following topics, each one of which would probably correspond to several schemas: college roommates, lending money, friendship, big cities, letters, marriage, divorce, lawyers, and telephones.

Another possible way of finding correct word senses through association would be using the marker-passing scheme mentioned earlier. If an algorithm passed markers from "terminal" to all of its senses, and from them to related concepts, and if it did the same thing for, say, "airplane," it would find an intersection at something like "airplanes leave from terminals," or a proposition to that effect. The path to this intersection would go through a particular word sense, and that would be the word sense to choose for the example. A side benefit is that the same paths help out in motivation analysis (remember we mentioned marker passing there also). Unfortunately, any two concepts in an associative network will have a path connecting them. For example, computer-terminal and airplane would be connected via isa links to solid-object or something similar. If marker passing is to work such paths must be longer than the correct ones, or else can be ruled out on some simple grounds. We have already pointed out that nobody knows if this will turn out to be the case. Thus both marker passing and scriptal lexicons have flaws (and adherents) at the present time.

However, as we already noted, not all influences on word-sense disambiguation fall under the heading of associations. The other influences are the logical constraints from the story. One very important subclass are those constraints originating with the verb on the kinds of arguments it requires. So for example, "pick up" has several meanings besides "to grasp." It also has the meaning seen in "Fran picks up men at singles bars" as well as "Fran picks up difficult ideas quickly," and several others.

Note that each of these meanings of "pick up" takes a different kind of direct object (a physical object, a person, an idea), and we could disambiguate on this basis. In linguistics this technique has been associated with the terms *semantic markers* and *selectional restrictions*. The semantic markers are labels like "person," "idea," and so on that are used to disambiguate the verb. The idea is that each verb will have "selectional restrictions" on the kinds of arguments it can take, and we look for a match between the selectional restrictions required by the verb, and the semantic markers possessed by the noun phrase.

If we associate verbs with plan schemas, then the selectional restrictions would be the statements in the schemas saying what kind of object can fill the roles in the schema. So a schema for **read** would require that the thing read be of the type **written-language** of which **book** and **menu** would be subtypes. In this view, the semantic markers would be the classes of things in the isa hierarchy which we use to classify objects.

Finally, there are the logical influences that require more complicated inference than the rather simple-minded selectional restrictions. For example,

> The baby was in the pen.
> The baby picked up the pen.

Here knowledge of the size and weight of babies and pens (of all varieties) are needed to pick the correct sense. This would seem to suggest that we try something here like we did with noun phrase reference, namely let normal processing make the decision. However, very little work has been done on this kind of problem.

10.7 Where We Have Been, and Where We Are Going

We have now looked at many aspects of language comprehension, but the reader may still be wondering how all of this fits together. This feeling may be excused in part, since our discussion of language has been divided over two chapters, rather remote from one another. But in fact, there are deeper roots to the problem. Selecting a group of techniques that spans the problems, and yet fits together, is an active research question. We will briefly review where we have been, but we cannot promise a neat package.

Presumably everything starts with syntactic processing. We say "presumably" since at least one of the processes we have discussed, marker passing, has no need of any of the results of syntactic processing, and thus could come before, or be in parallel. As the parse is proceeding, an internal representation is being built up. This will require the techniques discussed in Chapter 4. However, it will also require the techniques discussed in the last section for determining referents and word sense disambiguation. The problem is that the latter two depend on already having at least some of the internal representation already built up. While this does not involve us in a logical circularity, it does mean that the understander must build up enough representation to support the disambiguation processes, while not asking for information which is not yet available. This calls for fancy footwork. The footwork becomes even more complicated when we add the processes that are expected to give the syntactic parser advice on which parses to follow, and which to cut off.

At any rate, for word sense disambiguation the algorithm needs to have the verb sense (for the logical constraints) and some contextual information, either from marker passing, or a scriptal lexicon. Then referents must be determined. We have presented two ways in which context can be brought to bear on this process, through the introduction of Skolem constants and by guessing the last-mentioned possibility until it requires making extra assumptions about the story. Either way, lots of details need to be filled in.

Assuming the internal representation is somehow produced, the result is passed on to the "understanding" component. In this chapter we have looked at one part of this process, namely motivation analysis, with brief glances at related processes, like abductive projection. At this point everything fits together well, at least as far as we know.

At the risk of depressing everyone, there are a lot of problems we have not mentioned. One classic problem is that of metaphor. Most of us are used to thinking of metaphor as something that occurs in poetry. But it is much more widespread than that. Indeed, it seems to seep in everywhere. Take the previous sentence, for example. There is currently work on the problem, but we are still a long way from a good theory.

Nor have we said nearly enough about pronouns. For one thing we have looked only at singular pronouns. Plural pronouns are much more difficult because quite often there is no "individual" mentioned in the text that corresponds to the referent. For example,

George went to the store. He met Bill. They left together.

Here the "they" refers to a group consisting of George and Bill, an object which has no explicit existence in the sentences. Even worse, it is not even necessary for the sentences to individually mention the objects that form the group.

Each child put on a uniform. They had been donated by a local manufacturing concern.

A standard representation of the first sentence might look like the following (where we are only concerned with the representation of "a uniform").

```
(forall (child) (if (member child group-22)
                    (exists (uniform) (puton child uniform))))
```

The problem with this representation is that there is no explicit group of uniforms for the "they" to refer back to. This might be the fault of the representation of the first sentence. That is, perhaps it should include a term which denotes the set of uniforms. On the other hand, perhaps the first sentence should stay the same and somehow the second manages to relate the "they" to the uniforms implied by the first.

But if these last paragraphs have you down, let us end this chapter on a more cheerful note. In many respects the theory of comprehension espoused here is a rather elegant one. The reader should review the chapter and note how often we were able to use ideas which had come from earlier chapters: the indexing methods from Chapter 7, the plan schemas from Chapter 9, etc. That is to say, the actual amount of new machinery needed to implement the ideas of this chapter is small because many of the spare parts can be stolen from other areas of AI. That is the mark of a promising theory.

10.8 References and Further Reading

The idea of connecting problem solving and language comprehension is a popular one. Probably the most extensive analysis is that of Schank and Abelson [Schank77], although it has also been suggested by Charniak [Charniak75] and Rieger [Rieger75]. The basic algorithm for finding motivation has been discussed by [Schmidt78] and [Wilensky78]. A similar algorithm, but joined with a problem solver that can use the same knowledge, has been suggested by [Wong81]. The work on subsumption goals is due to Wilensky, whose Pam program could handle them. The discussion of emotion, and understanding them is taken largely from the work of [Lehnert81] and [Dyer83].

The idea of marker passing, or spreading activation, has a long history. The earliest reference within AI is [Quillian66]. It has also had wide circulation in psychology. A good review article on the subject is that of Collins and Loftus [Collins75]. Recently, this idea has been revived within AI by [Charniak83c]. A rather different type of marker passing has been advocated by [Fahlman79], who has figured out how to implement pointer-following operations like those of Chapter 7 on parallel marker-passing hardware.

While there is no work exactly corresponding to our treatment of abductive pattern matching from the viewpoint of unification, the basic idea of a pattern matcher that will make "leaps of faith" and where making one such "leap" may, in general, require others has appeared in many places. One early description is by Moore and Newell [Moore74]. The idea subsequently became a central part of the KRL language of Bobrow and Winograd [Bobrow77].

The general idea behind performative sentences is generally attributed to Austin in his famous book *How to Do Things with Words* [Austin62]. These ideas were then extended by Searle in his book *Speech Acts* [Searle69]. The term speech acts is due to Searle. More generally, on the role of linguistics in philosophy, readers might consult [Rorty67]. Within AI, the work to fit speech acts into the general theory of problem solving has been primarily that of [Allen80, Cohen79] and [Perrault80]. A more "conventionalist" approach to indirect speech acts is found in Gordon and Lakoff [Gordon75]. The notion of conversational implicature is due to [Grice75]. Our discussion of more complex conversations was modeled on the work of [Grosz78] and [Reichman78].

There has been a large literature on determining reference: an excellent survey is that by [Hirst81]. The specific scheme of substituting a Skolem function for an unknown referent has appeared in various guises in the literature by [Charniak72, Rieger76], and [Wilks75]. The alternative of using the most recent referent until it requires extra hypotheses was first suggested by [McDermott74]. The idea of association for word sense disambiguation is a common one. The specific proposal for scriptal lexicons has been put forward by [Hayes78] and [Cullingford78]. The idea of using marker passing for this task is common to most of the marker passing and spreading activation literature. Last, the original ideas concerning semantic markers and selectional restrictions originate in a well-known paper by Katz and Fodor [Katz63], and have appeared in many AI implementations, perhaps the best known being Winograd's Shrdlu program [Winograd72]. Work by Hirst has attempted to synthesize several of these basic ideas [Hirst82, Hirst83a].

For some suggestions on handling plural noun phrases and the difficulties they present see [Nash-Webber77]. An extensive discussion of metaphor is found in [Lakoff80]. For an AI perspective on the problem, see [Carbonell82].

Exercises

10.1 *(Open-ended)* Given the algorithm for motivation analysis presented in Section 10.2 as well as the formalization of cigarette lighting presented there, describe what would happen in the analysis of a "story" like "Jack was going to light a cigarette. He set fire to his house." Which part of our theory is responsible for this behavior? Describe ways to prevent such conclusions from being drawn.

10.2 We suggested as a possible rule for deciding between possible motivations this: if we have several possibilities, and one requires the creation of a new object and the others do not, then restrict consideration to the ones which do not (unless overruled by the previous rule). Consider the action of getting an ice cube, and suggest how its possible motivations might contradict this rule.

10.3 *(Open-ended)* Assume

    (a) chewing something is a subevent of eating it,
    (b) eating is a subevent of restaurant dining, and
    (c) eating is done for its own sake.

What will our motivation-analysis algorithm do with the following "story"? "Gerry went to a restaurant. He chewed on his steak." (Remember, take the algorithm literally.) Suggest solutions to this problem.

10.4 In Section 10.2 we noted a problem involving stories like "Jack got a rope. He wanted to commit suicide." After the first sentence we have no way to guess at a motivation. Initially we suggested that in such cases we simply give up, throw out whatever work we did, and go on to the next sentence. However, given the motivation analysis algorithm presented, the second sentence would never connect up with the first. To remedy this we suggested that we retain our guesses, so that when the second sentence comes in we will note that it confirms an open guess about the first sentence, and thus establish a motivation. An alternative would be to keep the idea of tossing out inconclusive analyses, and instead change the motivation-analysis algorithm. Suggest one or more ways in which this could be done.

10.5   By borrowing the problem-solving predicates of Chapter 9 for use in
       motivation analysis we assumed that (sub-event *super sub*) not only
       meant that *sub* was a subtask of *super*, but also that *super* was the reason
       for doing *sub*. This is reasonable, but raises an interesting question with
       regard to subsumption goals. Do we want to use this predicate to relate a
       subsumption goal *sub* to the task for which it was done? Discuss.

10.6   In our discussion of marker passing we recommended searching for a
       path between two concepts by marking from both concepts until a concept
       in the middle was "hit" by the waves of marks from both sides. An al-
       ternative is to mark from one concept until the other is hit. In each case
       the algorithm is to mark "breadth-first," that is, to mark all nodes at a
       distance n from the starting node before marking any at a distance $n+1$.
       Obviously, if either algorithm finds a node already marked, no further
       marks are propagated from it.

   a)   Show that both of these algorithms will find the shortest path
        between the two concepts.
   b)   Show that the first algorithm can be more efficient than the second.
        One way to model the situation is to assume that nodes representing
        concepts are arranged in a grid on a plane (or on a lattice in three-
        space if you prefer). Each node has four neighbors. If node 1 is n
        links away from node 2, how many nodes will be marked by the
        first algorithm? How many by the second?

10.7   In Section 10.2 we pointed out that marking from two concepts simul-
       taneously is not always feasible. In processing a sentence, we will mark
       from each word successively as it comes in, detecting previous marks as
       we do. Show that with such a method one will still find the shortest path
       between two concepts first. You should suppose that some method has
       been installed to prevent each wave of marker propagation from marking
       the entire database.

10.8   In our discussion of emotions, we developed a rule for explicating the
       emotion of gratitude. Show that the rule as finally developed is still nei-
       ther necessary nor sufficient. That is, give situations that fit the rule, in
       which the person will plausibly not feel gratitude; and some that do not fit
       the rule, in which the person will feel gratitude anyway.

10.9   Consider this story

       Aravind found an old book while visiting his grandparents. He wanted to
       read it, so he learned Sanskrit.

       Explain how our **prereq** mechanism (Section 10.3.2) accounts for under-
       standing this story. Unfortunately, it might account for too much; sup-
       pose we added the line "John beckoned to a Chinese friend he recognized
       sitting in the corner" to the story of John and the Chinese menu. Suggest

a way to keep the algorithm from inferring that John wants to learn Chinese.

10.10 In Section 10.3.2 we presented the story of Fred looking for his mother for money to buy ice cream. Reread that story, with the clause "he couldn't find her" replaced by "she had gone shopping."

    a) Explain why it is harder to understand this version. How can Fred's switch to a new plan be explained now? Will the methods of Section 10.3.2 be adequate? If not, suggest improvements.

    b) In the new version of the story, how would you answer the question, "Why did Fred's mother go shopping?" How would you extend our motivation-analysis model to handle multiple characters' goals and plans?

10.11 One issue we have not dealt with at all is revising abductive hypotheses. This story is due to Allan Collins:

> He plunked five dollars down at the window. She tried to give him two-fifty back, but he wouldn't take it. So when they got inside she bought him a large bag of popcorn.

    a) Explain how your understanding of this story changes halfway through. Suggest changes to our abduction algorithms to make such revisions.

    b) Try switching the genders of the pronouns. Give each version of the story to a different subject, and see if they differ in their interpretations. What does this say about sex-linked defaults in our culture?

10.12 One problem we have not considered is how our scheme could handle stories where the actions were presented out of sequence.

> Jack ate his meal and went to pay.
> He had ordered a lobster so the bill was large.

Assume that our English parser can sort out the tense problems and give us **seq** statements like those used in plan schemas. (See Figure 10.1.) Suppose someone wrote an odd story in which a particular **sub-event** of a task was done twice. Ideally we would want our program to at least notice this, although what it should do about it is by no means clear. Explain how a general process like that described in Section 10.4.1 for validating assumptions of equality might handle this.

10.13 Section 10.3 got quite a bit ahead of Section 10.4. The technical details in the later section failed to deal with the revised "goal-tracking" algorithm we discussed in Section 10.3. Instead, it went back to the assumption that all we wanted to do was instantiate a schema. How would those technical details have to be revised to handle goal tracking? In particular, suppose a plan is executed halfway, when an insuperable obstacle appears. How could things be changed so that "half a schema" was instantiated in a case like this?

10.14 In Section 10.6.1 we discussed how to handle the noun phrase "the horn" in "I bought a used car. The horn did not work." In light of this discussion, how will the following example be problematical: "The car I bought had no horn." Discuss.

10.15 Sections 10.2 and 10.4 can be viewed as a high-level description of a project to create a program capable of establishing motivations for actions it is given. To simplify matters, assume that the input is already in internal representation, so that you do not have to worry about handling real English. Before you start, you should give some thought to the representation of plans that you will use. In the text we have been quite cavalier in our use of various plan notations, ranging from the high-level plan-for: to lower-level implicit quantification forms. Probably you want to use the implicit quantifier form because that will make the matching the easiest. Another critical issue is how individual parts of a plan will be related to the plan as a whole. The most obvious way is to require that programs like the matcher (which require information from various places in the plan) be given a pointer to the entire plan. Alternatively, each plan step could be indexed separately, and have as one of its properties a pointer to the plan. This way you could give the matcher just the relevant plan step, and it could access the plan via this pointer. Another possibility is to index all of the relevant plan information separately, so that if the matcher needed to know what sort of object a (fire-source ?cigarette-lighting): was, it could look it up without looking through the entire plan.

a) The first program to write should probably be the matching program. It will take as input two event descriptions (and possibly the plan) and output either a signal saying that they cannot be made to match, or else a list of assumptions that must be made for the match to go through.

b) Next in line might be the indexer. This can be as simple as a list of available plans, plus a program to look through each one, sending each sub-event to the matcher for an accept/reject decision, or it could be something like the more complicated indexing method described in the text.

c) Next, write a program that, given a successful match, does the necessary work to hook the incoming statement to the plan of which it is a part. This will involve asserting that this statement corresponds to some particular plan step, as well as adding any new := statements for objects in the plan.

d) Write the overall control structure that connects up these elements, and calls the whole thing recursively on the resulting goal, so that several levels of motivation will be established.

e) The above program will not handle situations in which there is more than one possible motivation. Add a module that given several possible motivations, will pick the best one.

11

This chapter depends on Chapters 6 and 7. Besides that, Section 11.3 depends on Chapter 9, Section 11.4 depends on Chapter 8, and Section 11.6 depends on Chapter 4. Any or all of these three sections could be skipped.

Learning

11.1 Introduction

It must seem to many readers that we have completely omitted the essence of intelligence from our account so far, this essence being the ability to *learn*, that is, to extract deeper and deeper insights into a repeated type of situation. No matter how often our problem solvers and reasoners encounter a problem, they will always try exactly the same series of moves, even if these end in failure every time. A person would at least learn to give up.

There are lots of things people do not learn to do. No one learns how to compute Gaussian convolutions better in low-level vision. But we certainly improve on "high-level" skills like reasoning and problem solving. In fact, many students, on first exposure to AI, act as if learning explained most of what we do in these fields. For instance, they suggest that an engineer solves problems by bringing "experience" to bear on them. Sometimes they talk as if there is some kind of direct link between the past and present, but of course what must happen is that experience changes the state of an organism in such a way that the new state enables it to do better in subsequent situations:

experience → state → performance

Each half of this diagram can be studied independently. So far we have been concentrating on the second half. The "state" has included things like plan libraries, and we haven't worried too much about where they came from.

One idea that has fascinated the Western mind is that there is a general-purpose learning mechanism that accounts for almost all of the state of an adult human being. According to this idea, people are born knowing very little, and absorb almost everything by way of this general learner. (Even a concept like "physical object," it has been proposed, is acquired by noticing that certain visual and tactile sensations come in stable bundles.) This idea is still power-fully attractive. It underlies much of behavioristic psychology. AI students often rediscover it, and propose to dispense with the study of reasoning and problem solving, and instead build a baby and let it just learn these things.

We believe this idea is dead, killed off by research in AI (and linguistics, and other branches of "cognitive science"). What this research has revealed is that for an organism to learn anything, it must already know a lot. Learning begins with organized knowledge, which grows and becomes better organized. Without strong clues to what is to be learned, nothing will get learned.

11.2 Learning as Induction

As we will see, the field of learning presents a diversity that can become bewildering. In the first half of this chapter, we will attempt to be systematic, by focusing on the subfield in which most of the research has traditionally been done. In later sections, we will tarnish the image by looking at a larger, less classifiable group of research efforts, but at least the resulting mosaic will be more faithful to the field as it actually is today.

The classical name for our topic in this section is *concept learning*, but we will be attempting to summarize a broader class of research efforts than are usu-ally subsumed under that name. The simplest choice of name for this field is simply *inductive learning*, or *induction*, and these are the terms we will use.

In the abstract, we can view the output of inductive learning as a set of *production rules*. You will recall from Chapter 7 that these are rules of the form

In situation *do* action.

The "action" may be something overt, or an internal action, or even an infer-ence. We will sometimes use the word *concept* for the right-hand side of such a rule, and the phrase *concept definition* or *pattern* for the left-hand side.

We schematize inductive learning as shown in Figure 11.1. From one or more ·instances in which *action$_i$* was the appropriate action in response to

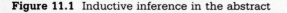

$$situation_1 \qquad action_1$$
$$situation_2 \qquad action_2$$
$$\cdots, \qquad \cdots$$

$$situation_{gen} \quad \rightarrow \quad action_{gen}$$

Figure 11.1 Inductive inference in the abstract

situation$_i$, we infer that the general version, *action$_{gen}$* is the appropriate type of action in response to the general situation type, *situation$_{gen}$*. As an example, consider Figure 11.2. Here the "action" is to make an inference, namely, that an object is black. (In this case, our "concept/definition" terminology is misleading, since being a crow is not part of the definition of being black. In some of our examples it will be more appropriate. In any case, it is traditional.)

The classic problem that philosophers have worried about is whether or in what sense general conclusions ever actually follow from specific observations in this way. Alas, AI research is unlikely to shed any light on this question, because it takes as its point of departure the fact that some inductive inferences are correct and some are not. The overall problem is to hit as many useful ones as possible, quickly eliminating or debugging the useless ones.

11.2.1 The Empiricist Algorithm

Debugging an if-then rule means making its antecedent more general or more specific, in response to feedback about how well the current version works. We will also use the terms *weakening* and *strengthening* respectively. (An antecedent is stronger if it "says more," that is, if it is true in fewer situations.)

Here is a fanciful example. Suppose that a robot has inferred this rule:

(inst ?x feline) → *should* (pet ?x)

from observations of several housecats. Suppose that the robot uses this rule when ?x is a tiger, and is rewarded with severe damage. This experience tends to disconfirm the rule. We will use the phrase "the teacher" to refer to the source of information like this, whether or not it is accompanied by pain or pleasure. In many cases, the teacher is just the environment.

When a rule is disconfirmed, the proper response is usually not to discard it, but to *specialize* it so that it applies to fewer situations. In this example, the program must find a way to distinguish situations involving felines in which petting was rewarded from those in which it was punished. Here is one way to do that:

---

object$_1$ is a crow.	*object$_1$* is black.
object$_2$ is a crow.	*object$_2$* is black.
. . .	. . .

| ?x is a crow. | → | ?x is black. |

Figure 11.2 Inductive inference of "All crows are black"

> (and (inst ?x feline) (size ?x small))
> → *should* (pet ?x)

Adding a conjunct to the antecedent of the rule strengthens it so that it is satisfied in fewer situations.

If a rule should have applied but did not, then the machine should *generalize* it. In our example, if the machine comes to realize (by being told or random experimentation) that petting a dog was the proper thing to do, then it may generalize thus:

> (and (inst ?x carnivore) (size ?x small))
> → *should* (pet ?x)

Of course, it can *overgeneralize*, but specialization can always fix things up.

To summarize, the problem is to find a pattern, or *concept definition* that applies to one set of situations (the *positive instances* of a concept), and does not apply to another (the *negative instances*); or, put another way, to generalize from the positive instances to a general pattern, but not so far that it includes any of the negative instances.

Many programs have been written that attempt this task. One of the most influential was that of Winston [Winston75a]. The rules it learned had conclusions of the form (inst ?x *category*), where *category* was some class of objects that could be built out of blocks, such as "arch." Put another way, it learned the "concept" of "?x being an arch," or just "the concept *arch*" for short. It would be given groups of blocks, some of which were arches and some were not. For instance, Figure 11.3 shows a blocks-world scene and its predicate-calculus description. The scene describes a typical "arch." Figure 11.4 shows

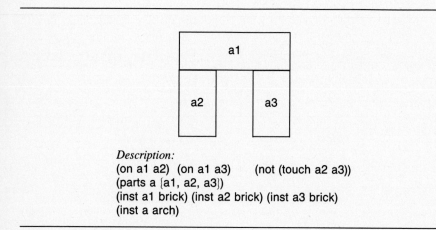

Description:
(on a1 a2) (on a1 a3)   (not (touch a2 a3))
(parts a {a1, a2, a3})
(inst a1 brick) (inst a2 brick) (inst a3 brick)
(inst a arch)

Figure 11.3 An arch

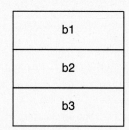

Description:
(on b1 b2)   (on b2 b3)
(parts b {b1, b2, b3})
(inst b1 brick) (inst b2 brick) (inst b3 brick)
(not (inst b arch))

Figure 11.4 A nonarch

a scene depicting a nonarch. Winston's program, given enough positive and negative instances of a concept such as "arch," could infer its definition, shown in Figure 11.5.

Once it gets started, a learning program can be thought of as maneuvering around the space of possible generalizations. To get started in the first place, it must know that there is a rule to be learned, and must generalize a few observations. For example, from the first two instances of an arch, it might conclude that three objects were all that was required:

```
(if (parts ?x {?x1, ?x2, ?x3})
    (inst ?x arch))
```

But counterexamples such as that of Figure 11.4 would invoke "specialization," which adds conjuncts to the left-hand side. With the right sequence of cases, the program could learn the correct definition.

Similar ideas have been pursued by [Dietterich81] and by [Vere78]. But they go back before that to the behaviorist psychologists and the great empiricist

```
(if (and (parts ?x {?x1, ?x2, ?x3})
         (on ?x1 ?x2)
         (on ?x1 ?x3)
         (not (touch ?x2 ?x3)))
    (inst ?x arch))
```

Figure 11.5 Definition of arch learned from training instances

philosophers, from Locke to James. For this reason, we will call the generalize-specialize algorithm the "empiricist" algorithm.

11.2.2 Generalization and Specialization

In the abstract, there seem to be only a few ways that a concept definition can be generalized or specialized. These two operations are inverses of each other, so we can present each generalization/specialization method as a progression that can be run either way.

Variables are more general than constants. Consider the set of situation descriptions shown in Figure 11.6. (Throughout this section we will be giving examples of "concept definitions," or left-hand sides of production rules. Bear in mind that in the antecedents of such rules the Skolemization conventions of Chapter 6 are reversed, so that variables marked with "?" are existentially, not universally, quantified.)

Within the progression of Figure 11.6, formula 1 is maximally specific. Formulas 2, 3, and 4 are all more general in the sense that 1 is subsumed by each of them. (See Chapter 6.) Similarly, each of 2, 3, and 4 is more specific than formula 5 because each subsumes it. The more general formulas match more situations; formula 5 is true if ?x is on anything, and ?y is on anything. Formula 1 is true only if both ?x and ?y are on a particular object, table1. Formulas 2, 3, and 4 are in the middle. Note in particular formula 4, which is true if ?x and ?y are on the same object.

We can use the term *variabilization* for the process of generalizing a formula by replacing a constant with a variable. This process is important because virtually all empiricist programs start by variabilizing their inputs. For instance, Winston's program began by assuming the definition of the concept to be learned was identical to the original scene except for having variables where the scene had constants. Hence it just replaced every constant with a variable.

An important observation about generalization and specialization is that they provide a *set* of methods for revising rules. We will show this more abundantly below, but already we can see that merely knowing in which direction to revise a rule does not tell us much about how to revise it. In the example, if we

---

1.   (and (on ?x table1) (on ?y table1))   *Specific*

2.   (and (on ?x ?z) (on ?y table1))
3.   (and (on ?x table1) (on ?y ?z))
4.   (and (on ?x ?z) (on ?y ?z))

5.   (and (on ?x ?u) (on ?y ?v))   *General*

Figure 11.6 Variables are more general than constants.

discover that formula 5 is too general, we have a choice of at least four ways to make it more specific. To know the right move to make toward the correct rule, one would have to know the correct rule already. In other words, we have here a *search problem*, in the sense of Chapter 5, where the correctness of a step toward increasing or decreasing generality cannot be judged until the final goal is reached; and so false steps are unavoidable.

The problem only gets worse as we think of new dimensions of generality. Predicates and classes tend to come in families with more and less general members. The progression from feline and canine to carnivore in the last section is an example. We can call this *isa-hierarchy generalization*. Here is a related example using predicates instead of classes:

1.   (epoxied ?x ?y)   *Specific*

2.   (glued ?x ?y)

3.   (attached ?x ?y)   *General*

Another example [Michalski83] is *numerical generalization*:

1.   (= ?x 3)   *Specific*

2.   ($\in$?x [2,5])   *General*

This could be useful if ?x values of 2, 3, and 5 had been observed to cause the rule to be appropriate.

Two open-ended ways to weaken or strengthen a pattern are *disjunct manipulation* and *conjunct manipulation*, as exemplified by this progression:

1.   (and (on ?x table1) (touch ?x wall1))   *Specific*

2.   (on ?x table)

3.   (or (on ?x table) (suspended ?x ceiling))   *General*

Adding disjuncts makes a condition more general; adding conjuncts makes it more specific.

As a final method of generalization, we have *universalization*, which shifts from lists of specific formulas to quantified combinations. For example, Figure 11.7 shows a generalization from two examples of a concept in which some spheres are on a table to the pattern, "Everything on the table must be a sphere." This generalization illustrates the general schema, shown at the bottom of Figure 11.7.

Although it is possible to think of other generalization operators, these should be enough to make it clear that the search space of possible generalizations is huge.

On top of that, we have the problem of figuring out what constitutes the "current situation." We cannot take this to be the set of everything the machine believes, because this covers its entire model of the world, past, present, and

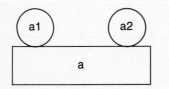
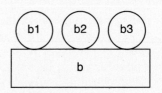

Description:

(on a1 a) (on a2 a)

(inst a1 sphere)

(inst a2 sphere)

(inst a table)

Description:

(on b1 b) (on b2 b) (on b3 b)

(inst b1 sphere)

(inst b2 sphere)

(inst b3 sphere)

(inst b table)

Generalization:

(and (inst ?x table)
    (forall (y)
       (if (on y ?x) (inst y sphere))))

Universalization schema:

1. $(p\ x_1)$ $(q\ x_1)$ *Specific*
     $(p\ x_2)$ $(q\ x_2)$
     $\cdots$
     $(p\ x_n)$ $(q\ x_n)$

2.   (forall (x)   *General*
     (if $(p$ x) $(q$ x)))

Figure 11.7 Universalization example and schema

expected. Normally, we expect attention to be focused on a narrow set of facts. For instance, in trying to infer the rules for dealing with possibly dangerous animals, we focus on their physical characteristics, their proximity, etc. We know to ignore the time of day, the contents of our pockets, and what we had for breakfast yesterday. Figuring out what features of the situation to ignore in revising rules is called the *situation-identification problem*.

For instance, consider learning that the two blocks of an arch must not touch. We included that datum in our description of Figure 11.3, but it seems somewhat suspicious that we did so. In any real scene, there will be thousands of true but irrelevant facts. Any algorithm based on generalization and specialization will bog down unless given just a few facts to work on. Whatever filters those facts automatically constrains what can be learned.

A related problem is the *description problem*. Consider the concept of "magic number." The following are magic: 7, 60, 70, 546, 627. The following are not magic: 364, 9, 626, 708. Is 628 magic? 69? 71? If the numbers are described in base 9, then the answer gets clearer:

Magic: 7 60 70 546 627
           base 9: 7 66 77 666 766

Not magic: 364 9 626 708
           base 9: 444 10 765 866

Queries: 628? (*base 9:* 767?)
           69? (*base 9:* 76?)
           71? (*base 9:* 78?)

This is roughly the same message we delivered in Chapters 1 and 6, that good representations make inferences smoother. The twist here is that the machine must be clairvoyant. It can't wait until the inductive generalization has been discovered to choose the representation.

In other words, the notation used for expressing concept definitions must have the property that *similar situations should have similar descriptions in the notation.* That way, there is a reasonable chance that a short generalization will capture all the positive instances. In the example, the generalization we want is "Every digit is a 6 or 7 in base 9." In base 10, the best we could do is "The number is 6 or 7 or 60 or 61 or 69 or 70 or . . .," listing every possibility.

Another headache is the *credit-assignment problem.* Consider a chess program that has just lost a game. This is one "bit" of information (in the information-theory sense), which tells the program that it made one or more mistakes along the way. Unfortunately, it doesn't say where the first big mistake was, which is what the program really needs to know. If it knew where that mistake was, then the rule or rules responsible for making it could be revised so as to avoid similar mistakes in future.

There are two places from which high-quality information like this can come: careful experiments, or, more likely, someone who already knows. In a careful experiment, one uses exactly one rule of dubious certainty and sees what happens. To avoid chance effects, one may have to run the experiment several times.

Even better than experiments is just asking someone who knows. For instance, if you are a novice chess player, your opponent will almost always tell you what you did wrong, and what you might have done instead. These hints can serve as the bases for generalization and specialization. This is the topic of Section 11.4.

When the situation-identification problem, description problem, and credit-assignment problem have natural solutions, then the empiricist algorithm works well. A good example of this is Mitchell's Lex program, which learns how to do symbolic integration [Mitchell83]. This is the problem, in calculus, of finding a formula that, when differentiated, yields a given formula. If you haven't studied calculus, you will not know exactly what this means, but suffice it to say that this process gives rise to a search through the space of possible formulas, and that many integration problems have no solution. Lex starts off knowing a set of operators to try, and when they are legal, but not knowing when they are appropriate. Hence the learning task here is to figure out, for each operator, a rule of the form

If -facts about formula-
→ *should apply* operator.

Such a rule is called a *heuristic*. Lex is given problems to solve, and initially can try only a breadth-first search. See Figure 11.8. After finding a solution path, it has more information. It knows that an operator on the solution path was executed correctly, while an operator that took it away from the path should not have been executed. This solves the credit-assignment problem. For each operator, such information gives it positive and negative instances of its correct application. There is no question about what information is relevant. The structure of the mathematical formula being operated on is all that can be relevant. The time of day, or the amount of free storage left, can be ignored. This solves the situation-identification problem.

Lex uses the idea of *version spaces* to keep track of the search through general and specific versions of a heuristic. Rather than guess at the correct version, and revise this guess, it keeps track of all versions that are permitted by the data so far. (This is a little misleading; see below.) Consider the example shown in Figure 11.9, taken from [Mitchell83]. After seeing one example in which a given operator ("integration by parts" or IBP) was the right thing to do to the formula $\int 3x \cos(x)dx$, several different versions of the general rule are in

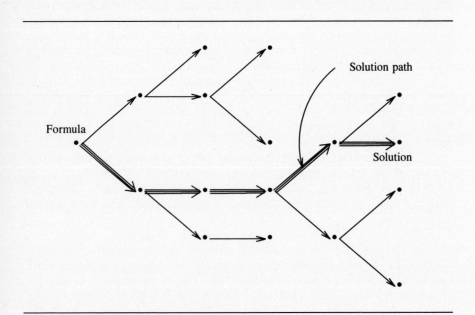

Figure 11.8 Lex's search for a solution

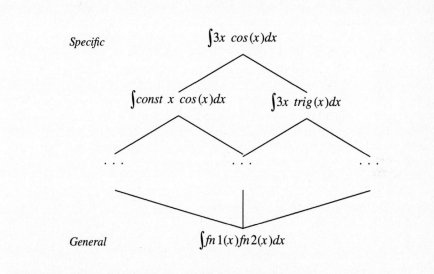

Specific

$\int 3x \ cos(x)dx$

$\int const \ x \ cos(x)dx$ $\int 3x \ trig(x)dx$

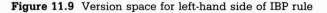

. . .   .

General $\int fn\, 1(x)fn\, 2(x)dx$

Figure 11.9 Version space for left-hand side of IBP rule

the running. The figure shows four of them. (The right-hand sides are always the same, "Apply IBP," so we show only the left-hand sides.) The different versions are related by *isa-hierarchy generalization*. The most specific says that the rule applies just to the particular problem in question. The most general says that it applies to any product at all. The truth lies in between. As new problems are tried, and more positive and negative instances are encountered, the gap narrows between the most general and most specific versions permitted by those instances. A positive instance, in which the rule is applicable, causes the more specific versions to be discarded in favor of generalizations that cover all the positive examples. A negative instance, in which the rule turns out to be a mistake, causes the more general versions to be discarded.

It is impractical in general to keep track of all the elements of a version space. (The one in Figure 11.9. is artificially small.) Fortunately, it is sufficient to keep track only of the "boundaries," the most specific versions and most general versions that have not been ruled out. As new negative instances of a heuristic are encountered, the general boundary is made more specific. As new positive instances are encountered, the specific boundary is made more general. Eventually the boundaries meet, and the process converges on one or more patterns that lie in the middle. Whether this pattern is actually correct depends on how well Lex's pattern-description language fits the domain. (More on this below.)

An interesting feature of Lex is that it can propose problems that will help it narrow the version space, by providing crucial experiments that distinguish between more general and more specific cases. For instance, given the version space of Figure 11.9, it might be led to try the problem $\int 5x \cos(x)dx$ in order to see whether the constant 3 was an important feature of the original problem. See [Mitchell83] for details.

Note in Figure 11.9 how the description language constrains the learnable rules. There is a class of functions *trig* containing both sin and cos ("sine" and "cosine"). Having seen sin and cos, Lex immediately generalizes to *trig* because that's all its notational machinery allows for. It is not able to try "sin *or* cos" as an intermediate. Similarly, from 3 and 5 it generalizes to *constant*. *Odd constant* is not allowed, even though in some cases it is the correct generalization. Hence the remarks we made above, that the version space represents all and only the still-possible versions of the heuristic, is an idealization. A more correct statement would be that it represents the still-possible versions *that are expressible in a notation chosen a priori*.

One is tempted to look for an "ultracautious strategy," using a notation that would allow the program to avoid ever jumping to a conclusion not sanctioned by the data so far. Alas, such a notation is all too easy to find. If unlimited disjunction is allowed in the language, then the most specific hypothesis that accounts for all the situations seen so far is just "*situation 1 or situation 2 or . . . or situation N.*" This will never match any novel situation, and will make the whole operation pointless. Hence to get anywhere a program must be willing to risk overgeneralization, and, when necessary, compensate with specialization later. One drastic way to make sure this happens is to eliminate disjunction from the notation.

Unfortunately, forbidding disjunction makes it impossible ever to learn a concept whose correct definition is actually disjunctive. This is the famous *disjunctive-concept problem*. Here is how it arises in the version-space terminology: Suppose that the correct pattern for a heuristic is (or P Q), where P is neither more general nor more specific than Q. To be concrete, take P to be the pattern $\int const \ x \ \cos(x)dx$ and Q to be the pattern $\int 3x \ trig(x)dx$ as shown in Figure 11.9. What we are picturing is that there is some operator that should trigger on anything matching either of these patterns, but there is no more general pattern that subsumes both P and Q without counterexamples. (Needless to say, such an operator is in reality implausible.) Now suppose that Lex has been trained on a sequence of problems that cause it to converge on P as the proper left-hand side for its heuristic. Then we give it a problem in which the operator is appropriate in a situation matching Q but not P. Normally, having an example that fails to match an element of the version space should cause that element to be eliminated in favor of something more general, but that is impossible here.

To solve the disjunctive-concept problem, Lex departs from a pure version-space strategy. When this strategy breaks down as described in the previous paragraph, Lex decides that the concept must be disjunctive, and it starts a new version space for the (hitherto unnoticed) disjunct. The new space is from the beginning disjoint from the old one, so there is never any question about where a new positive instance belongs.

11.2.3 Matching

We can generate variants of the empiricist algorithm by exploring different ways of processing the parts of Figure 11.1. We focus on a detail of this figure in Figure 11.10. We have drawn arrows between the parts to indicate important relationships. The arrow from the general situation to each individual is called the *abstraction mapping*. Going from the abstract pattern to the individual one is just instantiation, replacing variables with constants. Going back is a sequence of generalizations (Section 11.2.2). We will talk about the other mappings in the figure later.

When the correct abstraction has been arrived at, then the relationship between the general and particular patterns is straightforward. To test whether the general pattern applies to the particular situation, you do a deduction. The following query would be useful for checking whether an object A is an arch

(Show: (and (parts A {?x1, ?x2, ?x3})
 (on ?x1 ?x2)   (on ?x1 ?x3)
 (not (touch ?x2 ?x3))))

given the definition of arch that we presented in Figure 11.5. Now suppose that

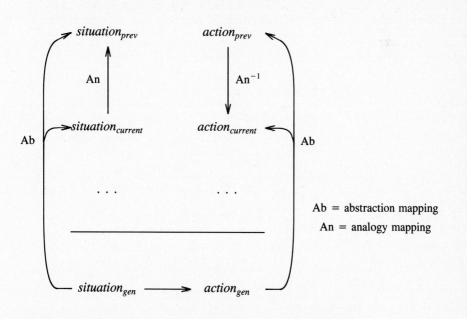

Figure 11.10 Relationships among parts of induction schema

the correct generalization has not been arrived at. In Mitchell et al.'s approach, this would mean that the version space for the concept of arch was still ambiguous; that is, there were untried cases whose "archhood" could not be deduced or refuted. In other algorithms, such as Winston's, the machine does not keep around a representation of all versions of a rule, but makes a guess as to the correct one, and revises it as it goes. Much the same issues arise in each case, but we will phrase our discussion in terms of the "guess" algorithm.

Suppose that, having seen the scene of Figure 11.3, Winston's program decided that the proper definition of the concept was

```
(if (and (parts ?x {?x1, ?x2, ?x3})
         (on ?x1 ?x2)
         (on ?x1 ?x3)
         (inst ?x1 brick)  (inst ?x2 brick) (inst ?x3 brick)
         (not (touch ?x2 ?x3)))
    (inst ?x arch))
```

Now suppose it is given the scene of Figure 11.11. The antecedent of the rule fails to be verified by the scene, and so the program concludes that it is not an arch. If it is told by the teacher that c is an arch after all, then it must generalize the antecedent so that it will be verified.

It is clear to a human observer that the required generalization is to delete the requirement that ?x1 be a brick. For the algorithm to figure this out, it must *match* the overly specific concept definition with the new example, looking for places where they differ. You can think of matching as a modified deduction

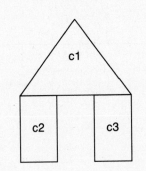

Description:

```
(on c1 c2)  (on c1 c3)      (not (touch c2 c3))
(parts c {c1, c2, c3})
(inst c1 wedge) (inst c2 brick) (inst c3 brick)
(inst c arch)
```

Figure 11.11 Another arch

in which goals are allowed to fail. Failed goals become noted as differences.
This is exactly the operation we discussed in Chapter 9, in connection with the
Strips problem solver. There we defined *maximal match substitution*, the substitution θ that satisfied as many conjuncts in a set G as possible. If G is taken to
be a (Skolemized) tentative concept definition, and S is a database representing
the current situation, then let $G\theta - S$ be the subset of $G\theta$ that is not deducible
in S.

In the case of the tentative arch pattern, we get the maximal match substitution:

{x1 =c1, x2=c2, x3=c4}
with difference set {(inst c1 brick)}

because (inst c1 brick) is not deducible. (See the next section for the details of
the matching algorithm.) In the Strips application, we were trying to change the
world to eliminate differences; here, we are trying to eliminate them by changing the concept definition. The simplest way is simply to delete the offending
conjunct from the description. However, all of the other generalization operators are at our disposal.

To see how they apply, define, for each element f of the difference set,
$N_\theta(f)$ to be the elements of S that prove that (not f). In the example, $N_\theta($(inst
c1 brick)) = {(inst c1 wedge)}, because (inst c1 wedge) is the reason why c1
is known not to be a brick. Clearly, a good way to generalize would be to find
some common superclass of brick and wedge, like prism, and replace the conjunct (inst ?x1 brick) with (inst ?x1 prism). Or we could be cautious and
replace it with a disjunction: (or (inst ?x brick) (inst ?x wedge)).

As in Section 11.2.2 one is tempted to look for an "ultracautious strategy," and go up the isa hierarchy only when forced to by the data. But, as
before, this idea leads nowhere. It could always turn out that c1 was the only
exception to an otherwise perfect rule, and that the proper revision was to (or
(inst ?x brick) (= ?x c1)). If such a strategy is followed repeatedly, then eventually all we will have is a long disjunction of exceptions.

Matching can tell a program when and how to generalize but, unfortunately, it cannot tell the program how to specialize. Specialization is needed
when the pattern matches, but shouldn't. In that case, the learner must find
some fact that is true of the negative instance, and not implied by the pattern,
and conjoin it with the pattern. The number of candidate facts to conjoin is
determined by how situations are identified and what the descriptive notation is;
there are few other constraints. Hence situations must be narrowly circumscribed for the algorithm to have a chance of finding the proper specialization.

So far we have discussed matching as a relationship between an abstract
pattern and a concrete one. We have assumed that the first step in induction is
to throw away constants that can't possibly be important, and replace them with
variables. From then on, we can use our match algorithm. But deciding which
constants are irrelevant is not always easy. We assumed in Figure 11.3 that
constants like a1 and a2 should be variabilized, while brick should not. We

pulled this decision out of thin air. There are plenty of constants that would be hard to classify. Suppose that the blocks were on table1. Can we just assume that this is irrelevant, and they could be on any object? Or should we leave table1 in as a key part of the description? If we do decide to variabilize, should we replace every occurrence of a constant with the same variable?

One way to solve these problems is to postpone any variabilization until two or more instances of the pattern have been seen. Then we perform a different sort of matching, in which constant patterns are matched against each other, with a correspondence being established between constants. If two distinct constants are placed in correspondence, then that is a strong indication that one should variabilize.

11.2.4 A Matching Algorithm (Optional)

We have made use of the maximal-match algorithm here and in Chapter 9. Since it seems to be so generally useful, we will pause to sketch how it works. It is given as input a set of conjuncts. The idea is to deduce as many as possible. This is like the goal-tree search of Chapter 6, up to a point. It still must look for solutions to the first conjunct, and try them on the remaining conjuncts. There are two important differences:

1. If there are no answers to a conjunct, the algorithm does not fail, but notes the conjunct as a difference, and continues on the remaining conjuncts.
2. More subtly, it may be necessary to ignore answers to a conjunct.

To see how this second issue arises, suppose that $G = \{$(color ?x red), (size ?x large), (shape ?x cube)$\}$, and suppose S includes the following data:

(color ob1 red)	(color ob2 green)	(color ob3 blue)
(size ob1 small)	(size ob2 large)	(size ob3 small)
(shape ob1 sphere)	(shape ob2 cube)	(shape ob3 cube)

The best match has $\{x = ob2\}$, with just one difference, (color ob2 red); but if we start with the answer to the first conjunct, we will wind up with $\{x = ob1\}$, with two differences, (size ob1 large) and (shape ob1 cube).

The solution to this problem is to try all orderings of the conjuncts. But this must be done carefully, or the machine will find the same solutions over and over. After trying an ordering in which $conjunct_1$ comes first, it must also try orderings in which $conjunct_2$ comes first, and $conjunct_1$ is not allowed to match at all. Hence the algorithm must keep track of a list of conjuncts that must *not* match. When a conjunct is skipped, it is added to this list, committing the matcher to seeing it ultimately as a difference. If it ever matches, the algorithm is in danger of finding the same solution again, so it aborts the partial solution so far.

We will suppose that the list of conjuncts is divided into two (possibly empty) classes, *mandatory* and *desirable*. The mandatory conjuncts must be satisfied for the match to make any sense. For instance, we might take the conjunct (parts ?x {?x1, ?x2, ?x3}) as mandatory in the arch example, because we can decide *a priori* that physical grouping is a prerequisite to taking three objects as forming another one. The mandatory conjuncts do not complicate matters much, because all the answers to them can be found at the outset. These answers may supply some variable bindings, but not necessarily all.

The algorithm is shown in Figure 11.12 and Figure 11.13. This version finds all the answers, not just the maximal one. Changing it to concentrate on the maximal match is left as exercise for the reader (Exercise 11.7).

Work a few examples to see the fate of the skipped first conjunct under various conditions. In the arch example, suppose that the program skips (color ?x red). On the next conjunct, it will bind ?x to ob2, and verify that (color ob2 red) is not deducible, and hence belongs to the difference set. On this same call, however, the program will try skipping (size ?x large). Now the next recursive call will have the following set of parameters:

conjuncts = ((shape ?x cube))
answer-so-far = *no binding*
must-not-match = ((size ?x large) (color ?x red))

Even though the program will find the answer {x = ob2}, this answer will be rejected because (size ob2 large) will be deducible, and it is in the *must-not-match* list. The answer is perfectly okay, but it is already being discovered. On the other hand, {x = ob3} will lead to a new answer (but not the optimal one).

Finally, note that first conjuncts that are skipped and never fully instantiated must fail at the very end, after all conjuncts have been processed. For instance, if (on ?y ?x) had been one of the conjuncts, and ?y appeared nowhere else, then at the end there must be no object deducibly on top of ?x; that is, (Show: (on ?y *ob*)) must fail, where *ob* is the object found for ?x.

In case it has escaped your notice, matching is expensive. In spite of our optimizations, the algorithm still tries essentially all possible subsets of conjuncts in its search for a match. There is no way around this (although in Exercise

---

Function: match
Arguments: mandatory — a list of conjuncts that must match
    desirable — a list of conjuncts as many elements
        of which as possible should match
Algorithm:
  Call the deductive retriever on the mandatory conjuncts.
    For each substitution sub obtained collect matches
      produced by applying match-many to desirable
      and sub with must-not-match = nil.

Figure 11.12 Match algorithm — top-level function

Function: match-many
Arguments: conjuncts — the conjuncts to try to instantiate
           answer-so-far — the substitution obtained by
                           matching previous conjuncts
           must-not-match — a list of previously skipped conjuncts
                           that are not allowed to match in
                           completing the current answer
Algorithm:
If no more conjuncts,
    then if there is no answer to any element of must-not-match,
        then return answer-so-far as substitution, and
        must-not-match as the corresponding difference set.
Else call the deductive retriever on the first conjunct.
    For each substitution sub obtained,
        go through must-not-match list. For each element,
            if the bindings in sub instantiate all the
            remaining variables in this element, call the
            deductive retriever to see if the instantiated
            pattern is true in the current situation.
        If any element of must-not-match matched,
            then ignore sub.
        Else recursively call match-many on the rest of
            the conjuncts with answer-so-far augmented by
            the bindings in sub and must-not-match as before.
    If the first conjunct has variables,
        then include answers found by skipping it, thus:
        Recursively call match-many on the rest of the
            conjuncts with answer-so-far as before
            and with must-not-match augmented with the
            the first conjunct.

Figure 11.13 Match algorithm — main function

11.7 you might experiment with heuristics for giving up on very unpromising partial matches).

11.2.5 Analogy

At the end of Section 11.2.3, we discussed a different sort of matching in which constants were matched against constants in an effort to decide what to variabilize. Actually, once we open the door to constant-constant matching, all sorts of other possibilities appear, including predicate-predicate matching, matching several objects to one object, and so forth. At this point, we must (apparently) abandon our view of matching as a kind of "deduction with gaps," and shift to a somewhat vaguer picture of matching as finding "correspondences" between aspects of a two situations. We will use the term *analogy matching* for this idea. In Figure 11.10 we have labeled with the symbol *An* the analogy mapping between the two situations.

Intelligent beings often see a new situation as similar to an old one. If the old situation includes a recommended course of action, then the right thing to do in the new one might be similar in the same way to the old recommendation. For instance, suppose you are in a chess game, under a certain sort of attack. You are reminded of a previous situation in which you unsuccessfully used such an attack against an opponent. There is a simple *mapping* between the two situations:

> my pieces now → opponent's pieces then
> opponent's pieces now → my pieces then

This mapping need not make the situations identical, but perhaps the differences can be ignored. Some are easy to ignore; if you were playing the black pieces in both situations, then the mapping reverses the colors of the pieces, and this is certainly irrelevant. But other differences, such as the positions of the king and queen, may be important.

This mapping may be applied to the opponent's successful defense last time, generating a proposed move for you. We schematize this in Figure 11.10 by inverting the mapping An to get An^{-1}, which, applied to the proper course of action then, gives the proper course now.

One difficulty with analogy is that the mapping may not be uniquely invertible (which, if you think about it, is just another reflection of the nondeterminism of generalization). Consider the example of Figure 11.14, due to [Anderson83], which shows two geometry problems solved by a student. In problem 1, the student showed that RN=OY by the following argument:

> RO=NY
> ON=ON
> Therefore, RO+ON=ON+NY

Problem 2, seen soon afterward, reminded the student of Problem 1. She found the correspondence:

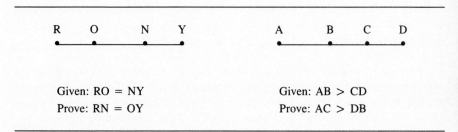

Given: RO = NY
Prove: RN = OY

Given: AB > CD
Prove: AC > DB

Figure 11.14 Two geometry problems

$$An = \begin{array}{l} A \rightarrow R \\ B \rightarrow O \\ C \rightarrow N \\ D \rightarrow Y \\ > \rightarrow = \end{array}$$

Note that part of the correspondence is between the *predicates* "=" and ">," not between constants. When the student inverted the mapping, she produced this attempted proof:

AB > CD
BC > BC
Therefore, . . .

which she quickly rejected as absurd. What had happened was that she had replaced *every* occurrence of "=" with ">." The original mapping turned *one* occurrence of ">" into "=." Unfortunately, because we lack a good account of just what an analogy mapping is, we can't say much about what counts as a legitimate inversion of one.

Once again, let us examine Figure 11.10. Over the past few paragraphs, we have focused on the mapping *An* between specific situations, and ignored the abstraction *Ab*. Even so, one may conjecture that, if *An* is to express more than a coincidental similarity between situations, then there must be some abstract schema that subsumes both. (Here we are assuming abstraction mappings have been generalized to include predicate-predicate mappings and such.) The work of Winston [Winston80a, Winston81, Winston83] is based on using analogy matching to discover such abstract schemas.

On the other hand, analogy is too slippery to be seen as just another road to induction. Often analogy matches are so slipshod that they merely suggest solutions to the present problem. By the time the proposal has been debugged, it may have strayed far from its original structure, and there may be no general principle left to induce. See [Carbonell82a, Carbonell83, Carbonell83a] for some interesting studies of this kind of analogy.

Then, too, analogies may be found between abstractions rather than between concrete situations. A theory that relies on this idea is that of Burstein [Burstein83]. He developed a psychological model of a student learning about computer programming for the first time. Many textbooks introduce the concept of *variable* with statements like, "A variable is like a box. You can put the number 5 in the variable X by telling the computer X=5."

Statements like this tell the student that the brand-new concept of *using programming variables* resembles in some ways the concepts of *using boxes*, *telling someone something*, and *manipulating algebraic equalities* (assuming the student has seen the "=" sign before). We can fit this to the model of Figure 11.10, but only by having *An* map among several different abstract schemas, and only by forgoing the expectation that a yet more abstract level will emerge. In fact, not only is there no general theory that subsumes all four domains but the An^{-1} mappings from the familiar domains to the new one are quite unreliable. There are lots of things one can do with boxes that one cannot do with variables, and vice versa. So, for instance, the student, given the statement $X=Y$, might guess that it causes the variable Y to be placed into the variable X, since putting one box into another is feasible (provided the containing box is bigger).

In fact, there are few inferences that carry over unscathed from the analogical domains to the new one. Nonetheless, the analogy is useful because it serves as initial framework for developing the new concept. It provides guesses about what things mean that, by being debugged, quickly evolve into useful concepts. Eventually the new domain grows familiar, and becomes independent of the domains it was attached to. For an experienced programmer, the only time the "box" analogy comes to mind is when the programmer needs to tell a novice about programming!

11.2.6 Indexing for Learning

The discussion so far has been artificial in one respect: it has assumed the machine always knows which concept it is generalizing or specializing. For Lex, this assumption is automatically guaranteed by the prior organization of knowledge into operators; the program knows by definition which heuristic it was trying to learn. For other programs, we simply posit a teacher who has told the student which concept is being taught, but from then on clams up and delivers only rewards and punishments. In Section 11.4, we will look at more interesting teachers. In this section, we ask what happens if there is no sentient teacher at all, but just an environment.

Much human learning occurs in circumstances in which no hint is given that "now we are learning what an arch is." Often, you simply become aware that the situation you are now in resembles ones you have experienced before, and this enables you to formulate or confirm a generalization. We take this ability so much for granted that we do not notice how hard it is to implement it. For example, one day we were going to get cat food from the pantry, and noticed there were only a few cans left. The question occurred to us whether we shouldn't head for the basement to replenish the stock. We were instantly reminded of experiences in playing tennis when, having used two of three balls, the novice is tempted to chase them down. Most tennis players figure out or are told that a better strategy is to play all the balls before retrieving any of them. Once reminded of this experience, one can form a generalization using the methods of Sections 11.2.2 and 11.2.5.

Why does the cat-food experience remind one of tennis balls? At a superficial level, the events are about different objects, used in different ways, at different time scales. But it seems overwhelmingly clear that the old experience must have been "indexed" in such a way in memory that it could be accessed easily during the new one. In this case, it could have been stored under "situations involving replenishable resources." This means, of course, that "tennis balls ready to hand" must have been classed as a replenishable resource, *at the time the tennis experience happened.* It is obviously too late to go back and classify them this way during the later experience; to find the old experience, it had to have been described this way already. The lessons to be drawn are that

1. Experiences must be described and indexed in abstract ways.
2. Experiences must be filed under many descriptions, most of which will probably never be used.

In case you doubt that people file experiences under many different indices, try using yourself as a subject for a couple of days. Catch yourself being reminded of a prior experience, and ask, "What did that experience and the current one have in common?" This exercise is guaranteed to increase your awe of the power of the human memory.

To take another example, one self-observed subject came across the following sentence in a research paper: "We will now try to get a larger picture, to see the forest for the trees, so to speak." After musing on how the author had misunderstood the expression "not seeing the forest for the trees," the subject was reminded of an advice column in which a youthful reader asked whether she should continue to hang out with the drug users at her high school. The columnist responded, "Stay away in droves." For this memory to be retrieved, it had to be filed under some category like "misunderstood idioms," or perhaps, "other people's language mistakes."

Schank and his colleagues have done much of the work on reminding and its uses in memory organization. See [Schank82, Riesbeck81, Kolodner83a] and [Lebowitz83]. To see the type of reminding their theory is supposed to explain, we must re-examine some of our ideas on memory organization and processing, developed in Chapters 7, 9, and 10, where we developed the idea of a *schema*, in particular, of *plan schemas* and *scripts*. We focused mainly on indexing, planning, and abduction, and neglected the important question of where new schemas come from.

In Chapter 7, we briefly mentioned the idea that the McDonald's script might be stored as a *virtual copy* of the restaurant script, with some modifications. In fact, there will be an entire hierarchy of possible types of restaurant schema, as shown in Figure 11.15. This hierarchy is not just a way of saving storage, but a way of organizing abduction (Chapter 10). A story understander, processing a restaurant story, should try to find the most specific schema in the hierarchy that applies. Schank et al. use the term "Mop" (*memory organization packet*) for this kind of hierarchy of schemas, so we will call this the "Mop theory" of learning. The hierarchy may be thought of as a *discrimination tree* (see Chapter 3). The understander attempts to find clues that guide it to the most specific applicable schema. Actually, the transition between levels must involve several discrimination trees because there are a variety of different clues that can be used. For instance, to figure out that the fast-food schema is appropriate, one could see (or, in story understanding, hear about) the sign in front of the building, the utensils used, the order of payment and eating, the fate of the dishes, etc.

People are not born with the restaurant hierarchy in their heads; it is learned. Presumably, it emerges as the best way to organize a set of similar

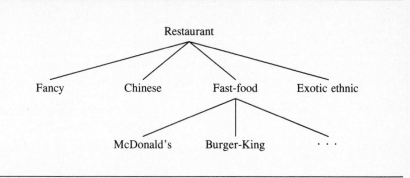

Figure 11.15 Restaurant hierarchy

experiences. Within the framework of inductive learning, the growth of this hierarchy can be seen as the spawning of new right-hand sides of rules of the sort schematized in Figure 11.1. That is, each schema type can be described using a rule of the form

> (if (and (?x *comprises several events*)
>   *description of event 1*
>   *description of event 2*
>   · · ·
>   *relations among events*)
>   (?x *is an event of type* restaurant))

Each node in the hierarchy represents a new *right-hand* side of such a rule, a new subtype of restaurant. Within each node, induction proceeds as usual, generalizing and specializing the *left-hand* sides.

Two programs that implement this sort of discrimination-tree growing are IPP [Lebowitz83] and Cyrus [Kolodner83a], which process newspaper stories about terrorists and American secretaries of state, respectively. We will draw our examples from Cyrus's domains. One of the schema trees it uses concerns diplomatic trips. Figure 11.16 shows a hypothetical discrimination tree Cyrus might have developed. At the nodes of this tree are schemas for processing stories about diplomatic trips by the secretary of state. At the leaves are particular episodes that fit all the descriptors leading to them from the root of the tree. It is not necessary to store each episode in its entirety, but only those aspects that cannot be inferred from the schemas the episode is classified under.

Cyrus uses the schemas in the tree to make default inferences about facts it cannot explicitly remember by filling in facts that are true in general for things matching a schema. For instance, if asked whether there was a state dinner at some meeting with the foreign minister of Russia, it would conclude that there had been if its schema for "meetings with foreign ministers" mentions a state dinner as a norm.

Cyrus grows its trees as new stories come in. When two or more episodes have settled to the same point, the program looks for some distinction between

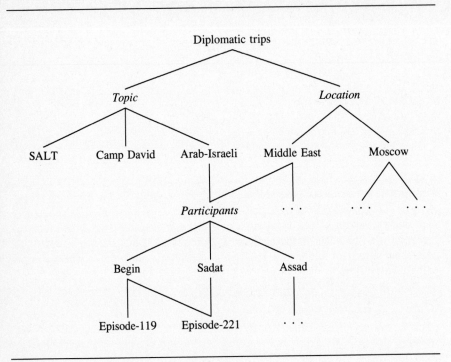

Figure 11.16 Cyrus-style discrimination tree

them and introduces a new discrimination. (This idea originated with Feigenbaum's Epam [Feigenbaum63].) For instance, if several meetings have taken place in Moscow, Cyrus will look for some distinguishing feature, and further classify each meeting.

There are two criteria for choosing a good discriminating feature. The feature should be likely to be available during later retrieval, and it should convey as much information as possible. The first criterion is important because it does no good to organize the tree around a key that will never be used. For instance, suppose it is known whether every meeting in the past eventually led to better or worse relations between the two countries involved. "Long-term consequences of meeting" is not a good discriminator, because in understanding accounts of future meetings, this information will not be available (at understanding time), and hence the program will never go down this branch of the tree.

What we mean by the requirement that the key "convey information" is that future experiences clustered according to feature value will tend to have other things in common. Recall that the nodes of the tree represent schemas, and the leaves represent particular episodes fitting these schemas. When a group of episodes is discriminated according to some feature, subgroups will emerge, which become new schemas. (Our original example was subgroups corresponding to types of restaurants; in Cyrus's domain, the subgroups might correspond to types of diplomatic meeting.) Sometimes as more information is gained these subgroups dissolve; that is, a group of episodes that had some feature value in common turned out to have nothing else in common. But some features tend to give rise to interesting new groups.

For instance, it does little good to classify diplomatic meetings by, say, the middle initial of the main participant, even if this information uniquely identifies all meetings recorded so far. On the other hand, if the meetings are discriminated by the *rank* of the main participant, then the program may find that all meetings in Moscow involving the defense minister concern arms control. This generalization is a fact about the world that may allow some new default inferences, and may aid in future processing.

A similar example is IPP's behavior after seeing several stories about terrorism in Northern Ireland, when it formed the generalization that it is usually the work of the IRA. Hence, given this story:

Irish guerrillas bombed hotels and shops in six towns in Northern Ireland today.

it would decide that "Irish guerrillas" meant members of the IRA.

Another example of a program that created new concepts out of noticed regularities was that of Soloway [Soloway77, Soloway77a]. It was intended to learn the rules of a sport by watching it being played. The program would read a low-level description of a baseball game and infer, for instance, that the goal of the batter was to get to first base. This program exemplifies several interesting techniques. At the lowest level, its biggest problem is to extract important features of its (simulated) sensory input. This causes it to focus on the actions of players rather than unchanging features of the environment. It then attempts to explain the players' actions by relating them to general schemas for playing games. For instance, if it observed someone doing something difficult (like hitting a rapidly moving ball), it would conclude that doing this was an important goal of that person. From several such experiences, it would make general hypotheses about the goals of people playing this game, and hence arrive at guesses about what the rules were. Like the other programs described in this section, it collected similar experiences, looked for commonalities, and created new concepts (such as "getting on base").

11.2.7 Assessment

In this section we want to repeat certain observations as a caution about the power of learning systems. Inductive learning is the classification of a set of experiences into categories, or "concepts." The concepts to be learned are given by the teacher or emerge as similarities in experience are noticed. Each concept definition is then "debugged" by searching through its generalizations and specializations until its definition exactly captures a set of experiences. The operators in this search space make patterns more general or more specific in order to include an experience that belongs in the set, or exclude one that does not. There is no hope of getting through this search space in a particular domain unless the following problems are solved:

1. The *situation-identification problem*: Only a few aspects of each experience can in practice be considered.
2. The *description problem*: The language in which the experiences are described must make the common pattern easy to express. All of the relevant factors should be captured in a short formula. The need for disjunctions should be minimized.
3. The *credit-assignment problem*: It must be clear which rules new information is relevant to. Often it is blame for failures that is being assigned rather than credit for successes.

Solving these problems requires imposing *a priori* constraints on the learning problem, and hence, inevitably, constraints on what can be learned. There is no way around this requirement. Or as William Martin put it, "You can't learn anything unless you almost know it already." (Quoted in [Winston84], p. 401.)

Not surprisingly, there is evidence that human beings and other animals are subject to these constraints in the real world. One example is language learning, the topic of Section 11.6. A more simple example is the "unfamiliar food" heuristic. If an animal eats an unfamiliar food and soon after gets sick, it will never eat that food again [Garcia66, Domjan83]. It does not matter what other unusual experiences it had before the nausea.

In our terminology, the situation is this: The animal is learning a rule of the form $(Q \ ?x) \rightarrow ?x$ *is edible*. There is an innate initial definition of Q, which is phrased in terms of sensory criteria ($?x$ should be sweet, should not smell rotten, etc.). If the animal ever gets sick, it always blames the most recent application of the rule to an unfamiliar $?x$, thus solving the credit-assignment problem in this case. It then amends Q to exclude some description of the offending object's sensory qualities. The situation-identification problem is solved by attending only to the taste and smell of the object. Obviously, we don't know anything about the descriptive notation (if any) employed by the brain of such an animal, but one can imagine a notation in which tastes and smells are classified along various dimensions. The animal files this object away as having values along these axes, presumably generalizing it somewhat, since it is unlikely to encounter exactly the same taste again. We can think of this as a kind of numerical generalization, which we looked at in Section 11.2.2. This notation solves the description problem for this domain. The next time the creature smells something falling within the generalization, it will fail to be counted as edible.

This set of constraints serves the average animal well. It means, however, that the animal is simply unable to learn to stay away from nuclear reactors after exposure to radiation makes it nauseous.

One issue we have neglected completely is the issue of *noisy data*. Suppose that the teacher or environment occasionally lies about a concept, or that the learner occasionally misidentifies the rule that gets the blame for a failure.

Most of the algorithms we have discussed so far will fall apart under these circumstances because they take every positive and negative instance of a concept equally seriously. Hence they will generalize or specialize the pattern to account for this anomaly, and the resulting alteration to the pattern will last forever. A related problem is that a concept may *change* over time. An animal learning the concept of "good places to look for food" will find that this set of places changes gradually; hence a strategy that retains all positive and negative instances, and tries to find an eternal pattern that accounts for all of them, is probably on the wrong track. The goal of most learning programs is to find necessary and sufficient conditions for something to fall under a concept. The goal of a problem solver trying to cope with the real world ought really to be to maximize its chances of success. Unfortunately, this goal is harder to formalize.

In the rest of the chapter, we will be looking at kinds of learning that do not fit the inductive-learning model so well. Nevertheless, the same techniques of generalization and specialization will come up repeatedly, and so will the constraints on them.

11.3 Failure-driven Learning

In Section 11.2.6, we looked at learning schemas ("Mops"). The novel aspect of that section was the production of new concepts. The debugging of their definitions was "induction as usual." However, the Mop theory is usually combined with an entirely different approach to debugging plan schemas, in which the learner attempts to execute them, and observes how they fail. The resulting bugs can then help revise the concept definition or produce new concepts. Such a paradigm is called *failure-driven learning*.

In addition to Mop-based programs, Sussman's Hacker is the primary example of failure-driven learning [Sussman75]. Hacker operates in the same world as many other problem solvers, the blocks world. It solves problems by looking up plan schemas in its Plan Library, and fitting them together. (Many planning ideas originated in this research.) There is a "gallery" of "critics" that do plan criticism. Hacker analyzes problems in terms closer to standard computer programming. (The word "hacker" means an obsessive, accomplished programmer.) The plan it is to execute looks at all times like a program, that is, a linear object containing conditionals and loops, rather than a task network. However, the program is still hierarchical: problems are solved by programs, whose steps become new problems. Once the program has been completed (down to primitives), Hacker executes it. If execution is halted by a bug, then Hacker corrects the program that led to it. The next time this program is used, this particular bug will not occur again.

For example, suppose Hacker is given the problem to get **a** on **b** in the situation shown in Figure 11.17. Assuming it is a total novice, the only program it will know will be this:

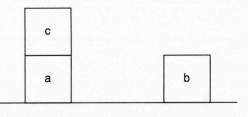

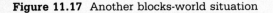

Figure 11.17 Another blocks-world situation

    (to-do ?task (achieve (on ?x ?y)) *; To get something on something else,*
        (move ?x ?y))   *; use the move primitive.*

It tries this schema, getting the plan (move a b). During execution, a bug occurs. The plan fails, and furthermore the (simulated) effector system reports that the reason for failure was that something was on block a. So Hacker looks for a way to make sure that one thing is not on another, and it revises the plan schema thus:

    (to-do ?task (achieve (on ?x ?y))   *; To get something on something else,*
        (prog (for-each ?z (on ?z ?x)*; get rid of everything on top*
            (get-rid-of ?z))   *; of the target.*
        (move ?x ?y)))   *; Then do the move.*

(The construct (prog $action_1, \ldots , action_N$) is carried out by doing the *actions* in the given order.)

    Generating and revising plan schemas was one way Hacker learned. Compiling new critics was another. In Hacker, a *critic* is a program that looks at a completed plan and revises it if necessary. For example, Hacker is able to learn a new critic that says (informally), ''If one step of a plan is of the form (achieve (on *a b*)), and a later step is of the form (achieve (on *b c*)), and the two conditions achieved are to be protected until the same subsequent step, then reorder the two steps.'' This is just a special case of the protection-violation-elimination algorithm we looked at in Chapter 9.

    Critics are learned by summarizing the experience of bug analyzers. The critic of the previous paragraph is learned when Hacker tries to solve a conjunctive goal problem. Suppose we take the classic (achieve (and (on a b) (on b c))). Hacker has a rule that says that a plan for a conjunction may be obtained by concatenating the plans for each conjunct. Note that it insists on a total ordering at every step, unlike the problem solvers we looked at before. So it produces this program:

    (prog (achieve (on a b)) (achieve (on b c)))

Each step is then figured out as before, and Hacker executes the resulting plan. Everything goes fine until the second phase is reached, when the code to get b on c removes a. This causes a protection violation which the bug analyzer decides is (abstractly) a case of a prerequisite (**clear b**) of one step ("get **b** on **c**") interfering with a brother goal ("get **a** on **b**"). This class of bug is referred to as **prerequisite-clobbers-brother-goal**. Hacker solves the problem by reordering the two steps. Furthermore, it summarizes schematically what it has learned, replacing the constants **a**, **b**, and **c** with variables. The result is a critic that will work in any syntactically similar situation, reordering the steps before execution.

Hacker stimulated a lot of work on problem solving, but not much work on learning. The problem is that it is not exactly clear where its sort of learning comes up in the real world. The critics that Hacker could learn turn out to be special cases of more general critics that may as well be wired in. Actually, this line of research has persisted, under the name "automatic programming," the attempt to automate as many as possible of the tasks associated with computer programming. But computer programming tends to be an unsatisfying model for what goes on when a creature learns about a world like the blocks world. Inside a computer it is reasonable to assume that one has complete knowledge of the reasons for a bug. (This assumption is less reasonable for intermittent bugs in complex software, but automatic programming is hard enough without worrying about such bugs.)

In the real world, it seems a little implausible that an effector system could diagnose the reasons for its failures so tidily, as we assumed it could when it failed to move block **a**. Suppose that in our first example the effector system had not provided a diagnosis of the problem ("**a** not clear"), but had simply failed. It is easy to imagine not getting any error message at all, just pictures back from the vision system showing block **a** in an unexpected place. There are several possible reasons for the bug, from a power failure or defective arm, to block **a** being glued to the table. To figure out what's going on, the learner needs to be a "physicist," not a computer programmer. That is, it has to be able to induce theories about the way its world works. By this we don't mean deep scientific theories, but shallow ones, with "laws" such as "You can't lift a block if another block is on it." Nonetheless, the scientific method — hypothesize and test — would be as useful as in real physics. This idea brings us back full circle to the "learning as induction" theory we started with. In the blocks-world example, the concept to be learned is "Situations when (**move** x y) will not get x on y." After several experiences, and some generalization and specialization, a description such as (**exists** (**z**) (**on z** x)) might emerge, and our hypothetical physicist could then get back on Hacker's track, debugging its plan schemas to cope with this anticipated kind of failure.

The Mop theory of Section 11.2.6 is an example of an attempt at this sort of "physicist." Many new schemas in a hierarchy like Figure 11.15 arise when old schemas prove inadequate to guiding behavior. For instance, suppose you go to an ethnic restaurant of some kind, and discovers you are supposed to eat with your fingers. This actually conflicts with the expectation from the schema, which is that you would use a knife and fork. In Chapter 10, had we considered such a possibility, we would have said that this kind of contradiction is evidence against the current hypothesis, which should therefore be changed.

But this attitude neglects the possibility that the current experience represents something new, which should be filed for future generalization. The right place to file the unexpected experience is in the memory schema, at the point where it occurred. Hence we would expect the ethnic novice to file it under the "eating" portion of the schema. All that gets filed there initially is a description of the occasion on which eating was done with fingers instead of forks.

The reason why this is the right place is that the next time a similar event occurs, the description of the first event will be ready to hand. Suppose that you are in another restaurant, and are surprised to find yourself eating with your fingers. Since you are once again engaged in understanding what is going on, we would expect the restaurant schema to be active again. Now when you see the unexpected event, you can compare it with previous events that violated expectations at that point. You will be reminded of the previous experience, and may note that both restaurants were Ethiopian. As time goes by, you will elaborate a new subschema concerning Ethiopian restaurants, with eating utensils and other unique features marked. This portion is just induction again; the novel aspect is the discovery of a new concept as a variant of an old one. Riesbeck [Riesbeck81] proposes a model based on this idea in the domain of economics. His program collects and analyzes economic arguments from the popular press. Arguments which depart from expected conclusions are remembered, so that the program learns to take more things into account in evaluating such arguments.

We have used the phrase failure-driven learning to talk about Hacker and the Mop theory, because they learn from failures of expectations about what will happen when schemas are used for planning or understanding. However, in a sense, all learning is failure-driven. A creature must change its rules whenever it does something it should not have done, or fails to do something it should have done. Such errors of commission or omission cause rules to be specialized or generalized. This seems obvious, but runs counter to classic behaviorist doctrine, which teaches that "positive reinforcement" causes a rule to be "strengthened," while "negative reinforcement" has little effect. The reason for the discrepancy is that behaviorists were relatively uninterested in where rules (or, in their terminology, "stimulus-response pairs") came from. They focused on how rules come to be dominant. They assumed that rules appear by an uninteresting trial-and-error process. Computational studies show just how inadequate this assumption is.

11.4 Learning by Being Told

Now let's swing to the opposite extreme, and assume that there is a teacher who has an interest in getting the learning system to learn something. Such a teacher would find many learning programs frustrating to deal with. Many of them can be told to start learning, and when they are right or wrong, but nothing else. Imagine trying to teach a student calculus using only a carrot and a stick.

Typically, a teacher wants to tell the student not just whether the student is on the wrong track, but also *why*. Early in the history of AI [McCarthy58] coined the term *advice taker* to describe a program that could learn from a helpful teacher. But progress toward actually implementing McCarthy's dream has been slow. The reason is that it is hard to devise wide enough channels of communication from the teacher to the advice taker. Ideally, communication should be in English. This raises all the problems, and then some, that we discussed in Chapters 4 and 10. Most natural language programs have dealt with simple stories, not general rules. The problems of ambiguity, pronoun reference, and so forth can only get worse as the sentences to be understood get more complex.

One problem in particular stands out. Suppose our program is designed to play Risk, the game discussed in Chapter 9. Suppose that the teacher tells the program, "It's better to take small, isolated continents." How is this to be translated into an internal representation? The program has several sets of rules, to be brought to bear at different phases of the game. This sentence should give rise to rules that belong in several of these sets (such as the rules for *plan generation* and *plan editing*). The natural language component must be able to translate "It's better" into rules whose antecedents summarize the phase of the game at which they're appropriate.

Such examples remind us that the person giving natural-language advice is often unaware of the internal structure of the system receiving the advice. The natural-language understander must be able in this situation to relate the advice to the internal structure by itself.

This is the approach taken in Mostow's Foo/Bar program [Mostow83, Mostow83a]. It reasons about a card game, the game of Hearts, rather than Risk, but the same problems come up. It does not accept natural-language input, but the advice it gets is close to terms the advice giver understands, and far from terms that can be directly used by the program. An example is the advice, "Avoid taking points," or (avoid (take-points robot)). This advice must be *operationalized* by transforming it into detailed rules like, "On each trick, play the lowest card you can." The program does not carry this process out all by itself, but needs help from a human being. Another example is Burstein's program, discussed in Section 11.2.5. You can think of it as taking advice of the form "A variable is like a box," and painfully transforming it, with help from a teacher, into something useful.

The alternative is to require the teacher to understand thoroughly at which points advice is sought, and roughly what the advice format is, so that he can make his advice fit the required form. Even for a program as straightforward as our Risk player, this is a discouraging requirement.

As an example of a practical program that achieved an interesting compromise in this area, we will describe Davis's Teiresias [Davis82a], an "advice-taking" interface to Mycin (see Chapter 8). The nice thing about Mycin is that it has a rather straightforward model. All questions are solved by a process of backward chaining through rules of a restricted format. Therefore, the teacher can understand the gap in Mycin's knowledge from roughly the same perspective as Mycin views it.

Teiresias operates by working on sample problems given it by the teacher. The teacher who disagrees with its conclusion on a problem is invited to follow the chain of reasoning that led to that conclusion. If the chain is unsound, then there must be some conclusion that was reached when it shouldn't have been, or wasn't reached when it should have been. Teiresias works back along the chain, from supergoal to subgoal, until the teacher recognizes that this point has been reached. That is, one of two things can be seen to have happened:

1. Some rule concluded P from premises that are all correct, even though P does not actually follow from those premises.
2. Some conclusion P should have been reached, even though each existing rule that could have concluded it failed to fire, because of some unsatisfied premise.

Once again, we are back in the world of induction, if you take "situations in which P should be concluded" as the concept to be learned. In the first case, the program must specialize, that is, the rule that concluded P must be changed so that it does not conclude it in this case. In the second case, the program must generalize, either by adding a new rule that concludes P in the current situation, or by weakening some antecedent of an existing rule that concludes P. Although Teiresias could tell which of these two approaches to take, it did not attempt to guess at the correct generalization or specialization itself. Instead, it asked the teacher to supply it.

Here is an example, a simplified extract from [Davis82a]. Suppose that Mycin has worked on a problem, and come up with recommendations based on two hypotheses about an unknown infection, **organism-1**:

> The identity of **organism-1** is either
> *E. coli* or *Pseudomonas aeruginosa*

Now Teiresias steps in, and asks, "Are there any hypotheses missing?" and "Are there any hypotheses that shouldn't have appeared?" The teacher responds yes to both questions, and goes on, when prompted, to say that

> *Klebsiella pneumoniae* and *Proteus non mirabilis should* have appeared
> while *Pseudomonas aeruginosa* should *not* have appeared.

Teiresias retrieves the rule which concluded that *Pseudomonas aeruginosa* was a suspect. (It keeps track of the rules as it goes.) Here is the rule, adapted to our notation:

```
(← (identity ?x pseudomonas-aeruginosa)
    (and (not (known (category ?x)))
         (gramstain ?x gramneg)
         (morphology ?x rod)
         (aerobicity ?x facultative)))
```

(As explained in Chapter 8, the actual rule attaches "certainty factors" to its conclusions, but that is irrelevant here.) If the rule arrived at the wrong conclusion, then there are just two possibilities: the rule itself is wrong, or it was fed wrong information, that is, one conjunct of its antecedent was satisfied incorrectly. Teiresias asks the teacher which of these possibilities is the case, and is told that the rule is correct, but conjunct 1, satisfied in this case by (not (known (category organism-1))), should not have been satisfied. The teacher tells the program this in response to simple questions like these:

> *Program*: Is this rule correct?
> *Teacher*: YES
> *Program*: Which clause of the antecedent should have been false?
> *Teacher*: 1

This dialogue tells Teiresias to look at rules that could have been used to conclude a category for organism-1, and so the same process is repeated until a culprit is identified. As we said before, either this is a rule that should not have applied but did, or a conclusion that should have been reached and wasn't. The latter category requires either a new rule or weakening an existing rule.

As we have emphasized, most of the time Teiresias is relying on short-answer questions or menus to manage the dialogue with the teacher. The only time it must depart from this style is when it is assimilating a new rule or a new conjunct for an existing rule's antecedent. Then it must accept the new material as natural language. Here is an example. What the teacher types is in upper-case:

> The new rule will be called RULE383
> If: 1- THE PATIENT'S INFECTION IS PRIMARY-BACTEREMIA
>   and 2- THE SITE IS ONE OF THE STERILE SITES
>   and 3-

> Then: THE CATEGORY IS ENTEROBACTERIACEAE

Teiresias translates this into its internal representation using simpler methods than those we developed in Chapter 4. It relies on strong expectations about what it is going to hear, and on strict constraints about what the words could mean. Even so, it is likely to get the meaning wrong. Therefore, having produced an internal representation, it retranslates it back into English, and checks with the teacher that the meaning is the same. If the teacher says no, then Teiresias tries alternative translations, or invites the teacher to rephrase.

In the example, the retranslation module prints out the following as its understanding of clause 1 above:

> Primary-bacteremia is an associated infection for which
> therapy should cover

Here the parser has gone astray, so the teacher indicates dissatisfaction, and Teiresias produces as its second guess:

> The infection is primary-bacteremia

It is obvious even to the nonexpert that this is a better translation, but not obvious to the program.

In summary, Teiresias performs teacher-guided specialization and generalization of its rules, based on two simple ideas:

1. It relies on menu-driven dialogues that make its internal structure as clear as possible to the teacher.
2. When natural-language input is necessary, it checks with the teacher to make sure the input has been translated correctly.

11.5 Learning by Exploration

In this section, we will look at two remarkable programs, AM and Eurisko, both developed by Doug Lenat [Lenat82, Lenat83, Lenat83a]. These programs explore domains, looking for interesting patterns and generalizations. AM works in the domain of elementary mathematics; Eurisko works in a variety of domains, including three-dimensional VLSI circuits and the design of battle fleets for a space warfare game. Eurisko is more complex than AM, and was designed to overcome some of AM's flaws. But both programs operate similarly, and we will often refer to them as "AM/Eurisko," as if it were a single program.

   This program works roughly as follows. It maintains a large, growing database of "concepts," such as *set* and *function* in the mathematics domain, or *spaceship* in the battle fleet domain. Each concept is represented in *slot-and-filler* notation (see Chapters 1 and 3). For example, here is a piece of the concept *set*, as used by AM:

> Name: Set
> Specializations: Empty-set, Nonempty-set, . . .
> Generalizations: Unordered-structure, . . .
> Examples:
>   Typical: {{}}, {A, B}
>   Boundary: {}
> Worth: 600

The slots point to other objects (often, other concepts). For instance, the *Specializations* slot points to a list of concepts that are subcases of this one.

   AM/Eurisko operates by creating new concepts and filling in their slots. The hope is that these concepts and the facts represented by the slot fillers are interesting. In fact, starting from concepts of set and "bag" (sets with duplicate elements allowed), AM was able to discover numbers, addition, and multiplication, and to make conjectures about these things. For instance, it conjectured that all numbers have unique prime factorizations. Eurisko was able to design battle fleets that won a nationally organized tournament two years in a row. (It had help from Lenat in pruning bad ideas.)

   The program is unique in that it *explores* a space rather than searching it (in the technical sense we have used throughout this book). It has a large number of operators for modifying concepts, but no well-defined goal-state description; instead, it is just trying to make more and more interesting discoveries. The space is much too large to try to do this exhaustively. Instead, it maintains an agenda of *tasks* to try to do. A task is always an attempt to fill in some slot of a concept, but it usually creates more concepts, slots, and tasks along the way. This use of the word "task" is similar to our use in Chapter 9, except that the activities are more introspective. Also, the tasks are not organized into a network because tasks are not planned before being executed. There is no reason to plan because tasks do not clobber each other in this domain; there are no protection violations. Instead the main issue is what to expend computing resources on. If the system has a choice between thinking about prime numbers, and thinking about "sets with an even number of elements," then it would be a mistake to dwell on the latter. In fact, the program can generate many more tasks than it will ever find time to work on, so some tasks are bound to be neglected completely. The problem is to make sure those tasks are worth neglecting.

The program maintains an *agenda* of tasks, and keeps them sorted in decreasing order of "interestingness." Its basic control cycle is to select the first task from the agenda, work on it (which may add new tasks), and repeat. Working on a task is done by rules called heuristics. Figure 11.18 shows an example of a heuristic from [Lenat82]. One case AM applied this heuristic to was checking examples of the concept of "odd prime numbers" (which it had created already). The heuristic was retrieved (with X = odd prime numbers), and evaluating the antecedent bound Y to "prime numbers," because Y, while apparently more general than X, is, except for the boundary case "2," coextensive with X. Hence AM concludes that all primes (except 2) are odd.

Note that the heuristic fills some slots, and also creates a new task to check examples of Y. The rationale for this new task is that, just as Y turned

---

If the current task is to Check Examples of X
    and for some Y, Y is a generalization of X
    and Y has at least 10 examples,
    and all examples of Y (ignoring boundary cases) are
    also examples of X

Then print the following conjecture: X is really no more
    specialized than Y
    and add it to the Examples slot of Conjectures
    and check the truth of this conjecture on boundary
        examples of Y
    and add X to the Generalizations slot of Y
    and add Y to the Specializations slot of X
    and add the following task to the agenda: Check
        examples of Y, with rating
            0.4(No. of Examples of Generalizations of Y)
              + 0.3(No. of Examples of Y)
              + 0.3(Rating of current task)

Figure 11.18 An AM heuristic

out to be basically the same concept as X, perhaps some generalization Z of Y may be turn out to be basically the same as Y. The rating depends on how many examples there are to look at. It also depends on the rating of the current task, so that the new task will be somewhat interesting if the current one is. The full rating for a task can grow if it is suggested again, for different reasons. In addition, the rating for a task depends on how interesting the concept is that it is concerned with.

It often happens that none of the tasks on the queue look very interesting. To deal with this situation, AM maintains a "Suggestions" slot on every concept. The contents of this slot are heuristics for generating some new tasks concerned with this concept. When all the tasks on the queue fall below some threshold of interestingness, all the suggestions heuristics are run (there may well be hundreds of them). The effect is to beef up the queue again, noting new tasks and increasing the estimated interestingness of old ones when they are proposed for new reasons. One might think that running all the suggestions heuristics would be worth doing only once, but each time they are run they find new material from the last wave to work with. In fact, one can view the control structure of AM as a multipass process in which the suggestions are tried repeatedly until no new interesting discoveries are being made. For details, see [Lenat82].

We should point out that AM never proved the theorem that all primes but 2 are odd, or any other theorem. Its machinery was oriented toward finding conjectures, not proving them. (Although its control structure looks as though it might be good for exploring the space of proofs, it has not been applied to that task.)

In some ways, AM/Eurisko is like the other learning systems we have examined, especially the Mop theory. It classifies things into hierarchies, and notes patterns and discriminations involving things that are currently classified close together, which leads to new classifications, and so on. The main novelty is that AM and Eurisko are active rather than passive. They don't wait for newspaper stories to appear, but start generating things themselves.

Of course, this difference is mainly due to a difference of domain. AM/Eurisko works only in domains that can be simulated faithfully inside the computer. This includes finite mathematics and computerized games. This constraint may sound like a serious limitation of the program, because it seems that the person creating the simulation already understands the domain, and the best AM/Eurisko can do is catch up. But in fact it is easy to mechanize domains without knowing all the empirical regularities that will appear in them, and this is where AM/Eurisko shines. Although it never found a completely new mathematical conjecture, it did find several that Lenat had never seen, and the team of Lenat and Eurisko completely outclassed every unaided human being in designing battle fleets for the war game.

One feature that AM/Eurisko must have, given its exploratory structure, is the ability to generate new things. For instance, when it produces a new concept, it must be able to generate examples of it. It often sets itself the task of producing a generalization or specialization of a given concept. One way to generate examples of a concept is to go through examples of its generalizations, and see if any of them just happen to be examples of the concept itself. However, methods like this would not get very far because they would have only the examples supplied with the initial stock of concepts.

To be able to create new entities, AM/Eurisko must be able to *mutate* existing objects. In particular, to create new concepts, it must mutate the definitions of old ones. For example, here is part of one of AM's heuristics for generalizing a concept [Lenat82]:

If the task is to fill in generalizations of concept X,
then take the definition D of X
     and replace it by a generalization of D.
   If D is a concept, use its generalizations.
   If D is a conjunction, remove or generalize a conjunct.
   If D is a disjunction, add or generalize a disjunct.
   If D is a negation (not D'), specialize D'.
     . . .

This rule uses several of the operations we talked about in Section 11.2.2, but uses them in a different way. It is not trying to generalize the concept to fit the input data, but in order to see if it gets an interesting new concept.

Definitions of concepts play several key roles in AM. The system keeps track of one or more definitions of concepts, expressed as Lisp functions. Hence, when this heuristic speaks of D being a conjunction, it means a Lisp program of the form (and . . .). Other heuristics manipulate Lisp programs in other ways. For instance, one way to generate examples of a concept if its definition is recursive is to instantiate the base step.

It is hard to describe AM and Eurisko without falling into anthropomorphism, something we have tried strenuously to avoid throughout this book. At the present stage of AI research, it is never correct to explain the operation of a system by assuming an "intelligent interpreter" at the outset. AM/Eurisko's control structure is seemingly so undirected and yet so productive that it is hard not to do this. As an antidote, let's look in some detail at how AM discovered the concept of *number*. It was given at the outset definitions of list, set, and bag, and equality on these domains. Equality on lists is defined as you might expect. Figure 11.19 shows the algorithm in our usual style, but remember that in the machine it is stored as a Lisp program, and hence as a Lisp list structure. AM tries to generalize this definition, by mutating pieces of it. In particular, it considers weakening the clause

     then check (recursively) the two lists containing
          the rest of their elements . . .

by discarding the first half of it. The resulting function, shown in the second half of Figure 11.19, does not test for equality, but for some weaker property, which we will call *shmequality*. Think for a minute about what the relationship *shmequal* is. The answer is that two lists are *shmequal* to each other if they have the same length. AM doesn't know this, because it has no previous

Original definition:

> To test if list |1 is *equal* to list |2
> > If they are both empty, then *yes*.
> > Else if they are both nonempty,
> > > then if their first elements are equal,
> > > > then check (recursively) if the two lists containing
> > > > > the rest of their elements are equal, and if so,
> > > > > then the answer is *yes*.
> > > > Else the answer is *no*.
> > Else the answer is *no*.

Mutated version:

> To test if list |1 is *shmequal* to list |2,
> > if they are both empty, then *yes*.
> > Else if they are both nonempty,
> > > then check (recursively) if the two lists containing
> > > > the rest of their elements are *shmequal*,
> > > > and if so then the answer is *yes*.
> > > Else the answer is *no*.
> > Else the answer is *no*.

Figure 11.19 Mutating the definition of equality

concept of length, but it is able to find examples of pairs of lists that satisfy this predicate, that is, have the same length, and hence labels it an interesting concept.

The next step is to apply a heuristic that says: "If weakening a definition leads to an interesting concept, then look for a canonical form for objects in the domain of the original definition." That is, suppose that R is an equivalence relation over a set of objects A, and suppose R' is a weakening of R that the program has found: if $R(x,y)$ is true, then $R'(x,y)$, but not necessarily vice versa. However, there may be a "canonizing" function C such that if $R'(x,y)$ then $R(C(x),C(y))$ In the present case, R is "equality"; R' is "shmequality." A good candidate for $C(x)$ would be $length(x)$, because if two lists are shmequal, then $length(list1) = length(list2)$. The lists (a b c) and (d e f) satisfy "shmequal," and *length* maps them both into 3.

AM can't arrive at this canonizing function by meditating on length, because it doesn't have the concept of number yet. It must produce C by finding a transformation on inputs to the equality tester that would cause the dropped part of its definition to be satisfied every time, thus producing the same result on the transformed data that shmequal has on all data. It has a rather special-purpose heuristic that knows that to make "The first elements of the two lists are equal" always come out true, you can make sure the first elements of the arguments are always the same constant. Hence, the wanted canonizing function is:

> $C(x) =$ If x is empty then return (), the empty list.
> Else apply C to the list of the all the elements of x
> but the first, and put a constant t at the front
> of the result.

If we apply this function to (a b c), (d e f), or any other three-element list, we get (t t t) every time. This is the canonical form AM arrives at instead of 3. But if you think about it, (t t t) is just as good as 3. In fact, AM creates the concept "list of t's" as a specialization of "list," and fills in examples by canonizing all the examples of lists that it knows about. It finds the new concept interesting enough that it continues to explore it. One heuristic tells it to consider restrictions of operations to new subsets of concepts; here that tells it to concentrate on restricting list concatenation to lists of t's, thus inventing addition. Eventually it discovers multiplication, and (by inverting multiplication) divisors, and primes, and ultimately the unique factorization conjecture mentioned above.

It is apparent from the way it discovers numbers that AM is just squeaking by on its ability to understand Lisp code. Its heuristics are able to do simple code mutations, and sometimes to foresee their effects, but would have trouble with long programs with many side effects. Unfortunately, much of the structure of AM was represented as just such code, namely, the heuristics themselves. Hence it was never able to perform very many experiments on its own heuristics. Eurisko is an effort to fix this problem by putting more structure into the heuristics. They become concepts themselves, with their Lisp code separated into small chunks appearing in slots with useful labels. For instance, if a heuristic prints anything, then in Eurisko it is represented as a concept with a "Print" slot containing the code to do the printing. This organization allows the program to mutate heuristics in interesting ways. Consult [Lenat83a, Lenat83b] for details.

Box 11.1

Research as Learning

Of the various programs we have considered in this chapter, AM/Eurisco seems the closest to what scientists do. This is in part because it has discovered things about mathematics, rather than more mundane areas, but primarily because of the way it explores its domain.

Because of the major role science has played in our civilization for the last two or three hundred years, the nature of science and scientific research has received a lot of attention, primarily from historians and philosophers. Until recently these two groups had only occasional things to say to each other. While the historians were interested in questions like "Who discovered oxygen?" or "When did Newton think of universal gravitation?", such questions had little relevance to the philosophers. For their part, the philosophers were interested in knowing why it is that science can progress in ways that other disciplines (such as philosophy) cannot. As they posed the question it was (and is) a purely logical one — whether or not any scientist ever behaved like the philosophers of science postulated was of no concern. Since the philosophers of science said little about the way scientists actually behaved, their theories were of little concern to the historian.

Fortunately, this state of affairs has changed, and both parties have moved more toward common ground. So, for example, in cases where several people came up with similar ideas at about the same time (the idea of conservation of energy is a classic example), the historian is less concerned with who discovered it first, and more concerned with the historical context which made the idea so much ''in the air.''

It is, however, the shift within philosophy which speaks more clearly to us in AI. At one time, philosophers thought that the reason behind science's unique history of progress is its ability to prove (or confirm) its theories. As such, science could be viewed as accumulating knowledge, where each block in the structure was secure because it was proven true.

While this model has a certain plausible ring (what are experiments for, after all?), it is hard for us in the twentieth century to take it seriously. The two great accomplishments of twentieth century physics, quantum mechanics and relativity, together overturned one of the great intellectual structures of all times, classical physics. If science proves its theories, then there were a lot of very sloppy physicists who somehow made a mistake when they thought that they had proven classical physics.

The best articulated response to this dilemma was put forth by Karl Popper, who suggested that the purpose of experiments was not to prove theories, but to disprove them. He noted that while any set of experiments could not prove a theory (any set of data is consistent with an infinite number of possible theories), experiments could *disprove* a theory. That is, if the numbers do not turn out the way the theory predicts, then the theory must be wrong. Thus the reason science progresses is that scientists propose testable theories, and then proceed to run experiments. If the numbers come out wrong, then new theories must be found. Viewed in this light, the switch from classical to modern physics was not a scandal of sloppy thinking, but a triumph of scientific method. A firmly entrenched theory was put to some tests to which it could not measure up, and was therefore replaced. This philosophy of science is called *falsificationism*.

Falsificationism is still around, but a more recent idea has largely supplanted it. This view, which is commonly associated with [Kuhn62] and [Lakatos70] sees science in a somewhat different light. According to this view, the battle is not between the theorists (proposing) and the experimentalists (disposing), but rather between theorists. That is, theories are not killed off by experiments, but by other theories (admittedly with the help of the experimentalists). In this view an established theory is overthrown only when there is a better one to replace it with — not before.

Historically this seems to be the case. Again looking at Newtonian mechanics, there were several long-standing problems with the theory — places where the experimental results could not be brought into line with the theory: the orbit of the moon, the orbit of Mercury, and the speed of sound in water come to mind. If experiments disprove theories, any of these should have been enough to get rid of Newtonian mechanics. Indeed the problem of the moon's orbit caused some to suggest that gravitation laws might be different when distances are large. But not much came of such suggestions. Rather scientists put the problems aside, assuming that one day they too would be fit into the Newtonian paradigm. They were two-thirds correct. The orbit of the moon and the speed of sound were solved. However, the orbit of Mercury served as the first experimental results to support a rather radical replacement for Newtonion mechanics — general relativity.

Furthermore, even when experimental results support one theory over another, it is rarely as cut and dried as it has been made to seem. It is always possible to suggest that the experiment was not carried out properly, or that the results were due to some spurious effect. When this is not possible, the defenders of the ''losing'' theory can usually make slight modifications to their theory to save it from the damaging results. In fact, it is hard to imagine what else could be the case. It simply makes no sense to give up a major theory without a fight.

This also has an AI perspective. In Chapter 7 we discussed data dependencies. One extension to this idea is called *dependency-directed backtracking*. In traditional chronological backtracking (see Chapter 5), a contradiction or failure causes the system to look for the last made choice, and try alternatives. In a dependency-directed backtracker, the system looks at the data dependencies of the rules involved, and only undoes decisions which were implicated in the failure.

Should a dependency-directed backtracker encounter a contradiction (e.g., it believes that Fred has appendicitis, but then discovers his appendix has already been removed), it will try to repair the contradiction. It does so by looking for *assumptions*, where we are using this as a technical term meaning a belief which is supported by our inability to disprove some fact. So we *assume* that Fred, a bird, can fly because we are unable to prove that Fred is a penguin, or has a broken wing. Then should the backtracker ever learn that Fred cannot fly, it will try to eliminate the contradiction by assuming that he is either a penguin or that he has a broken wing.

One issue which arises in such systems is what happens when, as in the flightless bird example, there is more than one way to get rid of the contradiction. Which one should the backtracker choose? Actual implementations of dependency-directed backtracking simply pick one assumption ''at random.'' But this is clearly an unrealistic simplification. If Mr. Jones reports that he hardly has anything to eat or drink, but he is gaining weight fast, we can resolve the apparent contradiction by, say,

1. doubting Mr. Jones's word, or
2. doubting the connection between food intake and weight gain.

Most of us would first assume (1), and not (2).

Thus a dependency-directed backtracker really should make a choice about what assumption to doubt. Is there a uniformly best way of making this choice? The lesson from the history and philosophy of science, at least to date, is that there is no such method. If you think about it, the problems of repairing a contradiction and responding to damaging experimental results are the same problem. There are many ways to respond to the results and get rid of the contradiction between theory and experiment. If there is a uniformly best way, then everyone should adopt it, and we could avoid the disagreements which loom so large in the history of science between the defenders of the old orthodoxy and the supporters of the new.

11.6 Learning Language

11.6.1 An Outline of the Problem

Language learning is an incredibly complex business and to keep things manageable we will have to simplify our discussion in many ways. We will ignore language generation and, as in Chapter 4, assume that the information comes in as distinct words. The result of the process will be a procedure that maps a string of words to the meaning of the sentence.

If the only input to the learning program were a string of words, the problem would be unsolvable. There is simply no way of deciding out of context on the correct internal representation for a string of words like ''Fermez la porte.'' Thus the learning program (sometimes referred to as ''the child'') must have two pieces of information: the string of words and the ''context.'' To make this concrete, we will assume that the language-learning problem is broken down into two parts. First, the child is somehow able to decide on the meaning of the sentence pretty much independently of the string of words. Then a second process takes the meaning and the words and tries to work out the correct mapping procedure. This is shown in Figure 11.20. We will further assume that the module labeled ''meaning guesser'' is also capable of linking individual words with pieces of the internal representation. We have indicated this by replacing some of the terms in the internal representation with the associated English words (the typeface is different). The ''meaning guesser'' must get the sentence as input in order to make the word concept connections; thus the dashed line in Figure 11.20. (The line is dashed because the major source of information to this module is not the words, but the general context.)

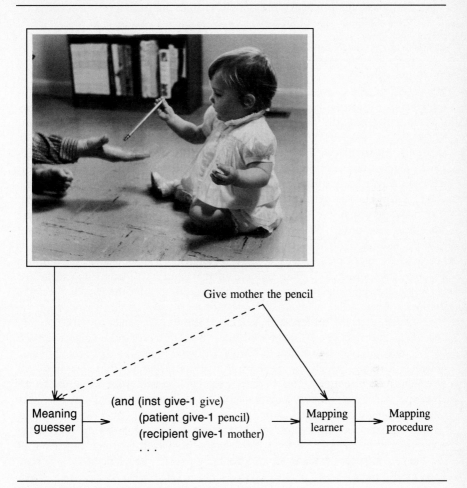

Figure 11.20 The language learning process

11.6.2 Determining the Internal Representation

We are assuming that the internal representation of a sentence is available independently of the sentence. Even at first glance, this is a major assumption, and a second thought reveals further complications.

- The child might not even have the appropriate concept for the spoken word (e.g., the child does not have a single concept corresponding to "daughter," having instead, say, "female child").
- The words used might be ambiguous, causing previous occurrences of the word to be actually misleading.

- The meanings of some words might change the meanings of others (e.g., "toy elephant" is not an elephant).

We will ignore all of these problems.

Even so, the problem of determining the internal representation without the mapping procedure is presumably impossible for the general case. (If it were possible, there would be no point in having a language comprehension program at all.) Thus the language learner must encounter language in a very special environment. Recent work in developmental psychology indicates that this is indeed the case [Clark78a]. People do not speak to children the way they do to adults. Particularly with very young children (one or two years old), sentences tend to be about objects that are in view and actions that are being performed. Given such constraints, it seems at least possible that the child could make reasonable guesses about the meaning of a sentence just given the context. [Selfridge80] postulates a number of rules for doing just this. His rules are something like these: "If someone performs an action following an utterance, then the utterance might be a description of the action" and "If the utterance is heard in an interrupted sequence, then it might be a command to do the next action in the sequence." For example in the context of setting the table and being handed some silverware, it might be possible to infer the meaning of "Put the forks on the table" without knowledge of the words.

Given that the process of language learning depends so crucially on "meaning guessing," one might well ask where this procedure came from. It seems unlikely that it was itself learned, since it must be in place prior to language learning, which for a child means prior to the first birthday or so. If we look at the mental faculties we have postulated so far, it seems closest to the abductive capability in story comprehension discussed in Chapter 10. To take but one example, the problem faced by a child trying to predict the meaning of "Open the door" seems close to that faced by an adult trying to respond appropriately to "Door!" when a bepackaged individual is trying to get out of the house. However, this is all very tentative, since very little work has been done in this area.

11.6.3 Learning Phrase-structure Rules

With all of this out of the way we are almost in a position to look at the problem which comes to mind first when one talks of language learning — how to devise a mapping between strings of words and an internal representation. However, we must still make a few more simplifying assumptions to get things going. They are

1. We will initially consider only phrase structure rules — that is, we will ignore learning transformational rules.
2. We will assume all words have an associated part of speech, and necessary syntactic markers indicated in the dictionary.

3. The system has one built-in rule of grammar — s → np vp, plus the knowledge that nps must contain nouns, and vps, verbs.

The first of these we will relax later when we consider how transformational rules might be added. The second we will not relax, but let us point out how it could be relaxed. The idea is that for simple cases such as those a child is initially exposed to, nouns correspond to objects, and verbs to actions. (This does not hold in general. For example "flight" and "fly" both denote actions.) Then for the simple cases it is reasonable to assume that the child has at least three word classes — nouns, verbs, and "the rest." Then the trick would be for the child to note distribution differences that cause "the rest" to break up into subgroups. That one sees "The red ball" but not "Red the ball" suggests that "the" and "red" belong to different classes. [Berwick82] discusses how this might be accomplished. He also shows how the last of the three above assumptions (that s → np vp is built in) can be relaxed as well.

Now let us consider how our system might learn phrase structure rules. Besides the sentence, our procedure has the internal representation and knowledge of the mapping of words to terms and predicates in the representation. As before we will indicate this informally by replacing predicates and terms with the English words that mapped into them. Thus, a sentence like "The big girl dropped the red block" might have a representation like this:

```
(and (inst drop-1 drop)
     (agent drop-1 girl-1)
     (inst girl-1 girl)
     (size girl-1 big)
     (patient drop-1 block-2)
     (inst block-2 block)
     (color block-2 red))
```

This is useful because its structure is not very distant from the syntactic trees used in Chapter 4. This may not be obvious from the way we have written it, but suppose we translate it into associative net formalism as in Figure 11.21. This still does not look like a typical syntactic tree, but this can be fixed by simply redrawing the arcs and nodes to conform to the notation for syntactic trees. Figure 11.22 shows how close the two can be made to look. In particular, with only one exception the groupings proposed by the two representations are the same. The exception is that in the syntactic tree, the verb and the last np are grouped together into a vp — a grouping not found in the associative net formulation. It would obviously be convenient if our learning program could assume that the two groupings are identical. Anderson calls this the *graph deformation condition* [Anderson77]. This could be achieved by modifying the syntactic tree to look like the associative net, or vice versa. Anderson does the latter. However we assumed a built-in rule of s → np vp, so for us the graph deformation condition can hold except for this special case.

Given the graph deformation condition, plus the rule s → np vp, the phrase structure for "The big girl dropped the red block" is determined up to the placement of the second "the," which could go two places.

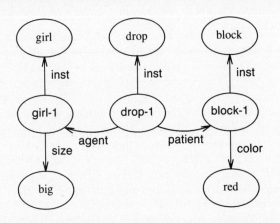

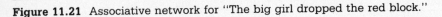

Figure 11.21 Associative network for "The big girl dropped the red block."

((the big girl) (dropped the (red block)))
((the big girl) (dropped (the red block)))

The point here is that one can imagine a procedure of two arguments (the internal representation and the sentence) which starts parsing the sentence using a standard ATN grammar such as we saw in Chapter 4. Any time it finds itself stuck, it postulates some new rule of grammar that would allow it to parse the sentence. (We will assume that the child is not given ungrammatical sentences.) When new rules are postulated, they are made as specific as possible; initially they would allow only the particular word for which they were designed. There would be a separate module which would attempt to collapse two rules into one by generalizing the preconditions. A first cut at such a program is shown in Figure 11.23. We should stress that this and its subsequent refinement both have lots of defects, most of which we will not mention. They are meant only to give some idea of what a language learning program might look like. Also, this algorithm does not specify how to learn rules for actually creating the internal representation. Given the assumption that meanings are only additive, this would not be too hard to fix.

11.6.4 Learning Transformational Rules

Although the constraints we have proposed are not adequate for determining the phrase structure of even simple sentences, let us now turn to the problem of sentences that are not interpretable by simple phrase structure rules, but rather were handled in Chapter 4 with transformational rules.

The first problem we must address here is how this extension will affect the suggestions we made for the phrase structure case. In particular, we implicitly assumed that the system would be given sentences that could be parsed

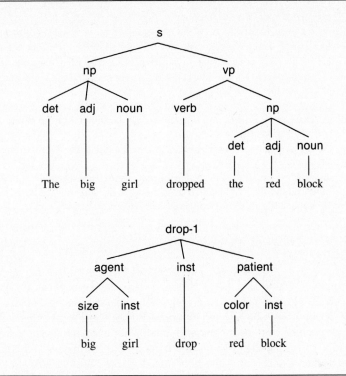

Figure 11.22 Associative nets as syntactic trees

using only the phrase structure rules. Suppose it tried to process something which should be done with a transformation. What is to prevent it from making up a new phrase structure rule and using it? For example, suppose the system were given the sentence ''Did the big girl drop the red block?'' The system we have proposed would simply see the ''did'' at the front of the sentence and assume that it must be part of the initial np in s → np vp. How is this to be prevented?

One possibility is to constrain the phrase-structure rules so that the newly desired rules will be illegal. One such constraint, called the *X-bar theory*, (where X-bar is written $\overline{X}$) has been proposed by some linguists. The motivation for this new theory is the observation that noun phrases and verb phrases can look remarkably similar in English. For example: ''flights from Chicago to Boston'' vs. ''flies from Chicago to Boston'' or ''believes that the world is flat'' vs. ''the belief that the world is flat.'' This has led to the hypothesis that all phrase structure rules have the following form:

$$\overline{X} \rightarrow \{ \text{ specifiers X complements } \}$$

Here the ''{}'' brackets are meant to indicate that the items enclosed are unordered, and the X is meant to be a variable over the *head* parts of speech, which

1. Start parsing with the current grammar.

2. Any time a subnet is called, see if the next thing in the internal representation is a subgrouping, and if it is, descend into it. Do similarly when a subnet is finished.

3. If no rule in the ATN is applicable, create one specific to the situation at hand:

    3a. If the next input in the internal representation is a group, then start a new phrase for that group.

    3b. If a group in the internal representation has just finished, then indicate that the current place in the ATN grammar can be the end of the phrase currently being processed.

    3c. Otherwise put in an instruction to parse the particular word from the sentence.

4. Generalize the networks. In particular, if two **word** commands are for the same part of speech, and the commands start and end at the same places in the network, these two commands should be collapsed into a single **category** command.

Figure 11.23 A ''language learning'' algorithm

for English might be **noun, verb,** and **preposition.** An $\overline{X}$ is a phrase of type X. For example a $\overline{\text{noun}}$ is a noun phrase; $\overline{\text{verb}}$'s are verb phrases. A phrase may not contain (except indirectly through subphrases) a second kind of head. (Typically, it is not allowed to have two heads of the same kind either.) We will assume a ''specifier'' is a single word modification of the head word. For example, if $X = $ **noun,** then the specifiers could be determiners and adjectives. If $X = $ **verb,** then a specifier might be a modal verb. (There are several formulations of the $\overline{X}$ theory, and we are not following any of them very accurately. This is meant to be impressionistic.)

The *complements* are themselves phrases (e.g., an **np** or **pp**) that fill the arguments of the head. If we use a case grammar approach as we did in Chapter 4, then we can think of the complements as specifying the fillers of various cases. For example, in ''the flight to Chicago'' the **pp** ''to Chicago'' is a complement that fills the **destination** case. The basic claim is that all of the phrase structure rules used by natural languages have this form. Furthermore, although the sections of the right-hand side (head, specifiers etc.) are unordered, once an order is decided for one phrase structure rule of the language, all other phrase structure rules in that language must have the same order. Thus once it is determined that in English specifiers come first in, say, **nps** this must also hold for **vps,** etc. However, this does not prevent Arabic, say, from having the opposite order.

We should stress that this theory is by no means unanimously upheld within the linguistics community. The linguists are hardly more unified than AI researchers on such things. However, linguists *are* unified in the belief that finding such constraints is one of the major tasks they face. We will adopt this constraint here because one language-learning program in AI uses it [Berwick80, Berwick82] and because it offers a case study on how such constraints make the problem of language learning more manageable.

Given such a constraint, two problems that we commented on above go away. First, remember that our scheme had no clear-cut way to decide that the second "the" in "The big girl dropped the red block" belonged to the vp or to the phrase that included "red block." With the $\bar{X}$ theory there is only one way it can go. After the system decides that "the" is part of the np for the subject, this constrains all phrase structure rules to start with specifiers (which are single lexical items in our version of the constraint). Thus in the vp there can be no single lexical items after the head of a phrase structure rule (the complements are all phrases). Since "the" is a single lexical item, it must go at the start of the next constituent, and not directly after the verb in the vp.

Second, we asked how the language learner would know not to postulate a phrase structure rule to handle "Did the big girl drop the red block?" To some degree this is solved by assuming that the rule s → np vp is the only rule for expanding an s node. But it does not explain why "did" is not part of the first np. Given the rule that a head of type Y cannot be part of a phrase structure rule for type X (e.g., we cannot have a verb as part of a noun phrase), this problem is solved, because "did" is a verb. In Figure 11.24 we have extended our learning algorithm. Sections (3b) and (3c) have been modified to be in accord with the $\bar{X}$ theory.

With the $\bar{X}$ theory we can prevent phrase structure treatment of examples that should be handled with transformations. This leaves us free to concentrate

---

1. Start parsing with the current grammar.
2. Any time a subnet is called, see if the next thing in the internal representation is a subgrouping, and if it is, descend into it. Do similarly when a subnet is finished.
3. If no rule in the ATN is applicable, create one specific to the situation at hand:
   3a. If the next input in the internal representation is a group, then start a new phrase for that group. *If the new phrase contains a head word (e.g., noun), then it must be a phrase of that type (by the $\bar{X}$ theory).*
   3b. If a group in the internal representation has just finished, then indicate that the current place in the ATN grammar can be the end of the phrase currently being processed.
   3c. Otherwise put in an instruction to parse the particular word from the sentence *provided it is consistent with the $\bar{X}$ theory. If it is not, and the word is a head word, then start a new phrase of the appropriate type. Otherwise see if the word can be attached to a higher level phrase.*
   3d. *If none of the above work, try parsing two constituents from the input (e.g., an aux and a np) and put them back into the input stream in reverse order.*
   3e. *Finally try putting a dummy np into the input stream.*
4. Generalize the networks. In particular, if two word commands are for the same part of speech, and the commands start and end at the same places in the network, these two commands should be collapsed into a single category command.

Figure 11.24 A better "language learning" algorithm

on the more difficult question, "What transformations?" Transformational rules unfortunately are much more powerful than phrase structure rules. Whereas a phrase structure rule can basically do only one thing — propose that a constituent of a certain type appear next in the sentence — transformational rules have a much larger repertoire. In Chapter 4 we said that transformational rules can

- add or modify features on the nodes of the syntactic tree;
- add or delete constituents;
- move constituents from one place in the tree to another.

This gives our learner a lot of possibilities to investigate and, as we have already noted, the search spaces generated in this fashion are rather large.

Probably the best way to attack this problem is to reduce the power of transformations. The less they can do, the smaller the search space. For example, while the transformations of Chapter 4 can assign an arbitrary feature to an arbitrary node, this may not really be necessary for a grammar of English (or other languages). To see why, consider one place where we used this ability. In the grammar of Chapter 4 it was used to flag a sentence as a command, statement, etc. This is shown in Figure 11.25. There the lines like

> (: = (the mood of $s-maj) 'command)

assign the feature **command** to the **s-maj**. It happens to be the case that everywhere else in the grammar, features are transferred from node to node. It is only this one place that new features are added from the outside. If we could get rid of this one occurrence, the grammar would no longer use the ability to add new features from outside the sentence and such use could be removed from the possibilities the learner needs to search through.

It may indeed be possible to remove these lines from the grammar. Assume that whenever a rule of the grammar applies (like *dative-movement*, or *aux-inversion*) the sentence is marked to indicate that this rule has applied. So a sentence that underwent *aux-inversion* would automatically be given the feature **aux-inversion**. If it underwent *you-insertion*, it would have **you-insertion**.

```
(def-net s-maj
  (seq (either
        (: = (the mood of $s-maj) 'statement)      ; A sentence is either
                                                    ; a statement
        (seq (peek verb)                           ; ------------------
             (= (the tense of $last)               ; or a command.
                'tenseless)                         ;
             (insert (the word you))                ; You-insertion rule
             (: = (the mood of $s-maj 'command))   ; ------------------
        . . .))
```

Figure 11.25 A piece of ATN showing feature assignments

Our ATN currently does not do this (it does not even distinguish where one rule starts and another stops) but this would be easy to change. The point of this change is that then we could identify **commands** with sentences that were marked with **you-insertion** and **questions** as sentences that had **aux-inversion** or **wh-movement**. As we pointed out in Section 4.2.1, since all of the differences between languages will be accounted for in the grammar, we may assume the parser is innate. Therefore, by moving the feature marking to the parser, we have removed one thing that a child must learn.

This is but one example of how the grammar might be simplified. If we could do this in a lot of other examples, we might reduce the power of transformations so that there would be only a very limited number of things they could do. We could then have the learning mechanism try *all* of them to see which worked. This is what the language learning program by [Berwick80] does. He managed to get a transformational component which could do only two things:

- reorder the first two things in the input stream;
- put in a dummy np into the input stream.

The first is intended to be used for a rule like *aux-inversion* while the second takes the place of rules that move or add noun phrases, like *wh-movement*, or *you-insertion*. We will not go into exactly how such a grammar would work. Our point is rather that if these are the only things that a parser can do (other than parse a normal phrase-structure constituent), then the learner has very little to try, and the search problem is under control. These two rules have been added as (3d) and (3e) to the language learning algorithm of Figure 11.24.

11.7 References and Further Reading

For many years, AI researchers stayed away from learning because earlier traditions, especially behaviorism, had focused on it to excess. Part of AI's early appeal was that it legitimized studying mental skills without studying how they were acquired. More recently, more and higher quality attention has been given to this area, as exemplified by the ongoing series of machine learning workshops [Michalski83, Michalski83a, Michalski83b].

Early work in the field of "concept learning" was done by Bruner, Goodnow, and Austin [Bruner56]. Winston's work [Winston75a] extended their ideas to descriptions of systems with interrelated parts. A good survey appears in [Dietterich81]. See [Shapiro81] for a theoretical treatment.

Quinlan has done interesting research on special cases of the discrimination-tree-building problem, investigating how to achieve optimal performance, and how to tolerate noisy data. See [Quinlan83, Quinlan83a]. The Mop theory is described in more detail in [Schank82]. For more on analogy, see [Carbonell82a, Carbonell83a]. Sussman and Lenat's Ph.D. theses describing Hacker and AM have been published; see [Sussman75] and [Lenat82].

Exercises

11.1 In Section 11.2.2, we mentioned that Winston's program started by replacing constants with variables. So it might replace (inst a1 brick) in Figure 11.3 with (inst ?x1 brick). What's the difference between the two constants a1 and brick? Can you formulate a general rule about which constants should be variabilized? Are there exceptions to your rule?

11.2 In Section 11.2.2, we described *numerical generalization*, in which a general rule of the form "?x should lie in interval [*l, h*]" is proposed to cover a set of observations of legitimate ?x values lying between *l* and *h*.

    a) Suppose the machine observes that values 3, 5, 7, 9, and 11 work. In what sort of domain is it legitimate to infer that any value between 3 and 11 is correct?

    b) Suppose that in addition ?x values of 6 and 8 had been shown *not* to be correct. Is there a patch to the generalization operator that will always find the simplest pattern that covers the examples of a numerical concept and excludes the nonexamples?

11.3 Suppose an empiricist algorithm was learning the concept "snorfle," and its current hypothesis about the concept was described by the pattern

        (if (and (parts ?x {?x1, ?x2, ?x3})
             (inst ?x1 circle)
             (inst ?x2 square)
             (inside ?x3 ?x1))
        (inst ?x snorfle))

Figure 11.26 shows positive and negative instances of the concept. Note that the current hypothesis matches all three, and so will have to be specialized. What is a reasonable specialization? What does this say about what properties of the objects must be included in the "identified situation" for this concept to be learned?

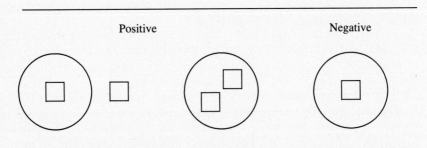

Positive   Negative

Figure 11.26 Two snorfles and a nonsnorfle

11.4 Figure 11.8 shows how Lex solves the credit-assignment problem: by classifying operators as staying on or straying from the correct solution path. Why won't this work for the domain of chess moves?

11.5 The Lex program represents heuristics as rules with schematized algebra terms on the left-hand side, such as

$$\int const \ x \ \cos(x)dx \ \rightarrow \ \cdots$$

Elsewhere, we assumed that the antecedents of rules were predicate-calculus expressions that were either satisfied or unsatisfied in each situation. Explain how to translate Lex's rules into this format. Would the match algorithm of Section 11.2.4 work on them?

11.6 In Section 11.2.2, we explained how the boundaries of *version spaces* are moved by positive and negative instances of a concept. Sketch an algorithm for doing this in the algebra domain of Lex. Do these ideas carry over to the general predicate-calculus rule format used by the match algorithm of Section 11.2.4?

11.7 Change the match algorithm of Section 11.2.4 so that it finds only the best match (the one with the fewest differences), not all of them. This will require keeping track of a queue of "matches in progress," and working on the most promising one.

11.8 The astute reader may find a gap in our argument (Section 11.2.3) that matching was no help in specialization. In the abstract, finding the pattern underlying the negative instances is the same kind of task as finding the pattern underlying the positive instances. Hence, we should be able to run the matcher of Figure 11.12 and Figure 11.13 on the negative instances as well as the positive ones. Then we could just conjoin the tentative hypothesis arrived at by the positive process with the negation of the tentative hypothesis arrived at by the negative process, and be fairly sure of having a better hypothesis.

Fill this gap by explaining why the negations of naturally occurring concepts are often harder to learn than the concepts themselves. (Hint: think about the *disjunctive-concept problem*.)

11.9 Write a version of the match algorithm of Section 11.2.4 that works on two situations rather than a pattern and a situation. It must pair up constants where the original bound variables to constants.

11.10 In the Mop theory of *failure-driven learning* (Section 11.3), where has the credit-assignment problem gone? What solution to it is presupposed?

11.11 In Chapter 7, our translation of schemas into predicate calculus were of the form "If *schema-name* then *event-description*." In Section 11.2.6 we put them the other way around. Is this just an example of the authors being inconsistent and confused?

11.12 In Section 11.5, we explained how AM discovered numbers by weakening the definition of list equality. Find other ways to weaken the same definition. Do any other interesting concepts appear?

11.13 Actually, the graph deformation condition is not sufficient to produce the syntactic tree of Figure 11.22 given the internal representation shown in Figure 11.21. One needs both the associative net and the name of the topmost node. For the version in Figure 11.22 this would be drop-1. Show what the tree would look like if one selected block-1 as the topmost node for the tree.

11.14 In French, adjectives typically come after the noun, as in "le moulin rouge," which means "the red windmill" but word-for-word is translated as "the windmill red." Since the $\bar{X}$ theory is presumed to hold for all languages, explain why this observation might be a problem for the theory as we formulated it.

11.15 How well will the language learning algorithm of Figure 11.24 do on the sentence "The girl dropped the block?" Assume that it had already seen "The big girl dropped the red block."

11.16 How well will the language learning algorithm of Figure 11.24 do on the sentence "Drop the red block?" Again, assume it had already seen "The big girl dropped the red block."

References

Agin72.   Agin, G.J., "Representation and Description of Curved Objects," Report 173, Stanford University Artificial Intelligence Laboratory (1972).

Aho72.   Aho, Alfred V. and Ullman, Jeffrey D., *The Theory of Parsing, Translation, and Compiling,* Prentice-Hall, Englewood Cliffs, N.J. (1972).

Allen80.   Allen, James F. and Perrault, C. Raymond, "Analyzing intention in utterances," *Artificial Intelligence* **15**(3) pp. 143-178 (1980).

Allen81.   Allen, James, "Maintaining Knowledge about Temporal Intervals," Report TR-86, University of Rochester Department of Computer Science (1981).

Allen83.   Allen, James and Koomen, Johannes, "Planning using a temporal world model," *Proc. Ijcai* **8** pp. 741-747 (1983).

Allen84.   Allen, James, "Towards a general theory of action and time," *Artificial Intelligence* **23**(2) pp. 123-154 (1984).

Anderson77.   Anderson, John R., "Induction of augmented transition networks," *Cognitive Science* **1**(2) pp. 125-157 (1977).

Anderson83.   Anderson, John R., "Acquisition of proof skills in geometry," pp. 191-219 in *Machine Learning: An Artificial Intelligence Approach*, ed. Ryszard Michalski, Jaime G. Carbonell, and Tom M. Mitchell, Tioga, Palo Alto, Calif. (1983).

Austin62.   Austin, J.L., *How to Do Things with Words,* Oxford University Press, London (1962).

Bach74.   Bach, Emmon, *Syntactic Theory,* Holt, Rinehart & Winston, New York (1974).

Ballard82.   Ballard, Dana and Brown, Christopher, *Computer Vision,* Prentice-Hall, Englewood Cliffs, N.J. (1982).

Barrow78.   Barrow, H. and Tenenbaum, J.M., "Recovering intrinsic scene characteristics from images," in *Computer Vision Systems,* ed. A. Hanson and E. Riseman, Academic Press, New York (1978).

Barrow80.   Barrow, H. and Tenenbaum, J.M., "Interpreting line drawings as three-dimensional surfaces," *Proc. AAAI* **1** pp. 11-14 (1980).

Barrow81.   Barrow, H. and Tenenbaum, J.M., "Computational vision," *Proceedings of the IEEE* **69**(5) pp. 572-595 (1981).

Beck82.   Beck, Jacob, "Textural segmentation," pp. 285-317 in *Organization and Representation in Perception,* ed. Jacob Beck, Lawrence Erlbaum, Hillsdale, N.J. (1982).

Berliner80.   Berliner, Hans, "Computer backgammon," *Scientific American,* (June 1980).

Berwick80.   Berwick, Robert C., "Computational analogues of constraints on grammars: A model of syntactic acquisition," pp. 49-53 in *Proceedings of the 18th Conference of the Association for Computational Linguistics,* Association for Computational Linguistics (1980).

Berwick82.   Berwick, Robert C., "Locality Principles and the Acquisition of Syntactic Knowledge," Ph.D. thesis, MIT Department of Electrical Engineering and Computer Science (1982).

Bledsoe77.   Bledsoe, W.W., "Non-resolution theorem proving," *Artificial Intelligence* **9**(1) pp. 1-35 (1977).

Bledsoe78.   Bledsoe, W.W. and Ballantyne, A.M., "Unskolemizing," Report ATP-41A, University of Texas at Austin Department of Mathematics and Computer Sciences (1978).

Bobrow69.   Bobrow, Daniel G. and Fraser, Bruce, "An augmented state transition network analysis procedure," *Proc. Ijcai* **1** pp. 557-569 (1969).

Bobrow77.   Bobrow, Daniel G. and Winograd, Terry, "An overview of KRL, a knowledge representation language," *Cognitive Science* **1** pp. 3-46 (1977).

Boden77.   Boden, Margaret, *Artificial Intelligence and Natural Man*, Basic Books, New York (1977).

Boyer79.   Boyer, R.S. and Moore, J S., *A Computational Logic*, Academic Press, New York (1979).

Brachman79.   Brachman, Ronald J., "On the epistemological status of semantic networks," pp. 3-50 in *Associative Networks: Representation and Use of Knowledge by Computers*, ed. N.V. Findler, Academic Press, New York (1979).

Brooks81.   Brooks, Rodney A., "Symbolic reasoning among 3-D models and 2-D images," *Artificial Intelligence* **17**(1-3) pp. 285-348 (1981).

Brooks82.   Brooks, Rodney A., "Solving the find-path problem by good representation of space," *Proc. AAAI* **2**(1982).

Bruce75.   Bruce, Bertram, "Case systems for natural language," *Artificial Intelligence* **6** pp. 327-360 (1975).

Bruner56.   Bruner, J.S., Goodnow, J.J., and Austin, G.A., *A Study of Thinking,* Wiley, New York (1956).

Bruynooghe80.   Bruynooghe, M., "Analysis of dependencies to improve the behavior of logic programs," pp. 293-305 in *Proceedings of the 5th Conference on Automated Deduction*, ed. W. Bibel and R. Kowalski, Springer-Verlag, New York (1980).

Burstein83.   Burstein, Mark, "Concept formation by incremental analogical reasoning and debugging," pp. 19-25 in *Proceedings of the International Machine Learning Workshop*, University of Illinois (1983).

Campbell82.   Campbell, A.N., Hollister, V.F., Duda, R.O., and Hart, P.E., "Recognition of a hidden mineral deposit by an artificial intelligence program," *Science* **217**(3) pp. 927-929 (1982).

Campbell83.   Campbell, Murray and Berliner, Hans, "A chess program that chunks," *Proc. AAAI* **3** pp. 49-53 (1983).

Carbonell82.   Carbonell, Jaime G., "Metaphor: an inescapable phenomenon in natural-language comprehension," in *Strategies for Natural Language Processing*, ed. W.G. Lehnert and M.H. Ringle, Lawrence Erlbaum, Hillsdale, N.J. (1982).

Carbonell82a.   Carbonell, Jaime, "Experiential learning in analogical problem solving," *Proc. AAAI* **2** pp. 168-171 (1982).

Carbonell83.   Carbonell, Jaime, "Derivational analogy in problem solving and knowledge acquisition," pp. 12-18 in *Proceedings of the International Machine Learning Workshop*, University of Illinois (1983).

Carbonell83a.   Carbonell, Jaime, "Derivational analogy and its role in problem solving," *Proc. AAAI* **3** pp. 64-69 (1983).

Chakravarty79.   Chakravarty, Indranil, "A generalized line and junction labeling scheme with applications to scene analysis," *IEEE Transactions on Pattern Analysis and Machine Intelligence* **PAMI-1**(2)(1979).

Chang73.   Chang, C.L. and Lee, R.C.-T., *Symbolic Logic and Mechanical Theorem Proving*, Academic Press, New York (1973).

Charniak72.   Charniak, Eugene, "Context and the reference problem," pp. 311-331 in *Natural Language Processing*, ed. R. Rustin, Algorithmics Press, New York (1972).

Charniak75.   Charniak, Eugene, "Organization and inference in a frame-like system of common sense knowledge," *Theoretical Issues in Natural Language Processing* **1** pp. 42-52 (1975).

Charniak76.   Charniak, Eugene and Wilks, Yorick (Eds.), *Computational Semantics: An Introduction to Artificial Intelligence and Natural Language Comprehension*, North-Holland, Amsterdam (1976).

Charniak78.   Charniak, Eugene, "On the use of framed knowledge in language comprehension," *Artificial Intelligence* **11** pp. 225-265 (1978).

Charniak80.   Charniak, Eugene, Riesbeck, Christopher K., and McDermott, Drew V., *Artificial Intelligence Programming*, Lawrence Erlbaum, Hillsdale, N.J. (1980).

Charniak81.   Charniak, Eugene, "The case-slot identity theory," *Cognitive Science* **5**(3) pp. 285-292 (1981).

Charniak81a.   Charniak, Eugene, "A common representation for problem solving and language comprehension information," *Artificial Intelligence* **16** pp. 225-255 (1981).

Charniak83.   Charniak, Eugene, "A parser with something for everyone," in *Parsing Natural Language*, ed. M. King, Academic Press, London (1983).

Charniak83a.   Charniak, Eugene, "The Bayesian basis of common-sense medical diagnosis," *Proc. AAAI* **3** pp. 70-73 (1983).

Charniak83b.   Charniak, Eugene, "The Frail/Nasl Reference Manual," Report CS-83-06, Brown University Department of Computer Science (1983).

Charniak83c.   Charniak, Eugene, "Passing markers: A theory of contextual influence in language comprehension," *Cognitive Science* **7**(3)(1983).

Chomsky57.   Chomsky, Noam, *Syntactic Structures,* Mouton, The Hague (1957).

Chomsky65.   Chomsky, Noam, *Aspects of the Theory of Syntax,* MIT Press, Cambridge, Mass. (1965).

Clark78.   Clark, Keith L., "Negation as failure," pp. 293-322 in *Logic and Databases*, ed. H. Gallaire and J. Minker, Plenum Press (1978).

Clark78a.   Clark, E.V. and Clark, H.H., *Psychology and Language,* Harcourt Brace Jovanovich, New York (1978).

Clocksin81.   Clocksin, W. and Mellish, C., *Programming in Prolog,* Springer-Verlag, New York (1981).

Cohen79.   Cohen, Philip R. and Perrault, C. Raymond, "Elements of a plan-based theory of speech acts," *Cognitive Science* **3** pp. 177-212 (1979).

Collins75.   Collins, Alan and Loftus, Elizabeth F., "A spreading-activation theory of semantic processing," *Psychological Review* **82**(6) pp. 407-428 (1975).

Cox80.   Cox, P.T. and Pietrzykowski, T., "On Reverse Skolemization," Report CS-80-01, University of Waterloo Department of Computer Science (1980).

Cullingford78.   Cullingford, Richard E., "Script Application: Computer Understanding of Newspaper Stories," Report 116, Yale University Department of Computer Science (1978).

Davis77.   Davis, Randall, Buchanan, Bruce, and Shortliffe, Edward, "Production rules as a representation for knowledge-based consultation program," *Artificial Intelligence* **8** pp. 15-45 (1977).

Davis82.   Davis, Randall and Lenat, Douglas B., *Knowledge-Based Systems in Artificial Intelligence,* McGraw-Hill, New York (1982).

Davis82a.   Davis, Randall, "Teiresias: Applications of meta-level knowledge," pp. 227-490 in *Knowledge-Based Systems in Artificial Intelligence*, ed. Randall Davis and Douglas B. Lenat, McGraw-Hill, New York (1982).

Davis84.   Davis, Ernest, "Representing and Acquiring Geographic Knowledge," Report 292, Yale University Computer Science Department (1984).

Dean83.   Dean, Thomas, "Time Map Maintenance," Report 289, Yale University Computer Science Department (1983).

deKleer77.   deKleer, Johan, Doyle, Jon, Steele, Guy L., and Sussman, Gerald J., "AMORD: Explicit control of reasoning," *Sigplan Notices* **12**(8) pp. 116-125 (August 1977).

deKleer79.   deKleer, Johan, "Qualitative and quantitative reasoning in classical mechanics," pp. 11-30 in *Artificial Intelligence: An MIT Perspective*, ed. P.H. Winston and R.H. Brown, MIT Press, Cambridge, Mass. (1979).

deKleer82.   deKleer, Johan and Brown, J.S., "Foundations of envisioning," *Proc. AAAI* **2**(1982).

Dietterich81. Dietterich, T.G. and Michalski, Ryszard, "Inductive learning of structural descriptions," *Artificial Intelligence* **16**(1981).

Domjan83.   Domjan, Michael, "Biological constraints on instrumental and classical conditioning: Implications for general process theory," in *Psychology of Learning and Motivation*, ed. Bower, G., Academic Press, New York (1983).

Dowty81.   Dowty, David R., Wall, Robert E., and Peters, Stanley, *Introduction to Montague Semantics,* Reidel, Dordrecht (1981).

Doyle79.   Doyle, Jon, "A truth maintenance system," *Artificial Intelligence* **12**(3) pp. 231-272 (1979).

Duda76.   Duda, R.O., Hart, P.E., and Nilsson, N.J., "Subjective Bayesian methods for rule-based inference systems," in *Proceedings of the 1976 National Computer Conference*, AFIPS Press (1976).

Duda78.   Duda, Richard O., Hart, Peter E., and Sutherland, G.L., "Semantic network representations in rule-based inference systems," pp. 203-221 in *Pattern Directed Inference Systems*, ed. D.A. Waterman and F. Hayes-Roth, Academic Press, New York (1978).

Duda80.   Duda, Richard O., Gaschnig, John G., and Hart, Peter E., "Model design in the Prospector consultant system for mineral exploration," pp. 153-167 in *Expert Systems in the Microelectronic Age*, ed. D. Michie, Edinburgh University Press, Edinburgh (1980).

Dyer83.   Dyer, Michael G., "The role of affect in narratives," *Cognitive Science* **7**(3)(1983).

Elliot82.   Elliot, R.J. and Lesk, M.E., "Route finding in street maps by computers and people," *Proc. AAAI* **2** pp. 258-261 (1982).

Ernst69.   Ernst, G. and Newell, Allen, *GPS: A Case Study in Generality and Problem Solving,* Academic Press, New York (1969).

Fahlman74.   Fahlman, Scott E., "A planning system for robot construction tasks," *Artificial Intelligence* **5**(1) pp. 1-49 (1974).

Fahlman79.   Fahlman, Scott E., *NETL: A System for Representing and Using Real-World Knowledge,* MIT Press, Cambridge, Mass. (1979).

Feigenbaum63.   Feigenbaum, Edward A., "The simulation of verbal learning behavior," in *Computers and Thought*, ed. Edward A. Feigenbaum and Julian Feldman, McGraw-Hill, New York (1963).

Feldman77.   Feldman, Jerome and Sproull, Robert F., "Decision theory and artificial intelligence II: The hungry monkey," Technical Report, University of Rochester Department of Computer Science (1977).

Fikes71.   Fikes, Richard E. and Nilsson, Nils J., "STRIPS: A new approach to the application of theorem proving to problem solving," *Artificial Intelligence* **2** pp. 189-208 (1971).

Fillmore68.   Fillmore, Charles J., "The case for case," pp. 1-88 in *Universals in Linguistic Theory*, ed. E. Bach and R.T. Harms, Holt, Rinehart, and Winston, New York (1968).

Fillmore77.   Fillmore, Charles J., "The case for case reopened," pp. 59-81 in *Syntax and Semantics 8: Grammatical Relations*, ed. P. Cole and J.M. Sadock, Academic Press, New York (1977).

Findler79.   Findler, Nicholas V., *Associative Networks: Representation and Use of Knowledge by Computer,* Academic Press, New York (1979).

Finkel75.   Finkel, R., "An overview of AL, a programming language for automation," *Proc. Ijcai* **4** pp. 758-765 (1975).

Forbus81.   Forbus, Kenneth, "A Study of Qualitative and Geometric Knowledge in Reasoning about Motion," Report 615, MIT Artificial Intelligence Laboratory (1981).

Forbus84.   Forbus, Kenneth, "Qualitative process theory," *Artificial Intelligence*, (1984).

Forgy79.   Forgy, C.L., *On the efficient implementation of production systems,* Carnegie-Mellon University Department of Computer Science (1979).

Freuder80.   Freuder, Eugene C., "Information needed to label a scene," *Proc. AAAI* **1** pp. 18-20 (1980).

Friedland84.   Friedland, Peter and Iwasaki, Y., "The concept and implementation of skeletal plans," Unpublished, submitted to *Artificial Intelligence* (1984).

Gallaire78.   Gallaire, H. and Minker, Jack, *Logic and Databases,* Plenum Press (1978).

Garcia66.   Garcia, J. and Koeling, R.A., "Relation of cue to consequence in avoidance learning," *Psychonomic Science* **4** pp. 123-124 (1966).

Gazdar81.   Gazdar, Gerald, "On syntactic categories," *Transactions of the Royal Society* **B-295** pp. 267-283 (1981).

Gelernter59.   Gelernter, H., "Realization of a geometry theorem-proving machine," in *Information Processing: Proceedings of the International Conference on Information Processing,* UNESCO (1959).

Gelernter77.   Gelernter, H., "Empirical explorations of SYNCHEM," *Science* **197** pp. 1041-1049 (1977).

Genesereth83.   Genesereth, Michael R., "An overview of meta-level architecture," *Proc. AAAI* **3** pp. 119-124 (1983).

Gibson50.   Gibson, J.J., *The Perception of the Visual World,* Houghton Mifflin, Boston (1950).

Gilchrist77.   Gilchrist, A.L., "Perceived lightness depends on perceived spatial arrangement," *Science* **195** pp. 185-187 (1977).

Gordon75.   Gordon, D. and Lakoff, George, "Conversational postulates," in *Syntax and Semantics 3: Speech acts*, ed. P. Cole and J.L. Morgan, (1975).

Grice75.   Grice, Paul, "Logic and conversation," pp. 41-58 in *Syntax and Semantics 3: Speech Acts*, ed. P. Cole and J. Morgan, Academic Press, New York (1975).

Grosz78.   Grosz, Barbara J., "Discourse knowledge," pp. 229-347 in *Understanding Spoken language*, ed. D. Walker, North-Holland, New York (1978).

Hart68.   Hart, P.E., Nilsson, Nils J., and Raphael, B., "A formal basis for the heuristic determination of minimum cost paths," *IEEE Transactions on Systems Science and Cybernetics* **SSC-4(2)** pp. 100-107 (1968).

Hayes77.   Hayes, Patrick J., "In defense of logic," *Proc. Ijcai* **5** pp. 559-565 (1977).

Hayes84.   Hayes, Patrick, "The second naive physics manifesto," in *Formal Theories of the Commonsense World*, ed. J. Hobbs, Ablex, Hillsdale, N.J. (1984).

Hayes84a.   Hayes, Patrick, "Liquids," in *Formal Theories of the Commonsense World*, ed. J. Hobbs, Ablex, Hillsdale, N.J. (1984).

Hayes78.   Hayes, Philip J., "Mapping Input onto Schemas," Report TR-29, University of Rochester Department of Computer Science (1978).

Hayes-Roth79.   Hayes-Roth, B. and Hayes-Roth, F., "A cognitive model of planning," *Cognitive Science* **3**(4) pp. 275-310 (1979).

Hendrix73.   Hendrix, Gary, "Modeling simultaneous actions and continuous processes," *Artificial Intelligence* **4** pp. 145-180 (1973).

Hendrix75.   Hendrix, Gary G., "Expanding the utility of semantic networks through partitioning," *Proc. Ijcai* **4** pp. 115-121 (1975).

Hewitt71.   Hewitt, Carl, "PLANNER: A language for proving theorems in robots," *Proc. Ijcai* **2**(1971).

Hinton79.   Hinton, Geoffrey, "Some demonstrations of the effects of structural descriptions in mental imagery," *Cognitive Science* **3**(3) pp. 231-251 (1979).

Hirst81.   Hirst, Graeme, *Anaphora in Natural Language Understanding: A Survey,* Springer-Verlag, Berlin (1981).

Hirst82.   Hirst, Graeme and Charniak, Eugene, "Word sense and case slot disambiguation," *Proc. AAAI* **2**(1982).

Hirst83.   Hirst, Graeme, "A foundation for semantic interpretation," in *Proceedings of the 21st Annual Meeting of the Association for Computational Linguistics*, Association for Computational Linguistics (1983).

Hirst83a.   Hirst, Graeme, "Semantic Interpretation against Ambiguity,"
                 Report CS-83-25, Brown University Department of Comput-
                 er Science (1983).

Hopcroft69.   Hopcroft, John E. and Ullman, Jeffrey D., *Formal
                 Languages and their Relation to Automata*, Addison-Wesley,
                 Reading, Mass. (1969).

Horn77.   Horn, B.K.P., "Understanding image intensities," *Artificial
                 Intelligence* **8** pp. 201-231 (1977).

Hummel83.   Hummel, Robert A. and Zucker, Steven W., "On the foun-
                 dations of relaxation labeling processes," *IEEE Transactions
                 on Pattern Analysis and Machine Intelligence* **PAMI-5**(3) pp.
                 267-287 (1983).

Julesz71.   Julesz, Bela, *Foundations of Cyclopean Perception*, Universi-
                 ty of Chicago Press, Chicago (1971).

Julesz75.   Julesz, Bela, "Experiments in the visual perception of tex-
                 ture," *Scientific American* **232** pp. 34-43 (1975).

Kahn77.   Kahn, Kenneth and Gorry, G.A., "Mechanizing temporal
                 knowledge," *Artificial Intelligence* **9** pp. 87-108 (1977).

Karp83.   Karp, Richard M. and Pearl, Judea, "Searching for an op-
                 timal path in a tree with random costs," *Artificial Intelli-
                 gence* **21**(1,2) pp. 99-116 (1983).

Katz63.   Katz, J. and Fodor, J.A., "The structure of a semantic
                 theory," *Language* **39** pp. 170-210 (1963).

Kay80.   Kay, Martin, "Algorithm schemata and data structures in
                 syntactic processing," in *Proceedings of the Symposium on
                 Text Processing*, Nobel Academy (1980).

Kender80.   Kender, John R. and Kanade, Takeo, "Mapping image pro-
                 perties into shape constraints: skewed symmetry, affine-
                 transformable patterns, and the shape-from-texture para-
                 digm," *Proc. AAAI* **1** pp. 4-6 (1980).

Keyser76.   Keyser, S.J. and Postal, P.M., *Beginning English Grammar*,
                 Harper & Row, New York (1976).

Knuth70.   Knuth, D.E. and Bendix, P.B., "Simple word problems in
                 universal algebras," pp. 263-297 in *Computational Problems
                 in Abstract Algebra*, ed. J. Leech, Pergamon Press (1970).

Knuth73.   Knuth, D.E., *Sorting and Searching*, Addison-Wesley, Read-
                 ing, Mass. (1973).

Knuth75.   Knuth, D.E. and Moore, R.N., "An analysis of alpha-beta pruning," *Artificial Intelligence* **6** pp. 293-326 (1975).

Kolodner83.   Kolodner, Janet, "Reconstructive memory: A computer model," *Cognitive Science* **7** pp. 281-328 (1983).

Kolodner83a. Kolodner, Janet, "Maintaining organization in a dynamic long-term memory," *Cognitive Science* **7** pp. 243-280 (1983).

Korf82.   Korf, Richard, "A program that learns to solve Rubik's Cube," *Proc. AAAI* **2** pp. 164-167 (1982).

Kosslyn75.   Kosslyn, Steven M., "Information representation in visual images," *Cognitive Psychology* **7** pp. 341-370 (1975).

Kosslyn77.   Kosslyn, Steven M. and Shwartz, Steven P., "A simulation of visual imagery," *Cognitive Science* **1**(3) pp. 265-295 (1977).

Kowalski79.   Kowalski, Robert A., *Logic for Problem Solving,* Elsevier North-Holland, Amsterdam (1979).

Kripke63.   Kripke, Saul, "Semantical considerations on modal logic," *Acta Philosophica Fennica* **16** pp. 83-94 (1963).

Kuhn62.   Kuhn, Thomas S., *The Structure of Scientific Revolutions,* University of Chicago Press, Chicago (1962).

Kuipers78.   Kuipers, Benjamin, "Modeling spatial knowledge," *Cognitive Science* **2**(2) pp. 129-154 (1978).

Kuipers82.   Kuipers, Benjamin, "Getting the envisionment right," *Proc. AAAI* **2** pp. 209-212 (1982).

Lakatos70.   Lakatos, Imre, "Falsification and the methodology of scientific research programmes," pp. 91-196 in *Criticism and the Growth of Knowledge*, ed. I. Lakatos and A. Musgrave, Cambridge University Press, Cambridge (1970).

Lakoff80.   Lakoff, George and Johnson, M., *Metaphors We Live By,* University of Chicago Press, Chicago (1980).

Lebowitz83.   Lebowitz, Michael, "Generalization from natural-language text," *Cognitive Science* **7**(1) pp. 1-40 (1983).

Lehnert78.   Lehnert, Wendy, *The Process of Question Answering,* Lawrence Erlbaum, Hillsdale, N.J. (1978).

Lehnert81.   Lehnert, Wendy, "Affect and memory representation," *Proceedings of the 3rd Conference of the Cognitive Science Society,* pp. 78-83 (1981).

Lenat82.   Lenat, Douglas B., "AM: Discovery in mathematics as heuristic search," pp. 1-225 in *Knowledge-Based Systems in Artificial Intelligence*, ed. Randall Davis and Douglas B. Lenat, McGraw-Hill, New York (1982).

Lenat83.   Lenat, Douglas B., "Theory formation by heuristic search," *Artificial Intelligence* 21(1,2) pp. 31-59 (1983).

Lenat83a.   Lenat, Douglas B., "EURISKO: A program that learns new heuristics and domain concepts," *Artificial Intelligence* 21(1,2) pp. 61-98 (1983).

Lenat83b.   Lenat, Douglas B. and Brown, John Seely, "Why AM and Eurisko appear to work," *Proc. AAAI* 3 pp. 236-240 (1983).

Letovsky83.   Letovsky, Stan, "Qualitative and Quantitative Temporal Reasoning," Report 294, Yale University Computer Science Department (1983).

Lewis73.   Lewis, David K., *Counterfactuals,* Basil Blackwell, Oxford (1973).

Loveland76.   Loveland, D.W. and Stickel, M.E., "A hole in goal trees," *IEEE Transactions on Computers* **C-25**(4) pp. 335-341 (1976).

Lozano-Perez77.   Lozano-Perez, Tomas and Winston, Patrick H., "LAMA: A language for automatic mechanical assembly," *Proc. Ijcai* 5 pp. 710-716 (1977).

Lozano-Perez81.   Lozano-Perez, Tomas, "Automatic planning of manipulator transfer movements," *IEEE Transactions on Systems, Man, Cybernetics* **SMC-11**(6) pp. 681-698 (1981).

Luenberger73.   Luenberger, David G., *Introduction to Linear and Nonlinear Programming,* Addison-Wesley, Reading, Mass. (1973).

Marcus80.   Marcus, Mitchell P., *A Theory of Syntactic Recognition for Natural Language,* MIT Press, Cambridge, Mass. (1980).

Marr78.   Marr, David and Nishihara, H. Keith, "Representation and recognition of the spatial organization of three-dimensional shapes," *Proceedings of the Royal Society* **B-200** pp. 269-294 (1978).

Marr79.   Marr, David and Poggio, Tomaso, "A computational theory of human stereo vision," *Proceedings of the Royal Society* **B-204** pp. 301-328 (1979).

Marr80.   Marr, David and Hildreth, Ellen, "Theory of edge detection," *Procedings of the Royal Society* **B-207** pp. 187-217 (1980).

Marr82.   Marr, David, *Vision,* Freeman, San Francisco (1982).

Mason81.   Mason, Matthew T., "Compliance and force control for computer controlled manipulators," *IEEE Transactions on Systems, Man, Cybernetics* **SMC-11**(6) pp. 418-432 (1981).

McCarthy58.   McCarthy, John, "Programs with common sense," in *Proceedings of the Symposium on the Mechanization of Thought Processes,* National Physical Laboratory, Teddington, England (1958).

McCarthy60.   McCarthy, John, "Recursive functions of symbolic expressions and their computation by machine," *Communications of the ACM* **7** pp. 184-195 (1960).

McCarthy69.   McCarthy, John and Hayes, Patrick J., "Some philosophical problems from the standpoint of artificial intelligence," in *Machine Intelligence 4,* ed. B. Meltzer and D. Michie, Edinburgh University Press, Edinburgh (1969).

McCorduck79.   McCorduck, Pamela, *Machines Who Think,* Freeman, San Francisco (1979).

McDermott74.   McDermott, Drew V., "Assimilation of New Information by a Natural Language Understanding System," Report 291, MIT Artificial Intelligence Laboratory (1974).

McDermott77.   McDermott, Drew V., "Flexibility and Efficiency in a Computer Program for Designing Circuits," Report AI-TR-402, Massachusetts Institute of Technology, Artificial Intelligence Laboratory, Cambridge, Mass. (June 1977).

McDermott78.   McDermott, Drew V., "Planning and acting," *Cognitive Science* **2** pp. 71-109 (1978).

McDermott80.   McDermott, Drew V. and Doyle, Jon, "Non-monotonic logic I," *Artificial Intelligence* **13**(1,2) pp. 41-72 (1980).

McDermott82.   McDermott, Drew V., "A temporal logic for reasoning about processes and plans," *Cognitive Science* **6** pp. 101-155 (1982).

McDermott82a. McDermott, Drew V. and Brooks, Ruven, "Arby: diagnosis with shallow causal models," *Proc. AAAI* **2**(1982).

McDermott83.   McDermott, Drew V., "Duck Reference Manual," Unpublished, Yale University Department of Computer Science (1983).

McDermott83a. McDermott, Drew V., "Contexts and data dependencies: A synthesis," *IEEE Transactions on Pattern Analysis and Machine Intelligence* **PAMI-5**(1983).

McDermott84.   McDermott, Drew V. and Davis, Ernest, "Planning routes through uncertain territory," *Artificial Intelligence* **22** pp. 107-156 (1984).

McDermott81.   McDermott, John, "R1: The formative years," *AI Magazine* **2**(2) pp. 21-29 (1981).

Mendelson64.   Mendelson, Elliott, *Introduction to Mathematical Logic,* Van Nostrand, Princeton, N.J. (1964).

Michalski83.   Michalski, Ryszard, "A theory and methodology of inductive learning," pp. 83-134 in *Machine Learning: An Artificial Intelligence Approach*, ed. Ryszard Michalski, Jaime G. Carbonell, and Tom M. Mitchell, Tioga, Palo Alto, Calif. (1983).

Michalski83a.   Michalski, Ryszard, Carbonell, Jaime G., and Mitchell, Tom M., *Machine Learning: An Artificial Intelligence Approach,* Tioga, Palo Alto, Calif. (1983).

Michalski83b.   Michalski, Ryszard, Carbonell, Jaime G., and Mitchell, Tom M., *Proceedings of the International Machine Learning Workshop,* University of Illinois Department of Computer Science (1983).

Michener78.   Michener, Edwina R., "Understanding understanding mathematics," *Cognitive Science* **2**(4) pp. 361-383 (1978).

Miller83.   Miller, David, "Scheduling Heuristics for Problem Solvers," Report 264, Yale University Department of Computer Science (1983).

Miller82.   Miller, Randolph, Pople, Harry, and Myers, Jack, "Internist-1, an experimental computer-based diagnostic consultant for general internal medicine," *New England Journal of Medicine* **307** pp. 468-476 (1982).

Minsky75.   Minsky, Marvin, "A framework for representing knowledge," in *The Psychology of Computer Vision*, ed. P.H. Winston, McGraw-Hill, New York (1975).

Mitchell83.   Mitchell, Tom M., Utgoff, Paul E., and Banerji, Ranan, "Learning by experimentation: Acquiring and refining problem-solving heuristics," pp. 163-190 in *Machine Learning: An Artificial Intelligence Approach*, ed. Ryszard Michalski, Jaime G. Carbonell, and Tom M. Mitchell, Tioga, Palo Alto, Calif. (1983).

Montague74.   Montague, Richard, *Formal Philosophy,* Yale University Press, New Haven, Conn. (1974).

Moore74.   Moore, J. and Newell, A., "How can Merlin understand?,"
                in *Knowledge and Cognition*, Lawrence Erlbaum, Hillsdale,
                N.J. (1974).

Moore75.   Moore, Robert, "A serial scheme for the inheritance of pro-
                perties," *Sigart Newsletter*, (53) pp. 8-9 (1975).

Moore80.   Moore, Robert, "Reasoning about Knowledge and Action,"
                Report 191, SRI Artificial Intelligence Center (1980).

Moravcsik80.   Moravcsik, Edith A. and Wirth, Jessica A., *Syntax and Se-
                mantics 13: Current Approaches to Syntax,* Academic Press,
                New York (1980).

Mostow83.   Mostow, D. Jack, "Machine transformation of advice into a
                heuristic search procedure," pp. 367-403 in *Machine Learn-
                ing: An Artificial Intelligence Approach*, ed. Ryszard Michal-
                ski, Jaime G. Carbonell, and Tom M. Mitchell, Tioga, Palo
                Alto, Calif. (1983).

Mostow83a.   Mostow, D. Jack, "A problem-solver for making advice
                operational," *Proc. AAAI* 3 pp. 279-283 (1983).

Nash-Webber77. Nash-Webber, Bonny and Reiter, Raymond, "Anaphora and
                logical form: On formal meaning representations for natural
                language," *Proc. Ijcai* 5 pp. 121-131 (1977).

Nau82.   Nau, Dana, "An investigation of the causes of pathology in
                games," *Artificial Intelligence* 19 pp. 257-258 (1982).

Nevins74.   Nevins, A.J., "A human-oriented logic for automatic
                theorem proving," *Journal of the ACM* 21 pp. 606-621
                (1974).

Nilsson80.   Nilsson, Nils J., *Principles of Artificial Intelligence,* Tioga,
                Palo Alto, Calif. (1980).

Paul77.   Paul, Richard P., "WAVE: A model-based language for
                manipulator control," *The Industrial Robot* 4(1) pp. 10-17
                (1977).

Paul81.   Paul, Richard P., *Robot Manipulators: Mathematics, Pro-
                gramming, and Control,* MIT Press, Cambridge, Mass.
                (1981).

Pearl82.   Pearl, Judea, "Reverend Bayes on inference engines: a dis-
                tributed hierarchical approach," *Proc. AAAI* 2 pp. 133-136
                (1982).

Pereira80.   Pereira, L.M. and Porto, A., "Selective backtracking for logic programs," pp. 306-317 in *Proceedings of the 5th Conference on Automated Deduction*, ed. W. Bibel and R. Kowalski, Springer-Verlag, New York (1980).

Pereira80a.   Pereira, F. and Warren, D., "Definite clause grammar for language analysis -- A survey of the formalism and a comparison with augmented transition networks," *Artificial Intelligence* **13** pp. 231-278 (1980).

Perlmutter79.   Perlmutter, David M. and Soames, Scott, *Syntactic Argumentation and the Structure of English,* University of California Press, Berkeley (1979).

Perrault80.   Perrault, C. Raymond and Allen, James F., "A plan-based analysis of indirect speech acts," *American Journal of Computational Linguistics* **6**(3-4) pp. 167-182 (1980).

Pierce66.   Pierce, John R., "Language and Machines: Computers in Translation and Linguistics," Publication 1416, National Academy of Sciences/National Research Council (1966).

Plotkin72.   Plotkin, G.D., "Building-in equational theories," pp. 73-90 in *Machine Intelligence 7*, ed. B. Meltzer and D. Michie, Halsted Press (1972).

Pople75.   Pople, Harry, Myers, Jack, and Miller, Randolph, "DIALOG: A model of diagnostic logic for internal medicine," *Proc. Ijcai* **4** pp. 848-855 (1975).

Pople77.   Pople, Harry, "The formation of composite hypotheses in diagnostic problem solving: An exercise in synthetic reasoning," *Proc. Ijcai* **5** pp. 1030-1037 (1977).

Pople82.   Pople, Harry, "Heuristic methods for imposing structure on ill-structured problems: The structuring of medical diagnostics," pp. 119-190 in *Artificial Intelligence in Medicine*, ed. P. Szolovits, Westview Press, Boulder, Colorado (1982).

Pylyshyn73.   Pylyshyn, Zenon W., "What the mind's eye tells the mind's brain: A critique of mental imagery," *Psychological Bulletin* **80** pp. 1-24 (1973).

Quillian66.   Quillian, M. Ross, "Semantic Memory," in *Semantic Information Processing*, ed. Marvin Minsky, MIT Press, Cambridge, Mass. (1968).

Quinlan83.　　Quinlan, J. Ross, "Learning efficient classification procedures and their application to chess end games," pp. 463-482 in *Machine Learning: An Artificial Intelligence Approach*, ed. Ryszard Michalski, Jaime G. Carbonell, and Tom M. Mitchell, Tioga, Palo Alto, Calif. (1983).

Quinlan83a.　　Quinlan, J. Ross, "Learning from noisy data," pp. 58-64 in *Proceedings of the International Machine Learning Workshop*, University of Illinois (1983).

Raiffa68.　　Raiffa, Howard, *Decision Analysis: Introductory Lectures on Choices under Uncertainty,* Addison-Wesley, Reading, Mass. (1968).

Reichman78.　　Reichman, Rachel, "Conversational coherency," *Cognitive Science* 2(4) pp. 283-327 (1978).

Reiter80.　　Reiter, Ray, "A logic for default reasoning," *Artificial Intelligence* 13(1980).

Reitman78.　　Reitman, W. and Wilcox, B., "Pattern recognition and pattern-directed inference in a program for playing go," in *Pattern-Directed Inference Systems*, ed. D.A. Waterman and F. Hayes-Roth, Academic Press, New York (1978).

Rich83.　　Rich, Elaine, *Artificial Intelligence,* McGraw-Hill, New York (1983).

Rieger75.　　Rieger, Chuck, "The commonsense algorithm as a basis for computer models of human memory, inference, belief and contextual language comprehension," *Theoretical Issues in Natural Language Processing* 1 pp. 180-195 (1975).

Rieger76.　　Rieger, Chuck, "An organization of knowledge for problem solving and language comprehension," *Artificial Intelligence* 7 pp. 89-127 (1976).

Riesbeck75.　　Riesbeck, Christopher K., "Computational understanding," *Theoretical Issues in Natural Language Processing* 1 pp. 11-15 (1975).

Riesbeck78.　　Riesbeck, Christopher K. and Schank, Roger C., "Comprehension by computer: Expectation-based analysis of sentences in context," in *Studies in the Perception of Language*, ed. W.J.M Levelt and G.B. Flores d'Arcais, Wiley, New York (1978).

Riesbeck80.　　Riesbeck, Christopher K., "You can't miss it: Judging the clarity of directions," *Cognitive Science* 4(3) pp. 285-303 (1980).

Riesbeck81.   Riesbeck, Christopher K., "Failure-driven reminding for in-
                 cremental learning," *Proc. Ijcai* **7** pp. 115-120 (1981).

Robinson65.   Robinson, J.A., "A machine-oriented logic based on the
                 resolution principle," *Journal of the ACM* **12**(1) p. 23
                 (1965).

Robinson80.   Robinson, J.A. and Sibert, E.E., "LOGLISP -- An alterna-
                 tive to PROLOG," Report 7-80, Syracuse University School
                 of Computer and Information Sciences (1980).

Rorty67.   Rorty, Richard, *The Linguistic Turn: Recent Essays in Phi-
                 losophical Method,* University of Chicago Press, Chicago
                 (1967).

Rosenfeld76.   Rosenfeld, Azriel, Hummel, Robert, and Zucker, Steven,
                 "Scene labeling by relaxation operations," *IEEE Transac-
                 tions on Systems, Man, and Cybernetics* **SMC-6** p. 420
                 (1976).

Sacerdoti75.   Sacerdoti, Earl, "The nonlinear nature of plans," *Proc. Ijcai*
                 4 pp. 206-214 (1975).

Schank75.   Schank, Roger C., *Conceptual Information Processing,*
                 North-Holland, Amsterdam (1975).

Schank77.   Schank, Roger C. and Abelson, Robert P., *Scripts, Plans,
                 Goals, and Understanding,* Lawrence Erlbaum, Hillsdale,
                 N.J. (1977).

Schank79.   Schank, Roger C. and Carbonell, J.G., "Re: The Gettysburg
                 Address: Representing social and political acts," pp. 327-362
                 in *Associative Networks: Representation and Use of
                 Knowledge by Computer*, ed. N.V. Findler, Academic Press,
                 New York (1979).

Schank80.   Schank, Roger and Birnbaum, Lawrence, "Memory, Mean-
                 ing, and Syntax," Report 189, Yale University Department
                 of Computer Science (1980).

Schank82.   Schank, Roger, *Dynamic Memory: A Theory of Learning in
                 Computers and People,* Cambridge University Press, Cam-
                 bridge (1982).

Schatz77.   Schatz, Bruce R., "The Computation of Immediate Texture
                 Discrimination," Memo 426, MIT Artificial Intelligence La-
                 boratory (1977).

Schmidt78.   Schmidt, C.F., Sridharan, N.S., and Goodson, J.L., "The plan recognition problem: an intersection of psychology and artificial intelligence," *Artificial Intelligence* **11** pp. 45-83 (1978).

Schubert76.   Schubert, Lenhart, "Extending the expressive power of semantic networks," *Artificial Intelligence* **7**(2) pp. 163-198 (1976).

Searle69.   Searle, John R., *Speech Acts: An Essay in the Philosophy of Language,* Cambridge University Press, London (1969).

Sedgewick83.   Sedgewick, Robert, *Algorithms,* Addison-Wesley, Reading, Mass. (1983).

Selfridge80.   Selfridge, Mallory G.R., "A Process Model of Language Acquisition," Report 172, Yale University Department of Computer Science (1980).

Shannon50.   Shannon, Claude E., "Automatic chess player," *Scientific American* **182**(1950).

Shapiro81.   Shapiro, Ehud, "Inductive Inference of Theories from Facts," Report 192, Yale University Computer Science Department (1981).

Shapiro79.   Shapiro, S.C., *Techniques of Artificial Intelligence,* Van Nostrand, New York (1979).

Shapiro79a.   Shapiro, S.C., "The SNePS semantic network processing system," pp. 179-203 in *Associative Networks: Representation and Use of Knowledge by Computer*, ed. N.V. Findler, Academic Press, New York (1979).

Shapiro80.   Shapiro, S.C. and McKay, D.P., "Inference with recursive rules," *Proc. AAAI* **1** pp. 151-153 (1980).

Shelley81.   Shelley, Mary, *Frankenstein,* Regents, New York (1981).

Shepard71.   Shepard, Roger N. and Metzler, Jacqueline, "Mental rotation of three-dimensional objects," *Science* **171** pp. 701-703 (1971).

Shortliffe75.   Shortliffe, Edward H and Buchanan, Bruce G., "A model of inexact reasoning in medicine," *Mathematical Biosciences* **23** pp. 351-379 (1975).

Shortliffe76.   Shortliffe, Edward H., *Computer-Based Medical Consultations: MYCIN,* American Elsevier, New York (1976).

Siklossy76.   Siklossy, Laurent, *Let's Talk LISP,* Prentice-Hall, Englewood Cliffs, N.J. (1976).

Slate77.   Slate, David J. and Atkin, Lawrence R., "CHESS 4.5 - the
                  Northwestern University chess program," pp. 82-118 in
                  Chess Skill in Man and Machine, ed. P.W. Frey, Springer-
                  Verlag, New York (1977).

Slobin66.   Slobin, Dan I., "Grammatical transformations and sentence
                  comprehension in childhood and adulthood," *Journal of Ver-
                  bal Learning and Verbal Behavior* **5** pp. 219-227 (1966).

Smith83.   Smith, David E., "Finding all of the solutions to a prob-
                  lem," *Proc. AAAI* **3** pp. 373-377 (1983).

Soloway77.   Soloway, Elliott and Riseman, Edward M., "Knowledge-
                  directed learning," *Sigart Newsletter*, (63)(1977).

Soloway77a.   Soloway, Elliot and Riseman, Edward M., "Levels of pat-
                  tern description in learning," *Proc. Ijcai* **5** pp. 801-811
                  (1977).

Soloway82.   Soloway, E., Ehrlich, K., Bonar, J., and Greenspan, J.,
                  "What do novices know about programming?," in *Directions
                  in Human-Computer Interactions*, ed. B. Shneiderman and A.
                  Badre, Ablex, Hillsdale, N.J. (1982).

Stefik80.   Stefik, Mark J., "Planning with Constraints," Report
                  STAN-CS-80-784, Stanford University Computer Science
                  Department (1980).

Stevens78.   Stevens, Kent, "Computation of locally parallel structure,"
                  Biological Cybernetics **29** pp. 19-28 (1978).

Stevens79.   Stevens, Kent, "Representing and analyzing surface orienta-
                  tion," pp. 103-125 in *Artificial Intelligence: An MIT Perspec-
                  tive*, ed. P.H. Winston and R.H. Brown, MIT Press, Cam-
                  bridge, Mass. (1979).

Stockman79.   Stockman, G.C., "A minimax algorithm better than alpha-
                  beta?," *Artificial Intelligence* **12** pp. 179-196 (1979).

Summers82.   Summers, R.H., Taylor, P.D., and Meyer, J.M., "AML: A
                  manufacturing language," *International Journal of Robotics
                  Research* **1**(3) pp. 19-41 (1982).

Suppes57.   Suppes, Patrick, *Introduction to Logic*, Van Nostrand,
                  Princeton, N.J. (1957).

Sussman75.   Sussman, Gerald J., *A Computer Model of Skill Acquisition*,
                  American Elsevier, New York (1975).

Tate77.   Tate, Austin, "Generating project networks," *Proc. Ijcai*
                  5 pp. 888-893 (1977).

Taylor79.   Taylor, Russell H., "Planning and execution of straight-line manipulator trajectories," *IBM Journal of Research and Development* **23**(4) pp. 424-436 (1979).

Thompson77.   Thompson, Alan M., "The navigation system of the JPL robot," *Proc. Ijcai* **5** pp. 749-758 (1977).

Thorne68.   Thorne, J., Bratley, P., and Dewar, H., "The syntactic analysis of English by machine," in *Machine Intelligence 3*, ed. D. Michie, American Elsevier, New York (1968).

Turing53.   Turing, Alan, "Part of Chapter 25," pp. 288-295 in *Faster Than Thought*, ed. B.V. Bowden, Pitman, London (1953).

Turing63.   Turing, Alan M., "Computing machinery and intelligence," pp. 1-35 in *Computers and Thought*, ed. E. Feigenbaum and J. Feldman, McGraw-Hill, New York (1963).

Udupa77.   Udupa, S., "Collision detection and avoidance in computer manipulators," *Proc. Ijcai* **5** pp. 737-748 (1977).

Ullman79.   Ullman, Shimon, "The interpretation of structure from motion," *Proceedings of the Royal Society* **B-203** pp. 405-426 (1979).

Vere78.   Vere, Steven, "Inductive learning of relational productions," pp. 281-295 in *Pattern-Directed Inference Systems*, ed. D.A. Waterman and F. Hayes-Roth, Academic Press, New York (1978).

Vere83.   Vere, Steven A., "Planning in time: Windows and durations for activities and goals," *IEEE Transactions on Pattern Analysis and Machine Intelligence* **PAMI-5**(3) pp. 246-267 (1983).

Waltz75.   Waltz, David, "Understanding line drawings of scenes with shadows," in *The Psychology of Computer Vision*, ed. P.H. Winston, McGraw-Hill, New York (1975).

Warren77.   Warren, D.H.D., Pereira, L.M., and Pereira, F., "PROLOG -- The language and its implementation compared with LISP," *Sigplan Notices* **12**(8)(August 1977).

Waterman70.   Waterman, D.A., "Generalization learning techniques for automating the learning of heuristics," *Artificial Intelligence* **1**(12)(1970).

Waterman78.   Waterman, D.A. and Hayes-Roth, F., *Pattern Directed Inference Systems,* Academic Press, New York (1978).

Weissman67.   Weissman, Clark, *LISP 1.5 Primer,* Dickenson, Belmont, Calif. (1967).

Whitehead25.　Whitehead, A.N. and Russell, B., *Principia Mathematica,* Cambridge University Press, Cambridge (1925).

Wilensky78.　Wilensky, Robert, "Why John married Mary: Understanding stories involving recurring goals," *Cognitive Science* **2**(3)(1978).

Wilensky83.　Wilensky, Robert, *Planning and Understanding,* Addison-Wesley, Reading, Mass. (1983).

Wilensky84.　Wilensky, Robert, *LISPcraft,* Norton, New York (1984).

Wilkins80.　Wilkins, David, "Using patterns and plans in chess," *Artificial Intelligence* **14**(2) pp. 165-203 (1980).

Wilkins84.　Wilkins, David, "Domain independent planning: Representation and plan generation," *Artificial Intelligence*, (1984).

Wilks75.　Wilks, Yorick, "An intelligent analyzer and understander of English," *Communications of the ACM* **18**(5) pp. 264-274 (1975).

Winker81.　Winker, S., Wos, L., and Lusk, E., "Semigroups, antiautomorphisms, and involutions: A computer solution to an open problem, I," *Mathematics of Computation* **37** pp. 533-545 (1981).

Winograd72.　Winograd, Terry, *Understanding Natural Language,* Academic Press, New York (1972).

Winograd83.　Winograd, Terry, *Language as a Cognitive Process, Volume I: Syntax,* Addison-Wesley, Reading, Mass. (1983).

Winston75.　Winston, Patrick H., *The Psychology of Computer Vision,* McGraw-Hill, New York (1975).

Winston75a.　Winston, Patrick H., "Learning structural descriptions from examples," in *The Psychology of Computer Vision*, ed. P.H. Winston, McGraw-Hill, New York (1975).

Winston80.　Winston, Patrick and Horn, Berthold, *LISP,* Addison-Wesley, Reading, Mass. (1980).

Winston80a.　Winston, Patrick H., "Learning and reasoning by analogy," *Communications of the ACM* **23**(12) pp. 689-703 (1980).

Winston81.　Winston, Patrick H., "Learning new principles from precedents and exercises," *Artificial Intelligence* **19** pp. 321-350 (1981).

Winston83.　Winston, Patrick H., "Learning physical descriptions from functional definitions, examples, and precedents," *Proc. AAAI* **3** pp. 433-439 (1983).

Winston84.   Winston, Patrick H., *Artificial Intelligence* (2nd ed.), Addison-Wesley, Reading, Mass. (1984).

Witkin80.   Witkin, Andrew P., "A statistical technique for recovering surface orientation from texture in natural imagery," *Proc. AAAI* **1** pp. 1-3 (1980).

Wittgenstein53. Wittgenstein, Ludwig, *Philosophical Investigations,* Basil Blackwell, Oxford (1953).

Wong81.   Wong, Douglas, "Language comprehension in a problem solver," *Proc. Ijcai* **7**(1981).

Woods68.   Woods, William A., "Procedural semantics for a question-answering machine," *AFIPS Conference Proceedings (Fall Joint Computer Conference)* **33** pp. 457-471 (1968).

Woods72.   Woods, William A., "An experimental parsing system for transition network grammars," pp. 113-154 in *Natural Language Processing*, ed. R. Rustin, Algorithmics Press, New York (1972).

Woods75.   Woods, William A., "What's in a link? Foundations for semantic networks," in *Representation and Understanding*, ed. D.G. Bobrow and A. Collins, Academic Press, New York (1975).

Wos67.   Wos, L., "The concept of demodulation in theorem proving," *Journal of the ACM* **14** pp. 698-709 (1967).

Wos83.   Wos, L., "Automated reasoning: real uses and potential uses," *Proc. Ijcai* **8**(1983).

Index